More praise for

THE INFORMANT

"READS LIKE AN ED McBAIN CRIME NOVEL . . . within a few pages the reader is hooked. I knew how the story ended, but I still couldn't put the book down."

—*New York Times* (daily review)

"A REMARKABLE, FASCINATING AND FAST-PACED BOOK . . . The strange details that emerge would be laughable in the context of a novel. In *The Informant*, they just leave a reader breathlessly amazed."

—*Portland Oregonian*

"A NEAR MASTERPIECE . . . thrilling, far-reaching, and significant . . . a fast-paced, accessible, race car of a book."

—*Salon.com*

"I WOULD SAY *THE INFORMANT* READS LIKE GRISHAM, ONLY NO-BODY EVER COULD HAVE INVENTED THESE CHARACTERS. A tale this riveting and this strange could only have been built from truth."

—Sherry Sontag, coauthor, *Blind Man's Bluff*

"SUSPENSEFUL . . . a book that can double as an attractive movie proposal."

—*Washington Post*

"A GRIPPING READ . . . ONE OF THE MOST COMPELLING BUSINESS NARRATIVES SINCE *BARBARIANS AT THE GATE*. *The Informant* offers an inside picture of a part of the corporate world that outsiders almost never see— one full of covert meetings, secret codes, and industrial espionage. Usually the pulp of airport fiction, here such shadowy doings become the stuff of sound investigative nonfiction . . . A great cops-and-robbers drama—leavened by occasional touches of screwball comedy . . . This is box-office material, and Eichenwald has written a book that reads a lot like a screenplay."

—*Business Week*

"A THRILLER, filled with espionage, double-crosses, and deceit, where nothing is quite what it first seems."

—*Dateline NBC*

THE
INFORMANT

THE INFORMANT

A TRUE STORY

KURT EICHENWALD

BROADWAY BOOKS   NEW YORK

To ADAM, RYAN, and SAM,
my wonderful and beloved boys.

And to my wife, THERESA,
Always.

You too must not count overmuch
on your reality as you feel it today,
since, like that of yesterday,
it may prove to be an illusion tomorrow.

—LUIGI PIRANDELLO

Six Characters in Search of an Author

This book is based on about eight hundred hours of interviews with more than one hundred participants in these events, as well as tens of thousands of confidential corporate and government records, including secret grand jury testimony. Much of the dialogue comes from publicly unavailable transcripts of secret recordings made by a cooperating witness with the FBI over more than two years. Other conversations are based on contemporaneous records of the events or the best recollections of participants. While I have disguised the identities of one witness and of some people mentioned in passing on the tapes, everything else in this book—no matter how unbelievable—is real.

Every scene, every name, every crime.

And every lie.

The Main Characters

WITH THE ARCHER DANIELS MIDLAND COMPANY

DWAYNE ANDREAS, *chairman and chief executive*

MICHAEL "MICK" ANDREAS, *vice-chairman*

JAMES RANDALL, *president*

TERRANCE "TERRY" WILSON, *president, corn processing*

BARRIE COX, *vice president, food additives*

G. ALLEN ANDREAS, *vice president and chief executive, ADM International*

RICHARD REISING, *general counsel*

MARK CHEVIRON, *head of security*

REINHART RICHTER, *president, ADM Mexico*

HOWARD BUFFETT, *assistant to the chairman*

JAMES SHAFTER, *of counsel*

RONALD FERRARI, *former product manager, protein specialties*

IN THE BIOPRODUCTS DIVISION

MARK WHITACRE, *president*

MARTY ALLISON, *vice president*

SIDNEY HULSE, *vice president*

DAVID PAGE, *director of market development*

ELIZABETH TAYLOR, *secretary*

ON THE SPECIAL COMMITTEE OF THE BOARD

BRIAN MULRONEY, *former prime minister of Canada*

F. ROSS JOHNSON, *former chairman, RJR Nabisco*

JOHN DANIELS, *former chairman, Archer Daniels Midland*

RAY GOLDBERG, *professor of agriculture, Harvard Business School*

ADVISORS TO DWAYNE ANDREAS
ROBERT S. STRAUSS, *partner, Akin, Gump, Strauss, Hauer & Feld, Washington, D.C.*
ZEV FURST, *principal, First International*

WITH THE FEDERAL BUREAU OF INVESTIGATION, WASHINGTON, D.C.
LOUIS FREEH, *Director*
WILLIAM ESPOSITO, *Assistant Director, Criminal Investigative Division*
NEIL GALLAGHER, *Deputy Assistant Director of the Criminal Investigative Division*
EDWARD HERBST, *Supervisory Special Agent*
ALIX SUGGS, *Supervisory Special Agent*

WITH THE RESIDENT AGENCY, DECATUR, IL
BRIAN SHEPARD, *Special Agent*

WITH THE RESIDENT AGENCY, CHAMPAIGN, IL
JOE WEATHERALL, *Special Agent*

WITH THE FIELD OFFICE, SPRINGFIELD, IL
ROBERT HERNDON, *Special Agent*
DONALD STUKEY, *Special Agent in Charge* (SAC)
JOHN HOYT, *Assistant Special Agent in Charge* (ASAC)
DEAN PAISLEY, *Supervisory Special Agent*
KATE KILLHAM, *Supervisory Special Agent*
KEVIN CORR, *Principal Legal Advisor*
THOMAS GIBBONS, *Special Agent*

WITH THE FIELD OFFICE, CHICAGO, IL
MICHAEL BASSETT, *Special Agent*
ANTHONY D'ANGELO, *Special Agent*
ED WORTHINGTON, *Assistant Special Agent in Charge* (ASAC)
ROBERT GRANT, *Supervisory Special Agent*

WITH THE FIELD OFFICE, MOBILE, AL
CRAIG DAHLE, *Special Agent*

WITH THE UNITED STATES DEPARTMENT OF JUSTICE, WASHINGTON, D.C.
JANET RENO, *Attorney General*
JAMIE GORELICK, *Deputy Attorney General*
SETH WAXMAN, *Associate Deputy Attorney General*

IN THE ANTITRUST DIVISION, WASHINGTON, D.C.
ANNE BINGAMAN, *Assistant Attorney General*
GARY SPRATLING, *Deputy Assistant Attorney General*

IN THE ANTITRUST DIVISION, MIDWEST FIELD OFFICE, CHICAGO, IL
JAMES GRIFFIN, *Chief*
MARVIN PRICE, *Assistant Chief*
ROBIN MANN, *attorney*
JAMES MUTCHNIK, *attorney*

WITH THE UNITED STATES ATTORNEY'S OFFICE, SPRINGFIELD, IL
FRANCES HULIN, *United States Attorney*
BYRON CUDMORE, *First Assistant United States Attorney*
RODGER HEATON, *Assistant United States Attorney*
JOSEPH HARTZLER, *Assistant United States Attorney*

WITH THE UNITED STATES ATTORNEY'S OFFICE, CHICAGO, IL
SCOTT LASSAR, *First Assistant United States Attorney*

IN THE FRAUD SECTION, WASHINGTON, D.C.
MARY SPEARING, *chief*
DONALD MACKAY, *attorney*
JAMES NIXON, *attorney*
PETER CLARK, *attorney*

WITH THE DISTRICT ATTORNEY'S OFFICE, ZURICH
FRIDOLIN TRIET, *Investigating Magistrate*

WITH THE LAW FIRMS

AT WILLIAMS & CONNOLLY, WASHINGTON, D.C.
AUBREY DANIEL, *partner*
BARRY SIMON, *partner*

AT SIMPSON THACHER & BARTLETT, NEW YORK, NY
RICHARD BEATTIE, *chairman*
CHARLES KOOB, *partner*

REPRESENTING THE INDIVIDUALS
JOHN BRAY, *King & Spaulding, Washington, D.C.*
REID WEINGARTEN, *Steptoe & Johnson, Washington, D.C.*
JAMES EPSTEIN, *Epstein, Zaideman & Esrig, Chicago, IL*
BILL WALKER, *solo practitioner, Granite City, IL*
JOHN DOWD, *Akin, Gump, Strauss, Hauer & Feld, Washington, D.C.*
SHELDON ZENNER, *Katten Muchin & Zavis, Chicago, IL*

WITH AJINOMOTO INC., TOKYO
KAZUTOSHI YAMADA, *managing director*
HIROKAZU IKEDA, *general manager, feed additives*
KANJI MIMOTO, *deputy general manager, feed additives*
KOTARO FUJIWARA, *engineer*

WITH THE EUROPEAN DIVISION, EUROLYSINE
ALAIN CROUY, *president*
JACQUES CHAUDRET, *vice president*

WITH A EUROPEAN AFFILIATE, ORSAN
PHILIPPE ROLLIER, *president*

WITH KYOWA HAKKO KOGYO CO. (BIOKYOWA), TOKYO
MASARU YAMAMOTO, *general manager, bioproducts*

WITH SEWON CO. LTD./MIWON (SEWON AMERICA), SEOUL
JHOM SU KIM, *president, Sewon America*

WITH CHEIL JEDANG LTD., SEOUL
JOON MO SUH, *executive*

WITH KROLL ASSOCIATES
JULES KROLL, *principal*
ANDREW LEVETOWN, *investigator*

THE INDUSTRY CONSULTANT

DAVID HOECH, *president, Global Consultants, Hallandale, FL*

THE ASSOCIATES

GINGER WHITACRE, *wife of Mark Whitacre*

RUSTY WILLIAMS, *groundskeeper for the Whitacre family*

BEAT SCHWEIZER, *money manager*

DR. DEREK MILLER, M.D.

PROLOGUE

June 27, 1995—Decatur, IL

The Country Club of Decatur loomed ahead, and Brian Shepard slowed the pace of his 1994 Dodge Dynasty. Beside him in the passenger seat, Bob Herndon sat in silence, gazing at the club through the windshield. Herndon checked his watch again, although he already knew the time, 6:00 P.M. Right on schedule.

Shepard turned onto the club's inclined driveway, heading to the parking lot as another car followed him up the hill. Passing the club on the right, the midsize sedans maneuvered into two parking spaces, out of place amid the array of Mercedes and BMWs.

Without a word, Shepard and Herndon popped open their doors and watched as Kevin Corr emerged from the second car. In an instant, Corr joined them, and the three men walked in step toward the club. Despite their differing ages and backgrounds, the three somehow looked strikingly similar. They wore short trimmed hair and dressed in dark suits with dark dress shoes. Their suit jackets fit loosely, masking the stainless steel automatic pistols that they carried.

They turned away from the small crowd milling outside near the pro shop. As expected, most every club member was there, enjoying the food and ambience of a night at the grill. The upstairs dining hall was sure to be virtually empty, a refuge for local businessmen looking for a quiet place to talk. It was perfect for the plan. Tonight there would likely be no witnesses to get in the way.

The three men headed toward the club's canopy-covered entryway. On the horizon, the sun threw a deep reddish glow across the Illinois countryside. Even here, far from the giant milling factories that dominate Decatur, a pungent aroma hung in the air. Newcomers to town usually found the smell disagreeable. But for Decatur residents, the ever-present odor produced by drying corn feed and toasting soymeal at the powerful Archer Daniels Midland Company had become part of the landscape, no different than the trees or the sky. Locals often joked it was just the smell of money being made.

The men pushed open the club's glass door, walking left toward the dining hall. The room was not Decatur's largest meeting place, but it was certainly among the most elegant, with chandeliers, a grand fireplace, and oceans of white linen draped across circular tables. This night, only one table was occupied, on the far side of the room, where three executives were chatting over drinks. Two of the men were well known in town—even their waitress recognized them as Terry Wilson and Mark Whitacre from the nearby ADM headquarters.

Corr waited in a foyer outside the dining hall as Shepard and Herndon walked briskly toward the businessmen. The diners barely noticed the approaching men until they came to a stop at their table.

"Mr. Wilson? Mr. Whitacre?" Herndon said.

The youngest of the diners, a blond man in his mid-thirties with a moustache and a baby face, looked at Herndon with a puzzled expression.

"Yes?" he said. "I'm Mark Whitacre."

Herndon and Shepard reached inside their jackets, bringing out matching leather cases. Two gold shields flashed in the light of the dining hall.

"I'm Bob Herndon, and I'm an FBI agent. This is Brian Shepard; he's also an FBI agent. We need to talk to both of you privately, right now."

Wilson, in his fifties with white hair, set down his glass of Dewar's and water. "What's this all about?"

"Well, Mr. Wilson, the best thing would be if Agent Shepard and I could talk to you over here," Herndon said, pointing to the foyer where Corr was waiting.

Wilson glanced across the table at his second dinner partner, Steven Yu, a visiting executive from ADM's division in China. With an almost imperceptible shrug, Wilson excused himself. He and Whitacre began to stand when Wilson abruptly stopped.

"Do I need an attorney?" he asked.

"That's up to you," Herndon said. "You're not under arrest, you're not in custody, you can leave any time. But you may want to hear what we have to say."

Wilson nodded. He and Whitacre left the dining hall, leaving behind their bewildered colleague.

As they reached the foyer, Herndon introduced Corr. "Agent Corr, why don't you find a place to talk to Mr. Whitacre?"

Corr looked at Whitacre. "Is that all right with you, sir?"

Whitacre nodded, his face a seeming mixture of astonishment and confusion.

Corr escorted Whitacre outside as Wilson found a seat in the foyer. Herndon and Shepard took chairs on either side. Herndon leaned in just a few feet from Wilson's face, his elbows resting on his knees.

"Mr. Wilson, we're here to see you because you're very important to ADM," he said. "This is a serious matter. It involves an international investigation regarding price-fixing. There are many companies involved, including ADM."

Herndon watched Wilson carefully. The man didn't flinch; his eyes held steady. But the color was draining from his face.

The FBI had used a number of investigative techniques in developing the case, Herndon said. He paused for an instant, and then dropped the bomb.

"We have tapes in this case," he said. "We have tapes of competitors getting together to fix prices."

Tapes? Jesus.

For several minutes, Wilson listened, reeling, as Herndon spoke. The agent said that the FBI knew ADM and its competitors had conspired to rig worldwide prices of its products and had formed bogus industry associations as a cover for their illegal meetings.

"Excuse me, sir, 'cover'?" Wilson interrupted. "What do you mean by 'cover'?"

Herndon and Shepard suppressed smiles. They knew Wilson understood exactly what they meant. The time had come to make that clear.

"We've heard you say over and over that the associations are the perfect cover," Herndon said. "We've heard you say it on tape. We've seen you agree to fix prices. We've seen you tell others to do it."

Herndon paused, staring into Wilson's eyes. Seconds passed, seeming like minutes. The moment grew unnatural. Wilson said nothing.

Finally, Herndon broke the tension. "There are going to be indictments. People will be going to jail. Right now you have the opportunity to make a decision, and we would like you to make the right decision."

This was Wilson's chance to admit his mistakes, Herndon said, a chance to someday be able to look his grandchildren in the eye and say that he had done the right thing by confessing and helping the government.

"It's tough, it's hard, but it will be tougher if you don't cooperate," Herndon said. "We're giving you the chance to make a difficult decision, probably the most difficult you've ever made. But it begins now by being honest about your activities at ADM."

Suddenly Wilson interrupted.

"I'm surprised you didn't go through the company attorneys," he said. "I know the antitrust laws, and I haven't done anything wrong. And don't think I don't recognize the pressure tactics you're using."

Wilson stood up. "I haven't done anything wrong," he repeated. "And this interview is over."

Herndon glanced at Shepard. Just as expected. The agents rose and thanked Wilson. Herndon handed him a subpoena, pointing out the name of the government attorney who would be available to answer any questions.

The two agents headed out the door. Almost immediately, they saw Corr and Whitacre heading back from the agent's car. It appeared that interviewing Whitacre had been as fruitless as confronting Wilson.

Herndon stared at Whitacre as they passed on the sidewalk. "Goodbye, Mr. Whitacre," he said. "Thank you for your time."

"Sure," Whitacre replied hastily. "I just don't think I know anything that can help you guys."

Herndon and Shepard walked to their car and climbed inside.

The show was over.

It was 6:17 P.M. Right on schedule.

"Mark, stay calm," Wilson said. "Stay calm."

It was about thirty minutes later. Wilson and Whitacre were hustling across the club parking lot, having finally ended their dinner with Steven Yu. They had attempted to hide their anxiety, with little success. Every few minutes, Wilson had headed to the phone in a frustrating effort to track down ADM's general counsel, Richard Reising. Between calls, he had sat at the table in near silence, slamming down scotches. When he finally found Reising, the lawyer sounded panicked: FBI agents were fanning out across Decatur, interviewing executives and seizing documents. Reising said Wilson and Whitacre should immediately head out to the house of Mick Andreas, ADM's vice-chairman. He would meet them there.

Before scurrying out the door, Wilson and Whitacre had muttered apologies to Yu, promising that someone would pick him up. Now, as they climbed into Whitacre's company-issued Town Car, Wilson was doing his best to calm his colleague and himself.

"This isn't going to be pleasant, so . . ."

"Oh, shit!" Whitacre interrupted, the tension of the moment exploding.

"I know."

"I did everything I could to stay calm around Steven."

"I know, I know," Wilson replied.

Wilson took a breath. His hands trembled. "Shit, I'm—I'm having trouble staying calm," he said.

The moment seemed unreal. Here they were, two senior executives at a company of immense influence, known in the corridors of power from Washington to Moscow. This was a company that *helped* the FBI for God's sake; some of its executives were even sources for the Central Intelligence Agency. And now these agents were confronting *them*? Telling them their own words, telling them that they were *on tape*?

On tape. Where the hell did the tapes come from? Maybe, Whitacre suggested, the FBI had tapped some of their telephones.

"Well, that may be," Wilson replied, "but what have they got? They got nothing."

"Well," Whitacre said softly, "I get calls from time to time."

Wilson nodded. "I know that, Mark."

As Whitacre drove, Wilson described his meeting with the agents and the tactics they had used. Whitacre said the same things had been done to him.

They pulled into Mick Andreas's driveway, stopping just past the entryway to the large, two-story stone house. As they got out of the car, Wilson tried guessing which other companies may have been raided.

It seemed too much for Whitacre. "Oh, God," he said. "I'm glad my wife's not around."

"Yeah," Wilson said. "Stay calm. Stay calm."

At that instant, Wilson saw Andreas walk out of the house, carrying a drink in his hand and with his shirt untucked. Whitacre was surprised by how calm he appeared; Wilson knew better. He could tell Andreas was in a panic.

Andreas told them that the meeting had been moved to Reising's house. He took a sip of his drink.

"They've been everywhere," Andreas said.

"Yeah, I know," Wilson replied.

"They hit pretty hard on me," Whitacre said. "Jesus."

Andreas nodded. "I bet. Me too."

In his confrontation with the FBI, Andreas said, the agents had played a tape with his voice on it, talking to some Japanese competitors.

Andreas eyed his colleagues evenly. "Well, I think the main thing is we'll get a good set of lawyers and we'll fight it."

All they needed to do, Andreas said, was stay cool and head to Reising's house.

"He's gonna be in all his grandeur," Andreas joked as Wilson chuckled. "I mean he's a lawyer, so he's gonna save us all."

Whitacre again brought up the telephones, asking if they were safe. Andreas shook his head.

"The phones are all tapped."

"God, that really scares me," Whitacre said. "I'll tell you, the phone conversations I've had in the last couple of weeks . . ."

"Don't—don't worry about it," Wilson said.

Andreas shook his head. "I really think they haven't got a lot," he said.

Besides, ADM had been through problems like this before with the government. In the end, thanks to its scorched-earth tactics, the company had always won.

"It'll be a ten-year thing," Andreas said. "And eventually they'll dig their way out, and that'll be the end of it."

The conversation dwindled to a close. Whitacre and Wilson headed back across the yard to the car.

"To the lawyers," Wilson said.

Hours later, just after nine P.M., Whitacre was driving west on U.S. Highway 36, away from downtown Decatur. By this time on most nights, he would be heading to his estate in the nearby town of Moweaqua. But tonight he had other responsibilities.

Whitacre saw his destination ahead—the Holiday Inn in Decatur. Putting on his blinker, he turned onto a side road that led to the hotel and then veered right, toward the back of the parking lot. He drove past the courts for tennis and volleyball, pulling into a space overlooking the neighboring fishing pond. He left the motor running and waited in the darkness.

He heard two car doors close. Suddenly, both passenger-side doors on his car opened. Squinting from the glare of the inside light, Whitacre watched as Shepard and Herndon climbed in, their faces stern. He started talking before the two FBI agents could sit.

"Hey, you guys were good," he said, the words rushing out. "You scared Terry. He doesn't really show it, but he's scared. And he thinks I was interviewed, too."

"That's super, Mark," Shepard said.

"Yeah, I just went off with Kevin Corr and chitchatted. But they think I was interviewed."

"Good."

"And Mick told us there's nothing to worry about, that the lawyers will take care of everything."

Shepard nodded. "Did you make a tape?"

Whitacre reached inside his jacket, bringing out a microcassette recorder. It was one of several government recording devices that he had been secretly carrying almost every day for more than two years.

"Yeah, yeah. I did just like you guys wanted me to," Whitacre said, handing over the recorder. "I got the tape of everything they told me."

Whitacre smiled. "And it's good stuff," he said. "It's real good."

———

It was a criminal case unlike any in the history of law enforcement. For years, a top executive with one of America's most politically powerful companies worked as a cooperating government witness, providing evidence of a vast international conspiracy. With little obvious incentive, Mark Whitacre secretly recorded colleagues and competitors as they illegally divided world markets among themselves, setting far higher prices for their products than free competition would allow.

In the end, the tapes showed that a company whose executives hobnobbed with presidents and prime ministers had organized a scheme to steal hundreds of millions of dollars from its own customers. With Whitacre's help, the FBI had been there—sometimes with video cameras rolling—as the conspiracy unfolded between ADM and its foreign competitors.

By the night of the raids in June 1995, the government had amassed an arsenal of evidence unprecedented in a white-collar case. Despite the secrecy of the criminals, despite their ability to spend millions of dollars on a defense, despite the political influence they could bring to bear, the possibility that they could beat back the prosecution seemed ludicrous. They were trapped—trapped by their own words and images, forever captured on miles of magnetized plastic ribbon. The government agents did not know whether Whitacre would emerge as a hero or an unemployed martyr, but they felt sure of their investigation. That night, they could hardly be blamed for believing that this case was all but over.

But it would be their last night of confidence and celebration for years to come. For despite all of the evidence the agents had collected, critical information had escaped them. Before dawn broke, they would sense that something had gone terribly awry. Years later, they would understand that the evening had not signaled the end of the case, but rather the beginning of events that eventually touched the highest reaches of government and industry around the world, events that no one could have imagined.

For on that night in the summer of 1995, almost nothing was what it appeared to be.

BOOK ONE

VERGE OF
TRUTH

CHAPTER 1

The large gray van, its windows tinted to block the glances of the curious, pulled away from the Decatur Airport, heading toward Route 105. Inside, four foreign visitors watched as images of the modest town came into view. Working-class houses. An Assembly of God church. A man-made lake. The vast fields of corn that could be seen from the air were no longer visible, replaced instead by an entanglement of industrial plants and office buildings.

These were the sights of a thousand other blue-collar neighborhoods in a thousand other Midwestern towns. Still, on this day, September 10, 1992, it was hard not to feel a slight sense of awe. For years, world leaders had seen these images, perhaps from this very van, in a virtual pilgrimage of power. In the last few months alone, this road had been traveled by Mikhail Gorbachev, the former Soviet leader, and by Dan Quayle, the American vice president. Those men, like leaders before them, had been drawn to this out-of-the-way place in the center of America largely by one company and often by one man: Archer Daniels Midland and its influential chairman, Dwayne Andreas.

Few Americans were familiar with who Andreas was or what he did. But among the world's moneyed and powerful, he and his grain processing company were known well. In Washington, anyone who mattered was acquainted with Andreas—or more likely, with his money. For decades, he had been one of the country's foremost political contributors, heaping cash almost indiscriminately on Democrats and Republicans—this year alone, Andreas money would be used by both George Bush and Bill Clinton in their battle for the presidency. The largesse helped transform Andreas into one of Washington's most important men, even as he remained comfortably ensconced in its shadows. But it also thrust him into controversy. It was the $25,000 from Andreas that operatives of President Nixon laundered into the bank account of a Watergate burglar. Following the wide-ranging investigations that stemmed from the Watergate scandal, Andreas was tried and acquitted on charges of violating campaign-finance laws—but that was for the $100,000 he gave to Nixon's 1968 rival, Hubert Humphrey.

The foreign visitors traveling to ADM on this day hoped for an opportunity to meet Andreas but were uncertain if they would. At this point, they were scheduled only to speak with others in ADM management, the people who ran its day-to-day business.

If all went well, the visitors expected the meeting to last some time. After all, before the day's end, there were several important things that they needed to learn. But there was also one important thing that they needed to steal.

The van turned onto Faries Parkway, heading directly toward ADM's homely, sprawling complex. Yellow flowers planted along the side of the road did little to soften the effect of the property's jagged barbed-wire fence. At the main gate, the driver gave a nod to the guard before turning right toward the squat, nondescript building that housed ADM's top brass. The van came to a stop beside the seven-foot bronze statue of Ronald Reagan, mounted on a two-ton granite base, that Dwayne Andreas had erected to commemorate a 1984 visit by the then-president.

Hirokazu Ikeda stepped down from the enormous vehicle, trailed closely by Kanji Mimoto, both senior executives from Ajinomoto Inc., a giant Japanese competitor of ADM. Two other Ajinomoto executives followed—one Japanese, one European. Shading their eyes from the morning sun, the men headed into the building's lobby and introduced themselves to a receptionist. She placed a call, and within seconds a young, energetic man came bounding down a hallway toward them. It was Mark Whitacre, the thirty-four-year-old president of ADM's newest unit, the Bioproducts Division. He was a man whom in recent months they had come to know, if not yet to trust.

Whitacre smiled as he stepped into the lobby. "Welcome to Decatur," he said, shaking Ikeda's hand. "And welcome to ADM."

"Thank you, Mr. Whitacre," Ikeda said in halting English. "Happy to be here."

Whitacre turned and greeted Mimoto, a man closer to his own age who spoke English fairly well. The other two men were strangers; they were introduced to Whitacre as Kotaro Fujiwara, an engineer at the company's Tokyo headquarters, and J. L. Brehant, who held a similar job at its European subsidiary.

With introductions complete, Whitacre escorted the executives down the hallway toward ADM's huge trading room, the corporate nerve center where it purchased tons of corn, wheat, soybeans, and other farm products for processing each day. On the front wall of the vast room, a screen flashed up-to-the-minute commodity prices. At row after row of desks, an army of traders barked buy and sell orders into telephones.

Around the edges of the room were various executive offices, most with the doors open. Whitacre stopped at one office and tapped on the door frame.

"Terry?" he said. "They're here."

Terry Wilson, head of the company's corn-processing division, looked up from his desk and smiled. The expression was more a reflection of strategy than delight; he was hoping to finish with the Ajinomoto executives quickly, in time for an early afternoon round of golf. Like many American businessmen, Wilson often felt frustrated with the Japanese. In negotiations, they seemed loath to horse-trade; they would listen but often retreated into ambiguity, making no specific commitments. Such tactics were considered a sign of virtue in Japan, the vague responses praised as *tamamushi-iro no hyōgen o tsukau,* or "using iridescent expressions." Whatever its elegant description in Japanese, for Westerners like Wilson, a hard-drinking ex-marine, the approach was tiresome. He was not looking forward to it today.

Wilson stepped from behind his desk, past a television that was broadcasting the day's news.

"Mr. Ikeda, Mr. Mimoto, it's been a long time," he said. "You've come on a day with such nice weather, it's a shame you're not here to play golf."

The men chatted about their golf games as Whitacre led them to the executive meeting room, where they found their places around a conference table. A kitchen staffer appeared, serving iced tea, water, and orange juice. As everyone settled in, Whitacre walked to a wall phone and dialed 5505—the extension for Jim Randall, the president of ADM.

"Jim, our guests are here," Whitacre said simply. He hung up and returned to his seat.

Everyone knew this could be a tense moment. Randall had been at the company since 1968. His skills as an engineer were indisputable;

his hands-on role kept the huge processing plants running. Still, the sixty-eight-year-old Randall was no Dwayne Andreas. As much as Dwayne's smooth and polished style made him the perfect Mr. Outside for ADM, Randall's gruff, plainspoken approach ensured that he would remain Mr. Inside. He often rubbed people the wrong way, whether he was boasting about his sports cars or ADM's market dominance. The visitors today expected to hear about the company's might; they knew that ADM's invitation to visit was partly for the purpose of scaring them.

Randall walked into the room a few minutes later, introduced himself, and took his place alongside Wilson and Whitacre. Instantly he took control of the meeting and the conversation, describing how ADM was transforming itself into a new company.

Over slightly less than a century, ADM had grown into a global giant, processing grains and other farm staples into oils, flours, and fibers. Its products were found in everything from Nabisco saltines to Hellmann's mayonnaise, from Jell-O pudding to StarKist tuna. Soft drinks were loaded with ADM sweeteners and detergents with ADM additives. Americans were raised on ADM: Babies drinking soy formulas were downing the company's wares; as toddlers, they got their daily dose of ADM from Gerber cereals. The health-minded consumed its products in yogurt and canola oil; others devoured them in Popsicles and pepperoni. While most people had never heard of ADM, almost every American home was stuffed with its goods. ADM called itself "the Supermarket to the World," but in truth it was the place that the giant food companies came to do their grocery shopping.

Now, Randall said, ADM was entering a new era. Beginning three years before, in 1989, ADM had taken a new direction, creating the Bioproducts Division. No longer would the company just grind and crush food products. Instead, it was veering into biotechnology, feeding dextrose from corn to tiny microbes. Over time, those microbes, or "bugs" as they were known, convert the sugar into an amino acid called lysine. As people in the business liked to say, the bugs ate dextrose and crapped lysine. In animal feed, lysine bulked up chickens and pigs—just the product needed by giant food companies like Tyson and Conagra.

Until ADM came along, the Japanese largely controlled the market, with Ajinomoto the undisputed giant. Start-up costs alone kept out potential competitors—tens of millions of dollars were required just to develop the proprietary, patented microbes needed to ferment lysine. But ADM abounded in cash; it had already invested more than $150 million in the new business. Now, the world's largest lysine plant was in Decatur, ready to produce as much as 113,000 metric tons a year. And running it all was Whitacre, a whiz-kid scientist who was almost certainly the first Ph.D. ever employed at ADM as the manager of a division.

"We're going to be the largest biochem company in the world," Randall said. "It just makes so much sense for us. We have the raw materials available, we have cheap utilities. It's just a natural."

The Japanese executives listened skeptically but said little. If ADM could produce that much lysine, it would have to gobble up much of the existing market. Building such a huge business struck them as irrational, foolhardy. ADM would have to keep large portions of the plant idle while waiting either for the market to grow or competitors to leave the business. Still, the executives didn't mind hearing the boasts. They knew that listening as ADM rattled its saber would give them the chance to learn other, truthful information about the company.

As Randall spoke, Whitacre and Wilson did their best not to cringe. For all of Randall's swagger, they knew the most important fact about ADM's new effort was being left untold: *The company couldn't get the damn plant to work.* The bugs went in the vats, the dextrose went in the bugs and out came—very little. In recent months, a virus had turned up repeatedly in the giant fermenters where the lysine was produced, killing the bugs before they produced much of anything. While ADM was producing enough to have a presence in the market, the virus contamination had cost as much as $16 million so far in lost production time alone. And the pressure was really on: Dwayne Andreas had recently suggested shutting down the plant and trying again with a test model. Meanwhile, Dwayne's son, Mick, who ran much of ADM's daily business, had been pounding Whitacre for weeks to fix the problem. But after each attempted solution, the virus returned. It was not something to mention to ADM's chief competitor.

Ten minutes into his monologue, Randall pushed himself back from the table.

"That tells you about our plant, in a nutshell," he said. "Now, Mark's going to give you a tour, and we'll see you back here later for lunch."

The Ajinomoto executives thanked Randall and followed Whitacre out the door. He escorted them to his Lincoln Town Car for the short drive to the plant. There, everyone donned hard hats and safety glasses.

They started the tour in the upstairs lab, where a handful of tiny flasks were being automatically shaken. Inside each of them was a mixture of dextrose and soy flour feeding a small number of microbes. Even as the group walked past, the microbes were multiplying rapidly. The irony was that those tiny cells of bacteria were the multimillion-dollar heart of this giant operation. They were ADM's proprietary biological secret that had allowed the company to break Japan's control of the business.

Fujiwara and Brehant asked questions and jotted down notes. The group left the lab, walking past the control room and into the main area of the plant.

The Ajinomoto executives hesitated, awed. In front of them was a plant unlike any they had ever seen, a vast acreage of fermenters. Dozens of them were spread across the plant, stainless-steel giants rising ninety feet toward the ceiling.

The group headed out onto the plant floor, then down a metal staircase. Fujiwara and Brehant walked near the plant manager as he described the operations. Whitacre and Ikeda were a few steps back.

Mimoto, already behind the rest of the group, slowed his pace. He waited until he felt sure that no one was looking. Quickly, he reached into his pocket and pulled out a plastic bag, removing the moist handkerchief inside. He placed the handkerchief on the staircase banister, rubbing it as he walked down the steps. Before anyone noticed, he slipped the handkerchief back into the bag, sealed it, and casually placed it back in his pocket.

Mimoto knew that the multimillion-dollar bacteria used by ADM to produce its lysine was growing everywhere in this plant, even places where it could not be seen. He could only hope that, with the handkerchief, he had successfully stolen a sample of it for Ajinomoto.

Weeks later, Whitacre was at his desk when the intercom buzzed. It was Liz Taylor, his secretary who sat just a few feet outside his office.

"Yeah, Liz, what's up?"

"Somebody's on the phone for you, but I can't pronounce his name. But he sounds Asian."

Whitacre picked up the telephone.

"Mark Whitacre."

"Hello, Mr. Whitacre?" Liz was right. The caller's Asian accent was thick.

"Yes?"

"I do not know if you remember me," the caller began.

At about six-thirty in the morning, Whitacre stepped off the staircase that brought him up from ADM's basement garage. He walked past the trading floor, straight for Mick Andreas's office. Mick was at his desk when Whitacre walked in, looking flustered.

"Mick, you're not going to believe what the hell's happened," he said. "I think I know the reason why we've been having all these problems in the plant."

Andreas leaned back in his chair. "Well, I've only been asking you to come up with one for eight weeks," he said. "I'm all ears."

Whitacre was jumpy and breathless. He clearly thought he had latched onto something explosive, and told the story to his boss in a rush of words. The recent contaminations in the plant, he said, were not the result of mistakes. Instead, he had just learned that they had been caused by a competitor. Ajinomoto in Tokyo had engineered an incredible plot of corporate espionage. The Japanese were behind the viruses plaguing the ADM plant.

Andreas listened silently. He wanted to hear everything before asking questions.

Pacing as he spoke, Whitacre explained that he had received a call at his office the previous day from an Ajinomoto executive named Fujiwara, one of the group who had toured the plant a few weeks before. During the call, Fujiwara had asked for Whitacre's home number. The request had seemed innocuous, he said; because of the time difference from Tokyo to Decatur, it made sense that Fujiwara might need the number.

"So last night, the guy called me at home just after eight o'clock," Whitacre said. "And Mick, he knew everything. Almost first thing, he said to me, 'Do you remember the total nightmare during May, June, July, and August that you had in your plant?' And when I asked him what he meant, he said, 'Those months when ADM was losing about seven million dollars a month in the lysine business.' "

The statement had taken him by surprise, Whitacre said, and faster than he could respond, Fujiwara began listing ADM's lysine production for the past three months.

Both Andreas and Whitacre knew *that* was serious. Those numbers were proprietary, and no one outside the company was supposed to have heard about the problems in the plant. How could this Fujiwara person have found out?

Before he had been able to raise that question, Whitacre said, Fujiwara began toying with him, asking coyly why he thought the ADM plant was having so many start-up problems.

"I couldn't believe what he said," Whitacre fumed, his voice unnaturally high. "He told me that one of our highest-paid employees is an employee of Ajinomoto, and is sabotaging the plant."

Andreas sat expressionless as Whitacre spelled out the ugly details: The mole was acting on instructions from Tokyo and had been ordered to inject a virus into containers of dextrose for the purpose of wreaking havoc on the plant.

As he spoke, Whitacre seemed to vacillate between anger and dismay. This Fujiwara call reinforced every bad thing he had heard about Japanese corporations.

"I'll tell you Mick, it's like *Rising Sun*," Whitacre said, referring to the Michael Crichton best-seller about intrigue at the American headquarters of a Japanese corporation. "Just like *Rising Sun*."

The idea of using the mole, he said, had come from Ikeda, the top man who attended the plant visit. Fujiwara seemed frightened of the senior Ajinomoto executive, Whitacre continued, and had openly expressed fears that Ikeda might have him killed or deported if he learned of the phone call.

"I couldn't understand why he would talk to me, so I finally asked him why he was calling."

Andreas anticipated the answer before Whitacre even said it: money.

Fujiwara wanted $10 million, Whitacre explained. For that, he would identify the saboteur, give ADM some new microorganisms immunized against the virus, and describe where and when the sabotage had occurred.

"He said that, with his help, in three days we could solve the infection problems we've been wrestling with for four months," Whitacre said.

Whitacre finished, and Andreas paused before asking his first question.

"How well do you know this guy?"

Whitacre stumbled with the answer, again mentioning Fujiwara's visit to ADM a few weeks before. Andreas pressed the question, and Whitacre conceded that he didn't know Fujiwara well at all.

Andreas thought for a moment. What Whitacre was describing sounded crazy. Still, it fit the reports that Andreas had heard about the plant's problems—the sudden appearance of the virus, the futile effort to stop it. Fujiwara couldn't simply be ignored.

"I gotta get this clear in my mind," Andreas said. "Go through it again."

Whitacre repeated the story. Andreas asked a few more questions.

"Okay, if you hear from this guy again, I want you to talk him down on the price," Andreas said. "I want you to find out the least amount of money he'd settle for." Maybe, he reasoned, they could just strike a deal for the bugs that were resistant to the virus.

Also, Andreas said, keep this quiet. If there was a mole inside the plant, the last thing they wanted was to give any sign that ADM was onto him.

A pause. "Keep me informed," Andreas said.

"Okay, Mick," Whitacre replied, nodding.

Whitacre headed out the door, while Andreas sat at his desk in thought. Had the news come from anyone but Whitacre, he might have dismissed Fujiwara's bizarre call as a clumsy extortion plot. But Whitacre understood the plant better than anyone else did. Without him, ADM's "Mr. Lysine," the company could never have moved so quickly into the business. If he was taking this Fujiwara call seriously, then Mick figured *he* had better be worried, too.

Andreas reached for the phone to call his father, Dwayne, who was staying at his apartment in Florida. This was just the kind of threat the ADM chairman needed to know about. With everything Dwayne had done to build his company and his influence, he would not sit back and let his new business be wrecked by a competitor. No one who knew the history of ADM or its iron-fisted chairman could expect that.

———

The modern era of ADM was set in motion on October 21, 1947, when Shreve M. Archer sat down for a meal of cooked chicken. The fifty-nine-year-old ADM chairman and descendant of its cofounder was enjoying his meal in the company's hometown of Minneapolis when he abruptly stood, gasping for air. A bone had caught in his throat. Archer turned blue, then grimaced in pain as he swallowed the bone. He was rushed to nearby Miller Hospital, but it was too late. Twenty days later, he died of complications from the incident.

The sudden, disturbing death of Archer left a void at the company he had directed since 1924. In his years at the helm, Shreve Archer had in many ways become ADM. He had pushed the company to acquire competitors, providing a diversified product line that helped it weather the darkest days of the Great Depression. Most important, he had made an open-ended commitment to the promise of the soybean, a farm staple that had gained prominence only since World War I. Archer pushed ADM into the budding industry, building a giant soybean-processing plant in Decatur. That decision, and countless others like it, had helped transform ADM from a single Midwestern plant at the dawn of the twentieth century into one of the nation's big grain processors. Succeeding Archer would have been hard for anyone; with no one groomed as a successor at the time of his death, the task seemed all but impossible.

The man chosen for the job was Thomas Daniels, a descendant of the company's other cofounder. Daniels had an unlikely background for the position; he had planned on a career in the foreign service and was probably the first head of a grain-processing company who had taken his own polo ponies to college at Yale. But as Daniels took over, ADM was on the verge of a descent into disarray, one that would end almost two decades later in a desperate search for a savior.

In the same year as Archer's death, across town at rival Cargill Inc., a twenty-nine-year-old vice president named Dwayne Andreas was rising to power. He had joined Cargill two years before, when it had purchased his family's business, Honey Mead Products Company of Cedar Rapids, Iowa. Now Andreas, the fourth son of a Mennonite farm family, was a millionaire and Cargill's youngest senior executive. At first glance, he seemed unimposing, standing five feet four inches and weighing just 137 pounds. But his bosses marveled at his intelligence and tenacity. He seemed destined for great things at Cargill.

No one at that time could have imagined the unlikely pairing of this young, hard-charging executive with a midsized competitor on the verge of decline. For that to occur, Andreas and Cargill would have to part ways, an idea that surely seemed far-fetched. With Cargill's high hopes for him, it seemed only Andreas himself could derail his career there.

In the early 1950s, America was a place of paranoia and fear. The Soviet Union had obtained awesome nuclear weaponry. Communists had won control of China, the first major defeat of American interests in the nascent Cold War. In Washington, an array of demagogues stoked alarm with shouts of treason, destroying reputations often with little more than innuendo. Accusatory fingers pointed at Hollywood, industry, and government, creating the widespread impression of a wholesale national betrayal.

At the height of the hysteria, in March 1952, Dwayne Andreas presented an audacious idea to his colleagues at Cargill: He planned to fly to Moscow the following month to attend a trade conference. He thought it was the perfect first step toward setting up a deal to market vegetable oil in the Soviet Union. Obtaining a visa would be no trouble; in his few years at the company, Andreas had won enough political allies in Washington to take care of that.

Persuading Cargill was another matter. The company was already reeling from complaints brought against it by government regulators that charged the firm with violating commodities trading laws. The last thing it needed was the whiff of further controversy.

"I am *ordering* you not to go," Julius Hendell, the firm's dean of grain trading, told Andreas as they discussed the Moscow trip.

"Now, Julius," Andreas replied soothingly. "You know you don't mean that."

Later that day, Andreas received a note to call John Petersen from Cargill's top management group. Andreas ignored the instruction and left on his trip.

Andreas found Moscow an incredible experience and hurried back to Cargill with invaluable information about the Soviet market. His managers would have none of it; they were outraged, muttering darkly about insubordination and expressing fears that Cargill's banks might react poorly to news of the visit.

As internal wrath mounted, Andreas offered his resignation, and it was accepted. Andreas left for another family-owned company, in the vegetable oil business. He seemed destined for an anonymous life in an obscure corner of the agricultural world.

But Andreas had other ideas. He enjoyed life at the top. He was not about to give that up so easily.

Vice President Hubert Humphrey leaned forward on his gold upholstered chair before pulling his dark blue suit down to smoothness. On the television in front of him, the lead delegate from Pennsylvania stepped up to the microphone on the floor of the Chicago Civic Center. Humphrey's friends and supporters stood quietly about him in the large suite on the twenty-fifth floor of the Conrad Hilton Hotel, watching as Pennsylvania cast 103 ¾ votes for their candidate. At that moment, 11:47 on the evening of August 28, 1968, Humphrey was put over the top. He was the Democratic nominee for President of the United States.

The suite erupted into cheers. Humphrey rose from his chair, applauding.

"I feel like really jumping," he said. He leaned over and kissed the cheek of Mrs. La Donna Harris, the wife of his campaign cochairman.

Then Humphrey turned and kissed Inez Andreas. Nearby, her husband, Dwayne—a member of Humphrey's elite brain trust—beamed.

In the sixteen years since leaving Cargill, Andreas's reputation had grown immeasurably. The onetime Iowa farm boy had parlayed the lessons and connections from his Cargill days into a speaking role on the national political stage. He had met Humphrey back then, after sending a one-thousand-dollar contribution to the Minnesota politician's first Senate campaign. In time, the Humphrey family was joining the Andreases for vacations at the Sea View Hotel in Bal Harbour, Florida—a hotel owned by Andreas. Their friendship was cemented in 1948 with the birth of Dwayne's son, Mick; Hubert Humphrey was named his godfather.

Andreas had also extended his political connections through a friendship with another political powerhouse, Thomas Dewey, the former New York governor and two-time Republican presidential candidate. Again, Andreas had met Dewey while working at Cargill. But their friendship blossomed when Andreas hired Dewey as a legal advisor and arranged for him to become special counsel for a national association that promoted soybeans. Dewey, like Humphrey, became a frequent visitor to Andreas's Sea View Hotel.

Dewey also ensured that Andreas extended his contacts in both political parties. He advised Andreas to contribute heavily to election campaigns, providing money to politicians across the ideological spectrum. Andreas became what was known in Washington as a "swinger"— one of the big-time contributors who hedges their bets by making donations to both sides.

Even as his influence extended in Washington, Andreas became known in foreign governments as well. He often accompanied Humphrey and Dewey on overseas trips, at times blending their political goals with his own commercial interests. He cut deals with Juan and Evita Perón of Argentina and touted the benefits of soybean oil to Francisco Franco of Spain. In Yugoslavia, he stayed up into the wee hours with Tito and in the Soviet Union, chatted with Joseph Stalin about vegetable oil.

Andreas was constructing his own brand of international corporate diplomacy—at times thumbing his nose at Washington to get his way. In the mid-1950s, Andreas advocated the sale of surplus government butter to the Soviets through a complex barter deal. The arrangement would have signaled some primitive form of détente, all while strengthening Andreas's ties to Moscow. The American government saw it differently; the idea diverged too radically from administration policy. Commerce Secretary Sinclair Weeks refused to grant Andreas an export license.

Despite the administration's clear dictate, Andreas finagled his way toward a Soviet deal anyway. Only the American government had enough surplus butter on hand to meet the Russian demand. But Andreas knew that vegetable oil could be used for the same purposes as butter—and with his company, he had virtually unlimited access to it. Of course, American officials would block a shipment of vegetable oil from the United States to the Soviet Union, but Andreas decided to get around that hurdle by shipping the oil from Argentina. At the time, he knew Argentina was sending 150,000 tons of vegetable oil to Rotterdam to meet contracts in western Europe. With American approval, he sent a second boatload of oil there from the United States. Then, in Rotterdam, he quietly had the two shipments switched. The American oil was delivered around Europe to meet Argentina's obligations, and the tanker loaded with Argentine oil was sent to Russia. Through the switch, Andreas had not violated America's laws, although he had certainly ignored its policies.

As the Kennedy administration took office in 1961, Andreas became the Zelig of Washington—present for great events, rubbing elbows with the powerful, yet unknown to the public. He was by Humphrey's side the day they walked into a suite in Washington's Mayflower Hotel to find Bobby Kennedy on his hands and knees, writing names on a huge chart of federal jobs that needed to be filled. Together, Andreas and Humphrey helped get George McGovern appointed as head of the Food for Peace Program; Andreas himself was named to the board advising McGovern. In the aftermath of the Kennedy assassination, Andreas's influence grew in 1965, when Humphrey became Lyndon Johnson's vice president. Andreas emerged as a fixture in the White House, heightening his own security concerns—often, he refused to discuss the issues of the day by phone, even with family, because of his fear of wiretaps.

It was at this time that Andreas crossed paths with of the old-line Archer Daniels Midland Company of Minneapolis. By the fall of

1965, ADM was teetering, having never recovered from the death of Shreve Archer. Its finances were in such disrepair that it could not pay its dividends to shareholders. To survive, the company needed a huge infusion of cash and the support of someone with the clout to catapult it into foreign markets. In short, ADM needed Dwayne Andreas. A member of the Archer family invited Andreas in, offering to sell him one hundred thousand shares of stock. Over the ensuing months, Andreas snapped up 10 percent of the company. By early 1966, he was named to ADM's board of directors and executive committee. After surveying the company's prospects, Andreas decided ADM needed to be closer to the soybean business that Shreve Archer had started so long ago. The company moved its headquarters to Decatur.

As Andreas solidified his new role, his chief political mentor took a tumble. The 1968 defeat of Humphrey by Nixon's Republican machine might have seemed a setback to Andreas's ambitions. But he was protected. The night Nixon was nominated, Andreas was dining with Tom Dewey. When the nomination was official, Dewey called Nixon to offer congratulations and mentioned that he was with Andreas.

Dewey listened for a moment, then put his hand over the mouthpiece and turned to his dinner guest.

"You willing to go in the cabinet?" Dewey asked.

Andreas shook his head; he could not imagine the reaction of friends like Humphrey if he turned up in a Nixon administration.

By 1972 Andreas was a big contributor to Humphrey once again but also to his friend's Democratic challengers. At the same time, he secretly funneled oceans of cash toward the Nixon White House. Knowing that a Nixon operative planned to pick up the money, Andreas dropped $25,000 in bills into safe-deposit box 305 at the Sea View Hotel just before midnight on April 7, 1972—minutes before a new law made anonymous contributions illegal. Later that year, Andreas sauntered into the White House, carrying a folder stuffed with $100,000 in one-hundred-dollar bills. The cash, which Andreas gave to Nixon's personal secretary, was kept in a White House safe for months until Watergate led Nixon to decide it should be returned.

With Andreas having locked in his role as a Washington power broker, federal agricultural policies began to align smoothly with ADM's interests. Federal sugar programs became one of Washington's most sacred cows. Through price supports and quotas, the programs kept the cost of sugar high—gifting billions to sugar producers while pushing consumer-product companies to save money by using high-fructose corn syrup, a sweetener made by ADM. In time, that created a billion-dollar-a-year market for ADM, which sold its product at a higher price than would have been possible absent government intervention. In the decades that followed, many Americans would comment that the Coke or Pepsi they drank as children somehow tasted different, not knowing that the change had been largely the result of a switch of sweeteners dictated by government policies that favored ADM.

During the same time, Washington issued a federal subsidy for ethanol, basically corn-derived moonshine used as a relatively clean fuel for cars—albeit at a higher price and with lower octane than gasoline. To promote its use, the government taxed gasoline mixed with ethanol at a lower rate than pure gasoline. Through that decision, Washington directed hundreds of millions of dollars each year to the coffers of ADM.

A wide swath of political and corporate interests opposed the tax break, yet it remained untouchable for decades. Lobbyists marveled at Andreas's skill in massaging government policy without leaving fingerprints. While struggling to reverse the federal law, they never saw Andreas but felt his influence. His clout seemed unprecedented.

No one could have guessed that Andreas was on the verge of increasing his political potency to almost unimaginable heights.

Mikhail Gorbachev smiled broadly as the American congressional delegation stepped into the Kremlin meeting room. It was April 10, 1985. Soviet-American relations were at a bitter point, an "ice age," Gorbachev liked to say. President Reagan had yet to meet a Soviet leader during his four years in office. Gorbachev, who had assumed power months before, was set on changing that. He intended to use this day's meeting, his first with a group of high-level American politicians, to indirectly prod Reagan for a summit.

Thomas P. "Tip" O'Neill, the American Speaker of the House and the head of the delegation, grinned as he thrust out a beefy hand and introduced himself.

"Oh, yes," Gorbachev said through an interpreter. "Your friend Andreas tells me you're a good fellow."

"Dwayne Andreas, the Soybean King?" O'Neill replied. "I played golf with him a couple of months ago, and he told me you were going to be the next Soviet leader. But I had never heard of you."

"Well," Gorbachev said, smiling, "Russia is a big country, with many places to hide. But Andreas told me about you, too."

The moment perfectly captured the international role that Andreas had achieved by the mid-1980s. No longer was he a tagalong for Humphrey or Dewey or Nixon; with his political sponsors long dead or deposed, Andreas had come into his own, using his connections to establish relationships with new heads of state—at times, before the American government had. He was one of the first Americans to hold extensive conversations with Gorbachev, back when the Soviet leader was the Secretary for Agriculture. He would also be among the first Americans to meet with Boris Yeltsin, when the future Russian president visited Andreas in Florida. His list of influential friends seemed endless: O'Neill, Bob Dole, the Senate majority leader; Yitzhak Rabin, the once and future prime minister of Israel; Bob Strauss, the Democratic Party superlawyer; Brian Mulroney, the prime minister of Canada; David Brinkley, the television newsman. Some were Dwayne's neighbors; Andreas helped Dole, Strauss, and Brinkley find apartments at the Sea View.

With his travels and connections, Andreas had expanded his role as diplomat without portfolio. That same year, 1985, he had helped broker a meeting between Reagan and Gorbachev, working back channels to pass messages between the two men. He assured Gorbachev of Reagan's good intentions, despite the president's brusque rhetoric about the Soviets; he eased Reagan's concerns about the new Soviet leader by passing along word that Gorbachev was a churchgoer.

"Well," Reagan responded after hearing the message, "I think I'll meet with him."

With such unusual access to world leaders, Andreas and ADM had also become an important source of intelligence for Washington. He channeled information about world markets to the Agriculture Department; his tips about opportunities overseas often arrived at the Commerce Department. His briefings even reached the White House and the State Department.

But the most important—and most confidential—of Andreas's government contacts were with the American intelligence and law-enforcement communities. The CIA and other government intelligence agencies developed particularly close ties with Andreas and his company. Often, at the end of meetings with foreign leaders, Andreas would pass detailed notes to the government for review. Briefings flowed both ways; ADM often relied on information from the intelligence world for meetings with foreign dignitaries.

Andreas's relationship with federal law enforcement, particularly

the FBI, was more complex. He and his company were financially supportive of law-enforcement causes. Still, for some agents, there were
lingering questions about ADM's commitment to the law. Enough
agents were around from the Watergate days to remember Andreas's
role, one questionable enough to lead to charges. Then there were the
cases against ADM itself: In 1978 the company pleaded no contest to
charges that it fixed prices on contracts in the Food for Peace program;
in 1981, the Feds had filed an ultimately unsuccessful civil case charging it with fixing the prices of fructose.

On top of that, whenever ADM executives chose to cooperate with
the Bureau, they seemed to always demand the right to set the terms.
One episode with ADM quickly entered FBI lore. In the mid-1980s,
Andreas became convinced that his company was being cheated by
dishonest traders at the Chicago commodities exchanges. Dwayne
sought the FBI's help and agreed to participate in a sting operation to
catch dishonest traders. Agents traveled to Decatur and trained in how
to trade. Then, they were sent out on the exchange floors, wired with
recorders to tape the misdeeds of others. Andreas was delighted with
the plan, which was known to only a handful of executives.

Such secrets could not be kept for long. Dwayne's son, Mick, who
ran ADM's trading operation, heard everything and hit the ceiling.
ADM's relationship with the exchanges had long been strained. By sic-
cing the Feds on them, Dwayne had run the risk of shutting ADM out
of business there in the future. Mick demanded that the agents—who
by then were working on the exchange floor—no longer pose as ADM
employees.

The sting operation continued, but the agents could no longer rely
on ADM for cover. The decision angered some at the FBI, which had
already invested enormous sums of money in the investigation.

Years later, in 1991, some of that anger became suspicion. The
FBI's Chicago office had heard that ADM's treasurer, Thomas Frankel,
had been involved in financial irregularities. ADM had done its best to
keep the information secret, but by September of that year admitted
that *something* had happened. Company officials disclosed that they
had uncovered more than $6 million in trading losses dating back
years and that Frankel was resigning. Fraudulent trading records were
discovered, and the total losses eventually exceeded more than $14
million. But when the Bureau investigated, ADM dragged its feet on
providing information, crippling the case. It was an unusual response
from a potential crime victim and left agents scratching their heads.

Some couldn't help but wonder whether ADM and Andreas had something to hide.

With suspicions running deep, one thing seemed clear: If Andreas ever again thought his company was the victim of a crime, he probably would not turn to the FBI for help. By the early 1990s, Dwayne Andreas had the power to go elsewhere.

———

Allen Andreas's phone rang in his cavernous London town house sometime after seven P.M. It was October 1992. Darkness had already settled over London, but Allen, who oversaw ADM operations in Europe, had more work ahead of him that night. He picked up the phone.

"Do you still have your friends in Europe?"

There had been no introductions, no pleasantries. But Allen immediately recognized the voice of his uncle, Dwayne Andreas. Something important had to be up. Dwayne had never become comfortable speaking openly over the telephone, particularly on overseas calls. Now, here he was, asking about Allen's "friends"—an oblique code for his London contacts at the Central Intelligence Agency.

"Yes, I do," Allen replied.

"We have a problem," Dwayne said. "Mick will call you about it. I want you to speak with him."

With that, the call ended. But Dwayne's terse, transatlantic message was clear: Something serious was happening in Decatur. Whatever problem Mick was about to discuss, Dwayne wanted the CIA to take care of it.

Allen placed the telephone back in its cradle. Almost before he could pull his hand away, it rang again. Mick and Dwayne had obviously coordinated their telephone calls for maximum impact.

"Hey, Mick," Allen said. "What's happening?"

"We've got a potentially serious situation going on here," Mick said. "We need your help."

For the next few minutes, Mick repeated everything he had heard about the Fujiwara call. The story left Allen's head spinning. Maybe Fujiwara was telling the truth. Maybe it was some sort of con. Maybe Ajinomoto had concocted a sting to get ADM in trouble with the Japanese government. Whatever the answer, Allen understood why his relatives were concerned.

"We don't know what's going on, but obviously there are implications for Japanese-American relations," Mick said. "Dad and I talked it over, and we'd like you to call your friends at the Agency."

Now Allen understood why they were calling him. Dwayne and Mick didn't know whom they could trust. Allen was family, a lawyer, and had ties to the CIA. There was no one better situated to help.

Regardless of what the Agency did, Mick said, the most important thing was to get the plant on-line. If that meant buying the "superbug" from Fujiwara, so be it. Maybe the CIA could help in the transaction.

"We're ready to do it," Mick said. "Tell the Agency we're ready to give them the money to put into escrow to help get this plant up and running."

Minutes later, Allen had heard enough. "I'll take care of it," he told his cousin. He hung up.

Allen checked the time. It was too late to phone his CIA contact; morning would be soon enough. He wanted to meet in person to explain the fantastic story emerging from Decatur. It seemed a simple plan.

He had no idea of the events he was about to set into motion.

CHAPTER 2

Dean Paisley, a Supervisory Special Agent with the FBI, stepped off the elevator on the fourth floor of the Illinois Business Center and walked toward an unmarked wooden door. He punched a five-digit code into a keypad on the wall, taking care not to drop the bag of fast food in his other hand. The door's electronic lock clicked open on his first try.

Behind the locked door was a stairwell, but Paisley did not head to another floor. Instead, he walked past the stairs through a second door, into the FBI Field Office in Springfield. Striding down the hallway, Paisley looked like Central Casting's idea of an FBI supervisor. At forty-nine, he was still handsome and in the physical shape of a far younger man. Only his hair showed signs of age, with specks of gray sprinkling its sandy coloring.

It was the afternoon of November 3, 1992, Election Day. As always, the election had caused minor disruptions at the Springfield office. A group of agents was on standby to handle claims of voting fraud that might come in, and various staffers had requested time off to go to the polls. With the office humming with activity, Paisley had decided to have a late lunch at his desk. On days like this, he figured, it made sense to be around the office.

He passed some framed prints hung on the hallway's odd-looking blue-green wallpaper. The decorations were the most obvious sign of the changes that had been taking place in Springfield. The former office director—the Special Agent in Charge—had insisted on a number of unpopular rules, such as one forbidding decorations in work areas. But he had been replaced a few months back by Donald Stukey, an agent who made his name chasing spies in Washington. Stukey cleaned house, bringing in a new assistant to oversee daily operations and discarding many of his predecessor's edicts. Office morale had gone up faster than the new wall decor.

Paisley greeted his secretary, Barbara Howard, before continuing to his office. Taking a seat at his desk, he unwrapped his food, casually scanning papers. He was finishing his lunch when Howard called to him.

"Hey, Dean. Ed Worthington, the ASAC from Chicago, is on line two for you." Howard had been around the Bureau long enough to know that even though *Special Agent in Charge* was shorthanded by its letters, *S-A-C*, the title of that supervisor's assistant was always pronounced as a single word, *ay-sack*.

Paisley punched line two. He knew Worthington well. Both were the contacts in their offices for American intelligence agencies that needed help from the FBI. Because of that responsibility, Paisley had met Worthington at a number of Bureau meetings.

"Hey, Eddie, how's it going up there?"

"Pretty well," Worthington replied. "Listen, I just got a strange call from the Agency. They gave me some information, and I want to run it by you."

The Agency. Worthington didn't need to explain further. The CIA. Paisley cleared a space on his desk for a pad of paper and began taking notes.

The story Worthington told was bizarre. The CIA had received a telephone call from ADM. Worthington's CIA contact had told him—incorrectly—that Dwayne Andreas had placed the call himself. Apparently, ADM was the target of industrial espionage and extortion by someone from Japan. For reasons Worthington couldn't fathom, Andreas had turned to the CIA for help. The agency concluded that the matter fell under the authority of American law enforcement. A CIA official had called Worthington to route it to the FBI. The CIA already had told the Andreases of its decision, Worthington said. Mick Andreas was now waiting for a call from the Bureau.

Worthington didn't mention that, just a few minutes before, he had provided the same information to John Hoyt, Springfield's new ASAC. Worthington had warned Hoyt that his people should be careful; ADM had a history with the Chicago office of being difficult, particularly in a recent investigation into possible fraud by ADM's former treasurer. Hoyt had thanked Worthington for the information and passed the call onto Paisley, the supervisor of Squad Three, which covered Decatur and other central Illinois towns.

Worthington finished with Paisley in about five minutes. He left out his warnings about ADM. Telling Hoyt was enough.

"Okay, Eddie," Paisley said, laying down his pen. "If there ends up being anything in this that involves Chicago, we'll get back to you on it."

Paisley hung up. Worthington's information had been sparse, but already Paisley thought this had the potential of being a lot more interesting than the usual bank robberies and drug busts.

A case agent would be needed to handle the nuts and bolts of the investigation, and Paisley knew the perfect person. For nine years, Brian Shepard had manned the FBI's Decatur Resident Agency, or R.A., which reported through Springfield. Shepard knew the people at ADM, and they knew him. With a little luck, Paisley figured, Shepard could wrap up this case and be back to his regular duties in a matter of weeks.

He was wrong.

It could be argued that Brian Shepard got his start as an FBI agent by parking cars. After he spent three years as an aide in the documents section of the Bureau's laboratory, his agent's application had been accepted. He emerged from training in March 1976 as a newly minted Special Agent, eager for his first big assignment. To his dismay, he was dispatched to the Bureau's New York City Field Office, widely reputed as one of the most difficult places to work. On his first day, Shepard learned part of the reason why: Traveling to work by a maze of buses and subways, he got lost. He finally rolled into the office at nine o'clock, forty-five minutes late by FBI standards. A mortified Shepard was sent to his desk, where he shuffled paper and tried to look busy. Finally, he received the word that he had been waiting for: His supervisor wanted to see him. Shepard was certain he was about to receive his first case.

But when Shepard arrived at his supervisor's office, the man wouldn't look at him. Instead, he sat with his back to the new agent, staring out the office window. Staying in that position, the supervisor told Shepard about his task. It was important, the supervisor said, and if Shepard did a good job, he might be allowed to do it on a frequent basis. Shepard was full of anticipation until the supervisor handed over his car keys. Parking rules in New York City were difficult, the supervisor said. To avoid a ticket, his car needed to be moved a few times a day.

Shepard never asked if the degrading assignment had been

punishment for being late and handled it without complaint for several weeks. Eventually, he dug himself out of the hole and started working with what the agents called FCI, foreign counterintelligence. For the next several years, Shepard hunted spies in New York. He and his wife, Diana, moved to Matawan, a New Jersey suburb that was an hour's commute from the office. For seven years, Shepard reluctantly made the trek by public transportation. That was another black mark for the city, as far as Shepard was concerned: He was crazy about cars but lived in a place where driving was often a luxury. Finally, in 1983 Shepard was eligible for a transfer. He saw an opening in Decatur and snapped it up.

Decatur was perfect for him. Shepard was originally from nearby Kankakee and his wife was also from the area. In many ways, he was an all-American boy, born on the Fourth of July in 1949. Despite the years in New York, Shepard had never stopped considering the Midwest as home. That was the place he and Diana wanted to raise their two young children. For Brian, going back had an added bonus: He would finally be able to start chasing criminals. With only three agents in the Decatur office, every kind of case landed on his desk, from financial frauds to bank robberies, from extortions to drug investigations.

In no time, Shepard became a fixture in the dusty prairie town. It boasted of many labels—the Pride of the Prairie, the Soybean Capital of the World, the First Illinois Home of Abraham Lincoln—but its community spirit did not translate into personal pretension. Shepard fit in perfectly. With his rumpled, off-the-rack suits and inexpensive ties, he might have been taken as a down-on-his-luck salesman rather than as a member of the nation's top law-enforcement agency. But in Decatur, the look suited him fine. Tall and slender, he had the image of Decatur's own Gary Cooper, always available at high noon to combat the black hats.

By 1992 Shepard was a forty-three-year-old veteran agent who knew most everyone in town. His early partners in the office had long since retired; Brian Shepard *was* the FBI as far as Decatur was concerned. As an investigator, he was no chessmaster, just a by-the-book agent who studiously immersed himself in the details of a case. To the dismay of supervisors, Shepard's case briefings often overflowed with those details; more than a few eyeballs had rolled in Springfield on hearing Shepard utter his trademark opening "to make a long story short." He almost never did.

Like any agent in Decatur, Shepard had occasional contact with ADM; some of his neighbors even worked there. One tie to the company was through Mark Cheviron, a former member of the Decatur police department turned ADM's chief of security. Cheviron had received training from the FBI's National Academy, a program for local law enforcement. Some years Shepard crossed paths with Cheviron and other executives at ADM's local cookout. Shepard didn't know the executives well, but he knew them well enough.

So when he heard from Dean Paisley about ADM's troubles, Shepard wasn't surprised to get the assignment. Paisley's information—the Worthington call, the CIA, the extortion—was enough for Shepard to know this case would be his top priority. Paisley said arrangements had been made to meet Mick Andreas the following day; both he and Stukey would be there.

Shepard hung up, looking forward to the next day. This extortion case was sure to be interesting.

That night, Jim Shafter, the personal attorney for the Andreas family, settled into bed early. It had been a tough day, and Shafter had arrived at his home on North Country Club Road, on the shore of Lake Decatur, looking forward to an uneventful evening—dinner with his wife, Gigi, followed by watching some television in bed before going to sleep.

About eight-thirty, Shafter was flipping through channels when the telephone rang on his bedside table. He put down the remote and reached for the phone.

He heard a deep voice that he recognized. "We've got a situation at the plant we need to deal with."

It was Mick Andreas. Shafter spoke with him frequently, often several times a day. It was not unusual for Mick to call him at home; they were next-door neighbors. But this time, he had no idea what Mick was talking about.

"What's up?"

Andreas told Shafter everything he had heard from Whitacre about the Japanese espionage and the extortion. Andreas gave no indication how he had learned the information, and Shafter didn't press him to find out. The lawyer was too taken aback.

"Who have you reviewed this with?" Shafter asked. "Does Reising know?"

No, Andreas replied, no one had told ADM's general counsel. "We decided that we shouldn't discuss it within the company."

Now, Andreas said, things were coming to a head. The FBI had learned about the case, and agents were coming to his house tomorrow to find out what he knew.

"I've been talking to Dad about it," Andreas said, "and we thought it might be more comfortable if you sit in on this meeting tomorrow."

Thank goodness. "It's my belief that any time you meet with government officials, it certainly makes sense to have legal counsel there," Shafter replied.

"Well, that's why I called."

There was one other thing, Andreas said. In the calls, Fujiwara had offered to sell ADM some sort of Ajinomoto "superbug" that would be resistant to virus contamination. If it would help bring an end to the millions that ADM was flushing away each month, it sounded like a good deal. The only problem was, they wouldn't be buying the bug from Ajinomoto, but from some rogue employee.

"Can we do that?" he asked.

It was at times like this that Shafter was glad Andreas felt comfortable calling him at home.

"Mick, this is just off the top of my head," Shafter said, "but hell, no."

The next day, at about one o'clock, Brian Shepard was sitting in his Bureau-issued car, parked near downtown Decatur, when his radio crackled to life.

"SI-14 to SI-122."

Hearing his call signal, SI-122, Shepard reached for the radio microphone. From those few words, he knew that Paisley and Stukey were close to the prearranged meeting place just off Route 121. Paisley, whose signal was SI-14, was telling Shepard to get ready.

"This is SI-122."

"Yeah, Bry, we're right here," Paisley said. "I see you already. Go ahead and lead the way."

Shepard pulled out, just ahead of Stukey and Paisley. Maintaining the forty-mile-per-hour speed limit, he drove past the 206-foot tower built by the A. E. Staley Manufacturing Company in 1929 as a tribute to the grain processor's employees and customers. Turning left, the cars crossed a bridge on Lake Decatur and turned onto North Country Club Road. They traveled another mile before finding Andreas's house and parking in his driveway.

The three agents stepped up to the entryway and rang the bell. The wooden double doors were opened by a man in his late forties, with glasses and thinning dark hair.

"Mr. Andreas?" Paisley asked.

"Yes?"

Paisley stuck out his hand.

"Dean Paisley, with the FBI. I talked to you on the phone yesterday."

"Oh yeah, come on in."

As they crossed the doorway, Paisley nodded toward Stukey and Shepard, introducing them.

"Good to meet you," Andreas said. "Everybody come on in and find a seat."

The men walked through the house. The agents glanced at the artwork, the expensive furniture, the family photos on the grand piano. Andreas ushered them across the living room, through a pair of open French doors, and into a large addition built onto the back. The room had a bar, an oversized television, and a high ceiling rising up two stories. Huge windows afforded a gorgeous view of Lake Decatur and the Andreas pool house. On one side of the room, a dining table held pots of coffee, tea, and a basket of rolls.

A doughy, balding man was sitting at the table. He stood as soon as the agents walked in.

"This is my personal attorney, James Shafter," Andreas said. "I don't know if this is appropriate for him to be here, but he's a lawyer and he's a friend."

Stukey raised a hand. "Mr. Andreas," he said, "it's fine with us if Mr. Shafter stays here."

The men took their seats at the dining table. Shafter brought out a pen and notepad. Shepard pulled out a leather case, which held the pad he used to take notes. As case agent, he would dictate the notes for later transcription onto a form 302.

Andreas started speaking before the first question was asked. "A lot of what I'm about to say is only known by a few people at the company. It's been restricted to me, my father, Dwayne, my cousin Allen, Mr. Shafter here, and Mark Whitacre, one of our employees."

Speaking in a cool tone, Andreas explained the recent history of the lysine market. He told how the Japanese had controlled the business until ADM's entry a few years back. That had led the Japanese to drastically cut the price of lysine and close some plants. Eventually, ADM started experiencing contamination in the lysine fermenters. About that same time, ADM and some of the Japanese competitors had visited each other's plants.

Within days, Andreas said, Whitacre received a strange call from one of those visitors. Andreas no longer remembered Fujiwara's name but recalled every detail of the sabotage by Ajinomoto and the demand for $10 million. In the weeks since receiving that first call, he said, Whitacre had spoken to the Japanese executive just about every other day.

Andreas clasped his hands on the table. "Mark's got him talked down to six million." Three million would be paid to identify the saboteur; the rest would be for the superbug.

Still, the company was concerned. If ADM paid the money and took the bugs, Andreas said, the Japanese might take legal action or go to the newspapers, saying the microbes had been stolen. This whole thing, he suggested, might be just a sting designed to cripple ADM as a competitor by luring them into something illegal.

"Mr. Andreas, don't worry about that," Stukey said. "I'm granting you international immunity."

Shafter wasn't sure if Stukey was joking, but he didn't want Mick getting any wrong ideas. He scribbled something onto his notepad and slid it toward Andreas. Mick glanced at the paper. He saw a single word.

Bullshit!

Andreas said nothing. Shafter took back the note.

"ADM is willing to lose three million dollars to resolve this matter," Andreas continued. "But we can't pay the money directly. If there's a mole in the company, it might attract his attention. But my dad has told me that he's willing to personally guarantee any money paid to this Japanese guy if the United States Government puts up the cash initially."

Shepard studied Andreas as he spoke. He seemed businesslike and taciturn. He was describing this multimillion-dollar transaction with the government as though it was like any other business deal.

"Well, Mr. Andreas," Stukey said, "we obviously know who you are and who your father is. And this has the potential of being a truly international case. This is corporate espionage at the highest level. We want to do everything we can to work with you."

To start, Stukey said, they needed to interview Mark Whitacre. After all, he was the person who was receiving these calls from the Japanese executive.

"Do you know where Mr. Whitacre lives?" Stukey asked.

"I can tell you exactly where he lives," Andreas said. "He lives in the house my mom and dad used to live in. It's out in Moweaqua."

That house was almost symbolic of Whitacre's stirring personal history that was so well known around Decatur. Most everyone associated with ADM—the Andreases, Shafter, Jim Randall—had heard Whitacre tell the amazing story of his life: how he had been orphaned as a young boy in Ohio when his parents died in a car accident; how he had spent difficult times in a local orphanage, feeling unwanted; how he had been adopted by a wealthy man who owned a giant Ohio amusement park called King's Island. Whitacre had gone from having nothing to wanting for nothing. Now from a family worth millions, Whitacre seemed to have no need to work; he had been able to buy the old Andreas house when he first joined ADM. His work ethic, combined with his family's personal wealth, fascinated other executives.

"We'll need to go out there," Stukey said. "We obviously would like to tape one of these phone calls he's had with the Japanese."

Andreas told the agents to make any arrangements for Whitacre through Mark Cheviron, ADM's security chief. He would be fully briefed on this meeting.

Andreas paused, eyeing the agents. There was one more thing he wanted out on the table, he said. He was of course aware of ADM's role in the FBI investigation years before at the Chicago futures exchanges.

"It's also no secret that I didn't like it when I found out about it," Andreas said. "To me, it's repugnant to tape people when they don't know it. In this case, I don't want my people taped unless they know about it or I know about it ahead of time."

Stukey assured Andreas that he had nothing to worry about. Still, the sudden demand seemed odd. The FBI had come to help fight off a sabotage effort. The only executives who might be taped would be those suspected of damaging ADM. Why would Andreas be against that? What was he worried about?

The FBI. God, no.

Later that day, Mark Whitacre sat in his office, feeling numb. He had just emerged from a meeting with Mick Andreas and Mark Cheviron, where they had told him that the FBI wanted to speak with him about the Fujiwara calls. The two had made it clear that they didn't trust the Bureau and gave Whitacre explicit instructions on how to handle himself.

Until then, Whitacre had heard nothing about the Andreases' decision to inform the government about Fujiwara. Instead, he had been listening to Mick's instructions to string Fujiwara along, to negotiate him down in price. From all appearances, ADM seemed ready to pay the money and be done with it.

But Whitacre had been fooled. Now, ADM expected him to meet with the FBI and answer their questions.

Answer their questions! Jesus!

Whitacre shook his head; he had never felt so nervous. Since learning of the interview, Whitacre had ranted, threatened to quit, but got nowhere. He was petrified of the FBI agents. There were too many things that they could find out. Things that could destroy him. Things that could destroy ADM.

Whitacre paced in his office. The timing of this was so bad. His career had been coming together at ADM. He had successfully overseen completion of the lysine plant. He was a division president. And now, just in the last few weeks, his situation had improved even more. The company had announced a management reorganization, naming Mick to the title of vice-chairman. At the same time, Whitacre had been named a corporate vice president, one of the youngest in ADM history. Wall Street had correctly interpreted the moves as Dwayne Andreas's clear designation of Mick as the heir apparent. In a few years, he was almost certain to take ADM's top job, and Whitacre felt confident that he had a shot at being number two. Now, all that was at risk. All for this crazy interview.

Whitacre glanced at the telephone. He needed to call his wife, Ginger. He was sure she could help him think this through.

Ginger had always been there for him, since they met as teenagers on a bus at Little Miami High School in Ohio. The oldest daughter of factory workers, Ginger was the picture of solid Midwestern stock, the high-school homecoming queen who played whatever hand life dealt her. In those days, Mark lived up to his then-nickname "Corky," as he popped off in different directions. Throughout high school, he broke up with Ginger repeatedly, but she always took him back, convinced that someday her patience would pay off. Finally, in 1979, a few years after graduation, the couple married. When Mark pursued his doctorate at Cornell, Ginger went with him. In the years since, she never complained as Mark moved from job to job—from Ralston Purina in St. Louis to Degussa Corporation in New York and eventually to Degussa's world headquarters near Frankfurt. Before leaving the country, they had adopted two children, Tanya and Billy, and not long after gave birth to a third, Alexander. Their family had grown from two to five people in one year.

The move to Decatur had been difficult for the family. Mark, caught up in his new job, was no longer as attentive as he had been. Also, Ginger felt uncomfortable around some ADM executives, who struck her as crass and too impressed with their own wealth. Still, she understood that the job was too great an opportunity to pass up. As always, she stood by Mark.

Now, as Mark called home, he only hoped that Ginger could be strong for him again.

Ginger was stepping through the living room when the telephone rang. Almost as soon as she picked it up, she could tell Mark was in a panic. His normal breezy cheeriness was gone, replaced by a tone of desperation. Before she could say anything, his story spilled out. The FBI was snooping around ADM. His boss had told him to talk with an agent.

Ginger sat down, uneasy. Her experience with law enforcement was limited; none of her family had ever had a run-in with the police. To her, the FBI was some sort of fearful monolith, one that clearly scared Mark.

"I'm really uncomfortable about this," he said. "There are lots of things going on. I could be asked some tough questions."

Ginger wasn't sure what Mark was talking about and didn't think she should ask. But she knew he had better not lie to the FBI.

"Whatever you do, no matter what's going on, just be honest with them and tell the truth," she said. "Tell the truth no matter what the truth is."

Brian Shepard checked the time again. It was late that same afternoon, and he was getting tired of waiting. Already, he had received two calls from ADM postponing Whitacre's interview. There were plenty of excuses; Whitacre was busy, something had come up. Shepard wasn't sure of the problem, but he couldn't shake the sense that something odd was going on.

But interviewing Whitacre was critical to the next stages of the FBI's investigative plan. The trick was to use the prospect of a multimillion-dollar payment to lure Fujiwara to the United States, where he could be arrested. A meeting would be set up between Whitacre and the Japanese executive; the FBI would be there, recording every word. Under the current plan, Whitacre would turn over $3 million if Fujiwara revealed the saboteur's identity and other information. Fujiwara would be allowed to leave that meeting and then be invited back to deliver the superbug for another payment from Whitacre. Once Fujiwara handed it over, the FBI would arrest him.

For the plan to work, Shepard had to learn everything that Whitacre knew about Fujiwara. That interview was going to take time—and now it was starting late. Shepard decided to call Diana and let her know he would be late for dinner.

In a place like Decatur, the slightest whisper can rapidly echo around town into a shout. A saboteur at ADM, particularly one in a high-level position, had a better-than-even chance of learning about the investigation if word of Whitacre's meeting with the FBI leaked out. So Jim Shafter decided to go all out in protecting the interests of his best client.

Late in the afternoon, Shafter made the rounds of his law firm, Kehart, Shafter & Hughes, telling everyone to head home. There were some people coming who needed privacy, he said. The staff started clearing out of their offices on the fifth floor of the Citizen's Bank building in Decatur. They were happy to take advantage of an early Thursday.

With nothing to do but wait, Shafter started a pot of coffee and checked the conference room. Before the staff had time to leave, a receptionist buzzed. Whitacre and Cheviron were waiting in the lobby.

Shafter hustled out to the front. No one was supposed to have seen them arrive. After all the delays, *now* they were early. When he reached the lobby, Shafter was surprised at their appearance. Whitacre was pacing and sweating. Cheviron seemed frustrated.

The men said nothing until they were in Shafter's private office. Whitacre resumed his pacing, unable to sit down. It struck Shafter as bizarre.

This guy is more than kind of nervous. What was the matter with him?

"Mark, you don't have a damn thing to worry about," Cheviron said, in a tone that made it clear he was repeating himself.

Whitacre looked to Shafter. "Is it okay for me to meet with them?" he asked.

Shafter stared at Whitacre, trying to gauge what was going on. When he spoke, his tone was calm.

"Look, Mark, let me clear one thing up for you. I represent the company here; I don't represent you. If you want a lawyer, we'll get you a lawyer. I can only give the company advice, and what I can tell you is that the company has requested that you meet with the FBI and cooperate with them."

Whitacre showed no reaction. "Fine, that's fine," he replied. "I'm a loyal employee."

A minute later, the receptionist buzzed again. Special Agent Shepard from the FBI was out front. So much for sending everyone home first.

Shafter brought Cheviron and Whitacre to the reception area and escorted everyone to the windowless conference room. It was as private a place as could be found in Decatur on short notice. Shafter excused himself and headed back to his office.

The situation was odd for Shepard. Cheviron had asked to sit in on the interview, a request that left the agent uncomfortable. Usually, FBI interviews are conducted privately. At times, a witness will bring along a lawyer, but no one else. That way, the witness could be assured any information would remain confidential. That seemed particularly important in this case. But Shepard decided not to make waves. ADM was the victim; if the company wanted Cheviron along, Shepard could agree, even if he didn't like it.

Shepard studied Whitacre. With his unlined, boyish face and blond hair, he looked as innocent as an altar boy. Still, Whitacre seemed anxious. For people in law enforcement, the reaction was not too unusual. Most everyone interviewed by an FBI agent or a prosecutor is, one way or another, probably having a bad day. Shepard began by trying to calm Whitacre.

"Let me introduce myself," he said amiably. "My name's Brian Shepard. I'm a Special Agent with the FBI."

Shepard put out his hand. Whitacre took it, feeling Shepard's strong grip.

"Hey," he said. "I'm Mark Whitacre."

"I met with Michael Andreas this morning, and he told me you were president of the Bioproducts Division," Shepard said. "We hope you can help us out. I'm not sure where this case will be going, but I want to listen to what you have to say."

The men took their seats. Already, Whitacre felt more at ease. Shepard wasn't what he had expected. Maybe this wasn't going to be like on television, where some growling G-man sweats information out of the reluctant witness. Instead, Shepard seemed down-to-earth, more neighborly than confrontational.

Whitacre leaned forward in his chair as he told the story about

Fujiwara. Shepard listened, taking notes and occasionally asking questions. After the first thirty minutes, Shafter stuck his head in the room. He was heading home, he said, and asked the men to shut off the coffeepot and lock up when they left.

In no time, Shepard's notes contained the broad outline of the case. Whitacre described how the Ajinomoto executives had been invited to Decatur so that ADM could persuade them to shut down their American plants. He told of the bizarre phone call he had received from Fujiwara on his off-premises office extension that ADM had installed at his house. He discussed his subsequent conversation with Mick Andreas and the efforts to haggle Fujiwara down in price. Since then, Fujiwara had called every few days.

"He told me that he wanted his payments deposited by wire transfer to numbered bank accounts in Switzerland and the Caribbean," Whitacre said.

"When was your last contact with him?"

"Three days ago. He said he would call three or four days after that. But I think he's getting suspicious, since he hasn't gotten a positive response from us yet. I've dragged this out as long as I can. If we don't get back to him soon, he may back out."

Whitacre said he expected to receive the next Fujiwara call that very evening. He mentioned two ADM executives who previously worked for Ajinomoto; perhaps they were the saboteurs. Shepard said he needed a phone directory for the Bioproducts Division so that he could obtain numbers for those executives. As the meeting wrapped up, Shepard said an agent would be coming by Whitacre's house with a recording device to tape the next Fujiwara call. But first, Shepard said, he needed approvals. It might take another day.

Sometime after eight-thirty, more than three hours after it began, the meeting broke up. Whitacre and Shepard shook hands again before stepping out of the room.

Whitacre seemed delighted to be going home.

"Now my family's being threatened! I can't put up with this!"

Whitacre was rambling, nearly hysterical. He had called Cheviron at home, shortly after leaving Shafter's office. From the instant Cheviron heard his voice, he knew something strange must have happened.

"Mark, what are you talking about?" Cheviron asked. "Calm down."

"They're threatening my daughter! I don't want to talk to Fujiwara anymore. This thing is affecting my family. It's not right."

Cheviron pushed Whitacre to explain what had happened. The story came rushing out.

As soon as he had arrived home, Whitacre said, he had heard horrible news. His fifteen-year-old daughter, Tanya, had received a call at her boarding school in Indiana. An Asian-sounding man was on the line, telling her to write down a message. The man had told her that Fujiwara would no longer wait. He wanted a deal now; he wanted his multimillion-dollar payment. If that didn't happen, the man had told her, *she* would be in trouble.

Whitacre was wild as he told the story. "I'm not going to be involved in this anymore! I don't want anything to do with it."

In an even tone, Cheviron tried to calm Whitacre. Eventually, they agreed to talk again the next day.

The ADM security chief hung up, bewildered. The problems stemming from this Fujiwara situation were escalating. But this time Whitacre's story was illogical. Why would anybody threaten his daughter? How would the Japanese even know to call her? It was an improbable, amateurish move, coming at a time when Whitacre desperately wanted this investigation to end.

Cheviron thought Mark Whitacre was lying.

The next morning, November 5, Cheviron left his house early, driving in the gray half-light of dawn toward the belching smokestacks at ADM. This was going to be a busy day. After Whitacre's call the night before, Cheviron had kept working. Mick Andreas had heard from Whitacre about the call to his daughter, and then phoned his security chief. Mick had said he wanted Cheviron to brief him and his father first thing that morning on everything Whitacre was saying.

Not long after arriving at the office, Cheviron was called to a meeting with Mick and Dwayne. He told them about his doubts, and the men decided that ADM's top lawyer, Rick Reising, needed to be involved. For the rest of the morning, the senior management of the company shuttled from meeting to meeting.

The strangest was between Reising, Cheviron, and Whitacre. Gently, Whitacre was pressed to run through the story of the phone call to his daughter. It sounded less believable the second time around. Cheviron made it clear he thought it was all a lie, pushing Whitacre with questions. How did they find his daughter? Why go to the trouble? If they wanted to threaten Whitacre, why not call him directly?

Finally, Whitacre broke down.

"All right, I'm sorry," he said. "I made it up."

Reising and Cheviron stared at Whitacre as he explained his lie. He was scared of the FBI, he said. He didn't want to be part of this investigation. Somehow, he had gotten it into his mind that if ADM thought his family was threatened, they would pay Fujiwara or tell the FBI to go away. Either way, the whole mess would end. He saw now it had been a stupid idea; it was just a sign of how upset he was.

Whitacre finished speaking. An uncomfortable silence hung in the air.

Reising told Whitacre that he and Cheviron needed to speak alone for a moment. Whitacre headed out, closing the door behind him.

About an hour later, James Randall, the ADM president, stormed in to Cheviron's office burning with anger.

"Whitacre came by my office," Randall said. "He says you're out to get him, that you want him fired."

Cheviron stared back at Randall, floored. He asked Randall what was going on.

"Whitacre's all excited," Randall said. "He's talking about sabotage in the plant."

The secret was out. Cheviron asked Randall what he thought. Randall scoffed. Even though Whitacre was the lysine expert, Randall didn't believe the Japanese had managed to get into the plant.

"There's no sabotage," he said. "We just don't know what we're doing. It's start-up problems."

Randall was particularly contemptuous of Fujiwara's promise to deliver some superbug. Even Dwayne was saying that once ADM obtained the bug during the FBI sting, the plant's problems would be solved. The whole idea was ridiculous, Randall said.

"They couldn't even transport the damn bug unless it was at extreme temperatures," he scoffed.

Over the next few minutes, Cheviron answered Randall's questions. Finally, Randall calmed down and left. Cheviron dialed Mick Andreas and told him that Randall now knew about the investigation. Mick muttered, "Okay," and hung up.

A few hours later, Cheviron received a call from Shepard. The agent said that he was making the arrangements to have a recording device placed on Whitacre's telephone. To get the recording underway, he said, Whitacre should contact a Springfield agent named Tom Gibbons. Cheviron promised to pass along the message.

Cheviron dialed Whitacre's extension and repeated Shepard's message.

"All right," Whitacre said, sounding angry. "I'll call him."

He hung up without another word.

Ginger Whitacre stepped into the crowded formal dining room at the Country Club of Decatur and looked for her husband. It was just after six P.M. that same day. Most of the tables were filled, but Ginger found Mark and his guests quickly. He saw her, clad in one of her nicest dresses, and stood to greet her.

The dinner had been planned for some time. An ADM vendor was visiting Decatur with his wife. Whitacre had a close relationship with the man; after hearing the family enjoyed horses, the vendor had presented the Whitacres with an expensive riding saddle.

Dinner was relaxed and elegant, with wine and laughter flowing freely. Late in the meal, Ginger excused herself to make a trip to the ladies' room. As she stood, placing her napkin on the table, Mark reached out with a business card in his hand.

"Here's that phone number you wanted," he said.

Ginger smiled as she took the card, uncertain what he was talking about. She headed past the dining room's entryway and looked in her palm. She was holding one of Mark's business cards for ADM. She flipped the card over and felt her heart drop as she read words written in Mark's familiar scrawl.

The FBI is coming by the house tonight at 10:00.

With all the back and forth that day, Mark had not been able to tell Ginger what was going on. He had spoken to the FBI repeatedly, trying to schedule a time for them to stop by. He had finally agreed to allow someone to come over to the house once dinner was over. Shepard would hook up the device himself.

Our house. Ginger felt a chill. Over the past two days, Mark had given her some hints about what was bothering him. Nothing in much detail, but enough to worry her. She had hoped that the previous day's interview was going to be the end of it. Now, some agent would be coming out to their home, standing with them, probably asking them questions. Ginger could not think of the last time she had been so frightened.

Ginger returned to the table with a smile plastered on her face. She tried to keep the mood light, to laugh at the jokes, to have a good time. But she could not stop thinking about the FBI agent out there right now, getting ready to visit her home.

Dinner broke up just before nine o'clock. In the parking lot, the guests joined Mark in his Town Car for a lift back to the Decatur Club, a nearby building where ADM owned an apartment. Ginger said her good-byes, climbed into her Grand Cherokee, and started the drive home.

Minutes later, her car phone rang. She knew it was Mark calling from his car. He had just dropped off their guests and finally had a chance to talk.

"This is really going to be something," Mark said over the car speaker, sounding terribly nervous again. "I don't know what to do."

"I know what you're going to do. You're going to tell the truth."

"You don't understand. These guys are more powerful than the government. I'm more scared of ADM than I am of the FBI."

"If I were you, I'd be more fearful of the FBI," Ginger replied. "You don't mess with the FBI. ADM's nothing compared with the FBI."

As far as Ginger was concerned, ADM was just another company. But Mark said she didn't understand how powerful ADM was and what it could do.

"I could tell Brian Shepard everything I know, and tomorrow morning I'll probably be fired from ADM, and they're a lot more powerful than the government."

Ginger sighed. "Mark, you only have one choice. Don't worry about ADM. You have to tell everything."

As she spoke, Ginger passed a thick, wooden sign. On it, red letters blared, "Welcome to Moweaqua. The One and Only." Ginger paused as she pulled onto Main Street in Moweaqua. Her husband's nervousness had made her more wary.

"Mark," she said gently, trying to mask her concern. "Have you broken the law?"

Whitacre was quick to answer. "No," he said. "I haven't broken the law at all."

"It doesn't matter if you did or not," Ginger said. "You need to tell me everything."

"Ginger, I'm telling you, I haven't done anything wrong. I haven't broken the law. Definitely."

There was a pause. Ginger said she was near home.

"Okay," Mark said. "I'll see you there soon."

Ginger disconnected the call and pulled into the driveway, stopping in front of the house. She needed to check on the children, then drive their housekeeper home. After that, Ginger would have nothing else to do but come back to the house, sit with her husband, and wait for the arrival of the FBI.

• • •

Moweaqua was a town that flourished on a promise that became a tragedy. It was founded in 1852 by Michael Snyder, the operator of a local sawmill, and for thirty years grew steadily. But it was not until 1886, when settlers discovered vast coal reserves buried beneath the Illinois countryside, that Moweaqua was transformed by an influx of new money. It seemed destined for giddy economic growth.

Those hopes were dashed on Christmas Eve, 1932, at the height of the Great Depression. That day, dozens of miners were hard at work beneath the earth, heaving their pickaxes and shovels in the search for coal. Many were putting in extra hours, hoping to raise a few dollars to pay for Christmas presents.

Unknown to everyone, the mine was filling with methane gas. In a horrible instant, the miners' open-flame carbide lights sparked a deafening explosion. Those not killed instantly were buried beneath tons of earth. Fifty-four miners died, leaving behind thirty-three widows and seventy fatherless children in the small town.

The great disaster closed the mines for years, choking the local economy and dousing its aspirations with misery. But remnants of that promising time still stood in town, solid homes and buildings constructed when Moweaqua seemed blessed with limitless possibilities and luck.

Chief among them was "the Old Homestead," a Georgian Colonial mansion first constructed by Michael Snyder. During Moweaqua's days of prosperity, the home had been expanded with two-story pillars and several porches. Nestled between acres of cornfields, the property cemented Moweaqua's connection to Decatur's growth when Dwayne Andreas bought it in his early days at ADM. That link continued with the arrival of Mark Whitacre in 1989. The Old Homestead seemed likely to remain something of a landmark to the history of Moweaqua and its 1,900 residents for decades to come.

There was little doubt that on the night of November 5, 1992, Brian Shepard would find his way to the house. Anyone out walking in the cool autumn air in Moweaqua that night would be able to direct the agent to the Old Homestead, a quarter-mile off Main Street.

About ten P.M., Shepard approached a blinking red light in the center of Moweaqua. He turned right, passing a series of modest homes. As he headed west, large maple trees and bushes obscured Whitacre's house. The two-story home—with multiple white awnings, pillars, and decks—was visible only in spots where dense foliage had never grown. Finally, the bright interior lights of the house cut through the darkness. Shepard turned onto the driveway, passing a black gate supported by brick pillars.

Inside, Mark and Ginger were upstairs in the master bedroom, where they had continued discussing the impending FBI visit for another half an hour. Mark had opened up a bit, telling her details of what he knew. Ginger was more convinced that he should talk.

"Just tell them everything," she said. "We'll just leave. I don't like what this company has been doing to you. This is a chance to go somewhere else."

Mark, sitting on the bed, looked up at her. "I may tell them at some point, but not now. Right now I'm going to follow the company line."

Ginger's face was a mask of determination.

"Mark," she said firmly. "If you don't tell them, I will."

The room fell silent. Mark stared at her; he just wasn't ready. He needed more time.

"I can't," he said softly. "Not now."

At that moment, Shepard's car headlights appeared in the bedroom window as he pulled up the driveway. Together, Mark and Ginger headed downstairs.

Shepard knocked lightly, and Mark opened the door. Shepard was dressed in khaki pants, a sports shirt, and a windbreaker. In his hand, he held a case—the recording device for the telephone was inside.

"Good evening, Mr. Shepard," Mark said.

"Call me Brian," Shepard replied.

Mark invited Shepard in and introduced him to Ginger. Shepard shook her hand. He apologized for the hour, saying he would be done in a few minutes.

Shepard noticed that the Whitacres seemed nervous. In some ways, Mark appeared worse than he had the previous night. Perhaps if he just installed the recorder and went on his way, they would feel better.

"Where's that line where you're getting the calls?" Shepard asked. He was looking for the ADM off-premises extension that Whitacre had mentioned.

"The OPX line," Mark replied. "It's upstairs."

The two men headed to a large room adjoining the master bedroom. Whitacre led Shepard in, showing him a small telecommunications setup, with phones and a fax machine. Shepard brought out the recording device and hooked it up to the phone.

Downstairs, Ginger was straining to listen by the staircase. She wanted to be sure Mark opened up.

Five minutes after he had arrived, Shepard had returned to the front door, thanking the Whitacres for their time. Mark opened the door and Shepard walked out, crossing the porch toward his car.

Inside the doorway, Ginger looked at her husband.

"Are you going to say something?" she asked softly. "Or am I?"

Mark didn't respond and started closing the door. Shepard had almost reached his car.

Ginger turned away from her husband. She shoved past him, pushing open the door and heading outside.

"Brian!"

Shepard turned when Mark called his name.

"Yes?"

Mark took a few steps outside.

"You have a minute?"

The two men sat in darkness.

Whitacre had been too uncomfortable to talk inside. Sometime before, workmen had found multiple phone lines coming into the house—leftovers apparently, from the time Dwayne Andreas owned it. Mark and Ginger both feared that somehow ADM could listen to what they said. About the only place that seemed safe to have a conversation was inside Shepard's car.

Shepard sat in the driver's seat, with Whitacre beside him. The car was off; the brisk evening air chilled both men.

"There are things I know," Whitacre said. "But if I decide to tell you what's going on, could I be prosecuted for it?"

The sudden shift surprised Shepard. Whitacre was talking like a potential target instead of a victim.

"I can't provide you with immunity," Shepard replied. "But any information you tell me about your involvement in criminal activity would be discussed with the U.S. Attorney's office."

Whitacre stared forward. A moment passed.

"Everything I told you yesterday about Fujiwara was true, except one thing," Whitacre said. "I never received a call from him on my OPX line."

Shepard looked at Whitacre. This made no sense.

"Why did you tell me that you did?"

"Before I spoke with you, Mick Andreas and Mark Cheviron met with me. They coached me on what to say. They told me to tell you that the calls came in on my OPX line, instead of my home line."

"Why?"

Whitacre paused again. It was too late to turn back. He had made his decision.

"What I'm about to tell you involves something very large," he said. "This extortion attempt by Fujiwara is nothing compared to it."

Shepard said nothing.

"It involves price-fixing in the lysine business," Whitacre said. "I've been involved in several meetings with our Japanese and Korean competitors, where the sole purpose is to fix prices. I've been instructed to go by the company."

No one understood ADM's business philosophy, Whitacre said. "They always say, 'The competitors are our friends, and the customers are our enemies.'"

Struggling to see in the darkness, Shepard wrote down the phrase. His mind raced; he had never been involved in a price-fixing investigation. At that moment, he wasn't sure if the FBI handled such cases.

"That's why they wanted me to lie about the OPX line," Whitacre said. "Fujiwara's calling my home line. But so are the people we're fixing prices with."

Whitacre knew the FBI planned to check which executives had frequent calls to Japan. That would be strong evidence of the saboteur's identity.

"That scared me," Whitacre said. "You check those records, nobody's going to have more phone calls with Japan than me. That's the price-fixing."

Even though he was acting on ADM's instructions, Whitacre said, he knew he could have become the fall guy if Shepard stumbled onto the price-fixing.

Shepard thought through what Whitacre was saying.

"Who told you to participate in these talks?"

Whitacre answered in a clear voice.

"I'm doing this at the direction of Mick Andreas and Dwayne Andreas."

Ginger Whitacre, dressed in a nightgown and robe, looked down at her sleeping seven-year-old son, Alex. She rearranged the covers, making sure he stayed warm. Stepping away from his bed, she walked to the window. She could see Shepard's car from there.

They were still talking. Ginger had heard enough from the doorway to know Mark was finally ready to tell the truth. Just seeing him out in the car with Shepard lifted her fears from the past few days.

She headed out to the hallway. She knew her son probably wouldn't be sleeping in that bedroom much longer. After tonight, their time in Moweaqua was limited. The family almost certainly would have to move when Mark took a new job.

The conversation continued for hours. Shepard jotted notes as Whitacre spoke, but far fewer than during the previous day's interview. He had been taken off guard by this sudden confession.

In time, Whitacre veered into new topics, describing crimes at ADM beyond just price-fixing.

"We've been stealing microorganisms from other companies," he said. "Jim Randall, the president of the company, told me everything about it."

One theft, he told Shepard, involved a man named Michael Frein from International Minerals Corporation in Indiana. The story he had heard from Randall, Whitacre said, was that Frein had been paid to steal a bug from IMC and bring it with him to ADM. That, he added, was part of the reason he was so concerned during his first interview with Shepard. He feared Cheviron was there to make sure he didn't talk.

Other efforts were more involved. Months back, he said, Randall had told him to write up a list of people at Ajinomoto's plant in Eddyville, Iowa.

"When I gave the list to Randall, he told me Cheviron had arranged for some women to get friendly with these guys. He wanted technical questions the women could ask the guys on the list."

Shepard looked up from his notes. Women? Was ADM hiring prostitutes to conduct corporate espionage?

"What did they call these women?"

Whitacre looked at Shepard, puzzled. "They called them 'the women.'"

These conspiracies were the reason ADM was keeping a tight leash on the investigation, Whitacre said. For some reason, they seemed to feel confident that Shepard would never figure any of it out as long as things died down. To accomplish that, Whitacre said that he had been instructed to wave off Fujiwara.

"I called Fujiwara today," he said. "I told him not to call for a while because things were too hot."

Periodically, Shepard turned on his car, letting the heater warm them. At one point, he called his wife to explain that he had been delayed. Then, he returned to Whitacre, who slowly seemed to be transforming from a reluctant witness to an eager cooperator.

"Can you give me a tape recorder?" he asked. "I can prove this if you give me a tape recorder."

No, Shepard said. He needed approvals before sending someone out to tape. Whitacre persisted, saying he was also willing to take a polygraph test. Finally, after two in the morning, Whitacre finished.

"I want to thank you for being honest with me," Shepard said. "You've done the right thing. I'm going to need to go back and talk to my supervisors. But we'll be back in touch."

Whitacre expressed fears that Shepard would drop by ADM, asking questions about what he had said. No, Shepard said, their conversation was confidential.

"But when you go to work tomorrow, if they ask, tell them I did come here tonight," Shepard said. "Tell them I put the machine on and left." He should just act as if everything else was the same.

Whitacre nodded, thanking Shepard before leaving the car. Shepard watched him head inside, then turned the key in his ignition.

The agent pulled around the circular driveway. He turned left, heading home to Decatur, the town whose first citizen, Dwayne Andreas, was now the subject of a criminal investigation.

Dean Paisley woke first, before his wife. The bedroom telephone on a nearby dresser was ringing. He threw back the covers. Naked, he padded across the bedroom to the dresser and picked up the phone.

"Dean? This is Brian."

Paisley quickly shook off sleep. "Yeah, Brian, what's going on?"

"I just got back from talking to Whitacre."

Shepard paused.

"There's something much bigger going on here."

CHAPTER 3

The intercom buzzer on the desk of John Hoyt, the Assistant Special Agent in Charge for the Springfield FBI, sounded promptly at 9:30 the next morning, a Friday. It was Don Stukey, with word that Shepard had arrived to brief his bosses on the Whitacre interview. Hoyt scrambled out to the hall. He wanted to collect a few other supervisors to hear what Shepard had to say.

The Springfield supervisors were energized that morning. Already they had learned bits and pieces from Dean Paisley, enough to know that Shepard may have stumbled onto something big. It was just what the office needed. Historically, the headline-grabbing cases turned up in Chicago, leaving Springfield with something of an inferiority complex. Over the years, some in the Bureau had even suggested just shutting down Springfield. The case Paisley had described—if true—was sure to silence the critics and give the Springfield agents a much-needed boost in morale.

Hoyt gathered up Kevin Corr, the office's principal legal advisor, and Bob Anderson, the squad leader in charge of most white-collar cases. In less than a minute, the three men appeared in the doorway of Stukey's large, wood-paneled office. Shepard was already there, sitting beside Paisley on one end of a dark brown leather couch. Stukey was in a matching chair, talking with the two men.

Stukey looked up as Hoyt and the others walked in. "Why don't you guys find a spot?" he said.

Hoyt glanced at Shepard as he took a seat. The man looked terrible. His usual rumpled appearance had a harried edge to it that morning. Hoyt couldn't help thinking that the agent looked somewhat like a deer caught in the headlights of an oncoming car.

Paisley opened the meeting.

"As most of you know, Brian met last night with Mark Whitacre from ADM," he said. "Things didn't go quite as expected."

Paisley looked over to Shepard. "Brian, why don't you tell everybody what's going on."

Shepard looked at his notes. "Well, as you know, yesterday I was attempting to go to Mark Whitacre's house to place a recording device on his phone line."

For several minutes, the words came tumbling out. Shepard's lack of sleep worked against him. He had never been given high marks as a briefer, but his effort this morning was particularly rambling. He had trouble focusing on Whitacre's words, instead drifting repeatedly into the atmospherics of the interview. It was proving immensely frustrating to his supervisors.

"The meeting went on just very, very late," Shepard said. "We were out in the car for three or four hours, and it was really dark. It was hard to take notes. And I knew I had a meeting this morning . . ."

Stukey broke in. "Brian, just start at the beginning again and tell us specifically what happened. What did the man say?"

Under gentle questioning, Shepard recounted the story. He described Whitacre's uneasiness, his concern about being found out. This was a man, Shepard said, who was scared to death. Shepard listed everything that Whitacre had described, from the price-fixing to the theft of microbes to the effort to mislead the FBI.

The supervisors reeled. They were uncertain what charges all this involved. Probably obstruction of justice for conspiring to lie to the FBI. Maybe interstate transportation of stolen property for the theft of microbes. Regardless, there was little doubt Whitacre was describing *something* illegal.

One potential problem, Shepard said, was Mark Cheviron. The security chief was pushing to be briefed on developments in the Fujiwara investigation. He had even scheduled an appointment for that afternoon with the Springfield supervisors. Everyone understood they would have to be circumspect, to avoid tipping off the investigation's new direction.

As the supervisors discussed the Cheviron meeting, Shepard glanced out the window, catching a glimpse of the state capitol dome a few blocks away. He was having trouble hiding his anxiety about this case. Whitacre's statements had bothered him deeply. He knew the case had to be investigated but wasn't eager for the job. He had lived in Decatur almost ten years; he was part of the community. He went to church with ADM employees; his kids played with their kids. How could he take on the company and still be part of the company town? What would happen to his family?

Hoyt could see the wheels turning in the agent's mind. He decided to corner Shepard later and find out what was bothering him.

After more than an hour, Shepard finished his briefing. No one spoke for an instant.

The silence was broken by Stukey. "I'll tell you," he said, "this doesn't surprise me."

Stukey related his experiences as a young agent, when he played a small role in the Watergate investigation. He had never forgotten that it was Dwayne Andreas's money that had been laundered into the account of a Watergate burglar. While Andreas had known nothing about it, the event had left Stukey suspicious. These were people who worked at the edge of the law, he said. Now, his team had to figure out if they had not just bent, but broken the rules.

Stukey divvied up the assignments.

"Brian, get some rest if you can, but prepare a 302 of your interview," he said.

Anderson was given the job of writing a teletype to inform FBI headquarters about what was happening. Shepard and Corr, the legal advisor, were told to examine the price-fixing laws and figure out what role the FBI played in such investigations.

"Once you finish all of that," Stukey said, "let's take a look at what we get, and we'll make a decision on exactly how to proceed."

The meeting ended, and the agents all scattered. They had a lot of work to do. And the first thing was to learn about price-fixing.

For 102 years before that day, American law prohibited price-fixing—at least on paper.

The law was a logical outcome of the industrial revolution, as capitalism blossomed while also plumbing its worst extremes. The birth of cross-country railroads—and with them, the flourishing of industries from banking to energy—had exacted change at a stomach-churning pace. Never before had possibilities seemed so limitless—for travel, for economic growth, for national supremacy.

But those opportunities came at a terrible price. Vast corporate empires, known as trusts, had been constructed by industrial robber barons such as J. P. Morgan and John D. Rockefeller Sr. Prices were set in backrooms by secret agreements, not by battles in the marketplace. The country was quietly being robbed of capitalism's promise. For the first time, it became evident that a free market left to its own devices would not be free at all, but enslaved to the whims of the powerful.

Shopkeepers and small distributors railed against the trusts. Amid the outcry, Congress stepped in with the Sherman Antitrust Act in 1890, prohibiting conspiracies "in restraint of trade or commerce," with violators subject to fines and imprisonment. The public interest appeared to have defeated the trusts.

But the sense of victory was short-lived; the law quickly became derided for its insignificance. Its language was vague, its enforcement spotty. It was riddled with so many loopholes that it was commonly mocked as "the Swiss Cheese Act." For all the good it did, the law may as well have not been adopted at all.

Then came the turn of the century and with it the onset of the most active period of the Progressive Era. Americans came to realize that the conditions bringing great wealth to the few were also bringing misery to the many. Child labor, grim working conditions, tainted foods—these were the ancillary products of unfettered capitalism and misplaced faith in the benevolence of corporate despots.

In the White House, Teddy Roosevelt capitalized on the public sentiment. In February 1902, Roosevelt revived the moribund Sherman Act by filing suit against the Northern Securities Company, a railroad that was part of the J. P. Morgan empire. Four years later, the government filed suit under the Sherman Act to dissolve Rockefeller's Standard Oil. By 1911, with the Supreme Court's affirmation that the once powerful oil trust should be broken up, the dominance of the law was unquestioned.

In the years that followed, price-fixing emerged as one of the principal accusations leveled in cases brought under the Sherman Act. The concept was simple enough. Say there are two companies that manufacture washing machines. If the quality of the machines is the same, the companies can compete for customers mostly over price. If one company wants more business, it will drop its price; if the other wants to keep customers, it will match the price. In theory, that competition serves to keep prices low, to the benefit of consumers and the most efficient corporations.

All of that changes with price-fixing. Under such schemes, companies secretly agree on the price for each washing machine. To insure neither loses business, they might divide up markets, planning which company gets to offer the agreed price to which customer. In the end, the scheme strips consumers of their power. No matter what customers purchase or prefer, prices remain the same, dictated by companies set on evading the rigors of the capitalist system that gave them birth.

With price-fixing so corrosive to markets, the Supreme Court ruled in the early twentieth century that all such schemes—regardless of motivation—are illegal. As a result, since the adoption of the Sherman Act, most criminal antitrust prosecutions have been for price-fixing or related charges.

But there is a big difference between charging a violation of the law and proving it. Because of the secret nature of price-fixing, cases pursued by the government often relied on complex economic analyses to confirm the existence of the scheme. Frequently, FBI agents were called in to interview witnesses and review documents. But in the end, proving a price-fixing scheme was often like confirming the existence of black holes in space. Neither could be seen directly; their presence had to be deduced by examining the surrounding environment. Rarely in the history of the Sherman Act had a price-fixing conspirator voluntarily stepped forward, offering to record other participants as the crime was planned.

By the time Shepard and Corr finished their review of the antitrust laws on that day in 1992, they knew that this nascent case had the potential to be historic. Mark Whitacre was a rare find. His continued cooperation would have to be cultivated carefully.

Whitacre tried to look natural that morning as he strode into ADM's hangar at the Decatur Airport. Jim Randall was waiting for him, looking irked. The two were supposed to fly to North Carolina by corporate plane so that they could check on a new plant. Randall liked an early start and was annoyed that Whitacre hadn't been there, ready to go. On top of it all, Randall had received a message that Whitacre should call the office before takeoff. There was no telling how delayed this flight was going to be.

"Hey, Mark," Randall growled. "Call Cheviron. He wants to talk to you right away."

Whitacre felt his heart drop. Had Cheviron already found out about what he had said to Shepard?

"What does he want?"

"I don't know. Just go call him."

Whitacre nodded. The walk to the telephone seemed to last an eternity. He dialed ADM's main number and asked for Cheviron, but he couldn't get through. He called again as Randall stewed. Finally, he was connected to Cheviron's home.

"What happened last night?" Cheviron asked. Whitacre felt relieved. Maybe the security chief didn't know anything.

"Brian Shepard came over and put a recorder on my line."

"Okay. They put a recorder on your line?"

"Yeah. I was instructed that when Fujiwara calls, I'm to record the conversation."

Cheviron paused. He didn't believe that the FBI would just leave the decision about what to record to Whitacre. He figured there was a good chance the line was tapped so that Shepard could check it out.

"Make sure if Fujiwara calls that you record it," Cheviron said, "because they may be checking to see if you're going to or not."

Cheviron's message was clear. He didn't trust Whitacre. He thought the man was up to something.

At almost that very moment in Lund, Sweden, Harald Skogman of ABP International was leafing through a contract from ADM. Under its terms, ABP, a Swedish agricultural firm, would supply the microbe needed by Whitacre's division to start a new venture—manufacturing threonine, a feed additive. In exchange, ADM would pay $3 million.

Skogman flipped the contract closed and placed it on his desk. His company's president, Lennart Thorstensson, had signed the document two days before. Skogman himself had sent two copies out yesterday by overnight courier to Rick Reising, ADM's general counsel. Last night, he had personally faxed a note to Whitacre, letting him know that the contract would be on Reising's desk today, waiting to be signed. Still, he had heard nothing in response.

Reaching for the telephone, Skogman decided to call Whitacre and press him. The calls continued back and forth until finally, late in the day, Skogman secured a signed contract, ready to be filed away.

For almost three years, the contract would remain largely unnoticed in filing cabinets at the two companies. Until then, no one would recognize the ultimate significance of the obscure document in the rapidly unfolding criminal investigation of ADM.

Shepard sat on a couch in Hoyt's office. He had tried to bury his feelings about the investigation, to hide his concerns. But now Hoyt was pressing him.

"I'm just not sure if I'm the best person to handle this," Shepard said.

All the misgivings came out, as Shepard described his apprehension about being a member of a company town while simultaneously investigating its company.

"This case is going to be bigger than one agent could handle," he said. "Maybe it would be best if somebody else did it. I could help with introductions. I could introduce them to Whitacre." Maybe, Shepard suggested, he should be left to do the other cases that came into the Decatur Resident Agency.

Hoyt studied Shepard as he spoke. Right now, he appeared fragile. Like many agents who had spent years in a small office, Shepard seemed to have become accustomed to dealing with day-to-day criminals. His confidence was lacking for the big-time case.

But Brian Shepard was a good investigator, and in this case, he was the best person for the job. Finding agents to handle the normal Decatur caseload would be easy; finding someone who knew the community as well as Shepard would not. Already, Whitacre had trusted Shepard enough to open up. Changing agents now might cause their new cooperator to shut down.

Hoyt leaned in on his chair. "Brian, you are simply the most knowledgeable person in the FBI about ADM," he said. "That is a tremendous resource. We can't waste it. We have the full trust in you that you can do this investigation. And you won't be alone. There is no individual or company that is bigger than the FBI. We will stand behind you one hundred percent."

Shepard nodded. He wasn't comfortable, but knew that as long as he had the Bureau's backing, he would probably get whatever support he needed. He was not alone; his ASAC had now made it clear that the resources of the government were standing behind him.

Over time, that would prove optimistic.

"We don't want the FBI going through all of ADM's closets."

As he said the words, Mark Cheviron stared across Stukey's office, into the eyes of the Springfield SAC. The meeting between the Springfield supervisors and ADM's security chief had begun at 2:30 that afternoon. With every statement he made, Cheviron made clear ADM's concerns about the investigation. In part, he said, that stemmed from the fallout after the sting operation at the commodities exchanges a few years before.

"Our reputation suffered because of that, and that has made us very reluctant to cooperate with the FBI," he explained. "Our reputation is more important to us than a couple-of-million-dollar extortion."

ADM wanted limits on the investigation, Cheviron said. Without them, the company might not cooperate.

"Dwayne Andreas is concerned about the FBI going off and investigating high-level ADM executives. We're also not sure we want to cooperate to the extent of allowing you to monitor our phone calls."

The agents listened carefully. With the information from Whitacre, they knew that this conversation could have hidden meanings. Sure, ADM might not want the FBI eavesdropping on its business. But maybe the truth was that the company was afraid its price-fixing and other conspiracies might be overheard.

Stukey assured Cheviron that the only phone being monitored by the FBI was Whitacre's off-premises extension—the OPX line. Cheviron nodded.

"Now, I believe what Whitacre's said about Fujiwara," Cheviron said amiably. "But you have to understand, Whitacre is a young Ph.D. who's paranoid. All this has an effect on him."

Cheviron looked at the agents around the room. "Our bottom line is, we have a business to run. We don't want our executives getting caught up in this to the extent that they can't do their jobs. That would not be worth our continued assistance. So, for us to keep helping, we need to know what's going on."

Stukey's response was the model of politeness.

"We appreciate your concerns, but please understand that we don't need a complainant to pursue this," he said. "If we have knowledge of a crime, it's the FBI's responsibility to pursue an investigation whether we have the cooperation of a complainant or not. Now, we will keep you advised of what is happening as much as possible, but there will be certain things that cannot be disclosed to you."

The conversation moved to the next stage of the Fujiwara investigation. Kevin Corr handed Cheviron a rough draft of a contract between ADM and the FBI. It said that the FBI would provide $3 million to ADM to use in the Fujiwara sting. If the money was not recovered within twelve hours, ADM would reimburse the government. Cheviron said the contract needed to be reviewed by ADM lawyers; they would come back with a response.

The meeting ended. Cheviron stood to shake hands, all smiles and pleasantries. The message he was conveying was simple: He understood law enforcement. He was a former cop. Maybe they differed on this investigation, but beneath it all, they were the same.

Stukey escorted Cheviron to the front lobby. Smiling, the SAC pushed open one of the glass doors. In a moment, Cheviron was on an elevator, heading down to the street.

Shepard gathered his notes from the meeting. Stukey wanted Cheviron's statements written up in a 302 while memories were fresh. He knew that someone might have to testify someday about everything the ADM security chief had just said.

Just back from North Carolina, Whitacre walked into his office that afternoon and headed for the phone to check his messages. He picked up the receiver and dialed into the company voice-mail system.

Among the first messages was one from Ginger, asking him to call. She rarely phoned the office unless something important was going on. Whitacre felt a rush of anxiety.

What's happening now?

He clicked off the line and dialed home.

Cheviron had been back at his desk for less than an hour when Whitacre burst in.

"You told me they were only going to tap one line!" Whitacre exploded.

Cheviron didn't need any explanation. He knew Whitacre was talking about the FBI.

"They *are* only monitoring one line, Mark."

"That's not true. That's not true. I just talked to Ginger. She got a call from some woman named Regina at the Inland Telephone Company. She told her both of our lines are tapped. They've tapped my home phone."

Cheviron stared at Whitacre. This was ridiculous. The phone company was not about to start calling people with word that the FBI was tapping their lines.

"Mark, that's not possible. I just came back from meeting the FBI. We talked about this. They assured me that they were only monitoring the OPX line."

"That's not true! Why would this Regina say they're tapping both lines unless it was true?"

Cheviron was enraged. He was sick of Whitacre's antics. He had no doubt the man was lying, just as he had with the story about his daughter. He let Whitacre know that he didn't believe a word.

"Then call my wife!" Whitacre shouted. "She'll tell you what happened. Or call Regina at the Inland Telephone Company. Ask her what she told my wife."

Cheviron looked up at Whitacre impassively. "Fine, Mark. I will."

For an instant, Cheviron just stared at Whitacre, saying nothing. Whitacre turned and stalked out.

Whitacre's latest story crackled through the senior reaches of ADM within the hour. But most everyone who heard it was concerned, not dismissive. Soon, Cheviron was meeting with Reising and Whitacre. The general counsel wanted to know what was going on.

"This is impossible," Cheviron protested. "I just met with the Springfield SAC. He told me only one line—the OPX line—was being monitored."

Cheviron had firmly planted himself on dangerous ground. Regardless of what he thought of Whitacre, the man outranked him. He ran one of ADM's most important divisions. And here he was, the head of corporate security, telling top management that their wonder boy was a liar—all on the say-so of Don Stukey. By the time he returned to his office, Cheviron had decided that he had to check out this new story. He looked up Whitacre's home phone number and called Ginger.

"Hi, this is Mark Cheviron at ADM," he said. "Your husband came by earlier to tell me about a telephone call you received. I was wondering if you could tell me who called."

"It was an employee of the Inland Telephone Company. She identified herself as Regina."

A flicker of hesitation.

"What did she want?"

"She said that it was the company's responsibility to let us know that some sort of device had been placed on our phone line."

Cheviron asked a few questions before hanging up. Ginger's story seemed to match Mark's. Still, Cheviron had trouble believing it. It didn't make any sense. Why would the phone company place such a call?

And if it was true, why had the FBI lied to him?

That evening, Shepard drove back to Whitacre's house. The night before, Whitacre had been petrified about returning to work, concerned that everyone would know what he had told. Shepard wanted to review Whitacre's day and make sure he was calm. It was important for him to know that he was not alone.

Whitacre came outside as Shepard pulled up. He was composed; it seemed as if opening up the night before had allowed his anxiety to slip away. Now, he was not as concerned about listening devices in the house and agreed to speak with Shepard in an eight-sided room near the outdoor pool. It was immense, filled with furniture, a piano, and a fireplace. Long ago, Whitacre said, the room had been a barn.

The relaxed atmosphere made it easier on both men. With his notepad out, Shepard asked Whitacre about his day. Whitacre described his morning call to Cheviron and the subsequent trip to North Carolina with Randall. He mentioned working with Reising to finalize the contract with the Swedish company ABP International. And he brought up the call his wife had received from Regina with the phone company.

"She told Ginger that my home telephone line was tapped or taped," Whitacre said.

Shepard wrote down the words, surprised. The FBI *had* placed "trap and trace" devices and "pen registers" on both lines at Whitacre's home. The devices would record the date, time, and number for every outgoing and incoming call, but the FBI couldn't listen in. Later, Shepard spoke with Ginger and straightened out the story. She had received the call but had misunderstood the devices to be wiretaps. Still, the phone company never should have said anything. If Whitacre had been under investigation, a slipup like that could have undermined an entire case.

Regardless, Whitacre's reaction had been just right. No one would suspect he was helping the FBI at the same time that he was complaining about the Bureau's investigation.

Before the interview ended, Whitacre said there was something else he wanted to discuss.

"After the evening when you first interviewed me, I called Cheviron at his home," he explained. "I told him that my daughter had received a telephone call at Culver Military Academy."

For the next few minutes, Whitacre recounted his conversation with Cheviron. Then he described the meeting the next morning with Cheviron and Reising.

"Cheviron asked me if the story about my daughter was true," he said. "I admitted it wasn't."

Shepard didn't press Whitacre on what he had been thinking, on why he had told the lie. He had enough experience as an investigator to know that cooperating witnesses do odd things. Being caught up in crimes while speaking with an FBI agent can throw people off. Pushing a witness about a lie or a strange decision can strain a developing relationship.

Still, as he pulled out of the driveway later that night, Shepard could not shake an uncomfortable feeling about the daughter story. It was all very confusing to him. Very confusing.

Two nights later, on November 8, Dean Paisley slipped into the passenger seat of Shepard's car for a trip to Moweaqua. This Sunday night would be the first chance for someone besides Shepard to size up Whitacre—to figure out his motivation for talking and to see how far he might be willing to go in his cooperation.

The two agents pulled into the driveway just after eight o'clock. Whitacre emerged at the front door, bubbly and excited, insisting that Paisley call him "Mark." He gave the agents the grand tour of the house. He took them through both of his garages, showing off his many cars. In the six-car garage, Whitacre stopped next to a red Ferrari and put his hand on it.

"I bought this one not too long ago," he said. "In fact, I bought it used from Jim Randall, the president of ADM. He gave me a good price."

Paisley and Shepard both chimed in with praise for the cars and the huge garage. The compliments continued as Whitacre escorted them through the rest of house, toward the room off the pool. Whitacre described the mansion's past, again relating how Dwayne Andreas had once owned it. Paisley, intrigued, asked a number of questions about the history and architecture of the place.

Shepard stayed in the background, letting Paisley set the pace. But at one point, he decided to get to work. Earlier, he had asked Whitacre to bring the business cards of lysine competitors who had attended price-fixing meetings. Shepard interrupted and asked if he had remembered them. Whitacre smiled and reached for his briefcase, taking out a small brown notebook.

"They're in here," Whitacre said as he handed the notebook to Shepard.

Shepard took the notebook to a nearby couch. Flipping through the pages, he saw mostly Japanese and Korean names. He began writing down the information.

Paisley and Whitacre stood by the sliding glass doors that led to the pool. Outside, bright spotlights glowed across the property, giving it a look of ethereal elegance. The lush yard was perfectly manicured. Even in the fall, not a leaf was out of place. The atmosphere was calming, conducive to conversation. It was having its effect on Whitacre. Somehow, it was comforting to know that an FBI supervisor had come. He felt like they were sending a message that the FBI was looking out for him.

As the two men gazed out across the yard, Paisley veered the discussion toward the investigation.

"Well, I've heard about these things that you told Brian the other night," Paisley said. "We appreciate your assistance and your openness. We've got a few questions for you tonight. Some might seem repetitive. We want to make sure we fully understand and make a good record of what you're telling us."

"I understand," Whitacre said. "That's fine."

The ensuing conversation was free-flowing. Sometimes they sat; sometimes they paced. But over time, Whitacre described a series of crimes.

"Until last April, I really had no contact with the business end of ADM," he said. "My only concerns were in the technical aspects of lysine production and other activities like that. But in April, I got called into a meeting by Mick Andreas. He told me then that I was going to be working with Terry Wilson."

Whitacre said the news had angered him. Wilson ran corn processing and knew nothing about lysine. As far as Whitacre was concerned, Wilson was a poorly educated boor, a man who only liked to drink, curse, and golf. Whitacre had complained, but Mick had told him that this was his chance to learn how ADM did business.

In their first meeting, Whitacre said, Wilson asked nothing about the division's employees, nothing about its products. All he had wanted to know were names of the company's competitors and how well Whitacre knew them.

"A couple of weeks later, we were on a plane to Japan. It was the first time I ever traveled as a businessman rather than as a technical person. I had no idea what to expect on this trip, no idea at all."

Paisley brought his hand up to his chin. "When did you learn the purpose of the trip?"

"Pretty quickly. We were there to set prices and production volumes with our Asian competitors."

Paisley nodded knowingly. He already understood that an effective price-fixing agreement would have to control total production. Otherwise, the market could become flooded with unsold goods, forcing down prices. The fact that the lysine competitors were discussing both prices *and* volumes was a strong sign that these people knew what they were doing.

In Tokyo, Whitacre continued, he and Wilson had met with executives from Ajinomoto and the Kyowa Hakko Kogyo Company. Then they flew to Maui, Hawaii. There, they met again with the Japanese executives and were joined by officials from a Korean company, Miwon.

"The first day there was spent socializing," he said. "We went to social settings, played golf, stuff like that. The second day was when we started negotiating price and production volumes."

Paisley broke in. "Who was running the meetings for ADM?"

"Terry. Terry Wilson. He was actively advising everybody else on production and price levels."

Whitacre sat back. "It didn't take long for me to understand why I had been assigned to work with Terry. He was supposed to be showing me how things occur at these price-fixing meetings."

The next meeting, Whitacre said, had been in June—about five months ago—and had taken place in Mexico. In September, executives from Ajinomoto had come to Decatur to tour ADM's plant so that they could learn whether the company was bluffing about its capacity. That was important for the negotiations over production. Afterward, he said, Whitacre and Wilson had toured plants owned by Ajinomoto in the United States.

"A few weeks ago we had another meeting in Paris, to discuss prices and volumes," Whitacre said.

Shepard leaned in. "Did you bring the copies of your expense reports that we talked about?"

Whitacre nodded. "Sure. They're right here."

Opening his briefcase, Whitacre pulled out his expense records and handed them to Shepard. The agent pored through them. He could see they documented trips to Tokyo, Mexico City, and Paris. This was the first evidence corroborating Whitacre's statements.

"Who schedules these meetings?" Shepard asked.

"Mr. Ikeda," Whitacre said. "He's the owner of Ajinomoto."

"When's the next meeting?"

"Sometime in January," Whitacre said. "It's going to be somewhere in Asia. The final arrangements are probably still being worked out by Mr. Ikeda."

The price-fixing had been an enormous boon to ADM, Whitacre said. In just the past month, the lysine business brought in $2.5 million in profits; a few months before, the company had been losing that much.

"All that profit is due to price-fixing," Whitacre said.

The agents pressed him. Had Whitacre heard about price-fixing in any other ADM products?

Whitacre nodded. "Just this weekend, Mick Andreas and Terry Wilson traveled to Florida to meet with competitors at the Corn Refiners Association. They have formal meetings during the day, but at night they meet in private rooms for pricing talks."

"How are those meetings set up?" Paisley asked.

"I don't know. I don't know details. But I've been told the pricing discussions occur that way."

Paisley's thoughts raced. This case sounded incredible. Whitacre was a source unlike any he had ever met. Even the room they were in underscored that. This was not the flophouse of some mope or the apartment of some embittered ex-employee. This was a man in reach of ADM's top rung. His financial rewards were obviously substantial. Personally, he seemed to have nothing to gain by stepping forward, and potentially everything to lose. Paisley had never even *heard* of a situation like that in law enforcement.

"Mark," Paisley said softly, "there's something else I have to ask you."

"Sure."

"Why are you doing this? We know you lied to us about the phone line and you're afraid of that. But now you're telling us all this other stuff out of the blue, so to speak. Why are you doing this?"

The look on Whitacre's face was grim.

"Things are going on I don't approve of," he said. "I don't like it. I mean, I'm a biochemist. I'm a technical guy. But now they've pulled me into the business side, and they're doing things that are illegal. I don't like it, and they made me be a part of it because they said it's part of the business."

Neither agent moved.

"They said that if I'm going to grow with ADM, I gotta be part of the business," he said. "I knew what they wanted me to do was illegal, and that weighed on me. When they told me to lie, I had to lie."

Whitacre cleared his throat. "I know I lied to you guys. I felt bad about that. I wanted to correct that. I wanted to come clean. But there was no way to explain that I'd lied without explaining why, without explaining that there are things going on in the business that are illegal. I didn't like those things, but I felt like I had to go along. Now I want to tell you about it because it's bothering me. It's the wrong thing to do. I want to do the right thing."

Paisley nodded. This made sense and explained Whitacre's earlier nervousness that he had heard so much about. The words didn't ease all of his concerns, but they made Paisley feel more comfortable.

"So," he said. "You look at yourself as wearing a white hat and they're wearing the black hats."

"Yeah," Whitacre said. "Something like that."

They had reached a turning point. This was the time to see how far Whitacre was willing to take this.

"Well, Mark," Paisley said, his voice almost fatherly, "do you think you'd be willing to go a few steps further in helping us?"

"Sure. What do you mean?"

"Would you be willing to help us by wearing a wire to show this is true? We don't have other sources we can go to at this time. We need your help."

Paisley knew he was asking Whitacre to risk a lot. He decided to be up-front.

"I realize what I'm asking you to do here," he said. "Sometime down the line, you're going to be the guy who has to testify against your fellow executives. That won't be easy. You'll be risking a lot."

Whitacre blinked. "Yeah," he said, "but I feel like, if everybody else went to jail or whatever, at least I did the right thing. I'll be the guy who did the right thing. That's how the company will look at me. They'll reward me for doing the right thing, and I'll probably end up being president of the company."

Paisley listened in disbelief. Whitacre was in a fantasy world, with no idea what he was getting into.

"Mark, you gotta realize that when these stockholders and directors find out that you're the one that caused all of this embarrassment, they're not going to look at you as the guy in the white hat. They're going to be mad at you. Do you really think they're going to make you president of the company?"

"Yeah, I think so. Because I'm the one who's doing the right thing."

I wouldn't count on it, Paisley thought. But he had warned Whitacre, and the man was still willing to proceed. He was sure Shepard would come back to the issue again at some future meeting.

There were still operational details to iron out, Paisley said. A method needed to be set up so Shepard could contact Whitacre without being detected by ADM.

"Tell me about the voice-mail system at your office," Shepard said.

It was normal voice mail, Whitacre shrugged. Worked pretty much like any other system.

"All right," Shepard said, pulling a pager off his belt. "Here's what we're going to do. If I need to speak with you, I'll call your voice mail. When the message records, I'll turn the pager on, like this."

A shrill beeping sound echoed in the large room.

"So whenever you hear that," Shepard continued, "you find a safe phone and call me back."

Whitacre nodded. The idea sounded good to him.

Shepard brought out a small slip of paper. "This is my office number. Put this in a safe place, and when you hear the pager, call me there."

Whitacre took the slip and escorted the agents to the door, where they thanked him again. Whitacre nodded, obviously feeling good about his decisions.

Shepard again cautioned Whitacre to act normal at the office the next day, as if nothing was going on. He said he would contact Whitacre during the day to see about setting up a place for the first recording.

Whitacre smiled.

"Okay, buddy," he said. "Talk to you then."

Paisley stared blankly out the car window, studying the surrounding fields as Shepard pulled out of Whitacre's driveway. He waited until they had left Moweaqua before asking the question on his mind.

"What do you think of this guy?" he asked. "Think he's telling the truth now?"

"Right now I'm taking him at face value," Shepard responded. "Why would somebody lie and then ask to wear a wire? That doesn't make any sense."

"Yeah, but why would somebody in his position do this? I mean, he's basically cutting his own throat with the company as soon as this comes out."

The two agents were quiet. Neither had an answer.

"Well, if he's willing to do it, we'll go ahead and do it," Paisley said finally. "I'll just have the SAC sign off on it and we're in business."

Paisley sat back. "You know, Brian, we're not going to wait too long for this guy to produce. Especially where we're just taking his word for it, and we've got a wire on an executive at ADM. We can't wait too long for results."

Shepard stared ahead. "I know," he said.

The next morning, Whitacre tore into Cheviron's office before eight. He had the same look of anxiety that had been on his face for days.

"Have you been able to get hold of Regina at Inland Telephone Company?" Whitacre asked, fuming.

Cheviron tried hard not to look too dismissive. He had thought this issue was done with.

"No, I haven't."

Whitacre could usually control his anger. But that morning, he looked ready to explode.

"Don't you care?" he snapped.

"Well, I care, but what's the problem?"

"I think you're setting me up, or ADM's setting me up!" he shouted, trembling in anger. "You're lying to me! They've tapped both my phones."

The moment was rife with deceit. Whitacre's frenzy was mostly an act—he already knew from Shepard that no listening devices were on his phone. But at ADM, he had to avoid raising suspicion by pretending that he knew nothing. For his part, Cheviron was tired of Whitacre's ravings. He had already openly attacked Whitacre's truthfulness. His career didn't need this.

Cheviron sighed. "Get me Regina's phone number and I'll call her."

"Fine," Whitacre said. He charged out of the office. Within thirty minutes, he was on the phone to Cheviron's secretary, giving her the number.

Just after ten-thirty, Whitacre reappeared. From the way he was acting, anyone would think this phone call was the most important thing Whitacre had to deal with. Whitacre certainly seemed to believe it was the *only* thing on Cheviron's plate.

"Did you call Regina?"

"No," Cheviron replied. "Haven't had a chance."

That was all Whitacre needed to hear.

"Don't think I don't understand what's happening here," he yelled. "You're working with the FBI!"

Cheviron held up his hands.

"This is ridiculous," he said. "I'll call Brian Shepard, and I'll just ask him, Mark."

Whitacre sat in a chair in front of the desk. Cheviron looked up Shepard's office number and punched it into the phone, trying hard to control his anger.

"FBI."

Cheviron recognized Shepard's voice.

"Brian, it's Mark Cheviron. I've been talking with Mark Whitacre, and he's having a problem."

Cheviron, glancing at Whitacre, quickly related the story of the phone call from Inland Telephone.

"Now, I asked you guys which lines you were monitoring on Friday, and you told me just the OPX line. But have you tapped both lines?"

Shepard paused.

"I really can't answer," he said. There were no taps, just the "trap and trace" and "pen registers." But that was not something he could discuss.

For Cheviron, the nonresponse spoke volumes. He felt convinced the FBI had lied to him on Friday.

"You don't have to answer," he said. "That's enough." He hung up the phone.

Cheviron looked over at Whitacre. "Well, Mark, you're probably right," he said. "I believe they've probably tapped both of your phones."

Whitacre jumped up. "But that's not right!" he blurted. "I was promised that both phones wouldn't be tapped! I was promised!"

"I know, Mark," Cheviron said, holding up his hands again. "I know that's what we were told. But I think they've been lying to us."

"I knew it! I knew it! I knew we never should have done this! It was a bad idea talking to the FBI. I told everybody that, but nobody listened to me!"

Cheviron did his best to calm Whitacre but failed. After Whitacre left, Cheviron walked to Reising's office to brief the general counsel. Reising eyed Cheviron carefully before replying.

"What it sounds like to me is that you're not doing your job," he said, "since you can't keep track of what the FBI is doing."

Cheviron felt beaten. By the time he left Reising's office, the decision had been made: ADM was pulling out. They would no longer cooperate with the FBI.

Later that morning, Cheviron called Shepard again and told him everything—how he had branded Whitacre a liar to his bosses, based on the FBI's word, how his own job now seemed threatened. Management didn't trust him anymore.

"ADM just wants out of this investigation," Cheviron said. "We are not going to cooperate any further with FBI requests, and any further requests should be referred to Reising."

The call ended quickly. Cheviron was not in the mood to talk. Four hours later, at 3:25, Cheviron's phone rang. Dean Paisley was on the line.

"I just talked with Brian about your telephone conversation," he said. "What is exactly your concern? What is your heartburn?"

Cheviron lashed out like a wounded animal.

"I understand you can't tell me everything," he said. "But I told Brian the only thing I don't want is lying. You don't lie to me, and I don't lie to you."

He recounted the Regina story, emphasizing how this contradicted what Don Stukey had said. He told how he had called Whitacre a liar—he had even told *Dwayne Andreas* that Whitacre was lying. Now, Cheviron said, it ended up that the FBI had made him into a fool.

"They don't trust me here," Cheviron said. "They want me out of it, and it's going to be handled by the legal department."

Paisley explained why Cheviron could not be told everything. Someone at ADM was potentially a saboteur, he said. Information had to be closely held. But now, he needed to know what ADM's role would be.

"Are you saying your company is formally telling the FBI that you will no longer cooperate at all in this investigation in which you are the victim?"

"Yes," Cheviron said.

"And you have that authority to tell me that from your people?"

"From our legal department. Rick Reising said he would be glad to tell you that."

Paisley pressed. "What you are saying is that any request that we have of your company to help us in this criminal investigation, you're not going to cooperate in any way. Is that what you're saying?"

Cheviron's antennae went up. Why was Paisley pushing him? He answered cautiously.

"I don't know if that's what he's saying. I think what he said is we want to withdraw our complaint."

"You know better than that," Paisley scoffed. "You don't do that in a federal investigation. Once an investigation is started, we have to play it out."

Something told Cheviron to hedge his answers.

"All I'm saying is that they're not going to let me be involved anymore," he said. "You can work it out with Rick Reising. I get the feeling they don't believe me anymore, and that's not my fault."

Paisley wrapped it up. He said he would contact Reising, and the call came to an end. Cheviron eyed the phone. He didn't know what Paisley had been up to, but something about the conversation bothered him.

About forty miles away, Paisley placed his phone in its cradle. He reached across the desk to the tape recorder that had been hooked up minutes before and jabbed the Stop button. The spools that had been turning during his call with Cheviron stopped moving.

That morning, beginning with Cheviron's second call to Shepard, the FBI had started taping ADM. It seemed obvious to the agents that the company was trying to shut down the Fujiwara investigation, maybe to cover up the other crimes Whitacre had described. But to prove an obstruction of justice, they needed evidence. That meant, from now on, the FBI's conversations with ADM executives were going to be on tape.

Paisley popped the cassette out of the recorder. Soon, the tape was sent down the hall to the office of the "ELSUR clerk"—an FBI staffer who maintained recordings from electronic surveillance. There, it was logged as number 1B2. Paisley had little doubt that it would be needed later.

That afternoon, Whitacre called the in-house voice mail and entered his code. He listened to a few messages, then dialed a number for the next one.

Beep.

Before the second tone from Shepard's pager could sound, Whitacre pushed two buttons on his keypad.

Deleted, the electronic voice said.

Whitacre headed out of the office to a nearby conference room. He felt sure it was a safe place to talk. He figured it wouldn't take long to find out from Shepard where they would be meeting for the first secret taping of the price-fixing conspirators.

Whitacre pulled off Pershing Road into the parking lot for the Best Western Shelton Inn, just outside downtown Decatur. He drove past the lobby, parking near a Shakey's pizza parlor that shared the same lot. The two-story beige-and-green hotel was nothing much to see—just one of thousands of faceless inns dotting the country that boasted of free cable and air-conditioning for weary travelers.

After locking his car, Whitacre walked toward the hotel, pulling his coat tight. Even though it was before 6:00 p.m., the lot was getting dark. Whitacre felt relieved when he reached the lobby. Outside, he felt too exposed; anyone driving by could see him.

He looked around the lobby and crinkled his nose. *What a shady place.* It was small; the recessed lights were dim, giving a dark, dingy feel. In some ways, the appearance made Whitacre comfortable. He felt sure none of the people from his circles would drop by.

"Can I help you?" the front-desk clerk asked.

"No, no thanks. I'm just waiting for someone."

A minute later, Whitacre saw Shepard, wearing a trench coat, come in through the side door. The agent walked down a short hallway, stopping by some pay phones. Whitacre approached him.

"Hey," Whitacre said in a soft, nasal tone. "How's it going?"

"Fine, fine. Listen, we're not going to be able to get a room tonight. But I still need you to make some calls."

Whitacre fixed him with a puzzled look. "Okay," he said cautiously. "What phone are we going to use?"

"One right here," Shepard said, nodding toward the lobby's bank of pay phones.

Here? In public? Whitacre thought. He didn't understand what was going on. Did Shepard's credit card not work?

Shepard wasn't comfortable with the idea, but it had been thought up at the last minute, when someone in Springfield raised concerns about using a hotel room phone. There were some legal and technical concerns. What if the conspirators had caller ID? They might become suspicious.

Whitacre looked around the small lobby. "This seems a little awkward," he said.

"It's the best I can do right now."

The side door to the pool opened. A hotel guest walked by the two men, excusing himself as he passed on his way to the Chestnut, the hotel's restaurant. When the man was gone, Shepard looked at Whitacre.

"Let's go out to my car and talk."

The two men headed back to the lot and got inside the car. Shepard looked at Whitacre intently.

"We really need these conversations, Mark," he said. They needed proof that Whitacre was telling the truth.

Whitacre nodded. "Okay. What do we do?"

Reaching into his pocket, Shepard pulled out a small recording device. It looked like any other microcassette recorder, but it was only available from the FBI. A wire was attached, with a small, sensitive microphone at the end.

"Hold this microphone on the receiver. There's a clip on it, but don't worry about that. It doesn't clip to the phone. You hold the microphone on the receiver, and I'll hold the recorder."

"Okay."

"Do you have the phone numbers with you?"

"Yeah, I brought them with me."

Whitacre took out the numbers. Shepard glanced at them, and the two men discussed their plan of attack. They agreed to first try a Kyowa Hakko executive named Masaru Yamamoto, or "Massy," as Whitacre called him.

Opening his briefcase, Shepard brought out some documents known as FD-472s. Shepard explained that the forms authorized the FBI to record the phone conversation. Then, Shepard handed Whitacre an FD-473, explaining that this would provide authorization to place a tape recorder on his body. Shepard said he would give Whitacre a recorder the next time they met.

The two men walked back to the lobby. Shepard held the tape recorder, while Whitacre fumbled with the microphone. He picked up the phone and dialed zero.

An Illinois Bell operator answered. Whitacre asked for help dialing Japan, and she transferred him to an AT&T operator. He told her the eleven numbers she needed and recited his fourteen-digit calling-card number.

A man answered the phone in Japanese, identifying himself as working with Kyowa Hakko's special pharmaceutical division.

"Uh, yes," Whitacre responded. "May I speak with Mr. Yamamoto, please."

The Japanese man shifted to English. "May I have your name, please?"

"Yes, the name is Mark Whitacre."

"Mark. Okay."

The man put Whitacre on hold. Light, syrupy music played for a moment. Yamamoto came on the line.

"Hello,"Yamamoto said in accented English.

"Mr. Yamamoto?"

"Hi. Yamamoto speaking. How are you?"

The two men traded pleasantries. Whitacre apologized for the delay in calling back. He had been traveling and would be leaving again tomorrow.

"I will pretty much be unreachable this week,"Whitacre said.

"Oh, I see. Ah, how is your sales?"

In less than thirty seconds, the conversation had already veered into sales.

"Sales are doin' pretty good," he replied. "How 'bout yours?"

"It's good."

Yamamoto complained about certain lysine prices that he had heard were being offered. As Whitacre listened, an older woman walked past, staring at him as he held the microphone to the receiver. Whitacre felt enormously uncomfortable—he figured she thought he was taping his wife. He shifted the microphone, trying to look less conspicuous. He didn't know that he had just caused his own voice to amplify on the tape.

"So Mr. Ikeda told me you guys would have a meeting November thirtieth—yourself and the Koreans."

"Yes."

"In Korea, I think, isn't it?"

"Yes, yes, Seoul."

This was working.

"And then we meet again with myself involved and maybe someone else from our company involved. Maybe even Mick Andreas. That would be early January?"

"Yeah, maybe so," Yamamoto said. "Then we discuss ninety-three, for ninety-three."

They were close. Whitacre decided to push Yamamoto on what they would be discussing about 1993.

"Right," he said. "For ninety-three pricing and volume."

"Ah."

"In Hong Kong or Singapore. Is that correct?"

"Yes, yes."

Whitacre had said it, but Yamamoto hadn't denied it. Competitors were meeting to discuss prices and volumes. That should prove something to the FBI.

Yamamoto mentioned that customers were claiming that ADM

was offering low prices—something that couldn't be done under price-fixing.

"We don't know is the customer making a trick," Yamamoto said in imperfect English. Maybe, he was suggesting, the customers were lying.

"Customers can be tricky," Whitacre replied.

Still, Yamamoto said, something had to be done for the best customers.

"It's very, very important how we can keep a good price for the big customers, don't you think?"

"Yeah, I think you're right."

Then, Yamamoto opened up.

"It's better to talk, you know, see how we maintain the price at $2.50, you know, in other countries, and $1.05 in the United States."

Jackpot. Yamamoto just admitted everything. The competitors were working together to control the prices. Whitacre felt a rush, a thrill.

The conversation proceeded for a few more minutes, with Yamamoto congratulating Whitacre on his recent promotion. Finally, it came to a close.

"Anyway, congratulations, and see you soon," Yamamoto said.

"Okay, Massy."

"Bye-bye."

Whitacre pulled the microphone away and hung up the receiver before turning to Shepard. He couldn't wait to let him know everything Yamamoto had said.

Around six-forty-five, Shepard and Whitacre came out of the hotel, walking to the parking lot. Whitacre had placed several more calls but only reached Ikeda and Mimoto from Ajinomoto. Ikeda confirmed the upcoming meetings; Mimoto hadn't said much, and the tape ran out near the beginning of the call. Still, Whitacre felt happy.

The two men climbed into Shepard's car and for a few minutes, Whitacre described the calls.

"Mark, this is exactly what we needed," Shepard said. "It really verifies what you've said."

Whitacre smiled.

There were still more forms required for the tape. Shepard filled out an FD-504b, indicating the date and time he had taken custody of the tape. When the paperwork was done, Shepard asked if anything else had happened recently. Whitacre recounted his day.

There was another issue, Whitacre said.

Shepard looked up from his notes. "What is it?"

"Well," Whitacre continued, "it's somewhat common knowledge among the executives at ADM that Mark Cheviron is responsible for secretly recording customers when they're staying at the Decatur Club."

"What do you mean?"

"ADM has a place at the Decatur Club, and out-of-town customers stay there. I've heard we have taping equipment hidden there. So when we negotiate some deal, we hear what the other side really thinks."

"How have you heard about this?" Shepard asked.

"Well, it's been the talk around ADM. And my secretary, Liz, used to work for Cheviron, and she told me one of her jobs was transcribing the recordings."

Shepard reviewed his notes. If ADM was conducting secret surveillance, that could result in another investigation. After a few follow-ups, he was done.

"Thanks for your time," Shepard said. "I'll go over this tape in more detail and be back in touch."

Whitacre hopped out and hurried across the lot. In no time, he was in his car. As he veered left toward Route 51 South, he ran the evening's events through his mind. Now the FBI knew that he was telling the truth about price-fixing. He felt confident Shepard had everything he needed to crack open this case.

He smiled. This would be over soon. The FBI would be done with him, and he could get back to his job.

Probably, he thought, in a few days the FBI wouldn't even need his help anymore.

As he headed down Pershing Road, Shepard was excited. Everything had worked out well. Now, they had strong evidence to prove that price-fixing was occurring. Still, the investigation had a long way to go. To make a criminal case, Whitacre would have to help develop more evidence, more tapes.

The FBI, Shepard knew, was probably going to need Whitacre's help for some time to come.

CHAPTER 4

Acres of farmland stretched across flat Illinois plains, disappearing into darkness. A nighttime wind sent raindrops sideways, providing a last burst of energy before they splashed the windshield of Dean Paisley's car. The wipers, on low, did little to improve visibility. Moderate rain had fallen throughout the day, and now a patchy fog hung over the highway. Usually, few drivers could resist exceeding the sixty-five-mile-an-hour speed limit on the monotonous drive from Decatur to Springfield on Interstate 72. But this night, the treacherous weather commanded patience. Paisley slowed to fifty-five.

It was shortly before eleven on November 9, 1992. More than three hours had passed since Shepard had taken custody of Whitacre's recording. Now it was inside Paisley's briefcase on the front seat of his car. Shepard had contacted Paisley almost immediately after the evening's success, and the supervisor had driven to Decatur for an update. Shepard's briefing dispelled most of Paisley's doubts about the price-fixing conspiracy. And now, Whitacre had tipped them to another potential criminal scheme: the taping at the Decatur Club.

Paisley drove past the Macon County border. Normally, by this point in such a long drive, he would have switched on the radio to hear some of the late-night talk shows he enjoyed. But on this evening, he drove in silence, lost in his thoughts.

Whitacre mystified him. Paisley remained uneasy about the man's blasé willingness to cooperate. If nothing else, Whitacre was sure to be a fragile witness. A time would come—probably soon—when he would decide the risks of cooperating were too much. Paisley knew that Shepard would have to watch for that.

Paisley stared ahead, the white lines of the highway glowing in his headlights, as he considered Whitacre's latest tip. The lead on the Decatur Club seemed shakier than the rest. Whitacre had no solid details, just rumors and second-hand information. If the FBI pursued that investigation now, ADM was sure to catch wind of it—and that would surely raise suspicions. The company might even call off the price-fixing if they suspected someone was talking.

Let's just let this one hang out there for a while, Paisley thought. Price-fixing was the bigger case. Plus, they still had Fujiwara, along with Whitacre's allegations of ADM's industrial espionage. Those investigations couldn't all be pursued at the same time. Instead, Paisley figured they could pick up the Decatur Club investigation later; maybe Whitacre would even come up with some better information by then.

Still, the investigation was too sprawling; no agent could handle it alone. If this case had originated in Chicago or New York, a half dozen agents would have already been assigned. Shepard needed help.

By the time he crossed the Sangamon River outside Springfield, Paisley had made up his mind. Tomorrow, he would appeal for more manpower. If his supervisors turned him away, Paisley could shift around other agents who reported to him. One way or another, Shepard would have a co–case agent by the next night.

But as he pulled off Route 72, Paisley was still struggling with a thought: Who should be the other agent?

"Sales are doin' pretty good. How 'bout yours?"

Whitacre's taped voice hissed out of a playback device resting in the center of Don Stukey's desk. It was early the next afternoon. The Springfield SAC was leaning back in his chair, while John Hoyt, the ASAC, stood beside the desk. Paisley sat in front of the desk, his eyes flitting from the tape recorder to his supervisors. This, he hoped, was all the proof he needed to show that the ADM case required more agents.

After almost an hour, the tape ended. Stukey, who had been fiddling with a pen, sat up in his chair.

"Well, it looks like there might be something to what the source has been telling us," he said, looking at Paisley. "So what's your plan?"

"Well," Paisley said, "if this is what we think it is, we need Brian on this full-time, and we need someone with him. I'd recommend three people on it."

Stukey looked uncomfortable. "Do we need three?"

If not, Paisley said, then at least there needed to be a backup. There would be days when Shepard was sick, on vacation, or testifying in some other case.

Topping it off, the case was expanding again. Earlier that day,

Kevin Corr had taped a call with Richard Reising, ADM's general counsel, who had said that the order to stop cooperating with the Fujiwara investigation had come from Dwayne Andreas himself. It was no leap of logic that an obstruction case might lead to the top of the company.

Hoyt joined in, agreeing with Paisley.

"Well," Stukey said, "why don't we just go with one more right now, and see how things progress."

Paisley nodded. It was a start.

"So," Stukey said, "who do you think should be working on this with Brian?"

Paisley had been pondering that question all night and was ready with an answer.

"Well, we have to pick somebody we think can do the best job, but it also has to be somebody who can work with Shepard," he said. That meant they couldn't pick a young agent or somebody new.

"So who do you recommend?"

"Joe Weatherall," Paisley answered. "He's meticulous and he's worked with Shepard before."

Everyone in the room knew Weatherall, a no-nonsense, Joe Friday type. He was the senior resident agent in the Champaign office, which reported through Springfield. The office was more than forty miles from Decatur; while he had worked cases in Decatur, Weatherall probably would be unknown to ADM.

The fifty-year-old agent had been with the FBI for decades—in fact, he was eligible for retirement, but seemed to have no intention of leaving anytime soon. A balding man with large, bushy eyebrows, Weatherall stood six feet three inches and weighed about 220 pounds. With the right glare or tone, he could be frightfully intimidating but usually came off more like a gentle giant. A West Point graduate and former member of the army, Weatherall was a man without pretense— his name in many ways reflected his character: he was never Joseph or Joey, just Joe. That, in fact, was the name listed on his birth certificate. Joe Albert Weatherall, Jr.

As an agent, Weatherall was a stickler for detail. He would continually wring his hands over everything that might go wrong in an investigation. If a fellow agent failed to account for possible flaws in a plan, Weatherall would quietly upbraid the colleague. Failure to consider details was how soldiers got hurt in Vietnam, he would say. The tone of the simple statement, propelled by the force of Weatherall's character, was withering.

Stukey and Hoyt jumped at the suggestion. Paisley headed back to his office and called Weatherall.

"Hey, Joe, how's it going?" Paisley asked. "Listen, I've got something that I'd like for you to consider doing."

Two days later, shortly before six P.M., Shepard and Weatherall walked silently down a fifth-floor hallway at the Holiday Inn in Decatur. Stopping at a door, Shepard took out the electronic key card he had picked up from the front desk. After he swiped the card through the lock, the agents stepped inside.

Shepard headed for the telephone and dialed Whitacre's voice mail. He listened for the tone.

"Five-forty-seven," he said.

Then he hung up.

Across town, Whitacre was pulling away from the ADM underground garage. Soon, he turned west onto Eldorado Street, heading out of town. A few minutes after six, he checked the clock. Following Shepard's instructions from earlier in the day, Whitacre called his voice mail on his car phone. He went through his messages quickly, paying little attention. Finally, he heard someone say a number.

Whitacre disconnected the call. Now he knew the hotel room where the FBI was waiting for him.

Weatherall sat quietly at a small table in the back of the hotel room. Nearby, Shepard was having trouble sitting still. He was jumpier, more nervous than Weatherall, and it showed.

There was a knock at the door. Whitacre ambled into the room as soon as Shepard answered.

"Hey, bud," Whitacre said. "Sorry, there were some people in the hallway. I had to walk back and forth a couple of times before I knocked. I didn't want you opening the door with people seeing it."

"That's okay, Mark," Shepard said. "Good thinking."

Whitacre looked across the room and saw a hulking man. Shepard had told him a new agent would be at tonight's meeting, but still the man's presence was disquieting. There was something about him, something more than just his size. He carried himself with a precision and exactness that reminded Whitacre of his preconceptions of federal agents.

"Mark," Shepard said, "this is Special Agent Joe Weatherall. He's from the Champaign office. He's going to be working with me on this case."

Whitacre smiled and took Weatherall's hand.

"Hey," he said, "how's it going?"

"Going fine. Good to meet you."

Weatherall's words were short and clipped. He was never much for small talk and not nearly as animated as Shepard. Still, he seemed friendly enough. Whitacre's anxiety about the new agent eased up.

Weatherall sat on the bed, and Whitacre took a seat at the table. Shepard sat across from him.

For several minutes, Shepard and Whitacre chatted—about families, the rain, whatever. The pleasantries went on a little long for Weatherall's taste; he wanted to get started. Still, he recognized that Shepard had his own style, and it seemed to work.

Finally, Shepard got down to business. He asked Whitacre to reconstruct the portions of his conversation with Mimoto that had not been taped. Shepard listened, writing down Whitacre's words. Finally, he flipped the page in his notebook.

"Anything else we should know about?" he asked.

Whitacre nodded.

"ADM is real concerned about you guys," he said. "Ever since you started talking to people at the company, they've been worried about it."

Two days before, Whitacre had flown to Mexico with Jim Randall and a group of other ADM executives.

"We were walking to the customs area," Whitacre said, "and Randall told me that ADM was going to do things by the book from now on."

Whitacre looked at the two agents. "He still said that he thought the company could beat the FBI. He told me, 'We're ADM, we're a lot stronger than the FBI.' He told me that Dwayne is more powerful than anybody could imagine."

Despite Randall's hubris, Whitacre said, there was no doubt that ADM had decided to start playing straight.

"This is a big policy switch," Whitacre said. "Randall told me I was supposed to hear about it from Mick tomorrow. It's supposed to be a big secret, so he told me to act surprised when I heard."

Whitacre glanced over at Weatherall. The agent was watching, not saying a word.

Around two o'clock that day, Whitacre said, he had called the office and spoke with Mick. "Mick started talking about how much ADM had invested in my division and how much I mean to the company. He spent a lot of time telling me about my potential to become president of ADM, because his father and Randall are getting old."

Shepard wrote down the words.

"After telling me all that, he said things were going to be different from now on," Whitacre continued. "He said, 'Mark, we're going to start doing things your way. You're not going to have to go to Japan in January. As a matter of fact, you're not going to be calling these guys anymore.' "

"What about the price-fixing?" Shepard asked.

"It's over," Whitacre shrugged. "Mick told me, 'We're not going to be fixing prices anymore.' "

Shepard asked more questions, while Weatherall sat silently on the bed. Finally, Shepard told Whitacre that he had brought a recording device and wanted to show him how it worked. It was a micro-cassette recorder and looked just like one from an office-supply store. Shepard showed Whitacre what buttons to push and how to tell if it was working.

Shepard slid the device into Whitacre's inside pocket of his suit jacket. Then, he clipped a tiny microphone to the top. No one would ever know a recorder was there unless they looked inside Whitacre's jacket.

"Now, Mark, be relaxed, be normal when you talk to people at the office," Shepard said. "Don't think about the recorder. But let's talk about some scenarios, what you should do in certain situations."

By the evening's end, Whitacre felt somewhat comfortable with the device. He pulled his suit straight, and shook the agents' hands. Shepard said he would be back in touch soon. Whitacre nodded and headed out into the hallway.

After Whitacre was gone, Shepard pulled down the bedcovers; he didn't want the maids wondering why the guest in this room never slept. For security, he and Weatherall decided to wait around a few minutes.

Weatherall looked over at Shepard.

"So," he said, "how much of that story do you believe?"

The telephone rang at Shepard's house the following Monday night at 9:10. On the line was Gene Flynn, a switchboard operator from the FBI office.

"Brian," Flynn said, "I have a call from Mark Whitacre, who says he's working with you on a case."

Shepard had left a page for Whitacre earlier in the day and never heard back. Probably this was the return call. He asked Flynn for the number. In a minute, he had Whitacre on the line.

"Yeah, Mark, it's Brian. What's going on?"

Whitacre abandoned any pretense of civility. "Brian, what do you want now?" he snapped, holding his voice down. "When does this end?"

Shepard took a breath. Whitacre had been pulling away, starting with his claims that the price-fixing had come to an end. Obviously, he was reaching some sort of breaking point. Shepard murmured a few calming comments, but Whitacre would have none of it.

"I've told you everything I know," he said. "I've proved I was telling the truth. That tape proved it. I've done what you asked of me, and now I've got a job to do. I don't know what else you want from me."

"Mark, there's a lot more that we have to do," Shepard said. "Right now you're our only witness. You're the only person we have to talk to. You know this is important, and we still need your help."

Whitacre sighed. He was standing at a pay telephone in the offices of Coors Brewing Company in Golden, Colorado, where he had traveled that day to negotiate a possible business deal. He had enjoyed the day—it had been all business, not law enforcement. But then he had checked his messages and heard Shepard's pager. The guy was like a dog with a bone.

"Well, Brian, I don't know how much I'm going to be able to help," Whitacre said. "I've been talking with Ginger, and we've decided that I should try and get a transfer to Mexico. And if I don't get the transfer, then I'm just going to quit the company."

"Okay, Mark," Shepard said. "But what does getting a transfer to Mexico accomplish?"

Whitacre was breathing heavily. Clearly, he wanted Shepard to go away and was thrashing about for any excuse to get that done.

"I'm going to contact an attorney," Whitacre hissed. "You guys are destroying my family."

"Who is, Mark?"

"The FBI."

"What do you mean?"

"The way you're treating me is unfair. I've been honest with you, and I've told you everything I know."

Shepard started to speak, but Whitacre interrupted him.

"I'm out here at a business meeting, a legitimate business meeting," he said. "You guys have got to realize that I've got a business to run and I just can't be working with you all the time."

"I know that, Mark, and that's something that we need to talk about," Shepard said, sounding calm.

Whitacre interrupted again.

"You guys don't care who you hurt. You're going to hurt me, and you're going to hurt Mick Andreas and a lot of other innocent people."

Shepard, who had started jotting down some notes, wrote the word *innocent*.

"I just did what I was told to do," Whitacre continued. "And I'll bet if I talked to an attorney, he would tell me I didn't have to talk to you anymore. All I'm going to do is go back and do business the right way. That's all I care about."

"Mark, that may be what you want to do," Shepard said. "But you know you're just going to get dragged back into the price-fixing."

"No, I'm not. Everything's changing, like I told you. The FBI being around reminded us that we can't be running the company with the kind of maneuvers and tactics that we've used in the past. It's a different attitude; it's a different approach."

"Mark, you know they aren't changing everything from what it was just a week ago. The company's not going to change overnight. You're just saying this because you want us to go away."

"No, you're wrong. The price-fixing is stopping. Definitely. We're even going to be dropping lysine prices, so we can do business the right way. And I can tell you, when we do that, all the competitors are going to be upset, especially the Japanese. There's not going to be any more price-fixing."

"What about other divisions? What about the other things you know are going on there?"

"I don't know anything about how other divisions handle their business. I don't know anything."

Now Whitacre was contradicting himself again. A week before he had told Shepard and Paisley about possible price-fixing by corn refiners. Suddenly, he knew nothing about it. Shepard decided to press him.

"Mark," he said. "You've already told us a lot of things. You've told us about problems in other divisions. You know more than you're saying now."

Then he closed his eyes, seething.

"Look," he said. "I don't know anything else. And I don't want anything more to do with the FBI."

Then he hung up the phone.

He stood by the pay phone, shaking. Everything was getting away from him. He never imagined that the FBI would latch onto him like this. What did they want from him? For God's sake, he didn't want to become some professional FBI agent. He wanted to get back to his job. He gave them the tape. He'd done enough.

Why can't Shepard just leave me alone?

On the third floor of an anonymous-looking office building in downtown Springfield, a forty-year-old federal prosecutor named Byron Cudmore was reviewing records from a criminal case. As First Assistant to the United States Attorney for central Illinois, Cudmore saw most of the paperwork from the big criminal cases in that part of the state—and generated a good deal of it himself.

To keep the heavy document traffic under control, more than half a dozen oak filing cabinets lined his office, each brimming with burgundy accordion folders. Everything about the room was meticulous. Cudmore himself, dressed as always in a starched white shirt and dark suit, had no tolerance for untidy desks or untidy minds. The law-enforcement agents who worked with Cudmore knew to come prepared if they wanted his help or counsel. The athletic prosecutor was all business, with little time for pleasantries or idle chat. Even defendants called him "Stone Face."

One of his lines rang, and Cudmore kept an eye on the extension light as his secretary answered. The light began blinking, and she buzzed Cudmore. Brian Shepard from the FBI was on the line.

"I'll take it," he said.

Before answering, Cudmore slid his rolling chair toward one of the filing cabinets and opened a drawer, removing the folder for the ADM investigation. The case had landed on his desk weeks before, the day after Whitacre first told Shepard about price-fixing. Since then, Cudmore had served as something of a shadow agent, providing input whenever Shepard needed it. Cudmore had worked with Shepard before and respected him; besides being hardworking, the agent always kept his appointments. He felt sure that if Shepard was calling, something important was up.

Cudmore placed the file on his desk, brought out a notepad, and wrote down the date. Prepared, he pushed the blinking light on his phone.

"Brian, this is Byron. What do you need?"

"We're having some trouble. The source is getting hinky. He's going all over the chart."

Cudmore was not surprised. Cooperating witnesses, he knew, usually get very shaky in the early days. Most start dealing with the government without understanding the terms: Cooperation is total immersion, all or nothing. Those who try to limit the details they share with law enforcement are playing a very risky game, one that can result in their being transformed in a flash from witness to defendant.

In this case, Cudmore already knew from Shepard that Whitacre was an intelligent, high-strung person. It was hard to tell if the problems described by Shepard were the result of connivance or Whitacre's own emotional volatility.

"Well, maybe that's just the way he is," Cudmore said. "But maybe there's more that he's hiding."

There were other concerns, Shepard said. The Fujiwara case was still the primary investigation. But Whitacre had yet to tape any calls with the Japanese executive. He had offered excuses—Fujiwara had developed cold feet; Cheviron had forced him to forward calls from his home line with the recorder onto the ADM off-premises extension. But the stories struck Shepard as illogical. On top of that, even though Whitacre had been trained days ago to use a body recorder, not a single tape had come in from ADM. It was frustrating.

"Any suggestions?" Shepard asked.

"Yeah. Maybe back off him a little bit, see what happens. But if things don't straighten out, tell it like it is. Let him know he can't have it both ways."

Cudmore held the receiver close.

"He can be a witness or he can be a target," he said. "It's his choice."

Whitacre closed the door to his office and walked over to his desk. He needed to talk to somebody, somebody he could trust.

He dialed the Atlanta sales office. He didn't need to look up the number; he knew it by heart. The executive who ran the office, Sid Hulse, was his top lysine salesman and a good friend. Whitacre called Hulse many times a day—to talk business, to discuss personal finances, or just to shoot the breeze.

Karen Sterling, an assistant to Hulse, answered.

"ADM Atlanta."

"Yeah, hey, it's Mark."

"Just a moment. I'll get him."

Sterling put the call on hold and turned toward her boss. Even though she had been working for Hulse only a few months, she felt petrified of him. He was physically and emotionally intimidating; she found his sexual harassment to be unrelenting. Unknown to Hulse, Sterling had begun carrying a loaded gun to protect herself from him.

"Sid," she called tentatively. "It's Mark."

Hulse grabbed the phone.

"Hey," he said. "What's up?"

"Got some problems, bud," Whitacre said. "Got some things happening I wanted to talk to you about."

Hulse asked what was wrong.

"You know we've been having trouble in the plant," Whitacre said. "Well, it ends up we might have somebody inside who's sabotaging the place. Dwayne called in the FBI. They're investigating."

Hulse didn't think this sounded too bad. "Well, they'll probably get to the bottom of the problem."

"But that's not all, bud. There's other things going on here. We've been fixing prices for lysine."

For a few minutes, Whitacre described the price-fixing. For all his calls to Hulse, this was the first time he had told his friend about the illegal scheme.

"So, what, you think the FBI's gonna find out about that?" Hulse said.

Whitacre paused. "They already know," he said. "I told them."

"What?"

"Yeah, that's my problem. I told them about it. Now they want me to help them investigate it."

Hulse didn't know what to say.

"I'm in turmoil over this," Whitacre said. "I didn't know what to do, so I thought I'd call you to talk it over. I knew you wouldn't say anything."

The two men hashed through Whitacre's options. Nothing sounded good.

"This just isn't fair, being placed in the middle of all this," Whitacre said. "I mean, I don't want to fix prices. But I don't want to lose my job, either."

As he spoke, Whitacre's distress grew. "I don't know, Sid," he said. "Where do I turn?"

Hulse listened to his friend's concerns but said little. He had no idea how to clean up this mess.

• • •

The blue waters of Camelback Lake were still and calm in the afternoon air. Usually, the forty-four-acre lake in Scottsdale, Arizona, was alive with motion, as windsurfers skimmed past brightly colored sailboats. But the approaching winter brought a chill this day, November 18, 1992. With the water too cold for swimming, the adventurous played golf instead on one of the championship courses of the lakeside resort, the Regal McCormick Ranch.

Whitacre glanced across the lake from a table at the Piñon Grill, an award-winning restaurant at the resort. He had just arrived in Scottsdale for an industry meeting and was eating lunch with executives from a food company. The talk was casual, the atmosphere relaxing. Whitacre felt calm and happy.

Lunch came to an end. Whitacre said his good-byes to his luncheon companions and wandered out of the restaurant to the hotel lobby. Ahead, he saw a bank of pay phones; he hadn't checked his voice mail for more than an hour. He called in and found that several messages were waiting. He had just finished deleting one message, and pushed zero to hear the next.

Beep. Beep.

Whitacre quickly deleted Shepard's pager tone and slammed down the receiver. He couldn't take the tension anymore. Something had to make this come to an end. He picked up the receiver again and called the Decatur Resident Agency. It rang just a few times.

"FBI." Shepard, as always, answered the phone.

"It's Mark," Whitacre said sharply.

Whitacre said incorrectly that he was calling from Phoenix—the city where his plane had landed that morning. Shepard asked about meeting again.

"Look, I'm here on business; I've got a lot of work to do," Whitacre said. "I'm really having trouble with all this. I've really been very distraught and working under a lot of pressure for the last couple of weeks."

"Why? What's going on?"

"Everybody's turning against me."

"Who?"

"Everybody. My superiors at ADM. They're all denying any knowledge of wrongdoing. Everything's against me."

Shepard asked a few more questions, trying to soothe his witness. But Whitacre wouldn't listen.

"You know, I'm a biochemist," Whitacre said. "I have access to lots of biochemical books. And I've taken a bunch of them home so I can research the lethal doses for a bunch of different chemicals."

Shepard paused. "Why would you do that, Mark?"

"Because I'm considering committing suicide," he said, his voice choking. "I've been an upbeat person my whole life, but not now. Not now. For the last couple of weeks, I've been very depressed."

The words flowed out as Whitacre grabbed at everything. Something, he thought, would make Shepard back off. But Shepard didn't believe a word.

"Mark, you know you're not serious," he said evenly. "You're not going to commit suicide. You're just upset, and you're trying to get away from this."

"Brian, I can't keep living two lives. I mean, when does it end?"

"It ends after you help us. Look, right now we need your help, and you're the only one who can do it. It's the right thing to work with us. But we're going to keep investigating, whether you help or not. That's the way it is. And if you're not helping us, if you're not with us, then you could end up a defendant."

Shepard paused to allow his statement to sink in.

"Now, you're telling me people are denying knowledge of wrongdoing," he said. "I gave you a tape recorder. Where's the tape of that conversation?"

Whitacre glanced around the lobby.

"I didn't make it."

"Why not?"

"If I record any conversations with my bosses, all it would do is implicate me. I mean, they could make me the fall guy. It's me against the Andreas family, and I don't see any way I can win that."

"Mark, you're not alone in this. We—"

"It would never work," Whitacre interrupted.

"Mark—"

"I talked to a friend of mine. He's twenty years older than me, but he's a high-level guy, president of a company outside Illinois. He knows the Andreases, and doesn't like them. I told him about this situation."

Was Whitacre telling outsiders about the FBI? "What's this friend's name, Mark?" Shepard asked.

"I'm not going to tell you. But he said there's no way the Japanese would ever trust me in this because I've only been with the company three years."

Shepard wrote down Whitacre's comments.

"And besides, you can't do anything to me," Whitacre said. "My friend gave me the name of an attorney, a former attorney with the Federal Trade Commission, as somebody to contact who knows all about price-fixing laws. I called the guy."

Shepard paused. "You've hired an attorney?"

"I'm not paying for him. My friend is paying for him. And I'm going to pay him back, with interest. In one year. I'll pay him back. My friend said I should never meet with the FBI without an attorney present."

"Okay," Shepard said. Things could be difficult now. Few lawyers would allow Whitacre to continue as a cooperating witness, and Shepard could not ethically press Whitacre to disclose his lawyer's advice.

"I spent five and a half hours with the attorney, and he says everything I've been doing is legal," Whitacre said. "It's all legal. He said it might be leading to illegal stuff. But for now, it's legal."

Shepard doubted what he was hearing. Any lawyer who said such a thing had not been told the truth, at least based on the tape that the FBI already had in hand. Maybe this lawyer didn't even exist. Shepard challenged Whitacre's statements.

"No, that's what he said," Whitacre insisted. "He told me I can legally contact competitors and talk about prices and volumes that we quote to customers."

Shepard reminded Whitacre of everything he had told him in the past. Whitacre *knew* what was going on, Shepard said. The FBI was only involved in this because Whitacre had been so troubled by it all. He had wanted to help clean everything up. What happened to that? Why was ADM so upset about the FBI being around if nothing illegal had been going on?

Hesitating, Whitacre shifted gears, saying that Mick Andreas was upset by the FBI's poking around in the Fujiwara case because he had told Whitacre about meetings in Florida and Europe.

"Were those price-fixing meetings?"

"I think so. And Mick was upset because Dwayne didn't know he had told me about the meetings."

Even though the lysine talks were probably legal, he continued, Mick was worried that if the FBI overheard Whitacre's calls to competitors, the agents might get suspicious and start investigating.

"So it's not that they're afraid of lysine," Whitacre said. "They're afraid that the FBI might uncover stuff about meetings in the other divisions."

Shepard listened carefully. Talking with Whitacre was like trying to grab smoke. He always had another reason, another explanation.

"Well, Mark, there's only one way to convince us of this," Shepard said. "You've got to cooperate fully. You have the recording device. You're going to have to start taping these conversations."

Whitacre paused.

"Fine, Brian," he said finally. "I'll tape it."

The following Tuesday, November 24, Whitacre sat in room 545 at Decatur's Holiday Inn, across from Shepard and Weatherall.

The meeting started badly. No, Whitacre said, he hadn't been able to tape anyone at ADM yet. And no, he had no tapes of Fujiwara, either. He had been on the road too much. After Arizona, he had traveled to Lake Charles, Louisiana, to meet with Chris Jones and Tim Hall, two former colleagues from Degussa whom Whitacre was consulting about a new project at ADM.

Without any tapes, Shepard asked Whitacre for details of meetings he had already described between ADM and the other lysine competitors.

The talks had indeed taken place, Whitacre said—in Tokyo, Maui, Mexico City, and Paris. But they were legal. They had discussed pricing and production simply in an effort to form an industry association. The companies wanted to work together to expand the lysine market, he said, and an association seemed the way to go. Maybe the meetings might lead to price-fixing, he added. But at this point, everyone was trying to follow the law. They had even discussed the idea of bringing lawyers to the association meeting to make sure everything was on the up and up.

Sitting on the bed, Weatherall watched Whitacre. He didn't believe a word. It was all too neat, too contradictory with his other statements. Suddenly, now that Whitacre was consulting an attorney, everything he said exonerated him from wrongdoing.

Weatherall had little doubt what was going on.

This guy, he thought, has been coached.

At home, Whitacre was up late, pondering his problems with the FBI. His family had noticed something was wrong; he had been more distracted and inattentive than usual. But he couldn't talk to Ginger about this. She had already made it clear that she wanted him to leave ADM or work with the FBI. Neither option seemed acceptable. But now, finally, Whitacre had come up with a plan, a way out.

Whitacre smiled to himself. Outsmarting Shepard wouldn't be so tough. In a short time, he wouldn't have to worry about the FBI anymore.

Best of all, he felt sure that no one would ever figure out his role in the events about to occur.

The next day, Whitacre was at his desk when he reached for the phone to call Sid Hulse.

"We've got volume building up in the plant," he said. "So we're going to stop worrying about getting prices up. In fact, I want you to drop 'em."

Hulse sounded uncertain. Not long ago, Whitacre was telling him about the illegal efforts to drive prices up, now he wanted to push them down. But Whitacre implied that the change of strategy was being ordered by ADM's top management. Hulse asked a few specifics about where the prices should be.

"Do whatever you have to do," Whitacre said. "Just sell as much volume as you can."

Hulse cautioned Whitacre that the new strategy could lead to a collapse in prices.

"I know that," Whitacre said. "But our warehouses are filling up, and our production costs will be lower if we sell more."

"Okay," Hulse replied.

Whitacre replaced the receiver and smiled. The FBI thought that they were in control, that they could decide what Whitacre would do. They were wrong.

I've got control of this whole thing.

In Decatur, no one but Whitacre understood the marketing of lysine. If anyone wanted a price, they asked Whitacre. If anyone wanted to know what the Japanese were doing, they asked Whitacre. He could decide what others knew, and what they didn't.

And he wouldn't tell them anything about what was happening now: He was seizing control of the world lysine market; he was ordering prices into a free fall. To flood the market with volume, ADM would have to drop its price every time the Japanese or Koreans tried to match it. The competitors would respond in kind, and a race to the bottom would ensue. Since the Asian competitors always called Whitacre, he could blame the move on his bosses. When his bosses asked, he could blame the Asians. This would take the wind out of the recent trend of price increases. After that, it might take a few weeks, but Whitacre felt confident he could push everyone toward a price war.

It was the first stage of his plan, and it was perfect. With a price war, there couldn't be price-fixing. And without price-fixing, the FBI wouldn't need a witness.

Whitacre felt gleeful. Now, all he had to do was keep up appearances for a few weeks.

He was almost free.

About a week later, the Whitacres were in the family room when the phone rang. Ginger answered; it was for Mark. He walked to the living room, sat on the couch, and picked up a cordless phone.

"Mark Whitacre."

"Ah, yes, Mr. Whitacre? This is Mr. Mimoto."

Whitacre shifted in his seat. He hadn't been expecting his counterpart from Ajinomoto to call.

Mimoto continued before Whitacre could respond. "I wanted to speak to you about lysine sales in Japan," he said.

"Excuse me, Mr. Mimoto, I'm sorry," Whitacre said. "We have a bunch of people over at the house tonight, we're having a party here. I was wondering if maybe we could talk about this another time?"

"Oh, yes," Mimoto said. "Sorry. We can speak another time."

Whitacre said he would call on a more convenient day and hung up. He headed back to the family room. Ginger was on the couch, reading a book. The kids were watching television.

There were no guests. There was no party.

But if the FBI was listening in on his calls, he had just made sure that they would have nothing to hear.

Byron Cudmore parked his light-blue Chevy Silverado pickup truck a short distance from the lobby of the Holiday Inn in Decatur. It was about six o'clock on the evening of November 30. Picking up his briefcase from the passenger seat, the prosecutor hustled across the lot to the hotel's entrance. Inside, Cudmore saw Shepard waiting in a lobby chair. The two men greeted each other, and Shepard said that everything was set. Cudmore nodded.

Without another word, Shepard led the way past the glass-paneled Greenhouse Restaurant, toward the elevators. After almost a month of talking about Shepard's cooperating witness, Cudmore would finally be meeting him.

Shepard had called Cudmore earlier that week to request the

meeting. Things with Whitacre were falling apart; the agent didn't know what to believe. Whitacre kept talking about some lawyer he was consulting, and at first, the agents had feared he was being coached on his answers. But now Shepard wondered whether the lawyer even existed. What lawyer would allow his client to keep meeting, alone, with the FBI?

To help get Whitacre under control, Shepard wanted him to sign a cooperation agreement with the U.S. Attorney's office. Most cooperating witnesses work without such agreements. But often—particularly when a witness is being difficult—the terms of cooperation are put in writing. That way, one document describes the witness's obligations to the government and the legal consequences if those terms are not met. In the call to Cudmore, Shepard said that he had mentioned the idea to Whitacre, who had agreed to meet with the prosecutor to discuss signing an agreement.

Cudmore followed Shepard to a guest room, where Weatherall was already waiting.

"When is Whitacre supposed to get here?" Cudmore asked, setting his briefcase on the hotel room table.

"He should be on his way," Shepard said.

The knock came a few minutes later. Shepard let Whitacre in and introduced him to the prosecutor. Whitacre struck Cudmore as awfully young; he looked more like a scientist than a top-level executive. Cudmore asked Whitacre to take a chair at the table.

"What we're trying to do today is get a chance to eyeball one another, and see what makes each other tick," Cudmore said. "That will give us a chance to develop some level of trust, and for you to ask me any questions to flesh out a cooperation agreement."

Cudmore asked if Whitacre had any worries.

"Well, I'm concerned about myself and my family and my new home," Whitacre said. "I mean, we just bought our house not too long ago, and it's the house that Dwayne Andreas used to live in. And I'm worried about the expenses because I have to pay for it."

Just days before, Whitacre said, he had been granted a one-hundred-thousand dollar raise and forty thousand additional shares of stock options. His job was lucrative, and he didn't want to risk it.

Cudmore listened, incredulous. Clearly, Whitacre did not fully understand his situation. Regardless of the risks, he didn't have many options.

"You know, there are no guarantees," Cudmore said. "But you've basically put yourself in a situation where cooperation is the logical way for you to proceed. You can't take yourself out of this situation; you can't make it go away."

Whitacre sat erect and didn't speak.

"If you're not cooperating, you could end up being a defendant," Cudmore cautioned.

"No, that's not right," Whitacre argued. "I've told Brian, there hasn't been any price-fixing yet."

"That's not the only issue that could lead to a criminal prosecution," Cudmore said gently. "You've told us a lot of things. In fact, you've told us so many things that there have to be some lies somewhere. Lying to a federal agent can be the basis for a prosecution. That's a felony, and I think the penalty is five years in prison and a big chunk of money."

Cudmore let that sink in for a second.

"You have to understand," he said. "I don't care if you're the defendant, or the price-fixers are the defendants. It doesn't matter to me."

The prosecutor leaned in.

"But I can assure you, somebody is going to be a defendant. If the case is against you, it'll be a good strong case. If the case is against them, it'll be a good strong case. I don't try bad cases."

Whitacre blinked through his glasses.

"Okay," he said.

Cudmore glanced at his briefcase on the table. He had a copy of the cooperation agreement with him but decided that the time was not right to bring it out. Better to let Whitacre absorb what was happening.

"Now, I'm going to tell you about the cooperation agreement," he said. "It's an agreement that I drafted and I've been using for years. It's the only cooperation agreement that we offer."

"Would it guarantee that I won't be prosecuted for anything?" Whitacre asked.

"It doesn't make any promises. And we've never struck a cooperation agreement with anyone that promised anything. Because someday you're going to have to be on the stand and testify that the government hasn't promised you anything. It's basically a 'trust me' situation."

Whitacre continued asking questions. Cudmore answered but felt increasingly uncomfortable. Whitacre showed little emotion; it was almost as if the man wasn't connected to what was happening.

"The bottom line here is, cooperate or be a target," Cudmore said. "Get yourself a lawyer and talk to him. Verify what I'm saying, and do the right thing for yourself."

Cudmore stood. He wanted to get home.

"You tell the agents when you want to meet and review an actual cooperation agreement," he said.

Again, Cudmore and Whitacre shook hands. Shepard escorted the prosecutor to the door. There, Cudmore turned to the agent.

"Keep me posted," he said softly.

Shepard switched on the tape recorder at his desk as soon as he heard that Richard Reising was on the phone. He had called Reising that morning, December 1, but only now, hours later, had the ADM general counsel called back.

Shepard asked if ADM's position was still that it was unwilling to cooperate with the Fujiwara investigation. The FBI was turning up the heat on the obstruction investigation and wanted to see if Reising would lock himself in. But ADM had decided to back down and pretend nothing had ever happened.

"I don't think we ever said we wouldn't cooperate," Reising said, having no idea he had been taped saying exactly that a few weeks earlier, in a conversation with Kevin Corr. "We have cooperated with the FBI numerous times in the past, and we want to cooperate in this matter."

Reising listed his conditions. Whitacre could not be involved. Cheviron was the only person who would respond to FBI requests. ADM had a business to run, Reising said, and that came first.

"Andreas doesn't want to put his executives at risk, nor their families. That is the only reason we want to get Whitacre out of this. That is not his job. You have your job; we have our job. Your job is law enforcement; ours is not law enforcement."

Shepard replied that Whitacre was already involved since he had spoken many times to Fujiwara.

"As far as I know, there have been no further telephone calls from Fujiwara," Reising said. "It's certainly our intention to let you know if there is a telephone call. Hell, you'll know."

The call ended in a few minutes. After almost a month of blocking the investigation, ADM was professing itself willing to cooperate. But only under terms that kept the FBI away from Whitacre.

Later that day, at an airport security checkpoint, Whitacre dropped his keys into a bucket and lifted his carry-on luggage onto a conveyor belt. The bag rumbled into an X-ray machine as Whitacre walked through a metal detector. He glanced at his watch before retrieving his belongings.

He had close to an hour until his flight. Walking through the terminal, he searched for a phone.

Minutes later, he was dialing the number for the Decatur Resident Agency. Shepard answered.

Whitacre got right to the point. Nobody at ADM was talking to him, he said. And now he had proof.

About an hour before he left for the airport, Whitacre said, he had seen a phone message on Reising's desk, saying that an FBI agent had called. But Reising had told him nothing about it.

"I mentioned the note to Randall, and he just changed the subject. They won't talk to me about it. It's just more examples of me being cut out of the loop. I mean, I'm willing to cooperate with the FBI. Definitely. But they don't trust me."

Whitacre mentioned that he was traveling to Europe and would be out of town at least a week. Shepard wished him a good trip, and the call ended.

Hefting his bag off the ground, Whitacre headed to his gate. His plan, he thought, was working perfectly. Soon, the FBI would *have* to give up on him.

After all, what good is a witness if none of the potential targets will talk to him?

At that same moment, Shepard phoned Weatherall in Champaign to brief him on Whitacre's call. The news worried Weatherall; problems were piling up.

After hanging up, Weatherall sat down to write a teletype to Bureau headquarters. It would not be a hopeful message.

With ADM's top officers apparently distrustful of Whitacre, Weatherall wrote, his usefulness as a cooperating witness might be limited.

The next morning, in Germany, Whitacre stepped bleary-eyed into a steaming shower in his suite at the Sheraton Frankfurt Hotel, across from the airport. Usually he traveled well, but this morning he felt the effects of the seven-hour time difference.

After his shower and a shave, Whitacre wandered out into the suite, one of thirty at the hotel. He glanced at the bedside alarm clock and saw that the local time was almost eight A.M. Making some mental calculations, he figured out the time in Tokyo.

Whitacre sat at a desk in his room. The hotel offered international direct dialing, and Whitacre took advantage of it. Probably no one would be checking his hotel bills for calls.

Minutes later, in Tokyo, Kanji Mimoto was at his desk when one of the young men who answered his department's line let him know that Mr. Whitacre was holding. Mimoto reached for the telephone. He was anxious to talk to Whitacre, to find out why ADM was forcing prices down around the world.

"Hello?" he said.

"Mr. Mimoto?"

"Yes, good afternoon. Or is it good evening?"

"Ah, actually it's good morning," Whitacre said. "I'm calling from Frankfurt."

"Frankfurt, ah. You have business in Frankfurt."

"Just some meetings with our European staff."

The men exchanged a few more pleasantries.

"Listen, I wanted to apologize about the other night," Whitacre finally said.

"Oh, no apology necessary."

"No, I wanted to apologize. Because I didn't have people over that night. We weren't having a party."

"No?" Mimoto was confused.

"No, but that's why I'm calling you from my hotel," Whitacre said. "I didn't want to talk to you because I was afraid my telephone might be tapped."

"Tapped?"

"By the FBI. They're conducting an investigation into our pricing in the CO_2 business."

FBI? This made no sense. Carbon dioxide—CO_2—is the ingredient that gives soda its fizz. Mimoto said he had no idea Whitacre worked in that business.

"Oh, I don't," Whitacre said. "But I was called into the FBI office."

"Why?"

"All high-level executives were interviewed by the FBI. And they talked to us about the possibility of recording our telephone calls."

This made Mimoto uncomfortable. He knew that his pricing discussions with Whitacre had been illegal; the last thing he wanted was federal agents snooping around, planting wiretaps. This could be a disaster.

"Then it is good we did not speak that night."

"Yes, that's why I'm calling. I don't think you should call my home anymore. It's just too dangerous."

"Yes, yes."

Whitacre offered an alternative. Mimoto could call his office voice mail and leave a message.

"I don't like that," Mimoto said. "I don't want to leave my name. I want to use another name."

Whitacre thought for a second. "How about Mr. Tani?" he asked. "Tani is an ADM sales representative for ADM in New York. No one but me would recognize his voice, and a message from him wouldn't raise suspicions."

"Good," Mimoto replied. "That's good."

The conversation continued for hours. At the end, the executives reviewed their new system for contacting each other. Mimoto would leave messages; Whitacre would call back from a safe phone. Mimoto thanked Whitacre for his caution and said good-bye.

Placing the phone in its cradle, Whitacre felt a sense of power. Mimoto had been his main contact in the price-fixing, the one who called with every update and question. Now, Whitacre had all but guaranteed that the man would never call him directly again. From now on, they would use pay phones.

Whitacre smiled. The FBI could tap any phones they wanted. There was nothing left for them to hear.

"Let's review the background on the Fujiwara calls," Shepard said. "How many did you receive?"

Whitacre glanced at the hotel room ceiling as if in thought. "It was like half a dozen," he said.

"Six?"

"From five to eight."

Shepard nodded. The Fujiwara investigation had been under way for more than a month, but Whitacre still had not recorded a single call from the Japanese executive. Shepard wanted to use this meeting to review the details of the extortion case again.

"Where did the calls come in?"

"Most of them to my home, but the first one came to my office," Whitacre said.

"And you've had no calls in the past few weeks?"

"He called one other time to the office, but I couldn't record that. Mick Andreas stopped by while I was on the phone with him."

Shepard began asking another question, when Whitacre changed the subject.

"Something you guys would want to know. A guy named Wayne Brasser was fired today. ADM told him to pack up and leave before the end of the day."

"Why was that?" Weatherall asked.

"I think because he knew a lot about price-fixing," Whitacre said. "I think that he was considered a liability, because he thought it was wrong and made his feelings known."

Shepard wrote down Brasser's name with little enthusiasm. Whitacre hadn't backed up any lead in more than a month. Why should this one be different?

In Decatur, Shepard was on the phone with Cudmore. His frustrations with Whitacre were getting to him. Whitacre seemed to think he was smarter than everyone else and could lie with impunity.

"Things are falling apart, and I don't know what to believe," he told Cudmore.

He had contacted the Behavioral Science Unit—the FBI's experts in profiling and psychological analysis. They offered insights and a suggestion. Cudmore listened as Shepard explained the idea.

"Sounds good," the prosecutor replied. "Get it going."

Two weeks later, Whitacre drove to the Holiday Inn for another meeting with the FBI. He was feeling calm and confident. The once-steady growth in lysine prices had slowed to a halt. Calls from Japan had stopped. The FBI seemed concerned about how little ADM trusted him. And Whitacre had kept up his act of cooperating, even pressing for a written agreement. This investigation, he felt sure, would collapse soon. His plan had worked better than he could have hoped.

Whitacre parked and headed inside. He already knew from his voice mail that the agents were in room 515. He arrived upstairs and tapped on the door.

Shepard let him in. The agents greeted Whitacre and shook his hand. That was when Whitacre noticed something was different. This time, a dark-haired man was busy in an adjoining room. The man, who looked younger than Whitacre, came through the doorway.

"Mark," Shepard said, "this is Special Agent Ed Hamara. He's going to be helping us this evening."

Another agent. No matter. Whitacre greeted Hamara warmly.

Shepard and Weatherall eyed their witness. Apparently, he had no idea what was happening.

"Agent Hamara is one of the Bureau's polygraphers," Shepard said.

Whitacre shot Shepard a perplexed look.

"Polygrapher," Shepard repeated. "He conducts lie detector tests."

CHAPTER 5

"Is your first name Mark?"

Agent Hamara brought his pen down on the chart paper rolling through the polygraph machine, marking the moment he finished his first question. Whitacre, in a chair beside him, answered yes. Hamara wrote a small plus sign beneath the wavy ink tracings.

Whitacre sat still. Rubber tubes wrapped his chest and abdomen, measuring his breathing. On his ring and index fingers, two small clips monitored his skin for changes in the flow of electricity. A blood-pressure cuff, at about eighty millimeters of mercury, checked the brachial artery in his arm for variations in blood volume. He faced a window that looked out onto the highway. The curtain was closed.

Shepard and Weatherall had surprised him with the polygraph, but Whitacre did not even consider making a fuss. Without saying so directly, Shepard had made it clear that a refusal in itself would be considered an admission of deceit. So Whitacre had walked to the adjoining room with Hamara, stripped off his jacket, and sat patiently as he was hooked up to the machine. Hamara had closed the door, leaving them alone.

Hamara's manner was soothing; to eliminate anxiety that might contaminate the results, he had told Whitacre the questions to expect. None of the relevant questions involved price-fixing, only Fujiwara.

"Were you born in 1957?" Hamara asked.

"Yes."

Hamara marked another plus sign on the paper. Whitacre's breathing was steady, at about eighteen breaths per minute. His heart rate was consistent, and the electrical resistance of his skin had stabilized. Hamara waited about twenty seconds before proceeding.

"Regarding the phone calls from Fujiwara, do you intend to answer each question truthfully?"

"Yes."

In itself, the question was meaningless, a sacrifice. It was intended to bleed off any anxiety about the exam's two relevant questions.

Twenty seconds passed.

"Are you concerned I will ask you a question on this test that we have not already reviewed?"

"No."

Hamara marked down a negative sign and glanced at Whitacre's response. He was telling the truth. Whitacre was properly prepared. The results would not be influenced by anxiety about the test.

"Before this year, did you ever lie to better your own position?"

"No."

A lie, but an expected one. The question was another control. Most anyone asked so general a question would have to say yes—no one ever fibbed to their parents about that late night in high school? But when Hamara discussed this question in the pretest interview, he had stressed the importance of being a truthful person. It was a technique designed to force a dishonest answer, one that could be measured against other deceptions that might occur.

Twenty seconds.

"Did Fujiwara ever telephone you at home and tell you there was a mole at ADM?"

"Yes."

A relevant question.

Whitacre glanced at the ink tracings. *Nothing*. To him, they looked exactly the same as before.

Hamara wrote a plus sign. He noticed an almost imperceptible change in the location of the dichrotic notch, a tiny tick in the cardio-vascular tracing coming from the pressure cuff.

Twenty seconds.

"Before this year, did you ever lie to someone that really trusted you?"

"No."

Another control.

Twenty seconds.

"Did Fujiwara say he would tell you who the mole was for X amount of dollars?"

"Yes."

Relevant.

Whitacre watched the tracings. It looked unchanged to him.

Twenty seconds.

"Are you married?"

"Yes."

Hamara wrote down a plus sign.

The first portion of the test was over.

"All right, Mr. Whitacre, now I'm going to ask the same questions again," Hamara said, flipping pages. "We want to make sure the results are consistent."

Whitacre nodded, feeling comfortable. "Okay."

After a moment, Hamara started over.

Shepard and Weatherall waited in the adjoining room for more than an hour. Finally, they heard a doorknob click. Whitacre walked in first, followed by Hamara. Both men seemed relaxed.

"Can I speak with you?" Hamara asked the agents.

Shepard and Weatherall stepped into the next room and closed the door. Whitacre sat down in a chair. He had no worries. He had watched the tracings and never saw them change. He was sure he had passed easily.

In the other room, Hamara picked up the numerical scoring he had completed after the exam.

"How did he do?" Weatherall asked.

Hamara flipped through the results and looked up.

Whitacre, he said, had splattered the walls with ink.

After ten minutes, Shepard and Weatherall returned to the room where Whitacre was waiting. Their expressions said everything; the test had gone badly.

As Weatherall sat down on the bed, he studied Whitacre. The agent was not a big believer in lie detectors; he had seen plenty of bad guys pass a polygraph and just as many innocent people fail. But this time, the whole picture—particularly the lack of any Fujiwara recordings— left him with little doubt that Whitacre was hiding something.

Shepard sat next to Whitacre.

"Mark, there were some problems," he said.

Whitacre fidgeted. "Wait a minute, I watched the machine," he said. "I didn't see any changes."

They spoke to him gently. Let's try to look at this, let's try to understand it. Whitacre held fast to his story. His words trailed off. He'd had enough.

He changed the subject.

"You know, there's stuff that happened today that you should know about," Whitacre said. "They're worried about Wayne Brasser."

Weatherall and Shepard listened, allowing the tension to ease. Everyone was exhausted. They would let it go tonight, let everyone rest. It was best for Whitacre to reflect for a day. Let his psychological distress do much of the agents' work for them.

Whitacre had mentioned Brasser days before; supposedly, he had been fired after objecting to price-fixing in ADM's business in sodium gluconate, a chemical used in industrial cleansers. Afterward, Whitacre said, ADM panicked and gave Brasser a big severance to keep quiet. Still, Whitacre said that ADM officials were asking if he knew about a file Brasser may have taken with him. The reason they were asking, Whitacre explained, was that he and Brasser were friends; they spoke often.

Shepard decided to take advantage of the moment.

"Mark, I'm interested in this information about Wayne Brasser," he said.

"What else do you want to know?"

"You say you talk to him all the time?"

"Yeah, all the time," Whitacre said eagerly.

"And he talks to you about what happened?"

"Yeah, yeah, he does."

Shepard leaned in.

"Then let's call him," he said.

Whitacre paused, breathing lightly. He had the look of a man who had just been cornered. He glanced from Shepard to Weatherall and back again.

Finally, he nodded his head. "Sure."

The line was ringing.

Whitacre sat on a bed with the receiver to his ear. In one hand, he held the microphone wire from the microcassette recorder to the earpiece. Shepard sat across from him, while Weatherall stood by the table. The agents were avoiding looking at Whitacre directly. They didn't want to unnerve him.

A woman answered, and Whitacre asked for Brasser.

"Hello?"

"Wayne?" Whitacre asked.

"Yes?"

"This is Mark Whitacre."

"Mark, how are ya?"

Brasser sounded sleepy, as if he had just woken up. Whitacre noticed the time. It was past eleven-fifteen.

"Hope I didn't get you up."

"Ah, no. What's goin' on?"

The two men chatted, saying little but obviously circling around something. Several executives, Whitacre said, had been talking about Brasser's file. But Brasser said he had no file; it had been given to Barrie Cox, who ran ADM's business in citric acid, an ingredient used in everything from soda to detergent.

Whitacre pressed about the file. What product was that about? he asked.

"Oh, that was on gluconate," Brasser said. "What they . . . you know. They came back with the information. I just . . . you know. They got the reports back."

Brasser was being evasive, never saying anything specific. It was the language of conspiracy. But Whitacre knew that Brasser needed to be more specific.

Were these reports from meetings with other gluconate producers? he asked.

"Yeah."

Whitacre had been instructed to push Brasser on every possible product, looking for confirmation. The agents were particularly interested in citric acid. To Whitacre, the moment felt right to bring it up.

"They seemed to be worried too, what you know about on, on citric," he said, nervous as he probed further. "The question's been going around a lot, 'What does Wayne know about what went on there?' "

Brasser listened calmly. "Barrie told me," he said.

"Same thing as on the gluconate business?"

"Sort of, yeah."

Whitacre felt a rush: Barrie Cox had told Brasser that price-fixing was taking place in his multibillion-dollar market.

Whitacre brought up Brasser's pay package. "They hoped they made a deal sweet enough that they wouldn't have to worry about it."

"Yeah." Brasser's answer was noncommittal.

Whitacre glanced at Shepard. The agent had told him before the call to ask if Brasser had attended price-fixing meetings. Whitacre returned to the topic, discussing how citric prices had risen from fifty-eight cents to eighty-two cents in just a few months.

"You were never at those meetings, were you?"

"No."

"So Barrie just told you about those?"

"Yeah."

What about gluconate? Did he go to those meetings? Did Terry Wilson or Barrie Cox attend?

"I went to one. After that, they went."

"What do you mean, Barrie and Terry?"

"Yep," Brasser said.

Whitacre laughed once.

"I went there because I was invited and I didn't know, you know, what it was," Brasser said. "And I got there and I thought, 'Holy shit!' "

"Well, they were worried about you knowing about that then. That makes some sense now."

"You know, what they're doing is, you know, playin' with fire," Brasser said.

Whitacre looked over at Shepard. The agent was watching him now, expectantly.

"Whenever those things happen, it seems the same guys are involved, doesn't it?" Whitacre asked.

"Yeah," Brasser said. He switched topics. Was there any chance he could get back to the company?

Whitacre sidestepped the question and asked about ADM's payment to Brasser. Although he had worked there about five years, Brasser said, he had received eighteen months' severance plus a company car. But everything that was happening at ADM still bothered him; Brasser said he had warned Wilson of the dangers.

"I said, 'You realize that you're gambling, you're really gambling a lot here.' "

"Well, it's a big deal in my opinion," Whitacre said. "It's unethical, and it's definitely illegal."

"I'm sure if Mick and them are aware of it, they're far enough away from it that, you know, they can't get the problems."

Whitacre agreed.

Brasser sounded resigned. "They're gonna get caught sooner or later."

"Well, if they get caught on that one, it will just lead to one product right after another. And then it will be about every product that ADM's into. You know?"

"I don't know what would happen," Brasser said.

The agent listened to Whitacre's side of the conversation, already able to tell that the men were expressing their disgust at ADM's illegal activities. Brasser said that Wilson was even interested in fixing prices for lactic acid, another additive.

"You mean, he wanted to make deals like that on lactic, too?" Whitacre asked.

"Yeah," Brasser said.

But Brasser said first they would have to go to war with competitors so that ADM could grab market share. Whitacre understood the strategy; low prices make everybody willing to talk.

"Boy," Whitacre said.

"Well, he said, 'Don't worry about it.' He said, 'Anybody has to go to jail, it will be Barrie Cox and myself.' "

The statement jolted Whitacre. Trying to keep from blurting anything out, he sniffed.

"He said that, huh?"

"I said, 'I don't want to know about it.' "

"He actually said jail and everything?"

"Yeah," Brasser replied, laughing.

Whitacre looked at the clock; it was past eleven-thirty-five. He told Brasser that he needed to sleep, but still the conversation continued. Five minutes later, it wound down, with Whitacre promising to keep in touch.

"Have a good Christmas and all the best to the family," Whitacre said. "All right?"

"Let's call, let's talk before Christmas."

Whitacre agreed, and the men said their good-byes. Whitacre breathed out as the call disconnected.

He looked at Shepard and Weatherall.

"Boy," he sighed.

Less than twenty minutes later, Shepard escorted Whitacre to the hotel room door, his hand touching the executive's shoulder. They needed to speak again tomorrow, Shepard said, and he'd leave a message with the room number. Whitacre nodded, looking wrung out. He opened the door and left.

Shepard turned to Weatherall, shaking his head. They had heard enough to know this tape was fabulous.

Their witness—this lying, manipulative man who had just failed a polygraph exam—was in the middle of a massive criminal conspiracy.

And, even with all of Whitacre's wild tales, the scheme seemed bigger than they had dared imagine.

• • •

At the stoplight just outside of the Holiday Inn, Whitacre turned left, heading home to Moweaqua.

He still didn't believe that he flunked the polygraph. It didn't make sense. None of the lines on the paper moved differently, regardless of the question. Probably, he thought, the agents just told him he had blown the exam to get leverage over him. Probably so.

He took a breath, letting out some of the anxiety from the evening. That tape of Brasser had come out better than he had expected. Now the FBI agents knew that there was somebody else who could tell them a lot about price-fixing. Maybe they might be interested in trying to flip *him* to be their witness.

Best of all, Brasser didn't know a thing about lysine. Whitacre decided to talk a lot more about him in the days to come.

The next day, Shepard and Weatherall were back at the Holiday Inn, ready for a rough meeting. This time, they had to push Whitacre on the Fujiwara story. Something wasn't right, something wasn't true. They were committed to finding out what their witness was holding back.

Confronting a cooperating witness with evidence of deceit is a delicate job. Threats can backfire; after all, the idea is to get the witness on board again, and fear is a poor motivator. The agents had decided that Weatherall would handle this confrontation. He was a skilled interviewer, and Whitacre seemed more off balance with him.

When Whitacre arrived, the three men fell into their routine: Everyone shook hands, Shepard asked about Whitacre's family, and Whitacre did the same. Finally, Whitacre took a seat. Weatherall sat across from him. Immediately, Whitacre knew something was up.

"Mark," Weatherall said, "we need to talk."

Whitacre nodded. "Okay."

"I want to talk to you regarding your truthfulness about the Fujiwara extortion."

Whitacre looked taken aback. "I've told you the truth," he said.

"Well, Mark, when you had that polygraph exam last night, it indicated that you weren't telling the whole truth about that. It indicated that you've got something more to tell."

Whitacre shook his head vigorously.

"No, I've told you everything," he said. "I've told the truth."

"Mark . . ."

"Look, I've heard these lie detector tests aren't accurate anyway. I mean, I've heard that."

"Mark . . ."

"No, I've been telling the truth. Definitely."

Weatherall leaned in. It wasn't just the lie detector, he said in his most grandfatherly voice. The Fujiwara story didn't make complete sense. There hadn't been any calls recorded since the FBI came onto the case. Extortionists didn't just leave their names and forget about it. There were millions of dollars on the line; he would have been in contact.

Whitacre protested, but each time Weatherall methodically explained why his story couldn't be true.

"Mark, I know it's hard," Weatherall said. "I know you're in this position where you've told everyone this story. You've told it to the company; you've told it to us. But it doesn't make sense."

Whitacre stared at the table, his expression vacant.

"You know there's more to tell," Weatherall continued. "I know it's tough, keeping it all bottled up inside, keeping it secret."

Weatherall gave Whitacre a long look. "Now it's time to be truthful. It's time to be completely honest."

His eyes watery, Whitacre breathed in.

"Okay," he said, his voice strained.

That's it. The first admission. By agreeing to finally tell the truth, Whitacre had all but confessed that he had misled the agents about something. That admission, Weatherall knew, was always the hardest.

"Good, Mark," he said. "That's good. So tell me, it's true you haven't been completely honest about Fujiwara, isn't it?"

Whitacre nodded.

"Did you lie to us?"

"Yeah," Whitacre sighed.

"Did you lie to ADM?"

Another nod. "I lied to Mick."

Weatherall took a breath. "Mark, did Fujiwara ever call you about a saboteur in the plant?"

Hesitation. Whitacre said nothing.

"Mark . . ."

"I'm sure there's been a mole in our plant," Whitacre said. "Randall thought so, too."

A nonresponse. His voice trailed off.

"Mark," Weatherall said, "did Fujiwara ever call you about a saboteur? Did he ever demand money?"

Nothing.

Then, gently, Whitacre shook his head.

"No," he said softly. "I made it up."

The conversation dragged on for hours. Just as Weatherall had expected, once Whitacre confessed to his deception, the explanations just kept flowing. As he spoke, he alternately seemed relieved and wrecked.

There had not been a sabotage call or an extortion attempt, Whitacre admitted, but he never thought things would go this far. There had been problems in the plant, with viruses causing shutdowns, and everyone was on him to solve the problem. Millions of dollars were being wasted. His bosses were angry.

Sabotage seemed to explain the unending problems. But whenever he raised the idea as a possibility, no one took it seriously or would look into it. Then in September, Whitacre said, Fujiwara called.

"Why was he calling?" Shepard asked.

"He had a technical question," Whitacre replied. "He wanted to know the status of our patent application on a drying process we use for our products. I didn't know the answer, so I told him I would call him back."

But the call had given him an idea, Whitacre said, that could force ADM to listen to his suspicions. So, he went to Mick Andreas and told him that Fujiwara had called about a saboteur and wanted money.

Mick had not seemed too concerned at first, Whitacre said. But he was interested in the prospect of dealing with Fujiwara to get some of Ajinomoto's microorganisms. After some talks, Whitacre said, Mick made it clear that he would be willing to pay as much as $6 million for those bugs.

"Fujiwara called back a few nights later. I told him that I thought Ajinomoto had a mole in our plant."

"How did he react?" Weatherall asked.

"He seemed surprised. But he didn't deny it."

In the conversation that followed, Whitacre said, he did just as Mick wanted. He told Fujiwara how valuable the Ajinomoto microbes would be to ADM, and how the company was willing to pay for the bugs.

"Fujiwara was surprised at the offer," Whitacre said. "He seemed like he had no interest in a deal. I told him to think about it, and asked for his home number. But he didn't want to give it to me."

Over the next month, he said, Fujiwara called several times but never agreed to sell the bugs.

"That got Mick worried that we were getting set up by the Japanese. So he asked me to stall because he was going to do something. The next thing I knew, you guys were involved in this."

Once the FBI arrived, Whitacre said, everything changed. In no time, ADM told him to inform Fujiwara that the deal was off.

"I called Fujiwara at Ajinomoto. I told him the heat was on and we needed more time."

Whitacre looked from Shepard to Weatherall. "There haven't been any talks with Fujiwara since," he said. "There hasn't been anything."

The agents flipped through their notes. This story had the ring of truth. The idea that ADM had tried to buy a competitor's bug was similar to Whitacre's other allegations about industrial espionage.

"So," Shepard said, "the major motive for telling Mick this story in the first place was?"

"The major motive was to prove to Mick something I've been saying for eighteen months," Whitacre said. "I think we had a mole in the plant, causing contamination and information-flow problems."

"And why did you agree to try and obtain the organisms?"

Whitacre shrugged. "I wanted to be on the team. I thought it would help my relationship with Mick."

The agents questioned Whitacre again from the beginning, writing it all down in longhand. They wanted to be sure Whitacre was committed to this version. Weatherall showed him the written statement.

"So, this is the full story?"

Whitacre nodded.

"Mark, if there's anything else you want to add, now's the time. The truth matters here."

"That's the full story."

"Now, this document and anything else you say can be used in court. Do you understand that?"

"Yeah, I understand."

"And you still want to sign? Nothing to add?"

Whitacre shook his head.

"Okay," Weatherall said, sliding the document across the table to him.

Whitacre signed the statement. Weatherall and Shepard both signed as witnesses.

"Okay, Mark," Weatherall said. "I'm proud you told the truth. You're doing the right thing."

The meeting ended twenty minutes later. Whitacre had finally opened up. Maybe now his real work as a cooperating witness could begin.

Ginger Whitacre, wearing a nightgown and a robe, carried two glasses of lemonade into the family room. Mark had brought wood in for a fire before changing for bed; now the flames were giving the room a warm glow. She walked toward the couch where Mark was sitting, handed him a lemonade, and sat down beside him.

She took a sip, staring into the fire.

"Mark," she said, "it's the right thing to do."

He drank his lemonade.

"I know," he said.

"You've started something; now you've got to finish it."

"I could always leave."

"Yes, you can just walk away, go work for somebody else," she said. "I'd be happy with that. But as long as you work for ADM, you should cooperate. You should sign the agreement."

He took another sip. "It's not like I'd be doing a lot of things different. I meet with them whenever they want; I make tapes for them. I guess all I'd be doing is putting everything in writing."

Ginger knew nothing about Mark's confession of his deceit to the FBI. She knew nothing of his plan. He still hoped he could upend the investigation and get away from the FBI. But until then, it seemed to make sense to sign the cooperation agreement. At least that way, no one could prosecute him.

"Okay," he said finally. "I'll call Brian. I'll tell him I want to sign."

Ginger leaned her head on his shoulder. She was proud of her husband. He was doing the right thing.

Christmas came and went, and afterward Shepard and Weatherall received one additional present—news of Whitacre's decision. The night of his confession seemed to have been a breakthrough. Now, he talked about how eager he was to help. Shepard called Cudmore in the prosecutors' office to let him know. They needed to get together again—and this time Cudmore could take the agreement out of his briefcase.

They met at the Holiday Inn on Tuesday, December 29. Whitacre arrived late; he had been at the store, purchasing seven cans of caramel popcorn as late presents for business associates.

"I brought the agreement," the prosecutor said, bringing out the three-page document. "You'll find it's exactly as I told you. I want to go over it with you and make sure you don't have any questions."

Whitacre read through the cooperation agreement's thirteen terms. It said that the government could not prosecute Whitacre on the basis of information he provided. In exchange, he was required to offer "complete and truthful" details about his crimes and the crimes of others. If he failed to meet that requirement, either by lying or omitting information, anything he said could be used against him in the prosecution of any crime, including perjury.

"For instance, you must neither conceal or minimize your own actions in any offense," it said. "You agree that you will not engage in any criminal activity of any kind without the prior knowledge and approval of FBI agents and this office."

Whitacre noticed a term forbidding him from telling anyone information about the investigation without FBI approval. Repeatedly, the document discussed Whitacre's "covert role" and "covert capacity." Whitacre asked how far that role would go.

"There's going to be a lot of undercover work," Cudmore replied. "Tape recordings, obtaining notes, those kinds of things."

Whitacre finished reading and looked up.

"Do I have to sign this now?" he asked.

"No," Cudmore said. "Take some time with it. Have a lawyer look it over. But this is the deal. It's not open to negotiation. And like I said before, we don't care how we proceed here, it's either you or them. The way to have us focus on them is to sign the agreement and prove you're being truthful."

Whitacre nodded. "Okay."

Sometime in early January, Cudmore said, he should let the agents know if he would be signing. With that, Cudmore packed up his briefcase.

"You're making the right decision," he told Whitacre as he shook his hand.

Cudmore headed to the door, stopping before he opened it. He looked back into the room.

"Happy New Year, everybody," he said.

The next Monday, Shepard studied Whitacre as he glided into the hotel room. Expensive suit. Garish tie. Gregarious demeanor. He looked calm and confident, with no sign of anxiety that might signal he was planning to back out.

Whitacre and Shepard sat at the table. Whitacre opened up the discussion, saying that he had not brought the agreement. He was still looking it over.

Shepard asked if he had any information about price-fixing. Nothing to report, Whitacre replied.

"But I've been thinking," he said. "I think it might be good for you guys to interview Wayne Brasser. He knows a lot about price-fixing at ADM."

"He's somebody we're going to want to talk to, Mark," Shepard said.

"You should do it soon. He's gonna forget stuff if you let too much time slip by."

The main thing now, Shepard said, was for Whitacre to come in with whatever information he could on price-fixing. Whitacre said he would try, but it was difficult. Everyone was still wary.

The conversation drifted away from price-fixing, toward the allegations of industrial espionage. Whitacre had earlier mentioned that ADM had hired an executive named Michael Frein from International Minerals Corp. Shepard asked about that again.

Randall had told him all about it, Whitacre said: ADM had hired Frein and paid him to bring along one of IMC's microorganisms, a bug used to manufacture an antibiotic called bacitracin.

"Are you going to be with Randall anytime soon?" Shepard asked.

"I see him every day."

"Next time you do, ask him about this on tape. See what he says."

Jim Randall stretched out his legs as he sat on one of the pillowy, upholstered seats in an ADM corporate jet. Despite the roar of the jet engine, this was a moment for Randall to relax. There were no phones ringing, no meetings to attend. Nursing a drink, he slouched in his seat and loosened his tie.

Nearby, Whitacre watched the ADM president. It was January 6, 1993, a Wednesday. Whitacre had been traveling with Randall for two days, as part of an effort to start a business in a new product called methionine—an amino acid, like lysine, that promotes animal growth. For much of the trip, they had been accompanied by Chris Jones, a former Whitacre colleague from Degussa who was now consulting with ADM on the project. The ADM plane had just dropped off Jones in Lake Charles, Louisiana. Randall and Whitacre were finally alone.

For a few minutes, the two executives chatted. Whitacre mentioned an executive he had met the other day from American Cyanamid, a company with dealings in the bacitracin business. Whitacre watched as Randall leaned his head back, seeming to rest.

Whitacre slid his hand into his inside left breast pocket. Looking in, he saw the indicator light on the top of the FBI's microcassette recorder. He flicked the switch. The indicator light glowed red.

Whitacre leaned toward Randall.

"You know, one thing the Cyanamid guy asked me," Whitacre said, "he asked me, 'Where did you guys get your technology?' "

Days later, Shepard slid a copy of tape number 1B13 into the TASCAM playback device on his desk. Slipping a set of puffy earphones over his head, he glanced at the paperwork for the tape.

Shepard cued the tape. Instantly, he heard the sound of a jet engine. Already, he could tell this would be a troublesome recording; there was too much background noise. He heard Whitacre's voice, saying something about a guy at Cyanamid asking where ADM obtained its technology.

"I said, well, we got it from Korea," Shepard heard Whitacre say. "The bacitracin technology."

Vaguely, Shepard could hear Randall say something. The engine drowned out the words.

"Huh?" Whitacre asked. Apparently, it was hard to hear on the plane, too.

"Got it from where?" Randall was speaking up.

"Korea," Whitacre said, "which is the standard lie we've always been sayin' when we're asked. You know, we don't get asked that much."

"Yeah," Randall replied.

Shepard played the section back. Randall hadn't jumped up, asking why Whitacre was lying about how ADM obtained the bug. That might mean something. Shepard turned on the tape again. Whitacre was talking.

"And he goes, well, ah, the IMC guys felt that you got it from this, from a guy that left their company named Mike Frein, that Mike Frein stole the bug," Whitacre said. "That's what he said."

"Yeah," Randall replied.

An indifferent statement. No shock. Interesting.

The conversation meandered. Randall mentioned a man named Scott who had done business with ADM.

"He used to be friends with Mike Frein," Whitacre said.

"Oh, yeah, he was."

"Is that how you got Mike Frein? From him, wasn't it?"

"Right."

"Did Frein come to us looking for a job?" Whitacre asked. "Or Scott told you about him?"

"I don't know, I can't remember exactly how . . ." Randall's words dipped, drowned out by the jet engine.

A second later they were clear again.

"I paid him fifty thousand dollars per bug."

"Cheapest bug we ever got," Whitacre responded, as both men laughed.

The middle section of Randall's statement had been unintelligible. Try as he might, Shepard could not understand those few words. But the words after that were clear as a bell.

I paid him fifty thousand dollars per bug.

Soon, Whitacre sent the conversation in another direction.

"It's a shame we got Frein, ah, the bacitracin bug," he said. "What we need is Ajinomoto's lysine bug."

"Do you think it's better than ours?"

Shepard listened closely. This had come up several times. That first night Whitacre spoke in the car, he had said that ADM hired women to hang around near the American offices of an Asian competitor in search of employees willing to sell a bug or answer questions. There was a chance that topic would come up.

Randall and Whitacre discussed the technical differences between the two bugs. Suddenly, Whitacre brought up the women.

"Cheviron never did have any luck with girls and stuff?" he asked.

"No, we pulled him out," Randall replied, "because then we were starting to deal with the Japanese." They had been getting friendly with their competitors, he said. New strategies were necessary.

Shepard stopped the tape and rewound it.

Cheviron never did have any luck with girls and stuff?

No, we pulled him out.

Unbelievable.

Shepard listened to the rest of the tape; its quality was terrible. But by the time he finished, Shepard was beginning to suspect that Whitacre's stories about ADM's industrial espionage might well be true.

• • •

After two days of rain in Decatur, the sun broke through the clouds on January 9. With the weather on his side, Shepard made good time to the Holiday Inn parking lot. Tonight, he would not be going inside.

A short time later, Whitacre pulled alongside. Shepard climbed out of his car; in a second, he was sitting in Whitacre's passenger seat.

"You have that agreement?" Shepard asked.

"Yeah, right here," Whitacre replied.

In a call that day, Whitacre had said that he was ready to sign the cooperation agreement. Shepard wanted it as soon as possible, so Whitacre agreed to meet. He wouldn't be around much of the next week; he had business to take care of in the Cayman Islands.

Whitacre handed the agreement to Shepard, who looked it over. Everything appeared to be in order. The two had a short conversation, and Whitacre decided to add one item to the agreement. He brought a pen out of his pocket and flipped to the last page.

"Furthermore," he wrote, "I promise to take a 'polygraph test' at any time."

Dwayne Andreas worked on the sixth floor of ADM's corporate head-quarters, in a large corner office next to the boardroom. In a company that prized its secrecy, Andreas's office was the inner sanctum. Few went there uninvited; rarely did anyone stand by listening while Andreas worked the telephones, networking with political and indus-trial leaders.

In that office, the final rulings were made on any tough issue for ADM. Dwayne would take input, but in making his decision he stood alone, unchallenged. Such was the prerogative of the chairman. But the decision this day was particularly tough.

Should Mark Whitacre be fired?

The entire Fujiwara episode had been a disaster. After a while, no one believed that there was a saboteur. Whitacre, they figured, had made the whole thing up to buy time so he could get the plant run-ning. But what about this lie involving threats to his daughter? What was going on with him?

Whitacre had finally been confronted by Reising and danced around the question of whether the original call from Fujiwara ever took place. He still insisted a saboteur had been in the plant but was less clear about whether he had proof.

The whole situation was too strange. Thankfully, the FBI didn't seem to be taking the investigation seriously. Shepard checked in occasionally, but with no new Fujiwara phone calls, the whole thing appeared to have faded away. Dwayne didn't want to reveal ADM's conclusion to the government. He didn't like airing the company's dirty laundry.

Dwayne figured that Whitacre should go. He called Randall and asked him to his office. The ADM president worked closest with Whitacre. He should have a say.

Randall was stunned when he heard the news. "Dwayne, you can't be serious. We need this guy. He's the best there is."

Sure, Randall said, Whitacre was odd, and this whole Fujiwara episode had been bizarre. But Whitacre had panicked; he was immature. Besides, the bottom line should be the bottom line, and Whitacre's division was finally showing profits.

"The margins are bigger than any other business line," Randall said. "We can't do it without him."

Randall kept up the lobbying, promising he would personally keep an eye on Whitacre. Dwayne finally decided to let the young lysine executive keep his job. Whitacre, he was convinced, played too important a role in the company's business.

A sense of fantasy permeated Chicago's "Magnificent Mile," the famed shopping district dotted with posh shops, mock-Gothic newspaper headquarters, and world-class hotels. On January 22, white Christmas lights twinkled in the trees along Michigan Avenue, as if the city was desperately clinging to the faded holiday season. The decorations were a concession to a Hollywood studio filming a movie, but the city embraced the illusion. Remnants of holiday cheer were a helpful tonic as Chicago struggled through another cold, blustery winter.

In the heart of the shopping district, two Asian executives headed into a hotel, the forty-six-floor Chicago Marriott Downtown. The men wore elegant suits and muted ties. They looked like nothing more than the visiting businessmen that they were. But Kanji Mimoto and Hirokazu Ikeda of Ajinomoto were in town to commit a crime. They wanted to see if the illegal price-fixing conspiracy among lysine manufacturers could get back on track.

As part of that effort, a meeting had been arranged with a senior executive of ADM, the newest competitor in the business. They weren't looking forward to the encounter; they viewed ADM management as reckless and ill-mannered. The Americans had rushed into the lysine business like cowboys, upending a cooperative price-fixing agreement that had existed for years among Asian competitors. The comfortable, familiar way of doing business was gone.

Making it worse was their suspicion that ADM was a corporate thief. Ajinomoto knew how long it took to develop the microorganisms required for the business. Yet ADM had become a big player almost overnight. There was only one way that the company could have moved so quickly, the Japanese executives were convinced: ADM must have stolen Ajinomoto's bug and used it as their own.

The September meeting in Decatur, when Ikeda and Mimoto had toured ADM's plant with two Ajinomoto engineers, had provided the perfect cover to prove their suspicion. During the visit, Mimoto had attempted to steal one of ADM's microbes by wiping a damp handkerchief along a staircase. The handkerchief had been taken to a lab, where it was searched for the bugs used by ADM. Ajinomoto had hoped to examine the bacteria for the telltale genetic markers embedded in its own proprietary microorganisms. That way, Ajinomoto would have proof that ADM had stolen them.

But no success. If the handkerchief had ever held any bugs, they had died before arriving at the lab. Ajinomoto's hopes of quickly pushing ADM out of the business with a patent-infringement suit were put on hold. Cooperation was the only option. For now.

Ikeda and Mimoto walked through the Marriott lobby to the elevators. They rode upstairs, wandering the hall in search of the conference room where they were supposed to meet the ADM executive.

Finally, they found the room. The ADM executive was there, sitting alone at a table. He stood as the Japanese executives walked in.

"Mr. Whitacre," Ikeda said. "Good to see you."

Whitacre grinned, shaking Ikeda's hand eagerly.

"Good to see you again, too."

The men sat. They talked amiably as they enjoyed a catered meal. The Ajinomoto executives hammered their position—regardless of any agreements, their company would have to remain the market leader. Whitacre turned that aside, saying that they needed to meet Mick Andreas and negotiate a lysine-production agreement. Otherwise, the scheme would never work.

Nothing seemed extraordinary to the Japanese executives. The talks involved the same issues, with the same hard-nosed positions from the past.

But the meeting itself was unusual. For this time Ikeda and Mimoto were discussing their plans with a cooperating witness for the government, a man who had signed an agreement to inform his FBI handlers of every illegal act. That way, such meetings could be taped and agents could surreptitiously observe them.

None of that, however, was taking place. Whitacre was not taping. No agents were present.

In fact, no one from the government knew what Whitacre was doing in Chicago. He had told the FBI nothing about this price-fixing meeting.

Whitacre felt sure he could keep it secret.

Rusty Williams set down his yard tools when he saw Whitacre walking toward him. Williams had been the Whitacres' groundskeeper for about six months and already liked his new employer. Whitacre, in fact, had rapidly become more of a friend than a boss. When Whitacre had heard that Williams owed seven thousand dollars in debts, he had handed over the money as a gift. Rather than ignoring Williams or talking down to him, Whitacre often discussed his work and daily life, like any other friend.

Whitacre stepped over the grass, toward the white fence where Williams was standing.

"Hey, bud," Whitacre said.

"Hey, how's it going?"

The two men talked about the yard. As always, Whitacre was concerned about keeping the driveway clear. After a few minutes, Whitacre changed the subject to his work at ADM. Williams had heard earlier from Whitacre that he was the top man in charge of ADM's lysine production. He had been impressed.

On this day, Whitacre said he had dreams for his job, a way to become very rich.

"I've got plans, bud, I've got plans," he said.

"What kind of plans?" Williams asked.

"I'll tell you, if I could control gas prices, I would be a millionaire."

"Yeah?"

Whitacre nodded knowingly.

"But if I could control the price of lysine and other products at ADM," Whitacre continued, "I'd be a billionaire by age fifty."

Six weeks passed.

The criminal investigations of ADM were going nowhere. Shepard had officially notified the company that the FBI was dropping the Fujiwara inquiry. With no new calls, he explained, there was nothing to investigate. The company seemed relieved.

Whitacre was proving to be a disappointing witness, despite the cooperation agreement. The agents had spoken with him only about a half dozen times since late January but he was always empty-handed, with no new information about price-fixing. One of the topics he wanted to talk about was Wayne Brasser. It was obvious Whitacre was hoping that Brasser would become their witness. They had made an attempt, interviewing Brasser as part of the Fujiwara investigation and asking at the end if he had other issues to discuss. Brasser didn't take the bait, and the agents weren't going to push. The more people who knew of their interest in price-fixing, the greater the risk that ADM might get tipped off.

Making it worse was the poor quality of the few tapes Whitacre did record. The agents had enough experience to know the types of recordings that should have been coming in, but it wasn't happening. Some recordings—such as the Randall airplane tape—were hard to hear. Oftentimes, there were televisions or other distractions drowning out the discussions.

The conversations they *could* hear were of little help. They didn't want to listen to any more tapes of Brasser; they wanted to hear what people *inside* ADM were saying. But again and again, Whitacre insisted there was nothing to record.

Finally, Shepard ran out of patience.

"Whitacre acts like he's cooperating, but I don't think he is," Shepard told Weatherall. "I think he's trying to wriggle off the hook."

Weatherall agreed; Whitacre was still hiding something. The two agents again contacted the Behavioral Science Unit and spoke with Special Agent Steven Etter, who for months had been providing them with advice on how to handle Whitacre. Shepard bounced his plans off Etter, who offered a few suggestions. Then, Shepard called Byron Cudmore, describing his concerns about Whitacre.

"So what's the plan?" Cudmore asked.

"We're going to put him on the box again."

The box. Another polygraph.

"Sounds good," Cudmore said. "Let me know what happens."

Twenty seconds.

"Are you lying about any aspect of your involvement in ADM's price-fixing operations?" Agent Hamara asked.

Whitacre glanced at the chart paper. It was March 10, sometime after seven o'clock at night. Whitacre had been surprised to see Hamara; again, he had been given no warning. Whitacre had tried being casual, telling the agents he was hiding nothing and was willing to take the test. Again, he had been told the questions in advance. This was the one that concerned him.

"No," he said in a strong voice.

As best as he could tell, the ink tracings stayed steady. Whitacre felt relieved. This was the fifteenth question he had been asked during the test and the second about his knowledge of price-fixing. Only two other questions seemed relevant; one asked whether Mick Andreas had directed him to buy bugs from Fujiwara and another whether Cheviron had told him to forward his home phone to the ADM off-premises extension. Whitacre had answered both questions yes.

Hamara asked a final control question and marked the paper with the response. He did not look up.

When Hamara finished with his two sets of questions, he studied the results, translating the tiny movements in the tracings into a numerical equation. Once he toted it up, he had no doubt: Each relevant answer was indicative of deception.

Whitacre had blown the box again.

The agents met behind closed doors for just a few minutes while Whitacre waited in the adjoining room. The agents were quiet; Whitacre could hear nothing. Finally, the door opened and Whitacre stood. The looks on everyone's faces told him all he needed to know. He started speaking before they could sit down.

"Guys, I'm really tired and I've got some stuff I've got to do early tomorrow morning. I need to go home."

Shepard and Weatherall paused before responding.

"Really, I need to go home," Whitacre repeated. "I've got a lot of stuff tomorrow. And I'm really tired. So I really need to go home."

If Whitacre wanted to leave, there was little the agents could do to hold him.

"Okay, Mark," Shepard said. "Head on home."

Whitacre walked to the door. Shepard and Weatherall watched, silent and frustrated. Whitacre certainly knew he had failed the polygraph. Weatherall felt sure that once their witness was out the hotel room door, he would never return. Even if he did, he would probably keep telling his lies.

The covert investigation, Weatherall thought dejectedly, was all but over.

The telephone rang in the Decatur Resident Agency early the next day. Shepard answered.

"Hey," Whitacre said, his voice a twangy whisper. "It's Mark."

Shepard was stunned to hear from him.

"I want to get together," Whitacre said. "I've got more to tell you."

"Well, Mark, we've . . ."

"Brian, just listen to me one more time. I really think you should."

Shepard paused.

"Sure, Mark," he said. "I'll get a room."

Whitacre arrived that night seeming particularly hyperactive. Shepard and Weatherall listened as he protested that he had told the truth, that he was still working with them, that they could trust him. Over the past day, he'd studied up on polygraphs; he knew they weren't reliable. People telling the truth failed all the time. He'd read that. He knew.

The agents weren't buying; the game was over. Whitacre could spend all the time he wanted arguing that the polygraph was wrong; it would get him nowhere.

Soon, Whitacre seemed spent. Weatherall moved in.

"Mark, I know this has all got to be hard, working in an organization where this is happening. I know it's hard to be reporting on your friends and colleagues. There are no easy choices, and I know that's tough."

Whitacre said nothing.

"But there's only one good choice for you. That's all there ever has been. We're not going away. There's only one way to protect yourself and to do what's right. And that's to start telling the truth."

For several minutes, Weatherall tried to get inside Whitacre's head, trying to empathize with him.

"Now, Mark, I know the truth is tough," he said. "But there's something you're hiding, something you're keeping from us. And I know that's got to be hard, to be carrying around a burden like that."

Whitacre stared at the table.

"Mark, that's true, isn't it?"

Finally, slowly, Whitacre nodded.

Connection.

"I'll tell you, Mark, the only thing that relieves that burden is to be honest. Can you do that? Make it easier on yourself, Mark. Just talk about it."

Weatherall leaned in. "You've got to stop worrying about your colleagues, Mark, and start worrying about yourself."

Whitacre looked at Weatherall. He was trapped. The meetings with the Asians were starting again; the price war was falling apart. His plan had failed.

He cleared his throat. Nothing had shaken these guys. He was sure they were at the final break point. They were getting ready to prosecute him.

He had only one option.

"For the past five weeks," he said, "I've been personally involved in efforts to fix lysine prices."

For the next hour, Whitacre talked about price-fixing. He told of his meetings with Ajinomoto and Kyowa Hakko, another major Japanese competitor.

"Does anybody know about these meetings?" Shepard asked.

"Mick Andreas. He's fully aware of them."

The talks were far along, Whitacre said. The Japanese had agreed to fix the price at about $1.10 a pound—almost double the recent cost—if ADM would cut its volume. More talks were scheduled on April 30, when a top Ajinomoto executive was coming to Decatur to meet with Mick Andreas. Whitacre said he would be participating in many of the discussions.

The agents listened, feeling a rush. After so many months, a breakthrough. Whitacre was personally confessing to specific crimes. This had to be true. Only a fool would lie like this to an FBI agent.

More important, Whitacre's demeanor had changed. He wasn't nervous, didn't seem shifty. Instead, he was energetic, seeming excited about the prospect of working with the FBI. He had either turned the corner, or he was the greatest actor the agents had ever seen.

"Well, Mark," Shepard said, "I want you to get these things on tape and bring us up to date on lysine. I don't want to just have your word, I want to hear this on tape. Are you going to do it?"

Whitacre paused. The agents were right. It had become a simple choice: his colleagues or him.

"Yeah," he said, nodding eagerly. "I'll give you all the tapes you need."

BOOK TWO

Honor amongst Thieves

CHAPTER 6

The blue Lincoln Town Car approached gate number three in front of ADM headquarters on March 17, St. Patrick's Day. A guard inside the gate's security booth peered through the driver's window. Whitacre lifted a hand off the steering wheel, giving a slight wave. As the guard nodded his recognition, Whitacre slowly eased the car past the fence.

Driving past the Ronald Reagan statue in front of the office, Whitacre tapped the electronic door opener attached to his windshield visor. By the time his car came around the curve, the metal door to the underground executive parking garage was opening. Whitacre felt a rush of tension as he drove in. The microcassette recorder hidden in his coat felt huge. He had used it before, but never like he would today.

Whitacre pulled into his reserved spot. Reaching inside his jacket, he slid the switch on the recorder. Was it on? He looked inside his pocket and saw the red light glowing. He smoothed out the jacket, putting sounds of rustling on the tape.

"It's currently seven-thirty A.M. on Wednesday; Wednesday, March seventeenth," he said into the recorder, staring at a wall as he spoke. "I'm just getting ready to go into my office."

Whitacre explained that he had turned on the device now because he felt sure that Wilson and Randall would want to see him immediately. The night before, he was supposed to have spoken with Masaru Yamamoto of Kyowa Hakko, the Japanese lysine company second in size to Ajinomoto. Yamamoto, whom ADM executives called Massy, had not been in, but Wilson and Randall might want a report first thing. It was easier, he told the tape, to turn on the device now rather than later, in front of his colleagues.

Whitacre opened his car door.

"Just getting out of my car and going to the office now," he said.

He spoke to no one as he made his way to his office. Sitting at his desk, he looked at his watch.

"Seven-thirty-three A.M.," he said. "Wednesday, March seventeenth."

He shuffled some papers, glancing up when he heard someone approach.

"Well, Terrance Wilson," he announced.

Wilson was in no mood for pleasantries. "Did you talk to Massy?" he asked.

"Yeah, I called, uh, Massy. He wasn't in."

Whitacre mentioned that afterward, he had heard from Kanji Mimoto of Ajinomoto. Apparently, Mimoto thought ADM had promised in September to cut production if prices went up. But no commitment had been made, Whitacre said. Instead, he and Wilson had promised to raise the idea with ADM management if lysine reached $1.10 a pound. But that never happened—ADM was only receiving ninety-three cents a pound now.

"I said, as long as prices are as low as they are, we had nothing," Whitacre continued. "We're not gonna go to our management and look silly to 'em."

"What'd he say?"

"He said, 'We understand it's a promise. We feel you've reneged on your promise.' "

As they spoke, Jim Randall walked into the room. The ADM president sat on the desk, arms folded across his chest. Whitacre started his story again.

"We got a call last night," he said.

"You did?" Randall asked. "From the Japs?"

"Yeah."

"About what?"

"Got a call on my voice mail to call, and I did from a pay phone. This was Ajinomoto."

Randall scrunched his nose. "Your, uh, tap's off your phone, you know," he said. There was no need to keep using pay phones.

"You think so?" Whitacre asked.

"Cheviron told me it was. The FBI is out of it, and they took the tap off the phone."

"Okay," Whitacre said. "I still think the pay phone is the way anyway."

Whitacre told Randall of the Mimoto conversation.

"He was pissed," Whitacre said.

"Kind of hard to keep him from being pissed," Randall replied.

Randall raised a few issues regarding lysine, mentioning a technical development used by "the Jews." Eventually, he returned to the Mimoto call and Ajinomoto's belief that ADM had broken its promise.

"What'd he threaten to do?" Randall asked.

"He said there'd never be peace, and the price would stay where it is," Whitacre said.

Randall asked a few more questions, then headed out. Whitacre looked at Wilson, and again mentioned Mimoto's concern about the agreement.

"He said he'd like to talk to you about it at some point, and I said, well . . ."

"Be right there lookin' right at 'em," Wilson muttered. "Say, 'Listen here you little mousy motherfucker.' "

Wilson laughed. Neither of them was much concerned about Mimoto's complaint. They figured it was all just negotiating strategy. There was no promise.

"They're tricky, you know," Whitacre said.

"Bet you they are," Wilson responded.

"And you know Ikeda's right there, telling him what to say."

"Yeah," Wilson said. "Plus, in 1992, we did exactly what we said we'd do, volume-wise. Exactly."

Whitacre fiddled with a pen, trying to contain his excitement. Wilson had just admitted that ADM had promised Ajinomoto to hold to a set volume in 1992.

The executives brought up an out-of-town sales meeting for the lysine division, questioning whether Wilson should attend.

"It'd be unusual for you to do that, wouldn't it?" Whitacre asked.

"Yeah," Wilson said. "It's not like I'd get laid or something. That'd be a reason to go."

Whitacre set down his pen as the conversation came to an end. Wilson headed out the door; Whitacre said nothing as he watched.

"Just had Jim Randall and Terry Wilson in my office," he announced to the tape recorder. For a few minutes, Whitacre summarized the conversation.

"By the way," he added, "there was no discussion with Mimoto last night. That was for illustration purposes only. That was all that was for. Illustration purposes only. So I wanna make that very clear. There's no discussion with Mimoto last night."

Whitacre was starting to repeat himself; his excitement was getting to him. But Whitacre was always hyperactive when he threw himself into a new job.

Whitacre was at his desk the next morning at 11:00. After turning on the tape recorder in his pocket, he opened a black leather case embossed with a gold ADM logo. A pad of paper was inserted on the right side; a calculator and a world map were affixed to the left. Whitacre pulled a pen out of a holder in the case, at the same time pushing down a tiny white switch. He couldn't see it, but knew the microcassette that the FBI had hidden behind the map was turning.

The previous day had imbued him with an awesome sense of power. He had walked around ADM taping, and no one had suspected. Now, he had an unvarnished portrait of ADM's corporate ethic for the FBI.

Whitacre headed to Wilson's office. Mick Andreas was there discussing a recent business deal. For several minutes, the men hashed it through.

"Now, on the lysine thing, totally different subject," Andreas said, looking at Whitacre. "When do the Japanese see you?"

"The small company wants to see me the fifteenth in Chicago," Whitacre said, referring to Kyowa Hakko.

"That's a month from now?" Andreas asked.

"Yeah. In Chicago."

"We got a month to think about it."

"Yeah."

"In the meantime," Andreas said, "they're callin' and dropping hints."

"Definitely." The Japanese, Whitacre complained, were pushing on this supposed promise by ADM to cut back. But no such promise had been made, he said.

"I think that's a good line for you," Andreas said. "When they come to me, I'm just gonna say, 'Look, first of all, we don't make deals.' "

That, Andreas continued, should be followed up by blaming the Japanese for poor prices in the market. "You should just say to him, 'Look, these prices are so shitty, and you guys are so disorganized that I don't know what kind of shit you're managing.' "

Whitacre nodded. "And it's gotten shittier."

Andreas's words were perfect for the case. ADM's vice-chairman was telling him to chastise a competitor for bad prices. Whitacre felt excited again. The FBI was sure to believe him now.

From behind his desk, Wilson spoke. "The market's bigger than we originally said it was. We just took it. So we're not in violation of nothin'."

"Yeah," Whitacre said.

"Fuck 'em," Wilson said.

The men changed subjects, discussing a request from Howard Buffett, the assistant to the ADM chairman and son of Warren Buffett, the famed Omaha investor. Howard often heard from politicians and their money men when they wanted campaign contributions from ADM.

"Howie called us," Whitacre said, "and asked us for funds for somebody, Tommy Thompson or whatever."

Thompson, the governor of Wisconsin, was a rising star in the Republican Party. He was in the midst of a fund-raising drive, ostensibly for his 1994 re-election campaign. But party officials were touting him for national office—maybe even a White House run. A war chest to scare off potential in-state challengers was widely seen as a necessary first step in that effort.

But Whitacre said there was a problem.

"Terry and I went up there and told 'em we're already at our limit and we couldn't give," he said. "We're at our limit."

Andreas shrugged. "You can go over the limit. Just a small fine."

"Yeah," Wilson said, "that's what we were saying."

Whitacre laughed. Andreas was blithely advising that they intentionally violate campaign-finance laws—and Wilson was agreeing. Already, Whitacre was imagining what the world would think about the Andreas family's political giving if this tape became public.

"If they want a thousand dollars," Wilson said, "you give a thousand dollars."

Whitacre laughed again.

"So it costs us nine thousand," Wilson continued, adding an estimated fine for violating election laws.

"Twelve thousand after tax," Whitacre laughed.

Andreas nodded. "That's true," he said. "You know, if the guy's up there asking you for money, just don't give it to him and see what happens."

Wilson joined Whitacre in the laughter.

Andreas looked at the two men. "If you wrote a check, you make sure Dad is behind it," he said. "Is Dad asking for 'em?"

"Oh, yeah," Wilson said, as Whitacre agreed.

"Okay," Andreas said.

The meeting broke up and Whitacre wandered back to his office. Sitting down, he glanced at his watch.

"Eleven-fifteen A.M.," he said to the tape. "Bingo!"

Days later, Shepard set down the headphones for the TASCAM device. For hours, he had been listening to the two tapes Whitacre had finally recorded inside ADM. The sound quality was poor, and Whitacre talked too much. Shepard needed to speak to him about that.

Still, everything was falling into place. Whitacre's statements now tended to be corroborated by tapes—devastating tapes. A nonchalant attitude inside ADM about lawbreaking—whether on price-fixing or campaign finance—was unmistakable. Whatever else could be said for this evidence, it would certainly have impact on a jury.

The state of the lysine conspiracy seemed clear from the tapes. A price agreement of sorts had been reached the previous year at meetings in Mexico and Paris. But the conspirators did not trust each other. So when prices faltered, everyone sold more to keep up their revenues. Apparently, Ajinomoto had believed that ADM would unilaterally cut production. The tapes made it clear that was not going to work—Ajinomoto wanted ADM restricted to forty-five thousand tons a year; ADM wanted every manufacturer to limit production, with its own allocation set at sixty-five thousand tons a year.

A production limit was critical to the scheme. Price-fixing often won't hold unless the manufacturers take control of the market's natural forces—the laws of supply and demand. The higher a product's price, the smaller the number of consumers who are willing to buy it. That's why fewer people buy high-priced steak than low-priced hamburger, even if everyone prefers steak. By setting prices high, companies are limiting their market to the steak buyers—consumers whose purchases are not determined by price. But if the companies manufacture more product than the steak buyers want, problems begin. Warehouses and store shelves overflow with unpurchased items. Steak buyers can't be forced to buy more, leaving the companies with one choice for unloading the backlog: attract hamburger buyers by cutting the price. In the end, price-fixing without a side agreement to limit production will last only as long as it takes to fill a warehouse with unsold items.

Shepard knew that, for the scheme to work long-term, the conspirators were going to have to hammer out a production agreement. And, if everything went well, the FBI would be listening in.

Gathering evidence of price-fixing in products other than lysine was going to be difficult. The separate schemes were organized like classic "hub-and-spoke" conspiracies. Wilson and probably Mick Andreas were at the center, coordinating the price-fixing of every ADM division involved. Whitacre was only immersed in lysine—other executives played his role for other products. Making it more complicated, different products meant different co-conspirators. So, if there was price-fixing in citric acid, ADM would be meeting with other corporate conspirators, not the Japanese and Korean lysine producers. For now, the only way to develop evidence of those other schemes was through the hub—Whitacre had to push his bosses to talk about other divisions.

Shepard phoned Cudmore. Now that they had a sense of the case's scope, they agreed the time had come to beef up their resources. They needed to call the government's top antitrust experts for help.

In the southern section of Chicago's Loop area stands an ensemble of buildings that make up the federal contribution to the city's architectural rhythm. Encircling a plaza adorned with a fifty-three-foot red steel sculpture by Alexander Calder, the buildings are the epicenter for Chicago's federal law-enforcement effort, housing everything from the district courts to the United States Attorney's office.

In the spring of 1993, one group of little-known prosecutors worked on the thirty-eighth floor of the John C. Kluczynski Federal Building, the tallest of the steel-and-glass high-rises ringing the plaza. Unlike most federal prosecutors in town, these lawyers were not with the U.S. Attorney's office and rarely took part in highly publicized cases. They worked instead for the Midwest office of the Justice Department's Antitrust Division, which enforced the Sherman Act and related laws. Partly because of their complexity, price-fixing and related crimes are often prosecuted by the division, which has the expertise to sift through thousands of documents when piecing together evidence of economic conspiracies.

In March, Cudmore's request for assistance landed on the desk of Kent Brown, the chief of the Midwest office. In a phone call, Cudmore laid out the history of the ADM case while Brown took notes. Brown said he wanted to talk over the case with one of his lawyers, Robin Mann, and would have her get back to Cudmore.

Hanging up, Brown gathered his notes. He felt confident Mann was perfect for the assignment. A veteran antitrust prosecutor, Mann had handled a number of price-fixing cases, some involving tapes—albeit on a far smaller scale than this new case. The daughter of a struggling salesman and a receptionist, Mann grew up in Chicago with little money and drifted into a legal career after years of working in a state welfare office. Her arrival at the Antitrust Division had been almost serendipitous; wary of the stifling atmosphere of law firms, Mann searched for a job after law school by flipping through a book of government agencies and calling the ones that seemed interesting. While she hardly arrived at the office with a fervor for antitrust enforcement, Mann soon became indispensable. She was a stickler for detail, who could drive colleagues to distraction with her concerns. But by fretting over the minutiae, Mann often uncovered weak points in cases that needed to be airtight.

Notes in hand, Brown found Mann. A cooperating witness was turning over evidence of possible price-fixing by ADM, he told her. Would she take the case?

Mann gave Brown a quizzical look.

"What," she asked, "is 'ADM'?"

Whitacre was back in a hotel room, meeting with the FBI. This time, though, the mood was upbeat.

"Mark, you're doing a great job," Shepard said. "These are just the kind of tapes we need."

Whitacre beamed. He was part of the team.

Still, there were problems, Shepard said. Whitacre shouldn't narrate what was happening, just let the tape speak for itself. And there was no need to rush; he didn't have to catch everyone on tape in just a few days. And never make things up, like the Mimoto call—that might cause trouble later.

"We don't want you to go in and have a conversation unless you would do it normally," Weatherall said. "Let the conversation come to you."

"Guys," Whitacre said, "I'm an executive. They want me to handle this. If I don't go to them, they might not come to me. They'll figure everything's under control."

The agents thought for a second. What kind of contact would a boss expect from an underling?

"All right, try this," Weatherall said. "Contact them before the big meetings. It would make sense for you to go to them then."

"You'd be getting your marching orders," Shepard said, picking up on the idea. "Ask them what they want you to do before a big meeting, then brief them on the results afterwards. That's perfectly natural."

Whitacre nodded. "Okay."

There was one other issue, Shepard said. Someone in Springfield had offered a suggestion. Maybe there was another way to gather evidence.

Whitacre listened carefully as Shepard described the plan that the FBI wanted to try.

Dusk had changed into night, and the executives from ADM's headquarters had headed home. A cleaning staff was making its rounds, and a guard stood watch in the lobby. Sometime after seven-thirty, Whitacre came in the front door, accompanied by a man the guard didn't recognize. The man was dressed in a suit and carried a large briefcase. Probably just another executive.

"Just bringing in one of our clients," Whitacre said to the guard. "Have some things to show him."

The guard nodded with disinterest, and Whitacre signed in. On the next line of the sheet, he wrote a name for his guest: Dwight Armstrong, an executive with Carl S. Akey Inc., an Ohio feed company.

The two men walked through the lobby, heading to Whitacre's office. Shutting the door, Whitacre pulled a curtain across the glass wall at the front and then closed the window drapes. He glanced at his guest.

"Just talk about business," the guest said.

"You know, Dwight, our lysine business is really going great," Whitacre began, sitting at his desk. "And I've got to tell you, we're really delighted with Akey's business. You're one of our best customers."

As Whitacre spoke, his guest stood on a chair and pushed up a ceiling tile. His head disappeared into the ceiling. Whitacre watched as his guest shifted a foot onto his desk.

"And I'm really glad you could come out here, Dwight," he said. "I think you're going to be impressed with our plans and how they're going to fit in with your business."

The guest replaced the tile and climbed down.

"Now, are you guys going to be growing your business in Ohio more in the swine industry or in poultry?" Whitacre asked.

"Oh, we're growing in swine," the guest said, turning to a wooden cabinet in the back of the office. He opened the doors, inspecting everything inside.

"How's that experimental farm you're working on?" Whitacre asked.

"It's good. It's going real well."

The guest opened his briefcase, removing an electronic device. Switching it on, he analyzed a radio frequency.

Ten minutes later, the men left Whitacre's office and headed down the hall to a conference room.

"I've got a little slide show that I think will give you a lot of useful information," Whitacre said. He dimmed the lights and turned on a projector. On the screen, yellow letters spelling out *ADM Bioproducts Division* appeared against a blue background.

Whitacre looked out across the room. "This presentation will tell you about ADM's Bioproducts Division, and how we are vertically integrated in the company."

As Whitacre spoke, the guest scrambled up to the ceiling again, lifting several panels and looking inside. Climbing down, he turned on the device he was using to analyze the radio signal. Whitacre droned on, clicking through the slides as he watched his guest maneuver all over the conference room. After about thirty minutes, the man put his equipment away.

"That was an excellent presentation, Mark," the man interrupted.

"Thanks," Whitacre said, shutting off the projector and turning up the lights.

The men headed out, wandering to ADM's computer center. After a glance, the tour was over. About an hour after arriving, they were back in the parking lot, climbing into Whitacre's Town Car. Whitacre drove past the front gate, heading toward a local hotel.

"So," said Whitacre, "any luck?"

The guest, Special Agent Thomas Gibbons, a technology specialist with the FBI's Springfield office, shook his head.

"Nothing we can do," Gibbons said. "We can't broadcast a signal out of the building."

Whitacre nodded. The FBI had hoped to place a transmitter inside ADM that would allow agents to monitor price-fixing meetings. But something was blocking the signal, probably some low-frequency device used to prevent potential bugging by corporate competitors. A transmitter would give the agents nothing but static.

The FBI would have to rely on Whitacre's tapes.

• • •

Whitacre was back in his office, staring out the window at the Ronald Reagan statue, when the phone rang. He spun around and reached for the receiver.

"Mark?" a voice said. "David Hoech."

Whitacre smiled to himself. Hoech was one of those people who operated in the shadows of every industry, gathering market information like a detective and using it for clients of his agricultural consulting firm. Whitacre had met him years before, when Hoech came to Decatur for a tour of ADM. During that trip, he had learned a lot about Hoech, and knew that he had lived in Japan. Whitacre also knew that even now, Hoech was in frequent contact with Yamamoto of Kyowa Hakko, one of the consultant's best clients.

Weeks had passed since Whitacre had heard from Hoech, so they spent the first few minutes chatting. Then, Hoech began subtly pumping Whitacre for information. What was up with the lysine business?

"Things are great, David. We're all set to start producing seventeen million pounds of lysine a month by June. We're ready to have a price war."

"That'll be new," Hoech drawled sarcastically.

"We can win this one, David. At that production level, our cost will be fifty cents a pound. We can ride the price down, and still make profit."

The boast intrigued Hoech, and he drilled Whitacre with questions. Whitacre answered with a confident, almost arrogant tone.

By the time he hung up, Whitacre felt pretty clever. The information he had revealed wasn't public, so he knew Hoech would write it up and send it to Kyowa Hakko. Yamamoto would read it, maybe panic.

It was all a tactic. Whitacre was using a back channel to pressure Yamamoto to the negotiating table. After all, the faster the price-fixing became serious, the faster Whitacre would be done with the FBI.

St. Mary's Hospital rises beside Lake Decatur like a gleaming white manor. With ample parking, the hospital is a secluded spot right on the way from ADM to Moweaqua, a perfect location whenever Shepard needed a quick meeting with Whitacre.

As Whitacre headed home one evening, he veered onto Lake Shore Drive, toward St. Mary's. His briefcase rested on the floor in front of the passenger seat. Shepard had asked him to bring it.

Whitacre spotted Shepard's car in the lot and parked beside him. The agent got out of his car and quickly hopped into Whitacre's front passenger seat.

"This should only take a minute," Shepard said.

Shepard picked up the brown briefcase and wrote down its specifications.

"We're going to fix you up with a briefcase like this one," Shepard said. "But we're going to put a recording device in it, a better one than you have."

"Will I use that as my new briefcase?"

"Only sometimes, only when you need it," Shepard said. "Most of the time, you'll keep your regular one. But it will make taping a lot easier for you."

Whitacre nodded. All these new toys were making the job more exciting.

John Hoyt, the Springfield ASAC, pounded the telephone receiver on his desk after disconnecting with Bureau headquarters.

"Incompetent bureaucratic nincompoops!" he shouted, banging the receiver on each word.

For weeks Hoyt had been pushing headquarters for an additional agent or two. The ADM case was moving rapidly, and his agents were wearing thin. Shepard and Weatherall handled everything—interviewing Whitacre, picking up tapes, listening to tapes. They were working fifteen-hour days, most every day. For goodness' sake, the agents were spending time *transcribing* the darned tapes. Plus, the loss of two agents from Springfield's relatively small contingent was rippling across the office. A new agent had been moved to Decatur; somebody else had picked up the work in Champaign; and other agents were needed to replace the agents replacing Shepard and Weatherall. This was a case, Hoyt felt certain, that called for more manpower and attention from the Bureau.

He had called Washington with his pitch, laying out the investigation's magnitude and the demands being placed on his agents.

"Well," the Washington supervisor had replied, "that sounds like a great case. Why don't you send me an air-tel and tell me when you expect to indict. Maybe we can work it into a national press release."

An air-tel? Hoyt had been around long enough to know that a request for such a written communication was just a brush-off. They weren't ready to indict, Hoyt had said. They needed agents to investigate, recording devices to gather evidence, maybe money to pay sources. They needed resources to get the job done.

But the words had flown past the Washington supervisor. Antitrust investigations were not something that set hearts racing at the Bureau. They rarely generated headlines, big fines, or lengthy prison terms. Hoyt had heard those unspoken words as the supervisor prattled on about hiring freezes and the needs of larger offices. His protests were pointless. When the call had ended, Hoyt was seething.

After pounding the desk, Hoyt slammed the receiver in its cradle. He remembered the promise he had given Shepard many months ago: *The Bureau would give him all the support he needed.*

Hoyt was beginning to realize how hard it would be to keep his word.

Yard cuttings were strewn across the Whitacres' driveway, and Rusty Williams was using a gas-powered blower to clean up the mess. The groundskeeper saw Whitacre driving past the gate, and stepped out of the way. Whitacre stopped the car and climbed out.

"Hey bud, come on over," Whitacre called. "I want to show you something."

Whitacre opened the back door and pulled out a briefcase. Walking behind the car, he set the case on the trunk. When Williams reached him, Whitacre opened the briefcase and smiled.

"What do you think?" Whitacre asked.

Williams looked inside. Nothing.

"It's a nice briefcase."

"Ah, but wait," Whitacre said excitedly.

He reached inside, grasping a pocket at the top. Williams heard Velcro tear as a secret compartment lifted. Behind it was a silver tape recorder. Williams didn't know it, but he was looking at a Nagra, one of the best recording devices used by the FBI.

"How do you like that?" Whitacre buzzed.

Williams didn't know what to say.

"Just start calling me 014," Whitacre said.

Williams looked at him. "Why 014?"

Whitacre smiled. "Because I'm twice as smart as 007."

Around eight-fifteen on the morning of April 15, Whitacre walked into Mick Andreas's office. He was there to talk about a meeting scheduled in Chicago later that same day with Yamamoto of Kyowa Hakko. The microcassette recorder in his pocket was already running.

"Well, today's the big day," Whitacre announced.

Andreas looked up, smiling. "Today's the little day," he said in a low voice. Kyowa Hakko was the little Japanese company, Ajinomoto the big one.

"The little, yeah, the little day," Whitacre said. "The little Jap."

"You're just goin' up there to listen, aren't you?"

"Yeah, that's what Terry and I just talked about."

Just listening did not mean he should forget to let Yamamoto know ADM's position, Andreas said.

"Tell him how terrible it is that they never got the price up," he said. "How disorganized they are, or how disappointed we are."

"Yeah," Whitacre said.

"And you know, our plan is supergood," Andreas continued. "Everything is fine, except those guys fucked up the market so that nobody could play."

Yamamoto had to be kept on the defensive. "Go up to him and say, well you know, we tried pulling back," Andreas said, "and all that happened was the price went down."

"Yeah," Whitacre said, "the price went down."

"Who's leading the price down?" Andreas asked rhetorically. "They're leading the price down."

"Especially Ajinomoto," Whitacre said. "I think it would be fair to say that, don't you?"

"Yeah, sure, I would say it."

"Put the blame on the other guy?"

"Absolutely," Andreas said.

"Let them lose a little trust in the big guy."

Andreas nodded. "Exactly. That's right."

Whitacre glanced at Andreas's saltwater aquarium, absentmindedly watching the fish. After a few minutes, the meeting broke up. Whitacre headed back to his office.

Sitting down at his desk, he checked his watch. "Eight-thirty A.M., April fifteenth," he announced. "Just saw Mick Andreas. For the, for the marching orders."

A few hours later, Shepard and Weatherall glanced around a room on the eighteenth floor of the Chicago Marriott Downtown. The Chicago technical team had done a good job. Everything looked normal, nothing out of place. The table lamp, with the hidden FBI video camera inside, matched the decor well.

The agents went to the FBI command center in room 1817. The technical team was hooking up a monitor that would allow them to watch the Yamamoto meeting. When they turned it on, Shepard and Weatherall noticed that the room's furniture was not set up properly. The camera was stationary, but no chair was in front of it. They walked back to the meeting room, moving furniture around until they were satisfied.

Soon, Whitacre showed up at the command center. After introducing him to the technical agents, Shepard and Weatherall took him to the meeting room.

"Now, Mark, the camera is right over there," Shepard said, pointing at the lamp.

Whitacre wondered how heavy it was. He walked over and started to pick up the lamp.

"Don't lift that!" Shepard said.

Whitacre put the lamp back down.

Shepard walked over to one of the chairs. "This is the spot. Make sure Yamamoto sits right here."

"Okay," Whitacre said.

There were a few other points to remember, Shepard instructed. The FBI could only tape when a person who had consented to the recording was present. If Whitacre left—to go to the bathroom, anything—the FBI had to shut off the camera. So if he was leaving the room, Shepard said, Whitacre should say something to tip off the listening agents. Whitacre said that he understood.

Shepard glanced at his watch. It was 5:45. Time for everyone to take their places.

Whitacre waited in the lobby for fifteen minutes when, at 6:05, Yamamoto came through the revolving door.

"Massy," Whitacre said, "good to see you again. Welcome back to Chicago."

"Thank you, good to see you too."

Whitacre guided Yamamoto to the hotel bar, where they sat down and ordered drinks.

For eighteen minutes, an FBI agent conducting surveillance watched as the executives talked, drank, and ate dinner. Finally, at 6:25, the agent terminated the surveillance. It would be picked up again later.

· · ·

Just past seven-thirty, Whitacre and Yamamoto paid their bill, walked to an elevator, and stepped in. As the doors closed, an agent posing as a hotel guest picked up a house phone and dialed the FBI command room.

"On their way up," the agent said.

Whitacre and Yamamoto stepped off on the eighteenth floor. Another surveillance agent followed. Once the two executives walked inside the meeting room, the agent picked up his pace. He slid a card key into the electronic lock for the FBI command room and opened the door.

"They're in," the agent said.

An agent sitting in front of the black-and-white television monitor turned a knob and pushed down buttons on a video-recording device.

It was 17 seconds past 7:40 P.M. The grainy image of chairs in the next room appeared on the screen. Whitacre was standing beside them.

"Have a seat, Massy," Whitacre said. He positioned himself perfectly, effectively blocking the only other seat in the room. Yamamoto would have to take the chair directly in front of the camera.

"Good," Yamamoto said from across the room.

"Would you like another drink?"

"I don't think so," Yamamoto said.

"Okay, then we'll get started. If you'd like one at any time, you let me know."

At that moment, Yamamoto appeared on camera. He sat down exactly where the FBI wanted him to be.

In the command room, Shepard and Weatherall stood beside the monitor, watching the flickering images. Shepard listened to the conversation on headphones.

Even without hearing a word, Weatherall was impressed at how easily Whitacre had navigated Yamamoto into the right chair.

Good job, Mark, he thought. *Good job.*

Whitacre's back was to the camera as he casually walked Yamamoto through the high points of every major price-fixing meeting that the FBI had missed.

"I realize there wasn't much business discussed in Hawaii," he said, "but it was a lot of business discussed in Mexico and Paris."

Yamamoto grunted in agreement.

"Like you said, Terry Wilson said if the price, at that time of sixty cents a pound . . ."

"Yes," Yamamoto agreed.

"And he said if the price got to a dollar-five, maybe we could talk to our management. And we said we could maybe convince our management to go to a lower volume."

Yamamoto grunted.

He and Wilson had informed his management of the discussions, Whitacre said, but the worldwide price never reached $1.05 a pound.

"Our management saw it as a very messed-up market," he continued, "and they just felt like there's no incentive to reduce volume."

Whitacre was following Mick Andreas's instructions to the letter.

Shepard listened to Whitacre's words. He was doing a great job recapping earlier meetings. Yamamoto was not objecting to Whitacre's characterization. This tape would be good evidence. Whitacre was following his instructions perfectly.

The talks dragged on for almost two hours as the men debated production limits. At 9:33, they stood, having agreed only to meet again.

"Okay, Massy," Whitacre said.

"See you again," Yamamoto said.

The two men walked off camera.

On the headphones, Shepard could still hear the executives talking as they headed toward the door.

"Okay, bye-bye. Have a good trip back."

"Thank you!" Yamamoto replied.

Silence.

Shepard slid off the headphones. "That's it."

Minutes later, a knock came at the door of the FBI command room. It was Whitacre, looking excited and proud. He walked over to Shepard.

"Did you hear how we talked about all the other meetings?" Whitacre said. "We went into all of them. He talked about everything."

Shepard clapped Whitacre on the shoulder.

"Excellent job, Mark," he said. "Fantastic."

• • •

Every successful federal criminal case is the product of teamwork between investigators and prosecutors. The relationship can be delicate; at some point, agents have to hand off their case and hope that the lawyers can carry it across the goal line. But, until then, prosecutors stand by as critics, letting the agents know if their work will hold up under the harsh realities of the courtroom.

As a result, the greatest moments of tension emerge when the agents trot out evidence for their prosecutors. Often, those can be days of high expectations; the agents hope to hear praise for their hard-won information, all the time fearing that their work will be greeted with a dismissive wave.

The day for the first presentation of evidence in the ADM case arrived on April 27, a Wednesday. That morning, Robin Mann arrived at the offices of the Springfield FBI accompanied by Tracy Meares, another Antitrust Division lawyer. Both had come to town eager to review the tapes that they had heard so much about.

The two prosecutors pushed open the glass doors to the FBI office and headed into the lobby. Byron Cudmore was already there, waiting. Cudmore knew this would probably be his last direct involvement in the case for some time. The Clinton administration, through Attorney General Janet Reno, had just demanded the resignations of almost every U.S. Attorney in the country—Cudmore's boss among them. Cudmore had been sworn in as acting U.S. Attorney the day before, and expected to have less time for the ADM case.

John Hoyt came out and escorted the prosecutors to the SAC's conference room. Stukey, the SAC, was not available that day, Hoyt explained, but plenty of other agents would be attending.

Shepard and Weatherall arrived a few minutes later, followed by Paisley. The agents were brimming with excitement. They discussed the case, saying that they had secured the cooperation of a highly placed source.

Mann threw in some caution. "It's good somebody's cooperating. But we're going to need more. We're going to need documents and witnesses to corroborate everything to bring this as an antitrust case."

Hoyt felt flustered. He broke in.

"Well, we were thinking this was more than an antitrust case," he said, realizing only after making the statement that he might be insulting his guests.

He decided to try again. "There's a lot more than just antitrust violations going on," he said, spelling out each possible charge, from obstruction of justice to corporate espionage. "We really think this has good potential as a racketeering case, or something else broad like that."

Mann said little in response. The racketeering laws dated back to the government's efforts during the 1970s to combat organized crime, but in recent years they had been applied to white-collar cases. Using the law's vast powers, the government can seize assets of a criminal enterprise—in this case, potentially ADM itself. It would be an enormous undertaking, requiring approval from the highest levels. That decision was not going to be made today.

Shepard and Weatherall proceeded with the history of the investigation, including the backgrounds of ADM's lysine business and of their cooperating witness. Mann could sense that the agents were wary of her; even though everyone in the room knew Whitacre's identity, they wouldn't refer to him by name, instead calling him "the source." It struck her as unusual.

At one point, Mann said that she would be interested in meeting the witness herself. But the agents batted the idea away. He had been skittish for months and only recently had become cooperative. Meeting another government official, they cautioned, might cause problems. Mann reluctantly agreed to wait.

Finally Shepard, with videotape in hand, stepped over to a VCR that had been set up in the room.

"We want to show you excerpts from a consensual recording made last week in Chicago," he said.

Shepard explained that there would be two people visible in the video: the source, whose back would be to the camera, and Yamamoto. He turned on the video and stepped back, giving Mann an unobstructed view.

The grainy image of a man appeared on the screen. "Have a seat, Massy," the man said.

Mann watched carefully, occasionally writing quotes on a yellow pad. After a few minutes, she grew concerned about the tape. Yamamoto's accent was too thick. She couldn't understand what he was saying.

"What was that?" she asked at one point.

Shepard stopped the tape. He explained what Yamamoto had just said, and rewound the tape so Mann could hear it again. She listened for another few minutes, and exhaled heavily.

"Stop, go back," she said. "I'm really having trouble with this."

Again, Shepard explained what had been said. His comprehension of Yamamoto's words was undaunted by the accent. But whether the FBI could understand the tape was not particularly important to Mann.

"I don't know," she said. "We're going to have some real trouble with this in front of a jury. It's really hard to hear."

There were other problems as well. To convict on price-fixing, a jury would have to find that there had been an agreement; this tape seemed all dispute, no agreement. On top of that, Whitacre was making many of the strongest statements, with Yamamoto's acquiescence. Any good defense lawyer would argue that the Japanese executive had simply misunderstood. The words had to come from the potential defendant's mouth.

The room was turning testy. The agents had planned for Mann to be blown away. All they seemed to be hearing, though, were problems.

After struggling with the tape, the group reviewed other case details. Shepard mentioned that Whitacre and Wilson were scheduled to meet in Chicago the next day with two French executives from affiliates of Ajinomoto. Because the meeting was taking place in a restaurant, videotaping would be too difficult, but Whitacre would be wearing multiple recorders. Mann nodded, saying she would be interested in hearing those tapes as soon as possible.

The meeting wound down by the end of the day. Mann and Meares were shown to the lobby. As she rode down the elevator, Mann couldn't help but think that the case looked fairly promising.

Back upstairs, the agents gathered in Hoyt's office. The mood was sullen and disappointed. They had hoped for cheers and whistles and had received only questions and concerns.

"Well," Hoyt said, "that was a whole lot of nothing."

The first floor of the Best Western Shelton Inn in Decatur was empty early on the morning of April 28. Whitacre walked down the hallway looking for room 143. Finally, he saw it. He glanced back to see if he was still alone before tapping on the door; Shepard answered almost instantly.

"Hey, how you doin'?" Whitacre said before the door was closed. "I've got to hurry."

Walking into the room, Whitacre nodded a hello to Tom Gibbons, the agent he had recently escorted on the nighttime tour of ADM. Gibbons, who was by the bed fiddling with some electronic equipment, returned the greeting. Whitacre knew he was about to receive his best recording equipment yet. Wilson would be at the meeting today with Philippe Rollier and Alain Crouy—two executives with Ajinomoto's European affiliates. It would be the first chance to tape Wilson with competitors, and no one wanted to miss a word.

Shepard brought out shaving cream and a razor. "Mark, I'm going to need you to take off your shirt."

"Oh, yeah," Whitacre said, removing his jacket.

Shepard had told him a few days before that this new reel-to-reel recorder, called a body Nagra, would be strapped onto his back under his shirt. Small wires with multidirectional microphones would run from the device to his chest. Recordings from a body Nagra would be far better than from the pocket microcassette and would minimize the problem of clothing brushing the microphone. Plus, unlike the brief-case or notebook, he could carry it anywhere.

Whitacre laid his shirt across the bed and Shepard smoothed dabs of shaving cream on his chest. He stared straight ahead as the agent ran the razor across his skin until it was smooth. Gibbons handed Shepard the microphones, which he secured to Whitacre's chest with pieces of tape.

Using a white belt lined with Velcro, the agents strapped the body Nagra around Whitacre. The device, resting in the small of his back, felt huge; Shepard assured him it was difficult to detect, but warned him to be careful when sitting down. The device could make a clunk-ing sound if it hit the back of a metal chair.

"Now, we're going to need to cut a small hole inside your pants pocket," Shepard said. "It will help you operate the device."

Whitacre hesitated. "Okay," he said finally.

He took off his pants and handed them over. Gibbons quickly snipped open a front pocket. Then, he slid a tiny wire from the body Nagra into the pants and through the hole before handing the pants to Whitacre.

Once Whitacre zipped his pants, Gibbons instructed him on how to use the recorder. In his pants pocket, Gibbons said, was a tiny switch.

"So when there's something to record, just put your hand in your pocket and turn it on," he said.

Gibbons suggested trying out the device. He and Shepard walked behind Whitacre as he slid his hand into his pocket and flicked the switch.

"Ummm," Shepard said, studying the recorder.

"On," Gibbons confirmed. "On."

His hand still in his pocket, Whitacre turned off the device.

"Okay," he said, "that seems easy."

As Whitacre dressed, Shepard brought out the FBI briefcase. They wanted Whitacre to use two recorders that day to insure that nothing was missed.

"Okay," Shepard said. "We can meet back here tonight and I'll pick up the tapes."

He shook Whitacre's hand. "Good luck."

The Beech King Air B300 turboprop gently touched down on runway 18/36 at Merrill C. Meigs Field near downtown Chicago. The pilot taxied the ADM corporate plane to the hangar just before five o'clock. Seated in the spacious cabin's rich leather chairs, seven company executives waited for the propellers to stop spinning before heading for the exit.

The first off was Richard Reising. The ADM general counsel had come to Chicago with other company lawyers for a dinner with investment bankers. Whitacre and Wilson had tagged along, agreeing to meet later for the flight home. Whitacre was the last to reach the tarmac. With the body Nagra strapped on, he didn't want anyone behind him as he walked off the plane.

The executives headed out of the terminal in search of a taxi. With everyone else distracted, Whitacre leaned down, as if checking something in his briefcase. As instructed, he touched the latches.

Inside the case, things began to happen. Behind a false top, the Nagra recorder sparked to life, draining power from the commercial batteries that Gibbons had installed that same day. The magnetized tape moved through the recording heads.

Every sound within range was now being taped.

Whitacre stood. "Not easy to get a taxi down here, is it?" he said.

"Well, there's one right there," one of the ADM lawyers responded.

Wilson looked over to the cab and raised his arm. "There's one, yeah."

"We've got plenty of time," the lawyer said. "Why don't you take that one?"

"Yeah, thank you," Wilson said.

Whitacre and Wilson walked to the taxi. Whitacre climbed in first and scooted across the backseat.

"Remember," the lawyer said, "we take off before dark, or we don't get out of here."

"We'll be here about nine to nine-thirty," Whitacre responded.

Reising leaned toward the taxi.

"Pat 'em down for wires," he said to Wilson.

What was that? Whitacre couldn't see who was talking, but he had heard something about wires.

"Huh?" Wilson said.

"Pat 'em down for wires," Reising repeated.

Wilson laughed as the cab pulled away.

Whitacre looked at Wilson. "What'd he say?"

"Pat 'em down for wires," Wilson said.

Is this serious? Whitacre thought. If ADM insisted on pat-downs, the Europeans might reciprocate. It wouldn't be hard for them to find the recorder strapped on his back.

"Probably should," Whitacre laughed.

Wilson instructed the driver to take them to O'Hare International Airport, where they were scheduled to meet the two French executives. Whitacre slid his hand into his pocket, found the switch for his body Nagra, and flicked it on. He wanted a backup, to be sure that this conversation was recorded.

"So Reising must know who we're meetin' with, huh?" Whitacre asked.

"I didn't tell him," Wilson replied.

"I didn't tell him," Whitacre said.

Wilson laughed. "He just figures who we're meetin' with."

"He must have thought we were meeting with Ikeda. He said 'pat 'em down for wires.' "

"Oh, I don't know," Wilson grumbled.

"I don't think we'd have to worry about that with Rollier."

For more than an hour, the cab crawled through stop-and-go traffic. Whitacre shut off his recorders to save tape. Finally, they pulled up to the O'Hare Hilton Hotel. After paying the fare, they headed through the lobby toward the Gaslight Club, the restaurant where they were scheduled to meet the French executives. Whitacre slid his hand into his pocket and turned the body Nagra back on.

The restaurant seemed a surreal holdover from the 1970s—part Playboy Club, part Edwardian steakhouse. The bordello-red decor was highlighted with generous amounts of velvet; the waitresses dressed in fishnet stockings, heels, and sequined black bodysuits. Older businessmen seated around the room chose their dinners from a circular steel platter holding cuts of raw meat. Among them, a smattering of FBI agents from the Chicago surveillance unit posed as diners.

Whitacre excused himself, heading to the bathroom. As expected, an FBI agent was waiting. Whitacre identified himself and told the agent that he and his group were seated in the smoking section.

Outside the bathroom, Whitacre ran into the French executives and took them to Wilson. After they sat at the table, a scantily clad waitress appeared.

"Good evening," she said. "I'm Teri. I'll be your Gaslight girl this evening. May I get you something to drink?"

In a few minutes, the men were offering toasts and were ready to talk business.

"Well, how about you guys?" Whitacre asked. "Are you satisfied the way things are going for lysine?"

"Not completely," Crouy said. "I mean, we have restricted our quantities to try to keep prices, and uh, the prices were satisfactory."

"Especially in Europe," Whitacre said.

True, Crouy agreed, but prices were now going down, so his division was stepping up sales to compensate for the lost revenue.

"Price is going down in Europe?" Wilson asked.

"In Europe, very much so," Crouy said. "I mean, pushed by you."

Whitacre's effort months before to derail the price-fixing scheme was catching up with him. He glossed over it, offering up a few explanations.

The men haggled over prices and volumes around the world. Rollier and Crouy blamed ADM for most every problem. Wilson, already on his second scotch, fought back by reminding them of an earlier meeting.

"We told everybody as plain as we could tell them that by the end of October 1993, we intend to be as big as Ajinomoto. We said it openly."

The fact that prices held for a while in Europe was meaningless, Wilson continued. "Alain, we cannot have one section of the world where it works and the rest of the world where it doesn't. It will not last. It cannot last. It just doesn't."

Getting close. Without using the words, Wilson was openly talking about price-fixing. The liquor seemed to be loosening everyone's tongues.

Teri the Gaslight girl returned, carrying a platter of meat. The executives indulged themselves, selecting racks of lamb, shrimp, and steak. When she left, they resumed their conversation.

Crouy said that he had left the Paris meeting in October with the impression that few competitors wanted an agreement to limit production. The men argued about the responsibility for falling prices.

"Well, one can point a lot of fingers," Whitacre said, setting down his glass of Chardonnay. "I guess the thing is, what's the solution?"

Wilson agreed. At the first big Mexico meeting, getting an agreement on a target price was easy.

"We went out and we said, 'Okay, our price is going to be at . . . ,' " he said, holding up his hand to symbolize the selected price. "That's what we agreed on. And we did it. And we did it across the board without hesitation."

Then, Wilson continued, excuses started piling up. The Japanese complained they were having trouble preventing their salesmen from competing for customers by offering lower prices.

A strategy could be adopted, suggested Wilson, in which each company reported sales numbers to the other producers. That way, competitors would know which company was pushing down prices by selling too much. That company would be allocated fewer sales for the following month. If the companies cooperated, everyone would receive a fair share and prices would hold.

"You have monthly reporting," Wilson said.

"Which means that you have to see each other very often," Rollier said.

"I don't know if you have to see each other often," Wilson countered. "I just think you gotta have the figures monthly, that's all."

Whitacre knew that Wilson was describing the system used by ADM and its competitors to fix prices in the huge market for citric acid. Shepard had been pushing him to tape Wilson talking about citric. Whitacre figured this was his opening.

"That's how it's done in citric, isn't it?" Whitacre asked.

"Yeah," Wilson replied.

Confirmation.

Crouy didn't like the idea of sharing numbers. "That doesn't work with Asian people," he said.

Rollier agreed. "We would obviously play that game. But, uh, the Koreans and the Japanese—"

"You will never get them," Crouy interrupted.

"You will never get them from the Koreans," Rollier continued. "They'll cheat, or they'll say yes and they'll, uh . . ."

"Never do it," Crouy said.

Wilson sat back. "It'll never work, then."

The men sifted through their positions again. Wilson became frustrated. Occasionally, he broke the tension by flirting with the waitress.

If everyone shared sales numbers, Wilson repeated, they would know exactly who was producing too much. Throughout the year, each company would be allowed to adjust sales as each month's numbers were distributed.

"If we're ahead, then we've gotta cut back," he said. "Oh, shit, it's so goddamn simple. How the hell else will you do it?"

Again, the French executives said that the Koreans would not cooperate. They would cheat. Whitacre suggested that sales numbers could be audited by an accounting firm hired by the lysine producers.

"We do that in citric," Wilson added.

Rollier and Crouy encouraged Wilson and Whitacre to attend more meetings. Even without agreements to limit volume, the meetings helped.

Wilson's face was hard. "Well, I don't know."

Crouy leaned in. "Let's not forget that if prices went up in Europe, it's because we talked in Mexico first."

"That's right," Wilson agreed.

"Then because we talked in Europe a lot after."

"You made it happen," Wilson said.

"I mean, it didn't just go up like that."

"You made it happen," Wilson repeated.

Whitacre tried not to breathe. Crouy and Wilson had just confessed: Lysine prices went up because competitors met in Mexico. *They made it happen*.

The executives drank coffee after dinner. Past eight-thirty, Whitacre checked his watch. He and Wilson needed to leave, or they would miss their plane. Whitacre picked up the $267 dinner bill, and the men parted ways. Wilson and Whitacre hurried to a cab.

As the cab made its way to Meigs Field, Whitacre decided to make one more point for the tape. He mentioned that he had paid the bill for dinner.

"On my expense report, should I put dinner with Philippe Rollier and Alain Crouy of Eurolysine?"

"Nah," Wilson said. "Probably not."

"I did that one time and Randall kicked my ass."

"Yeah, yeah. Well, better not."

Whitacre relaxed in his seat. It was the perfect close for the evening.

• • •

Later, shortly before eleven-twenty, Whitacre was back at the Best Western, barely able to contain his excitement.

"Brian, you're not going to believe it," Whitacre breathed. "They talked about everything. They talked about Mexico. Terry told them all about citric, how they do it. And it's just like I told you."

Shepard held up a hand. Whitacre was a little too excited. He needed to slow him down.

"That's great, Mark," he said. "Let's take this one step at a time. Did you get everything on tape?"

"I used the recorder, just like Tom said. I think it was fine, I think everything worked fine."

"That's super. Why don't we get the recorder off first, and then we can talk."

"Okay, Brian."

Whitacre shucked off his suit jacket.

"Man, Brian," Whitacre said, grinning. "You're gonna love it. You're just gonna love it."

That night, Ginger Whitacre was awakened by the sound of her husband coming up the stairs. She glanced at the bedside clock and saw it was past one. She could scarcely believe his days; she knew he would be getting up in just over four hours. Between ADM and the FBI, he was barely sleeping anymore.

Ginger leaned up on her elbows as Mark quietly pushed the door open. His tie was already loosened and the top few buttons of his shirt were unfastened.

"I'm awake," she announced.

"Hey," he said softly. "How you doing?"

"I'm fine," she said.

"Chicago went well," said Mark, as he unbuttoned the rest of his shirt. "Just finished up with Brian."

Ginger took a deep breath, saying nothing. In recent weeks, her attitude had soured toward the FBI. They were demanding a lot of her husband.

"Hey," Mark said as he took off his shirt, "look at this."

He walked over to a small brass lamp on the bedside table and turned it on.

Ginger stared at him, aghast. *Somebody had shaved his chest hair.* The hair they always joked about, because it had taken most of their marriage to grow. Now, there were strips of bare skin across his chest.

"Oh, my God," she gasped.

"Now I've got a chest like a woman," Mark laughed.

"Why did they do that?"

Mark explained as he took off his pants.

"Hey, that's not all," he said, turning his pocket inside out. "They cut a hole right here, too. Can't carry change in that pocket anymore."

"Are you joking? Not your good pants!"

Ginger seethed. The FBI was taking over her husband's life. It was one thing to cooperate. It was something else when the government was shaving her husband's body and cutting up his clothes.

"This is ludicrous," Ginger said. "Why does this have to be you? These FBI agents are trained to put their lives on the line. You're not. If somebody needs to do all this, let it be them."

Mark laughed, telling her not to worry. But Ginger knew he was just as bothered as she was.

"Mark, you've got to get out of this," she said. "Why don't we say you got a job offer? They can't make you stay just to tape, can they? Can't you leave?"

Whitacre sat down on the bed.

"I don't know," he said softly. "I don't know."

The next morning, Shepard and Weatherall drove to Springfield to turn in the latest tapes. They arrived at the ELSUR office by 10:40 and obtained duplicates. Soon, they were listening to the tapes, noting the best phrases.

Pat 'em down for wires.

That could spell trouble. They needed to make sure everything was being done to protect Whitacre.

We do that in citric.

Perfect. Now the larger case involving citric acid was making progress.

If prices went up in Europe, it's because we talked in Mexico first.

Mann would want to hear about that portion. It was as close to an admission as anyone could hope.

By about three, Shepard and Weatherall were hustling down the hallway to find John Hoyt or Dean Paisley. This was a huge breakthrough.

Hoyt was in his office. For several minutes, the two agents briefed him on the new tape. The ASAC offered congratulations and hand-shakes.

After they left, Hoyt pulled out his daily planner, where he kept a record of important meetings. He flipped to the page for April 29.

"Brian and Joe re: ADM," he scribbled.

Hoyt smiled. He could summarize the briefing in one word. He brought his pen back down on the page.

"Homerun!!" he wrote.

CHAPTER 7

The receptionist on duty peered through the bulletproof glass in front of her desk, into the lobby of the FBI's Springfield office. A young stranger dressed in a conservative suit had just come through the public entrance and was walking toward her. He was a handsome man, standing more than six feet tall, with reddish brown hair and a confident manner. The receptionist watched as he took a small leather case out of his suit jacket and flipped it open. A badge and credentials—his "creds." The man was an agent.

"Good morning," he said. "I'm Bob Herndon. It's my first day."

To Herndon, the moment felt good. The thirty-year-old agent was back in an FBI office, showing his creds, identifying himself by name. It had been a long time.

For three years before this day in June 1993, Herndon had worked undercover, posing with a false name and identity in a long-running counterintelligence project. All that time, he and his wife had been separated from their friends and family. He couldn't carry real identification, couldn't walk into the office where he was assigned. It had been challenging work, but he had been ready to come in, to be Bob Herndon again. He wanted to go home to the Midwest; Springfield needed more agents. The match was perfect.

Herndon and his wife, Raelene, had just purchased a house nearby, and he was already boasting to friends about his three-mile commute. His phone calls with Bob Anderson, the supervisor who ran his new squad, left him feeling as though a good relationship was already developing.

Anderson appeared in a few minutes and escorted Herndon back to his office. The supervisor broke into a grin as he sat down.

"Well, I've got some news for you," Anderson said. "You've been traded."

A last-minute transfer had been ordered, Anderson explained. Herndon was being moved to the squad supervised by Dean Paisley, assigned to a complex financial investigation that had been under way for months.

"It definitely needs another person," he said. "And you'll be working with a couple of great guys."

Anderson said that the case involved ADM. Herndon stared across the desk blankly. He had no idea what Anderson was talking about.

For forty-five minutes, the supervisor provided a crash course in ADM, lysine, and price-fixing. He briefly mentioned other allegations from the cooperating witness, including the corporate espionage, the bugging of the Decatur Club, and the bogus extortion claim.

"Now, the case is being handled in Decatur," Anderson said. "That's about forty miles away, but it's an easy forty miles, with hardly any traffic."

He explained that Herndon could work in Springfield. But much of his time would be spent in Decatur, where he would also have a desk. Anderson finished up and paused for questions.

"Sounds great," Herndon said.

The supervisor stood and showed Herndon to his new desk. He gave his new agent the number for the Decatur Resident Agency, telling him to call Shepard and Weatherall. Probably he should head out there today, maybe catch lunch with them, Anderson suggested.

Sitting at his new desk, Herndon picked up the phone. He was excited about the case and eager to meet his new partners. Still, he couldn't shake the feeling that his bubble had been burst.

That three-mile commute was history.

Later that day, the three FBI agents were walking down a dusty Decatur road. Despite the hot sun, Shepard and Herndon wore their suit jackets to cover the guns holstered on their hips. Weatherall was in shirtsleeves; he had left his weapon inside his briefcase. The agents were heading to lunch at the Lock Stock & Barrel, about a mile away.

As they walked, Shepard and Weatherall questioned Herndon. The investigation had begun progressing smoothly; the last thing they needed was some young hotshot spooking Whitacre. Would he take shortcuts? Was he a know-it-all?

Answering the questions, Herndon poured out his story. He had grown up a strapping, middle-class kid in Overland Park, Kansas, the only child of a state auditor and a schoolteacher. In school he trained to be an accountant and worked with a Kansas City firm. But Herndon had always wanted to be with the FBI and applied in 1986. It was good timing; the savings-and-loan crisis was blossoming and the Bureau needed accountants. So, at the age of twenty-three, Herndon had been shipped off to the FBI academy in Quantico, Virginia.

After his training, Herndon had first been assigned to New Orleans, where he investigated possible fraud at a thrift. The case had been a success, with Herndon "flipping" a crooked bank officer, persuading him to plead guilty and cooperate. That was followed by a case involving a federal judge who took bribes. An FBI team that included Herndon had wired up a witness and planted listening devices in the judge's chambers, gathering the evidence to send him to jail. Coming off that case, Herndon had been chosen for the counterintelligence project.

Herndon began to worry that he was talking too much; he didn't want his new partners thinking he was out of line. He changed the subject.

"Well, Bob Anderson told me about your case," he said. "It sounds great."

"Let's not get into it here," Shepard said.

They arrived at the restaurant; it seemed nice and agent-priced. Weatherall and Herndon took advantage of the all-you-can-eat salad bar, while Shepard just sipped on black decaffeinated coffee. At the table, Shepard described his background. He mentioned that he had originally trained to be a meteorologist, setting off a slew of jokes about TV weathermen. Weatherall talked about growing up in Texas, his military background, and the types of cases he had handled since being stationed in Champaign.

The mood relaxed as the three men began to get a better sense of one another. This partnership seemed as though it might work.

During his first few days on the case, Herndon reviewed the files, now three volumes thick. He knew he had to hurry; the investigation was not going to wait for him. Already, another price-fixing meeting was scheduled in a few days for Vancouver, British Columbia.

As he flipped through, Herndon wrote down each name. Dwayne and Michael Andreas, as chairman and vice-chairman, were clearly the people in charge of running ADM, along with Jim Randall, the president. Mark Whitacre and Terry Wilson were most directly involved in the lysine price-fixing.

The names of the foreign competitors were the hardest to keep straight. Ajinomoto seemed to have the most contact with ADM, through Kanji Mimoto and Hirokazu Ikeda. They were the Japanese company's version of Whitacre and Wilson. The managing director at Ajinomoto, Kazutoshi Yamada, was the equivalent of Mick Andreas. About a month before, Yamada had flown to Decatur for a meeting with Mick Andreas. Whitacre had taped the conversation, but it wasn't of much use.

Yamada was easy to mix up with Yamamoto of Kyowa Hakko. But of the two, Yamada was far more important—both his company and his authority were bigger. One simple trick to remember who was who: The one with the shorter name was the bigger player.

Besides the Japanese, there were other foreigners involved—executives with European subsidiaries of Ajinomoto, as well as officers of two Korean companies, Miwon and Cheil Jedang Ltd. Over time, Herndon figured, he would get comfortable with the names.

He reviewed tapes from the investigation, which now numbered almost fifty. There had been a lot of meetings already; in just the past few weeks, ADM had met with the Japanese in both Decatur and Tokyo. As he listened to the recordings, Herndon thought he could help by writing summaries of them. He had used such a system in the case against the federal judge, and it had been helpful. Shepard liked the idea when Herndon proposed it, and gave him the go-ahead.

Throughout June 23, planes carrying executives from the world's lysine producers landed at Vancouver International Airport. A gathering on the American continent seemed only fair; ADM had traveled to Tokyo the month before. Plus, in Vancouver, they remained out of the reach of law enforcement from the United States, where antitrust laws were particularly tough.

The executives from each company arrived at different times. ADM from America. Ajinomoto and Kyowa Hakko from Japan. Miwon and Cheil Foods from Korea. Even the executives from Ajinomoto's European affiliates, Eurolysine and Orsan, flew in, heading to the meeting at the Hyatt Regency Vancouver.

As the men traveled through the terminals that day, no one noticed that they were being photographed and videotaped by the Royal Canadian Mounted Police. For while American law-enforcement officials had no authority in Canada, they did have an assistance treaty with their northern neighbors. And the RCMP was recording every public move made by the conspirators.

• • •

The next morning, June 24, Joe Weatherall was in his hotel room at the Hyatt in Vancouver. Weatherall had drawn the assignment for this trip, to serve as Whitacre's contact and to provide help to the RCMP. At about eight-fifty, the phone in his room rang.

"Joe?" a voice said. "Hey, it's Mark."

Whitacre described the morning's plans. He and Wilson would meet with Ajinomoto to discuss monosodium glutamate, or MSG, the additive best known for its use in Chinese food. Whitacre was not responsible for MSG; that product was handled at ADM by Barrie Cox, who also ran citric. The meeting would give Whitacre a chance to hear what kind of discussions took place with products other than lysine.

Throughout the morning, Whitacre called Weatherall with updates on the MSG talks. Ajinomoto wanted their executive in charge of MSG to meet with Cox. At one point, Whitacre said, an Ajinomoto executive had asked, "Can we do MSG like we do lysine?"

Whitacre said that the lysine meeting was scheduled for about one o'clock, and promised to call at the first break. Weatherall thanked him and hung up.

For a moment, the agent reviewed his notes.

Now it's MSG.

These companies wanted to rig the market for every product they sold.

Later that afternoon, Dean Paisley came out of his office and signaled to Herndon. "Hey, Bobby," he said, "Joe's on the line."

Herndon got up from his desk and hurried over. Paisley was already back at his desk.

"Okay, Joe, I've got Bobby here," Paisley said to the speakerphone. "So what's going on up there?"

"Well, our friend tells me it's been a good meeting," Weatherall replied slowly.

Weatherall provided a quick rundown of the developments. The meetings had taken place throughout the day; all five lysine producers attended. According to Whitacre, a pricing agreement had been struck, but volume was still a problem. ADM was pretty mad.

The agents discussed Vancouver excitedly. Even though the Canadians had refused permission for Whitacre to record, the FBI now had its first solid evidence that all lysine competitors—not just one or two companies—were gathering for secret meetings.

The agents ended their call feeling confident. It was good to hear

that after all of his early deceptions, Whitacre was finally playing it
straight.

Fake steer skulls and plastic cactuses lay scattered beside the multicolored wall at Carlos O'Kelly's, a popular Mexican café in Decatur.
Nearby, Whitacre was enjoying dinner with another executive. Whitacre
liked the food; he and his dinner companion, David Page, had also
eaten lunch there that same day.

As Mexican music played on a sound system, the two men talked.
Page was an operating manager with Vanetta USA, a vitamin K sup-
plier for ADM. The two had met years before, in the early 1980s, when
Whitacre worked for Ralston Purina and Page for Heterochemical
Corporation. As Whitacre's career blossomed, Page had kept con-
tact. Now, Whitacre had approached Page with a job offer at the ADM
Bioproducts Division.

Over their meal, Whitacre laid out the terms of Page's employment: He would be paid $120,000 his first year, along with a signing
bonus of $30,000. From then on, he would be considered for raises.
Whitacre emphasized that as division president, he had the full authority to make hiring decisions.

Page listened carefully. The pay sounded good, and the bonus was
particularly nice. But he still did not understand the job that Whitacre
had in mind.

"What would my responsibilities be?" he asked.

A fleeting smile passed over Whitacre's face.

"Nothing," he said casually.

Days later, Whitacre was at his desk, filling out his expense reports for
the week. He fished out the receipts from his two meals with David
Page and wrote them up. At the bottom of the report, he scribbled Page's
name into the blank space under the heading *Persons Entertained,*
mentioning that he had been interviewing Page about a job. The next
column was headed *Company Represented.* There, Whitacre was supposed to write the name of Page's current employer, Vanetta USA. Instead, he wrote *Heterochemical*—where his friend had been employed
six years before.

But Vanetta was an ADM supplier; Heterochemical was not. Interviewing a supplier's top employee might have raised questions inside ADM. And the last thing Whitacre wanted was for anyone to ask
about what he was doing with David Page.

• • •

The FBI brainstorming session thrashed through a single question: What would persuade the foreign lysine producers to come to America?

Without a meeting on American soil, there was a good chance that critical price-fixing decisions would never be recorded. But because of the tough American laws on price-fixing, the United States was the last place that any of them wanted to meet.

Weatherall sat up straight. "I've got an idea."

Most of these executives shared an interest in golf. Asian countries, and Japan in particular, were known for their paucity of good golf courses. But weren't some of the world's best courses in Hawaii?

The agents tossed around the idea. They would have to start now, using Whitacre to convince the other executives to fly to Hawaii.

They could only hope that lush golf courses were enough of an enticement to persuade the foreign lysine executives to risk jail.

North of Decatur, at the intersection of Interstate 72 and Route 51, lies the village of Forsyth. Founded in 1854 as the spikes were being driven for the Illinois Central Railroad, Forsyth had long been little more than an appendage to Decatur. But beginning in the late 1970s, a boom in economy hotels there followed the construction of the Hickory Point Mall. Forsyth soon emerged as a frequent stop for budget-minded travelers. By the summer of 1993, the Forsyth hotels had also become popular spots for the FBI's meetings with Whitacre.

Storm clouds were gathering on the evening of July 13 as Herndon drove his Bureau car to Forsyth. After more than a month on the case, tonight he would meet Whitacre for the first time.

Herndon put on his blinker when he saw the brown-and-white sign for the mall. He drove into the entrance and made a quick left. Ahead was the Hampton Inn, his destination. After parking, Herndon threw a floor mat over his red bubble light and stuffed his radio microphone under a seat. He didn't want passersby to wonder why law enforcement was at the hotel.

Upstairs, his partners were waiting. The three agents spent a few minutes testing the telephone-recording equipment they wanted to use that night. Shepard and Herndon took off their guns, putting them in their briefcases. There was no reason to make Whitacre uncomfortable.

Their witness arrived about forty-five minutes later. By then, a torrential downpour had begun.

"Hey, how you doin'?" Whitacre said as he walked inside the room, shaking off the rain. He glanced around. Weatherall was sitting on a couch. On the bed, Whitacre saw a young, athletic-looking man he did not know.

"Mark, this is Special Agent Bob Herndon," Shepard said. "Like I told you, he's transferred from another office and been assigned to this case."

Whitacre broke into a smile.

"Hey, very nice to meet you," Whitacre said. "Great to have you here."

The men shook hands. Herndon was impressed. Whitacre commanded a room, just lit it up. He was clearly a salesman, eager for everyone to like him. As he studied his witness, Herndon noticed that Whitacre's blond hair appeared to be almost two different shades; for a second, he wondered whether it was a toupee. Then he eyed Whitacre's clothing; his expensive suit and garish tie seemed chosen to attract attention. That struck him as a good icebreaker.

"Hey, that's a really nice tie," Herndon said.

"Thank you very much," Whitacre replied. "I got this one at Bachrach. That's a store I like a lot."

Herndon nodded.

"You know, you've got a nice tie there yourself," Whitacre said.

Herndon looked down. "Hey, thanks."

Coyly, Whitacre glanced at Shepard, dressed in his usual off-the-rack sports jacket and drab tie. He looked back at Herndon and the two men smiled. They shared the same thought. *We gotta work on that guy.*

Shepard picked up his notebook. "So, Mark, do you have any tapes?"

Whitacre reached into his pocket, removing two microcassetes. For the next few minutes, he recited the information about the tapes; both were of telephone calls with Ajinomoto. Once Shepard finished the paperwork, Whitacre sat at the table in the room. Weatherall took the seat across from him.

"All right, Mark," Weatherall said slowly, "what's been going on?"

For the most part, Whitacre said, he had been on vacation, traveling in Mexico. But he had spoken with Ikeda that morning; it was one of the conversations he had taped. The Japanese executive wanted to resolve the volume dispute through a meeting of top decision-makers from each company—in this case, Mick Andreas and Kazutoshi Yamada. While the two men had met in April during a visit in Decatur, they had not participated in any large gathering of the lysine producers. Weatherall told Whitacre that it was important to let the agents know as soon as a meeting was arranged.

Whitacre nodded.

"Mark, there's something else we need to talk to you about," Weatherall said. "We told you that we need to see if one of these meetings can be held in the United States, and we've come up with an idea."

Whitacre listened carefully as Weatherall described the golf proposal, and broke into a big smile. The idea might work.

"Put it on my calling card?" Whitacre asked as he picked up the telephone.

"Yeah," Shepard said.

It was twenty minutes later. Sitting on the bed, Whitacre dialed the number for Kanji Mimoto at Ajinomoto. He had rehearsed the conversation several times and was ready to suggest the Hawaii proposal. The recording device was hooked up to the phone.

"It's ringing," Whitacre told the agents.

A woman answered.

"Yes, may I speak to Mr. Mimoto, please?"

"I'm sorry, he's in a meeting now, and he'll be free at noon."

"He told me if he's in a meeting to call him out of the meeting, that it was very important."

The woman asked for his name. Whitacre waited on hold until the phone clicked.

"Hello?"

"Is this Mr. Tani in New York or Mr. Mimoto?" Whitacre was still using Mimoto's code name.

Mimoto chuckled. "Mr. Tani, yes, speaking."

"Well, how are you?" Whitacre asked.

"Is it Mark speaking?"

"This is Mark Tani speaking."

"Yeah," Mimoto laughed. "Mark Tani."

The two men discussed the possible effects of a planned price increase. ADM, Whitacre said, was concerned about drying up demand.

"Remember in Vancouver," Whitacre continued, "Terry Wilson made this very clear, that we'll wanna try to keep the levels of lysine usage as high as we can."

"Yeah, that's right."

"Not to get the prices too high where we shrink the market."

"Yeah," Mimoto said, "if we shrink the market, of course, we have to avoid such a price increase."

Whitacre glanced over at the agents. The time had come to lay the trap.

"Since you guys hosted the Vancouver meeting, I think ADM should host the next meeting, don't you?"

"Yeah," Mimoto said. "That's fine."

"And maybe we host it in, uh, Maui."

"Maui?"

"You know, have the group meeting like we had last time in Vancouver. Have it in Maui, Hawaii."

"Maui, Hawaii, is, uh, still in the United States," Mimoto said warily.

Whitacre had been told to push Mimoto if he objected, to force him to explain why he didn't want to meet on American territory. He glanced at Shepard.

"Yeah, but what's that mean? 'Still in the United States'?"

"Well," Mimoto said, " 'still in the United States' means, uh, United States is, ah, very severe for the control of antitrust activity, no?"

Whitacre's eyes lit up. That statement was going to be almost impossible to explain away. He brushed aside Mimoto's concerns.

"Hawaii, next to an eighteen-hole golf course?"

Mimoto laughed. "If your company judges no problem, maybe I will consult with our legal department."

Whitacre reminded him that the previous year, when the price-fixing scheme was in its nascent stages, there had been a meeting in Maui.

Well, Mimoto said, maybe the meeting could be held in Hawaii to establish the lysine association. Apparently, Ajinomoto was prepared to accept the idea of using association meetings as a cover.

"Yeah, that's right," Whitacre said, picking up the theme. "It'd be a formal association meeting."

"Hmm."

"And also would be a good distance for you and us both together."

"Yeah, yeah, that's right," Mimoto said. "And be on the golf course."

"Yeah."

"No big problem," Mimoto said.

That was it. Mimoto had taken the bait.

Whitacre hung up the phone a few minutes later.

"You guys gotta hear this tape!" he said, his words rushing out. "He let it all out! He knows this is wrong. He talked about American antitrust laws."

The agents, already excited from Whitacre's half of the discussion, removed the tape and punched out the tabs to prevent it from being accidentally erased. Then, after rewinding it, they listened to the conversation. Whitacre paced as the tape played.

"Here it comes, here it comes," he said.

Mimoto's voice could be heard clearly.

United States is, ah, very severe for the control of antitrust activity, no?

Whitacre jumped. "Hey, there it is! Did you hear it, did you hear it?"

The agents nodded, keeping their cool demeanor. But they knew the statement was big; it clearly established Mimoto's intent to violate American law.

They finished with the tape, and Whitacre received a round of congratulations. Afterward, everyone checked their schedules and arranged their next meeting. Then they were done.

"Okay, guys, thanks," Whitacre said, shouldering into his raincoat. "See you next time."

At a small restaurant in the historic castle district of Budapest, down the street from Hungary's Gothic coronation church, a group of lysine executives had just finished an expensive lunch. Wrapping up their discussions on global lysine prices and volumes, the group of Japanese, Korean, and European executives bid one another good-bye and headed off in different directions.

Walking with the group from Kyowa Hakko of Japan, Masaru Yamamoto was speaking with a more junior colleague. The battles that had been waged between the Japanese lysine producers and ADM appeared to be on the wane, Yamamoto said. Prices were rising all over; the cooperative relationship seemed to be working.

"It is all right to talk to ADM now," Yamamoto told his colleague. "ADM is no longer the enemy."

The first fireflies were coming out in Lincoln, Nebraska, as John Hoyt eased himself into a big porch chair beside his brother-in-law, J. R. Hovelsrud. The Springfield ASAC and his wife had taken some days off to visit family, and that night they had enjoyed a big dinner at Hovelsrud's farm. Everybody was full and content. The outside air was warm and sweet.

Hoyt stared up at the sky, watching as the stars appeared. He enjoyed visiting his brother-in-law and respected him. Hovelsrud had been a farmer most of his life, struggling almost every day to get the crops in. He had been dependent on banks, dependent on weather, dependent on feed companies. Then recently, Hovelsrud and a friend had decided to take more control of their futures by opening their own feed business. This was Hoyt's first chance to ask about the venture.

"So," he said, "how's the feed business going?"

"Okay," Hovelsrud said, disappointment in his voice. "But, boy, it's frustrating. How am I supposed to make ends meet when prices keep going up?"

"Prices of what?"

"Oh, it's this stuff we use called lysine."

Hoyt stared ahead. The criminal investigation was still secret. He played dumb.

"What's lysine?" he asked.

"It's an artificial amino acid that's used in hog feed and stuff like that," Hovelsrud said. "And, gee whiz, the price has just been going crazy."

Hoyt listened as his brother-in-law ticked off how lysine costs had been climbing. He already knew some of the numbers. In June, when the price-fixing scheme was still struggling, lysine had been available for as little as sixty cents a pound. But since Vancouver, when lysine producers sealed their deal, prices had soared to as much as $1.20 a pound by the end of July—a 100 percent increase in a few weeks.

As Hovelsrud described his financial difficulties, Hoyt's anger welled up. He knew that no company in the world was competing for his brother-in-law's business. No one was going to offer a lower price in hopes of winning a new customer. Everything had been rigged; no matter how hard Hovelsrud worked, the success or failure of his new business was being decided by a bunch of suits in fancy hotel rooms.

Just a few weeks before, Hoyt had been watching *This Week with David Brinkley* on a Sunday morning and saw one of ADM's ads proclaiming itself as the "Supermarket to the World." The attempt to project a squeaky-clean image had struck him as outrageous. Now, as he listened to Hovelsrud's troubles, the reason that the ad had bothered him seemed particularly clear.

Hoyt had heard stories about ADM executives racing up and down the roads of rural Illinois in their Ferraris and other expensive sports cars. He knew the company's customers, including untold numbers of struggling, middle-income farmers such as his brother-in-law, were being priced out of business. He knew that average Americans were being ripped off, too, paying pennies and dimes more for the weekly groceries just to satisfy the greed of ADM and its competitors.

For a while, Hoyt and his fellow agents had understood the

theoretical concept behind antitrust laws, the reason why price-fixing was illegal. But now Hoyt understood that the victims were real. They had a human face. They looked like J.R.

This case was not about some economic theory, he thought. It was about *thievery*. These executives were stealing. They were little different than some armed thugs who robbed a liquor store, except that they were already far richer than most of their victims.

Hoyt couldn't tell his brother-in-law that his problems were about to grow worse. The lysine companies were getting ready to reach volume agreements that could push up prices even more. Inwardly, Hoyt vowed to do what he could to solve the problem harming his brother-in-law and so many other farmers and agricultural workers. And as he thought about the true cost of ADM's crimes, he knew exactly what should happen to the company and its executives.

This bunch of crooks, he thought, *all deserve to go to prison.*

Every major FBI investigation is given a code name, allowing agents to discuss it without tipping off anyone on the outside. But, after more than eight months, the ADM investigation had yet to be named. Shepard had offered a couple of suggestions, but headquarters had rejected both. One had already been used, and the second—a wordplay on ADM's slogan "Supermarket to the World"—was too easily identifiable.

One summer afternoon, Paisley called in Herndon. They needed to come up with a code name, he said. "I mean, Bobby, this is getting ridiculous. Spend some time and come up with as many names as you can and give them to me tomorrow."

Back at his desk, Herndon flipped open his notepad. He thought for a minute.

Lysine, a feed additive for chickens. *Fowl Play, Fowl Ball, Fowl Out.*

A crime taking place in Illinois, the Land of Lincoln. *Ill Deal. Linc Con.*

Decatur, Pride of the Prairie. *Lost Pride.*

An agricultural company. *Feed Greed. Hot Commodity. Field of Schemes.*

Worldwide price-fixing. *Fixed Income. Trade Imbalanced. Global Illusion.*

After three hours, Herndon had a list of about sixty suggestions. The next morning, he brought them to Paisley. But his boss didn't look at them.

"Brian called with a suggestion that sounds pretty good," Paisley said. "I already forwarded it on to headquarters."

The answer came back fast. Headquarters approved.

The lysine investigation was now "Harvest King."

"Mimoto changed his mind," Whitacre said. "He doesn't think Hawaii is an acceptable meeting site."

It was the evening of August 24, and Whitacre was meeting with Shepard and Herndon in a Forsyth hotel. In the weeks since the idea of a Hawaii meeting had been raised, Mimoto had approached other lysine producers with the proposal. While the possibility of playing golf on world-class courses was tempting, the others thought it too risky. Instead, Whitacre told the agents, they wanted to meet in Paris on October 5.

Other conspiracies also seemed to be brewing, he said. Following the discussions in Vancouver, Wilson was scheduled to travel to Zurich, Switzerland, on September 23 to meet with Ajinomoto's European affiliate that manufactured MSG. Probably, Whitacre said, Barrie Cox would accompany Wilson. From what he had heard, a citric-acid meeting would also occur, involving Hoffman-LaRoche, the pharmaceutical giant.

"Mick also said I'm getting some new duties," Whitacre said proudly. "I'm going to be responsible for joint ventures and acquisitions worldwide. Mick said that at the next board meeting he was going to recommend me for a raise of one hundred thousand dollars or more."

Shepard and Herndon listened to Whitacre's story with skepticism. Why all of a sudden was Whitacre being paid so much more?

"Well, Mark," Herndon said, "do you think this is money to keep your mouth shut, or maybe additional compensation for the price-fixing?"

Whitacre looked offended.

"No, nothing like that," he said. "Guys, I work hard. I'm not spending all my time at price-fixing meetings. They're paying me for all the work I do."

The agents listened. Maybe Whitacre was right; maybe this raise was innocuous. But they decided to keep an eye on how ADM treated Whitacre financially. Maybe the payoff theory would eventually build into something that could be presented to a jury.

The young man walked down a snow-covered Washington walkway near the Vietnam Memorial, side by side with a Special Agent from the FBI.

"Let me get this straight," the man said, "I steal files from the firm, turn them over to the FBI, testify against my colleagues, and send them to jail?"

The actor Ed Harris, playing Special Agent Wayne Tarrance, glanced at the younger man, Tom Cruise.

"They suckered you into this," Harris said.

A nearly full house in the Illinois movie theater watched the screen as Cruise, in the role of a young lawyer named Mitch McDeere, showed his anguish at learning his law firm was involved with the Mafia. The FBI wanted him to cooperate with its investigation. Returning home, he told his wife. She was terrified.

In the audience that night in the summer of 1993, Mark and Ginger Whitacre began to feel a bit uncomfortable. This was all too familiar.

The movie version of *The Firm*, John Grisham's best-seller, was one of the popular releases that summer. Mark had been a fan of the book when he'd read it years before, and was eager to see the movie. As they watched, the Whitacres could not help but notice similarities between Mark's situation and McDeere's. Cruise plays the character as reluctant, unwilling to cooperate at first. Then the government gets tough, threatening him with prosecution; McDeere seems to have little choice but to inform on his coworkers.

Then McDeere turns the tables on the FBI. In the middle of the movie, Cruise meets Harris at a dog track and lays out his demands for his cooperation.

"A million dollars, in a numbered account in Switzerland," Cruise says. "IBG International, in Zurich."

Harris pulls back his overcoat. "You sure as hell turned greedy all of a sudden."

The McDeere character also demands that the FBI arrange for his brother, who had been convicted of manslaughter, to be released from prison. The agent rages, threatening McDeere with prosecution while acknowledging the charges would be bogus. But McDeere has the upper hand; he is wired and has taped the agent's every word. If his demands are not met, McDeere implies, the tape would be made public. By the movie's end, McDeere outsmarts the criminals and the FBI, and takes back control of his life. The credits roll.

The theater lights came up as the camera panned away from the Memphis skyline. Mark and Ginger stood, making their way to the exit. They talked about the movie as they walked; Mark had liked the book better. By the time they were in their car, driving toward home, the conversation had shifted. The number of similarities between the movie and Mark's life, they thought, was sort of spooky.

About the only big difference was that McDeere, with his demands for money and immunity, was a lot more exacting than Mark had ever been.

Shepard hung up with the Springfield office and dialed Whitacre's phone number. It was about seven-thirty on the night of September 26, and the switchboard had just called to say that Whitacre wanted to talk.

In recent weeks, flashes of potential problems had started to emerge with Whitacre—nothing significant, but the change was noticeable. Ten days before, Whitacre had told Shepard that he believed he had satisfied the terms of his cooperation agreement; he had wanted assurances that the FBI was trying to investigate other potential subjects without his involvement. Shepard was not surprised by the sudden recalcitrance; he just wasn't eager for another ride on Whitacre's emotional roller coaster.

Whitacre answered the phone. He sounded ebullient.

"I've learned some important things recently," he told Shepard. "I've been told I'm probably going to be the next president of ADM."

Shepard wrote the information down. With Jim Randall almost in his seventies, it was no surprise that ADM might be thinking about a successor. Whitacre had always seemed to believe he had a strong shot. Shepard asked what else Whitacre had heard.

"At least ten of the products produced by ADM are price-fixed," he said.

"Ten?"

"Yeah," Whitacre said, "and I would estimate that for all of the companies involved, the total extra profit is in the range of eight hundred million to one billion dollars. That's just profits from the price-fixing."

As he wrote down Whitacre's statements, Shepard pressed him about the information. Whitacre offered few details but said that each company involved in the price-fixing had two or three people who negotiated prices and volumes.

"You know, Brian," Whitacre continued, "if all these companies are charged with price-fixing, they're going to be paying an awful lot in fines. Don't you think?"

"Mark, I don't know. Under the law, if they plead or are found guilty, they might pay large fines. But nobody knows how this will turn out."

"Sure, sure I know that."

There was a moment's pause.

"You know, Brian, I've taken a lot of risks," Whitacre said. "And I need to think about my family."

"What do you mean?"

"Well, I'd like it if, in their fine, ADM was ordered to pay me ten years' salary."

"Well, Mark . . ."

"I mean, Brian, it's only fair."

"Mark . . ."

"Also, one other thing," Whitacre said. "I never expected this investigation would last as long as it has. And I think I should get total immunity from prosecution if I agree to cooperate through the end of this investigation, however long it lasts."

These requests were what the call was really about. Whitacre had demands and wanted them known.

"Listen, Mark," Shepard said, "I can't grant you immunity. And I can't give you any answer regarding any type of fine that might be imposed on ADM. But I can tell you that this will all be discussed with the U.S. Attorney's office at some point."

Whitacre raised objections. But Shepard repeated that at this point, there was little he could do.

"Okay, Brian," Whitacre finally said.

Two nights later, Whitacre met with Shepard and Weatherall at one of the Forsyth hotels. Plans were firming up for the lysine competitors to meet in Paris on October 5, the following week. Whitacre told the agents that Mick Andreas wanted him first to meet with the French and negotiate a volume agreement in Europe that would help keep prices high there.

"Mick wants the Europeans on board before he starts dealing with the Asians," Whitacre said.

The meeting sounded promising, but the agents had been unable to obtain authorization from the French government for Whitacre to make any tapes. Once again, a big meeting would go unrecorded.

Whitacre arrived home from a meeting with the FBI sometime after dinner. After greeting Ginger and the kids, he walked upstairs to his office.

He reached inside his suit jacket and removed the recording device in his pocket. Popping it open, he pulled out a microcassette. This was a tape that the FBI knew nothing about. This was one of his recordings of his meetings with the agents. He was just like Tom Cruise, taping the agents when they didn't know.

Feeling cocky, Whitacre opened the closet and placed the microcassette on a shelf. He found it amusing that he was using a recording device from the FBI to tape its own agents.

On October 5, at 11:53 in the morning, Philippe Rollier walked into the lobby of the Ritz in Paris. Rollier, the president of one of Ajinomoto's European affiliates, was joined by two colleagues. Almost fifteen minutes later, Whitacre arrived in the lobby, having just come down from his hotel room.

The four men met in the middle of the lobby, then headed down a hallway to the dining area. At that moment, Whitacre glanced quickly at one of the lobby chairs. Brian Shepard was sitting there, appearing to read a newspaper as he worked surveillance with a member of the French national police. Whitacre smiled to himself. Shepard *looked* like an agent.

We gotta get that guy some new clothes, he thought.

Later that same afternoon, Whitacre rushed from the lobby of Le Grand Intercontinental Hotel, toward a line of taxicabs. He jumped into the first one and pulled a piece of paper out of his pocket.

"I'm going to the American embassy," he told the driver, handing him the paper with the address.

As they pulled up to the embassy, Whitacre saw Shepard standing on the sidewalk. The taxi stopped abruptly. Whitacre paid quickly and jumped out. He and Shepard hurried toward the entrance. Whitacre had only a little bit of time until he was expected to join his co-conspirators for dinner.

Inside, Regina Superneau was waiting for them. Superneau was the embassy's assistant legal attaché, or ALAT. Superneau took Shepard and his witness to an elevator, whisking them to an upstairs office.

Whitacre quickly briefed Shepard on the day's events. At lunch, Rollier had accepted an ADM proposal to keep lysine prices higher in Europe, even if they fell in America. Afterward, the executives had traveled to Le Grand Intercontinental for the main meeting of lysine producers at 2:20. Formal presentations were made about the official lysine association, before turning to illegal activities. They agreed to set the lysine price at $1.20 a pound in America and $1.80 in Europe. But no resolution was reached on the volume dispute. The group agreed that a meeting between Mick Andreas from ADM and Kazutoshi Yamada of Ajinomoto was needed to break the logjam.

"That's great, Mark," Shepard said. "Now why don't you go ahead and make your call."

As Shepard turned on a tape recorder, Whitacre sat down at the desk and quickly dialed the number for Mick Andreas. He would give Andreas a briefing right in front of Shepard and Superneau. Nobody expected much from the tape; it would just be more evidence that Andreas knew the purpose of the Paris meeting.

Even though the French government would not allow the hotel meetings to be recorded, the agents could at least get one tape out of the meeting. Andreas was expecting to hear developments. And at the embassy, Whitacre was officially on American soil.

Here, they could legally record almost anything they wanted.

The FBI agents could feel it—Harvest King was moving toward a critical juncture. The time had come to step up their resources. They explained the plan to Whitacre, who eagerly agreed with the strategy.

It was first put into action on October 12. That morning at about six o'clock, Whitacre, wearing dark blue suit pants but no jacket, knocked on the door of room 121 at the Hampton Inn in Forsyth. Herndon answered.

"Hey, how you doing?" Whitacre said as he rushed inside the room. "I don't have much time."

"That's fine, Mark," Herndon said. "This won't take long."

Herndon brought out a suit jacket that matched the pants Whitacre was wearing. Whitacre smiled. His new recording equipment was ready.

For a week, Whitacre and Andreas had never been in the office at the same time, so today was the first opportunity for a face-to-face briefing on the Paris meeting. There was also a good chance that Andreas might discuss meeting with Yamada. This was a day that the recording devices could not fail.

A few weeks before, the agents had asked Whitacre for the jacket. A secretary in Springfield had sewn the small recording device into the lining, and tiny microphones had been placed under the lapels.

Whitacre slipped on the jacket. It seemed about the same as when he had turned it over to the FBI.

"Okay, Mark," Herndon said, "now when you want to turn it on, the switch is here, in the coat pocket."

The switch felt tiny, but it was easy to flick on and off. The FBI had done good work.

Whitacre handed Herndon his microcassette and notebook recorders, and the agent loaded them with batteries and tapes. Whitacre put the microcassette recorder back into his breast pocket and then picked up the briefcase. He was ready to go to work, carrying four different hidden recording devices.

At 9:15 that same morning, Whitacre and Wilson walked past the maze of desks in the ADM trading room, heading toward Mick Andreas's office. Mick had just called, asking for a face-to-face briefing on the Paris meeting. The recording devices hidden in Whitacre's jacket lining and his breast pocket were running.

"Where do they think we are?" Andreas asked.

"We're really at about sixty-eight thousand tons," Whitacre said. "They claim we're closer to fifty."

"Forty-five," Wilson growled.

Whitacre shook his head. "They'd like to see us at forty-five. But they think we're closer to fifty."

"And we're at seventy?" Andreas asked.

"We're at sixty-eight now," Whitacre said.

Andreas asked if it was possible just to give up the additional twenty thousand tons of production, but Whitacre said the problem ran deeper than that. The total production sought by the other manufacturers was bigger than the entire market. Prices were bound to collapse if the proposals were accepted.

"I think the problem is we're working with that Ikeda guy," Whitacre said. "Terry and I, we just can't work with that guy."

Wilson thought Whitacre was being naïve. "Shit," he said. "He's doing what Yamada tells him."

Fixing the problem, Whitacre said, was going to require Andreas to meet Yamada in person.

"He's the only one I'm worried about," Andreas said.

"That's right, and I think he's a reasonable guy," Whitacre said. "Ikeda's an asshole, and I think he started this whole problem."

"Yamada's like everybody else—he uses his asshole for negotiating," Andreas said. "He said, 'Go in there and be tough and don't give anything away.' "

"That could be part of it," Whitacre agreed.

"Did you get my message to Yamada?" Andreas asked. "That I would meet him anywhere?"

Whitacre nodded. "I'm going to tonight."

Something was going to have to be done soon, Whitacre said. Prices simply were not going to hold.

"I think for three or four months, we're all right, but I think eventually if we don't come to some terms . . ."

"Then we could all lose a lot of money," Andreas interrupted.

At 3:30 that same day, the three men met again. Andreas wanted to understand more about the size of the lysine market. Whitacre and Wilson described the opinions of the lysine competitors.

Wilson rubbed his chin. "The market could easily be off by as much as ten percent," he said.

"In the size?" Andreas asked, sounding surprised.

"Yeah," said Wilson.

"Yeah," Whitacre agreed, "that's right."

Andreas smiled and turned up his hands. "Then we gotta start lying. One thing about ADM, we know when we're lying."

Wilson nodded. That was the difference between ADM and the Japanese, he said.

Regardless of the market size, Andreas continued, ADM needed to plan its negotiating position. In a few months, the company should start complaining about its volume allocation—even if they were producing more and lying about it. If the time came that the competitors agreed to provide production numbers, then ADM should put up a lot of hurdles. That could give them time to cover up their lies.

"Hell," said Andreas, "we can delay that mess."

"That's right," Whitacre said.

"So," Andreas said, "maybe we oughta just start lyin'."

Whitacre and Andreas were alone, letting their hair down in Mick's office. The only sound was the air pump in Andreas's aquarium. It was 4:40 the same day, and Mick had just called Whitacre again, seeking more information about the Japanese. Clearly, Mick understood that they were at a make-or-break point. The options were either price war or profits.

Mick went back and forth on how he wanted to handle the situation. Lying was a good option if the competitors refused to deal. But if they would talk, well, that was different. In a way, Andreas relished his position. The Asians had all been together, fixing prices before ADM even came on the scene. Then, ADM started banging on the door, demanding to be part of the club. When no one answered, ADM drove down prices. The company's executives had made it clear that they could not be ignored.

Andreas leaned back in his chair. Now was the time to be quiet in the marketplace, he said. If demand fell, ADM would cut production.

"Tell 'em we're gonna go down with the market," Andreas said. "But we're not gonna stand for any poaching or anything."

ADM wasn't about to cut back if competitors started stealing customers. If they did, Andreas said, the competitors should just be told that any business ADM lost would be taken back when prices went higher.

"I don't think they'll try to screw with us, do you?" Andreas asked.

"No, I don't think so," Whitacre said.

"I mean, that takes balls."

"There's definitely a trust factor here, though," Whitacre said.

Andreas coughed. "I know."

"I mean, Terry scared 'em shitless."

"That's just like Ikeda," Andreas said, smiling. "Terry's our Ikeda."

Whitacre laughed. "Terry did what we needed done at the time."

"Yeah," Andreas said, leaning forward on his chair, "and Ikeda probably went back and said, 'I told those sons of bitches they're cutting back to half where they are or else.' And Yamada's saying to himself, 'Or else what, you dumb motherfucker?' "

Yamada had to know, Andreas reasoned, that a confrontational approach wouldn't work. ADM had crashed lysine prices before, and if the company didn't get its way, they could be crashed again.

"Let's face it," he said, "our track record is good."

"We drove it to sixty cents three times."

"Yeah, that's right. Third time is a charm."

Andreas moved to the edge of his chair. "I would enjoy havin' that meeting with Yamada."

Whitacre snapped to attention.

"You would?" he asked. "I think it's gonna be a necessity in the long run."

"I'd like to do it myself."

Whitacre shrugged and agreed.

"Just him and me alone in a room," Andreas said. "Just sit down and say, 'I've got stockholders.' "

"Did you want me to suggest that?" Whitacre asked. "Ikeda acts like he's gonna be there."

"We can do that at the last second."

Maybe, Whitacre suggested, it would be better to meet together for a while, and then Andreas could be alone with Yamada. That way, everyone would be happy.

Andreas nodded. "Probably better to sit and listen to their bullshit first," he said.

"Yeah."

"And then sit alone and say, 'Well, here we are. These guys are fighting, having a lot of fun cutting each other's throats, and you and I are losin' all the money. So maybe we oughta come to an agreement.'"

Whitacre laughed. "Yeah."

"Put me with him alone," Andreas said again. "I can talk a lot more freely."

"Yeah."

Andreas managed a tight smile. "Ikeda's probably wearing a wire on us," he said. "Under his jacket."

Whitacre blinked and laughed. The tape recorder running under his jacket suddenly felt very big.

"He's probably tapin' it that way so he can translate and then report it to the Japanese," Whitacre said, still laughing. He was making little sense; he wanted to change the subject.

"Okay, well, I appreciate everything you done," Whitacre continued, his grammar getting worse as his tension increased. "I definitely, definitely enjoyin' the hell out of it and we're gonna get there. We really are. It's not where citric is today, I'll be perfectly honest with you."

"No, no, I know."

Talking about citric reminded Andreas of something. He wanted to promote Barrie Cox to president of the citric group. That would open up the possibility for other promotions in the division.

"I want him to find out whether that means we could make that girl in there a vice president, and maybe the one in Canada that's supposed to be so good-lookin'," he said.

"Yeah."

"I may do that before the board meeting."

Whitacre leaned in; there was a woman in his division named Kathy who should be promoted as well. She was dedicated, a real career woman.

"I told Dad what I felt we should do is get an all-female sales force," Andreas said. "We'll put like Debbie* out there in charge of the West Coast. You know, there'd be more partyin' once a year."

Whitacre laughed.

"He says, 'Yeah, yeah, that's great. I'll come to the party,' " Andreas said, clearing his throat. "He wouldn't care if he gets sued. Shit, he's seventy-five years old."

Whitacre again pushed Kathy; she was just as good as Anna, the woman in citric. Andreas said he wasn't trying to help Anna. In fact, he said, Anna scared him. She had once pressed him with questions at a meeting, Andreas explained, asking him what he considered ADM's obligation to the community to be.

"And I said, 'Well, our obligation is to provide good-paying jobs to hardworking people.' "

Whitacre fiddled with his tie.

"She said, 'Well, that doesn't seem like enough,' " Andreas continued. "She's talking about day care centers, and I thought, 'Fuck this.' "

"Yeah, she's a women's libber," Whitacre said. "One's gotta be careful."

Maybe, Andreas suggested, he should promote a couple of women to vice president and make another woman president of the western department.

"What the fuck do I care?" he shrugged.

"Yeah, just a title, just a title," Whitacre said. "Don't mean anything. At least to the outside, it does mean something."

"Yeah," Andreas said, nodding.

That evening, Whitacre met with Herndon and Weatherall at the Hampton Inn, turning over the tape from that day. The meeting between Andreas and Yamada was getting close, he said. The only potential problem was Mick's desire to meet alone with Yamada. If that happened, the FBI's consenting party—Whitacre—would not be in the room, meaning they couldn't tape unless they received court approval. The agents instructed Whitacre how to head off that problem. Mick had been willing to meet everyone at the beginning; just make sure the Japanese demanded that.

The men checked their watches. It was almost seven-thirty; Ikeda would be in his office by now. Herndon set up a recording device on

*For privacy reasons, the names of every woman mentioned only in passing on the tapes has been changed.

the phone. Whitacre was going to try to make the arrangements right now.

The recorder on, Weatherall spoke into it.

"I am Special Agent Joe A. Weatherall Jr. I am here with Special Agent Robert K. Herndon, and Mark Whitacre at the Hampton Inn, Forsyth, Illinois. Mr. Whitacre is about to telephone Hirokazu Ikeda."

Whitacre dialed the number, charging it to his AT&T card. A secretary answered. Whitacre identified himself and asked for Ikeda.

"Hello? Hello?" Ikeda said a moment later.

"Hello, Mr. Ikeda."

"Yes, speaking. How are you, Dr. Mark Whitacre?"

Whitacre quickly got to the point.

"I had a chance to update Mick Andreas," Whitacre said. "He thinks, well, we made some progress, but we have much further to go yet."

"Yeah, that's right."

Whitacre laughed. He explained that Andreas wanted to meet with Yamada but would not have time to fly to Japan for many months. "He said he would meet him anywhere in the States."

Whitacre had left the Japanese with a stark choice. They could either come to the United States for this meeting or continue losing money in their lysine business from the lack of a volume agreement. Where golf failed, greed succeeded—Ikeda suggested meeting in California at the end of the year.

Whitacre hesitated. Now he had to make sure that he was in the room, too, so the FBI could tape.

"He felt it would be best if we met as a group: you and I, Mr. Yamada, and Mick Andreas. And then for a few minutes alone with Mick Andreas and Mr. Yamada after the meeting."

"Yes. That is our intention, too."

Whitacre smiled. *Problem solved.*

Ikeda suggested that he would speak with Yamada to come up with possible meeting dates and would send Whitacre a fax with the information.

"You are, you are at, uh, home right now, I think," Ikeda said.

The statement put Whitacre off balance. He hadn't planned how to respond.

"Yep, that's right," he said. Suddenly, he realized that Ikeda could be faxing him the letter immediately and might want to discuss it.

"No," he corrected quickly. "I'm at a, at a pay phone. I'm currently travelin'. And I won't be back home 'til tomorrow afternoon."

Ikeda sounded puzzled. "You will be at, uh, home right now," he said.

Did Ikeda have some sort of caller ID?

"No, no," Whitacre said. "I'm currently traveling in Chicago and I won't be back to Decatur 'til tomorrow afternoon."

"Oh, okay," Ikeda said.

The potential crisis seemed to have passed.

"Can I reach you at your hotel?" Ikeda asked.

This was getting bad. Whitacre had just locked himself into a story that he was in Chicago. But he was near Decatur. Ikeda might know as soon as he heard the area code. Whitacre was thinking fast. Herndon and Weatherall could do nothing but watch.

"Well, the only thing is, the only thing is," he stammered, "I'm staying with one of our distributors."

The lie was ridiculous. ADM was making its managers double up with company distributors? How far did attempts to cut corporate costs go?

Somehow, Ikeda accepted the explanation. "I see," he said.

"And I feel uncomfortable him bein' aware of what the discussions would be on," Whitacre said.

"Oh, yeah, sure," Ikeda said. "I understand."

Whitacre had fumbled, but survived. Ikeda promised to send the fax to his office, and Whitacre said he would speak with Andreas about it the next day. He hung up.

Everyone breathed a sigh of relief.

At 2:00 the next day, Whitacre picked up the Ikeda fax and scanned it quickly. Yamada was willing to meet with Andreas and Whitacre in Los Angeles on either October 25 or 26. A site for the meeting could be chosen when the date was set.

Whitacre walked down to Mick Andreas's office. He flicked on the recorder in his pocket.

"Mick?" he said at the office doorway. "You got a quick minute?"

Andreas looked up from his desk.

"Yep."

Whitacre walked in, holding out the fax.

"Ikeda's working quick for us," he said. "Yamada wants to meet in L.A. the week after next."

"No kidding?"

"Told me on the phone that he's coming with him."

"Ikeda's coming just for that?"

As Whitacre described the details, Andreas checked his schedule and saw he was free on the twenty-fifth. Whitacre said he would go make a copy of the Ikeda letter for Mick. The original, he was thinking, needed to go to the FBI.

When Whitacre returned, Andreas discussed the meeting arrangements. Who did they know in L.A. who might have ideas? Whitacre mentioned a former ADM employee named Tina, who had moved to southern California.

"She's gettin' married," Whitacre said.

"Well, what a waste," Andreas said.

Andreas checked with the ADM pilots; the flight to Los Angeles would take just over four hours. He suggested flying out at seven o'clock in the morning, Decatur time, for a nine o'clock Los Angeles meeting. They could be home by seven o'clock that same night. Whitacre said he would make the arrangements.

Since he had Andreas's attention, Whitacre decided to check on the promotion for Kathy, the woman in his division. He asked what had happened with Anna. Andreas said that her boss opposed promoting her.

"He says she wants so much," Andreas explained. "She'll say, 'Well, do I get a raise? Do I get a car? Do I get this? Do I get that?' "

Whitacre saw an opening. "Kathy's not that way," he said. "Kathy wouldn't ask for any of that."

"Well, see . . ."

"Kathy would appreciate what she's got," Whitacre said. "Anna is a little bit different."

"Yeah, she's a lot more aggressive."

Whitacre coughed.

"Oughta be a fantastic fuck," Andreas said, smiling. "But I think she'd be trouble with a capital *T*, don't you?"

"Yeah," Whitacre said. Kathy wouldn't be a problem, he added. She'd take what ADM gave her without complaint.

They spoke for another moment about promoting women. Andreas leaned back in his chair, smiling.

"So, my Tina is getting married," he said, referring to the woman who had moved to southern California.

"Yeah," Whitacre said. "Two or three weekends from now."

"That won't last for very long, do you think?"

"No."

"She's kind of a dodo-head, you know?" Andreas said. "She'll be back. I just hope she doesn't get pregnant. Fuck up her body."

"Yeah."

"Nice body," Andreas said. "It'd ruin her tits. She's got the greatest tits in the world."

Andreas smiled broadly. "In the world."

About an hour later, at 3:15, the telephone rang in the FBI's Decatur Resident Agency. Weatherall, sitting in the main room of the office, answered.

"Hey, Joe, how you doin'? This is Mark."

"Hey, Mark. What's happening?"

"Well, it's all set. I got the fax from Ikeda. They want to meet week after next."

Whitacre described Ajinomoto's meeting proposal and said that he had discussed it with Andreas.

"He's all set to do it," Whitacre continued. "He wants to meet with them on the twenty-fifth. So that's the date of the meeting. We're gonna be taking a corporate jet, a Falcon aircraft, about seven in the morning. And we're gonna come back the same day, probably after lunch, about one o'clock. So it's all set."

"Okay, Mark, that's great," Weatherall said.

They hung up, and Weatherall called to Herndon.

Twelve days. They had just twelve days to arrange everything—to find out where the hotel room would be, to get it wired up. A thousand things could go wrong. But this was the critical meeting.

Everything had to go right.

CHAPTER 8

A nine-foot bronze statue of John Wayne—dressed in full cowboy regalia and illuminated by floor lights—towered above a crowd of tourists. The travelers had just walked from their gates to the lower level of the main terminal at John Wayne Airport, on the edge of Irvine, California. The airport's décor projected a perfect Southern California image, with indoor palm trees stretching toward the ceiling and glass walls showcasing another sunny day.

On one side of the terminal, Brian Shepard and Joe Weatherall hefted their luggage off a baggage carousel. It had been just over a week since Whitacre's call about the meeting tentatively scheduled for Los Angeles. In the days that followed, the executives had settled on a Marriott hotel in Irvine as the site. The city was about thirty-five miles south of Los Angeles but was easily accessible by corporate jet. As soon as the FBI heard, Dean Paisley had called the Los Angeles Field Office for help; an agent with the Santa Ana Resident Agency was assigned as a local contact.

From the airport, Shepard and Weatherall headed straight to the Marriott, just half a mile away. The seventeen-story, gleaming white hotel was a tiny village unto itself, with 485 rooms, twenty-nine conference rooms, and two restaurants. For the meeting, Whitacre had booked one of the largest private rooms, suite 1538.

The agents headed to the suite after dropping off their luggage. A large table for banquets and business meetings was in the center. The executives were sure to do their haggling there. The agents set up the lamp with the hidden video camera; the shot included the whole table. The agents were not concerned about the executives wandering around; this camera came with a small remote control that would allow them to zoom in or rotate the shot from several rooms away.

Problems emerged in the first few days. A hotel security official had decided to double-check with the hotel's corporate parent, the Host Marriott Corporation. In no time, a Marriott lawyer was on the line, demanding that the entire operation be put on hold. The company wanted a briefing to be sure it would not be liable for the FBI's actions. It seemed like a lousy time for a joust; the FBI complied. The troubles were ironed out with a few phone calls.

By the morning of October 25, a Monday, everything was ready.

The Falcon 50 turbojet touched down that morning at John Wayne Airport just before eight-fifty, West Coast time. The sleek jet, one of the fastest in ADM's fleet, had made good time; besides some fog over Irvine, the weather had been beautiful all the way from Decatur.

As the pilot taxied toward an air hangar, Mick Andreas and Mark Whitacre gathered their belongings. Whitacre picked up his briefcase, feeling the extra weight of the Nagra recorder inside. He was wearing his blue suit with the recorder sewn inside the lining. In his pocket, he carried the microcassette device. None of the recorders was running yet; the agents had told him to save the tape for the lengthy meeting. This meeting was too important to miss because of some technical failure.

Andreas and Whitacre arrived at the Marriott and headed to the fifteenth floor.

In a nearby room, Brian Shepard sat in front of a black-and-white monitor, holding the camera's control device. Sony headphones covered his ears. Weatherall was never comfortable with high-tech equipment; he stood in another part of the room, watching.

Another agent signaled that Whitacre was in the suite. Shepard hit the VCR switch. It was 9:00.

Whitacre was speaking. "I was talkin', we just got some crazy guy back in Decatur wants to take this thing up to three hundred and fifty million pounds."

Shepard could see both men. An easel that Whitacre had ordered through the hotel soon arrived and was turned to face the camera— just the way the agents had wanted it positioned.

ADM was paying $24.50 for the easel. Before long, it would probably cost them a lot more than that.

For twenty minutes, Andreas and Whitacre knocked around by themselves, talking about the lysine market. Andreas wanted to be sure he didn't make any mistakes when he discussed the business with Yamada.

At 9:22, the door opened. Ikeda stepped in with Yamada, a tall, balding man with glasses.

"Well, there we are," Andreas said.

"Hi," Ikeda said.

"Good morning," Yamada said.

The executives talked about their flights.

"So it's the middle of the night for you still, isn't it?" Andreas asked.

Yamada laughed. "Oh, yes. It is."

"Well," Andreas said, "sorry to wake you up."

Everyone took seats around the table.

Shepard watched as the four men sat down. Andreas and Whitacre were almost facing the camera, but Shepard could still see Yamada and Ikeda from the side. The shot was perfect.

For more than an hour, the conversation ebbed and flowed through a range of topics: MSG, potential deals, other companies—almost everything except lysine. During the talks, a hotel employee arrived with coffee, tea, juices, breads, and fruit. The executives marveled at the quantities. It was enough, Whitacre laughed, for forty people.

At 10:39, Yamada glanced from Ikeda to Andreas.

"May I talk about the lysine association?" he asked.

"Um-hum," Andreas said, nodding.

"There is an official association," Whitacre said.

"Official association, yes," Yamada said. "And I think that is good for the development of the market."

Whitacre wrote a note on his pad and coughed.

"We already spent more than one year, uh, to getting a better market situation," Yamada said in broken English. The question now was whether they could have an understanding on volume, he added.

"Talked a little bit about it in Paris," Whitacre said, crossing his legs.

Andreas sat back. "My understanding of the meetings that have taken place," he said, "is that the market is larger than most of our competitors think it is."

He looked over at Whitacre. "That's my impression," he said.

As Andreas spoke, Shepard pushed the buttons on the control in his hand. The camera zoomed in.

Shepard looked at the monitor—the camera was centered on a lamp. He pushed the buttons again, moving the image to the right. Once Andreas was in the shot, Shepard used the control to zoom in again. The shot came in too low; the top of Andreas's head was almost off the monitor. Shepard struggled with the device for several more seconds. After a few adjustments, he had his close-up of Andreas.

"That's my impression," Shepard heard Andreas say. "Because the numbers that we keep hearing don't reflect what we're doing."

Shepard listened while Whitacre talked about ADM's production numbers. The camera stayed focused on Andreas; only Whitacre's hand was in the shot.

"I'm the vice-chairman of our board," Andreas said. "We have a big board of directors. We have public shareholders."

Yamada grunted an acknowledgment.

"Like you, we've suffered," Andreas continued. "Prices were nowhere near what we hoped they would be, and growth was very difficult."

ADM already had the plant capacity to take more than half of the market's growth if it wanted, Andreas said. But the company understood that it was in no one's interest for ADM to be greedy.

"If we're going to have any stability at all, to take seventy percent is probably too much. But for us to shrink is out of the question."

ADM's position had just been thrown out on the table. The company was not going to demand all the growth—but it also would not cut back. The proposal pushed by Ajinomoto for months was not negotiable.

Ikeda mentioned the possibility of arriving at a compromise figure.

Andreas looked at Whitacre. "Did you get some paper up here?" he asked.

Ikeda and Whitacre pointed past Andreas's head. The easel was behind him.

"Oh, we got it," Andreas said, looking over his shoulder.

Ikeda stepped up to the easel, while Andreas visited the buffet, picking up a plate of food and refilling his cup of coffee.

Whitacre stood.

"Is there a rest room in here?" he asked, hoping Shepard heard the warning that he was about to leave.

Ikeda was looking for the pens to use with the easel. Whitacre picked them up off the table and handed them to the Japanese executive. Ikeda started writing down production numbers.

Whitacre glanced toward the camera. "While you're writing those, I'll take a quick rest-room break here," he announced.

That should be enough. Whitacre walked out.

In the other room, Shepard reached for the VCR and shut if off. He'd missed Whitacre's first warning. The tape had continued rolling for four seconds after Whitacre left. Fortunately, no one had said a word.

Shepard waited. How long would Whitacre take in the bathroom? A minute and a half later, he turned the system back on. Whitacre was back, and Ikeda was still working. Andreas was in midstatement, discussing ADM's television advertisements.

"*Meet the Press*, and the Brinkley show," Andreas said. "Some of those."

An uncomfortable pause set in. Whitacre walked over to watch Ikeda at the easel.

Ikeda leaned in toward Andreas. "What is the basic idea of that 'Supermarket to the World'?"

Andreas glanced toward a picture on the wall.

"It was a phrase that someone else invented," he said. "But the idea is that we provide the food for people who sell the food. And really, over our history, that's what's been happening."

Ikeda turned toward the group.

"Sorry to disturb you," he said politely.

Ikeda had finished writing on the chart. The other executives turned to face him.

For several minutes, Ikeda discussed the production of the two previous years. Those numbers, he said, should be used to determine each company's 1994 production. Andreas and Whitacre periodically stepped up to the board, arguing over numbers. If all the figures were true, Whitacre said, then the total lysine market had to be bigger than anyone thought.

"And if that's true," Andreas said, "then the problem is not as great."

If everyone accepted the numbers, all they needed to do was estimate the market's growth for the coming year and divvy up that amount. Ikeda did some calculations and announced his answer. The market would grow by fourteen thousand tons.

"So we've got fourteen thousand tons of growth in one year," Andreas said as he wrote down the numbers. "So the question is, who gets that growth?"

. . .

It was happening. Right in front of Shepard's eyes. These men were sitting nearby—sitting in a *Marriott*—dividing up a multibillion-dollar market.

All while they casually drank their coffee.

Settling the first problem took only a few minutes. Kyowa Hakko, Miwon, and Cheil should each be allocated two thousand tons of growth, Andreas said. That left eight thousand tons for ADM and Ajinomoto.

"What would we be willing to accept?" Andreas asked. "And what would you be willing to accept? Isn't that the question?"

There was more to be considered, Ikeda said. The other producers still did not believe ADM's production numbers were real. Their projections depended on that number. They would have to come up with some explanation to support the numbers.

Whitacre walked away from the easel and sat down. His briefcase was in front of him on the table.

Wait a minute. What was that?

A click. Whitacre had definitely heard a click in his briefcase.

Andreas turned his back to Whitacre, looking at the easel.

There it is again.

The briefcase was making a noise. What if the others heard something?

Whitacre reached down and turned the case slightly away from the other three executives. He popped open the latches.

Shepard watched the monitor intently. Andreas was speaking.

"I would suggest we do the following," Andreas said.

Andreas was on the verge of making his proposal. In his excitement, Shepard was paying no attention to Whitacre. The agent didn't notice that his witness had begun fiddling with the hidden panel in his briefcase.

Whitacre tugged on the panel. A small amount of Velcro pulled apart, but the panel stayed in place, slightly farther from the recorder. Maybe that would stop the noise. He shut the briefcase.

"I'd suggest you tell the people that whatever they have in ninety-three, they can each have two thousand more in ninety-four," Andreas said. "And we get the rest between you and us."

Ikeda, still holding the pen, looked confused. "We have to give, uh, some specific number," he said.

"Whatever their number is in ninety-three," Andreas said. "Then we can agree on how we split the rest."

There it was.

Shepard had heard it. Andreas had just proclaimed that he was setting volumes for every lysine competitor, dictating sales for companies that weren't even in the room.

This was dynamite evidence.

Click.

There it was again. Whitacre looked up and saw everyone was at the easel. He opened his briefcase and gave the panel another tug. More Velcro tore.

Whitacre shut the case and looked up. Andreas was just a few feet away, walking straight toward him.

Shepard had noticed nothing about Whitacre. His witness sounded calm, in control. He had really come through this time.

The group was on the verge of a deal. Shepard watched as Andreas stepped out, toward the bathroom. The two Ajinomoto executives stayed in front of the easel, speaking in Japanese about Andreas's proposal.

Click.

Whitacre decided he had to do something drastic. Somebody would definitely hear this. How in the world would he explain noises coming out of his briefcase?

Whitacre scanned the room. Andreas was still in the bathroom, Ikeda and Yamada were talking with each other. No one was paying attention to him.

He opened the briefcase again and pulled hard on the panel. The Velcro tore. Whitacre lifted it and looked at the recording device inside.

If anyone came up behind Whitacre at that moment, they would see it.

Shepard could not tell what the Ajinomoto executives were talking about. They were speaking softly, in Japanese. He pushed the buttons on the remote control, making the camera zoom in. He didn't notice what Whitacre was doing.

• • •

The device looked okay. Whitacre closed the cover.

Click.

Whitacre opened the case again. Something on the back was rubbing against the recorder. He pressed it, and then snapped the panel closed. He shut the briefcase.

Andreas returned to the room, tugging his ear.

No one had noticed anything.

Yamada stepped toward the easel. The Asian companies had great difficulty accepting the argument that ADM deserved any lysine growth in 1994, he said.

"Their ground is, ADM has already eaten all the growth," Yamada explained.

"For the past three years," Whitacre said.

Yamada laughed. "And now ADM is trying to absorb all the growth. That is not fair."

The approach was a variation on a classic Japanese negotiating strategy known as *naniwabushi*. Yamada had adopted a victim mentality, complaining that the other side was unfairly taking advantage of the Asian companies' weakness. In Tokyo, the method is effective in resolving disputes without confrontation.

But for Andreas and Whitacre, the statement seemed beside the point. Andreas was frustrated. Everyone else was standing, debating the numbers. It was time to make ADM's position clear.

"There's another thing you gotta keep in mind," Andreas said, turning to the easel. "We have a lot more capacity than we're using."

This was Ajinomoto's big fear. Andreas was threatening to flood the market and start another price war.

Ikeda nodded. "Yeah, we understand."

"If in fact there becomes a free-for-all," Andreas said, "our numbers are liable to be a lot larger than five thousand tons."

Yamada put his hands behind his back. "Hum."

"Because we'll grow at twenty thousand tons instead of five," Andreas said.

Yamada nodded.

Two women dressed as waitresses walked into the room, rolling a table that carried lunch for Andreas and Yamada. One was an FBI agent.

"You think they oughta just leave that on that table?" Andreas said, glancing at the food.

"We can serve you if you like," a waitress replied.

Ikeda and Yamada walked to the easel, again discussing their plans in Japanese. Whitacre and Andreas stepped to the other side of the room as the women cleared the main table, laying out the lunch of salads and steak sandwiches.

Shepard knew the meeting was close to breaking up. Yamada and Andreas were scheduled to eat alone; Whitacre and Ikeda would be stepping out of the room for an hour. As soon as Whitacre left, Shepard would have to shut off the recorder. And the two sides hadn't yet reached an agreement.

There might be only minutes left.

Whitacre was signing the bill when Ikeda laid out Ajinomoto's proposal: ADM would be allocated its recent production—or about sixty-seven thousand tons—plus an amount he called alpha. That word meant, he said, a substantial portion of lysine growth. The proposal was vague, with few specifics.

But it sounded to Whitacre and Andreas as if they had a deal. All ADM wanted was sixty-seven thousand tons plus some growth. Whitacre said that Ajinomoto was now making the same proposal as ADM.

"This is just a way to say it," Ikeda said. "It's more agreeable to other people."

Andreas smiled. He didn't care what the Japanese called it, so long as ADM got what it wanted.

"You decide how to say it," he said.

Ikeda walked to the easel and tore off the piece of paper that contained all of the production numbers.

Andreas laughed. "We better keep that," he said.

Neither side said it out loud, but they seemed to have reached their illegal deal. Right in front of the waitresses, just as they were serving lunch.

Whitacre walked out of the room.

He had what he had come for.

Shepard had heard the words. Just before they broke, the companies had reached their deal. As soon as Whitacre left, the agent reached for the console, and pushed the buttons. The monitor screen went blank.

• • •

Quietly, the hidden camera shut off.

Andreas looked at Yamada. Now they were alone. This was his moment to be blunt, to underscore that ADM was not going to buckle.

"Look," he said, "I checked again after Mark just now. I don't care what your people think, our figures are right. So I don't care what you do."

"We have to present it differently," Yamada said. "The Asian way is different."

"I don't care what you do," Andreas said. "Do whatever you want."

Yamada said nothing.

An hour later, an agent informed Shepard that Whitacre and Ikeda had returned to the room. Shepard switched on the monitor and VCR. Whitacre was standing over the table. The sheet of paper that Ikeda had torn from the easel was still lying amid the clutter.

Shepard and Weatherall watched as Whitacre picked up the sheet.

"I guess I should probably keep this, huh?" Whitacre said, folding the paper.

Shepard and Weatherall watched as Whitacre reached down for his briefcase. Weatherall marveled at how smooth Whitacre had been. He had just taken a risk with a deft maneuver and managed to obtain a key piece of evidence for the FBI.

This guy, Weatherall thought, was the best cooperating witness he had ever seen.

Just before seven-thirty that evening, Herndon drove into the parking lot of a Pizza Hut near the Decatur Airport and pulled into a space. Minutes passed before he saw Whitacre's blue Town Car come around the corner. As soon as Whitacre parked next to him, Herndon hopped in on the passenger side.

"Hey, Mark. I hear you had a good meeting."

"Yeah," Whitacre said, looking excited. "I think you guys are really going to be pleased with this."

Whitacre was talking a mile a minute, repeating himself. He was obviously pumped.

"This is just what you guys have been driving home, as far as us showing Mick's involvement in the conspiracy," he said breathlessly. "It's clear as day. He's involved in the conspiracy. He divides the

market with Yamada. He just divided the market with Yamada. It's right
there. This should really help you with Mick, showing his involvement. Man, it's a good tape. Mick's dividing the market. This should
give you guys everything you need. Awesome, Bobby."

Herndon sat back. Whitacre needed time to decompress. This was
his first chance to talk about everything that had happened.

"Okay, we'll have to look at the tape and see what's there," Herndon
said. "We need to get you home to your family, but let me get the tapes
first."

Whitacre took out the microcassette recorder. Herndon removed
the tape and, using his pen, popped its plastic tabs to ensure it would
not be erased. He asked Whitacre questions about the tape as he filled
out the paperwork. Whitacre's suit jacket, with the small recorder
sewn inside, was already lying between them on the car seat. Herndon
picked it up, then grabbed the briefcase. He planned to remove the
tapes from the equipment the next morning.

About twenty minutes later, Herndon thanked him and said good
night. He watched as Whitacre swung out of the parking lot into late-
evening traffic. For a moment, he kept an eye out to make sure that
Whitacre wasn't being followed. Herndon was feeling protective of his
witness. Whitacre was helping them crack the conspiracy. He was part
of the team.

Days later, on Halloween, Herndon wheeled a kitchen chair into his
living room, in front of the television. He had finally received a copy of
the Irvine tape and wanted to work on a summary. He slid the tape into
his VCR, picked up the remote, and pressed the Play button. One of
his family cats, Mookie, jumped on his lap as the scene unfolded.

The recording was fabulous. Over and over, Herndon fast-forwarded
and rewound the tape, reviewing critical scenes as he listened and
watched.

The time counter, in white letters at the bottom of the video, was
approaching 11:00 when Herndon saw Whitacre head to the bathroom. Of course, he left his briefcase behind and it continued taping. Under the law, that portion of the tape couldn't be turned over to
prosecutors—no consenting party was present.

Later, Herndon watched as Andreas laid out his proposal.

Wait a minute.

On the screen, Herndon saw Whitacre lift the briefcase panel covering the recording device. It was out in the open, there for almost anyone to see.

What is he doing?

Herndon hit Rewind to watch the scene again.

What an idiot!

Herndon would have to talk to Whitacre about this. Later, he called Shepard in the Decatur R.A.

"You're not going to believe this, Brian," Herndon said. "But I watched the tape and it looks to me like Whitacre lifted up the panel on his briefcase, right there with everyone around him."

Shepard paused. "You're kidding," he said.

Herndon told Shepard the counter number on the tape where Whitacre had opened the case. Shepard hung up. He wanted to see this for himself. If there was a problem with the briefcase, Whitacre could have shut it off. They were going to have to talk to him. He couldn't be so reckless.

"Where's the agreement?"

Robin Mann was speaking to the three case agents by telephone. Days before, they had sent her a copy of the Irvine tape, then sat back waiting for the call of congratulations. But Mann had objections: Under the law, it was the *agreement* that constituted a crime, not the discussion. While Mann felt an agreement had probably been reached, she knew a jury would want to hear the participants declare a deal. Instead, the executives in Irvine had talked around a deal for hours, subtly sliding into an agreement in the last minutes before lunch. It was good evidence, but Mann felt it could have been better. Any good defense lawyer would notice the problems.

But as the agents listened on three phones in the Decatur R.A., they felt frustrated. How could Mann not see the agreement? Did she just not *want* to see it?

"If this isn't an agreement, then what are they doing there?" Weatherall asked. "Don't get bogged down in the words. Look at what the actions are."

"I've looked at it, Joe," Mann said. "I see a chart with a lot of numbers, and I can't really pinpoint what the agreement was."

Weatherall sighed. "It's right in front of you."

"It could just be a proposal," she said. "All the other companies weren't there. Nobody said they were in agreement."

Shepard picked up the argument, again explaining that the agreement was clear in the full context of the tape. Weatherall, feeling sour, put down the phone. He stood and walked to the doorway of the back office, where Herndon was listening on the phone.

Herndon glanced up. Weatherall waved his arm dismissively and stuck out his tongue. He was making his opinion clear. Herndon stifled a smile.

After hanging up, the agents met in the main room. What more did Mann want? Maybe, they theorized, she was getting cold feet about a trial. Finally, after several minutes of complaining, the agents decided to speak with Whitacre about trying to get the word *agreement* on tape. But that didn't mean they had to be happy about it.

On Monday, November 22, Whitacre was filling out his latest expense report. He had been out of town the previous week and now his desk was littered with receipts. On the form, he wrote that he had traveled to Chicago the previous Monday and Tuesday, attaching his bill from the Embassy Suites on North State Street. For the four days that followed, he wrote that he had been in Miami, at an industry meeting.

He included daily hotel expenses in Miami of $387.27, but attached no receipt—the bill, he wrote, was coming by mail. Whitacre listed several meals with members of the trade group and included receipts. But the top of each one had been carefully cut off—no one would ever be able to determine the name or location of the restaurants. In fact, nowhere in his expense report was there a single receipt with the word *Miami* on it. And even though Whitacre usually placed dozens of calls a day, anyone checking would have found no record of *any* during three of his days in Florida—either from his hotel or on his corporate phone card.

On his trip, Whitacre had been very careful to avoid creating a paper trail. It would be extremely difficult for either ADM or the FBI to realize that, during the time Whitacre was claiming to have been in Miami, he had not even been in the United States.

Nailing down proof of the Irvine agreement proved harder than the agents had expected. While ADM and Ajinomoto had walked away convinced that they had reached a deal, each side had a different opinion of the terms. Whitacre and Andreas—and the FBI, for that matter—had believed that the Japanese company had committed to allocating ADM its prior year's production, plus a big part of the expected fourteen thousand tons of growth in 1994.

But Yamada and Ikeda had never expressly said that. Instead, they had retreated behind a vague word—*alpha*—that they defined as a "substantial portion of growth." At no point, though, did they say what growth they were talking about. It was not, as ADM believed, the four-teen thousand tons of growth estimated for 1994. Instead, alpha was part of the growth that might occur *beyond* the predicted amount. The fourteen thousand tons would be divvied up among the Asian compa-nies alone. ADM's alpha would kick in only if the market grew beyond that—so, if fifteen thousand more tons were sold in 1994, ADM would receive a substantial part of just the *one thousand tons* exceeding the predicted growth. In effect, Ajinomoto was telling ADM that it could have most of the food on the plate, so long as everyone else first had a chance to lick it clean.

Ajinomoto had simply repackaged its earlier proposal. The vague terms that the Japanese had used were not meant to satisfy the other competitors, as Yamada appeared to have said. They were there to ap-pease the Americans. ADM's attempts to bombard Ajinomoto with logic had gotten nowhere; the Japanese were still convinced that their proposals were intrinsically correct.

In November, Whitacre taped several arguments with Ikeda about the Irvine agreement but got nowhere. On December 1, he went to Mick's office to update him on a call from the night before.

"We talked for like half an hour," Whitacre said, sounding livid. "We're at sixty-seven for ninety-four as far as they understand. I said, 'God, I can't believe you were at the same freakin' meeting.' I mean, these guys, it's goddamn *Rising Sun*."

Andreas nodded. He had discussed the Michael Crichton best-seller with Whitacre before.

In a matter of days, Wilson and Whitacre were scheduled to fly to Tokyo for the next price-fixing meeting. Whitacre was so angry that he was asking whether the meeting should be canceled.

Andreas was calm. The two sides were only five thousand tons apart. Maybe it wasn't worth the effort.

"I don't think we should argue with 'em, do you?" Andreas said.

Whitacre raised his hands. "I don't know. What do you think? I think they're tricky sons of bitches."

Maybe just tell them that ADM expected some growth in '94 and leave it at that, Andreas said. Alpha had to mean something more than zero.

The White House nomination for the new Springfield U.S. Attorney sailed through the Senate in weeks. Byron Cudmore, the first prosecutor to meet Whitacre, had been in the job in an acting capacity for more than six months. Now he would be replaced by Frances Hulin, a long-time Illinois prosecutor.

In the first days after her confirmation in early January, Hulin was briefed by Cudmore about Harvest King. He had passed much of the day-to-day responsibility for the case to another assistant in the office, Rodger Heaton, but had kept his eye on developments. The prosecutors had been working closely with the antitrust office in Chicago, he told her, and the relationship had been good. The potential significance of the case was obvious, and Hulin sought an immediate briefing from the FBI.

The meeting took place at 2:00 one afternoon, in the SAC's conference room at the Springfield office. Shepard made a presentation covering the investigation's background, while Herndon discussed the apparent effects of each price-fixing meeting on the lysine market. With a chart, he showed a graph that generally tracked the changing price of lysine over time, as well as when each meeting occurred.

Hulin was impressed. By the end of the meeting, she was telling the agents how much she was looking forward to working this case to completion.

The news was bad from the American legal attaché in Japan. Whitacre had taped an earlier price-fixing meeting in Tokyo for the FBI, and for an upcoming gathering, the agents had requested permission for him to use more sophisticated equipment. But the Japanese national police had become uncomfortable with the whole idea. This time, they would not authorize Whitacre to use *any* FBI recording devices in Tokyo.

Still, there was a loophole. The Japanese authorities said the restriction did not apply to a "businessman's recorder." If Whitacre wanted to tape on his own in Tokyo, no one would stop him. Theoretically, it would be a crime, and Whitacre could be arrested. But the Japanese almost seemed to be saying that they would look the other way.

The agents discussed the dilemma among themselves. They would have to talk to Whitacre about what was happening. The decision would have to be his.

Shepard's expression was grim as he looked across the hotel room table.

"Mark, we've got a problem," he said. "You can't take our equipment to Japan. We have no jurisdiction and the Japanese government won't authorize it."

Whitacre listened, nodding. Well, they had faced the same problem before.

"Okay," he said, "so I guess you want me to take notes like I did in Vancouver?"

"Well, sure, you can take notes. But there's something else I want you to think about. Like I said, we can't give you recording equipment. But if you tape on your own, and you just happen to give us those tapes, we can't stop you from doing that."

Huh? Whitacre looked at Shepard, puzzled.

"So, that means you want me to make a tape in Japan, right?"

"I'm not allowed to say that," Shepard shrugged.

Whitacre sat back. Shepard was essentially telling him to tape without saying it. What was this?

"Well," Whitacre said, sounding eager, "I'll go ahead and tape. I've decided to tape the meeting."

Shepard pulled a piece of paper out of his pocket. That day, Tom Gibbons, the Springfield technical expert, had told Shepard that some of the best commercial recording devices were made by Radio Shack. Shepard had written down the information.

"If you're going to tape, you might want this equipment," Shepard said, handing over the paper. "They have them over at the Hickory Point Mall."

Whitacre eyed the paper suspiciously. He started to speak, but stopped.

"Now, we can't buy any of the equipment," Shepard said. "If we did, it would belong to the Bureau. Then it couldn't be used legally in Japan."

"What happens if I get caught taping there?"

"I don't know anything about Japanese laws, but you could be in trouble. And if you're arrested, it's possible that we may not be able to provide much help in resolving the situation."

Whitacre contemplated that a few seconds. When he answered, he kept his voice level, his tone calm.

"Okay."

On December 2, Whitacre made his way through the Christmas crowds at the Hickory Point Mall and headed into Radio Shack. He waited a few minutes until a salesman was free.

"I'd like a tape recorder," Whitacre said, looking down at the sheet of paper in his hand. "It's the Radio Shack Micro-26."

The salesman disappeared, returning with the recording device. Whitacre ordered some triple-A batteries and three ninety-minute microcassettes. The total cost, with tax, was $149.82.

Whitacre headed to his car. He didn't mind spending the money but was uncomfortable with the risk that the FBI was asking him to take. Still, he figured that by taping in Japan, he would help end the investigation faster. Nothing mattered to him more.

He climbed into his car, tossing the bag with his new recorder onto the seat. As he drove out, he thought through his discussion with Shepard. He wished he had known about it ahead of time. Then he would have been sure to tape it. If he got into trouble in Japan and the FBI tried to cut him off, at least he would have something he could use to protect himself.

No matter. Probably he would just talk to Shepard later and re-create the conversation. The FBI had trained him on how to get people to repeat themselves. He was getting good at it.

The Imperial Palace sits in the center of Tokyo, built on the site of the Edo Castle where the Shoguns ruled until the dying days of the nineteenth century. To the southeast lies the spacious Kokyo Gaien, or "outer garden," a spot where the remaining Fushimi Turret, a watchtower of the old castle, can be seen over the double-arched stone bridge that crosses a moat.

The gardens were visible to Whitacre and Terry Wilson on December 7 as the car they hired at Narita Airport approached the hotel entryway of the Palace Hotel. Whitacre paid the driver in yen before he and Wilson headed into the hotel lobby. Wilson was looking tired and angry. The long plane trip on Japan Airlines had worsened the pain in his troubled back. These trips were getting to be too much for him.

Tensions were rising among the lysine producers, even before the Tokyo meeting began. Several of the companies were dissatisfied with the results from Irvine. The Korean companies—Miwon and Cheil—both believed that they were being cheated in the volume allocation. Executives from Cheil were so angry that they refused to come to Tokyo. The tussle between ADM and Ajinomoto had been only partly resolved, and both were wary of the other's honesty. Only Kyowa Hakko had not voiced a direct objection to the allocation.

Still, a stilted friendliness permeated the room as the executives arrived. The last to appear were Ikeda and Mimoto, on behalf of Ajinomoto. They arrived five minutes late, at 9:35, Tokyo time.

"Good morning," Ikeda said as he opened the door. "We are late."

"No problem, no problem," Whitacre said good-naturedly. "You lost twenty thousand tons, but . . ."

Everyone laughed.

For about forty minutes, the men discussed specifics of the lysine market, region by region and at times, customer by customer. It was tedious, but the tensions lowered. They were making progress.

Whitacre checked his watch. It was time to flip the tape.

"Excuse me," he said.

Whitacre headed to the rest room, walked into a stall, and shut the door. Out of sight, he reached into his jacket and removed the Radio Shack tape recorder. Popping it open, he flipped over the tape and pushed the Record button before dropping it back into his pocket. He flushed the toilet and came out of the stall. Jacques Chaudret, the executive from one of Ajinomoto's European affiliates, was there. He had come into the bathroom just seconds after Whitacre.

Whitacre smiled. "Same idea, a break, huh?"

The two headed back. Whitacre had missed only about a minute of the discussions.

Despite the initial friction, the major lysine producers were finally beginning to read off the same page. Finally, they were settling on volume allocations. A few points were left unresolved, particularly defining what was meant by ADM's "alpha." But, overall, the executives had reached their strongest agreement yet. Even without Cheil, production could be controlled. The price of lysine could well stay fixed for years.

Wilson saw his chance to impose structure on the disorganized scheme. Now was the time, he said, for the lysine producers to finally begin sharing production numbers. The figures could be collected every month by the trade association. Lots of industries did that to legally learn the size of their markets. But, while the trade association could tell them the total, it would have to keep the individual production numbers for each company a secret. Sharing those numbers would almost certainly be illegal.

That's where the scheme came in. No one would question why each company had collected monthly sales data if it was turned over to the association. Then secretly, the companies could swap the numbers among themselves to enforce the volume agreement. If one company sold more than it was allotted, it would be forced to purchase lysine from companies lagging behind. That would keep everyone on target, he said.

"Report every month," Wilson said. "Feedback every month."

Wilson suggested that the companies phone their numbers to Mimoto at Ajinomoto. He would then compile them and alert everyone to the results.

"So officially by association," Whitacre said, "and unofficially to Mimoto by phone."

Several of the executives were still confused. Whitacre and Wilson tried again.

"The association will give you one number, which is the total market, but not by company," Whitacre said.

"That's a legal number?" Mimoto asked.

Whitacre nodded. "That's a legal number, that's right."

"You want it illegally," Mimoto said.

Whitacre looked at the group. "Mimoto is illegal, and the association is legal."

Everyone laughed again. The idea sounded perfect.

Wilson reminded the group that there was reason to be cautious when phoning the production numbers in to Mimoto. Wiretaps were possible.

"We have to watch our telephones," Wilson said. "It can be done, but it must be very careful."

Inside Whitacre's pocket, the Radio Shack recorder picked up every word.

The evidence in the price-fixing case was getting better, but the prosecutors couldn't shake a sense of discomfort. Outside the FBI, the only person in law enforcement who had ever sat down with Whitacre was Cudmore—and he was expected to leave the prosecutor's office in months. Robin Mann discussed the problem with Rodger Heaton, who had taken over day-to-day responsibility for the case from Cudmore. They both decided to push the agents for a meeting with Whitacre.

Days later, in a conference call with the agents, Mann was asking questions about a recent tape. The agents' explanations were not helping much.

"Well, you know," she sighed, "if I could talk to Mark it would help things. You guys need to think about that. It's better sooner than later."

Mann had made the request before. Weatherall and Herndon fell silent.

"That's a valid point," Shepard said. "But as you know, we have some concerns about that, and we're kind of working through those. I'm sure it's going to happen soon; I just can't make any promises."

"What are your concerns?" Mann asked quickly. After sliding into the topic, she was ready to confront the agents on the issue.

For a second, no one spoke. The truth was that the agents didn't trust the prosecutors with Whitacre. Weatherall in particular feared that the lawyers would mess with his head, upsetting his delicate emotional balance. Whitacre needed kid-glove treatment, and the agents had seen how direct Mann could be. But diplomatically, another explanation was needed.

Shepard said that the agents had been using the prosecutors as scapegoats for months. Whenever Whitacre had a question about the future of the case—Would he be a witness in court? What would happen to the Andreas family?—the agents had simply replied that those decisions would be made by the prosecutors.

"We'd hate to have you all of a sudden be forced to answer questions from him that you're not ready to answer yet," Shepard said. "It's better for us to lay the blame on you, and that keeps him satisfied."

Mann remained adamant, but the agents would not bend. They would consider a meeting, Shepard said, sometime later. When the time was right.

Ginger Whitacre almost didn't recognize her husband anymore. Throughout their marriage, he had made his family a priority. He always had made time to raise rabbits with their youngest son for 4-H Club, and had attended all of the children's school shows. But now, between ADM and the FBI, the family seemed last on the list. One night, she argued with him about his absences. He needed to come home more, she told him. His children needed him; *she* needed him.

"I'm doing all this for you and the children," he protested. "I want to give you guys everything. That's why I'm working so much. It's for the family."

Ginger took a breath. Mark's tone was snippy. He had always been so bubbly and happy; these days, he was often just unpleasant and tired.

"Mark, this isn't for the family," she said. "We don't need all these things."

"What, you want to be somebody living in some small house?" he snapped. "You want to be like those people who can't afford cars for their kids?"

Ginger felt taken aback. It sounded as if he thought that money made him superior to people with smaller incomes. Something inside him had changed.

"You're not better than somebody else because you have more cars or a bigger salary," she said. "It has nothing to do with the kind of person you are."

She paused. "You used to know that," she said softly. "You used to know what mattered. You need to find that out again. You need to turn back to God."

Mark glared at her.

"I don't need God," he said. "I've got more power than God."

On February 2, 1994, Whitacre met with Shepard and Weatherall. In the weeks since Tokyo, he had recorded a number of tapes, mostly haggling with the Japanese. Still, the conspiracy was working: Whitacre estimated that ADM would go from a two-million-dollar loss in lysine for 1993 to a fifty-five-million-dollar profit in 1994.

That night, Whitacre seemed eager. "Our next price-fixing meeting's been scheduled," he said.

He paused. "It's gonna happen in Hawaii."

In his conversations with the Japanese in recent weeks, Whitacre had been talking up Hawaii. His message was always the same: the golf, the golf, the golf. Finally, with a new sense of trust emerging among the lysine producers, the Asian companies agreed. They would meet in Hawaii and play golf.

Everything was arranged, Whitacre said. They would be traveling to Hawaii in early March. A meeting of the official lysine association was scheduled to provide cover for the price-fixing meeting.

Shepard and Weatherall were delighted with the news. Their long shot had finally come in. And all thanks to Hawaii's world-renowned golf.

CHAPTER 9

Outside a terminal at Honolulu International Airport, Weatherall tossed his suitcase in the back of a rented convertible, feeling delighted with his luck. The convertible had been available at no extra charge; now he could soak up some Hawaii sun. Herndon hopped into the passenger seat, setting a case loaded with recording equipment on the floor. In a few minutes, the car top was down and the agents were starting the forty-five-minute drive to the Makaha Valley.

Soon, they were on a road between the rugged cliffs of the Waianae Range and Oahu's western shore. As they drove, they saw a gorgeous, eighteen-hole golf course, with views of the Pacific and Makaha Valley, framed by huge volcanic cliffs. Behind the course, quaint, cottagelike structures came into view—the luxurious 185-room Sheraton Makaha Resort and Country Club. This was the place, in an isolated and lush part of Hawaii, chosen by the price-fixing conspirators as the site of their next meeting, scheduled in two days.

Weatherall and Herndon left their hotel rooms early the next morning dressed like any other tourists, in slacks and open-neck shirts. They walked to the lobby and headed straight to the front desk.

"Excuse me," Herndon said to the desk clerk. "We're here for some meetings with Mark Whitacre of ADM. I understand he has some conference rooms reserved. Can we take a look at them?"

A hotel employee led them across the grounds to the cottages. They headed down an outdoor hallway to the conference room. The employee opened the door.

The room was a disaster. It was huge, giving the conspirators plenty of space to walk around—a potential problem for the videotape. Worse, the neighboring room where the FBI was supposed to work was separated by only a flimsy partition. Even if the agents were not heard, anyone could open the partition by pushing a button. Herndon glanced at Weatherall.

"I know," Weatherall said, "this is not good."

Weatherall looked over at the hotel employee.

"This room is simply not going to work," he said. "We need to do something about it."

The three men headed back to the hotel lobby. While Weatherall and Herndon were waiting, an agent from the Honolulu Field Office arrived, accompanied by members of the FBI's surveillance team known as the Special Operations Group, or SOG. The SOG members would never have been mistaken for FBI agents. Several were dressed in shorts, with open, brightly colored shirts. With their deep tans, they were not likely to stand out among the hotel guests.

The agents headed to the office of the hotel's head of security and explained the problem with the conference room. This was an FBI operation, they explained. They needed a smaller room, preferably connected to another room where they could work.

"This isn't easy, guys," the security chief said. "The hotel's full. But let me work on it."

The group headed out the door. Weatherall sighed.

"I'll tell you, Bob," he said. "Nothing simple is simple."

Later that afternoon, Herndon stood in one of the hotel suites. It was small and would probably be pretty uncomfortable as a meeting place for the lysine executives. But it was the best the hotel could do on short notice. Whitacre would stay in the suite's bedroom; that would provide a plausible explanation for why the meeting was being held there.

With less than twenty-four hours to go, new problems cropped up. The neighboring rooms were occupied, forcing the agents to set up far down the hall. For the camera to work, they would have to shoot microwaves through the walls of two rooms; it would be impossible to hide wires over such a huge distance.

After bringing in the first load of equipment, the SOG team ran a test. The signal went in and out—they were sure to miss parts of the meeting. The team dashed out of the room, coming back with several boxes of new equipment to boost the signal. Everyone held their breath as the equipment was turned on. The picture came through; the microwaves would work.

But unfortunately, the camera would not. Unlike the device in Irvine, this camera could not rotate or zoom in. Because the new meeting place was so small, the camera could not be placed far back enough to get a wide view of the room. Half the people in the room would be outside the shot. The SOG team placed an emergency call to a technical support group in Quantico, Virginia, asking for another camera.

As they waited for the delivery from Quantico, the agents did their best to arrange the room. They pushed the chairs into a circle, hoping to narrow the shot. They moved a table in front of the window, with plans to put the lamp there when it arrived. The room looked unnatural, but it would have to do.

The next morning, a box with the new camera was delivered to the FBI office in Hawaii. A technical agent drove it to the Sheraton Makaha. Herndon and Weatherall watched as an agent opened the box, pulling out a green-tinted glass lamp. It looked familiar.

"Yeah, we've seen this one," Weatherall said. "It's kind of been making the rounds in our case."

The lamp appeared identical to the one that had been used at the meeting in Irvine, California. But it was too late for a change. The agents could only hope that, if the executives noticed the similarity, they would just assume that some lamp company was doing a good job marketing to the nation's hotel chains.

The next morning, Whitacre came back from breakfast and walked straight to the FBI's command center, where he knew Herndon would be waiting.

Herndon studied Whitacre as he slipped inside. He showed no tension, no fear. This was a big day, but Whitacre was calm. The agents traded greetings with him, talking a bit about the quality of the hotel.

Bringing out a small bag, Herndon unzipped it and removed a razor and shaving cream.

"It's that time again, Mark," he said, an apologetic tone in his voice.

"Oh, sure, no problem," Whitacre replied.

As Herndon filled his hand with shaving cream, Whitacre pulled off his shirt. The agent smeared the cream across Whitacre's chest and carefully shaved his body hair. It was an uncomfortable moment.

Afterward, Herndon brought out the equipment. It was one of the earliest generations of a new device, known as F-Bird, after FBI

Research and Development. This was one of the first FBI investigations to use the new equipment. It was thin, about the size of a cigarette case. It did not need tapes; instead, the device recorded digitally using memory cards, allowing conversations to be uploaded later and played on a computer. There was no On/Off switch for Whitacre to worry about. Before a meeting, the agents would turn the device on, after programming it with a time limit for recording. The F-Bird would keep running until either the time ran out or the agents switched it off.

Herndon strapped the device onto the small of Whitacre's back, then attached the microphones and fed the wires to the front. He carefully taped them to the spots he had just shaved.

Whitacre dressed. "Bob, I really think this will be a good meeting," he said, pulling on his shirt.

"Think you'll have any problem with the room?"

"No, the room will work out. It'll be fine."

Herndon ran through a few last points before remembering the instructions from the prosecutors.

"Mark, one more thing," he said. "When you guys start agreeing to volumes and prices, I want you to poll the group and see if they're all in agreement. And I want you to use the word *agreement*."

Herndon expected Whitacre to object. People just didn't talk like that. Even Herndon thought the move would potentially be a tip-off, but the prosecutors were demanding it. Surprisingly, Whitacre calmly said he would have no problem taking the poll.

"Now, during the meeting I'll probably give you a call," Herndon said. "So just act like it's room service or the hotel management, checking to see if everything's all right. I'll call even if there aren't any problems, just to let you know we're in place."

"Okay."

Weatherall arrived in the room, looking serious. He was ready to get started.

Herndon turned back to Whitacre. "Everything will be fine, you'll be great," he said. "Remember to use the word *agreement*."

"Okay, Bob."

"And remember, don't talk too much. Let the action come to you."

"I gotta talk, Bob," Whitacre said, exasperated.

"I know that but . . ."

"I mean, I'm there representing ADM. I've gotta make sure our interests are portrayed. Otherwise, everybody would be suspicious."

"I understand, Mark. You can talk. Just don't dominate. We want to see the others' involvement."

"I got you. I got you," Whitacre said.

Whitacre was ready to go. At that moment, Herndon felt some level of affection for him, felt lucky to have Whitacre on his team. He was the reason they were here. He was the one allowing the FBI to collect the evidence of this crime. Without Whitacre's help, the case could never happen.

Masaru Yamamoto of Kyowa Hakko pushed open the glass doors to the lobby of the Sheraton Makaha and walked outside. He had enjoyed breakfast at the hotel restaurant and was now headed to the meeting in Whitacre's suite. Despite his casual dress of slacks and a sport shirt, Yamamoto looked almost formal compared with the many guests heading out for golf.

As he walked, Yamamoto did not notice the casually dressed man following him. Yamamoto reached the path going downhill to Whitacre's room, and the man stopped, touching the microphone on a concealed radio.

"I've got an Asian male, about forty years old, dressed nicely, and walking your way," the man said.

Yamamoto rounded the corner at the bottom of the hill, a few dozen feet from Whitacre's room. He walked near a window that appeared to be blocked by a blind.

Behind the blind, another agent aimed an automatic, motorized camera through a tiny opening.

The camera clicked repeatedly as Yamamoto passed.

Herndon took a seat in front of the blank monitor and slid the earphones over his head. The SOG agents came in, telling him that Whitacre and some of the other lysine executives were in the room. Herndon glanced at the clock; in a few seconds, it would be 8:55. He pressed down the buttons on the recording equipment. Images and sounds instantly emerged from the monitor. Terry Wilson was talking.

"We'll give you five percent of the market," he said. "That's what we'll give you."

Yamamoto was amused. "Five percent, oh yes."

"That should wake him up," said Henri Vetter, Eurolysine's representative to the meeting.

The men laughed.

Herndon wasn't positive what they were discussing. It didn't matter.

Manipulating the joystick, Herndon grew concerned. J. S. Kim, a Korean executive from Miwon, had placed a chair in front of the lamp. But almost as soon as it was there, it disappeared. Herndon watched Whitacre move the chair to another part of the room. Herndon smiled. Whitacre was paying attention.

Whitacre looked around the cramped room. The seats were unnaturally close together. The lamp—wait, was that the same lamp from Irvine?—was set up in front of the window and looked out of place. Whitacre had stayed the night in the suite but hadn't noticed how bad it was until he saw all the lysine executives crawling over each other.

He checked his watch. It was time to get started.

"I'd like to welcome everybody here to this meeting," he said. "Glad everybody could make it, and sorry for the ones who can't play golf tomorrow. We're gonna have a good time."

The nine other executives laughed as many sipped coffee or orange juice.

Whitacre said that in the morning the executives would discuss production volumes and the results from the group's last meeting in Japan. In the afternoon, they would deal with Cheil, the smaller of the two Korean companies involved in the scheme. Cheil was still refusing to agree to a reasonable volume allocation. The others had decided to keep its executives out of the morning meeting, figuring that might put pressure on them to accept a deal.

"We can discuss some of the pricing situation this morning, too, obviously," Whitacre said.

Wilson, sitting on a light-colored couch, grabbed a cigarette. Smoke filled the small room.

Whitacre turned the meeting over to Kanji Mimoto, who walked toward an easel in the corner of the room. For several minutes, he wrote a series of numbers on the board. These, he said, were the sales figures for February reported to him by each company. He compared them to the allocations that everyone had received.

"We are doing this, you know, to keep the price," he said. "And, uh, to keep the price, we have to understand each other."

For thirty minutes, the conversation continued. Whitacre was getting antsy. Herndon hadn't called. Maybe the phone was broken. Maybe the agents couldn't get to him. He didn't have the patience to wait.

At 9:34, Whitacre picked up the telephone, and dialed a number.

"I'm gonna order another orange juice," he said.

• • •

Herndon picked up the phone on the first ring.

"Is everything okay?" Whitacre asked. It was hard to believe that the man was placing this call right in the midst of the conspirators.

"Everything's fine," Herndon said. "That chair was a problem at first, but everything's fine now."

"Yeah, okay," Whitacre said. "Another orange juice. Thanks."

Both men hung up. Whitacre rejoined the meeting. Herndon fixed his eyes on the monitor once again.

None of the agents in the command center bothered to prepare any juice. If any of the executives ever noticed that the juice had not arrived, it would probably be blamed on lousy room service.

If they shared production numbers, how could the conspirators be sure they were true? Perhaps, one executive suggested, they should re-vive the idea of hiring auditors. That made Mimoto uncomfortable.

"If we, uh, we don't trust each other, then it must be audited," he said in fractured English. "But we don't want, clearly, because it, uh, is illegal thing we are talking and we don't want to—"

Wilson broke in. "It's not illegal."

Mimoto stared at him, astonished. "It's very illegal," he said.

Whitacre shook his head. "To audit, to have an auditor? Nah. You're going to have an auditor going through your financial figures anyway."

"You don't think this is illegal thing, no?"

"No," Wilson said. "Absolutely not."

"This is completely illegal," Mimoto said.

"No," Wilson repeated. "No, it's not."

This made no sense to the Japanese. *Of course* what they were do-ing was illegal. That was the reason for the clandestine meetings. They didn't understand that Wilson was making a distinction between the le-gal act of submitting numbers to an association and the illegal act of us-ing the data to fix prices. For the next few minutes, Wilson explained why associations were allowed to have sales numbers.

Yamamoto argued. What about after the numbers were submitted to the association?

"Submitting the numbers is legal," Whitacre said. "What we do with it is illegal."

Yamamoto pointed toward some data. "This number is illegal," he said.

Wilson raised his hand. "I won't even discuss that, Massy."

The whole group laughed.

Yamamoto remained insistent. "This is illegal," he said, pointing to one number after another. "This is okay. This is illegal."

Sitting back, Wilson joined in the laughter.

The SOG agents in the command room stood behind Herndon, watching in disbelief.

"Oh, man, did you hear that?" one of the agents asked. "This sounds like really good stuff."

Herndon almost shrugged. "Yeah, it's pretty good," he said. "But this is like a lot of meetings we've heard."

The SOG agents watched silently for a second.

"This is a great case," one said softly.

The Korean executives from Miwon eyed the rest of the group with suspicion. What auditors would check the sales figures? The group wanted each company to just turn over the job to their usual accountants. How could such an audit be trusted? Maybe, the Korean executives implied, the companies could pressure the accountants to lie. Perhaps a new accounting firm should be hired just for this project.

Sitting in a corner, Jacques Chaudret from Eurolysine shook his head. The idea was lunacy. Bringing in new accountants would signal to everyone in their company that something strange was going on.

"You're in Korea, but in the U.S. and in Europe, the antitrust law is very strong," Chaudret said to the Miwon executives. "I have a hard time to explain to the controller that we have to be audited by a different company than the normal auditing company. For what reason?"

Wilson nodded. "Yeah."

"The guys would be very, very suspicious," Chaudret said.

The discussion went around the room. Wilson listened, sucking on another cigarette. It amazed him how many risks these guys were willing to take.

"How the hell do you give it some cover?" Wilson interrupted. "We can't. We don't have any cover."

The debate raged on as Wilson listened, occasionally sipping coffee from a Styrofoam cup.

"Either we trust each other or we don't trust each other," Wilson said. "I have no problem with audits; we do it lots of places. But in the end it comes down to: Do you trust or don't you trust?"

The group finally agreed that they would rely on certifications provided by each company's usual auditor. The check would be looser than the system that the Miwon executives wanted, but it would involve far less risk.

The only major issue left to resolve was what to do with Cheil, the one company not at the morning meeting. J. M. Suh, one of the company's executives, would be allowed in later that day. What position should they take with him?

The amount in dispute was between two thousand and six thousand tons. Wilson said that Cheil should simply be given the percentage of the market it was demanding. Otherwise, the company could upend the conspiracy by offering lysine at a lower price.

"You have a rogue elephant out there that could destroy the market," he said. "Two thousand tons can take the market from a dollar-twenty to sixty-five cents."

Mimoto nodded. "That's right."

"I think we've got to remember that," Wilson said. "We have an old saying in the United States and at ADM. 'It's better to have 'em inside the tent pissin' out, than outside pissin' in.' "

Mimoto looked confused. "Outside piss?"

Everyone laughed.

"It's better that they be part of the group," Wilson explained. "It's better."

Whitacre leaned in. "It's better that they be one of our friends. Competitors are our friends, remember? Customer's the enemy."

The group agreed. They would offer Cheil more volume and try to bring them into the conspiracy. Mimoto pulled the sheet of paper filled with production numbers off the easel.

"Next subject," Mimoto said as he folded the paper. "How to use the Amino Acid Association."

Yamamoto laughed.

"We're usin' it," Whitacre said. "We're usin' it."

Mimoto turned the floor over to Jacques Chaudret, who handed out copies of an agenda for an association meeting. The agenda was a fake; it was simply paperwork to explain why the lysine competitors had gathered in the same hotel room.

"Everything we are doing today is legal," Chaudret said to laughter. "But just in case . . ."

"Did your lawyers tell you that?" Whitacre laughed. "Our lawyers didn't."

Whitacre scanned the paper. "This is an official agenda?"

"That's right," Chaudret said as he sat down. "That's an easy cover-up, at least for us."

"I agree," Wilson said.

For twenty minutes, the men reviewed each item on the bogus agenda, explaining everything that was supposed to have happened at the fictional meeting of the lysine association.

The morning session broke just after eleven. Whitacre stood. He thought it had been fabulous. He was dying to talk to Herndon about it.

"I wouldn't mind making a phone call," he said.

Whitacre slipped into his bedroom and picked up the telephone. The F-Bird was still recording.

Herndon was staring at the action on the monitor when the phone rang.

"Hey, Bob," Whitacre said. "It's Mark."

What the hell? Herndon glanced at the monitor. Whitacre wasn't on the phone in the room. *Whitacre wasn't in the room at all.* Quickly, Herndon shut off the video recorder. It was 11:13.

"Mark, where are you?"

"I'm in my room now, in my room."

Herndon groaned inwardly. The camera had been lined up so that he could see the front door. He felt sure he would know when Whitacre left. He'd never thought Whitacre would walk out the side into the bedroom. This was just going to create problems down the line.

Nothing simple is simple.

"Mark," Herndon said, trying to contain his frustration, "the tape was still running when you walked out of there."

"Can you turn everything off?"

"I already did. But, Mark, I didn't hear you say that you were leaving."

"I did say I was going to my room."

"Well, Mark, next time announce it."

"I did say it to those guys," Whitacre said defensively. "Said I'm gonna make some phone calls and see everybody at eleven-thirty."

In truth, Whitacre's statement had been far more ambiguous. Herndon tried speaking in a monotone, to hide his anger.

"Okay, Mark."

"That didn't affect anything, did it?"

"I don't think so. Everything's fine. Just next time when you leave, announce it real loud."

"Yeah, well I told 'em we were going to make phone calls and were meeting up at eleven-thirty."

"It's okay, Mark. I just missed it."

Whitacre paused. "Goin' pretty well, isn't it? You guys getting what you need?"

Herndon knew this was the reason for the phone call. Whitacre was excited about the progress at the meeting. He couldn't wait to chew over every detail.

"Yeah, we're getting everything. You're doing a good job, Mark."

"The chairs being moved around didn't affect anything?"

"No, that was fine."

"First he put his right in front of it, did you see that?" Whitacre asked. "And I moved him over. 'Cause he first had his back right to it, J. S. Kim."

Whitacre barely took a breath. "*Agreement* is used a lot, isn't it?"

"Yeah, Mark."

"Yeah, a lot. Lot. Yeah."

Whitacre talked about the plans for lunch and told Herndon not to worry about what he was missing in the room. Everyone, he said, was just socializing.

"Okay, Mark," Herndon said. "Now remember, later today if you leave, just announce it."

"I did," Whitacre said. "I told 'em I was going to use the phone and see 'em in fifteen minutes in the restaurant. I made it very clear to those guys. And I said it to three or four of them."

"I understand, Mark. I'm just reminding you."

"Okay."

Pause.

"You guys getting everything you need?" Whitacre asked again.

"Yeah, Mark, everything's fine."

"And you understand why I called you that time, right? For the orange juice. I didn't need orange juice. I really just wanted to say, 'Is everything okay setup-wise?' "

The two men discussed the dinner plans for that evening; Whitacre agreed that he would eat with the other lysine executives.

Pause.

"You're getting everything you need?"

A few minutes later, Whitacre caught up to Wilson downstairs in the hotel. The tape recorder strapped to his back was still running.

"I think it's going pretty well, don't you?" Whitacre said.

"Yeah," Wilson agreed.

All of Wilson's pleadings for trust had done the trick. The others were letting down their guard. Wilson had really built something, Whitacre said.

"Helped 'em get all the anger out," said Wilson.

Whitacre laughed.

Wilson shrugged. "Everybody's going to want to cheat anyway. Knowing Mick, we'll want to cheat."

Shortly after lunch, J. M. Suh of Cheil wandered into the meeting room with Whitacre.

"Do you play golf tomorrow?" Suh asked.

"We're gonna be playin' tomorrow," Whitacre said. "I think we're gonna play this afternoon also."

Several of the other executives strolled in.

"I came here just to play golf," Suh laughed.

Suh sank into the couch as the others found their chairs. The room was even more cramped than during the morning session. Not everyone had a seat.

Wilson looked around the room. "Surprised this wasn't bigger than it is."

"It's a whole lot smaller than expected," Whitacre said.

He stood, announcing that he was headed to the other room to fetch a chair. He said it as loudly as seemed natural.

Herndon turned off the recorder for a few seconds. At least his instruction had gotten through.

Suh scanned the room, resting his head on his arm. He was angry that his company had not been able to attend the morning meeting.

"I want to hear background why we were excluded," Suh said.

Mimoto seethed. "I told you already over the phone many times, no?" he snapped. "I explain many times, so I think it's useless to repeat this."

Suh stared back at him, saying nothing. If Mimoto was trying to intimidate him, the effort wasn't working. Even though Cheil was the smallest lysine company, Suh wasn't going to let himself be bullied.

"Anyway, forget about the past," Mimoto said. "We are ready to accept you also, of course, depending on the quantity."

The others asked what 1994 allocation would satisfy Cheil. Suh insisted on eighteen thousand tons.

"That is our position," Suh said.

Mimoto sounded exasperated. "What is the reason?" he asked.

In the next room, Herndon cracked a smile. Even though Suh was there to negotiate Cheil's role in a crime, Herndon couldn't help but admire him a bit. Suh was standing up to the biggest lysine players in the world; he seemed to know that his little company still had the power to wreck everyone else's scheme. Suh was playing on those fears to the hilt.

The guy, Herndon thought, was pretty ballsy.

For several minutes, Wilson explained his proposal. Cheil would be allocated the percentage of the market it was requesting. If the numbers were truthful, the company would be able to sell eighteen thousand tons—maybe more. If the market dropped in size, everyone would cut back. All the companies would stick with their percentages and adjust sales depending on the total market.

Suh listened impassively as the others explained the proposal for sharing production numbers. Suh asked about using auditors to check the figures.

"Our preference is to trust each other," Wilson said. "If we find somebody lyin'—death or something like that. Something very bad would happen. We would hire some Mafia figure or something, and rub you out."

The group laughed.

"If we can't trust each other in the end, it ain't gonna work," Wilson continued. "That's how I feel."

Whitacre nodded. "If we can't trust each other, it's not worth meetin'."

Wilson lit a cigarette. They had reached an end point. It was make or break.

Mimoto looked at Suh. "You are okay for that?"

Suh nodded. "Yeah, I'm all right."

"Okay, then, very good," Mimoto said.

He smiled and looked around the room.

"Fantastic," Mimoto said with a laugh. "So five companies agree on quantity for the first time."

• • •

Five companies agree.

"That's it!" Herndon said. "That's the one."

After more than a year, they finally had a conspirator pronouncing an agreement on tape. Robin Mann was going to love this one. So would a jury.

Herndon glanced around. Weatherall was standing behind him. Their eyes locked.

Weatherall smiled and nodded. He'd heard it.

From that moment, a tone of friendliness permeated the meeting. The group spent hours discussing regional prices and how to handle customers who falsely claimed that they had been offered a better price. If everyone held firm, the customers would have to pay the fixed price to somebody.

Wilson leaned forward on the couch. "You just say, 'The price is not gonna be less than x,' period. It's tough to do, but it can be done if you just trust each other that you're not cheating."

Mimoto agreed. "If we trust each other, we can enjoy the gain," he said. "Offer the simple price."

Wilson walked across the room for a can of soda, then trudged back to the couch. Some of the executives were still talking about their fears of being cheated.

"We are gonna get manipulated by these goddamn buyers," Wilson said, waving his hands. "They can be smarter than us if we let them be smarter."

Everyone listened in silence.

"They are not your friend," Wilson continued. "They are not my friend. Thank God we have 'em, but they are not my friends."

He looked around the room.

"You're my friend. I wanna be closer to you than I am to any customer, 'cause you can make it that I can make money or I can't make money. At least in this kind of market. And all I want is to tell you again, let's put prices on the board. Let's agree that's what we're gonna do and walk out of here and do it."

The pep talk had its effect. The executives were willing to give trust a chance. The men continued their talks, laughing and joking for an hour and a half. With warm feeling spreading, Mimoto invited everyone to join him for dinner at the hotel restaurant.

"We appreciate it," Whitacre said, following Herndon's instructions. "Take you up on it."

The group started chattering. Business was done; who was ready for some golf?

"I have to make a few phone calls first," Whitacre said. "I'll meet you on tee in about fifteen minutes."

The executives stood and headed to the door.

"I have to play golf," Suh said.

The phone beside Herndon rang just seconds after he shut off the monitor.

"Hey, is this Bob?"

"Yeah, Mark. It's me."

"What do you think?"

Herndon took a breath. "It's a good tape, Mark. It's a very good tape."

"Yeah, it's good, isn't it?" Whitacre said excitedly. "Kinda ties everything together, doesn't it? Kinda ties everything we've been talking about."

Herndon couldn't argue.

"You did a great job, Mark. Really great."

Herndon lifted his arms, pushing his shoulders back as far as he could. He breathed out as he held the position, stretching his muscles. He sometimes cheated himself on his warm-ups before he exercised, but today Herndon was going through all his paces. After hours of sitting, staring at a black-and-white screen, he badly needed to loosen up.

Once he was limber, he picked up a bucket of one hundred golf balls and headed to a tee on the hotel driving range. The place was relatively empty. He set up his first ball and took a swing.

He whacked the balls for ten minutes, moving through the bucket quickly. Herndon heard someone arrive behind him, but stayed focused on his swing.

Thwack.

A golf ball whizzed past him, about three feet from his left ankle. Herndon jumped back and turned around to get a look at who was golfing so carelessly.

It was Jacques Chaudret.

Chaudret, wearing a pastel sweater around his shoulders, walked over to Herndon, looking surprised.

"Oh, I am so sorry," Chaudret said. "It's a terrible mistake. Unfortunately, that's how my golf game is a lot."

Herndon smiled. "You kind of scared me."

"I know. I thought I was going to hit you."

"Well, okay," Herndon said. "Have a nice day."

"Yeah, you, too."

Chaudret turned. But there was something Herndon enjoyed about the moment; he couldn't let it go.

"Great weather, isn't it?" Herndon said.

Chaudret stopped.

"Yeah, it is," he replied, almost by rote.

Turning away, Chaudret walked back to his tee. Herndon watched, smirking to himself.

Boy, if only you knew who I am and what I just did, he thought.

"Okay," Mimoto said as he walked with a club in hand up to the first tee. "If I win, we get Tyson."

The other executives, gathered around the tee box, all laughed. It was in jest; no one was about to let their golf games decide who received the lysine contract for Tyson Foods or other customers. But the joke set the tone for all eighteen holes. *The winner of the next hole gets Hudson Foods. The loser has to give up five thousand tons. We already know Whitacre's score—sixty-seven plus alpha.*

As they laughed and played, no one noticed the man on a nearby hill, carrying what appeared to be a gym bag. The man, a member of the SOG team, looked through his sunglasses at the executives standing near the tee box. He turned his gym bag slightly. Without looking down, he gripped the button near his hand. The camera hidden inside the bag clicked.

Another executive stepped up to the tee. The agent readied his next shot.

Early that evening, Whitacre arrived at Wilson's bungalow, dressed casually in a sports coat with the microcassette recorder hidden in the breast pocket. Herndon had removed the F-Bird that afternoon.

With so much evidence on lysine, the agents had pushed Whitacre to use his time with Wilson to talk about price-fixing in citric acid. This would be Whitacre's only chance, when he and Wilson were alone.

Wilson headed out of the room and joined Whitacre. The sidewalk between the bungalows was almost like a tunnel, cutting down the natural light from the Hawaiian sunset. Wilson seemed happy; the golf game had relaxed him.

The two men stepped off the sidewalk, onto a blacktop parking lot leading to the hotel restaurant. This was the moment, Whitacre thought.

"So, is citric about where lysine is today?"

"Yeah," Wilson said.

"I thought citric was all perfected by now."

"No. It always goes back to trust."

"Same kind of trust factor there?"

"Trust is a little bit different."

The two men stepped over a curb.

"Do you submit the numbers?" Whitacre asked. "Has that helped out?"

"Yeah, yeah."

"Is it done by region or by country?"

"We do it by country."

"Boy, I don't know if we can do that."

"Nah," Wilson said, shaking his head. "Not right now 'cause you're not big enough."

Well, Whitacre asked, are the citric numbers called in to somebody similar to Mimoto?

Wilson looked thoughtful. "The numbers, let's see, the numbers go to Hoffman-LaRoche."

The two men walked under an awning and into a hotel lobby. Whitacre held back a smile. Wilson had just implicated one of the world's largest drug companies in the citric-acid price-fixing.

Whitacre breathed deep. It had been a good day.

Weatherall and Herndon were already seated at a table on the patio terrace of the hotel restaurant. A breeze came in as the skies darkened, rustling the surrounding palm trees. The evening was gorgeous.

Herndon was positioned near a glass wall, with a perfect view into the restaurant. He watched as Whitacre and Wilson walked inside and were joined quickly by the other lysine executives. A hostess steered them toward a large table.

"Looks like they're sitting inside, Joe," Herndon said.

From the corner of his eye, Herndon saw Whitacre standing. He was pointing outside, saying something. The others stood and began trooping toward the patio.

"Uh, here they come," Herndon said. "They're going to sit out here."

The agents studied their place settings as the lysine competitors emerged from the restaurant. None of the patio tables was large enough for them, so the executives moved several together.

Herndon looked up, catching Whitacre's eye for a second. Herndon broke the stare, glancing back down to the table. Knowing Whitacre, Herndon thought, he might start trying hand signals or something if they maintained eye contact. Plus now he had the added danger that Chaudret might walk over to talk about the mishap at the driving range.

The waitress set the agents' meals on the table and they dug in. They weren't there for surveillance; there was no reason to pay particular attention to the nearby table. At one point, Herndon noticed that Whitacre had stood, glancing toward him before heading inside. Did he want something?

"Well, he's getting up to go to the rest room," Herndon told Weatherall. "I think I'll follow him and see if there's something he needs."

Herndon wiped his mouth with his napkin and pushed back his chair. He headed to the rest-room door, and glanced over his shoulder. No one was coming. He walked in. Whitacre was washing his hands.

"Hey," Whitacre said. "Got something for you."

Herndon could tell that Whitacre was going to keep talking. He quickly looked under the stalls. They were alone. Herndon stood beside the door.

"Terry and I were talking about citric on the way over here," Whitacre said. "I got the tape. They're doing the same thing with citric. Just like I said. Same thing. We talked about numbers they exchanged. They're exchangin' numbers, country by country."

Whitacre was pouring everything out, right there in a public rest room. Herndon suggested holding off.

"It's fine, Bob," Whitacre said. "And it's a great tape. Just what you guys have wanted."

Herndon held up his hands. "Okay, that's good, Mark," he said. "Well, just go back to dinner and—"

"What time are you guys checking out tomorrow?" Whitacre interrupted.

Herndon started to answer, then caught himself. He didn't want to stay in the bathroom chatting.

"Look," he said, "let's get together later tonight. Give us a call and—"

"I don't know how late we'll be out with these guys," Whitacre said, interrupting again.

"That's fine. We'll be up. Just give me or Joe a call, okay?"

"Okay," Whitacre said, nodding eagerly.

Whitacre headed back into the restaurant, while Herndon walked to the sink, exasperated. Whitacre's excitement was leading him to take unnecessary risks again.

Why does he do this? Herndon thought

The next morning was cleanup for the FBI. The lamp had to be returned, the other recording equipment packed away. Before the morning was out, Weatherall and Herndon were in the lobby, packed and ready to go.

As the agents waited for the desk clerk, Yamamoto and some of the other Asian executives arrived. They were all checking out around the same time. Herndon and Weatherall noticed them in line, but said nothing.

It made sense that they were all leaving together. The executives had finished their illegal meeting. And the agents had finished recording it.

The lysine investigation was a wrap. With volume and pricing agreements in place, the conspiracy was finally on course; every meeting between the lysine producers from now on would just be an update.

Now, the case had to take another turn. The agents had gathered evidence indicating that price-fixing was a way of life at ADM. Many of the other possible products—citric and lactic acid, MSG, even high-fructose corn syrup—involved huge industries that dwarfed lysine. Whitacre still had no direct contact with those businesses, but could pick up secondhand information such as his conversation with Wilson in Hawaii. Even Dwayne Andreas's seventy-sixth birthday party at the company had offered Whitacre the chance to overhear discussions about the citric conspiracy. But he would never be able to develop enough information on his own to bring a solid case.

On April 14, the agents and prosecutors met to discuss their options for developing other cases. Herndon and Shepard arrived with a list of ideas. Perhaps the FBI could set up an agent as a supplier in the citric-acid business. Maybe the agents could approach the accountants who were auditing numbers from the citric conspiracy and persuade them to cooperate. The ideas seemed unlikely to succeed.

The meeting ended with a decision to pursue two tracks. The agents would push Whitacre for more information. At the same time, Herndon would work with Rodger Heaton, the prosecutor handling the case for the Springfield U.S. Attorney, on an application for wire-taps at ADM. There was a lot of information they needed for the application, and it would take a long time to develop. But if a judge approved it, the government would hear exactly what ADM executives said in their phone conversations with competitors.

Something bothered Herndon. The agent stared at Whitacre, who was sitting at a table in a Forsyth hotel as he spoke. His suit jacket was on; in fact, it seemed like Whitacre's jacket was always on.

Herndon glanced at Shepard. Shirtsleeves. His own jacket was hung up over by the door. It was a hot day; the room's air-conditioning unit was working hard, but still the room was toasty.

And Whitacre was wearing his suit jacket.

What's up with that?

"Hey, Mark," Herndon said. "It's kind of warm. Can I take your jacket?"

Whitacre smiled. "Oh, no, Bob, that's okay. I'll keep it on."

The conversation resumed, and Herndon sat back. Warning signals were going off in his head.

When Whitacre left, Herndon approached Shepard.

"Hey, Brian," he said. "You know, Mark hasn't been taking his coat off recently."

"Yeah?"

"You don't suppose there's a reason for that, like he's been taping us?"

Shepard considered that for a moment. Even if Whitacre was taping, confronting him could be a disaster for their relationship.

"I don't think he is, Bob," he replied. "He may be. But I don't think he is."

Herndon nodded.

"Yeah," he said. "I don't think he is, either."

Work was piling up for Whitacre. Not only was he still responsible for lysine, but now his duties had expanded to include setting up legitimate business deals with other corporations. Topping that off, some of his European salesmen were participating in regional price-fixing meetings. It kept him busy.

On May 3, Whitacre was scrambling to get a few things done. In just eight days, he would be leaving for Europe to meet with the top executives in his division's European staff, Marty Allison and Alfred

Jansen. While he was there, he also had an ADM corporate check that he wanted to deliver. But for that, he needed to put the paperwork through.

Whitacre fished out a copy of the standard request form for a check distribution. At the top, he wrote that the check should be made payable to ABP International, a supplier that had sold ADM the microbes needed for a feed additive called threonine. This payment, he wrote on the form, was for an improved microbe that ADM had agreed to purchase for $2.5 million—a fairly standard amount. Whitacre stapled the contract for the purchase to the form.

Before sending the records to accounting, he wrote a short note, explaining that he was leaving for Europe and wanted to personally hand the payment to the ABP executives during his visit.

Whitacre knew that Kirk Schmidt, the controller for the Bioproducts Division, would handle the request. Schmidt was a friend; just the other day, the two had enjoyed lunch together at the Country Club of Decatur. Even though the request was unusual, Whitacre felt confident he would have his check in no time. Schmidt wouldn't give him any trouble.

Heaton was running out of patience. More than a year had passed since he had begun working on the lysine case for the Springfield U.S. Attorney's office. He had reviewed the files and listened to the tapes. But he had yet to meet the chief witness. How would Whitacre appear to a jury? How would he work with the prosecutors? Heaton had no idea; the agents were still telling the lawyers to wait for a meeting.

The deadlock had been a large topic of conversation between Heaton and Robin Mann. Both had pushed the agents, but they got nowhere.

Heaton got up from his desk on the second floor of the Springfield federal building and headed to the office of Joseph Hartzler, one of the district's most respected prosecutors. Frances Hulin, the recently appointed U.S. Attorney for Springfield, had asked Hartzler to keep on top of the ADM case. Hartzler was a prized litigator. He had honed his skills with the Chicago U.S. Attorney's office before moving to Springfield in search of a slower pace that would allow him more time with his family. While no one had asked him to take the job of trying the case, Hartzler would be an asset if the ADM case ever went to court.

Hartzler was at his desk. Heaton scarcely noticed the motorized scooter that his vigorous colleague used to get around, the only outward sign of Hartzler's multiple sclerosis. Heaton asked if Hartzler had a minute to talk about the ADM case.

"Do you think it's odd that the agents appear not to want us to meet this guy?" Heaton asked.

Hartzler asked what the agents' explanation had been. Heaton described their concerns about Whitacre going south. Hartzler didn't like what he heard.

"They can't do this," Hartzler said. "You've gotta meet the guy, find out if he's for real."

Prosecutors, Hartzler knew, needed to look a witness in the eye, to figure out if he was trustworthy. But in this case, there was a question that made the meeting even more important. Whitacre was a top executive at ADM, had a big salary and a lot of responsibilities. That raised a question that gnawed at Hartzler, a question he thought a prosecutor needed to probe before this case went much further.

Why in the world was Whitacre doing this?

The agents and staff of the Springfield FBI devoured cake and coffee as they watched Joe Weatherall step to the front of the SAC's conference room. There was a smattering of applause.

"You know, in Spanish, *jubilarse* means 'to retire,' " Weatherall said. "When you think about it, the word kind of looks like *jubilee*. And that's kind of the way I feel about retirement."

It was June 3, 1994. After twenty-three years with the FBI, Weatherall had decided to take his pension. If there was ever a time, it was now. Lysine was done. Dean Paisley, the squad leader who had supervised the case since its inception, had retired himself just after the Hawaii meeting. A new squad leader would be taking over in a few months, handling a case that was set to go in new directions. This was the best opportunity to move on.

Weatherall had broken the news to Shepard and Herndon some time before and had hoped to keep everything low-key. He had turned aside efforts to put together a retirement party but had agreed to the small office reception. His colleagues presented him with a plaque, and soon the reception came to an end. Weatherall returned to Champaign, where he cleaned out his desk. At 5:00, he dropped off his keys with a colleague. After a few final good-byes, Weatherall walked out of the office for the last time.

The moment felt good. Weatherall was confident that Shepard and

Herndon had the investigation firmly in hand. With the lysine competitors all on tape, the surprises and challenges had been resolved. The case would almost certainly be smooth sailing from now on.

In Mobile, Alabama, Special Agent Craig Dahle reviewed the notes of his interview with an executive from the Degussa Corporation. Dahle was investigating possible corporate espionage by former employees of the giant German agricultural company. The company suspected that two former executives, Chris Jones and Tim Hall, had improperly taken proprietary information about Degussa's process for making an amino acid called methionine. Degussa had taken the allegations to the Justice Department, which referred the case to Mobile, where Degussa maintained offices.

An executive from Degussa had presented the company's information to Agent Dahle during a June 24 meeting at the Justice Department in Washington, D.C. The executive, Andrew Burke, had no direct evidence of any crimes, but had been contacted by a man who claimed to know a lot. The whistle-blower, Kyle Rountree, had told Burke that he had seen evidence suggesting that Hall had obtained confidential Degussa information about methionine; Rountree had also procured letters between Jones and an executive at the Archer Daniels Midland Company. Rountree believed that the Degussa information had been sold to ADM by Jones and Hall—he had even seen several ADM checks to Jones in the amount of $10,000 each. If a crime was taking place—and of that, Dahle was not yet sure—then ADM may have attempted to use stolen secrets from Degussa when it was planning a methionine plant of its own.

The ADM executive was possibly the key to the investigation. Was he knowingly trafficking in stolen information? Was he persuading the others to commit a crime? Dahle flipped a page of his notes and glanced at the executive's name.

Mark Whitacre.

Dahle had never heard of Mark Whitacre but felt confident that the name would soon be very familiar. After all, by the time his investigation was over, this Whitacre fellow could end up under indictment.

CHAPTER 10

Word of the Mobile investigation trickled back to the Springfield FBI office in little more than two weeks. The first heads-up came July 12, in a call from the FBI's fraud unit in Washington. Afterward, a supervisor in the unit faxed a copy of a memo detailing the allegations raised by Degussa against its former employees, Jones and Hall.

By that afternoon, copies of the three-page memo found their way to Shepard and Herndon. Both knew Whitacre's division was responsible for methionine—there were several tapes of discussions about the product. Herndon remembered an early tape of Randall and Whitacre, recorded when the two were on the corporate plane scouting sites for a methionine plant. Chris Jones had even been along for part of that flight, although Whitacre hadn't turned on the tape until he and Randall were alone.

The two agents spoke by phone early the next morning. By then, both had covered their copies of the fax with questions. Whitacre was not mentioned anywhere in it. Perhaps, the agents hoped, if a crime was taking place, Whitacre knew nothing about it. Maybe he could even cooperate on *this* case, too.

At the bottom of the memo, Herndon noticed that Tim Fuhrman, a squad leader with the FBI in Mobile, was listed as the case contact.

"Brian," Herndon said, "why don't we call this Fuhrman guy and see what's going on?"

Shepard agreed. Herndon pushed a button on his console for a conference call and dialed the number. Fuhrman answered, and the agents introduced themselves.

"How're you doing?" Shepard asked. "How's everything in Mobile?"

Fuhrman was not the type for chitchat, so Shepard got down to business. He described how he and Herndon were working a case involving ADM. Shepard began a long story describing the background of Harvest King.

"I'm familiar with the highlights of your case," Fuhrman interrupted.

The Springfield agents needed to speak with Dahle, Fuhrman said, since he was running the investigation. But he said Dahle wasn't in the office.

"But you both need to know," Fuhrman continued, "the latest information we have is that your guy Whitacre may be involved in this."

Shepard and Herndon were silent for a second.

"I think we need to talk with Craig Dahle as soon as possible," Herndon said.

"I think that's a good game plan," Fuhrman agreed.

Later that night, Robin Mann glanced around a large hotel room at the Holiday Inn in Decatur. It was dim and gloomy, the curtains pulled for secrecy. A light fixture hung over a circular table, casting shadows across the floor. With her briefcase in hand, Mann pulled out a chair and sat. Rodger Heaton took the chair beside her, while Shepard and Herndon stood.

After more than a year of prodding, the prosecutors were finally about to meet Whitacre. With the lysine investigation essentially complete, the case could go to a grand jury anytime in the next twelve months. That meant the prosecutors would need time with Whitacre to prepare his testimony. The get-acquainted sessions could no longer be delayed.

As they waited, the group reviewed the plans for the meeting. The agents had briefed Mann and Heaton on the developments from Mobile, although not a hint could be given to Whitacre yet. Shepard and Herndon first needed to coordinate their effort with Dahle.

Beyond that, the group agreed, the meeting would follow a script. Shepard would handle introductions; Mann would ask most of the questions. The agents urged the lawyers to be gentle. This wasn't cross-examination; it was establishing relationships.

Everyone stood when Whitacre arrived. He was his old self, gregarious with the perpetual enthusiasm of a teenager. Everything about him was pressed and tailored. The lawyers came from a world of dark suits and white shirts; Whitacre was wearing a light, double-breasted suit and a funky tie with geometric shapes. He struck Heaton as looking like something of a high roller. The prosecutor made a mental note to work on Whitacre's appearance. He didn't want him coming across to a jury as arrogant or flippant just because he was a flashy dresser.

"Mark, this is Robin Mann," Shepard said. "She's a prosecutor with the Antitrust Division in Chicago."

Mann smiled. "At last we meet."

Whitacre stuck out a hand and returned the smile. "Hey," he said, "good to meet you."

After introductions, everyone found a seat. Mann reached into her briefcase; she had prepared two sets of questions—one thirteen pages long and the other an abridged, seven-page version. She decided to take it easy the first time. She brought out the seven-page list.

"All right, Mr. Whitacre," she said. "Tell me about your professional background."

Hours later, the meeting wrapped up. The lawyers were impressed. As a witness, Whitacre came across as accomplished and articulate; he was intelligent and good with details. He was far different from the usual cooperating witness in a criminal case.

Whitacre shook hands all around and headed out the door. The lawyers and agents stayed behind to discuss how the meeting had gone. Everyone was happy with the results. Whitacre, Shepard said, seemed comfortable with the prosecutors.

"Don't you guys have enough yet?" Whitacre asked. "Why do you really need to keep involving me?"

It was two weeks later, the night of August 1, a Monday. Whitacre was back at a Forsyth hotel room, sitting across from Shepard and Herndon. He could not understand why the FBI still wanted his help. He had given them the lysine case. He had done his job.

"Can't you find another guy?" he asked. "Go to Barrie, he can help you out on citric. I can't do citric. It's not my product line."

"Mark, you're the only guy in the position to help us right now," Herndon said.

Whitacre threw up his hands. "Can't you just bug the office? If you did it for thirty days, you'd get all the evidence you'd need. You'd hear it yourself from Terry and Barrie. You wouldn't need me."

"Stop, Mark," Shepard said. "You need to understand something. There's things we can do as the FBI, but there's a lot of things we can't do."

Methodically, Shepard explained that the Bureau needed to file an application with a judge under the federal wiretapping statute before they put listening devices on the phones. They were working on such an application now, but it took time and effort. And there was no guarantee a judge would approve it. Plus, the FBI couldn't just float into ADM, install the devices, and disappear. It was a complex operation.

"Come on," Whitacre said, "you guys can do anything you want to do. You can get in there."

"Maybe we could," Shepard said, "but we don't want to compromise the case. It would take a lot of surveillance and a lot of practice."

Herndon leaned in. "Our goal, Mark, is to get you out of this. If we could flip somebody else, we'd do it in a heartbeat. It would make our case stronger if we had a second person for the next product lines. But to do that, we need to concentrate on the other products. Talk to Barrie more about citric. Talk to Terry about it. Talk to Mick about fructose."

"You know Mick's not gonna want to hear this from me," Whitacre protested. "He's going to tell me, 'Look at your business card, does it say anything about citric, Mark? Or fructose?' Guys, this could blow your whole case."

Herndon started to speak.

"I think Mick could harm me if I start testifying against him," Whitacre blurted out.

This had come out of nowhere. Herndon shifted to a technique he had learned from Shepard: When Whitacre barrels off the track, ask questions to slow him down.

"Well, Mark, what did Mick say to you that gives you the fear that he might harm you?" Herndon asked.

"I don't know. I just have that fear. He's just that type of guy. I just have that fear."

"What has he said to give you that fear?"

Whitacre tugged at his glasses. "I just know he's going to. He's powerful. I wouldn't put it past him."

Pressed, Whitacre admitted that he couldn't recall specific threats. Herndon started to respond.

"You have to find somebody else," Whitacre interrupted. "I don't have time for this. I've got a lot more responsibilities now. I'm responsible for acquisitions and joint ventures at ADM. We're gonna spend like six hundred or seven hundred million dollars this year investing in other companies. That's a big responsibility."

Herndon was struck with an idea. Was there any possibility that ADM would enter into a deal with another company in the citric or fructose business? Maybe the FBI could set up a relationship with a joint-venture partner to gather evidence.

"It would never happen, guys," Whitacre said. The government would never approve a merger giving ADM a bigger share of those markets.

"I'm doing all sorts of acquisitions, in other products," Whitacre said. "I'm the one bringing them before the board of directors. Like I handled a joint venture on methionine with Rhone-Poulenc."

Methionine.

Shepard and Herndon didn't look at each other, didn't breathe. They had never mentioned the Mobile case to Whitacre, but now they had the chance to hear his version. It had to be handled delicately; the agents couldn't seem too interested.

"Well, Mark," Herndon said casually, "what did that project involve?"

Whitacre smiled, launching into a monologue about methionine. He had been interested in the business, he said, because it would give ADM the widest selection of bioproducts for customers.

"I particularly had a real desire to develop a methionine plant because of my past experience with Degussa," he said. His former employer was a top producer of methionine.

Whitacre explained how he had hunted for plant sites and had also contacted suppliers that sold the raw materials ADM would need for the project.

"I found out which suppliers to call from some consultants I hired," Whitacre said. "They were these two ex-Degussa employees, Chris Jones and Tim Hall."

But the efforts proved unnecessary, Whitacre continued. ADM scrapped plans for the plant, instead investing in one owned by Rhone-Poulenc.

"Did Dwayne or Mick play any role in studying the idea?" Herndon asked.

"No, that was my project," Whitacre said.

Herndon nodded. "Okay, let's get back to our case."

About twenty minutes later, Whitacre headed home. Following their usual procedure, the agents waited a few minutes in the room. They had a lot to talk about.

If Whitacre had been involved in some wrongdoing in methionine, it seemed odd that he would bring the project up. Maybe that was a sign there was nothing to these Degussa allegations. Maybe Jones and Hall had simply shared their expertise in methionine, without divulging Degussa's secret process.

But as they talked it through, the agents began to wonder. Maybe that's just what Whitacre wanted them to think. Maybe he offered his side of the methionine story because, somehow, he had figured out that the government was on his tail.

Joe Hartzler sat in the grand jury room of the Springfield federal courthouse, eating his lunch. The prosecutor was filling in for Heaton at a meeting scheduled for shortly after one o'clock. For the first time, prosecutors in both the methionine and lysine cases would be in the same room, laying out their positions. Because Whitacre was a cooperating witness in one investigation and a potential defendant in the other, the two cases were hopelessly intertwined. The expectation was that by the end of this meeting, the two sets of prosecutors would be cooperating.

Shepard, Herndon, and John Hoyt were the next to arrive, accompanied by Robin Mann and two other antitrust lawyers, Marvin Price and Susan Booker. The six had just returned from lunch. The group greeted Hartzler, joining him around the conference table.

The agents had been pleased to learn a few weeks before that Hartzler was taking a role in the lysine case. Hoyt had worked with Hartzler fleetingly in the 1980s, when the prosecutor was bringing criminal cases in Chicago against Puerto Rican terrorists. Hoyt had been impressed with Hartzler's aggressive style.

As the group waited, they discussed strategies. They had plenty of time; Peter Clark and Jim Baker, prosecutors from the Justice Department's Fraud Section who were involved in the methionine case, had been delayed in their flight from Washington.

Hoyt was appointed to make the opening presentation. The group would have to be savvy; they had heard that Clark had a strong, aggressive personality and was not likely to bend if confronted.

The fraud prosecutors finally arrived and quickly took their seats. Hoyt smiled, asking about their flight and trying to set an amiable mood.

"Now, we've all kind of got an embarrassment of riches," Hoyt said as he segued into the main topic. "We've got two cases that both seem pretty important. But each one could cause the other trouble."

Hoyt began summarizing portions of Harvest King, stressing that it involved important allegations against a Fortune 500 company. Clark broke in.

"I've heard about your case," Clark said in a booming voice. "But our case is important, too. It involves the same Fortune 500 company. And the agent is finding the witnesses to be very credible."

With that, Clark seized control of the conversation. Shepard and Herndon were surprised; they had never seen anyone from the Justice Department so forcefully shove aside an FBI supervisor.

Over time, the two sides thrashed out their positions. They agreed that Shepard and Herndon needed to meet the cooperating witness in the Mobile case so that they could examine his story in light of other information they knew. They also resolved to include the Mobile allegations in Springfield's wiretap application. Springfield would also issue grand jury subpoenas in the Mobile case for bank records of individuals in their district—including Whitacre.

Robin Mann spoke up. Mobile had no looming statute-of-limitations problem that required filing charges anytime soon, she said.

"So can you give us assurances that you won't take any action in your matter until the completion of our investigation?" she said.

Clark stiffened. He had the look of someone who had been hit in the face with sand.

"I'm not giving you guarantees about anything," he snapped.

Mann and Clark stared at each other for a second, the air between them frigid. Finally, Mann pressed Clark again on the timing of a potential prosecution.

"If it comes down to it, the decision will be made by Assistant Attorney General Jo Ann Harris," Clark responded, his tone cold.

The room was silent. Invoking the name of Harris, the head of the Justice Department's Criminal Division, struck the antitrust team as excessive. All that these cases needed was coordination; there was no need to run to senior officials in Washington. Whatever else was going on, Clark was making it clear that he had no intention of being railroaded by Springfield.

Hartzler cleared his throat. "Well, Peter," he said, "couldn't you agree not to take action until the Springfield agents have an opportunity to meet with the Mobile agent? That way, we can coordinate, and that might influence how we do things."

Clark nodded. "Yeah, I'll do that. But I want you to understand. Any postponement of further action on this case is only temporary."

He looked at the assembled group. "We are not stopping this investigation," he said.

Just off Interstate 10 in the Louisiana town of Lake Charles, the Players Riverboat Casino floated dockside. The vessel appeared to be of the Victorian era, belying its true age of less than one year. A huge paddle wheel was visible behind it—a nicety required on all casino riverboats by Louisiana gambling laws, even though this one was powered by diesel engines and underwater propellers. In its first few months, the riverboat had brought an economic boom to Lake Charles, an oil town still struggling from the collapse of crude prices in the 1980s. Some folks in town had once considered the boat a sign of moral decay. But now, with money coming in, the casinos were mostly viewed as a blessing, the town's salvation.

On August 24, Shepard and Herndon drove past the riverboat and eyed its inviting polished chrome and flashing lights. Perhaps, the agents agreed, they would visit the casino later. But first, they had to stop by a hotel up the street, where Craig Dahle was waiting to introduce them to his cooperating witness.

Dahle met the two agents in the hotel's downstairs restaurant for dinner. Everyone was friendly, but the atmosphere was strained. The agents knew that one of the cases was probably going to be derailed before too long. The only question was whose.

After his meal, Dahle checked his watch.

"I better get upstairs in case my guy shows up," he said. Shepard and Herndon agreed to come up soon.

When they arrived, Dahle was still alone. The witness, Kyle Rountree, knocked on the door about ten minutes later. After the introductions, Dahle walked his witness through his story.

Rountree said that the former Degussa employees, Jones and Hall, now worked at a Lake Charles company called Kronos. Rountree worked with them and made no secret that he disliked Jones. A woman close to Jones had raised Rountree's suspicions about espionage. She showed him documents from a computer disk she claimed to have found on Hall's desk. The documents appeared to contain proprietary data on Degussa's methionine process.

Rountree mentioned that he had letters between Jones and Mark Whitacre, as well as check stubs documenting ten-thousand-dollar payments from ADM to the two former Degussa executives. A date on one check matched the date on a letter from Whitacre to Jones.

"You told me something last time about Whitacre and the sign-in sheet at Kronos," Dahle said.

"Yeah, I remember seeing his name on the Kronos visitor's log sometime around November of 1992."

Herndon blinked. "How do you remember a visitor's log from two years ago?" he asked.

"I just routinely check the visitors' log so I can know who's coming and going," Rountree said.

The answer didn't make a lot of sense to Herndon, but he dropped it. The interview lasted another hour, but Rountree offered no more details about Whitacre.

After it broke up, Shepard and Herndon walked down the street to the riverboat casino. They were feeling pretty good; there seemed to be no evidence that Whitacre had been involved in wrongdoing. Probably Mobile was nothing to worry about.

The effort to obtain authorization for wiretaps at ADM was moving ahead. As the lawyers explained it, they probably had enough P.C.—"probable cause"—to persuade a judge. But, for approval, they also needed to demonstrate that the FBI had the technical ability to tap specific company phones. It was a tall order, since the agents couldn't exactly walk into ADM and start asking about how the company's phone system worked.

But then again, maybe they could. At one of the meetings in Forsyth, Shepard told Whitacre that they wanted him to ask Mick Andreas a few questions. All it would take was a little playacting.

On the morning of September 12, Whitacre turned on the tape recorder in his coat pocket as he walked toward Mick Andreas's office.

"Mick, how you doin'?" he said at the doorway.

Andreas looked up from his desk. "Hey, how you doin'?"

For a few minutes, Whitacre discussed some proposed investments for his division. Eventually, he mentioned that one lysine competitor was worried about the security of ADM's phones.

"I said security shouldn't be a—for me to call on these phones—I don't see that as a problem," Whitacre said. "Do you?"

Andreas didn't understand. "What?"

"Like for them to call me on a lysine problem on our phones here at the office," Whitacre said. "I couldn't imagine these phones could be a problem."

"To tap these phones or get into these phones, you gotta get inside the building," Andreas said.

He pointed to the wire attached to his desk phone. "This phone line doesn't go anywhere. It goes down into a computer, and then comes out on one of a hundred or five hundred lines."

"That's what I thought."

"It just does it at random," Andreas said.

Essentially, the computer guaranteed that a single phone line could not be tapped. Plus, anyone trying to place a tap would have to get past the company's on-site telecommunications crew, who were on duty twenty-four hours a day. The phones were safe.

"But that doesn't mean we go around . . . ," Andreas said, waving his hand in the air. "Gotta be careful what we talk about."

The latest Andreas tape was a letdown for the government. ADM seemed to have a security system in place that was virtually impenetrable. The investigators wouldn't be able to show a judge that they could tap the specific lines they wanted.

The application for wiretaps was at death's door. The agents could still gather information about lysine—in October, meetings were scheduled in Chicago between Ajinomoto and ADM, and the larger group meeting was set for Zurich. But they might have to accept that they would be unable to prove ADM's involvement in other price-fixing conspiracies.

Howard Buffett bid good-bye to Congressman Dick Durbin and hung up the telephone. Buffett was feeling pretty good about himself. Maybe he had just saved ADM from being caught up in a scandal.

A few years back, Buffett had been recruited to ADM from his hometown of Omaha—the city where his famous father, Warren, presided over an investing empire. By the fall of 1994, Howard Buffett was serving as a director, as well as an assistant to Dwayne Andreas. Buffett was the company's chief spokesman and its prime contact for the nation's political elite. But Buffett also saw part of his job as helping to keep the company out of trouble.

The call with Durbin was part of that effort. Buffett had heard days before that the congressman was interested in going to a Chicago Bears football game. Buffett had mentioned that to Dwayne Andreas, who told him to make the necessary arrangements.

But then Buffett's secretary brought something to his attention.

That summer, a scandal had enveloped Mike Espy, the Secretary of Agriculture for the Clinton administration, because of gifts he had taken from companies—including a basketball ticket from the Quaker Oats Company. Setting up Durbin with seats at a Bears game, the secretary said, sounded awfully similar. Buffett thanked the secretary and telephoned a lawyer to ask about the situation. The lawyer came back with a strong answer—the tickets couldn't be provided unless Durbin paid part of the cost.

When Buffett informed Durbin, the response could not have been more gracious. The congressman thanked Buffett for his efforts and promised to pick up part of the tab himself. Buffet felt confident that he had just helped ADM dodge a bullet.

Not everyone saw it that way. Days later, Dwayne Andreas confronted Buffett. He had heard everything about the tickets. And he was livid.

"If a congressman asks you to do something, you do it!" Andreas snapped. "If there's something wrong with it, that's his problem!"

Buffett started to explain what the lawyers had said, but Dwayne waved him off.

"Howard," Andreas said sharply, "you're useless to ADM if you have to ask for an attorney's opinion every time you get a request."

The October 11 meeting in Forsyth was a reunion of sorts. Herndon's first child, a girl, had been born in September, and his participation in meetings with Whitacre had dropped off. So when Whitacre saw Herndon with Shepard in the hotel room, he beamed. For several minutes, they talked about the new baby.

When they finally got down to business, Whitacre seemed to have little new information. He shared some office gossip about how Dwayne Andreas was angry with executives traveling on company business without authorization. It seemed insignificant.

Suddenly, Whitacre smiled. "You're not going to believe what Howard Buffett told me," he said.

Howard Buffett? The name had been mentioned in the case before, but hardly with any frequency. The agents looked at Whitacre quizzically.

"You know, Howard Buffett," Whitacre said. "He's a corporate vice president in public relations. And you know who his dad is?"

The agents nodded. Who hadn't heard of Warren Buffett?

"Well, Howard doesn't like Dwayne and Dwayne doesn't like Howard," Whitacre said. "Dwayne told Howard that he's useless."

Whitacre looked at the agents expectantly.

"Howard was talking to me about it, complaining about the Andreas management style. And Howard told me this quote. He said, 'With what I know about the company, it's amazing what I could do with these people.' That's what he told me."

Shepard leaned in. Was there something here?

"What more do you know about here?" he asked. "Let's get more specifics. What does this involve?"

Whitacre shrugged. "I don't know," he said. "I didn't ask him about it."

The agents could almost feel the air draining out of the room. All this build-up for nothing? Herndon wrote it down anyway. Maybe sometime later they would interview Buffett and find out what he knew.

The meeting droned on, with little accomplished. The agents figured they would be breaking soon.

"Oh, by the way," Whitacre mentioned casually, "this friend of mine, Kuno Sommer. He's a Ph.D. He just replaced Mr. Hauri at Hoffman-LaRoche. He's in charge of their citric-acid business now."

The agents snapped to attention. From earlier tapes, they knew that Hoffman-LaRoche collected the production numbers in the citric-acid price-fixing conspiracy. And now the new head of that operation, this Kuno Sommer, was a friend of Whitacre's? With the chances for the wiretap application fading, suddenly Whitacre had presented a new avenue for investigation.

"Tell us about Kuno Sommer, Mark," Shepard said.

Whitacre brought out Sommer's business card, showing that his friend was head of global marketing for Hoffman-LaRoche's Vitamins and Fine Chemicals Division. Herndon and Shepard stared at the card, awed.

The timing was perfect. The next day, Whitacre was scheduled to accompany Wilson and Mick Andreas to Chicago for a meeting with Ajinomoto at the Four Seasons Hotel. Now Whitacre had another assignment. Herndon told him to ask Wilson about Kuno Sommer. If Whitacre's friend was collecting numbers on citric, Wilson would have to know about it.

Whitacre's face fell.

"Kuno hasn't been in the job very long," Whitacre said. "He won't know anything yet."

The agents pushed him, but Whitacre kept arguing. His message was clear: while he might be willing to record Wilson, Andreas, and the lysine competitors in their conspiracy, he wasn't comfortable laying a trap for his friend.

"Mark, who knows how the answer will come back," Herndon said. "Look, if Kuno Sommer is not involved, this might give him the chance to avoid getting caught up in citric. Just ask the question. Let's find out."

Eventually, Whitacre agreed to ask Wilson about Sommer. The meeting ended, and Whitacre headed out the door. A minute later, Shepard glanced at Herndon.

"Wow," he said, "this could be our break."

Whitacre opened the driver's side door on his new 1994 Lincoln Town Car. He liked the green color of this car better than the blue on his old model. When the doors unlocked, Mick Andreas climbed into the front passenger's seat, while Wilson struggled into the back. Wilson's bad back was troubling him; his doctor was advising surgery, but Wilson kept putting it off. Whitacre sat in the driver's seat, easing against the cushion gently. The F-Bird digital recorder was strapped on, and he didn't want to crush it.

Putting the car into reverse, Whitacre backed out of his parking place. Soon, he was headed toward the Decatur airport where a corporate plane was waiting.

"This is your company car?" Andreas asked.

"Yeah," said Whitacre. "Always get the used ones. Last one I had was Buffett's."

"Very impressive," Andreas joked.

Whitacre smiled. "Tryin' to save the company money."

Wilson and Andreas chuckled.

"Well," Andreas said, changing the subject to the upcoming meeting, "Mr. Yamada—"

"And Mimoto is there," Whitacre said.

"Who's that?" Andreas asked.

"He's the Ikeda replacement." Ikeda had retired sometime before.

"I've never seen him, have I?"

"Let's see," Whitacre mused, "was he in L.A.?"

"No," Andreas replied. "Ikeda was there."

Well, Mimoto had replaced Ikeda, Whitacre said. "And he's just as bad."

"Is he a jerk or is he—"

"He's a goddamn prick," Wilson growled from the backseat.

Andreas looked back. "Why is he a prick?"

"He wants everything his way," said Whitacre.

Andreas faced front again. "How are things shaping up now? What's our volume going to be?"

"Seventy-three thousand tons," Whitacre answered.

"What'd we tell 'em it would be?"

"Seventy-three thousand tons."

"Really?"

Whitacre nodded. "We're comparin' numbers every month by region," he said. "Every month, Mimoto gets them from everybody."

"Who gets 'em? Mimoto?" Andreas asked.

"Yeah."

"He's the quarterback?"

Whitacre pulled his car to a stop at the airport parking lot. "He's the quarterback."

"He's the butler," Wilson said.

The three men climbed out of the car. Whitacre sidled up to Wilson. This was his chance.

"Kinda like Roche is on citric, right?"

"Yeah," Wilson said.

"Big quarterback—is that Kuno?" Whitacre asked.

"Yeah."

"He's a good guy," Whitacre said, coughing. "You'll like Kuno. I even knew him from my Degussa days."

The three men headed onto the corporate plane.

About an hour later, the three executives were in an American-United cab, driving from Meigs Field in Chicago to the Four Seasons Hotel. They spent much of their time talking about plans for Whitacre's division to develop new products. One feed additive called tryptophan, Whitacre said, was proving particularly nettlesome. Considering how long it took for ADM to start manufacturing lactic acid in large quantities, he said, the company was still probably two years away from making tryptophan efficiently.

Andreas nodded. "We'll be able to run it."

"We may have some this year," Whitacre said. "Half a truckload or something."

Andreas turned. "What about lactic?" he asked. "Are we really ever gonna fix prices on it?"

• • •

It was an Indian-summer day in Chicago, and the crowds on the street were in shirtsleeves and light dresses. A small group was gathered in front of the Four Seasons, watching construction work on a nearby church. A cab pulled to the front of the hotel. Whitacre paid the twelve-dollar fare, and the three ADM executives hopped out. Whitacre glanced at the crowd watching the construction and quickly looked away. Bob Herndon was standing among them.

The executives pushed open the glass door to the lobby and walked in. Herndon turned and followed them, keeping up his surveillance.

After some initial confusion, the ADM and Ajinomoto executives met in the seventh-floor lobby of the hotel. Andreas grasped Yamada's hand.

"How are you?" he said. "Good to see you."

He turned to Mimoto. "Mick Andreas," he said, extending a hand. "How are you?"

Whitacre smiled, walking over to Mimoto. "My name's Mark Whitacre."

Mimoto nodded. "Oh, my name is Tani."

Everyone walked into the hotel restaurant and was shown to a table in a private room. The meeting started uncomfortably. A top executive—senior to Yamada—was supposed to have attended but did not. Subtly, the Ajinomoto executives made it clear that Andreas was being snubbed because he had failed to visit Tokyo. Whitacre worsened the tension by mispronouncing the top executive's name—it was Toba, but he repeatedly said "Tobi," even after he was corrected.

Andreas did his best to recover. "I know that meetings are very important in Japan. I will make sure we get that organized."

The men offered a toast and sipped their drinks. Mimoto mentioned that one of the Korean companies was creating problems. Miwon had experienced internal strife and had split into two companies—Miwon and Sewon. Lysine was now handled by Sewon, and the new boss was a man who had caused trouble before.

"They stopped reporting to us," Mimoto said.

"Oh, they have?" Wilson asked.

Mimoto nodded. "Yeah."

The Koreans were now demanding more volume and felt they were not bound by earlier agreements.

Wilson snorted. "It'll destroy the whole goddamn market."

The ADM executives were perplexed by the news. They had met with the Koreans not long before, and everything had seemed fine. They had not raised any complaints.

"Hopefully, they'll come to reason," Whitacre said.

Andreas stroked his chin. He remembered one thing the Koreans had said at the last meeting, when he had brought up the idea of having ADM invest in Sewon.

"Remember them commenting, 'Would that be legal?' " Andreas said to Wilson.

"Yeah."

"He asked that?" Whitacre asked.

"I wonder if that's got something to do with it," Andreas said.

Whitacre shook his head.

"No?" Andreas asked.

"You mean, worry about antitrust and so on?" Whitacre asked.

Andreas nodded. "Mmm-hmm."

"They're not concerned about that," Whitacre said.

The discussions continued over whitefish and salad, but nothing was resolved. Andreas patted his mouth with a white linen napkin as a waiter arrived to pour coffee. They skipped dessert and headed out of the restaurant. They had accomplished what they needed—updating each other on the conspiracy to make sure that it held.

Andreas shook Mimoto's hand. "Good luck in all your businesses."

"Thank you very much," Mimoto replied.

"We hope you make a lot of money," Andreas said. "And if you do, we will, too."

In the cab, Andreas reviewed the meeting with Whitacre and Wilson. The three laughed at how upset the Japanese executives had been about Andreas's failure to visit Tokyo.

Abruptly, Whitacre turned to Wilson. "Did Kuno Sommer call you this morning?"

Wilson ignored the question.

"He was getting a little bit irritating, really," Andreas said of Mimoto. "Sorta like I'm not coming over on purpose."

Whitacre agreed. "Mick Andreas took buying an acquisition and making money over coming to Japan to have dinner and sushi."

Wilson chuckled. Then they all laughed about Whitacre's repeated mispronunciation of Toba's name.

"I should have said, 'Tell Tobi hello for me,' " Andreas joked.

Whitacre turned to Wilson.

"Kuno Sommer call you this morning?"

About an hour later, the three were on the corporate plane nearing Decatur, still joking. Eventually, there was a long silence.

"Hey, Terry," Whitacre suddenly said. "From a business standpoint, is Kuno pretty reasonable?"

"Who?" Wilson asked.

"Kuno Sommer."

Wilson stared at Whitacre. What was all this about Kuno Sommer?

"I've only been around him once," Wilson said. "He seems to be pretty reasonable."

"Nothing like the Japs here," Whitacre said.

Wilson shifted in his seat. His back was killing him. Whitacre asked if it was true that Hoffman-LaRoche was stronger in vitamins than in citric acid.

Wilson changed the subject. He wasn't comfortable with all this talk about Kuno Sommer and citric.

At the airport, the three climbed into Whitacre's car for the drive to the office. From the backseat, Wilson stared at Whitacre's head. It looked funny.

"Whitacre, what are you doing?" Wilson asked. Whitacre's hair looked like it was two-toned, he said. Was he dying it?

"Kinda bleaches a little bit," Whitacre said. "Especially in the summertime."

"Has Sue told you it looks better that way?" Wilson asked, referring to a woman at the office. "Or what's the deal?"

"Sue likes that," Whitacre said.

Andreas smiled, half raising a hand. "I'm gonna ask you a few questions about that," he said. "Sue is getting married, right?"

Yes, Whitacre said. Sue was getting married and moving to Canada.

"What else is new around the office?" Andreas asked.

"Amy's divorced," Wilson said.

Whitacre asked if they were talking about the same Amy who used to spend time with another senior ADM executive.

"He used to fuck her, but he doesn't anymore," Andreas said. "She loves to give head and fuck."

Whitacre looked in the rearview mirror. "Is she really getting a divorce, Terry?"

"Yeah," Wilson said. "I've been tryin' to tell her how to—"

"How to give blow jobs?" Andreas interrupted.

"No," Wilson answered, smiling. "How to take care of the kids so she doesn't have any problems."

Andreas looked into the backseat.

"How about that little fat one over there by you?" he said.

"Anna?" Wilson asked.

"No, no. Yeah, Anna, too. Who's fuckin' Anna now?"

Wilson shook his head. "I don't know who's fucking Anna."

"You think she's pretty much of a rounder?" Andreas asked.

Whitacre smiled. "She's very, very, very friendly. I think she's very bored with her life here. I don't mean ADM, either; I'm talkin' after-ADM life."

"So," Andreas said, "she likes to just go out and fuck?"

A minute later, the men brought up another woman at the company. Andreas shot Whitacre a look.

"I know you fucked her a few times," he said.

"No, no," Whitacre replied.

Andreas smiled. "You look at her up close, she is not that attractive."

"No," Wilson said. "But she is built."

"I don't like her, though," Andreas said. "She's so masculine or something."

Wilson sat up. "She's got lips, look like a black. Sensual. You know they'd fit right around."

Whitacre coughed. He was painfully aware that this conversation was being taped.

"Her makeup disguises what she really looks like," Andreas said. "She's got kind of a flat face and oval eyes."

Wilson coughed. "I thought she might be somewhat Hispanic."

"Could be Hispanic," Andreas said.

"Latin," said Whitacre.

"She's got big lips," Wilson repeated. "Like a black."

Andreas smiled. "She'd give great head."

He turned to Whitacre, asking to hear about some of the new women at work. Whitacre mentioned a woman who had recently joined ADM.

"You were trying to get in her pants, and she wouldn't talk to you," said Andreas.

"She's just a quiet gal," Whitacre said.

"Sort of a little meek-lookin' gal," Andreas added.

"Yeah," Whitacre said. "But she looks like she's an—"

"Looks like a whore," Andreas interrupted. "Looks like a fuckin' whore."

Whitacre pulled into ADM, circling the car around to the parking garage. In an instant, the three executives—the vice-chairman and two division presidents of a Fortune 500 company—walked back into the corporate headquarters, smiling and politely bidding hello to some of the female employees they had just been tearing apart so venomously.

"Brian, I'll tell you, Terry was really angry with me today," Whitacre said over the telephone.

It was the next day. Whitacre was calling Shepard from Scottsdale, saying that Wilson had confronted him at 9:15 that morning, furious with him for speaking too openly during the taxi ride in Chicago.

"He told me, 'You never talk that openly because there could be undercover agents everywhere, especially in Chicago,' " Whitacre said.

He had argued that Andreas had been just as talkative, but Wilson didn't want to hear it.

"And, Brian, there was another thing bothering him."

"What?"

"Kuno Sommer."

"What about him?"

"He told me, 'Don't worry so much about me and Kuno. He may be your friend, but the part I'm talking to him about has nothing to do with you.' "

Shepard hung up the phone a few minutes later. If Wilson was getting this antsy about Kuno Sommer, they were going to have to figure out another way to develop information on Whitacre's friend.

Two days later, Whitacre glanced up at Mummy Mountain in Scottsdale as he walked past a sparkling swimming pool near the lobby of Marriott's Mountain Shadows Resort. Palm trees swayed in the breeze, but the scenic panorama didn't deter Whitacre from the business at hand. He headed into the hotel, toward a conference room reserved for a sales meeting. Near the room, Whitacre saw a few other ADM employees. Some of his best friends at the company were here with him.

By the doorway, Whitacre ran into two friends, Sid Hulse and Reinhart Richter. The three greeted each other effusively before heading in to find their seats. Whitacre had recruited both men to ADM.

Hulse ran ADM's lysine sales effort from Atlanta and was probably Whitacre's best friend at the company.

Richter was the head of ADM Mexico, but maintained frequent contact with Whitacre. In 1989, while the two had been palling around at an industry conference in Atlanta, Whitacre had told him about being orphaned at a young age and adopted by a wealthy man. Richter had listened, enraptured, as Whitacre told of his adoptive father's generosity—how he had given one million dollars to each of Whitacre's three children. At the time, Richter had cautioned that Mark and Ginger had a great responsibility in making sure that children blessed with so much remained motivated.

Richter took his seat on the left side of the room, across from Hulse. The room quickly filled with ADM staffers. Marty Allison, Whitacre's first hire at ADM who now was a top sales representative in Europe, slipped into the room. He traded a few laughs with Whitacre before settling into his chair.

Sunlight draped the room in a golden glow. Whitacre smiled.

"Okay, well, we've got a lot to talk about," he said. "So let's get started."

The discussion began with a review of general sales topics for the lysine market. The assembled executives took notes as they listened to Whitacre.

"Let's look at some numbers," Whitacre continued.

He turned on an overhead projector and a white light hit the screen behind him. Whitacre placed a chart on it, filling the screen with bar graphs that showed the production for each lysine manufacturer.

"Okay, these are the quarterly production figures we obtained in meetings with our competitors," Whitacre said.

Allison could not believe what he was hearing. He knew about the price-fixing meetings—he had already attended a regional meeting himself. But few others in the room had been told about them. And there was no way Whitacre could have obtained the numbers without breaking the law. Such quarterly production figures were not even disclosed to company investors, much less competitors. It was clear evidence that price-fixing was taking place.

Glancing up, Allison eyed the other executives in the room. All of them—Richter, Hulse, and six others—were staring at each other in amazement. The room was filled with seasoned sales professionals, and none of them had ever seen anything like this before.

"Now," Whitacre said, "I'm not handing out copies of this, 'cause I don't want them going around. But go ahead and take notes if you want."

The executives wrote down the once-secret numbers from ADM's competitors. No one objected; no one expressed discomfort at participating in a crime.

And no one from the FBI knew that this was happening.

The length of the Bahnhofstrasse in Zurich was jammed with shoppers marveling at store windows that beckoned with Sprungli chocolates, Cartier watches, and Tiffany jewelry. The road opened up at the Paradeplatz, the erstwhile parade ground that serves as the town square. There, a uniformed employee held open the door of the Savoy Baur en Ville, one of Switzerland's most elegant hotels. Whitacre emerged from the lobby, nodding his thanks.

Whitacre had arrived in Zurich the day before, October 24, in preparation for the next lysine price-fixing meeting, scheduled to be held that afternoon at the Dolder Grand Hotel. This time, there would be no recording, and neither Shepard nor Herndon had accompanied him. The meeting today was little more than another update on the conspiracy; a briefing from Whitacre would be ample evidence. For once, Whitacre was alone. He could do as he pleased.

Outside, Whitacre watched a train headed to Zurich's central railway station. Close by, a church bell tolled the hour. It was 10:00 in the morning. Whitacre picked up his pace as he headed toward a building on the edge of the Paradeplatz. The Zurich office of the Swiss Bank Corporation. His destination.

Whitacre headed briskly into the lobby. A hall porter dressed in a topcoat stood nearby.

"*Guten Morgen,*" Whitacre said to the porter. "*Ich möchte Herr Briel finden, bitte.*"

The porter pointed toward an elevator. "*Herr Briel ist nach oben am vierten Stock,*" he said.

Whitacre nodded. "*Danke schön.*"

As instructed, Whitacre headed across the lobby to the elevators, then pushed the button for the fourth floor. There, he approached a receptionist.

"*Guten Tag,*" he said. "*Wie geht es Ihnen? Ich suche Herr Briel, bitte.*"

The receptionist gestured toward a chair. "*Nehmen Sie Platz, bitte,*" she said.

Whitacre eased into the rich leather chair in front of the receptionist's desk. He watched as she walked back toward the bank offices. In a moment, she returned, followed by a young, clean-cut man with brown hair and a wide smile. Whitacre had never seen the man before but knew this must be Daniel Briel.

"Mr. Whitacre," the young man said enthusiastically as he extended a hand.

Whitacre stood, flashing a smile as he clasped Briel's hand. *"Jawohl. Guten Morgen, Herr Briel. Wie geht es Ihnen?"*

"Gut, gut," Briel said, inwardly wincing at Whitacre's pronunciation. *"Wie geht's? Gut daβ wir uns eben getroffen haben."*

Whitacre nodded, smiling.

Together, the two men headed back to a private area, toward a windowless office. Whitacre walked in, taking a seat. Briel quietly closed the office's heavy wooden door. No one outside the room could hear them. Their conversation wouldn't take long.

The news Whitacre brought back from Switzerland was incredible: The lysine conspirators wanted to meet again in the United States, this time in Atlanta.

At a meeting in Springfield, Whitacre told Shepard and Herndon that the others had been spooked by news of a price-fixing investigation of European cement manufacturers. Jacques Chaudret was particularly worried, saying he would not meet again without the cover of an industry meeting. Everyone agreed. The next such meeting was a mid-January poultry convention in Atlanta. Most of the executives were already scheduled to attend and agreed that it would be safe to hold a price-fixing meeting there.

The prospect of another American meeting set off an enormous debate among the antitrust team. Since they already had the evidence against the foreign nationals—but might not be able to extradite them later—should they all be arrested in Atlanta?

Quick arrests presented big problems: Indictments would have to be handed up within weeks. The prosecutors would have little time to use the grand jury as an investigative tool. Making it worse, once the executives were indicted, they could insist on a speedy trial. That could leave the government hanging—a thousand pages of tape transcripts were yet to be typed. The prosecutors could be forced to go to trial without being fully prepared.

The realities forced the decision: The foreign lysine competitors would be allowed to leave the United States. But the debate under-scored the need to begin massive transcription efforts. Right away.

Ginger Whitacre descended the staircase at her Moweaqua home, lis-tening as rain drummed loudly on the roof. A fierce weekend thunder-storm had just blown in, and it sounded particularly vicious. Strolling through the living room, Ginger wondered where Mark was. Despite all their years together, Ginger found that she no longer understood her husband. Something in him had changed, something had been lost.

It wasn't just his frequent absences anymore, or his repeated fail-ure to attend family events or to just come home for dinner. Those as-pects of his behavior had almost become accepted in the household as a given. But now, even when he was home, he wasn't completely there. Mark seemed to be drifting through his family, with the detachment of a commuter waiting for a train to take him away.

But there was more. Ginger didn't understand it, but Mark had just become *weird*. Over the summer, they had built horse stables across the street, and Ginger loved to relax with an occasional ride. But Mark would disappear to the stables for hours, often not returning until 2:00 in the morning. Usually he would come home saying that he had been brushing the horses. *Brushing horses for three or four hours?* Then, a few hours later, he would head for work. It just wasn't normal. He seemed to be getting almost no sleep.

Ginger was getting ready to call out Mark's name when she heard a gas-powered engine turn on outside.

"Oh, no!" she said, walking over to the window.

Mark's other obsession. He had been leaning on their gardener to keep every leaf off the driveway. It was no easy task—the leaves from a two-hundred-year-old walnut tree covered the property in the fall. But Mark couldn't stand them there, ever.

Ginger reached the window and looked outside.

Wind and rain rustled the walnut tree, sending leaves cascading onto the driveway. Waiting there with a leaf blower in hand was Mark. The rain soaked him as he aimed the blower at the sopping-wet leaves. Puddles of water blew into droplets as clumps of leaves tumbled off the driveway. A flash of lightning lit the sky. Mark kept working, drip-ping wet.

Ginger closed her eyes, feeling frightened and helpless. What in the world was wrong with him? What was happening to her husband?

• • •

In October of 1994, the Antitrust Division was making plans for how to handle the criminal trial of ADM. Raids of the company were expected in a matter of months, but the lawyers needed for the case were still not in place. The Chicago antitrust office did not even have a permanent chief. On top of that, while Robin Mann was talented, she was not among the division's most experienced litigators.

At that time, a prosecutor named James Griffin was returning to his job as Deputy Chief of the Atlanta antitrust office, having just wrapped up a stint as an American advisor on legal issues to the Hungarian government. A quiet, open-faced man with a full head of white hair, Griffin was an unusual mix of refined and rowdy. Few in the office would have guessed that Griffin, with his soft-spoken manner, could often be found at home, cranking up the latest grunge-rock music on his stereo. He seemed an unlikely person to be one of the Antitrust Division's top litigators.

Griffin was settling back in at his eleventh-floor office in the Atlanta federal courthouse when a call came from Washington. A receptionist told him that it was Joseph Widmar, Deputy Assistant Attorney General in charge of all criminal prosecutions in the Antitrust Division. Griffin picked up the phone.

After some idle conversation about the trip to Hungary, Widmar got to the point.

"I want to talk to you about our chief opening in Chicago," he said.

"Yeah, I understand that's open."

"I want you to consider it."

"Why?" Griffin asked. He was happy in Atlanta. Plus, he had once experienced a Chicago winter and wasn't too eager to live through that again.

Widmar spent some time describing the advantages of becoming an office chief. But, he stressed, the Chicago office offered some particularly appealing benefits. There were important cases going on there, Widmar said, and the division would want Griffin to play a hands-on role in those.

Griffin listened, intrigued. He knew about the cases; the division was small enough that it was easy to hear about promising cases in the pipeline. He was particularly interested in the ADM investigation. The chance to play a role in a case of that magnitude was attractive. He was sorely tempted and told Widmar that he would think about the offer. It would not be long before he accepted.

• • •

About the same day Widmar placed his call to Griffin, an aggressive young lawyer in the Chicago antitrust office was preparing to go to trial.

Jim Mutchnik, who had just turned thirty a few weeks before, had been working for about two years on an investigation of potential bid rigging at a Kansas City shopping mall. It had been a blast. He had traveled to Kansas City, working side by side with an FBI agent. Together, they found witnesses and recorded conversations among the targets of the investigation. Some targets had cut deals. Now, the trial of the remaining defendant was scheduled to begin in a few weeks. Even though Mutchnik had to get ready, no one expected the case to go to a jury. The defendant, whose health was failing, was sure to plead it out. The evidence against him was too overwhelming.

Mutchnik was typing on his computer, his back to the office door, when he heard a voice behind him.

"Hey, do you have a minute?"

Mutchnik turned in his chair. Marvin Price, the acting chief of the office, walked in and took a seat.

"Listen, Jim, it looks like your case might go away and you're going to need something to do," Price said. "I want to see about getting you involved in the Grains case."

Mutchnik recognized *Grains* as the division's odd internal code name—short for *Grains and Field Beans*—for the ADM case. He had heard bits and pieces about it from Robin Mann.

"It's a good case," Price said. "And it needs your help. You've obviously done a lot of work with the FBI. It's got tapes and you've done all that. Robin needs another person on the case."

Mutchnik nodded. This was just the kind of assignment he wanted.

"That sounds great, Marvin," he said.

Soon, Mann heard that Mutchnik had joined the case and came to see him. As she described the investigation, not a lot registered with Mutchnik. It was just a bunch of names and places. He was going to need to review the voluminous case records.

But now, a full team of antitrust prosecutors was finally forming for Harvest King.

At 3:45 on December 5 in Columbus, Ohio, Federal District Judge George Smith called a recess in the trial unfolding in his courtroom. He asked the lawyers for the government to come to his chambers.

The trial was the country's most prominent antitrust prosecution in more than a decade. The General Electric Company had been indicted, accused of fixing prices in the industrial diamond market. GE was fighting the charges, and just days before, the prosecution had rested its case.

Once the lawyers arrived in his chambers, Judge Smith gave them shocking news. Before the case went to a jury—before GE even presented a complete defense—he was dismissing the charges. Judge Smith found that, based on the government's evidence, no reasonable person could conclude that the company had committed a crime. GE had won, in the most embarrassing way possible for the government.

News of the government's crushing defeat crackled through the nation's courtrooms and law firms. Everywhere, the questions began to be asked: How could the Antitrust Division have fumbled so badly at the prosecutorial equivalent of the Super Bowl? Was this a group that choked when the stakes were high?

Those questions resounded in Springfield. For weeks, tensions had been building between the U.S. Attorney's office and the Antitrust Division. Often, the agents received complaints from one set of lawyers that they didn't know information the others had been told. The styles were starting to conflict—the antitrust lawyers were used to moving slowly, while the U.S. Attorney's office was more familiar with fast-moving, politically charged cases. But in this situation, neither side was completely in control.

In the weeks that followed the GE decision, articles critical of the Antitrust Division appeared in a variety of publications. The most damning, published in *American Lawyer* magazine, was faxed to the FBI's Springfield office. Agents and supervisors read the article with a growing sense of anxiety. Devastating phrases jumped out:

> The Justice Department antitrust division has had a reputation in recent years for not taking cases to trial—and when they do take them to trial, losing them. . . .
>
> A lot of lawyers distinguish between prosecutors and antitrust division lawyers.

By the time everyone had digested the article, the agents could not help but worry about what this meant for the ADM case. Was the Antitrust Division up to the job?

• • •

In Springfield, a train slowly pulled into the station. Rodger Heaton stood nearby, watching passengers step onto the platform. Finally, he saw them: Robin Mann, Susan Booker, and the new prosecutor on the team, Jim Mutchnik. The antitrust lawyers had arrived for their latest meeting with Whitacre.

Heaton greeted them and escorted them to his car. Popping open the trunk, he shoved some tennis balls and a racquet aside to make room for their luggage. The lawyers traveled to an inexpensive restaurant for lunch before driving to the Decatur Resident Agency to find Shepard and Herndon.

The meeting on this day was intended to help the lawyers write a search warrant in preparation for the raid of ADM. They needed descriptions of the office layout and details about the computer system. Whitacre had been preparing for days to answer their questions.

When the group arrived at the FBI offices, Shepard and Herndon were waiting for them. Mutchnik introduced himself, and the agents welcomed him. The lawyers walked into Shepard's office, and Mutchnik slid into the seat behind the desk. A spot in the center of the room was reserved for their star witness.

Whitacre arrived shortly afterward. The lawyers wanted to meet with him alone this time; Shepard and Herndon took him to another room for a few minutes to make sure he was comfortable with the idea. Afterward, they escorted Whitacre back to the office where the lawyers were waiting.

"Okay, Mark," Shepard said. "Just talk to these guys, and we'll be right next door if you need us."

Shepard and Herndon left, closing the door behind them. Whitacre sat down, looking confident. The lawyers greeted him; Mutchnik introduced himself.

The questioning began, with Heaton taking the lead. Whitacre was astonishingly prepared. He had even brought some ADM documents with him, spelling out internal details of the company.

Mutchnik sat silently behind the desk, impressed with Whitacre. He seemed to be a top-notch executive, involved in an array of important areas at ADM. As Mutchnik listened, he thought about Whitacre's salary—a few hundred thousand dollars a year, from what he understood. It seemed ridiculous, given the value Whitacre brought to ADM. As far as Mutchnik was concerned, Mark Whitacre was tremendously underpaid.

• • •

Herndon popped the latest tape into his TASCAM playback unit with a sense of anticipation. After weeks of being pressed by the agents, Whitacre had finally recorded a conversation with his friend Kuno Sommer from Hoffman-LaRoche. Herndon was eager to hear the man suspected of being at the center of the citric-acid conspiracy.

The conversation began at counter 123. Herndon listened as Sommer talked about a recent trip to China. Sommer mentioned that Terry Wilson had given him a tour of ADM's vitamin C plant and said that he wanted the two companies to talk about their situations with that business. Herndon listened, curious. What was Terry Wilson from the corn-products division doing involved in ADM's vitamin business?

The tape rambled on, with Sommer saying next to nothing about citric acid. Sommer also expressed concerns about talking on the phone—it was easier, he said, to speak in person.

Herndon shut off the TASCAM. Sommer wasn't going to trip up easily.

It was becoming obvious that there wouldn't be a simple way to crack open the citric conspiracy. There were still months of planning necessary before the lysine case could go overt. Other attempts to pursue price-fixing in citric or any other product might risk the secrecy of the lysine case. And right now, secrecy was paramount; if anyone learned what the government was doing, the whole investigation could be endangered.

Whitacre smiled as he walked into Howard Buffett's office on the sixth floor of ADM headquarters. The office was unlike any other in the building. Corporate toys decorated the room, from trucks emblazoned with logos from Coca-Cola or ADM to a plastic Coca-Cola bottle that played music.

"Hey, Howard," Whitacre said, leaning against a credenza behind Buffet's desk. "How's it going?"

Buffett looked at Whitacre, clasping his hands behind his head.

"Not so well, Mark," he said. "I'm thinking of leaving the company."

The news was a shock. Whitacre liked Buffett and considered him a good friend at ADM. They talked all the time.

Whitacre pressed him, hoping to change his mind. But Buffett was fairly well decided. He had been talking about the idea with his father, Warren. He didn't like handling investor relations or watching the way the company was run, Buffett said. The atmosphere at ADM made him uncomfortable.

Beyond that, even though Buffett was an ADM director, Dwayne Andreas often dealt with him like a child. He handled work for ADM in Mexico, where his title "assistant to the Chairman," had about the same prestige as "chief janitor." To gain credibility, he had asked for a new title—one beneath his true role. But Dwayne had refused.

Whitacre argued to no avail. Buffett's frustrations with the company and the Andreases were running too deep. But Whitacre was certain that as soon as the investigation went public, the Andreases would be gone. It was only a matter of months.

Taking a breath, Whitacre glanced at the office door. It was closed.

"I wouldn't leave if I was you," he said. "Things are going to be changing."

"Why?" Buffett asked. "What do you mean?"

Whitacre leaned forward.

"You never know what will happen, Howard," he said softly. "Not too long from now, you and I might be running this place."

CHAPTER 11

"M̲ark, are you an idiot?"

Ginger Whitacre sat on a couch in the family room, cradling a cool drink and staring at her husband in disbelief. For days, he had been endlessly upbeat, almost unreasonably so. But now he was going over the edge. For the past few minutes, as logs crackled in the fireplace, Ginger had listened to Mark describe the glorious future he saw for himself—at ADM.

"No, really," Mark replied earnestly. "When all this goes down, I'm going to be the only one left. Dwayne will be gone, Mick will be gone, Terry will be gone. I'm going to be the only one who can run ADM."

Ginger threw up her hands. "That's totally illogical," she said. "How can you possibly stay there when you've just taken down the company? You think they're going to pat you on the back?"

Mark shook his head. His pep talk with Howard Buffett had emboldened his own expectations. If someone like Buffett—an ADM director—was dissatisfied, other directors almost certainly would feel the same way. Buffett had postponed his resignation plans, so now Whitacre felt he was guaranteed at least one ally on the board. Once ADM's crimes were exposed, Whitacre was convinced, everything would change. He was sure his name would be high on the list of candidates for the permanent chief executive of the company—perhaps even the only one there.

"Ginger, they need me," Mark said. "They need me to run this company. I'm valuable to them. And I did the right thing. The board is going to understand that. They're going to respect that."

Ginger kept arguing, trying to persuade Mark of how irrational his beliefs were. But he wouldn't budge. He was convinced that he would soon be running ADM as a reward for his work with the FBI. He had expressed these thoughts in the first days of the investigation, but had dropped the foolish ideas. Now, somehow, the same unreasonable expectations had crept back into his mind.

The more Ginger saw that glint of excitement in Mark's eyes, the angrier she became. This sudden pipe dream could not have come from nowhere; something had to have triggered it. He was acting as if he had been brainwashed. As Mark argued about his bright destiny, she became certain of who was to blame.

Brian Shepard.

Ginger seethed at the FBI. They were lying to her husband just to keep him in line. They didn't care about him at all. Of that she was convinced.

"We're worried about our guy," Herndon said. "We want to make sure we look out for him."

On the other end of the phone, Jack Cordes from the FBI's contract review unit asked a few questions. What Herndon wanted was not unprecedented but would take time. There were lots of bureaucratic hurdles to clear before the FBI could pay someone who lost his job after working as a cooperating witness.

It was January 10, 1995. With planning under way for the raids on ADM, Shepard and Herndon were beginning to worry about Whitacre. He had become unrealistic, talking all the time about becoming a hero and running ADM. The agents did their best to brace him for the probability that he would be fired, but didn't press. At this point, Whitacre's feelings were bound to be complex. If he needed to believe in a bright future to get through the day, the agents couldn't rip that away. But they could make sure Whitacre wasn't abandoned if he ended up unemployed.

Shepard and Herndon had expressed their concerns to the prosecutors, who were split on the issue. Some wanted the matter resolved by the FBI; others vehemently opposed paying anything. Whitacre wasn't some drug dealer, they argued; he would find another job. But a jury would always look askance at a witness who had been given money by the government.

In the end, the matter was left to the FBI's discretion. By the end of the call with the contract unit, the agents felt more at ease. At least they had gotten the ball rolling.

Six days later, Shepard and Herndon flew to Atlanta to prepare for the price-fixing meeting scheduled for January 18 at the Atlanta Airport

Marriott. When they arrived, the sixteen-story hotel was exceptionally busy. The Cobb Room, where the lysine executives were planning to meet, was booked until 11:00 the next night, leaving Shepard and Herndon cooling their heels for hours. When the agents finally gained access to the room, they saw it had problems, as always. It was spacious enough, with a wood veneer conference table, plenty of padded chairs, and a small buffet cart against a wall. But there was no end table for the lamp; the only furnishing that could hold the camera was a large dresser in the wrong part of the room. Shepard and Herndon moved heavy furniture late into the night.

The room reserved for the command center also made the agents uneasy. It was connected by an inside door to the Cobb Room, meaning that the agents might be heard. Herndon grabbed a towel and stuffed it under the connecting door. It was hardly a high-tech solution. But it would work, so long as the agents whispered.

Early the next morning, Whitacre appeared at Shepard's hotel room, ready for the day. Herndon handled the briefing, again reminding Whitacre to announce if he was leaving the room and to let other executives do as much of the talking as possible.

As Herndon spoke, Shepard walked across the room to check the briefcase recorder one more time. He placed it on the bed and turned it on.

Nothing.

He tried again. Still nothing.

"We might have a problem here," he said evenly.

Herndon came over to look, and the two agents struggled with the case for several minutes. Shepard couldn't understand it. He had tested the device in Decatur, just before they had flown to Atlanta.

Whitacre stood by watching helplessly. Finally, he checked his watch.

"Hey, guys," Whitacre said with an uncomfortable urgency to his voice. "I should probably be in the room when everybody else arrives."

The agents agreed and Whitacre headed down to the meeting room. A few minutes later, the frustrated agents swept up the briefcase and hurried to the command center. Shepard dropped into the seat in front of the monitor, while Herndon called the Atlanta FBI in search of the agents assigned to provide backup.

The Atlanta agents arrived a few minutes later, and Herndon showed them the briefcase unit. After studying it, the group agreed that somehow, the new batteries had died. One of the Atlanta agents, Jay Spadafore, said he had a spare set in his car and rushed to get them. He needed to hurry—the meeting next door was starting. Shepard turned on the camera.

A Korean executive, J. E. Kim from Cheil, was laughing. He had just taken a cab to the Marriott from his hotel, the Renaissance. Kim hadn't realized until he arrived that the hotels were adjacent to each other. Whitacre walked with Kim to the window. The day was sunny and bright, affording a clear view.

"That's right next door," Whitacre said.

"Yes, I didn't know," said Kim. "So I only paid two dollars from Renaissance to here."

Yamamoto from Kyowa Hakko arrived minutes later, just before nine o'clock. Whitacre greeted him and then picked up the telephone, ordering breakfast and scheduling lunch. He hung up the phone as Yamamoto dropped his coat and other belongings near the camera.

"Here, Massy, I'll move this stuff out of the way for you," he said, picking up Yamamoto's belongings. "There has to be a space to hang that."

Kim folded himself into a chair. He mentioned hearing about an earthquake the previous day hitting Kobe, a city in western Japan. Yamamoto nodded, saying he had heard that as many as 2,500 people were dead.

"Yeah," Whitacre said. "They blew up a lysine plant there, too."

Yamamoto nodded, smiling. "Yeah."

Kim was confused. "Lysine plant?" he said, looking at Yamamoto. "Your plant?"

"Yes," Yamamoto said. "And we have to increase the price. A dollar-fifty?"

Yamamoto laughed.

Kim still did not understand. Was the plant partly destroyed?

Smiling, Yamamoto and Whitacre shook their heads.

"No," Whitacre said. "It's a—"

"It's a joke," Yamamoto interrupted.

Everyone laughed heartily.

In the adjoining room, the agents snapped the new batteries into the briefcase. Herndon touched the buttons and the tape started to spin. He hurried over to the phone and dialed the number for the Cobb Room.

• • •

Whitacre answered.

"Hey, it's Bob, I've got your briefcase," Herndon whispered.

"I'm sorry?"

"I've got your briefcase. It's working. I'm going to bring it to you."

"Yeah, that'd be great," Whitacre said.

"Now, I've got a story for what's going on."

"Yeah," Whitacre said. "I already ordered from the menu the other day."

"Good, okay," Herndon whispered. "I'm going to come to the door and say I'm with the hotel staff. I'm going to say I found the briefcase downstairs."

"Okay."

"Okay? So I'll see you in a couple of minutes."

"Thank you," Whitacre said. "Bye-bye."

Whitacre hung up and returned to the table.

By 9:05, the price-fixing meeting was ready to start. Mimoto had arrived and taken a spot at the head of the table. Beside him was a new executive from Ajinomoto, Hisao Shinohara. Jacques Chaudret had scurried in and was at the banquet cart, fixing a cup of coffee. Yamamoto and Kim were on either side. Only Sewon, the Korean company, was not represented.

"We have a couple of other people joinin' us, I think, don't we?" Whitacre asked.

"At, uh, ten-thirty," said Mimoto.

"Two more at that point?" Whitacre asked.

"Two more," Mimoto said.

"Well," Whitacre replied, "we've got plenty of space."

Kim spoke up. Two more were coming from Sewon?

Chaudret, still at the banquet cart, turned to face the others. "No, no," he said. "Two more from Sewon. One from Tyson. One from ConAgra."

The group laughed, amused at the idea of two big lysine customers attending a price-fixing meeting.

Mimoto smiled, staring straight at Whitacre.

"And one from FBI," he said.

Whitacre felt his heart drop, until he heard everyone laughing. It was a joke.

"And seven from the FTC," Whitacre laughed. The Federal Trade Commission, which also enforced antitrust laws, would be as interested as the FBI in what was happening in the Cobb Room.

"Yeah," Mimoto said, looking at his notes, "FTC."

"FBI," Whitacre laughed again, still anxious.

He checked his watch. *Let's get going.*

"Welcome to Atlanta," Whitacre said. "We've been so often to Asia, so often to Europe, it's good that everyone could come here at some point. I think Kanji is going to lead the meeting. And I think the topic here at the beginning would be more volume related."

A knock came at the door. The group paused.

"Yes?" Mimoto said in response. "FTC?"

Whitacre walked to the door and opened it. It wasn't the FTC.

It was the FBI.

Herndon stood in the doorway, briefcase in hand.

"I wonder if I have the right room," he said.

"Yes," Whitacre said.

"This was left down in the cafeteria," Herndon said, holding out the briefcase.

"Okay."

"The bellman thought it might belong to you."

Whitacre took the briefcase. The tape was already running. He shut the door and hurried to the table.

"Uh, the banquet people," Whitacre said as he scooted past Yamamoto. "I left my briefcase in the lobby. When I signed up for food and everything."

"You forgot your briefcase there?" Chaudret asked.

"Yeah."

"Wow!" Chaudret said.

"When I signed up for all the food and everything."

"Very honest, huh?" Chaudret said. "In Paris, it would have already been sold."

"Yeah," said Whitacre. "Luckily, I had all my passports and every-thing still in my room."

Yamamoto, his hand on his chin, looked at Whitacre. "You're keep-ing all document . . . in case?"

Whitacre shook his head. "No, no."

The group laughed again.

The Atlanta recording was another rousing success. For more than an hour, the executives reviewed their 1994 lysine production, praising one another for sticking to the agreed levels. Later, with the arrival of J. S. Kim from Sewon, more evidence of the illegal agreement piled up. Kim argued that Sewon needed a huge increase in its allotted volume. The others objected, saying the proposal would cause a price collapse. By the end, all but Sewon settled on new production levels for 1995—and every company agreed to hike the price to $1.30 a pound.

Days later, Jim Mutchnik, the new antitrust lawyer on the case, walked into a small conference room with a copy of the Atlanta tape. He was amused at how the meeting had just come and gone. This conspiracy no longer fazed the others; with so much evidence already collected, Atlanta was being treated as almost a bother.

But to Mutchnik, Atlanta was a hoot. The first minutes—with everyone joking about the FBI and the FTC—cracked him up. He couldn't believe these executives were sitting there, committing a crime, thinking it was the funniest thing in the world.

Mutchnik watched as, late in the meeting, the executives agreed to set the American price at $1.30. On screen, Mimoto looked at the assembled executives.

"Finished," he announced. "Canada is the same?"

The others wondered, what's the Canadian exchange rate? Jacques Chaudret fished out a newspaper, scouring the financial tables.

"Canada," he said. "What does it say?"

He found the number. The group recalculated $1.30 as $1.83 in Canadian dollars. Mimoto announced the new prices would go into effect the following week.

Mutchnik watched, blown away. In a little more than two minutes, the group had used a newspaper to fix the Canadian market—worth about $100 million.

I can't believe they're doing that, Mutchnik thought. *It can't be that simple.*

The J. Edgar Hoover Building sprawls along a full city block on Pennsylvania Avenue, standing out as one of the most hulking and unattractive parts of official Washington. There, in offices along an inner corridor on the seventh floor, the workings of the FBI are overseen by a group of deputies and assistants who report to the man at the end of the hall, the Bureau Director, Louis Freeh.

In early 1995, one of the newest officials on that corridor was William Esposito, the acting Assistant Director of Division Six, the Bureau's Criminal Investigative Division. He had been promoted the previous fall from Special Agent in Charge in the San Diego Field

Office to Deputy Assistant Director, but quickly moved up. Now, Esposito was responsible for knowing what was happening with every major criminal investigation being conducted by the FBI.

Not long after starting his new job, Esposito was working in his office when his secretary told him that Don Stukey, the SAC from Springfield, was on the line. He snatched up the receiver.

"So, Don, what can I do for you?" Esposito said.

"We've got a case going here that's pretty important," Stukey replied. "But I think we're going to need your help with DOJ."

What was the problem with the Department of Justice? Esposito asked.

The case was dragging, Stukey said. It was an antitrust investigation, and the agents had developed evidence that included excellent tapes. Indictments could have been brought months before, but the Antitrust Division still wouldn't commit to a timetable. Also, Stukey added, there were tensions between the Antitrust Division and the U.S. Attorney's office. The U.S. Attorney seemed prepared to go forward with the case quickly, but Antitrust was pushing to slow down. Stukey was considering going to the Justice Department to appeal for help.

"But before we ratchet this up, I want to make sure we have the backing of headquarters," Stukey said. "This is a very significant case involving influential people, so there's going to be a lot of pressure here. I think it's something that you and others in the division, maybe even the Director's office, need to hear about, so you know what we're getting into. Nobody outside Springfield seems aware of it. There really hasn't been anyone behind it."

Esposito was not surprised. Springfield was hardly a place known for turning out big cases. The name of that office on a case file would have led many at headquarters to pay scant attention. Plus, the Bureau's historical expertise was with violent crime; while white-collar investigations had expanded, headquarters had not yet been affected in any meaningful way. Often, investigations of corporate crimes still failed to attract much interest.

"Okay, Don," Esposito said. "Draft your case agent, bring your charts, bring your tapes, and I'll block out whatever time is needed."

Whitacre walked past the charcoal-gray legions of ADM commodities traders, oblivious to the punctuated rhythm of their barked orders. He headed toward his office, first bidding hello to his secretary.

It was the morning of January 31. Whitacre had returned from Atlanta more than a week before, but had yet to speak with the FBI or the prosecutors. Instead, he had fallen back into the flow of work, forgetting about price-fixing and law enforcement. After all, he still had a business to run.

At his desk, Whitacre picked up the telephone to check his voice messages. There were several, including one from Louisiana that sounded urgent. He called there first. A secretary answered.

"Dr. Jones's office."

"Chris Jones, please. It's Mark Whitacre returning his call."

"Just a moment."

Whitacre leaned back in his chair. He had known Jones at Degussa and had hired him as a consultant a couple of years before on ADM's methionine project.

"Mark," Jones said when he came on the line.

"Hey," Whitacre said. "How you doing?"

"Pretty well. How about you?"

"Fine, fine. What's so urgent?"

"We're having some problems," Jones said, sounding agitated.

"What do you mean?"

"Mark," Jones said, "are you aware of what the FBI is doing down here?"

Minutes later, the "hello" line rang in the Decatur R.A. The line was standard in most FBI offices, often for the use of cooperating witnesses. It was never answered by identifying the location; instead, agents simply picked up and said hello. That way, if any potential defendants checked phone records, the identity of the witness working with the Bureau would still be safe.

Shepard answered the phone.

"Hey, Brian, it's Mark."

"What's going on?"

"Listen, I just got a telephone call from Dr. Chris Jones," Whitacre said. "He's a guy I knew back from Degussa. ADM had him on retainer back when we were considering building a methionine plant."

This was interesting. "What did he want?"

"Well, he told me he was contacted by an associate, a guy named Tim Hall. Hall said that he'd been interviewed by an FBI agent named Craig Dahle."

"Okay."

"Jones told me that the interview was all about possible theft of technical information from Degussa, stuff about methionine-plant construction."

For several minutes, Whitacre reviewed the history of ADM's involvement in methionine. Jones, he said, had accompanied him on trips to evaluate possible sites for a plant. But ultimately, the idea was shelved, and ADM had done the Rhone-Poulenc deal.

"Well, Mark, tell me this," said Shepard, "are you aware if Jones provided you with any protected or proprietary information? Do we have a case on him?"

"No, definitely not. Definitely not."

" 'No, he didn't do it,' or 'No, you don't know'?"

"Well, I don't *know* that he did anything. I mean, back when he met with Randall and me, we asked if any of the information he had was protected or copyrighted. He told us it wasn't and that the patents had expired. That's what he told us."

Shepard tried a few more questions, but Whitacre insisted there was not a problem, adding that Jones had assured ADM that the methionine technology used by Degussa had been the same since 1949.

Shepard decided to push. "Mark, did you direct Jones to obtain any information that you knew to be proprietary or protected in nature?"

"Definitely not. Definitely not."

Jones had told him the investigation seemed to be spreading, Whitacre said. The FBI was planning to interview Jones, other ADM employees, and Whitacre himself. A grand jury was likely to be convened soon.

The call ended, and Shepard looked up the number for Craig Dahle. He wanted to let him know that there was no reason to keep his investigation a secret from Whitacre anymore.

Dahle flew immediately from Mobile to Decatur. Now that Whitacre knew all about the case, the agent wanted to interview him right away. Shepard and Herndon met Dahle and drove him to a Forsyth hotel. Whitacre arrived soon after, seeming eager and nervous. Shepard handled the introductions, telling Whitacre that Dahle would be asking all of the questions today.

Whitacre nodded. "Okay," he said.

He sat across the table from Dahle, who began by asking about the call from the previous day. Whitacre repeated the story he had told Shepard.

"Now, I haven't spoken to Chris Jones in something like a year and a half," Whitacre said, "so I was really surprised to hear from him."

"What did you think about what he had to say?"

"I didn't know what he was talking about. I was surprised to hear about all this."

Jones, Whitacre said, was incensed, arguing that the investigation was caused by a Degussa executive who was angry with him for leaving the company.

Whitacre said that he had ended the phone call by promising to get back to Jones in a couple of days. But already, Jones had left two more messages on Whitacre's voice mail.

Dahle flipped through his notes. "All right, why don't we back up a little bit," he said. "Tell me the chronology of ADM's efforts to build a methionine plant and how Jones and Hall relate to that."

Whitacre laid out the story again. He had decided to add methionine to ADM's product line and took steps toward that in 1992. Jones, he said, was a renowned methionine expert and the logical person to call.

"I asked Jones what it would take to get him involved. He told me he needed a ten-thousand-dollar-a-month retainer. That seemed acceptable, and it was the kind of arrangement that was very common for ADM."

They worked together for six months, looking for plant sites. At one point, Whitacre said, he became aware that he would need more of Jones's time and increased the retainer to $20,000 a month. At that time, Jones had suggested Tim Hall as a plant manager. Whitacre didn't know Hall but interviewed him and was impressed. Later, Whitacre said, Jones suggested putting Hall on retainer. He told the agents that he had agreed, and ADM had begun paying Hall $10,000 a month.

"Did you have reason to suspect that any of the information you were receiving was from Degussa?"

"Never," Whitacre said. "At my initial meeting, I asked Jones about infringement problems. He told me there were patents, but said if we built a methionine plant, we wouldn't want to use Degussa's procedure."

Whitacre wrapped up by describing how ADM had junked the project and instead bought into Rhone-Poulenc's methionine plant. Dahle had one question left: Would Whitacre be willing to tape a call with Jones right now? Whitacre shrugged. Sure.

The agents decided to place the call from Whitacre's car phone. Shepard and Dahle followed Whitacre out to the parking lot and hooked up the recording equipment. Afterward, they listened as Whitacre spoke with Jones. Nothing jumped out.

When they were done, Whitacre shook the hand of each agent and headed home. Once he was gone, the agents got back together. What did Dahle think?

"His story sounds believable," Dahle said.

Herndon pulled his coat closed, bracing against a bitter chill that had descended on Washington, D.C., in the first week of February. He was walking down Pennsylvania Avenue alongside Don Stukey and Kate Killham, his new squad leader. The day had arrived for the presentation to headquarters on Harvest King.

At a security checkpoint, the agents flashed their creds and signed in. After receiving visitor's identification cards, they were escorted to a conference room where a television and VCR were already set up. Herndon opened his briefcase, pulling out a videotape containing portions of several price-fixing meetings—the "greatest hits," as the agents liked to call them. He put the tape inside the VCR.

The room was soon filled with supervisors from the Bureau's Financial Crimes Section, including its chief, Thomas Kubic. Joining him was Alix Suggs, who had recently been assigned as the new Washington supervisor on Harvest King.

Once everyone was seated, Herndon took to the floor with a memorized speech.

"Hi, my name is Bob Herndon. I am one of the co–case agents working the Harvest King investigation."

He held up a small stick. "As you can see, I drew the short straw," he said to laughter.

Herndon outlined the case, telling the group it involved price-fixing of lysine.

"Lysine is fed to chickens, making them fat, dumb, and happy," he explained. "However, as consumers, you and I are not necessarily fat, dumb, and happy because each time we go to McDonald's and order Chicken McNuggets, we're paying slightly more than we would have."

After finishing his overview, Herndon hit the Play button on the VCR. The supervisors watched portions from Irvine, Hawaii, and Atlanta. As the scenes unfolded, a sense of delight was in the air.

When the video finished, Herndon took the floor again. Despite the quality of the evidence, there were still two issues of concern, he said.

"First, we need to see if we have enough prosecutors on the team," he said. There was no clear leader among the various prosecutors in the case. And the Chicago antitrust office was in transition, having just been assigned a new chief, Jim Griffin.

"It has become particularly confusing to brief everybody," Herndon said. "We don't always know which ones to go to."

Was the confusion about leadership causing any big problems? the supervisors asked.

"It's not really a big issue now," Herndon said. "But we can see a complication once this goes overt."

Stukey took over from Herndon, making a short presentation about the need to prepare a financial package for Whitacre in the event he lost his job. As Stukey spoke, Herndon handed out a package of materials that Whitacre had provided about his finances. The supervisors were awestruck as they glanced through it. Whitacre's expenses totaled $17,680 a month. It was hard to imagine that anyone could afford to spend so much.

Herndon flipped open his notebook case. Reaching inside the inner pocket, he removed a slender piece of paper and held it up for everyone to see. It was a Christmas card from the Whitacres, complete with a photograph of the whole family.

"I wanted everyone to see this," Herndon said. "This is our CW, Mark Whitacre, along with his family. I carry this picture with me all the time as a constant reminder that he is a real person with a real family dependent on him. He has taken some serious risks with his career to help us. The only reason we have the kinds of tapes that you've just seen is because of this man. We want to make sure that, if necessary, the Bureau is ready to stand behind him."

Tom Kubic held up a hand. "If he loses his job because of his cooperation, we'll be in line before you are, Bob," he said. "Don't worry about that."

Later that day, Alix Suggs, the Washington supervisor in charge of Harvest King, called around headquarters looking for Herndon and Kate Killham. She found them speaking with some Bureau computer experts.

"Bob, I've been looking all over for you," she said. Esposito, the Assistant Director, had just been told about the tape. "He wants to see it right now."

The Assistant Director? This had escalated to the seventh floor. Herndon's heart was in his throat.

Killham was all gung-ho when he told her. "Come on, Bob, let's go up there," she buzzed.

"*You* go up there," he said.

"No, Bob," she said, grabbing him by the arm. "You're coming, too."

About that moment, Esposito was settling into a chair in the seating area of his office. On one side of the room, Tom Kubic and Don Stukey were opening a wooden cabinet, revealing a television and video player. Stukey loaded the "greatest-hits" tape, while Kubic pulled over a chair for a better view.

Grainy black-and-white images filled the screen. Stukey tried describing the action but didn't have a case agent's familiarity with the players. To his relief, Herndon and Killham arrived soon afterward. Herndon immediately took over narrating the video.

At the end of the tape, Esposito stood up, a grin on his face.

"Listen, I'm no expert on antitrust matters," he said as he shook Herndon's hand. "But based on what I just saw, I think we've got a pretty good case here."

The agents thanked Esposito for his time and headed out the door. Esposito asked Stukey to stay behind for a minute. Both men sat.

"Jesus, is anybody else aware of this?" Esposito said. From what he had seen, this was one of the FBI's biggest white-collar cases—and nobody at headquarters knew a thing about it. Using just two agents was crazy; a dozen would have been reasonable.

"Your agents have done a good job," Esposito continued. "But knowing what's going to happen and the size of this company, you're going to have to put in for a lot of people. You need to think long-range. Figure out what resources you're going to need, and give me a game plan I can start supporting here."

Stukey promised to come back with a proposal.

"One more thing," Esposito said. "If you need help with DOJ, let me know. If necessary, I'll go across the street and try to take care of it."

Stukey thanked him. Across the street, he knew, were the main offices of the Department of Justice. Finally, FBI headquarters was ready to go to bat for Springfield and Harvest King.

Louis Freeh, the Director of the FBI, walked toward the conference table in his office. A group of assistant directors were taking their seats, ready for the 8:00 morning briefing. Freeh, in shirtsleeves, slid into a chair at the head of the table.

"Anybody have any news?" Freeh asked, glancing around the room. He mentioned an item he had read in the *Washington Post* that morning, and the group discussed the article for a moment. The meeting moved at a fast clip. Freeh liked to get things done.

He turned to an assistant director. "What have you got for me?" he asked.

This was a chance to update Freeh on events of the last twenty-four hours and to let him know what to expect for the next twenty-four. The assistant director described his division's recent activities, and Freeh followed up with a few questions.

He looked at Esposito. "All right, Billy," he said. "What have you got?"

Esposito looked down at his notes and described a handful of cases. He flipped a page.

"Also, I just had a briefing on the ADM case, out of Springfield," he said. "It's a significant case, and it's going to involve a lot of resources."

Esposito glanced up. Several of his colleagues were wearing baffled expressions. One leaned forward.

"What," he asked, "is ADM?"

"The Archer Daniels Midland Company."

More blank stares. "What's that?"

"It's a Fortune 500 company, one of the world's biggest grain producers."

Esposito glanced at Freeh, whose eyes were gleaming with recognition. The Director knew the name.

"How strong a case is it?" Freeh asked. "If it's ADM, it had better be good."

Esposito nodded. A company as powerful as ADM had the legal firepower to blow apart any weak case.

"It's got tapes, and I've actually seen some of them," he said. "They're excellent."

Esposito described the videos. Freeh peppered him with questions, the kind of reaction that signaled that this case had caught his attention.

"All right, that sounds good," Freeh finally said. "Let's stay on top of it."

He turned to another assistant director.

"What have you got?" he asked.

The tensions among the Harvest King prosecutors seemed to be escalating. As long as the case was in the investigative stage, their differences could be buried. But now, with the case moving toward going public, there was no more papering over the conflicts.

The antitrust lawyers wanted to move slowly and to participate directly in the interviews on the night of the raid. Their division often played a hands-on role during investigations, sometimes to the dismay of FBI agents unfamiliar with their approach. But the prosecutors with the Springfield U.S. Attorney's Office usually took the opposite tack. They wanted to leave the FBI alone and let the agents conduct the raids on their own—so long as they struck soon and struck hard.

In early February, the prosecutors and the agents were on a conference call, discussing plans for the raids. The group agreed that lawyers would be needed in a command center to field questions. Mann mentioned that she wanted to participate in some of the drop-in interviews with potential defendants. In particular, she wanted to take part in the meeting with Wilson.

The Springfield prosecutors had never heard of such an idea. Investigation was for the agents; prosecution was for lawyers. Joe Hartzler, on the phone in Springfield, spoke up.

"Look, Robin, Bob and Brian can do this themselves," he said. "They're much better at confrontational interviews, much better at going to someone's house and handling the unexpected."

"I still think it's important to have a lawyer along who understands the antitrust law," Mann said. "It would help."

Hartzler couldn't believe what he was hearing.

"How many confrontational interviews have you done?" he snapped. "How many doors have you kicked in? How many arrests have you made?"

Shepard and Herndon listened in, silently siding with Hartzler. They weren't familiar with the practices at the Antitrust Division and weren't comfortable with the idea of Mann tagging along. But Mann stuck to her position.

"Well, Joe, I've been on confrontational interviews," she said. "And I think it's smart for us to be on those interviews."

Hartzler did a slow burn. This was so far outside standard practice for a U.S. Attorney's office that he couldn't believe it. He thought Mann was snowing him.

"Robin," he said sharply, "we need people handling this who know what they're doing."

"Would that be you?" Mann shot back.

Everyone was uncomfortable, and one of the prosecutors changed the subject. A few minutes later, Mann raised a technical issue on another matter.

"Do you agree with that, Joe?" she asked Hartzler.

Pause.

Nothing.

Hartzler had left the conference call.

Frances Hulin, the Springfield U.S. Attorney, worried about the conflicts with Antitrust. Clearly, somebody needed to take charge. Bickering among prosecutors would only help the potential defendants.

Hulin was planning to travel to Washington and decided to use the opportunity to meet with Anne Bingaman, the Assistant Attorney General in charge of the Antitrust Division. Between them, she hoped, they would work out this problem. Hulin made the arrangements and then called a few of her assistants to her third-floor office to announce her decision.

"I'm going to meet with Anne Bingaman," she said. "I want to make a pitch to take over the case."

Hulin looked at her assistants and asked what they thought of the idea.

"Institutionally," Hartzler said, "the Antitrust Division would have to resist. If U.S. Attorney's offices around the country start picking up criminal antitrust cases, there would be very little reason for the Antitrust Division to handle them."

Well, Hulin said, such changes had happened before. The Tax Division used to prosecute all criminal tax cases; now many were filed by U.S. Attorneys. She turned to Rick Cox, her First Assistant.

"I've got to side with Joe," he said. "I don't think this is likely to happen."

But Hulin was determined to try. On Friday, February 24, she showed up in Washington at the Antitrust Division's offices at the Department of Justice. At first, Anne Bingaman was busy, and Hulin had to return a couple of times. When they finally got together, Bingaman was friendly and gracious, quickly whisking Hulin into her office. Both women sat down. After some initial chatting, Hulin got to the point.

"As you know, my office has been working for some time on the ADM investigation," she began.

That night, Herndon was eating out with his family at a local Applebee's restaurant. His parents were visiting from Kansas City to see their new granddaughter and for once, Harvest King was not in the forefront of his mind.

Herndon was sitting at the table when his pager went off. He checked the number; it was Rodger Heaton.

"I'll be right back," he told his family.

He headed to the restaurant's pay phone and had Heaton on the line in a few minutes.

"I just talked to Frances," Heaton said. "She says that Anne Bingaman just gave her the case. She told Frances 'You're in charge.'"

Herndon was stunned. "Are you sure, Rodger?"

"That's what Frances says. She said that Anne thinks Frances's plan to go to the grand jury in March and then go public soon after sounded great."

Herndon glanced around the restaurant, trying to collect his thoughts. This was too much, too fast.

"Does Antitrust know this?" Herndon asked. "I mean Antitrust in Chicago."

"There's going to be a meeting on Monday. Your bosses are all going to come over, and we're going to talk about this. But yeah, we're going forward."

The two men wrapped up the call. Herndon was astonished; after all this time, the tenor of the entire case had changed. Now, there was only one group of prosecutors in charge, and the raids were finally going to take place—quickly. Shepard needed to know right away. Herndon dropped more change in the pay phone and called his partner at home.

"Brian, you're not going to believe this," he said. "I just spoke with Rodger Heaton. Frances Hulin has the case now, and they're talking about grand jury next month and going public next month."

"You're kidding!" Shepard said. "No way. They didn't give up this case."

"How can there be a miscommunication? You would think something like this would be clear as day."

Shepard paused. "What are we going to say to Robin and Jim?" he asked.

At 1:00 on Monday, Shepard and Herndon showed up in Hulin's office along with Stukey, John Hoyt, and Kate Killham. Heaton and Hartzler were already there.

Hulin described her meeting with Bingaman, saying there was no doubt about the outcome. "We're in charge of the case."

Quickly, Hulin issued marching orders. She wanted the case

presented to a grand jury for indictment in two weeks. The raids would take place April 3.

"Let's hit 'em fast," Hulin said. "The case is not complicated if we keep it to lysine. A jury will convict off the tapes. We won't need many witnesses."

Everyone headed out, ready to put the plan into action. But almost no one believed that the Chicago antitrust lawyers would accept such a crushing defeat without putting up a fight.

In Washington, Bingaman was at her computer, typing an e-mail to her deputy and the Chicago office.

"Frances Hulin came to see me," Bingaman typed. "She's concerned that we coordinate this case appropriately, although it doesn't sound as if we have not. She just wanted to touch base with me to tell me her plans to take her cooperating witness before the grand jury on March 6."

Bingaman explained how, in their meeting, Hulin had stressed the importance of speed.

"It was a cordial visit, and she seemed genuinely interested in working closely together with us," she typed. "I was somewhat surprised that the March 6 date was coming so soon, because I had not previously been aware of that date."

Bingaman finished and hit the Send button.

News of Hulin's maneuver hit Chicago like a bomb. The prosecutors raged at what they saw as her high-handedness. Some even suspected that Herndon and Shepard had been behind the effort. The FBI had made no secret about its impatience with the division's slower pace. But this was an *antitrust* case. How could Bingaman not see what was happening?

Together, the prosecutors—led by the new office chief, Jim Griffin— composed their own e-mail to Bingaman's deputy, Gary Spratling.

"It was our understanding that we would not be presenting the witness in March," they wrote. "Ms. Hulin's proposal is precipitous."

They explained several reasons why the cooperating witness should not be put in front of the grand jury quickly, adding one note at the end.

"The important issue here is not when the CW testifies, but whether the Antitrust Division or Ms. Hulin makes this and other future litigation decisions."

• • •

By that afternoon, the turf battle between the Antitrust Division and the Springfield U.S. Attorney had spun out of control. No one—except perhaps Hulin—was sure who was running the case anymore. A conference call was scheduled among Hulin, the Antitrust Division, and the FBI supervisors in Springfield. Stukey and Hoyt went to Hulin's office, gathering at a table around a speakerphone.

For the first twenty minutes of the call, nobody raised the main issue. The call descended into chitchat, as everyone pledged cooperation. Bingaman eventually launched into a discussion of the Antitrust Division's accomplishments.

"We've made marvelous changes here, streamlining the department," she said. "We want strong prosecutions and nothing but the best attorneys."

As Bingaman droned on, Hoyt became restless. He decided to get to the point.

"Excuse me, Ms. Bingaman," he interrupted. "This is John Hoyt from the FBI. One of the confusions here for the FBI is, who is the head prosecutor? Who is going to be in charge of *this* investigation?"

Silence.

Hulin spoke up. "Remember, we discussed this? We talked about my office taking charge of the case?"

Silence.

Finally, Bingaman spoke.

"I have remade this Antitrust Division," she said. "I am the Assistant Attorney General responsible for antitrust cases. I have been personally appointed to that task by the President of the United States."

Pause.

"And it will be over my dead, kicking, screaming body before this case is taken away from the Antitrust Division. We have been in charge, and we will continue to be in charge. Thank you very much."

Hulin went pale. No one had expected Bingaman to lash out, or could understand how the two lawyers had miscommunicated so badly. A few perfunctory words were uttered, if only to put distance between Bingaman's sharp statements and the end of the call.

"Thank you all very much for your time," Hulin said as the conversation closed. She pushed a button on the speakerphone and closed her notebook.

"Well," she said to the assembled group, "I guess we're out of this."

• • •

After the conference call, the Chicago antitrust lawyers telephoned Spratling, the division deputy. Everyone was elated at Bingaman's performance.

"God, she's good," Spratling said. "When she wants to do something like that, she's fantastic."

The Chicago lawyers—Mann, Mutchnik, Griffin, Booker, and Marvin Price—felt happy and wrung out. After work, they headed to a bar at the John Hancock Center. There, they laughed and toasted with margaritas, ready to tranquilize their frayed nerves following the fervent, victorious fight.

The departure of Hulin's office from the case left Shepard and Herndon reeling. Not only were Heaton and Hartzler out of the picture, but now the prosecutors who *were* on the case seemed to believe that the agents had tried an end run around them. They felt like the children of a bad divorce.

Almost two weeks passed without a call from the antitrust lawyers. After years of almost daily contact, the change sent a strong message. Each morning, the agents discussed the strain. When were the lawyers going to call? Was today the day?

Finally, they decided to make the first move. Shepard and Herndon picked up extensions in the Decatur office and dialed Jim Mutchnik. He seemed approachable, and, unlike Mann, had not dedicated years of his life to ADM. Mutchnik, they figured, might give them the benefit of the doubt. Besides, they couldn't keep working the case without talking to *somebody*.

"Jim Mutchnik."

"Hey, it's Brian and Bob," Herndon said.

"Hi, guys," Mutchnik said. His tone was professional, maybe a bit wary.

The three men spoke. Gradually, the ice between them seemed like it was beginning to thaw.

For two weeks, the agents called Mutchnik every day, transforming him into their lifeline to the Chicago office. But the problems between them had never been faced head-on; the conversations at times were stilted and laced with an undertone of suspicion.

One day, the agents were speaking with Mutchnik when a click sounded on the line. The agents paused.

"Are you recording this?" Herndon asked.

The question had been sarcastic. But it was the wrong time to be joking.

"I can't believe you would ask me that question!" Mutchnik snapped. "I wouldn't do that to you. We've been talking for two weeks and you still don't trust me!"

Herndon backpedaled. "Jim, you're overreacting. I was joking, making light of this tension between us."

"You weren't joking."

"Yes, I was."

Mutchnik took a breath. In his mind, the agents had learned nothing. The conversations over the past two weeks had simply been their attempt to pump him for information.

"Fine," Mutchnik said. "Let's just finish up what we need to do."

The call ended uncomfortably. Soon, Herndon called back.

"Listen," he said. "I just want to apologize."

"I want you to understand something, Bob," Mutchnik said. "I'm not your inside guy. I'm not your cooperating witness. I don't want that role. I won't record you, but I won't be your inside guy here. If you want to understand what we do, great. But don't treat me the way you treat an enemy."

The blowout served its purpose. All of the emotions and anger were finally on the table. From there, their relationship had nowhere to go but up.

Later that month, Mann and Mutchnik traveled to Washington to brief Spratling and other top antitrust officials. Jim Griffin and Marvin Price, his deputy, both came along.

They met in Spratling's office in the Justice Department building. Spratling, a large man with an eager, friendly face, was waiting for them. He called in a few associates before the briefing began.

Robin Mann took the lead. She had brought along a copy of the greatest-hits tape, and loaded it into Spratling's video player. For more than an hour, Mann narrated the events on the screen. She seemed comfortable and confident.

His hand covering his mouth, Spratling shook his head, awed by what he saw.

"My God, I can't believe that," he said while watching Mick Andreas at Irvine. "This is amazing."

The video ended, and Mann wrapped up. She glowed as the assembled lawyers praised the case.

"You have just done a great job," Spratling said, shaking Mann's hand. "I can't say enough."

With the meeting over, Mann and Mutchnik headed downstairs for lunch, feeling pretty good. Promising to catch up with them, Griffin and Price stayed behind to discuss a few personnel issues. When they finished, Spratling asked to speak with Griffin privately.

"Jim, this a great case," Spratling said. "And you've had a lot of experience in twenty years."

Griffin listened, already knowing where Spratling was headed.

Mann and Mutchnik returned from lunch with the sense that something was up. Griffin had never joined them in the cafeteria. Spratling asked the two lawyers into his office, inviting them to take a seat.

"You have done a wonderful job on a very important case," Spratling told them. "Now that this is getting ready to move to the next stage, I tried to write down all the best trial lawyers in the division. I asked Joe Widmar to do the same thing. And we both had Jim Griffin at the top of our list."

Realization struck Mann and Mutchnik. They didn't even need to hear Spratling say the words.

"Jim's going to be your new lead attorney," Spratling said.

The two lawyers didn't know what to say. Mann felt crushed, but said little. Neither knew it, but Griffin had said he would step aside if Mann and Mutchnik handled the news badly. But both kept their own feelings buried as best they could.

Griffin came in and assured Mann and Mutchnik that their roles would still be significant on the newly constituted team. Mann and Mutchnik nodded and asked questions.

When the meeting was over, Mann, Mutchnik, and Price headed downstairs and flagged down a cab. They rode in silent anger for several minutes. Finally, as the cab approached L'Enfant Plaza, one of them gave voice to their shared suspicion. Appointing Griffin as lead counsel was not some new idea that had occurred to Spratling today. This whole meeting had been a setup, one that had been put in place a long time ago.

Griffin moved quickly to smooth over the raw feelings between the Chicago antitrust office and the FBI. He set up a meeting in Springfield, planning to introduce himself to the FBI supervisors. But first, on the evening of March 20, he arranged for a dinner between the lawyers and the agents.

The group gathered at the restaurant in the Holiday Inn South in Springfield, just past six-thirty. Sitting around a large circular table, the discomfort was palpable. Shepard, who usually opened meetings with a few comments, said little. The agents studied the new lawyer; his voice was soft and his demeanor charming. It was hard to imagine him playing hardball.

Griffin guided the conversation, talking amiably about how Chicago's cold weather was playing havoc with his running schedule; already, a ski mask had frozen to his face during a jog. Attempting to ease the tension at the table, Herndon and Shepard joined in, comparing their workouts with Griffin's.

There was a pause. Griffin shifted to the matter at hand.

"We're all in agreement on where we need to go from here," Griffin said. "Let's get this thing going, get this train on the track. We're going to get these guys, and we're going to do it soon. You've done a great job getting the evidence. My job now is to take all your hard work and not disappoint you."

Herndon and Shepard nodded, relief sweeping over them. Griffin was speaking their language.

On April 8, Kanji Mimoto picked up the phone in his Paris hotel room. He had just received an unusual urgent message to call Whitacre and had few doubts about what was on the ADM executive's mind.

In recent months, Ajinomoto had finally concluded that ADM's Bioproducts Division was indeed using one of the Japanese company's proprietary microorganisms. Since 1992—when Mimoto had failed in his attempt to steal ADM's lysine bug during a plant tour—Ajinomoto had continued developing proof for its suspicions. Evidence had finally turned up with another ADM microbe, used to produce an amino acid called threonine. Two days before, Ajinomoto had filed a federal lawsuit accusing ADM of illegally using the Japanese company's patented microbe. As Mimoto dialed the number, he could imagine Whitacre's fevered reaction to the litigation.

He didn't have to imagine for long.

"Kanji, I can't believe you guys would file a lawsuit without warning us first," Whitacre sputtered. "Mick Andreas is really angry about it."

Mimoto explained that Ajinomoto had to protect its interests, but

Whitacre didn't want to hear it. ADM's bug had nothing to do with Ajinomoto, he protested; it had been purchased from a Swedish company called ABP. And this suit was going to cause plenty of problems that Ajinomoto hadn't planned for.

"What problems?" Mimoto asked.

The next price-fixing meeting was coming up in Hong Kong on April 21, Whitacre said, and because of the suit, Mick Andreas was forbidding him to go.

Mimoto responded in soothing, reassuring tones, stressing the importance of their meetings. The price and volume agreements had been profitable for both companies; they shouldn't stop now. By the end of the call, Whitacre promised to be in Hong Kong but continued prodding for ways to work out this lawsuit. Mimoto muttered some reassuring comments before saying good-bye.

In Decatur, Whitacre hung up. There was no recording device to shut off. Even though he had been discussing price-fixing meetings with Mimoto, he had decided not to tape this particular call. This was a conversation that he didn't want the FBI to hear.

Bill Esposito, head of the FBI's Criminal Investigative Division, sat at his desk reviewing a communication about Harvest King. For weeks, he had been working to keep his promise to Don Stukey, making sure that bureaucratic snafus in Washington didn't hinder the case.

But still, something about Harvest King bothered him. The cooperating witness, given his position and authority, was unlike any Esposito had ever seen, and he felt perplexed. Why would Whitacre risk so much?

Before this case went public, Esposito thought, somebody in the Bureau needed to take a closer look at Whitacre, to try and get a better understanding of his motivations. The case agents would never have the time for the assignment; this was a management problem.

Esposito called Springfield, suggesting that an agent needed to be assigned to investigate Whitacre's background. The supervisors were cool to the idea. Esposito knew he would have to ride them a bit to make sure he got a full answer.

On the morning of April 19, a truck carrying a bomb made of fertilizer and fuel oil parked on the north side of the Alfred P. Murrah Federal Building in Oklahoma City. The driver, Timothy McVeigh, fled the vehicle. Within minutes, the bomb exploded, rupturing support columns and triggering a progressive collapse at the front of the building. By the time the rubble was cleared, 168 people would be dead.

Five days after the attack in Oklahoma, a mail bomb exploded in the offices of a timber industry lobbying group, killing one person. The device was quickly traced to the Unabomber, the then-anonymous architect of a two-decade campaign of terror.

The double-barreled terrorist assaults were unprecedented in American history and triggered a massive response from federal law enforcement. Hundreds of FBI agents from around the country were assigned. Louis Freeh and his division chiefs flocked to the command center on the Hoover Building's fifth floor. Esposito was there for weeks, eighteen hours a day, until he was dispatched personally to Oklahoma.

With two high-priority cases demanding unparalleled resources and attention, other investigations of less urgency were placed on the back burner. Esposito in particular had little time for much else. His desire to investigate the cooperating witness in Harvest King was all but forgotten.

Shepard and Whitacre sat beside each other in a car parked in the lot of St. Mary's Hospital in Decatur. Whitacre had been to Hong Kong for the latest price-fixing meeting, and Shepard had collected notes and other evidence from him.

As they wrapped up, Shepard handed Whitacre some tapes and other material that he might need. He suggested that Whitacre put them in his briefcase.

"That's okay, Brian," Whitacre said. "My briefcase is kind of loaded with work anyway."

Shepard nodded and said good-bye, pushing open the door and heading to his own car. Whitacre pulled away, relieved. He was glad Shepard hadn't forced him to open the briefcase. It would have been impossible to explain why it was stuffed with wads of cash totaling tens of thousands of dollars.

With Shepard assigned for more than two years to a single case, the daily work of the Decatur R.A. had fallen to another agent, John Bruch. Working at a nearby desk in the small office, Bruch was keenly aware of developments in the ADM investigation, but for the most part had little involvement. Instead, he handled other cases that were the lifeblood of the Bureau. The FBI couldn't shut down in this part of Illinois simply because of one large investigation.

At 9:55 on the morning of April 27, Bruch was alone in his office when he heard the hello line ring. He knew it was probably Whitacre calling. He walked over and picked up the phone.

"Hello?" he said.

There was silence for an instant. "Is this a federal government location?" a voice asked.

Bruch didn't hesitate. "You must have the wrong number," he said.

The caller hung up.

Twenty-five minutes later, Bruch was back at his desk when the main line rang. He picked up the phone.

"FBI," he said.

Hesitation.

"I must have the wrong number," the caller said before hanging up.

Bruch placed the phone back in its cradle, his stomach churning. The caller's voice had sounded familiar. It was, he thought, the same person who had just called the hello line.

Was somebody on to them?

Bruch dialed the Springfield office. He needed to speak to a supervisor right away.

CHAPTER 12

As he waited for an elevator, Whitacre glanced toward a gourmet delicatessen on the ground floor of a Chicago office building. The lobby was elegant, the space airy. Even though the skies were dark this day, May 18, 1995, a glass ceiling coaxed in light. The elevator arrived and Whitacre stepped in, punching the button for the sixth floor, the new location for the Midwest office of the Antitrust Division.

The planning for the raids had shifted into high gear. Whitacre was attending numerous meetings to answer the remaining questions. Prosecutors and agents wanted to know the comings and goings of executives, the design of the office, the location of records, anything. And they needed to prep Whitacre for his grand jury appearance, which was anticipated soon.

Now, on top of everything, the odd call to the hello line had jangled nerves in the government. Maybe someone was suspicious; time might be running out for the covert investigation. The Bureau had placed a pen register on the line, to record the number of anyone else who called. So far, no one had.

Whitacre stepped off the elevator, walking across a marble floor toward the antitrust office. Inside, he was whisked to a conference room with Mann and Mutchnik. Whitacre sat at one end of a large wood-veneer table, with Mutchnik on the opposite side. Mann handled the interview, tossing out questions. But Whitacre seemed distracted.

"Don't you think, guys, everything will be okay for me?" he interrupted at one point. "Don't you think they'll recognize I did a good thing?"

"We don't know, Mark," Mann said.

"They'll take out the bad guys, but I'll be okay, don't you think?"

"We don't know, Mark. There's no way we could know. But let's get back to what we're doing."

Mann turned to the beginnings of the case. This whole Fujiwara episode, where Whitacre claimed to have received an extortion call from the Japanese, what was that about? "Walk us through the story," she said.

Whitacre nodded uncomfortably.

"Well, we were having production problems," Whitacre replied. "And they just didn't make sense."

While there was no extortion call, Whitacre said, he did believe there was sabotage. But no one would take his concerns seriously, so he had made up the call to get people to look into the problem.

Mutchnik said nothing. To him, it sounded like Whitacre had bungled production and come up with this wacky idea to buy time. It had been a dangerous gambit, he figured, one that Whitacre had over-played.

As the meeting broke, Mutchnik glanced out the window and saw it was drizzling. His softball team was scheduled to play that night, and he was planning to be there, rain or shine. He hurried down the hall-way, changed into his sweats, and left. As he walked outside through the lobby door, he froze in his tracks.

Whitacre was beneath an overhang of the office building, staring across the street at a bank. Mutchnik walked up beside him.

"Share a cab?" he asked.

Whitacre, standing straight, continued staring at the bank.

"No, I'm meeting somebody."

The rain picked up.

"You sure?" Mutchnik asked. "I'm heading north; we can share a cab."

Whitacre's stare didn't break.

"No, I'm okay," he said, sounding detached. "I'll see you soon. It's nice getting to know you, Jim. I think you're a smart guy."

Whitacre continued to stand motionless as Mutchnik hailed a cab.

"Okay, Mark," Mutchnik said. "I'll see you."

As the cab pulled away, Mutchnik looked out the back. He watched as Whitacre moved from his sheltered spot and walked up the street, getting soaked in the rain.

The sight chilled Mutchnik. With the raids coming, he knew Whitacre's guts must be churning—about what he had done, about

what he faced. That night, Mark Whitacre had to be the most con-
flicted person on the planet.

What a confused, mixed-up guy, Mutchnik thought.

Mark Cheviron felt proud. The ADM security chief was to be honored
at a special meeting on June 29 at the Waldorf Astoria Hotel in New
York. Not only that, but Dwayne Andreas would receive a tribute, too.
Cheviron wanted to be sure everything went right. After all, it wasn't
every company that received accolades from the Federal Bureau of
Investigation.

At the meeting, Cheviron would be named chairman to an advisory
board of the FBI National Academy, a Bureau program for local law enforcement. Dwayne Andreas was to be named honorary chairman.

On May 31, Cheviron dictated a memo to Claudia Manning,
Andreas's secretary, spelling out details of the Waldorf celebration.
He listed the expected attendees, including executives from Merrill
Lynch & Co., Johnson & Johnson, and IBM.

"Thanks for all your help in getting this off the ground," Cheviron
dictated. The memo was typed and sent to Manning.

Cheviron didn't know it, but he had just inadvertently created the
only document that might obstruct the tidal wave bearing down on his
company.

"Bob? I've got something you'll want to see."

Special Agent Alec Wade approached Herndon's desk in
Springfield. Wade was involved with the National Academy and had
seen some paperwork for the upcoming celebration at the Waldorf. He
had just received a fax from ADM's security department, saying that
Andreas and Cheviron would be attending. The date—June 29—
jumped out; the raids were scheduled two days before.

Herndon scanned the fax and decided that Washington needed to
know about this. Already, he had sent several memos about "raid day"
to Alix Suggs, the Washington supervisor overseeing the case. He decided to include the fax from Cheviron. Suggs, he knew, would get the
information into the right hands.

After his infant son went down for his morning nap, Mutchnik headed
to his car. Dressed casually in an open-neck shirt, he drove his black
Honda Accord through morning traffic to Interstate 90, getting off at
the Cumberland Avenue exit. He pulled into the parking lot of a small
office complex.

Mutchnik felt nervous as he approached the third building in the complex. He was about to conduct surveillance of the Chicago office for Heartland Lysine, Ajinomoto's American subsidiary. The office was on the raid list, and prosecutors needed details of its appearance for the search warrant.

In the lobby, he checked a building index. *Heartland Lysine, Suite 650.*

"Who are you here for?" a security guard asked.

"A friend on the sixth floor," Mutchnik replied. The guard nodded.

Mutchnik rode the elevator up. He walked past the Heartland Lysine office, paying no attention. Down the hall, he stopped by another office near the bathroom and memorized the name on the door before walking back. He wandered past Heartland Lysine again, glancing inside. Finally, he strolled in.

No one was in the reception area. Mutchnik looked around. Desks, offices, filing cabinets, nothing special. He memorized the setup; this was the kind of bland information they needed for the warrant. Suddenly, a young Japanese woman appeared.

"Can I help you?" she asked.

"Yes," Mutchnik said. He was looking for a friend. He mentioned the name of the company located down the hall, next to the bathroom.

The woman struggled to explain the location of the company; her English was poor. Mutchnik thanked her, walked to the elevator, and headed back to his car. Inside, he picked up a pen and small notepad off the seat and sketched the office he had just seen.

When he finished, he put away the pad and pen, started the car, and pulled out of the lot. He wanted to get back home before his son woke up.

Dwayne Andreas was in his sixth-floor office when Jim Randall came in. Randall had recently undergone open-heart surgery but was now back at work full-time. The two men sat, talking business.

Suddenly, Randall's eyes clouded over. "Dwayne, I just wanted you to know, I owe everything I have to you," he said. "And I am loyal to you."

Surprised, Andreas thanked Randall and a few minutes later ushered him out. He returned to his desk, feeling odd. Despite their years together, he and Randall didn't have an emotional relationship. The display left Andreas feeling uncertain.

What was that all about? he wondered.

• • •

Who should they try to flip?

That question was debated ferociously among the antitrust team for weeks. There would be only one chance to turn a potential defendant into a witness. If it worked, the government could pursue price-fixing cases in other products. If it failed, there would be no choice but to proceed with the raids. It was an all-or-nothing gamble.

The investigators considered Barrie Cox, head of ADM's citric-acid business, but ruled him out. Their leverage with Cox was poor; he had never been caught saying anything particularly incriminating. Plus, beyond citric, he was unlikely to know much.

Wilson was the dark-horse candidate, but the arguments against him were compelling. He was dedicated to the Andreas family; it was hard to imagine he would turn on them. Plus, to use their leverage against Wilson, the agents would have to play a tape. But Whitacre was on all of them. If Whitacre's role in the case was going to be kept secret as long as possible, Wilson couldn't hear his own tapes.

That left one option.

On June 22, days before the raid was to take place, Herndon sent a teletype to headquarters, spelling out the plan.

"On Tuesday, June 27th in the early evening, co–case agents will interview subject Michael D. Andreas," he wrote. "The purpose of the interview is to flip Andreas in order to gather other evidence."

The following Monday, Bill Esposito, head of the FBI's Criminal Investigative Division, heard about some news in the Springfield information packet: Just two days after the scheduled raid on ADM, top Bureau officials would be attending a ceremony honoring Dwayne Andreas. Esposito called a deputy director at Quantico who was scheduled to go to the event.

"I'm not allowing you to attend," he said. "I mean, what the hell's going on here? We're getting ready to hit this guy's place."

Esposito headed down the hall to tell Freeh about the development. As Freeh sat at his desk, Esposito described the ceremony.

"What are they doing that for?" Freeh asked.

The last-minute notification by his senior staff irritated Freeh. For major takedowns, he usually received a full briefing first. He knew about Harvest King but had no idea until now that the raid was coming. ADM was not a company to be trifled with; Freeh wanted to know more.

The orders went out. Before the raids received a green light, somebody from Springfield had to personally brief Louis Freeh.

• • •

That same afternoon, John Hoyt hung up his phone, irritated. In about thirty hours, Springfield's biggest operation ever was scheduled to start. But now Stukey was ordering him and Kate Killham, the squad leader in charge of the case, to brief the Bureau Director. Hoyt called Killham to let her know.

"Get packed," he said. "Everything's on hold for tomorrow. We have to be in Washington by nine A.M. to brief Louis Freeh on the operation."

"What do you mean?" Killham asked. "Freeh doesn't know about it? What happened to all the material we've been sending to them?"

"I don't know," Hoyt said. "But apparently he doesn't know a thing about it. And nothing's going to happen until we brief him and he okays it."

Killham was thunderstruck. "What have they been doing back there?"

Thirty minutes later, the parking lot of the Hampton Inn in Forsyth was swarming with lawyers and agents. Three Chicago prosecutors— Mann, Mutchnik, and Price—were there for a final Whitacre briefing. But the lawyers agreed to give Shepard and Herndon a chance to first speak with their witness alone.

The agents, shaken, mentioned to the lawyers that Freeh had put the raid on hold. They would know tomorrow, they said, whether they could proceed.

Mann's face hardened. "I can't believe this," she said. "Do we need to send someone to Washington?"

"I don't think so," Shepard said.

"Damn, it's got to happen now," Mann said.

All the pieces were in place. A federal magistrate had signed the search warrant. Whitacre had testified before the grand jury. Shepard and Herndon had rehearsed their planned interviews with Mick Andreas and Terry Wilson. All of the ADM executives were in town. But now, everything hung on Freeh.

The agents headed upstairs, leaving the lawyers in the parking lot. Soon after, Whitacre arrived, bubbly and excited. Shepard met him at the door.

"Hey, Mark," Shepard said as Whitacre came in. "How are you feeling?"

"Good, I'm good," Whitacre said. "Guess we're ready to go ahead, huh?"

"Looks like," Shepard said. "How's your family doing?"

"They're good. They're going to be gone tomorrow, at an amusement park. We thought that would be best."

Whitacre sat, talking fast and using his hands. They had been bracing him for weeks, walking him through what was about to happen. The agents had cautioned that if there was anything in his background that could be used against him, ADM would find it. Whitacre said he understood, but there was nothing to find. Now, all that was left to do was review the plans.

"Okay, Mark," Shepard said. "There are some things we need to talk to you about."

Whitacre nodded. "Okay."

"First of all," Shepard said, "once this starts, ADM is going to be trying everything to find out about this investigation. How it started, who's involved, everything like that. So you need to be careful, be alert to their efforts to gather information about the investigation and your involvement in it."

"Sure. I understand that."

"It's going to be very intense, Mark. They're going to be looking around everywhere. They're going to know that somebody said something. They're going to do almost anything to find out who it is. So you need to lay low and pay attention to what's happening."

Whitacre nodded. "I understand. I understand."

The agents didn't let go of the point. Whitacre had been talking a lot about his fears of being discovered, but he needed to be careful if his role was to remain a secret as long as possible. He couldn't talk about things he knew only from being involved in the case. Whitacre insisted that he understood.

"Okay, Mark," Shepard said. "A few other important things. One of them is, we've been talking to our antitrust attorneys. As soon as possible, once we do the search, you need to make it clear to everybody that you have your own attorney."

Whitacre looked at the agents, confused. "Well, uh, do you want me to go and hire an attorney now?"

Herndon jumped in.

"No, no, not now. But you have to understand the law, Mark. You're viewed as twofold. You're part of the corporation, but you're also an individual. Once we go public, you can't tell us any of the legal strategy at ADM. If you have your own attorney, you're less likely to be exposed to ADM's strategies."

"That's right, Mark," Shepard said. "So just tell them you have your own attorney and that you're going to cooperate with the government."

"Wouldn't it be odd?" Whitacre protested. "I mean, why would I be telling them that? Won't they know right off that something's wrong?"

"It won't be odd, Mark," Herndon said. "It's perfectly reasonable for you to cooperate. It happens all the time. And you're a high-level executive. It's not unusual for you to have prior contacts, to know a white-collar attorney. They'll understand that."

Whitacre looked at them thoughtfully. "Well, I think I know a guy in Decatur I can hire."

Shepard stiffened. "No, Mark," he said. "The town's too small. You shouldn't hire somebody local."

Whitacre looked lost. The agents had discussed this with the prosecutors, and no one felt comfortable recommending a lawyer. It would give them too much control. Whitacre needed to make his own choice.

"Now, there's another thing, Mark," Herndon said. "We've been talking with the antitrust attorneys. They say the first thing that's going to happen is the company lawyers are going to come to all the executives with a list of attorneys to pick from, attorneys the company is paying for."

Herndon leaned in.

"Now, understand something, Mark," he said. "These attorneys don't represent you. They are being paid by ADM. They do not represent you. Do not take one of these attorneys that they offer you. That's when you say you have your own attorney."

An expression of discomfort swept over Whitacre's face. "That will seem weird," he said sharply.

"Mark, it's not weird," Herndon said. "You have a right to your own attorney. You can say it's somebody you've known a while. As far as they're concerned, you're in the same position they are. Just tell them you want somebody you trust."

The back and forth continued, but eventually, Whitacre's resistance fell.

"Yeah, okay," he said. "I guess it would work."

Down in the parking lot, the antitrust lawyers were getting restless. They had not expected to be hanging around so long, and now hotel guests were eyeing them suspiciously. Making it worse, Mutchnik had shown up with a new burr haircut. Mann thought he looked like something out of the movie *Natural Born Killers*. Anyone who saw them lurking around probably had reason to be nervous.

Finally, Shepard appeared. They would be a little longer, he said.

The lawyers didn't want to hang around, so they walked to the nearby Hickory Point Mall and found a candy store. Marvin Price grabbed a bag and filled it with several pounds of jellybeans. The next two days were going to involve plenty of waiting, he figured. They might as well have something to snack on.

Back in the hotel room, Shepard and Herndon were describing the plans for the following day. They told Whitacre about their strategy of visiting Mick Andreas first. If Andreas didn't flip, Herndon said, they would proceed with the interview of Wilson, who was scheduled to be at dinner with Whitacre and Steven Yu, an executive with ADM in China.

"Mark, here's what's going to happen at the country club," Herndon said. "There's going to be three of us. Brian and I will take Terry, and the other agent will take you. He'll tell you where to go, and make it look like you're being interviewed. And I'll say up front that I need to speak to both of you."

Whitacre smiled. "That's good. I like that."

A short time later, the agents finished up.

"Now," Shepard said, "the antitrust attorneys still want to talk to you. They're in a better position to explain the law, and they'll be up here after we leave."

Before taking off, Herndon said, they wanted to review. "Remember," he said, "when they give you a list of attorneys to pick from, don't take one. It's the company's attorney, not yours. Tell them you have your own attorney; tell them you're going to cooperate with the investigation. And tonight, think about who you're going to hire as your attorney."

"Okay, guys," Whitacre said. "I understand."

The three men shook hands. The agents wished Whitacre good luck and left.

The antitrust lawyers showed up a few minutes later. Whitacre smiled as soon as he saw Mutchnik.

"Hey," Whitacre said, "you got a haircut."

"Yeah," Mutchnik said. He walked toward Whitacre and leaned down. "You want to touch it?"

Whitacre laughed and rubbed the back of Mutchnik's close-cropped hair.

"This is for luck, Mark," Mutchnik said.

Mann took a seat across from Whitacre. Price sat in a nearby chair; Mutchnik flopped down on the bed.

Mann took the floor. "Mark, whatever happens tomorrow, here's our legal issue. We're concerned that if you're directly represented by ADM's counsel, you should know there may be a conflict. ADM's counsel is representing ADM, not just you. We want you to think about whether it's in your best interest to get an attorney who represents your interests alone."

It was the same message again: Get a lawyer.

"I understand," Whitacre said.

He scanned their faces. "Do you think everything will work out okay for me at the company?" he asked. "Do you think I'll be okay?"

"Mark, we couldn't know, and we're not here to talk about that," Mann said. "All you can do is do what's best for you. One of those things is, we think you should tell the company that you're going to cooperate with the government's investigation."

Whitacre had already heard this. He agreed with an airy wave of a hand.

As the prosecutors continued speaking, Whitacre began to seem downhearted. Reality was settling in.

"I really don't know whether I'll be around, whether I'll be okay at the company," he suddenly said. "You know, it's gone pretty far. Maybe, maybe they'll be okay, though. There are a lot of good people there. I don't know."

Whitacre paused. "I guess it really is coming to an end, isn't it?" he asked.

Mann nodded. "Yes, it is," she replied.

"Do you think I'll have to testify?"

"I don't know, Mark," Mann said. "It's too early to tell. Just keep doing your job. We don't know what the future's going to hold."

After almost fifteen minutes, Mutchnik reviewed their points. Whitacre needed to think about what was in his interest and who best could represent him.

"I understand," Whitacre replied. "I think I know somebody I'll call."

As they wrapped up, Whitacre smiled.

"You know, Jim, with that haircut, are you getting ready for the military or something?"

• • •

About eight-thirty the next morning, the captain on United Airlines flight 602 turned off the seat-belt light. John Hoyt removed a credit card from his wallet and popped the airplane telephone out of its holding case. He followed the instructions on the phone's tiny screen and swiped his card through.

The trip to Washington for the Freeh briefing had become a mad dash. With so little warning, there had been trouble finding a flight. The first available had been early that morning, with a connection through Chicago. There had been worries in Springfield that the two supervisors would miss the connection.

Hoyt put the phone to his ear. The SAC's secretary answered.

"Hey, Dot. It's John Hoyt. Is he there?"

"Just a minute."

Stukey came on the line. "John, how's it going?"

"We made the flight, Don. We're on our way."

"Okay. Keep me informed."

Hoyt replaced the phone and checked his watch.

This was no good, no good at all. He had been told that Washington wanted them to brief Freeh by nine, but they would never make it. They wouldn't even be landing until about eleven. Hoyt made some mental calculations. By the time they arrived, they would have a little more than six hours before the raids were scheduled to begin.

He breathed deep. They were cutting this close.

In Springfield, Herndon and Shepard couldn't stop checking the time. They had held a series of smaller briefings for some agents during the day. But the final briefing for all personnel involved in the raids was scheduled for 2:00. Agents had already arrived from all over, ready to help. Even the weather was perfect. If there was a delay, it might take months to put the pieces back in place.

It had to go today.

As soon as they reached the gate at Washington National Airport, Hoyt and Killham popped their seat belts open. They were not weighed down with luggage; they stood and waited for the crowds to move. They both glanced at their watches. Just after eleven.

Inside, the two hurried to the front and waited in line for a cab. Eventually, it was their turn.

"We're going to the FBI building in Washington," Hoyt said.

The cab pulled out.

•   •   •

Still no word.

Herndon and Shepard were in Stukey's office, pacing. They were getting close to the time for the final briefing, with no idea if the raids were going forward. They decided to start the briefing as planned, but with a warning that the operation was not yet approved. There was no time for any other option.

At the Hoover Building, Hoyt and Killham were cooling their heels. Since they missed the 9:00 slot, they were told to wait until Freeh's schedule had another opening. Just a couple of hours, they were assured.

Two o'clock in Springfield. Time was up.

Scores of agents crowded the SAC's conference room, waiting for their final briefing. Stukey stepped behind the podium.

"We need to say up front, this may or may not go on," Stukey said. "As we speak, John Hoyt and Kate Killham should be speaking to the Director. But we don't have final approval yet."

Herndon checked his watch again. What was taking so long?

"Well, I just want to open up by thanking everyone for your efforts today," Stukey said. "This is truly going to be a great moment for Springfield."

Stukey turned over the floor to Herndon and Shepard, who led the agents through the case.

Hoyt and Killham walked into the Director's conference room. Freeh and a number of his deputies were already there, waiting for them. The two Springfield supervisors took seats at the far end of the table. Freeh lifted a hand.

"No, no," he said. "John, both of you come on up here."

Hoyt and Killham stood and walked to the other side, sitting near Freeh.

"First of all," Freeh said, "I want to thank you both for coming here on such short notice. I apologize for the inconvenience this has caused you. I'm sure you both would rather be in Springfield, helping in this operation. You have a really good case, an important case here. And I'd like a briefing."

Freeh eyed the Washington officials in the room.

"That's something I should have had before now," he said pointedly. "But I'll deal with that later."

The room was silent in discomfort. Killham could almost hear the others sweating.

"All right, John," Freeh said, turning back to Hoyt. "Go ahead."

Hoyt looked down at some notes.

"This case concerns price-fixing by ADM. I know you're aware of it and you've seen our notes. We're ready to take this overt. This evening, we're planning to serve search warrants."

Hoyt described the broad outlines of the case, then Killham handled the particulars. Freeh asked a few pithy questions, but nothing much. Both agents were impressed with his knowledge of the case details.

"That sounds like an excellent plan," Freeh said. "Expect a lot of attention from the media."

The Director looked at the two supervisors. "So why are you still here?" he asked. "Wouldn't you rather be in Decatur, where the action is?"

Hoyt and Killham smiled. "Yes," they said in unison.

"Well, good luck with it," Freeh said.

Hoyt and Killham hurried for the door. They needed to find a telephone and get back to the airport.

"Bob and Brian, please come to the front."

Shepard and Herndon stood as soon as they heard the voice on the intercom. They hurried down the hallway, walking through Stukey's door without knocking. Stukey was at his desk.

"I just heard," Stukey said. "It's a go."

The agents felt a wave of excitement. *Yes!*

"So get going," Stukey said.

They walked out, with Herndon making a quick left into the conference room where some agents were still waiting. Shepard headed to the radio room with a message to be announced over the intercom.

A minute later, the intercom crackled to life.

"In the Harvest King matter," a voice said, "it's a go."

Two hours later, Shepard and Herndon were silently sitting in a Bureau-issued car in front of a Decatur convenience store. A cell phone plugged into the car lighter rang, and Herndon answered.

"Hey, it's Mark. I think Mick's on his way."

"Thanks."

A minute later, Andreas's Mercedes drove past.

"There he is," Shepard said.

They waited. They didn't want to confront Andreas in his drive-way; they wanted him to get home, loosen his tie, talk to his family. His defenses would be down. He would be vulnerable.

About ten minutes later, Herndon breathed in deep.

"I think this is a good time to go," he said.

Shepard turned the key in the ignition. "That's what I was think-ing, too, Bob."

Shepard pulled into the street. Herndon rubbed his palms; they were sweaty from nerves. In a short time, they were on North Country Club Road, headed to Andreas's house. Shepard saw the driveway and put on his signal.

Herndon picked up the car microphone. "Eight-oh-seven, this is SI-15," he said.

"SI-15, go ahead."

"We're going into subject number one's house right now."

Shepard pulled around the circular driveway and stopped. He paused for a second.

"This is it," Herndon said.

In silence the agents headed to the door and rang the bell. Sally Andreas, Mick's wife, answered.

"Good evening, ma'am," Shepard said. "I'm Special Agent Brian Shepard of the FBI. This is Special Agent Bob Herndon. Is your hus-band available?"

"Oh, yes. Won't you come in?"

The agents stepped into the front hallway while Sally Andreas found her husband. When Mick appeared, his tie, coat, and shoes were already memories.

"Hey, fellas, how're you doing?" Andreas said in a low, rumbling voice. "What can I do for you? Always interested in helping law en-forcement."

"Well, we just want to take a minute of your time," Shepard said. "We have something very serious we want to discuss with you."

Andreas almost shrugged. "Well, sure," he said. "Why don't you fol-low me?"

The agents walked behind Andreas as he led them through the house. On the way, they passed a den. A boy, one of Andreas's children, was watching television. Andreas brought the agents into his office and sat at his desk. The agents took chairs in front of the desk and showed Andreas their credentials.

"Okay," Andreas said. "So tell me about this serious matter."

Shepard took a breath. "You're the first person we've contacted. We're doing this because we respect your position; we understand your authority at the company. We'd like for you to listen to us for a little bit and hear what you have to say."

Andreas didn't move. "I'm all ears," he said.

"This involves an international investigation regarding price-fixing by many companies, including ADM," Shepard said. "We've used numerous investigative techniques during the course of this, some that include our latest technology. In fact, we've gathered more evidence than we ever thought we could. It's been a real learning experience for us."

Shepard turned to Herndon. "Special Agent Herndon is going to give you a sample of what we learned."

"We won't take much time; we're going to get to the punch, Mr. Andreas," Herndon said. "But we just want to give you the benefit of what we believe we know and see what your reaction is. And we're going to have to ask you for your help in the end."

Herndon ticked off a few facts. Trade associations as cover. The exchange of sales and production numbers. Audits to prevent cheating. He included a few facts that seemed to indicate that the case involved high-fructose corn syrup and citric acid. He never mentioned lysine. The agents were dedicated to protecting Whitacre as long as possible.

Andreas listened calmly, his hands clasped on the desk. He struck Herndon as an amazingly cool customer.

"We know a lot," Herndon said, "because we've seen it and we've heard it. We even have tapes."

Herndon lifted his soft briefcase off the ground. Opening the flap, he pulled out a tape recorder. For days, the agents had debated which tape to play at this moment. In the end, their hopes of keeping Whitacre's role a secret had driven the decision. They chose a recording of an Andreas meeting with Yamada on April 30, 1993. Whitacre's voice was not on the tape, and there were no direct references to price-fixing. If they were going to protect Whitacre, it was the best they could do. They hoped that Andreas would be frightened just hearing his voice on tape.

Andreas listened to the snippet and shrugged. "Doesn't sound like price-fixing to me," he said.

"We have other evidence, Mr. Andreas, other tapes," Herndon said. "We have a lot of tapes."

Herndon paused, feeling the weight of a great silence in the room. For a moment, he wondered whether Andreas was somehow recording this.

"Let me ask you a question, sir," Herndon said. "Have you ever heard the statement, 'The competitors are our friends and the customers are our enemies?' "

"Are you aware of our second motto at ADM?" Andreas asked. "It's 'We know when we're lying.' "

The agents didn't respond.

"You know," Andreas said, "I don't think you guys understand the business."

"Let me tell you why we're here," Shepard said. "This is probably the most impressive antitrust case in history. We've been speaking with the attorneys from the Justice Department's Antitrust Division, and I think you can expect jail time for people who participated in these schemes, including you."

Despite the many companies involved in the conspiracy, only ADM clearly fell within the easy reach of American law enforcement.

"Right now, ADM stands alone," Shepard said. "If you don't cooperate, the other companies will prosper or could prosper. Customers are going to continue to need high-fructose corn syrup or citric acid, and they may be forced to buy from other companies. The other companies won't have the black eye that ADM has."

Still no mention of lysine. Andreas would probably never think of Whitacre.

"You have an opportunity tonight to make a decision, and this decision is going to affect your life and your company. You have a chance to protect ADM and to influence the rest of the investigation. But you've got to make the decision tonight."

Shepard paused. Andreas didn't move.

"Here's the decision," Shepard said. "Your dad has worked long and hard to make this company. You know that, we know it, and we've got a lot of respect for your dad and you. But we need your help."

"I'm a law-abiding citizen," Andreas responded. "I always try to cooperate with law enforcement. But I can't make a decision to fully cooperate without consulting my dad and my attorney. ADM is publicly owned. I have a responsibility to the directors."

"Mr. Andreas, we believe you have the authority to make the decision to cooperate," Shepard replied. "We need your help gathering further evidence of price-fixing in citric acid, in high-fructose corn syrup, or in any other product where price-fixing is going on right now. If you decide to help us, we want to start making phone calls tonight. We know it won't be easy; it's a big decision. But we're telling you, if you don't cooperate, ADM will stand alone domestically."

Andreas said nothing.

"We think the decision is clear," Shepard continued. "To keep ADM from being singled out, to save everything your dad has worked so hard for, you should help us. This is a onetime opportunity for you to help us gather evidence on other companies."

Shepard stopped. That was the pitch.

"Honestly, guys, I don't think you understand the business," Andreas said.

Andreas denied that there could ever be price-fixing at his company. The products the agents had mentioned were commodities, he said, and it was impossible to rig those prices. He admitted talking with competitors; of course it happened all the time. It was like having two used-car salesmen with lots next to each other, he said. They're going to talk about how many cars they're going to sell this year.

"I know what an antitrust violation is," he said. "And I haven't broken any laws. What you've got on that tape is not an antitrust violation."

"Again, we have a lot more evidence than just this," Herndon said. "The tape was designed to show you that we have you on tape. It wasn't to convince you that this is a violation right here."

Herndon stared Andreas in the eyes. "You've got a decision to make," he said. "We're not going to stay here all night. You need to make a decision."

"I'm not going to do it," Andreas said abruptly. "I'm not going to be a spy. I'm not going to wear a wire, and my kid's not going to wear a wire."

Andreas sat back. "You guys need to leave. And the very first thing I'm going to do is call my dad and call the company attorneys."

"Well, that's fine," Herndon said as he reached into his briefcase. "Before we leave, though, we need to serve you with some subpoenas."

Herndon handed four subpoenas to Andreas, one for him and three for the company. Andreas set the documents down on his desk and stood.

"Well, fellows, I think it's time for you to leave," he said again.

Andreas walked to the office door. He stopped as he passed Shepard, a look of recognition in his eye.

"You owe me one," he said to Shepard.

"What do you mean?" Shepard asked.

"I recognize you," Andreas said. "We talked about another matter about two years ago."

The Fujiwara incident. Shepard didn't reply.

More than thirty minutes after the agents had arrived, Andreas showed them out. They climbed back into their car, and as Shepard turned the ignition key, Herndon picked up the radio microphone.

"Eight-oh-seven, this is SI-15," he said.

"SI-15, go ahead."

"Eight-oh-seven, please advise all other units to proceed with the other investigation."

The radio operator understood the meaning: Mick Andreas hadn't flipped. The word went out to agents around the country just before six o'clock.

The raids were on.

Minutes later, Shepard and Herndon pulled into a sandy area just off the road, parking in front of a waiting car. Kevin Corr, the principal legal advisor in Springfield, came out of the other car and walked over as Herndon rolled down his window.

"Well, you were gone so long I thought maybe you had him," Corr said.

"Nah, he's not cooperating," Herndon said. "So let's go do the next thing."

Corr nodded and walked back to his car. It was time to go confront Wilson.

At almost the same instant, FBI agents walked into the main headquarters of ADM brandishing search warrants and headed quickly up to the executive floors.

Allen Andreas, Mick's cousin who years before had worked with ADM in London, was at his new desk at headquarters. He watched as a group of agents swept across the office, packing documents and carrying them out. None of them was paying attention to Allen.

After a while, Allen decided this was a sign that the workday was over. He walked to the elevator.

The warm, breezy evening had attracted a crowd to the outdoor patio at the Country Club of Decatur. At one table was Jim Shafter, the lawyer for the Andreas family who had attended Mick's original FBI interview about the Fujiwara incident. He and his wife, Gigi, were relaxing over wine as they waited for their meal.

Just past six o'clock, two cars pulled up in the parking lot about twenty yards away. With his back to the lot, Shafter couldn't see Shepard, Herndon, and Corr as they walked from their cars into the club. Nor did he notice when Corr returned minutes later, escorting Whitacre to one of the cars.

A waitress set dinner in front of the Shafters. As the couple enjoyed their meal, Shepard and Herndon came out of the club. Almost on cue, Whitacre climbed out of the car and approached the two agents, appearing apprehensive. Whitacre and one of the agents said something as they passed.

Sometime later, the waitress returned to the table. "Mr. Shafter, when you finish with dinner, Mr. Reising would like to speak with you," she said.

"All right," Shafter replied. "Thank you."

Shafter thought nothing of the call. Probably ADM's general counsel wanted to line up a golf game. But soon, the waitress returned.

"Mr. Shafter, Mr. Reising would like you to call as soon as you can," she said.

"Okay, thanks."

Minutes passed. The waitress returned.

"Mr. Shafter," she said, "Mr. Reising wants you to call him right now."

Shafter considered using his cell phone. But if Reising had called three times, this was probably sensitive. He wiped his mouth with a napkin and stood.

"I'll be right back," he said to his wife.

Shafter walked inside the club to the men's locker room and found a phone. Reising's wife answered at his home. Her husband was at Mick's, she said, and was expecting Shafter to call him there. Shafter dialed Andreas's house, and Reising answered.

"Come over here right now," Reising said cryptically as soon as Shafter spoke.

"Well, Rick, give me some heads-up here," Shafter said. "What's—"

"Come over here right now," Reising interrupted.

Then he hung up.

After pulling away from the country club, Shepard drove to a small marina. He and Herndon had not yet had a chance to take a breath, to talk about their interviews. Neither wanted to be immediately thrown into the mix at the Decatur R.A.

Shepard pulled into a spot and shut off the car. He looked over at Herndon.

"Do you think it went well?" Shepard said.

"Yeah," Herndon said. "I don't think I would change a thing."

Neither could believe Andreas had given them so much time; they had obtained some good statements. Wilson was even better—he repeatedly contradicted his words on tape. A jury would see that.

The agents looked at each other and extended their hands.

"Good job," Shepard said.

At that moment, agents were fanning out across Decatur, confronting ADM executives at their homes.

Two older agents, Alec Wade and Steven Nash, pulled up in a Bureau car to the gate at the end of Dwayne Andreas's driveway. They phoned the house from the car, and the gates swung open.

Andreas met the agents inside. They told him that they were investigating possible price-fixing in high-fructose corn syrup, citric acid, and lysine. They asked if he had ever heard about the trade associations that existed for those products.

"I'm unfamiliar with those associations," Andreas shrugged. "I consider most trade associations as do-gooders anyway."

"Well, do you know if ADM sells any of these products to the government?" one of the agents asked.

"No, I don't. Do you?"

"No, sir, I don't."

The agents asked Andreas several questions about price-fixing, and he shook his head dismissively. It was impossible to fix prices in those products because too many variables were involved, he replied.

The agents circled around, asking about Andreas's contact with competitors and whether he was aware of any recordings of competitors that took place at the Decatur Club—a charge Whitacre had raised years before. Andreas calmly batted away each question.

"Well, sir," one of the agents said, "can you explain why Wayne Brasser was fired?"

Andreas looked back blankly. "Wayne Brasser? Who's Wayne Brasser? Was he an employee?"

"Yes, sir. And we've heard Wayne Brasser was fired from ADM because he wouldn't fix prices."

Andreas snorted a laugh.

"Fat chance," he grunted.

In another part of town, Barrie Cox, the head of ADM's citric business, had been surprised outside of his home by two FBI agents. The agents told him they were investigating possible price-fixing, and Cox good-naturedly invited them inside. Everyone was taking a seat in the living room when the telephone rang. Cox took the call. When he returned, his smile was gone.

"I don't understand your inquiry," Cox said suddenly. "And if you have any questions, I think you should call my boss, Terry Wilson, or the ADM corporate counsel, Richard Reising. Other than that, I don't have anything to say."

The agents stood to leave, and one of them handed Cox a grand jury subpoena. ADM was already locking up its employees, less than an hour after the operation began. Their lawyers moved fast.

Howard Buffett was at home, playing host to Special Agent Robert Schuler. Not only was Buffett willing to talk, he was dropping tantalizing tidbits.

"I don't believe Dwayne Andreas is a totally honest individual," Buffett said. "He would do anything to get what he wanted. He's authoritarian and very cunning."

The agent pressed for details. Buffett mentioned his confrontation with Andreas over the football tickets for the congressman. He said that he believed ADM misrepresented the size of its revenues from one business in order to disguise risks in the stock. But he said he had no direct knowledge of price-fixing and knew nothing about whether ADM secretly recorded visitors to the Decatur Club.

The interview lasted long into the night. Probably, Schuler thought, the case agents needed to follow up with Buffett.

Special Agent Ken Temples arrived at the home of Kirk Schmidt, the controller for the Bioproducts Division. Schmidt opened the door, and Temples flashed his creds.

"Oh yeah, come on in," Schmidt said. He seemed calm. Almost as if he had been expecting a visit.

Outside Mick Andreas's house, Rick Reising was slumped in a chair, reading subpoenas. Beside him, Andreas was reliving his FBI interview.

The two heard someone coming and looked up. Jim Shafter was walking across the yard toward them. Reising stood.

"Here," Reising said, thrusting the subpoenas toward Shafter. "Read this and we'll start."

For a few minutes, Shafter reviewed the subpoenas. "Okay," he said, looking up when he finished. "What's going on?"

"Right now," Reising said, "I don't know the number, but we've got twenty or thirty FBI agents going through the offices, carrying out documents."

"Do we have anybody there?" Shafter asked.

Reising nodded. "Yeah, Cheviron's people."

"Well, not to interfere, but obviously tell them to keep track of things as best they can."

Reising made a face. "Gee, thanks, Jim," he said sarcastically.

The men reviewed everything they knew. Agents were visiting executives all over town; even Dwayne's house had been hit. Reising looked at his watch.

"Listen, I'm sorry," he said. "I've got to go." Other executives were coming to his house to meet.

Shafter sat beside Andreas. "Mick, what the hell?" he said. "Why don't you tell me what the FBI talked to you about?"

Andreas looked calm. "It was about lysine."

Back at the Decatur R.A., the mood was hectic. Shepard and Herndon showed up after six-thirty and helped coordinate the flow of information that was coming in. In one part of the room, lawyers and agents were watching a computer rigged to pen registers and trap-and-trace devices on some executives' home phones. Every time a call was placed to or from one of those houses, the other phone number registered on the computer. The group then tried to figure out who the number belonged to.

Mutchnik was having a blast. He manned the phones, answering with a brisk "CP," for Command Post. He felt like a cop.

At one point, Mutchnik was out of his chair when the phone rang. An agent answered and called Mutchnik. "This guy needs to talk to you," he said.

Mutchnik grabbed the phone. "CP."

"Yeah, hey, this is Ken Temples."

"Hey, Kenny. It's Jim Mutchnik."

"Hey, Jim. Listen, we've got a problem out here."

Temples sounded floored by something. Mutchnik's antennae went up.

"What's wrong?"

"I was just out interviewing an ADM employee named Kirk Schmidt."

"Yeah?"

"Well, Schmidt knew we were coming," Temples said. "He said that Whitacre told him days ago all about the raid."

A few minutes later, Mutchnik hung up the phone, shell-shocked. He walked to another part of the office where Mann, Price, and Susan Booker, another antitrust lawyer, were working. He stopped in front of them.

"Mark told," Mutchnik said simply.

That grabbed everyone's attention. "What do you mean?" Mann asked.

"Mark told," Mutchnik repeated. "They knew."

Over the next ten minutes, the word from the field kept getting worse. Another agent phoned in with the same news, that Whitacre had told a woman in his division named Kathy Dougherty about the raid. The biggest shock came from the agent who had interviewed Liz Taylor, Whitacre's secretary. He not only gave her a heads-up on the raid, but had told her months earlier about his work with the FBI.

Shepard and Herndon were enraged. For months, they had held Whitacre's hand as he poured out his fears of being discovered. In their interviews, they had done everything to protect him, even avoiding the word *lysine*—the one bait that might have hooked Andreas. And now they learned it was all for nothing.

People at the company knew that Whitacre had been working for the FBI.

But now there were bigger concerns. How bad did this get? If ADM executives had received enough warning, they might have concocted a cover story or even planted fake evidence that could be used to exonerate them. This was a potential disaster.

Just past eight-thirty, the agents were angrily preparing to meet with Whitacre when the phone rang. Herndon answered to find an FBI supervisor from Washington on the line. Freeh, the supervisor informed him, needed a memo by 6:30 the next morning on every interview conducted that night by every agent around the country.

Herndon seethed, working the muscles in his jaw. This was a bunch of Washington bureaucrats in action. Freeh was too much on the side of the field agents to demand paperwork in the middle of an operation. Herndon argued, but got nowhere. The fight caught the attention of the antitrust attorneys, who walked over.

"Look, I'll try my best," Herndon said into the phone acidly. "I'll have something for you. But this isn't right. This isn't right."

"Well, Bob," the supervisor said, in a condescending tone, "I've got to be here all night, too."

Herndon hung up and looked at the lawyers. "You're not going to fucking believe this!"

The lawyers listened as Herndon explained. They told him not to worry about the memo. He and Shepard needed to meet Whitacre. The prosecutors would write the summary for Freeh themselves.

Herndon looked at the lawyers, feeling touched. After all the earlier tension, the group had solidified into a real team.

"Thank you," Herndon said, relieved. "You guys are just great."

With barely another word, he and Shepard hurried out the door.

The two agents sat in Shepard's car, looking out on to the fishing pond off the back parking lot of the Holiday Inn. As angry as Herndon was with Whitacre, Shepard felt even worse. He had known Whitacre the longest; he had stuck up for him and tailored the case for him. He felt deeply betrayed.

"Hey, Bob," Shepard said as they waited, "let me talk to Mark first."

Herndon nodded. "Okay."

Whitacre pulled beside them. The agents got out of the car, and Shepard opened Whitacre's front passenger seat. Herndon climbed into the back.

Whitacre seemed hyped up. He excitedly said that Wilson had been scared by the confrontation. He and Wilson had met with Mick, he said, and the whole conversation was recorded. He thought the tape was really good. Shepard mumbled a few compliments.

"So," Whitacre said, "how's everything going? Everything going okay?"

Shepard stared hard at Whitacre.

"Mark," he said abruptly, "who did you tell?"

Silence descended on the car for an instant.

"What . . . what do you mean?" Whitacre fumbled.

"Who did you tell?"

Whitacre stammered out a tangle of words.

"Well," he said finally, "I had to tell Liz Taylor."

Shepard's eyes flashed in anger.

"I told her a long time ago, like, three months ago," Whitacre said, the words rushing out. "I didn't tell her anything about what you guys are doing. I just said, 'Look, I'm working with the FBI on some things. I may be out of touch for a while.' I had to tell her where to contact me. I make a lot of decisions and a lot of times they need to find me. I had to let Liz know where I was going to be, so I told her I was involved with you guys on some things. But she didn't know anything about what you're doing."

Shepard stared at Whitacre, waiting for more.

From the backseat, Herndon could almost see Whitacre's mind turning. By Herndon's guess, Whitacre was trying to figure out how much the agents already knew.

"Well, oh yeah, you know I've mentioned Kathy Dougherty to you before," Whitacre said. "She's a dear friend and a trusted ally. I just didn't want her to be scared. So I told her a few days ago that some FBI guys would be coming by to talk to her this week and that she should just answer their questions."

"Why did you do that, Mark?" Shepard said forcefully. "Come on, Mark. That story doesn't make any sense. Why did you tell Dougherty?"

"It's just like I said: I didn't want her to be scared," Whitacre replied, working himself into a frenzy. "You guys don't know what it's like. I was just looking out for her interests. And I can trust her. Guys, I can trust her. I mean, nothing's going wrong tonight. Is anything going wrong tonight?"

The agents didn't answer. They couldn't explain their fears about fake evidence and false statements. Plus, Whitacre had messed with their careers. They had built him up to their superiors. They were supposed to be his controllers. And he was out of control.

"Who else, Mark?" Shepard snapped, his voice brittle. "Come on, don't jack us around. *Who else?*"

It took another minute before Whitacre offered up Kirk Schmidt.

"I wanted to let him know it was okay to talk to you, 'cause he might not 'cause he's loyal to me," he said. "You guys don't understand. I have to work with these people long after you're gone."

Shepard's anger got to him. "Mark," he growled, "you could have ruined this entire operation!"

Whitacre went white and babbled excuses. It was becoming obvious that the bizarre call received by Agent Bruch on the hello line was probably from one of Whitacre's friends, checking out his story.

From the backseat, Herndon didn't like what he was seeing. They needed Whitacre's head clear for the next day. Herndon put a hand on Shepard's shoulder, signaling that he was about to join the conversation.

"Time out, Mark," he said slowly. "You know what you did was wrong in our eyes."

Whitacre started to speak.

"Don't say anything, Mark," Herndon said. "Look, we can talk about this later, okay? We can get past this. But is there anything else we need to know?"

Whitacre shook his head. "No, no, I can't think of anything, Bob."

"Okay, so let's talk about tonight," Herndon said. "Did you tell anybody at the company that you're going to cooperate with the government?"

Whitacre paused. "Well, you've got to understand. After everything that happened, I was concerned about telling them. I mean, I was just scared."

Herndon held his anger. "Okay, Mark, but listen. You can't be walking around hearing their legal strategies. You've got to let them know first thing tomorrow that you're going to be cooperating. Okay?"

"Okay, okay," Whitacre said, nodding. "I'll tell them as early as I can."

The tension eased, and the agents told Whitacre about the evening's developments. By the time they finished up, Whitacre seemed back on an even keel. The agents said good night and headed to their car.

They drove back to the Decatur R.A., unable to shake the sense that Whitacre was holding back. Why had he disclosed the raids? Did he misunderstand something they had said? After thrashing it through, the agents felt sure they had done nothing wrong. Whitacre had simply been freelancing.

But that conclusion was even worse. If Whitacre had been foolish enough to disclose the raids, Herndon asked, what other surprises were still out there?

Rick Reising finished the meeting with his ADM colleagues with one clear conclusion: A major criminal investigation was under way. He needed to line up lawyers, right away. He dialed a contact with

Williams & Connolly, a Washington powerhouse with a take-no-prisoners reputation in litigation.

Founded by Edward Bennett Williams, the politically connected Washington "superlawyer," Williams & Connolly had become a firm feared by prosecutors and sought out by wealthy defendants. Michael Milken, the billionaire junk-bond king, was a Williams & Connolly client during the Wall Street scandals of the 1980s; so was President Bill Clinton as the Whitewater investigation unfolded.

Reising called Aubrey Daniel III, a tenacious Williams & Connolly partner whom he knew well. Daniel had made a national name for himself in 1971 leading the prosecution in the court martial of U.S. Army Lt. William Calley for slaughtering civilians in the Vietnamese hamlet of My Lai. Daniel, fresh from law school, delivered a fiery summation that riveted the nation. When President Nixon ordered Calley out of the brig and into house arrest, Daniel wrote a much-publicized letter of protest. That helped attract the attention of Ed Williams, who picked Daniel for his growing firm.

In the years since, Daniel had built up an impressive corporate clientele. He had done work for ADM—even handling an antitrust case involving possible price-fixing of carbon dioxide. But this time, the case was criminal; people faced prison. Reising needed Daniel in Decatur—right away.

"Aubrey," he said, "it's Rick Reising at ADM. We've got a problem."

Whitacre arrived home shortly before ten-thirty, shucking off his coat and tossing it onto the couch. Ginger was waiting up. He smiled and walked toward her, taking her into his arms. Everything was working out as well as he could have hoped. Perhaps soon, he would be in position to lead ADM into a new era.

"This is the end," he said. "Another couple of days and these guys are gone."

The next morning, ADM was in chaos. Howard Buffett sat in his sixth-floor office, still in awe over the events of the last sixteen hours. The raid. The tapes. Even his own FBI interview, at his house right after six o'clock. Everything had gone exactly the way Whitacre had promised so many weeks before, when he had told Buffett all about the price-fixing investigation.

Around ten, Buffett gaped as two longtime ADM staffers transported armloads of documents out of Dwayne Andreas's office and boxed them up. The movement of paper continued for almost thirty minutes; later, Buffett saw the records being carried away. He made a mental note to tell the FBI what he had seen.

Sometime later, Dwayne himself stopped by. "So, what did you tell the FBI last night?" Andreas asked before launching into a description of his interview.

Buffett stopped him. "I'm cooperating with the government," he said. "I've retained my own lawyer. Anything you tell me is the same as telling the FBI."

Andreas set his jaw, visibly upset. He said nothing more about the investigation.

Aubrey Daniel arrived that morning at Decatur Airport with a Williams & Connolly colleague. Shafter was waiting and drove the lawyers straight to ADM.

Once there, the lawyers reviewed the subpoenas. It didn't take long to figure out the targets—the Feds had cleaned out the offices of Mick Andreas, Wilson, Whitacre, and Cox. Daniel was convinced this was a covert operation. Somebody had cooperated.

Everyone needed their own lawyers, right away. Daniel, who was most familiar with the white-collar bar, made a series of suggestions. Shafter and Reising accepted each without question. The list was drawn up and the phone calls went out. The personal lawyers would begin arriving in Decatur by that evening.

In Washington, Bob Strauss hung up the phone, bewildered by the news from Decatur. Strauss, an ADM director, was the consummate Washington insider with roles among the power elite that transcended party labels. He was equally comfortable serving as Democratic Party chairman, or ambassador to the Soviet Union for the Republican administration of George Bush. Strauss was also a confidant and first friend to Dwayne Andreas, a man he had met decades before.

As usual, Strauss spoke to Dwayne that day, this time receiving an update on the raid. He heard about the search for lawyers to represent executives. ADM had even sent a plane to Washington to shuttle lawyers to Decatur. Strauss had suggested Bill Hundley, a lawyer with his firm, Akin, Gump, Strauss, Hauer & Feld.

But after hanging up, Strauss learned that Hundley was not around. There was no time to wait; the ADM corporate plane would be leaving for Decatur in just about thirty minutes. Who else fit the bill?

Strauss thought of John Dowd, another prominent lawyer at the firm. Dowd was a former prosecutor who was best known as the lawyer who led major league baseball's investigation into gambling allegations against Pete Rose.

Strauss reached for the phone.

The apparent targets of the investigation were called into Reising's office one at a time to meet with the lawyers. Whitacre was summoned in the morning. Daniel looked at Whitacre affably.

"Pleasure meeting you," he said. "I'm Aubrey Daniel; I'm representing ADM in this matter."

The lawyers questioned Whitacre about his FBI interview the night before, and he provided rehearsed answers. Afterward, the lawyers offered assurances. Whitacre shouldn't worry. ADM would stand by him.

Hours later, an ADM corporate lawyer stopped by Whitacre's office. The company had found criminal lawyers, the lawyer said, some of the best available. Many would be arriving in Decatur that night. Whitacre could meet them that evening at Jim Shafter's office.

The moment had unfolded just as the government had predicted. They had briefed Whitacre on exactly what to say. Now was his chance.

"Okay," Whitacre said. "I'll be there tonight."

Herndon and Shepard picked up extensions at the Decatur R.A. when they heard Whitacre was calling.

"Hey, Mark," Herndon said. "How's it going?"

"Good," Whitacre replied. "Listen, I wanted to let you know I've made arrangements to meet with an attorney. He's flying into Decatur right now."

"How long will it take him to get here?"

"About two hours. I'm already set to meet with him early this evening."

It sounded like Whitacre had done as he was told. He hadn't taken a company lawyer. The agents breathed easy.

The first wave of personal lawyers arrived in Decatur over the next few hours. That evening, they trooped over to Shafter's office for the meeting.

Before the potential targets had arrived, the lawyers debated among themselves. They had considered putting Whitacre with Reid Weingarten, a rising star of the white-collar defense bar. But now they were having second thoughts. Whitacre seemed shaky and probably could use the psychological boost of an older, father figure. Weingarten was basically a Whitacre contemporary. They decided that John Dowd, who was approaching sixty, was a better match.

The decision went over smoothly. Wilson met with Weingarten; Cox visited with William Taylor, another prominent Washington lawyer summoned for the meeting. Shafter offered his own office to Whitacre and Dowd. The two men walked in and shut the door.

Dowd settled behind Shafter's desk and began calmly describing his background. When he finished, Whitacre stared at him cautiously.

"Let me ask you," he said. "Who do you represent, me or the company?"

Waiting in the reception area, Shafter and the other lawyers became restless. Shafter was already on a caffeine high.

"I'll tell you," Shafter said. "I've drunk all the goddamned Coke I can stand."

The lawyers laughed. Shafter headed to his firm's refrigerator, returning loaded down with beer.

"At least we're a full-service firm," he said, passing out drinks.

The beer was nothing without food, so soon the lawyers were on the phone. The pizza arrived before the private meetings ended. Cox was the first to come out. Taylor, his new lawyer, walked beside him.

"Barrie," Taylor said, "I think you ought to just go home tonight, and we'll talk again tomorrow."

Cox nodded solemnly. "All right, thank you."

Sometime after ten o'clock, Wilson and Weingarten appeared. They settled in and enjoyed some of the food, while everyone waited for Whitacre and Dowd.

Eventually, Shafter's office door opened. Whitacre looked solemn; Dowd was pasty-faced. Whitacre walked toward Reising.

"Rick, I need to tell you that I'm going to be cooperating with the FBI."

Twenty-four hours late, Whitacre was finally doing as he had been instructed.

"Well, Mark," Reising replied, "you have a good lawyer. You need to do what your lawyer advised you."

Whitacre fleetingly looked back at Dowd. "I'm going to be getting another lawyer," he said. "John agrees that I should be getting another lawyer."

Walking closer to Reising, Whitacre shook his hand. Shafter stood nearby and heard Whitacre mention something about "hundreds of tapes."

Whitacre headed out the door, following Wilson. Shafter accompanied them; it was now so late that they needed an escort to get out of the building. When they reached the door, Whitacre shook Shafter's hand.

"I'm sorry for what's happened," Whitacre said.

Shafter nodded, uncertain what Whitacre meant.

Back inside, Weingarten watched Dowd; the man looked blown away. Given that Dowd had recommended that Whitacre find a new lawyer, he had obviously found a conflict. Weingarten had no doubt what it was.

Later that evening, the two lawyers returned to the Decatur Club, where they were staying. Weingarten and Dowd were sharing a suite and sat up enjoying a nightcap. Weingarten decided to test out his theory.

"You know," he said, "that SOB was probably wearing a wire on *you* tonight, too."

Dowd spilled his drink on his pants.

BOOK THREE

NOTHING SIMPLE
IS SIMPLE

CHAPTER 13

Brian Shepard gripped the steering wheel as he drove up a hill, stopping at the usual spot in front of his Decatur house. It was the afternoon following the raids, and the pressure of recent days had coupled with Shepard's natural demeanor, leaving him exhausted and glum. With only a few hours sleep since the previous morning, he wanted to get away from the case for a while. He trudged up the driveway, feeling ready for some well-earned family time.

Those hopes ended just past ten-thirty, when his pager sounded. It was Whitacre. Shepard returned the call.

"Hey, Mark," Shepard drawled. "What's going on?"

"Hey, Brian, how you doin'? Listen, I met with the attorney I told you about. I'm really not happy—"

Shepard interrupted, again cautioning Whitacre not to reveal confidences shared with his lawyer. "I know," Whitacre said. "Well, he's this guy named John Dowd."

Whitacre described Dowd's background, stressing that he had been a prosecutor for many years.

"I thought since he was a prosecutor he would be sympathetic with me helping the government," Whitacre said. "But I was disappointed."

Whitacre said that he had told Dowd details of his work with the FBI, including his role in recording tapes.

"Dowd promised everything I said would be confidential and that he represented me personally," he said. "I didn't say anything until he promised that."

As Whitacre spoke, Shepard slowly realized a painful truth: Dowd had been hired by ADM. Whitacre had seen him against the agents' explicit instructions.

And Whitacre had told everything.

. . .

Later that night, the Whitacres were in bed when the ADM off-premises extension rang in the next room. Mark threw off the covers, glancing at the clock as he climbed out of bed. Just past midnight.

Dressed only in sweatpants and a T-shirt, he padded into the other room and picked up the phone.

"Mark Whitacre."

"Mr. Whitacre, this is Aubrey Daniel. We met earlier. I'm the attorney representing ADM."

"They're telling me not to come back to work!"

It was early the next morning, Thursday, June 29. Whitacre was back on the phone with Shepard.

"Aubrey Daniel said I was a target of the investigation, and so I shouldn't come back to the office. That doesn't sound right. I mean, you don't think they're gonna tell Mick not to come in, do you?"

"Wait a minute, Mark," Shepard said. "Did anyone at ADM tell you not to come to work? Or just the lawyer?"

"I haven't heard from anybody at ADM. Definitely not."

Whitacre reached a decision.

"I'm going in," he said.

Briefcase in hand, Whitacre glided through the trading room toward his office, hoping to pass unnoticed. He had arrived at work a little later than usual, but not so much as to raise any eyebrows. He slid behind his desk and thumbed through some papers. No one had said a word to him.

For about an hour, the workday passed without event. But around nine o'clock, Scott Roberts, a young attorney in ADM's legal department, appeared in the doorway.

"Mark, I'm afraid you're going to have to leave," Roberts said. "They want you to take some vacation time."

Whitacre sat back. "Why do I have to leave?"

"I'm just delivering a message. You have to leave."

Whitacre at first refused to follow Roberts's instructions. But the lawyer did not allow himself to get caught up in an argument. He had his assignment.

"All right," Whitacre finally agreed.

He picked up his briefcase and walked past Roberts, heading to the elevator. The lawyer stayed with him until Whitacre got into his car and pulled away.

As he drove off, Whitacre reached for his car phone.

When they heard Whitacre was on the line, Shepard and Herndon picked up extensions at the Decatur R.A.

"Hey, how you doing?" Whitacre asked, sounding surprisingly up-beat. "Listen, I've got an appointment in your building and wondered if I could stop by."

"Sure," Shepard said. "How's everything at work?"

"Not good," Whitacre said, describing how he had been tossed out of ADM.

"I'm looking for another attorney," he said. "I'm really unhappy with Dowd."

Herndon had just heard the Dowd story from Shepard and was still burning about it. Whitacre said he was now thinking about hiring a Decatur lawyer. Herndon couldn't believe it. If there was any place he shouldn't hire a lawyer, it was in ADM's hometown.

"Mark," Herndon said, "why don't we talk about this more when you get here?"

Soon, Whitacre was knocking on the door to room 353 at an office building on South Water Street.

Shepard opened the door. "Hey, Mark, come on in."

Whitacre walked into the Decatur R.A. The toll of the day was etched on his face. The agents took him into Shepard's office, where they could talk.

As Whitacre told the story of being led out of ADM, his pager sounded—5413. Buffett's extension.

"Hey," Whitacre said. "It's Howard Buffett. Can I call him from here?"

"Sure, Mark," Shepard said.

The agents knew that Buffett was a friend to Whitacre. After his hard morning, he could probably use the support.

"Listen, go ahead and take the office," Shepard said.

Both agents stood. Whitacre nodded, thanking the agents as they stepped out of the room and closed the door. He reached for the phone and dialed.

"Howie," Whitacre said, "it's Mark."

"I can't talk long," Buffett said. "I've got something important to tell you."

• • •

In a few minutes, Whitacre emerged from the office, ashen-faced. Shepard was on the phone, so Herndon walked back without him. Whitacre took a seat behind the desk.

"Howard had a hot tip for me," Whitacre said. "He talked to Dwayne. He knows everything. Dowd told him.* Dwayne's saying I'm responsible for the FBI coming."

Whitacre looked at Herndon.

"Dwayne's repeating what I told my attorney. Can he do that, Bob? Isn't that some sort of violation?"

Of course not, Herndon thought. "I can run that by our attorneys, but I don't think Dwayne is under any attorney-client privilege. He can say whatever he wants."

"Well, that's not right," Whitacre said.

Shepard walked into the office, and Whitacre told the story again. The agents murmured soothing words, but inside they seethed. ADM wouldn't have figured out anything if Whitacre had followed instructions; he had blown *himself* up. The agents had always assumed that after the raids, ADM would be the enemy set on destroying the case. They never thought that their own witness would take that role first.

The antitrust lawyers gathered in Marvin Price's office when they heard that Shepard was calling with an emergency. Price pressed the button for his speakerphone.

"Okay, Brian," he said.

"I was saying, we're having problems and need help."

"What's happened?" Mann asked.

"Well, to make a long story short, Mark came by today. Like I told you, he got escorted out of ADM this morning."

The lawyers listened in disbelief as Shepard related the story of the meeting with Dowd, the call from Buffett, and the apparent discovery of Whitacre's work with the FBI.

"He's in a panic and needs a lawyer," he said. "Don't you guys know anybody?"

"We don't find lawyers for witnesses," Mann replied. "He has to choose one."

---

*Dowd has acknowledged telling ADM that Whitacre *would* cooperate with the FBI, but denies ever disclosing that Whitacre *had* cooperated with the government. Additional reporting confirms his account.

"Well, that hasn't worked," Shepard said. "Isn't there anything you can do?"

After some debate, there was an unspoken acknowledgment that things were getting out of control. The prosecutors agreed to put together a list of qualified lawyers available to represent Whitacre. But they insisted that he make the final selection. Shepard thanked them and said he would let Whitacre know.

Once the call ended, the lawyers stayed in Price's office, venting their anger. *We told him this! What was he thinking? How could he do it?*

As they spoke, Mutchnik noticed a subtle change. Days ago, whenever the lawyers had discussed Whitacre, they had always called him Mark. Now, in their anger, none of the lawyers would even mention his name.

Later that day, James Epstein was working at his Chicago law firm when his secretary buzzed. A federal prosecutor named Mutchnik was on the line.

"Yeah, I'll take it," Epstein said.

Epstein was accustomed to hearing from government lawyers. At forty-two, he was established as one of Chicago's most respected trial lawyers. In 1985, after six years at the Cook County public defender's office, Epstein had set up his own private practice. It quickly attracted more business than he could handle, so he brought in two friends who had worked as his partners ever since. Most kinds of cases came through the door: civil and criminal, federal and state, everything. Epstein liked to say that his firm was the type of practice that television viewers might see on *L.A. Law*—just without the sexy people.

Epstein answered and Mutchnik introduced himself.

"So what can I do for you?" Epstein asked.

"We're working with somebody in an investigation who needs to see a lawyer urgently," Mutchnik said. "Would you be willing to meet with him? His name's Mark Whitacre."

Epstein paused. He never made the first move. He didn't want to be accused of improperly soliciting clients.

"Give him my name," Epstein replied. "If he calls, we'll set up an appointment."

Mutchnik thanked the lawyer and hung up.

. . .

After a few hours, the prosecutors had drawn up a list of lawyers. In the afternoon, Whitacre called Mutchnik.

"Okay, we've got three possibilities," Mutchnik said in a direct tone. He ticked off the names, telling Whitacre a little about each lawyer's background.

"Oh, this is great, thank you," Whitacre gushed. "Should I go ahead and call?"

"Do what you want," Mutchnik said. "It's up to you."

Just before ten-thirty the next morning, Mark and Ginger arrived on the eleventh floor at 120 South Riverside Plaza in downtown Chicago. They found suite 1150, the offices of Epstein, Zaideman & Esrig, and spoke with the receptionist.

The lawyer appeared quickly. Ginger stayed in the lobby while Epstein escorted Mark to one of the firm's two conference rooms. A wooden table dominated the small windowless room, with seating for about six people. One of Epstein's partners, Bob Zaideman, joined them.

"First," Epstein said, "I want you to understand that our conversation is confidential. So why don't you go ahead and tell me why you're here."

With that, Whitacre was off, rushing through the story with the speed of a runaway train: ADM, price-fixing, audiotapes, videotapes, hidden cameras, strapped-on recorders, briefing the FBI, briefing the Justice Department.

Epstein listened in awe. *This whole thing sounds like a dime-store thriller,* he thought.

When Whitacre finished, Epstein went back, grilling him about missing pieces of the puzzle. Finally, he was satisfied that he saw the full picture.

"Look," Epstein said, "at this point you haven't hired me and I haven't said I'm interested. But I'll tell you anything about my background that you'd like to know."

Epstein handled Whitacre's questions nimbly. His first concern, Epstein said, would be to make sure that Whitacre met his dual obligations as a corporate officer and a cooperating witness. Did he expect to continue working for ADM? If so, why? They needed to discuss a possible severance agreement. Epstein suggested bringing in a consultant to help put together a financial proposal.

By meeting's end, Whitacre felt more secure than he had in months. He thanked Epstein and left.

Epstein looked to Zaideman. Neither had ever heard of a case like this. As soon as Whitacre was out of earshot, they broke out laughing.

The doorbell rang that same evening at Dwayne Andreas's Fifth Avenue apartment in Manhattan. A minute later, a familiar voice resounded from the doorway, greeting Andreas's longtime maid, Fatima.

It was Zev Furst, one of Andreas's trusted advisors. The men had become friends years before, when Andreas was looking for business opportunities in the Middle East and found Furst, who had numerous connections there through his work with the Anti-Defamation League. Since then, Furst had become a sounding board, helping formulate strategies for dealing with the press and the government. Days before, Furst had heard about the ADM raids while watching CNN during a trip in Germany. He had called Dwayne immediately, but tonight was their first chance to meet in person.

The maid escorted Furst to the study, where Andreas was waiting. Furst greeted him and sank into a wing chair.

"So, what the hell happened?" he asked.

Andreas was poker-faced. "We have a fellow named Mark Whitacre, who is president of our Bioproducts Division. Now it's clear that he has been working with the FBI for several years and wearing a wire."

He had always found Whitacre strange, Andreas said. At one point the company had caught him in lies involving threats to his daughter and sabotage at the plant.

"Randall convinced me not to get rid of him because his profit margins were so large," he said.

But since the raid, Andreas said, he was seeing events of recent years differently—and was even beginning to question things he had witnessed in just the past few weeks. He feared something secret was still going on.

"Many times I saw Whitacre go into Randall's office and shut the door, and I always wondered about that," he said. "Then a few weeks ago, Randall came to see me, crying and telling me he's loyal and owes everything to me."

Andreas looked Furst squarely in the eye.

"Now," he said, "I'm starting to wonder if Randall knew about this taping."*

Furst didn't like what he was hearing.

---

* There is no evidence that Randall knew anything about the investigation before it went public.

"Dwayne, if that's true, I don't care how close Randall is to you," Furst said. "He had an obligation to go to you and the board if he knew."

Andreas considered that.

"You know, Dwayne," Furst said, "there are two stories here. One is the government investigation. But the second part of the story could be an attempt by others to push the Andreas family out of ADM."

Andreas nodded. "You're right. Some people still view me as a carpetbagger from Minnesota."

The conversation lasted into the night, with both men discussing the possibility that others at ADM were working against Andreas. It was the first stage of the paranoia.

The next day, Shepard received another page from Whitacre. His calls had picked up since the raid; clearly he was reaching out to the agent for support.

"Hey, how you doing?" Whitacre asked a moment later. "Did you page me?"

"No, I'm returning your page."

"Oh, I just got a funny number on my pager, didn't know what it was. Figured you might be trying to get me."

"It wasn't me," Shepard said. "But how's it going?"

"Well, I met with a new lawyer, a guy named Jim Epstein in Chicago. I'm very satisfied with him."

Everything was working out, Whitacre said. Epstein had agreed to take the case.

Shepard clicked off the line a few minutes later. Whitacre sounded levelheaded again, more controlled. The agent felt relieved. Now that his witness finally had someone watching out for his interests, maybe everything would be all right.

Scott Roberts, an ADM in-house lawyer, thumbed through records at the office. Roberts had been assigned to handle some of the defense work in the lawsuit filed months before by Ajinomoto, accusing ADM of illegally using the Japanese company's threonine microbe. That day, Roberts had pulled documents related to ADM's purchase of the bug from ABP International, a Swedish company.

Roberts removed two ABP contracts. The first, for $3 million, was signed in November 1992—unknown to Roberts, during the week Whitacre first met Shepard. The second, for $2.5 million, was dated October 21, 1993.

Something about the records bothered Roberts. For one thing, there were too many invoices. Plus, the contracts seemed odd. Both Jim Randall and Lennart Thorstensson, the presidents of the two companies, had initialed each page of the first contract, but hadn't on the second. Why was that?

Roberts flipped to the last pages, where the signatures of Randall and Thorstensson appeared. To Roberts's eye, each man's handwriting looked similar from contract to contract. *In fact . . .*

Bringing the two pages closer together, Roberts laid the signature page of one over the other. He held them up to a light, allowing him to see both signatures together.

Slowly, he slid the two pages until the signature lines matched up. Randall's signature on the top page melded perfectly with the one on the bottom.

The signatures weren't just similar—*they were identical.*

Roberts set the documents down on his desk. He needed to find Rick Reising right away.

After dinner, Whitacre was at home, skimming an old copy of *National Geographic*. Outside, the evening was tranquil, a stark contrast to the emotions and thoughts swirling through his head. He set the magazine down when the phone rang. Lou Rochelli, an ADM controller and a friend, was on the line. Whitacre appreciated the call; he wanted desperately to know the gossip inside the company.

"Hey, Mark," Rochelli said. "I haven't seen you around. What's going on?"

"Why? Are people saying things about me?"

"They seem like they're angry with you. Do you know what's happening?"

"It's just this investigation," Whitacre said. "There was somebody in the company working for the FBI. But what are you hearing about me?"

For several minutes, Rochelli revealed everything he had learned behind the thick walls at ADM headquarters.

"Dwayne's going after me inside the company," Whitacre said to Shepard.

It was the next morning, Friday, July 2. Whitacre sounded ragged. The calming influence of Epstein had worn off. Hanging around the house was tearing him up.

"I've had like twelve phone calls from coworkers," he said, "and they tell me Dwayne's saying I was responsible for the investigation. But everybody calling is supportive of me. Definitely. I've got a lot of support."

Not only that, but Howard Buffett had told him he would be resigning soon. "He really feels the company has committed criminal acts and that they're going to be prosecuted," Whitacre said. "He's getting out."

The troops from Williams & Connolly arrived for their first meeting with the Chicago antitrust prosecutors that same day. Aubrey Daniel took the lead, accompanied by Barry Simon and other lawyers from the firm. The show of force seemed intended to send a message: ADM was ready to fight.

The meeting started casually, with Marvin Price providing a brief history of the building. The lawyers then assembled in the office's large conference room. The antitrust lawyers had prepared their seating arrangement in advance for the most strategic positioning. The defense team sat in a row on the far side of the table, their backs to a wall of windows. They were cordial but aggressive.

"Rick Reising has told me that Whitacre says he made thousands of audio- and videotapes," Daniel said. "We want the results of the entire investigation to date, including all of the tapes. Any tapes in this case are company property. An ADM officer made them, on company time."

The antitrust lawyers suppressed smiles.

No, Griffin responded, the defense lawyers would not be getting everything now. The tapes were the property of the government, not ADM. They would be turned over, as required, in preparation for any court trial.

Barry Simon of Williams & Connolly stood in a conference room across from Jim Epstein, jabbing a finger in the air as he spoke.

"Your client is an ADM officer," Simon said sharply. "He has obligations to this company. And he is going to meet those obligations."

Epstein raised an eyebrow and laughed. Whether intentional or not, Daniel and Simon were running some good cop/bad cop routine—and there was no doubt of Simon's assigned role. Epstein never liked being bullied and wasn't about to respond to the tactic.

The issue on the table was whether Whitacre would cooperate with an internal ADM investigation of price-fixing being conducted by

Williams & Connolly. Epstein doubted it would be objective—the chairman's son was facing prison, for heaven's sake. Rather, he felt sure it would be used to formulate ADM's defense. Before agreeing to help, Epstein first wanted to check with the antitrust lawyers. If they had no problem, Epstein would probably allow an interview with Whitacre as part of some severance agreement. That would clean up the loose ends.

Epstein raised his hands. "I've heard what you've said. I'll get back to you."

More than a week after the government raids on ADM, little about the criminal case unfolding in Illinois had captured the attention of the national news media. Fairly small articles, usually buried inside newspapers, noted that ADM had been served with search warrants, as had a few other companies. It seemed like small beer.

That was about to change. Two reporters with the Chicago bureau of the *Wall Street Journal* were about to propel the investigation to front pages around the globe.

On the evening of July 7, a Friday, Ginger listened as a car pulled around the driveway. A moment later the bell rang, and she opened the door. A bearded man was there.

"Good evening," he said. "Is Mark Whitacre home?"

Ginger stared at the man. "Sorry, he's out of town."

"My name's Scott Kilman. I'm a reporter for the *Wall Street Journal*."

Kilman explained that he and a *Journal* colleague, Tom Burton, were working on an article about the ADM case, and he laid out details of what they had learned. Ginger spoke for a short bit but insisted that her husband was not around. Eventually Kilman thanked her and headed back to the car.

Ginger listened as he drove away. Thank heavens a friend had called to warn that the reporter was on the way. Ginger crossed the room and picked up the phone, calling the stables across the street.

"Mark?" Ginger said. "He left. You can come back."

Over the days that followed, Kilman and Burton kept beating the bushes, trying to confirm their information that Whitacre had cooperated with the FBI.

Until now, Whitacre had been despondent. His life was in shambles;

nobody was congratulating him for doing the right thing. He was the white hat, but the black hats had run him out of town. Maybe if people knew the truth, Whitacre thought, it would help. Maybe Decatur, the industry—maybe even the ADM board—would back him up. These *Journal* reporters had already figured out a lot and were going to print it anyway; they may as well get it right.

Kilman returned early Sunday morning, driving his car to the Whitacres' stables. Whitacre was waiting inside. The time was finally right, he felt, to get his story out.

Later that day, Shepard took a call from Whitacre.

"Brian, listen," Whitacre said. "I heard from some reporters with *Wall Street*. They tell me *Wall Street* is running an article tomorrow or the next day. They said that it's gonna name me as cooperating with the government."

Shepard listened, uneasy. This was not good.

"Did you talk to them, Mark? What did you say?"

"They came by the house Friday. But Ginger told them I was out of town. One of them came by again this morning, and I was here. But I just told him I had no comment."

Soon afterward, Whitacre cradled the phone. He didn't feel bad misleading Shepard. As far as he was concerned, he'd helped the FBI enough. He didn't owe them the truth.

Mutchnik arrived at work early Monday morning and headed to the mailboxes. As always, several copies of the *Wall Street Journal*—brought up from the lobby by a receptionist—were stacked up. Mutchnik grabbed one, scanning the front. His eyes locked on the lead article.

SEEDS OF DOUBT: AN EXECUTIVE BECOMES INFORMANT FOR THE FBI, STUNNING GIANT ADM, the headline read.

A little more than halfway down the page, a sketch of a smiling Whitacre appeared. Mutchnik skimmed the article as he walked to his office; the reporters had learned a lot. The article told how Whitacre had begun working for the FBI in 1992, offered details about audio- and videotapes, and listed meeting sites in Tokyo, Hawaii, and Los Angeles. The reporters had even found out about the briefcase rigged with a recording device. Obviously, they had good sources.

Mutchnik was reviewing the article again when his phone rang. Shepard and Herndon were on the line. They had just seen the article and were very upset.

"How could this happen?" Shepard asked.

"Yeah," Mutchnik said. "What a shame for Mark."

That same morning, Whitacre was in his kitchen eating cereal as he watched the news on WAND, a Decatur television station. The weather segment had just finished and the anchor, Gayle Simpson, announced the top news story.

"Mark Whitacre, a high-level executive with the Archer Daniels Midland Company, has reportedly been a Federal Bureau of Investigation informant," Simpson intoned, crediting the news to a report in the *Wall Street Journal*.

Whitacre listened, swelling with pride.

"Hey, Ginger!" he called out. "Quick, get in here! You've gotta hear this!"

Ginger hurried in and listened to the news in wonder.

In Lake Charles, Louisiana, Kyle Rountree grabbed the top copy from a stack of *Wall Street Journal*s at a local store and paid the cashier. As he headed for the door, he glanced at the lead article.

Mark Whitacre.

Whitacre. From ADM. Rountree, the cooperating witness in the FBI's investigation into the possible theft of Degussa's methionine secrets, was very familiar with the name. This was a central figure in the methionine case, a man Rountree had discussed with the FBI. Now, it ends up Whitacre had been a cooperating witness, too? *Since 1992?*

Rountree found a phone and dialed Special Agent Craig Dahle at the FBI office in Mobile, Alabama.

"It's Kyle Rountree," he said when Dahle answered. "What the hell's going on here?"

Ron Ferrari was watching the television news at his house in suburban Chicago when a photograph of his old friend Mark Whitacre appeared on the screen. Ferrari listened as the newscaster described Whitacre's work for the FBI. Immediately he reached for a telephone.

Ferrari was a local hero back in his hometown of Moweaqua, thanks to five years as a linebacker with the San Francisco 49ers. His team had even traveled to the Super Bowl in 1985, although a knee injury had kept Ferrari off the field. But Ferrari had long known that he would never be a star and was prepared to fall back on his training in grain marketing. After his professional football career, Ferrari had worked at ADM, where he had met Whitacre. Ferrari had since left the company but kept in touch with Whitacre. He reached his old friend at home.

"Hey," Ferrari said. "I'm sitting here watching TV, and I saw you."

"Yeah," Whitacre replied. "What do you think?"

"What should I think? I can't believe this."

Whitacre described all of the events of recent days. Ferrari asked a question about Mick Andreas.

"He's not going to be with the company anymore," Whitacre said. "I'm going to be taking over. Mick's gone."

Just off the Whitacre's driveway, crowds of reporters milled about, some craning their necks for a look at the home of that day's most newsworthy corporate executive.

The steady drumbeat of news coverage was overwhelming. The Whitacres' name was on every television and radio station. It all left Ginger uneasy. Long a private person, she could no longer leave her own home without passing throngs of shouting reporters. Worse, Mark would tell her, anonymous threatening calls were coming to the house. She had never imagined it would come to this.

Still, for the first few days, Mark seemed happy with the way the story was playing out. Everywhere, he was being portrayed as a corporate hero, a golden boy executive who had been unwilling to tolerate wrongdoing. He liked that.

But on the third day of relentless coverage, the tide turned. That morning, Whitacre drove to a gas station where there was a newspaper box for the *Wall Street Journal*. He dropped in a few coins and took his copy, heading back to his car as he scanned the paper. A headline on the front page hit him like a sock in the stomach.

You dirty rat, says Decatur, Ill. of mole at Archer Daniels: People think Mark Whitacre betrayed them and ask why he turned to FBI.

Whitacre felt blinded by anger. When did it become time to dump on Mark Whitacre? This wasn't right. He climbed into the car and drove home, fuming and insulted.

Later that day, Herndon was in Springfield, listening on the phone as Whitacre angrily rambled.

"Dwayne and Terry have been bad-mouthing me at ADM," Whitacre ranted. "They're saying I'm not a good worker and can't be trusted! How can they be saying that?"

"Mark," Herndon replied soothingly, "why are you worried about that? You know you're a hard worker. You're a workaholic; you do a good job. Look, Mark, these guys violated the law. They're going to lash out at you."

"Yeah, but . . ."

"Mark, listen. Haven't we talked about this before? How many nights did we tell you how you had to expect the unexpected, that you might be attacked, you might be fired, that some people aren't going to like you."

"Well, it's not fair. They shouldn't be able to say these things. I'm thinking about bringing a slander suit."

"Mark, I'm not an attorney. I can't give you legal advice. But I don't know if this is a slander suit."

Whitacre took a breath. Herndon could tell he wasn't holding up well.

"Mark, you need to relax," Herndon said. "Hey, want to play some golf?"

"No, I'm not going to play golf."

"Well, why don't you guys take a vacation, just get out of the area. Look, this story is the big thing in Decatur. Get away from it. Go out of town."

Again, Whitacre turned away the suggestion. He had other concerns, he said. He might move sometime, to get away from all this. He had asked for the government's help in selling his house before but never received a response. What was happening with that?

Herndon said he still didn't have an answer. As long as ADM continued paying Whitacre, the government would resist giving him money. But Shepard and Herndon understood Whitacre's financial concerns. They wouldn't forget him.

Five days later, on July 18, two innocuous-looking letters arrived at ADM headquarters. Postmarked on July 13 in Knoxville, Tennessee, both had been sent with no return address and stamps that portrayed President Nixon. One was addressed to Dwayne Andreas, the other to Jim Randall. Even though they were anonymous, the letters contained allegations against Whitacre—and the FBI—that the company took very seriously.

After they were read and copied, the letters were sent to Aubrey Daniel. He would know how to use them to ADM's advantage in its fight with the government.

• • •

Franklin, Tennessee, nestled in the bluegrass hills twenty miles south of Nashville, is a town whose citizens like to boast of being comfortable not only living beside their history, but in it. The town is built around a fifteen-block Victorian commercial district, featuring at its center a towering statue of a Confederate soldier—one of many markers to the bloody Battle of Franklin in 1864.

But in 1995 the new battle of Franklin was being won. After years spent renovating the town, young entrepreneurs were beginning to join its citizenry. Property values were climbing. It was a good time to be a real-estate broker.

Among the brokers who handled Franklin was Gertraud Borasky, a top saleswoman at the Haworth Homes–Century 21. Business had been brisk for Borasky in recent months; the phone was always ringing. One afternoon, Borasky was at her desk when another call came in. She answered pleasantly.

"Hello," a woman's voice said. "My name is Ginger Whitacre. My husband and I live in Moweaqua, Illinois, and we're going to be coming to Nashville to look for a new house. I wanted to see what was available in your area."

"Of course," Borasky said. "What kind of home are you looking for?"

"Well, we need nine thousand square feet of living space and facilities for our horses."

Borasky smiled. This would be a big sale. The caller scheduled an appointment for late July. The Whitacres wanted to come down and do some house hunting.

At 3:19 on the afternoon of July 16, a Sunday, a fax machine for Dwayne Andreas hummed to life at ADM. A one-page typewritten memo scrolled into a tray. The fax "telltale," which normally prints the number of the sender at the top of the sheet, had been disguised. But the first words of the note made clear the intended recipients.

> TO: *Aubrey Daniels and ADM board members.*
> FROM: *ADM Shareholders' Watch Committee (ADMSWC)*

What followed was unbelievable. The author—or authors—claimed to be part of a shareholders' group formed to investigate companies whose stock they owned.

"We have been gathering information for years and were planning to present our findings at the upcoming shareholders' meeting," the note read. "Unfortunately, the FBI upstaged us. We were well aware of ADM's price-fixing activities."

The note accused an ADM officer of billing the company millions of dollars for personal travel on company planes. It also criticized Aubrey Daniel—incorrectly calling him Daniels—implying that he represented the interests of the Andreas family rather than those of the shareholders.

"We have moles, if I may use the word, inside every division of ADM. You see, this is our company, not the Andreases!" it read. "Fifty thousand shareholders are a sleeping giant that is waking up to the alarming actions of Dwayne and his den of thieves!"

At the bottom, it was signed, "The Lamet Vov."

Even as those words were printing out of Andreas's fax machine, the unlisted business fax number for another company director was ringing. Over the next forty-six minutes, the anonymous note would be faxed to more than a dozen sites around the continent—including Montreal, Springfield, Washington, and Minneapolis—to the offices of most every ADM board member.

Brian Mulroney, the former prime minister of Canada, smiled to his fellow directors as he walked into the sixth-floor boardroom at ADM on July 19. They took their seats around the large circular table dominating the room. Replicas of master artworks, painted through a technique involving computers, hung on the walls beside plaques and honors awarded to Dwayne Andreas over the years.

Mulroney looked around the table. Seated nearby was F. Ross Johnson, the former chairman and chief executive of RJR Nabisco who had lost a battle to buy the company but won national fame from his depiction in *Barbarians at the Gate*, the book and movie about the takeover fight. Bob Strauss, the dean of Washington insiders, occupied another seat. Happy Rockefeller, the widow of Nelson and a longtime friend of the Andreases, was chatting with Ray Goldberg, a Harvard University professor. John Daniels, a former ADM chairman, was reviewing material for the meeting.

The primary agenda item that day was the criminal investigation. Aubrey Daniel was there to make a presentation to the board. He laid out the relevant information developed by that point. Already, the company was facing numerous shareholder lawsuits claiming that price-fixing had damaged the stock value.

"Based on our experience," Daniel said, "if the directors do not appoint a committee to cope with the litigation, then a group of share-holders can become a self-appointed committee." In essence, if the board didn't handle this, the shareholders might.

The directors agreed to form a litigation committee. The newest director—Gaylord Coan, the president of Gold Kist Inc.—announced that he had a conflict of interest. His company was in a partnership with ADM and was a large purchaser of lysine. "I'm not going to sit on this committee," he said after explaining his problems.

Bob Strauss spoke up. "I also have some difficulties," he said. His firm represented ADM in some matters—and then there was the short-lived representation of Whitacre by his partner, John Dowd.

After several minutes, the group reached an agreement. Nine of the seventeen directors would serve on the committee, including Mulroney, Johnson, Daniels, and Goldberg. Mulroney was named chairman.

"It would be best," Aubrey Daniel suggested, "to have cochairmen."

The directors looked at one another. Several eyes settled on John Daniels. Would he take the job? Daniels thought for a second. His grandfather had founded this company; his father had been chief executive. The decision was easy.

"I'm horrified at what I have heard in the last few weeks," he said. "I feel a close affinity for this company and anything I can do to help I want to do."

Daniels looked at the assembled directors.

"So, yes," he said, "I will accept the nomination as cochairman."

The next sign of trouble for the government's investigation appeared the following morning, in the pages of the *Chicago Tribune*.

The article led with ADM's announcement that the board had formed a special committee to deal with the case. A few paragraphs later, it veered in a new direction. Millikin University in Decatur had provided the reporters with biographical information about Whitacre that had been turned over to the school when he was elected to its board. The information showed that Whitacre had earned a master's degree from the prestigious Kellogg Graduate School of Management and a doctorate in biochemistry from Cornell.

But, according to the article, the claims were false. Whitacre never received a master's from Kellogg, a school spokesman told the paper. And, while Whitacre was awarded a doctorate from Cornell, the article said, it was in nutrition, not biochemistry.*

---

*The degree was actually in nutritional biochemistry.

"Questions about Whitacre's credibility could become an issue in the government's grand jury investigation," the paper intoned.

That morning, Mutchnik laughed as he read those words on his usual 6:53 train to work. He had always thought that something about Whitacre exuded pretense; this story fit his opinion. When Mutchnik arrived at the office, he headed for the phone to call the agents. Herndon was at his desk.

"Hey, Bob," Mutchnik said, laughing.

"What's so funny?"

"Hold on," Mutchnik said. "Let me read this to you."

As he listened to the *Tribune* article, Herndon sighed.

"Oh, man," Herndon said. "What's he going to lie about next?"

That same day, Mark and Ginger Whitacre were down in Tennessee, walking through a large house with Gert Borasky of Century 21. The tour took more than an hour, but by then the Whitacres were ready to buy. Borasky phoned later that day with a bid of $890,000—$60,000 below the list price. The owners, Paul and Carole Myer, countered with a price of $935,000, and the two sides struck a deal.

The next day, the Whitacres came back to the house with the realtors, ready to go to contract. Everyone gathered around a table as Mark signed. Paul Myer watched, feeling good. The house had been on the market for more than a month. He was glad the sale was done.

"Listen, Mr. Myer," Mark Whitacre said after he finished signing. "Can I speak with you outside for a second? I have a question about your hot tub."

"Sure," Myer replied, standing up.

The men walked out to the deck. Whitacre stopped and looked Myer in the eye.

"Do you know who I am?" he asked in a near-whisper.

"I know you're the person who just spent almost a million dollars buying my house," Myer replied, instantly regretting the words.

"Well, I asked you that question because I was recently on the front page of the *Wall Street Journal*, regarding Archer Daniels Midland," Whitacre said. "I was an informant for the FBI. I was working with them in an investigation of ADM, my employer. For two and a half years I worked as an informant, taping evidence about price-fixing. Now the case is public, and Decatur is a very small community. So the FBI advised me that it might be good to relocate. That's why I'm moving here."

Myer stared at Whitacre. *Why are you telling me all this?*

"So I'm just wondering if you have any concerns," Whitacre said.

Myer shrugged. "As far as I'm concerned, I have no need for any of this information," he said. "My only concern is obviously getting the money for the house."

"Don't worry, I have the money," Whitacre replied. "The FBI's willing to help me financially, probably by providing a loan to cover the sale of my other house. The government's making it possible for me to move from Decatur."

A fleeting smile passed over Whitacre's face. "I have the money," he repeated.

It took only a few days for another unsigned note, mailed in San Francisco on July 17, to arrive at Williams & Connolly. This one was addressed to Aubrey Daniel, who by now was growing used to the flood of anonymous letters. It was as if there were two teams out there: "the Lamet Vov," who sent notes attacking ADM, and other writers who went after Whitacre. The latest note clearly came from someone on the anti-Whitacre side.

"Sir," it began, "ADM's Whitacre has some 'strange' allies—*and* a bit of blackmail *against* him. Check his family, 'friends' and *Justice people*."

The writer cautioned not to hire a "stumblebum investigator," but instead to find somebody "ruthless and smart," like G. Gordon Liddy, the famed Watergate burglar.

"You'll be surprised," the letter said at its close, "about who Whitacre *really* is."

Janet Reno, the Attorney General of the United States, stepped into a Justice Department conference room where Louis Freeh and his top deputies from the FBI were gathering. They had just arrived from Bureau headquarters for their biweekly meeting with the department's senior staff, including Jamie Gorelick, the Deputy Attorney General. The meetings were intended to keep communications open, and Reno tried to stop by whenever possible.

The conversation moved along quickly. After reviewing a number of agenda items, Reno spoke. "On the ADM matter, I've received letters from their counsel," she said. "They're represented by Williams & Connolly."

In recent days, Reno said, Aubrey Daniel had sent written complaints to her by messenger. Most everyone at the table already knew about them; Freeh had received copies, and Gorelick had also seen them. The most recent letter complained about press coverage, claiming that "agents of the government" had spoken with reporters. The letter clearly implied that the FBI, Whitacre, or both were the source of the leaks.

The group discussed the Williams & Connolly complaints, with the FBI taking the opportunity to brief Reno and Gorelick on the progress of the case. The discussion ended in a matter of minutes.

In the days that followed, the ADM case was increasingly a topic of conversation at the senior levels of the Justice Department. The frontal assault by Williams & Connolly made it painfully clear that ADM was preparing for war. The prosecution team was going to need reinforcements. Quickly, the decision was made. They needed to find a prosecutor with experience in high-profile cases involving top-notch defense attorneys.

In a onetime newspaper publishing office in Oklahoma City, Joe Hartzler was reviewing documents about the bombing at that city's federal building. Since leaving the ADM case months before, Hartzler had volunteered to come from the Springfield U.S. Attorney's office to lead the prosecution of Timothy McVeigh and his co-conspirators in the terrorist attack. Indictments were just weeks away.

The phone rang on Hartzler's desk. It was Merrick Garland, the senior Justice Department official who had personally handled portions of the bombing case. Hartzler and Garland spoke frequently every day, but this time Garland said there was also another matter on his mind.

"We have a complicated financial case out in Chicago," Garland said. "It involves some high-powered defense counsel, and I wanted to know if there was a lawyer in the U.S. Attorney's office you think could handle it."

Hartzler suspected this was his old case, Harvest King. And immediately, he knew that his friend Scott Lassar was perfect for it. Lassar was a federal prosecutor who had worked many major cases. At this point, Lassar was deeply immersed in Operation Silver Shovel, an investigation that used a corrupt waste hauler as a cooperating witness to collect recordings of Chicago city officials soliciting and collecting bribes. Lassar knew tapes, he knew informants, he could handle tough cases.

"I'd recommend Scott Lassar," Hartzler replied. "He's the First Assistant there, although I'm not sure he could take on a major battle that would be all-consuming."

"Well," Garland said, "without telling anybody else, could you call Lassar and find out if he'd consider it?"

Hartzler reached Lassar that evening after ten o'clock. Lassar relaxed in his family room while speaking on the portable phone; Hartzler was calling from his temporary quarters at the Embassy Suites in Oklahoma City.

"Scott, I got a call from DOJ, and they're looking for somebody to handle a complex financial fraud case. Your name came to mind. And I was wondering if it's something you would consider."

Lassar had no idea what case Hartzler was talking about or where it would even be tried. But he didn't hesitate for a second.

"Sure," he said. "I'm interested."

Outside a budget hotel in Bloomington, Illinois, Whitacre stepped out of his car, buttoning the jacket on his lightweight double-breasted suit. The drive north on Route 51 from Moweaqua had taken a bit more than an hour, pretty good time. Whitacre looked at his watch. Just before six o'clock. He might even be early.

For days, Whitacre had been coming apart. He had been bottling up secrets, holding back on information he knew. He was tired of it. He wanted to open up.

He walked through the lobby, heading for the prearranged hotel room, the site of his secret meeting. After so many years, all the stealth and sneaking felt like second nature. He arrived at the room and knocked on the door. A young man answered.

"Mark?" the man said, extending a hand. "Hi, I'm Ron Henkoff. Good to see you."

Whitacre smiled. Henkoff, a reporter from *Fortune* magazine, looked just the way he had imagined. Whitacre knew that *Fortune* was well trusted by Warren Buffett; Howard had told him so. And now *Fortune* was promising to let Whitacre tell his own story, in his own words. This was his chance to speak to Decatur—for that matter, to the world. Then everyone would understand the choices he had made. They would understand he had done the right thing.

Henkoff invited Whitacre to another room, where a photographer, Chris Sanders, was waiting. The blinds were closed; pieces of cloth were hung up as a background. Whitacre looked occasionally bemused as Sanders snapped shot after shot. One of these, Whitacre knew, was a photograph destined for the magazine's cover.

Once the photography session was over, Whitacre returned to Henkoff's room and sat at a table. For several hours under the reporter's questioning, Whitacre told his perspective on the price-fixing investigation, describing the roles of Wilson and Mick Andreas, the involvement of Kyowa Hakko and Ajinomoto, his first meeting with Shepard, volume agreements, the tapes.

Close to midnight, they were done. Many of the secrets of Harvest King had been revealed.

The Whitacres' purchase of the house in Franklin, Tennessee, was proceeding without a hitch. Gert Borasky, their real-estate agent, had heard from Whitacre that an associate would be helping him find a mortgage. During their conversations, Whitacre mentioned that he had been working for two years as an FBI informant, but insisted she not tell anyone. It was a secret, he said.

Borasky said she needed something attesting to the Whitacres' financing. A letter, written July 26, soon arrived at her office from Joseph Caiazzo, a New York lawyer. Caiazzo wrote that he represented a lender who had agreed to provide the Whitacres with financing of up to $930,000 for the purchase.

Everything looked in order. Only one item was curious. Neither Caiazzo nor Whitacre had told Borasky the name of the lender. But the oversight seemed inconsequential.

Nothing seemed to concern Whitacre more than the talk about him inside ADM. Every negative rumor left him arguing fitfully that the comment was a lie. Ginger begged him to stop calling old colleagues in search of scuttlebutt. Sometimes he seemed to agree—only to rush back to the phone minutes later and start his hunt again.

In July, Whitacre was visiting family in Ohio when he called Lou Rochelli, the ADM controller. Whitacre asked eagerly if anything was happening.

"Well," Rochelli said, "there's one thing happening you're going to be interested in."

"ADM's trying to smear my character!" Whitacre wailed to Shepard. "This isn't right!"

It was minutes later. Whitacre explained he had heard that Mick Andreas was instructing auditors to review Whitacre's expense statements and financial transactions in search of irregularities.

"And he's telling them if they don't find anything wrong, that they're supposed to make something up!"

"Mark," Shepard said soothingly, "we've talked to you about this in the past as something you should expect."

Despite Shepard's efforts, Whitacre stayed upset. He didn't like the way this was going. Definitely not.

A flurry of faxes and letters from the anonymous Lamet Vov continued to arrive throughout July to the homes and offices of ADM executives and directors. One went to Mark Cheviron, ADM's security chief, urging him to tell what he knew to the board. Another was sent to the company's chief pilot, urging him to report all improper travel by officers. Each was forwarded to Aubrey Daniel, who was growing angered by what he perceived to be threats.

On July 30, a new, more aggressive fax from the Lamet Vov was sent to ADM directors. It demanded the resignations of Dwayne and Mick Andreas, Terry Wilson, and Barrie Cox. It also insisted that Joe Hale, a company director, be named chief executive and that Mark Whitacre be selected as executive vice president.

"We suggest you get things moving in the right direction, and fast," the fax read. "We can have a book on the street in two weeks exposing our findings that will ruin many people and end careers."

Brian Mulroney had no illusions about the allegiances of Williams & Connolly. They were fighting for the company, which in this case could easily mean for the Andreas family. But now Mulroney was in charge of the board's special committee, a group that did not even exist when Williams & Connolly was retained. What if the committee needed to take an action that might harm the Andreases? How could Williams & Connolly provide objective advice?

Mulroney telephoned his cochairman, John Daniels.

"I'm concerned," he said. "I think we need our own counsel, because we may not be working on the same side of the street as Williams & Connolly before we're through."

Daniels agreed but had no suggestions for which law firm to hire. Mulroney came up with his own idea.

Beneath vast stretches of deep blue in Emigrant, Montana, a team of ersatz cowboys straggled out of the main lodge at the B Bar Ranch, ready for the day's activities. The summer haying and vegetable harvests were still under way at the nine-thousand-acre ranch in the heart of the Rocky Mountains. But there were plenty of other activities available for the wealthy clientele, from fly-fishing in the meandering Yellowstone River to saddling up for some work with cattle herds.

Richard Beattie, chairman of the New York law firm Simpson Thacher & Bartlett, was planning on taking advantage of the fishing. A soft-spoken ex-marine, Beattie was a man who traveled in diverse circles, from the political elite of New York's Democratic Party to the top deal-makers of Wall Street's investment community. Beattie had also gained fame from his longtime role as a legal advisor to Henry Kravis, general partner with Kohlberg Kravis Roberts & Co., the premier leveraged-buyout firm. Beattie had been a principal advisor in Kravis's successful takeover bid for RJR Nabisco, besting a competing offer from a group led by the company's then-chairman, F. Ross Johnson. Beattie, like Johnson and Kravis, had been prominently featured in *Barbarians at the Gate*, the best-selling book about the takeover fight.

On this day, Beattie was vacationing with an old friend, Kenneth Lipper, a renowned investment banker and former deputy mayor of New York. For the two men and their wives, the trip to the B Bar Ranch was a chance to get away from the hustle and ringing phones of Manhattan. But that morning, a message was waiting for Beattie at the ranch's front office. Brian Mulroney wanted to speak with him. Beattie found a phone and called right back.

"I called because I need someone to advise a special committee of directors with the Archer Daniels Midland Company," Mulroney said a few minutes later. "And you have come highly recommended to me."

Mulroney said he had spoken with one of his fellow directors, Ross Johnson, as well as with Henry Kravis, and both had sung Beattie's praises.

Despite the sketchy details, Beattie accepted the assignment. He and Mulroney agreed that they would get together at the next meeting of the special committee, at the Washington offices of Williams & Connolly.

The August morning was clear and bright, the hot sun tempered by a cool breeze. Herndon figured it was perfect golfing weather—and a great excuse to show Whitacre that the FBI still cared. He dialed Whitacre's home number.

"Hey," Herndon said. "It's Bob. How's it going?"

"Pretty good, pretty good," Whitacre mumbled.

Herndon took a breath. Whitacre sounded terrible, his voice heavy with distraction.

"Well, I just wanted to make sure everything's going okay," Herndon said. "I haven't seen you for a while, and I wanted to see if maybe you'd like to play some golf. I can take an afternoon off if you want to go—"

"I'm kind of busy," Whitacre interrupted.

"Well, how about Brian and I come by and let's go to lunch? We need to pick up that equipment, and we'd like to see you and see what's going on."

"Well, yeah, what's good for you?"

"Whatever's good for you, Mark. You tell me."

Whitacre flipped through his schedule. He suggested meeting in two days, on Wednesday, August 2.

"That'll be great, Mark," Herndon said. "We'll see you then at your house."

Later that afternoon, Jim Epstein's telephone rang. He had been representing Whitacre for less than a month, but already the case was taking up much of his time. He had reached the outlines of a $7.5 million severance agreement with ADM, which would require Whitacre to sit for an extensive exit interview. But those negotiations were not Epstein's only demands from the case. Between calls from ADM, the government, reporters, and Whitacre, it seemed he was spending most of his day on the phone.

This time, the caller was a surprise. It was Jim Randall, along with a Williams & Connolly lawyer.

"I am calling on behalf of ADM to demand that your client, Mark Whitacre, meet with company officials on the afternoon of August third, at five o'clock," Randall said.

What was this all about? Epstein asked.

"We want him to answer questions about certain financial transactions."

On the morning of August 2, Jim Griffin was at his desk in the Chicago office when he heard that Aubrey Daniel was holding for him. He picked up the phone.

"I have an urgent matter to discuss," Daniel said. "I want a meeting immediately, in Washington. And I want it with someone in the division who has the authority to make decisions about the investigation."

Griffin listened, intrigued. "What does this involve?" he asked.

"That's what I want to discuss at the meeting. I assure you, it's an important matter, and I wouldn't be making this request if it wasn't."

Griffin thought for a moment. There seemed to be enough urgency in Daniel's tone that he couldn't simply be put off. Griffin decided to take the lawyer at his word.

"I'll arrange something," Griffin said, "and get right back to you."

Shepard shook his head. "What do they think they have now?" he asked.

The news of Daniel's demands for a meeting hit like a dousing of cold water. Griffin had made arrangements to hold the meeting the next morning and had already booked his flight to Washington. The agents thought the response was excessive; probably this was just going to be another complaint about leaks in the press.

"Man, DOJ should refuse to talk to this guy," Herndon said.

"You're right," Shepard agreed. "They should say, 'If you want to talk to the government, Mr. Daniel, you go to Jim Griffin. He's in charge of this case.'"

The two agents groused another few minutes, until Shepard noticed the time. It was after twelve-fifteen. If they were going to drive over to Whitacre's for lunch, they needed to leave the office right away.

The drive to Moweaqua took about twenty-five minutes. The agents pulled the car into the driveway, weaving up to the front. Whitacre appeared on the porch. He seemed in good spirits. The three men greeted each other.

"Hey, listen," Whitacre said. "I thought we could go to this Chinese place I know in Taylorville. Nothing fancy, but the food is pretty good."

"Sure, Mark," Shepard said. "Sounds great."

The men decided to take Shepard's car. Whitacre got into the back. As they drove to Taylorville, Whitacre chatted about the restaurant. Eventually, he paused, leaning his arms on the front seat.

"Guys," he said, his tone serious. "There's something I want to tell you."

Herndon turned, while Shepard glanced in the mirror.

"My attorney's telling me not to say anything. It's something I've wanted to talk about for a while, but he wanted to see if ADM raised it. But I want to tell you."

This didn't sound good. Herndon held up a hand. "Mark, wait.

Don't tell us anything. You have an attorney. We need to make sure we're allowed to hear this."

"Bob's right," Shepard said. "This isn't like before, Mark. You're represented."

Whitacre sat back, looking disappointed. Both agents could tell he was going to have trouble holding back on his story. Herndon changed the subject.

"So," he said, "how was your trip to Tennessee? What's the new place like?"

Whitacre smiled. "Oh, it's great," he said, launching into a description of the house.

The idle talk continued for some time, as they drove down the small road, surrounded on both sides by cornfields. Eventually, the conversation ran out. Whitacre stared out the window.

He looked back at the agents. Jim Randall had contacted him, he said suddenly.

Herndon fixed him with an intrigued look. "Oh, yeah?"

"They want to talk to me. It's about money stuff."

"What kind of stuff?"

"Financial transactions. Stuff I haven't told you."

It had only taken Whitacre a second, but already he had slipped the conversation back to the topic that had been bothering him.

"Is this what you were referring to before?"

"Yeah."

Herndon wavered. He wanted to call the lawyers, to ask how to proceed. But that wasn't practical. He decided to make sure Whitacre knew what he was doing.

"Mark, you understand your lawyer has advised you not to discuss this matter."

"I know."

"And we're not asking you. So anything you say to us is a free and voluntary statement, against your lawyer's advice. If you tell us about this now, it means you'll be talking without representation present. You understand?"

"I understand. But I want to tell you."

Both agents sat silently in the front. They thought it was dangerous to say anything. Whitacre was on his own; whatever happened from here on was his decision.

"ADM's found some questionable financial things involving me. They want to meet with me and Epstein tomorrow to answer questions. If I don't cooperate, they say they're going to take 'appropri-ate action.' "

Whitacre sounded distressed.

"What does that mean, 'appropriate action'? I mean, are they talk-ing about going to the FBI? Are they talking about going to prosecu-tors?"

This was getting bad, rapidly.

Shepard looked in the mirror again. "It's difficult to know what the term means, Mark," he said. "It's hard to say whether law-enforcement agencies, if advised of the information, would open an investigation and whether they would ultimately refer it for prosecution."

For several minutes, Shepard continued a monologue about law enforcement. He talked about the differences between civil and crimi-nal cases, about state, local, and federal agencies, and about how the merits of a prosecution are judged. Herndon listened, hoping his part-ner could keep his speech going until they reached the Taylorville restaurant, where they could call the antitrust lawyers.

He did. As Shepard wrapped up his primer, they pulled in at the shopping center where the Chinese restaurant was located. After park-ing, the three men headed in, the conversation temporarily on hold. Herndon noticed a pay phone and hesitated, thinking about calling the lawyers. He decided to wait. A hostess approached the group and guided them to a table near the front.

Whitacre hesitated. "Umm, could we sit in the back?"

The hostess nodded, escorting the group to a large, round table. They took seats facing a wall, with Whitacre between the two agents. The three men studied the menu and ordered quickly; their food arrived in a few minutes. Herndon tasted his orange chicken. Whitacre was right—this place was pretty good.

The men chatted for a few minutes about the food and whatever else came to mind. No one was going to ask Whitacre anything about the financial issue. The conversation hit a lull. Everyone was uncom-fortable.

Whitacre looked down at his food for a moment.

"Let me throw out some hypotheticals," he said. "I'll talk about some financial stuff and you tell me if they're wrong and how serious they might be."

The agents continued eating, trying to seem casual.

"Suppose a company gave an executive a car, you know, a corpo-rate car," Whitacre said. "But instead of driving it to work, he drove his personal car and gave the company car to his daughter to drive. Would that be a problem?"

The agents almost wanted to laugh. After the big buildup, Whitacre's concerns sounded trivial.

"Mark, that may be against corporate policy and there may be IRS issues," Herndon said. "You may have to pay taxes on that, but it shouldn't be a big problem."

Whitacre nodded, looking serious. He paused.

"Well," he finally said, "just hypothetically, let me give you another example. What about if an executive used a corporate airplane for personal use?"

Basically the same thing, Herndon said. Maybe some tax issues, but it didn't sound like a major problem.

"Okay," he said when Herndon finished, "let me give you another one."

"Okay."

Whitacre paused again.

"What if, hypothetically, the activity involved was kickbacks by corporate executives?"

Herndon and Shepard didn't flinch.

"Well, Mark," Herndon said, "you know better than I do that there are plenty of ways companies try to attract business. I mean, you know, they buy meals at restaurants for potential customers; they buy them tickets to sporting events. They even buy them gifts. That happens."

Shepard chimed in. "I don't know if there would be federal violations involved in something like that. Maybe it's ethically not right, but it's done. I mean, it's widely known that businesses do that."

Whitacre pondered the agents' words. He appeared to be considering how to respond.

"Umm, I need to ask," Whitacre said. "Is this conversation on or off the record?"

"Definitely on the record, Mark," Shepard replied. "A report will be generated about whatever you say."

Herndon shoveled some orange chicken into his mouth, watching Whitacre as he ate. He could tell the man was uncomfortable and that they had some distance to go. But at this point, there was no telling where they were headed.

"Okay," Whitacre said. "Well, what if the kickbacks to executives were generally accepted in the company?"

"What do you mean?" Shepard asked.

"What if the company generally accepted kickbacks to executives? Like ten to twenty thousand dollars for low-level guys and more for higher-level executives."

Shepard set down his fork. "How much money are you talking about?" he asked.

Whitacre was slow to respond. "Like as much as five hundred thousand."

Shepard and Herndon stared at Whitacre, speechless.

"Well," Shepard finally said, struggling to recover, "taking cash in any amount is different from having meals paid for or receiving tickets."

Herndon glanced over at Shepard. *Thanks for the brilliant observation, Brian.*

"But this is a difficult question," Shepard continued. "The funds sound like they would be corporate, so I'm a little uncertain regarding possible violations."

As far as he knew, Shepard said, fraud cases handled by the FBI usually involved federally insured money. Herndon shook his head; he knew almost any embezzlement could be charged as a wire fraud and said so.

"Well, what if the money wasn't from the executive's company?" Whitacre asked. "Would it be any different if the transaction involved a foreign company?"

Where was this going? The conversation was driving both agents crazy. Whitacre was giving bits and pieces but never letting them see the whole picture. If a foreign company was involved, it could lead to more violations, Herndon said. But it was hard to say without specifics.

Shepard decided to push. "What do you mean by a foreign company being involved?" he asked.

Whitacre ignored the question. "Would it make any difference if it was solicited by a foreign supplier?"

"No, Mark," Shepard said. "It probably wouldn't."

Herndon couldn't believe the man was a Ph.D. He was acting like a simpleton. Why was he dragging this out? What was all that garbage about company cars? *And—oh yeah, what about half a million bucks in kickbacks, too?*

During the conversation, they had finished their food. They paid their bill and headed to the car. Herndon climbed into the back, and Whitacre took the front seat.

Herndon leaned up on the seat and looked at Whitacre.

"Let's not go home right now," he said. "Let's talk about this a bit more, okay?"

Whitacre nodded, saying nothing. They drove for a short while, going down a country road outside of Taylorville. Finally, Shepard pulled off the road, onto a small embankment beside a cornfield.

"Okay," he said. "When was this first transaction?"

Whitacre looked down. The "hypothetical" cover was being dropped.

"December of 1991."

The agents wrote that down. The meaning was not lost on them. Whitacre did this long before meeting the FBI.

"Did you receive money?" Shepard asked. "And if so, how was it paid?"

"By check. There were checks deposited in various accounts. But the amount was always under ten thousand dollars."

Herndon winced. The number had a meaning in law enforcement. To guard against money laundering, banks send currency transaction reports, or CTRs, to the government for every transaction involving more than $10,000. But structuring payments so that no check exceeds $10,000 could also be a crime, if the purpose was to avoid the CTR.

"Why below ten thousand?" Herndon asked.

"Big checks draw suspicion in a small town."

"Is that really the reason, Mark?" Herndon asked sternly. "Or were you trying to come under the level that would require the banks to report it?"

Herndon's tone shocked Whitacre. He told Herndon that he didn't understand. Herndon explained the law. Whitacre denied he had been trying to avoid reporting.

"When did you set up these accounts?" Shepard asked.

"Over a period of time."

Shepard didn't want to ask the next question. "Did you get any of these checks after meeting me in 1992?"

Whitacre looked back at Shepard blankly. He nodded.

"A couple may have been deposited after that."

The agents' faces showed their disbelief and anger.

"What are you guys gonna do with this?" he asked. "Is ADM going to find out? Is my attorney going to find out?"

The agents stared at him. *How can he think we wouldn't turn this over? Who does he think he's dealing with?*

They had to document everything, Herndon explained again. Those records would be turned over to the defense at some point, so yes, ADM would find out. And they would have to tell the prosecutors.

Shepard leaned in, trying to mask his feelings. "Who else knows about this? Who else have you told?"

"Nobody knows about this."

"Oh, come on, Mark," Herndon interrupted. The man who couldn't keep his role in the case secret didn't tell anybody about taking kickbacks?

"Really, no, honestly, I didn't tell anybody."

Pause.

"Well, when the transaction happened, Randall questioned me about the amount," Whitacre said. "He said, 'Looks like you'll be getting some of this yourself.' And when he said that he kind of snickered. Kind of snickered."

"Okay, Mark," Herndon said, an edge in his voice. "So first nobody knew, now Randall knew. Anybody else?"

"Nobody. I promise you. No one else at ADM ever said anything about it."

"Come on, Mark," Herndon said.

"No, really, I promise you. Nobody else would know."

Whitacre shifted in his seat. He looked frightened.

"How much could ADM find out?" he asked. "Do they have a way of investigating?"

Of course they could investigate, the agents said. ADM had the paperwork. They could trace whatever they wanted.

"Well, the company condoned this. I mean, Randall knew all about it. I'm not the only one. Other people do this."

There had been a treasurer years back, Whitacre said. A guy named Frankel. He had received money. ADM knew about that, too. The agents wrote down the name.

Whitacre stared into his lap, silent. The magnitude of what was happening appeared to be settling in.

Suddenly, he looked up. "Is this going to affect the price-fixing case?"

Shepard and Herndon answered in unison. "Yes."

Whitacre looked into his lap again.

"Well, you know," he said, looking up, "it was such a pervasive attitude at ADM. I mean, they really promoted this kind of stuff. It wasn't the same at Degussa."

That didn't change things, the agents said. If he broke the law, he would have to face the consequences.

"Okay, Mark," Herndon said. "Anything else that you're involved in that you need to tell us about?"

Whitacre shook his head. Just the $500,000.

"Okay," Herndon said. "This isn't good for the case, and it's not good for you. But if we know everything now, we can work with it better than if we don't have the full story. So, I'm asking again, is there anything else?"

"No. There's no more. Absolutely, that's for sure."

Silence.

Shepard spoke. "Mark, does Ginger know any of this?"

"No. Absolutely not. Not at all."

Shepard looked Whitacre in the eyes. "Tell her."

Herndon nodded. "Brian's right. You need to brace her before this becomes public. Tell her right away."

Whitacre nodded, saying nothing.

The conversation had gone about as far as it could. Shepard started the car. As they drove to Moweaqua, the agents pressed Whitacre on other issues. How many people did he tell about the investigation before the raids?

"Kirk Schmidt, Kathy Dougherty, Liz Taylor. Oh, and Ginger. But that's it."

Whitacre took a breath and waited. Nothing. Apparently, the agents didn't know that he had also told Buffett, Wayne Brasser, and several others.

Shepard asked if Whitacre knew how reporters were learning details of the case. He replied that coworkers had told him they were speaking with the press.

"They said that they're doing it because they want to help me," Whitacre said. He decided not to mention his interview with *Fortune* magazine. The article was still weeks from publication.

They arrived at Whitacre's house, and the agents said that they wanted to go inside for their equipment. They also wanted to see Ginger.

Whitacre trudged into the house. The family was bubbling with excitement about moving to Tennessee and getting away from ADM. The agents asked to speak with Ginger and walked to a distant part of the house.

"How's he holding up?" Shepard asked.

"Terrible," she said. "He's withdrawing from the family. He's having trouble with the negative press."

"Tell him to be patient," Herndon said. "His day is coming. The press is going to change when the tapes come out. The evidence is very explicit."

"I know, Bob," she said. "But he can be difficult. He's isolating himself from the family. Some days, he's said he wants to kill himself. This isn't easy."

The agents praised Ginger for keeping the family going. They told her that they understood how hard it was, without mentioning that they now knew it was about to get harder.

About thirty minutes later, the agents thanked Ginger and returned to Mark. They collected their equipment, and Mark followed them to the door. Outside, Shepard faced him.

"Mark, tell Ginger," he said. "She needs to know."

"Okay," Whitacre mumbled.

The agents headed to their car, saying nothing as they drove down the driveway. They continued in silence for about a quarter mile down the road.

"Unbelievable," Herndon finally muttered. "Just unbelievable."

He looked at Shepard.

"Well," he said, "I guess we know what Aubrey Daniel wants to talk about."

CHAPTER 14

A ubrey Daniel showed no expression the next day, August 3, as he flipped a page in a black notebook, turning to a photocopy of a check. He glanced across the desk of Gary Spratling, watching as the Deputy Assistant Attorney General studied the same document in an identical binder—one Daniel had given him moments before. Spratling did not speak or show emotion. This, both men knew, was a high-stakes moment. They were wearing their best poker faces.

Despite the impassive reaction, Daniel felt confident that this $2.5 million check could doom the price-fixing investigation. It was the proof, Daniel argued, that the government's cooperating witness, Mark Whitacre, had stolen millions from ADM—all while working with the FBI.

Every word on the document told part of the story. It was an ADM corporate check, payable to ABP International of Lund, Sweden. It had been cashed at the Union Bank of Switzerland in Zurich. Spratling passed the notebook to Jim Griffin, who examined it before handing it to Scott Hammond, the third government lawyer at the meeting.

Daniel and his colleagues had done their homework, and proceeded to reveal other documents that they said proved their case. They showed the original ABP contract and described a second contract that they said had recently been discovered. They produced affidavits from the people whose signatures appeared on the second contract—Jim Randall of ADM and Lennart Thorstensson of ABP—both saying they had never seen the document before. And they flashed a report by a handwriting expert who concluded that the signatures on the second contract were photocopies.

"The evidence is clear," Daniel said. "The contract is a fake."

It was Whitacre, Daniel said, who submitted the bogus contract and requested a check for hand delivery to ABP. Whitacre took the check, and the check was cashed—even though ABP was not owed money and never received it. Whitacre had stolen it, Daniel said.

"This is just the tip of the iceberg," Daniel said. "We have information indicating Whitacre was involved in other fraudulent schemes, beginning as early as 1991."

Daniel stared at the government lawyers evenly.

"And the FBI agents assigned to Whitacre may have been a party to his wrongdoing," he said.

What?

"What's your evidence?" Griffin shot back. He was burning; he knew Shepard and Herndon. These were two straight arrows.

"Two anonymous letters were sent last month to ADM," Daniel said.

He described the letters postmarked from Knoxville, Tennessee, that had been delivered to Dwayne Andreas and Jim Randall two weeks before. Both letters contained the same claim—that Whitacre had received $2.35 million at a Cayman Islands bank, paid in 1991 by rogue FBI agents in exchange for his cooperation.

This sounded thin. Not only that, but the date was wrong. Shepard hadn't even met Whitacre until late 1992.

The prosecutors pressed for details about other schemes, but the defense lawyers refused. At this point, information was power; they were not about to give it away.

As they asked their questions, the antitrust attorneys could not shake gnawing suspicions. ADM had known about Whitacre's role for only a few weeks, and suddenly he's a crook? It was too convenient, too perfect.

"How did you discover this $2.5 million transaction?" Spratling asked.

The scheme, Daniel replied, was first detected by an attorney reviewing documents relating to patent litigation between ADM and Ajinomoto. The attorney had examined the two contracts with ABP and became suspicious.

"What made him suspicious?" Griffin asked.

Daniel shrugged as he threw out some vague words in reply, seeming to sidestep the question.

"What was the timing of this?"

Daniel fidgeted. "I believe it was after the search of ADM," he said.

The government lawyers paused. Daniel's equivocal response

contrasted sharply with the exacting self-confidence he had exhibited moments before. The change reinforced their suspicions. Did ADM know about the alleged misconduct before the search? Had they kept it under wraps in the event Whitacre ever strayed from the company?

The Williams & Connolly lawyers pressed ahead, arguing that the evidence of Whitacre's crimes was irrefutable. And the government, Daniel said, was responsible. "That is clear from the unprecedented and unconscionable cooperation agreement between Whitacre and the government."

Daniel brought up paragraph eight in the agreement, which required Whitacre to act at the direction of the FBI and the Springfield U.S. Attorney's office. Then he raised paragraph nine, which said that Whitacre could only engage in crimes with the prior knowledge and approval of the FBI.

"The government appointed itself Whitacre's supervisor, and every act or failure to act by Whitacre is directly attributable to his FBI handlers," Daniel said. "The requirement that the FBI approve his crimes shows that the agents were either aware of Whitacre's theft or that Whitacre was violating the terms of his agreement."

The implications were obvious. The defense was prepared to argue that either the FBI was hopelessly corrupt or that Whitacre had deceived the agents—destroying the credibility of the chief government witness.

The entire investigation, the defense lawyers maintained, had been driven by Whitacre and motivated by his designs to take over ADM. He had implicated his superiors to eliminate competition for the top job. He had stolen millions. He had lied to the agents or enticed them into crime. The government had gotten into bed with the wrong man.

"Face it," Barry Simon said. "Whitacre's a psychopath."

About that time, Shepard was listening impassively as Whitacre rambled over the phone from his home in Moweaqua.

"Brian, I'm calling for advice," Whitacre said. "I think ADM's really going to come after me. So I was thinking, do you think maybe I ought to release a statement or grant interviews about this financial stuff?"

The idea was ridiculous.

"I'm thinking about doing that," Whitacre continued. "I think it might help to make a positive statement to the press before they start hearing ADM's side."

Shepard didn't pause. "Mark, I can't give you any advice," he said. "That's a matter that needs thorough consideration and discussion with your attorney."

"I understand," Whitacre replied. "I'm just asking because your advice tends to be sound and reasonable."

Silence.

"Mark," Shepard repeated, "I can't offer you any advice."

Work had come to a halt that day at the Chicago antitrust office. The night before, Shepard and Herndon had spoken with Mann and Mutchnik, telling them about Whitacre's confession to taking $500,000 in kickbacks. They were sure the same story—or one like it—was now unfolding in the Washington meeting with Aubrey Daniel.

By early afternoon, Griffin called with an update. He told them about Whitacre's apparent embezzlement of $2.5 million. All of his information came from his own notes; Aubrey Daniel had taken all the documents with him when he left. But before Griffin could get into much detail, he announced that he had another meeting. He clicked off.

Dazed, the lawyers kicked back in Price's office and informally declared the workday to be over. They discussed their suspicions about ADM's speed in uncovering the documents and railed some more against Whitacre.

But, in truth, their most overwhelming feeling was not about ADM or Whitacre. Rather, they were focused on the knowledge that, with a problem this big, Washington would meddle. After all their work, someone else would probably take charge. This case wasn't going to be theirs anymore.

It was gone.

Scott Lassar, the First Assistant U.S. Attorney from Chicago, flew in that same day to Washington National Airport for his first meetings at the Justice Department on the ADM case. Since first being contacted about the case days before, Lassar had learned more details of Harvest King and had agreed to join as co–lead counsel. He had already met with Griffin for lunch and reviewed a few tapes. They were impressive. He felt sure they would have impact on a jury.

As his plane winged toward Washington, Lassar could not help but wonder about what was happening there. He had heard the previous day about Daniel's demand for a meeting, but was still in the dark about what the lawyer wanted. After landing, Lassar headed out of the terminal and took a cab straight to the Justice Department. He arrived for a scheduled appointment with Seth Waxman, Associate Deputy Attorney General. After exchanging greetings, the two lawyers took their seats.

"Well, Scott," Waxman began, "you've come on an interesting day."

About forty-five minutes later, Mary Spearing, the chief of the Fraud Section in the Justice Department's Criminal Division, was headed down a third-floor hallway, rounding up prosecutors. She had just been notified that Waxman wanted the Fraud Section represented at a big meeting that was starting right away. Unfortunately, the section's offices were in the Bond Building, about ten blocks from main Justice. Even if Spearing and her lieutenants hurried, they were sure to be late.

Spearing stuck her head into the office of Donald Mackay, a compact fireplug of a prosecutor with a salty tongue and a devilish smile.

"Don, come on," she said. "We've got a meeting over at main Justice."

Mackay stood. "What about?"

"I don't know," Spearing said. "There's some case out in Illinois where the shit's hitting the fan."

Before they reached the elevator, the two prosecutors stopped at the office of James Nixon, a staff attorney. Spearing told him to grab his notepad; he was coming, too.

They headed to the street and started walking. None of them even thought to flag down a cab. With the traffic in downtown Washington, they knew they could hike the ten blocks faster than any car could drive them.

About that same time, John Hoyt was at his desk in Springfield. So far, it had been a lousy day. That morning, Kate Killham, the squad supervisor for Harvest King, had come by his office to brief him on Whitacre's confession. Hoyt could scarcely believe it. How did Whitacre think he could take $500,000 of kickbacks without being discovered?

The rest of Hoyt's day had been spent assessing damage, briefing his boss, and telephoning Justice Department officials. By 3:45, he had still heard nothing about the latest allegations from Williams & Connolly. At that time, he was speaking with Kate Killham when Don Stukey's secretary appeared at the office door.

"Excuse me," she said. "The SAC wants to see you."

The two supervisors walked across the hall to Stukey's office. Hoyt started to speak, but Stukey signaled them to be quiet. A voice came across the speakerphone.

"All right," the voice said. "Is everybody there?"

Nearly a dozen government attorneys sat around a huge wooden conference table in a fourth-floor room at the Justice Department, staring at a speakerphone as they waited for a response to Waxman's question.

"Yes," a voice from Springfield said. "My ASAC just joined me."

Waxman, who was sitting in the middle on one side of the table, explained that he had ordered this emergency meeting to assess where the ADM case stood in light of the allegations raised by Williams & Connolly.

"So what's the story with this Whitacre guy?" he asked into the speakerphone.

"Why didn't you let us know the source was involved in criminal activities?" a voice from Washington said. "Did you know about this?"

The words struck Hoyt as ridiculous. "What are you talking about?" he said.

"We've seen the affidavits from ADM that seem to show Whitacre forged a contract," Waxman said. "They have documents tracing it to banks in Switzerland. They have all sorts of documentation of his embezzling."

"*We* didn't have access to their corporate documents," Killham said.

"How could you not know?" a voice snapped. "Haven't you done anything to verify his financial status?"

Hoyt burned. For years, he had pushed for the manpower that the case deserved. But every request had hit a wall. Now, these lawyers were saying that the agents handling this case—often working nights and weekends for years—*should have done more?* That it was *their* fault?

"The agents in this case have worked hard under enormously trying circumstances," he began.

"Well," a voice said, "Brian Shepard either has to be in cahoots with this guy or he's the dumbest agent going."

"What do you mean?" Hoyt asked.

"Williams & Connolly said they have reason to suspect the agents were involved in Whitacre's wrongdoing."

This was becoming surreal. None of these people in Washington knew anything about Shepard—or Herndon and Weatherall for that matter. Yet they were willing to attack their characters, maybe ruin their careers—*because defense lawyers said so?*

"You don't know these agents," Killham said. "These guys are top drawer."

Hoyt asked for details of any evidence implicating the agents in wrongdoing. No one would answer the question—or say it was based on a couple of anonymous letters. The trust in Washington for the Springfield FBI had obviously taken a big hit.

"Look, the source has already started opening up about some of this," Hoyt said. "We're on top of it."

The Fraud Section prosecutors walked into the conference room at that moment. Don Mackay was surprised at the size of the crowd. This was no routine meeting.

Whatever this is about, it's a heater.

"Okay," Waxman said. "Mary Spearing and two of her lawyers from the Fraud Section are coming in."

The three found seats. No one explained what was going on or even what case was being discussed. They were left to listen in and piece together whatever they could.

Mackay, a former United States Attorney from Illinois, was surprised to hear lots of names he recognized, such as "ADM" and "Decatur." It didn't take long to understand why this case was attracting so much attention.

Under pointed questioning from the Washington lawyers, Kate Killham recounted the previous day's meeting with Whitacre at the Chinese restaurant. The story did not square with the allegations raised by Williams & Connolly—and many of those were documented. Some of the lawyers expressed their bewilderment.

"Well," Killham said, "we'll see Whitacre, and we'll get some clarification."

Waxman sat up. "No, don't contact Whitacre. Look, a few hours ago, nobody knew anything about this, and now it's a crisis. Let's wait until we figure out where we are."

"Wait a minute," Killham objected. "It's important for us to reach out to this guy. We've been involved with him for more than two years. He's emotionally very shaky, and he needs our support. We just can't cut him off."

"I hear you," Waxman said. "But my decision stands. This is a criminal matter now. But we'll revisit this."

"This is a mistake," Killham said emphatically. "I think you're wrong."

Don Mackay stifled a smile. He didn't know who Killham was but had to give her credit. Here she was, talking to an Associate Deputy Attorney General, and she wasn't intimidated in the least. That took guts.

"All right," Waxman said a minute later. "Thank you for your input."

He disconnected the call.

In Springfield the supervisors sat in Stukey's office and fumed. *What is this? Why are they saying agents may be involved? Why are they keeping information from us?*

Hoyt was the most outraged, in a white-hot fury. From the case's earliest days, he had been angling for the Criminal Division of the Justice Department to take over. But no one would give him the time of day.

Now, some high-powered Washington lawyers—from the firm representing President Clinton—come in with half-baked allegations of agent wrongdoing. And Justice falls all over itself to take the case into the criminal realm.

Hoyt shook his head. He was convinced that those people in Washington didn't know what they were doing.

After hanging up with Springfield, there was one main question for the Justice Department lawyers: Who should prosecute Mark Whitacre?

To Scott Lassar, the problem seemed modest. Cooperating witnesses usually get jammed up in criminal activity; experienced prosecutors faced the same problem all the time. At that very moment, his office was wrapping up a major public corruption investigation involving someone who had committed a series of crimes while working for the FBI. The prosecutors were planning to plead out the witness, then use him at trial. It was not a big deal. In fact, in Harvest King, Lassar figured that Whitacre might even be a better witness if a jury knew he was serving time and hadn't been let off the hook completely.

"My position is, before we start dividing up the case, why don't we ask Whitacre about this?" Lassar said from a far end of the table. "Maybe he'll admit to it; then we'll prosecute him for it in Chicago, and we'll proceed."

"Hold on," Waxman said. "Let's find out some more of the facts here first." The allegations against the agents in particular had to be examined. Everyone needed to know now if there was a problem at the FBI, one way or another.

"I know Whitacre's lawyer, Jim Epstein," Lassar said in a nasal voice. "He's a good lawyer and a reasonable guy. I can get in contact with him, get something going."

Mary Spearing didn't like what she heard. This case sounded as if it would be great for her section, but Lassar struck her as too eager to paper over the problem in order to salvage Harvest King. She needed him out of the way.

"It would look better if a separate group investigated Whitacre," she said. "That way, there are no conflicts. Everyone will be able to have faith in the results."

Some of the lawyers in the room were struck by the direction of the conversation. If the Williams & Connolly allegations were right, the crime took place in the Central District of Illinois. Technically, the case belonged to Frances Hulin, the United States Attorney there—not Chicago, not Washington. But no one even mentioned Hulin as a possibility. This case was already in a different realm.

As the meeting progressed, the lawyers wore down. Anne Bingaman, head of the Antitrust Division, at one point paced the room, wheezing and looking pale. She excused herself, heading back to her office.

The meeting ended late, with no final decision. But as the prosecutors filed out of the conference room, Mary Spearing was certain of one thing: She wanted her section to handle this case. She wanted it badly.

It had been a lousy day to start vacation.

Herndon had driven with his family to the southeast, to sightsee and visit friends. That day, they had traveled to Oxford, Mississippi, where the Herndons planned to stay with an old friend who was the new chief at the local FBI office.

On the way that Thursday afternoon, Herndon saw a Holiday Inn off the road. It seemed a good place to freshen up, change the baby's diapers, and check in with the office. Herndon parked the car. His wife, Raelene, took their daughter to the rest room while he carried his notebook to a pay phone. He called Kate Killham, his supervisor.

"Kate, it's Bob. What's going on?"

"It's not good," Killham said.

Herndon listened as Killham described the allegations about

the theft of $2.5 million. He wrote down some of the words in his notebook, feeling his anger well up again.

Million. Law-enforcement judges fraud by dollar amounts, and Whitacre had just crossed into the big leagues.

Two and a half million dollars.

Herndon thought about all those speeches he had given at the FBI about protecting Whitacre financially, the times he had showed the picture of Whitacre's family to gain sympathy for him. The phone calls and the meetings where Whitacre had pressed for money from the Bureau, even pressed for the government to buy his house. And he's got millions tucked away? What was wrong with this guy?

Herndon asked a few questions, but Killham had few answers. By the time he hung up, Raelene was already back in the car. Herndon joined her quickly. The motor was running, and the air conditioning was on.

"It's now two and a half million dollars," he said to his wife. He explained the details.

"This guy's just unbelievable," Raelene said. "He's so self-destructive."

"Yeah," Herndon said. "What's next?"

He shook his head and took a breath.

"You know, this guy's already ruined my case," he said. "I'm not going to let him ruin my vacation, too."

He put the car in gear and pulled out of the lot.

The next morning at 7:10, Seth Waxman was at his desk when a call came through from Aubrey Daniel. He wanted to bring over some documents related to the Whitacre situation. Waxman invited the lawyer to stop by.

Daniel arrived in fifteen minutes, accompanied by Barry Simon and a note-taker. Daniel handed a three-ring notebook to Waxman and proceeded to explain the documents it included. Most of the records related to the $2.5 million transaction in the name of ABP.

"This is a lay-down case," Simon said. "You could indict this very quickly."

Daniel added that the firm had already obtained other documents relating to ABP and to other crimes. But they were not ready to share that information.

"When would you be?" Waxman asked.

Simon spoke up. "Once we're contacted by a prosecutor handling this case, and we're sure that the information won't be going back to Whitacre's FBI handlers," he said. "We suspect they're complicit in Whitacre's misconduct."

"We received an anonymous letter," Daniel said. "It clearly states that Whitacre deposited large sums of money into a Caymans account with the complicity of the FBI."

"Could we see that letter?"

Daniel shook his head. "Not at this time."

The Williams & Connolly lawyers asked for a commitment that a prosecutor would be contacting them by the following week. Waxman replied only that the department intended to look into the matter promptly.

"In light of this, the department should look at the whole investigation," Daniel said, "including how it began and how the FBI related to Whitacre."

Waxman said nothing.

"We would like the department to come to a prompt determination about whether the antitrust investigation of ADM will continue," Daniel added.

"We'll pursue all allegations of wrongdoing," Waxman replied. "I can't commit to more than that."

As the meeting ended, Waxman was presented with a receipt to sign, to prove that Williams & Connolly had provided the records. Waxman picked up a black pen and signed, then escorted the lawyers to the door.

"By the way," Daniel said, "we've received some written threats from an organization called the Lamet Vov. I've provided some of them to Jim Griffin but haven't heard back. We're taking it seriously and would like a response."

Waxman nodded. "I'll make some inquiries."

The lawyers left the office at 7:50. Waxman hurried to his desk and wrote down everything the lawyers had said.

"What are they accusing me of?" Shepard asked sharply, shock framing his face. "What are the specifics?"

Hoyt shook his head. "I don't know, Brian," he said. "They won't tell me."

It was early the next morning, a Friday. Hoyt had asked Killham and Shepard to his office to discuss the previous day's call with the Justice Department. Hoyt was still simmering about the treatment he and his agents had received. Now, just as Hoyt had expected, the sniping from Washington was taking its toll on Shepard.

"Look, if they don't trust me, take me off the case!" Shepard snapped angrily.

"Brian, I understand how you feel," Hoyt said. "But let's think about this before we do anything."

Shepard paced. "How can they accuse me?" he said. "This makes no sense."

Hoyt was at a loss for words. Since the previous day's call, he had concluded that this "agent wrongdoing" allegation was almost certainly just a defense ploy; the law firm had probably developed a nickel's worth of information and used it to make fifty dollars' worth of accusations. He was sure it was designed to drive a wedge between the agents, the prosecutors, and the witness—all for the purpose of derailing the price-fixing case. And it was working.

Shepard flopped into a chair, looking spent.

"How can I not contact Whitacre?" he asked. "The guy's a basket case. How can I not talk to him?"

"That's what they're telling us to do," Hoyt responded.

"John, I've already got calls from him. He's left messages. Am I supposed to ignore him?"

Hoyt sat back in his chair. This whole situation was absurd. The FBI didn't just cut off sources. For all they knew, maybe ADM was setting them up so that Whitacre would see the FBI as the enemy and start helping the company.

"All right, Brian," Hoyt said. "Don't call him back. But if he calls you, you can listen to him."

That wasn't good enough. Whitacre had to be told why, Shepard said, in person. It was the right thing to do.

Finally, Hoyt relented. Shepard could go visit Whitacre to explain that they could no longer talk. Killham was ordered to ride along, to ensure that there was a witness to the conversation. There would be no discussions of the case, no instructions given. That way, Hoyt figured, they could argue later that they had followed the spirit of Waxman's instructions, even if they had ignored the letter.

That same morning, Mary Spearing was getting worried. The grapevine was already buzzing with the word that Lassar might be allowed to pursue the case against Whitacre. The only way that the Fraud Section would win a role in this headline-making case was if somebody pushed.

After discussing the situation with Don Mackay, Spearing picked up the phone and called Waxman. She explained that she strongly believed Whitacre should not be prosecuted by anyone involved in the price-fixing case.

"The big issue here is the appearance of propriety," Spearing said. The key witness in a major antitrust case had been found embezzling from the target. Anything the prosecutors on that case did would be suspect.

"They'd be open to exposure for being unduly harsh to the informant or being unduly lenient," Spearing said. "Somebody needs to handle this who is truly independent, to maintain public confidence in the results."

At one point, Spearing added a new wrinkle to the logic. Williams & Connolly was raising concerns of possible wrongdoing by the agents in Harvest King. They had made it clear that they would not cooperate unless they were assured those agents were cut out of the case.

What was needed, she argued, was a "Chinese wall," a sharp restriction in the flow of information to anyone in Harvest King. Whatever emerged from the investigation of Whitacre would be kept secret from them; they would be forbidden from seeing documents or interviewing witnesses.

Eventually, Spearing got the decision she wanted. The criminal investigation of Whitacre was assigned to the Fraud Section. On top of that, the Chinese wall was put into place. No information was to be shared with the case agents from Harvest King—or, to Spearing's delight, with Scott Lassar. No one would be able to meddle with the investigation. They could simply ignore the price-fixing case. Immediately, Spearing began arranging an interview with Whitacre for the following Monday, if he was willing.

Don Mackay was not as pleased with the results. Even though he said nothing to Spearing, he didn't think the Fraud Section needed to take the case. Lassar and his crew were professionals. They knew the players better; they were farther up the learning curve. This decision was just going to cause unnecessary delays in the investigation.

And maybe that was the whole point.

The government, Mackay feared, might just be playing into the hands of Williams & Connolly and its client, ADM.

Shepard put on his blinker as he drove the final yards toward Whitacre's driveway. As soon as Hoyt gave the authorization, Shepard had scheduled an appointment to see his witness. As ordered, Killham had come along with him. Shepard was glad to have the company for this Whitacre meeting. It was sure to be difficult.

They parked in front of the house, where Shepard spoke with Whitacre briefly. They decided to head across the street to the horse stables.

Whitacre brought along Ginger; as promised, he had already told her about his confession to the agents. The couple looked desolate and frightened. Shepard introduced Killham to them, and the Whitacres mumbled a greeting.

"My attorney advised against having this meeting with you two," Mark said calmly. "But I want to."

Shepard nodded. "Well, Mark, I want to tell you something. The nature of our contacts have to change as a result of your statements about financial transactions."

The agent said he would no longer be able to ask Whitacre about anything involving ADM. If Whitacre called and tried to give either Shepard or Herndon such information, he would be told to stop.

"And if you don't stop," he said, "we'll hang up."

Whitacre nodded.

"Now," Shepard continued, "you can call all you want to discuss personal matters, your family situation, your feelings. But no more than that."

Whitacre said nothing.

"Mark, please understand this isn't what I want," Shepard said. "I don't have any choice here."

The words passed by Whitacre, seemingly unnoticed.

"I'll tell you, Brian, my frustration and anger is all coming from my work with you," he said. "I mean, this stuff with the media is terrible. It's all just 'Dump on Mark Whitacre.' It's not right. I'm harassed by the media and ADM while Mick and Terry aren't harassed by anybody. They're still at the company, and I'm out here alone. And none of you guys are being supportive."

"Mark, remember, whenever you asked what would happen when the case went overt, I always told you it was impossible to predict. The press coverage was impossible to predict. We couldn't know what they would say."

"Well, what about Mick and Terry?"

"Any prosecution of them is going to take time. The case is continuing. But don't expect immediate action."

As Ginger listened, she wept. She didn't like what she was hearing. Her husband had given the FBI *everything*. And now they were leaving him hanging out to dry.

"You don't know what you're doing to him, you don't understand what he's going through," she shouted. "He worked for you for two and a half years, he risked his career for this case, and now you're turning your back on him."

"Ginger—"

"I don't think anything's ever going to happen to ADM!" she shouted. "They've got too much money and too much influence. And they're just terrible people."

Burying her face in her hands, Ginger was wracked with sobs. Mark sat nearby, watching. Shepard felt torn by what he was seeing and asked Mark to leave the stable for a moment. With barely a shrug, Mark stood and walked away.

"Ginger," Shepard said in a comforting tone, "we *are* concerned. The reason we came today was because of our concern for yours and Mark's well-being."

Ginger's eyes were icy. "Does everything he did for you people mean nothing?" she asked sharply. "He's just been used by the government, and now you're throwing him away."

"No, Ginger, his assistance meant a great deal."

"Well, who was really the target of this damned investigation? Was it Mick and Terry, or was it Mark?"

Ginger broke down again. "I don't know what's going to happen," she cried. "I don't know how to plan from day to day. He's just falling apart."

They couldn't tell her what to expect, Shepard said. She would have to take it one day at a time and reach out to the agents if she had personal matters to discuss. Ginger nodded, saying she believed that Shepard did care about their situation, even if the government generally did not.

"I'm so frightened for him," she said. "He's going to kill himself. And there won't be any case if he kills himself because the government turned its back on him."

"Help Mark any way you can," Shepard said. "Make the arrangements for the move to Tennessee."

Ginger nodded. "I'll do what I can," she said.

Once Ginger seemed better, Killham walked outside and brought Mark back. He sat on the couch.

"Mark," Shepard said, "there are probably going to be some very hard times in your future. Remember, focus on the important things: your health and your family. You're very fortunate to have a loving wife and family. Turn to them."

Whitacre nodded.

"But if you need to talk about any personal concerns," Shepard continued, "Bob and I are available for you. Remember that."

There was nothing left to say. The agents said good-bye and headed back to the car. As they turned onto the road, Shepard's eyes misted. The meeting had been one of the most wrenching experiences of his career.

What the hell were these agents thinking?

The response from the Fraud Section to Shepard's final visit with Whitacre was fast and furious. They had been *ordered* to stay away from him. Spearing was particularly angry, lashing out that *no one* in Harvest King was to contact Whitacre. An objection was raised that Whitacre was a cooperating witness who couldn't just be cut off.

"He's not a CW!" Spearing shot back. "He's a target!"

"I want to know everything you did," Epstein said, looking at Whitacre sternly. "I want to know who you did it with, when you did it, and what evidence you have of it."

Whitacre nodded. Epstein had been told that prosecutors from the Fraud Section wanted to meet Whitacre on Monday, August 7. The idea made Epstein horribly uncomfortable, but Whitacre was determined to attend and explain everything. He felt sure that the government would understand.

"Now, Mark, if you're not prepared to tell the truth and tell everything, then we're far better off not going," Epstein said. "It would be better not to go than to leave out one detail or, God forbid, say something you know is wrong. It will just get you deeper and deeper into this."

"I understand," Whitacre said. "I'm gonna tell the truth."

For hours, Epstein and his partner, Zaideman, debriefed Whitacre. He provided numerous details of his financial activities. One scheme, involving a $2.5 million check made out to a company called ABP, had been hatched with another executive, he said.

"I didn't get all of that money," Whitacre said. "One million dollars of it went to Lennart Thorstensson, the president of ABP."

"Why did he get the money, Mark?" Epstein asked.

"He was the guy behind it. A million was for him."

As they finished the briefing, Epstein was less comfortable than when they had begun. The story had holes.

"Mark, this just isn't convincing to me," Epstein said. "I don't believe it."

"I swear, I swear I'm telling you the truth."

"They're going to tear you apart on this. I don't think you should go in, because I don't believe it."

"I want to go in. I've gotta tell them."

Finally, Epstein relented. As a lawyer, his job was to give advice. He couldn't stop a client who insisted on destroying himself.

Bloomington, Illinois, was quickly becoming Whitacre's site of choice for secret meetings. That weekend, he traveled to a hotel there to meet with David Page, a man he had recruited for a position at ADM two years before.

Page's hiring had been one of Whitacre's secrets; Page still worked for a supplier of ADM, a fact that Whitacre had told him to hide on his application. When he had offered Page the job, Whitacre had promised it would entail no responsibilities. He had lived up to his word.

But now, Page was worried. He had read about Whitacre working for the FBI. Had Whitacre told the government about their dealings? He had called Whitacre in a panic, and Whitacre had agreed to meet. Page started by questioning Whitacre about his role as a government mole.

"David, don't believe everything you read," Whitacre said. "Most of what you're reading in the paper is untrue. I wasn't working as an informant."

Joseph Caiazzo, the lawyer representing the lender for Whitacre's home purchase, was ready. He had opened a trust account at a Fleet Bank branch in Brooklyn, calling it the I.O.L.A. account. On August 4, the final instructions for wiring the money to Fleet were faxed out. By Monday, $941,000 was to arrive in the I.O.L.A. account, just enough to pay for the house and a few additional expenses. The Whitacres were almost set to close.

Ginger Whitacre was beside herself. Mark seemed out of control. He brooded around the house, sneaking off at every opportunity to call some reporter—*any* reporter, *anywhere*—and rage about his ill treatment by ADM, by the government, by the press at large. This was their chance to get away from Decatur, to start anew, but Mark just wouldn't let it go. Now, having heard about his illegal financial dealings, Ginger's anger had boiled over.

With Mark grumbling about some other perceived injustice, Ginger screamed. *What about me? What about the family?* In a pique, she smacked Mark hard across the head.

"I can't take this!" she screamed. "You're not here anymore! You're not part of this family anymore!"

Ginger stared hard at her astonished husband.

"For all the good you're doing," she screamed, "you might as well be dead!"

The first public report appeared that Monday morning, August 7, in the *Decatur Herald & Review*: ADM planned to announce that day that Whitacre had been fired for embezzling at least $2.5 million. News organizations around the world picked up the story, reporting that the FBI informant was now accused of his own crimes. At the same time, ADM sent Whitacre a terse letter of termination.

His six-year career at the agriculture giant was over.

Passengers lined up that morning as their seats were called for the early flight to Chicago from Washington's National Airport. Don Mackay and Jim Nixon were near the front of the line, while Spearing stood farther back. Beside her was Supervisory Special Agent Edward Herbst, who was expected to conduct much of the Whitacre interview. Herbst, who worked in Washington, had been temporarily assigned to the job on Saturday, until full-time case agents could be found. He still knew little about the situation, but Spearing planned to brief him on the way.

Minutes later, after settling in their neighboring seats, Spearing handed Herbst the notebook of documents from Williams & Connolly. The agent flipped it open.

The records told the grim story. They showed that Whitacre had personally signed the check distribution request and had promised to deliver it by hand. The attached affidavits made it clear that the contract was a fake. Some banking documents showed that the money had gone to a Swiss account. And that account, the records indicated, was controlled by Whitacre.

Herbst looked over at Spearing.

"Boy," he said. "I wonder what he's going to say about all this?"

The lawyers gathered gradually at the Chicago U.S. Attorney's office, on the fourth floor of the glass and steel Dirksen Federal Building. Lassar played host, escorting Herbst and the Fraud Section prosecutors to a conference room across from his office. Nondescript art prints adorned the walls on either side of a huge cabinet stuffed with law books and legal mementos.

"We're still waiting for the antitrust lawyers," Lassar said. "They're going to make a quick presentation to Whitacre and then hand off to you."

A short time later, Jim Griffin showed up with Robin Mann. They chatted while waiting for Whitacre's arrival. The call came in soon after.

"They're here," Lassar said.

As he neared the conference room, Jim Epstein could not shake a terrible sense of foreboding. All weekend, he had pressed Whitacre on his story. But his client swore up and down that he was telling the absolute truth. The government, he kept saying, needed to hear it.

Now, Epstein and his partner, Bob Zaideman, were on either side of Whitacre, but still their client seemed alone in his thoughts. Epstein was heading into the conference room when he felt a tap on his shoulder.

It was Whitacre.

"Listen," Whitacre whispered, "I haven't been telling you the whole truth. I'll clear it up in there."

"What are you talking about?" Zaideman asked.

"Come on, let's go," Epstein barked, pushing back out of the room. There was no way Epstein would allow a prosecutor to hear his client's story before *he* did.

"No, no," Whitacre objected. "I want to tell them."

Whitacre walked in and found his seat. His lawyers reluctantly joined him at the table. Epstein took a breath. He couldn't believe this was happening.

As the meeting began, the antitrust prosecutors handed Epstein a letter for Whitacre. It was notification, Griffin said, that Whitacre had violated the terms of his cooperation agreement with the government.

"The Department of Justice is operating under the opinion that there is no agreement between the government of the United States and Mr. Whitacre," Griffin said. "Accordingly, any promises regarding immunity for him are void. The agreement was breached by Mr. Whitacre's criminal conduct and his failure to make full disclosure to the government of his criminal conduct."

"This is outrageous," Epstein responded. "My client is here. He's been great to you. He clearly made mistakes, but he's trying to make this right."

Epstein argued that the government was still bound by the agreement, but Griffin disagreed. Finally, Epstein tossed the letter on the table. "All right," he said, "this will be an argument for another time."

Griffin, Lassar, and Mann left the room. Now, the fraud prosecutors were in charge.

Herbst eyed Whitacre. He was pale and his tie was askew. He looked like someone on the verge of a breakdown—or maybe just returning from one.

"Mr. Whitacre," Herbst said, "I'm Ed Herbst from the FBI in Washington, D.C., with the Economic Crimes Unit. I'm here to discuss a case of fraud against you."

For several minutes, Herbst quizzed Whitacre about his background. Whitacre truthfully described his education, saying that in addition to his doctorate from Cornell, he had received a business degree from Kensington University, a correspondence school.

"When did your first criminal conduct begin at ADM?"

Whitacre shifted in his seat. "In early 1992."

His job was to build the ADM Bioproducts Division, Whitacre said, a $1.5 billion business. Over the years he handled that work, he had signed five hundred contracts.

"Now, I didn't get any kickbacks in more than ninety-nine percent of those contracts. More than ninety-nine percent."

"How did you start taking kickbacks at ADM?"

"Well, I learned it basically from Mick Andreas. He's the one who taught me how to use embezzlement and kickbacks as tax-free compensation."

Whitacre nodded. "He's the one."

For more than an hour, Whitacre spelled out details of the scheme. Fraud was integral to ADM's culture, he said. Almost everyone was involved in similar crimes.

"Now, I know the frauds that I committed are wrong," Whitacre said, "and I accept responsibility for them."

"How do you approach people on these kickbacks?"

"Well," Whitacre said, "you just go overseas and tell them, 'I'll give you a $1.5 million contract, but you've got to give five hundred thousand dollars back to me.' "

Whitacre brought out some notes. He hadn't reviewed any documents, he said, so some details might not be correct. He began ticking off the crimes. One of the first kickbacks, he said, took place in 1992 and involved a company called Eurotechnologies. The company was American owned, but headquartered in Switzerland.

"ADM contracted with Eurotechnologies, and we paid them seven hundred thousand dollars to get regulatory approval in Europe for some of our products," Whitacre said.

"Who did you deal with there?"

"Sid Hulse," Whitacre answered. "Sid was the representative with Eurotechnologies, and he paid me two hundred thousand dollars on the contract."

He cleared his throat. "Sid works at ADM now. He's a friend of mine."

Another kickback occurred in March 1992, Whitacre said. ADM was introducing products in Asia and hired a consultant for help with regulatory approval.

"I forget his name," Whitacre said. "Something Tarrapong. That's his last name. He's a veterinarian."

The contract, Whitacre continued, was worth $1.5 million, and he received a five-hundred-thousand-dollar kickback from Tarrapong.

"How did you receive the money?" Herbst asked.

"Primarily by check," Whitacre replied.

Spearing shook her head. "Come on, they paid a kickback by *check*?"

"Yeah, by check," Whitacre said, shaken by Spearing's tone. "I deposited them in my Decatur bank account."

He said that he also established a company in Switzerland as a place to store the money he obtained illegally. He started it up in October of 1993 with $70,000 in "seed money" that he had obtained in kickbacks.

"What was the name of the company?" Herbst asked.

"I don't really remember. It was something like Agriconsulting and Trading, something like that."

Herbst brought out some corporate records obtained from Williams & Connolly. The documents showed Whitacre had set up a Swiss company called ABP Trading and granted power of attorney over it to someone named Beat Schweizer. The company had then been used as part of the $2.5 million transaction involving the bogus ABP contract.

"Does this help your memory?" Herbst asked, sliding the records across the table.

"Yeah," Whitacre said. "That's it. ABP Trading."

Herbst studied Whitacre. He was convinced that the man was lying. He recalled every detail of small transactions but became forgetful once they crossed into millions of dollars. But Herbst didn't want to confront him now. First, let Whitacre lock himself into his story.

The lawyers weren't interested in that technique.

"You can't possibly be telling us you don't remember this transaction," Nixon said. "That's ridiculous."

"Come on," Whitacre said, sounding pained, "I've got a lot going on in my life."

Epstein leaned in. "Hey, we're coming to you guys. We're going to cooperate, and we're going to get the money back. What else do you want?"

"It's entirely reasonable for us to do this," Herbst said. "If you think we're being hard on him, wait until he's under cross-examination on the stand. They're going to kick the daylights out of him."

After several minutes, everyone cooled off. Herbst resumed his questioning.

"Tell us about Beat Schweizer." The person with power of attorney over ABP Trading.

"He's a Swiss guy, from Switzerland," Whitacre said. "He's in the business of setting up companies there. You know, just off-the-shelf businesses."

"How did you meet him?"

"Oh, he's a good guy. He doesn't know what's going on. And he tried to get me to do it legitimately."

Why are you protecting Beat Schweizer? Herbst thought.

"How did you meet him?" Herbst repeated.

"At Degussa. I met him when I was in Germany."

Herbst decided to change topics for a moment.

"So how did this transaction work?"

ABP had sold ADM a threonine microbe in 1992, Whitacre said.

But the first bug had problems, and Whitacre had insisted that ABP provide another at no charge.

"But I didn't tell ADM that I had talked them into giving it to us for free," Whitacre said. "I had ADM pay $2.5 million for it."

To make the transaction look legitimate, he had created a bogus contract based on the original. That's what Mick Andreas told him to do, Whitacre said. That was the way it was done. ADM couldn't go around cutting checks for that amount filled out to Mark Whitacre. They needed supporting documentation.

"Now, the contract had to be authorized by Jim Randall," Whitacre said. "But Randall doesn't read things too closely. He's a guy that signed anything put in front of him. So he signed the second contract."

No one said that they knew the second Randall signature was a fake. Without commenting, Herbst pulled out copies of the contracts. Whitacre looked surprised.

"Where did you get that?" he asked.

"These are ADM's records."

"Well, look at that," Whitacre said. "With all the contracts I signed, how did they know this was the one?"

He looked around the room again. "That's how they keep people under wraps. They pay us this money, then use it against us if we talk."

Whitacre went on to say that he had faked the signature of Lennart Thorstensson, the ABP president, by using a photocopy from the original contract. Then, it was a simple matter to fill out a request for the check.

"I called Beat Schweizer and told him I had a check for $2.5 million," Whitacre said. "I told him I needed his help to cash the check, deposit the money, and make disbursement to my various accounts."

"Where did you meet with Schweizer?"

"I don't remember. Either Switzerland or London."

What did Schweizer think of this check?

"He was very concerned," said Whitacre. "He asked for assurances that the check was from legitimate activities."

How much was Schweizer paid?

"Something like $350,000," Whitacre said. "We had an agreement that he would receive ten to fifteen percent of each transaction, depending on the work involved."

Fifteen percent? For cashing a check? The answer hit the room hard. Everyone was familiar with the world of fraud. If Whitacre was telling the truth, then Schweizer was receiving the going rate for a money launderer.

Spearing sat at one end of the table, shaking her head. Jim Nixon, who had been taking notes furiously during the interview, slammed his pen down. They didn't believe Whitacre was this naïve. He was lying.

Whitacre looked anxiously at the prosecutors before continuing. He explained that he had instructed Schweizer to wire $1 million each to two bank accounts he maintained, one in Hong Kong and one in the Cayman Islands.

"Umm, I have a few other things to tell you about," Whitacre mumbled. He described $20,000 in kickbacks he had received in 1992 from a person in Mexico.

"There's also some things I did with Marty Allison," he said. "He's a vice president at ADM. He received cash kickbacks from customers and split them with me."

The total amounts of the kickbacks, he said, were around $40,000.

"Did you have an agreement for him to do that?"

"No, he did it on his own," Whitacre replied. "We didn't have any agreement."

Spearing and Nixon let out soft, short laughs. This was ridiculous. *Hey, boss! I just got forty grand in kickbacks. Want some?*

"There was also a gift I got, you know, a bridle and saddle," Whitacre said. "It was worth like eight thousand dollars, from an ADM distributor in Venezuela. It wasn't a bribe or anything. But I wanted to tell you about everything."

"Anything else?"

Whitacre nodded. "With Sid Hulse. Before he worked at ADM, he worked at a vendor. He gave me one hundred thousand dollars on a three-hundred-thousand-dollar contract. We made it look like a loan. But I never made any payments, and we both knew the loan would be forgiven."

The prosecutors pressed with other questions, aggressively challenging Whitacre's recollections. Eventually, Epstein stood. It was time for a break.

Whitacre headed with his lawyers to another room. Epstein closed the door and turned toward his client. The lawyer's cool facade collapsed, replaced by open dismay.

"Mark, what is this?" he asked sharply. "What about Lennart Thorstensson?"

Whitacre shrugged. "He had nothing to do with this," he said evenly.

"Nothing to do with this?" Epstein repeated, throwing up his hands. "You were saying before this guy stole a million dollars! Now he has nothing to do with it?"

For a second, Whitacre seemed to consider Epstein's words. "I didn't like Lennart very much," he said softly.

Epstein sank into a chair.

"Well, Mark," he said, "if he knew you almost implicated him in a million-dollar theft that he had nothing to do with, I'm sure he wouldn't like *you* very much, either."

In the men's room, Herbst ran into Don Mackay.

"He's lying," Mackay said flatly.

"You think so?" Herbst asked.

Mackay laughed. "You're not buying this shit, are you?" he said. "He's lying!"

Herbst shrugged. He agreed that Whitacre was lying. But he wasn't sure that his story of a corporate scheme could be dismissed so easily. He had heard about what was on the ADM tapes. And as far as he was concerned, there was no telling what that company was capable of doing.

When the meeting resumed, the prosecutors circled back, asking about inconsistencies. Eventually, Whitacre was asked to explain his involvement in Harvest King. He gave a rambling answer. Hours after the meeting began, everyone was exhausted. They agreed to meet in two days, this time in Washington. Whitacre and his lawyers left.

Scott Lassar stopped back in, asking how everything had gone. Spearing ran through Whitacre's story. Before she finished, Herbst broke in. There was a problem that needed to be handled quickly. He was a supervisor, he reminded them, only at this interview on an emergency basis. As much as he would like to, he couldn't take the case.

"We're going to have to find agents to assign to this," he said.

The next afternoon, on the ninth floor of that same building, Special Agent Anthony D'Angelo reached for the ringing phone on his desk. An eleven-year veteran agent, D'Angelo was seated at his cramped bullpen area in the FBI's Chicago Field Office, where he had been preparing for an upcoming trial. D'Angelo worked on a squad called WC-1, handling mostly bank frauds, and in the last few years, he had hit the jackpot. An investigation of a neighborhood bank had led to a corrupt waste hauler, who flipped and provided evidence against a bank officer. Later, that witness became the chief cooperator in the public corruption unit's Operation Silver Shovel, the massive investigation of bribery in Chicago city government.

The thirty-seven-year-old D'Angelo didn't look up from the records on his desk as he brought the phone to his ear.

"FBI."

"Ed Worthington."

The acting Special Agent in Charge. A call from him was unusual. D'Angelo forgot about his documents.

"Tony, you busy?"

"Yeah, really busy. Getting ready to go to trial."

"Well, there's a big case coming," Worthington said. "It's politically sensitive, and you've had sensitive cases. So I want you to put everything aside and work on this. You're going to be working with somebody else."

This was odd. D'Angelo's squad leader almost always gave him his assignments, not the SAC. "Does this case have anything to do with WC-1?"

"No," Worthington said. "But I can't tell you more right now. I'll give you more information later."

Worthington hung up.

This was not normal procedure. It gave D'Angelo a bad feeling.

In the basement of his suburban Chicago house, Special Agent Michael Bassett was watching television as he pumped the pedals on an exercise bicycle. An accountant by training, Bassett, thirty-seven, had been with the FBI for twelve years. He had arrived in Chicago in 1987 as part of an undercover assignment after ADM had raised allegations of fraud at the Chicago commodities exchanges. Assuming the identity of Michael McLoughlin, Bassett had trained at ADM and later had traded bond futures at the Chicago Mercantile Exchange, maintaining his undercover identity until the case went overt in 1989. In the years since, his path had crossed with ADM again when he played a bit part in Harvest King, conducting surveillance at Chicago's Gaslight Club during a price-fixing meeting there.

Bassett was picking up the pace of his pedaling when he heard the distinctive, shrill sound of his pager coming from upstairs in the kitchen. He hopped off the bicycle, pulling a towel from the handlebars and draping it around his neck. The pager was still beeping when he reached the kitchen. It was Dave Grossman, his squad supervisor, calling from home. Bassett headed over to the wall phone.

"Yeah, Dave. It's Mike. What's up?"

"Mike, I need you to take a case here. You're going to need to be in Washington tomorrow to talk to a guy."

"Okay, what's the case?"

"Well, you know about ADM and this guy Whitacre?"

Bassett had read the newspapers. "What about him?"

"Well, there's been allegations that he's been stealing money while working for us," Grossman said. "We need to do a separate investigation of that. Tony D'Angelo will be working the case with you, but the two of you need to get out to Washington for this interview tomorrow."

Grossman gave Bassett a few more details, and the agent said he would take care of it. He disconnected the call, then dialed the travel service used by the Bureau. He needed to arrange a flight right away.

That evening, Whitacre called his longtime gardener, Rusty Williams. The Whitacres were staying nearby, with Ginger's parents. They had left Moweaqua once movers had packed the furniture for Tennessee. But Whitacre told Williams that he needed somebody at the old house early the next morning. ADM was coming by to pick up his company car at 6:15. Williams agreed to be there. Whitacre had done a lot for him; he had no problem returning the favor.

The next morning, Wednesday, August 9, Whitacre climbed out of bed early. He was scheduled to take the first flight to Washington for his next interview with the Fraud Section. By 4:30, he was showered, shaved, and dressed. In the darkness of the bedroom, he looked down on Ginger as she slept. He leaned over and hugged her.

"Good luck," she mumbled, half awake.

Mark gripped her for a few extra seconds. He seemed petrified.

"It'll be okay," she said soothingly, stroking his arm. "You'll do fine."

Finally letting go, Mark headed to the door. As he left the room, he picked up a small stack of envelopes. Before he did anything else, he needed to find a mailbox. He wanted to send some letters right away.

At about seven that same morning, Special Agents D'Angelo and Bassett met at the security checkpoint in the United Airlines terminal at Chicago O'Hare. Neither knew quite yet what to expect with this Whitacre interview. It seemed odd that both the witness and the agents were flying from Chicago to Washington. On one level, the agents figured that the travel just underscored the sensitivity of the case. But they feared that it also could be a sign that the prosecutors might be planning to micromanage everything.

As they waited, Bassett and D'Angelo compared notes. Neither of them had seen anything yet about Whitacre's interview two days before. But the acting SAC, Ed Worthington, had briefed D'Angelo more fully. Already, he knew this was a case where the agents would be stepping on the turf of the Springfield division; the agents there were sure to be livid. On the other hand, if Bassett and D'Angelo missed anything, ADM's lawyers would scream that they were trying to protect Springfield. It was a no-win situation.

But they would come out of this okay, D'Angelo said.

"If it doesn't work out," he said, "we can both still get jobs flipping hamburgers at Wendy's."

About that time, Rusty Williams crossed the road in front of the Whitacre house, walking toward their stables.

Whitacre had called his gardener again that morning, saying that ADM was not sending anyone to the house until 7:45. But Williams had already dressed, and said he would head over. Whitacre had continued to try and persuade him to stay home, but something about his boss's demeanor had bothered Williams. He had decided to go to the house around seven anyway. He had nothing better to do.

As he approached, Williams saw one of the horses with Terry Yonker, the stable manager. Williams waved and walked over to him. They had a lot to talk about: With the Whitacres leaving, both would soon be looking for work.

Just before seven o'clock, Williams started feeling uncomfortable again.

"I'm gonna go over and check out the house, make sure everything is okay," Williams said. "Want to come?"

The two men crossed the street, walking up the driveway toward the house. Williams headed toward the mudroom entrance. Whitacre had told him that a set of keys would be waiting for him, but Williams didn't see any. He ran his hand across the top of the door frame.

Nothing.

"Hold on," he told Yonker, walking toward the garage.

Williams heard a muffled sound coming from the garage. He opened a white gate and noticed a line of gas cans sitting outside the door.

Oh, my God. Something was wrong. He knew it.

Williams pulled open the garage door and was stunned. The place was full of fumes, the temperature stifling. The motor for the BMW convertible was running. And in the backseat of the car was Mark

Whitacre, his head resting on the boot of the convertible top. He was motionless.

"No!" Williams shouted.

He turned to Yonker. "Call 911!"

Williams ran into the garage and was overtaken by the fumes. He began coughing uncontrollably and was immediately chilled. Whitacre wasn't coughing at all, Williams noticed. It might be too late; Whitacre might already be dead.

Yanking open a door, Williams jumped into the driver's seat and threw the car into reverse, pulling out of the garage. He heard Whitacre sigh. He wasn't dead.

Williams looked over to Yonker. "Cancel 911."

Worried that he might be making a mistake, Williams got out and paced. He glanced at Whitacre, who was still in the car. His shirt was drenched. He looked terrible. Williams shook his head and turned away.

Yonker watched Whitacre as Williams paced away from the car. Suddenly, he saw Whitacre lift his head and look at Williams. When Williams turned back, Yonker saw Whitacre put his head back down. Yonker called Williams over and told him what he had seen.

Williams was confused but figured that Yonker didn't need to stay. He knew that the stable manager was a man who prized his privacy—and this was going to be anything but private.

"Look, why don't you go ahead and take off," he said. "I'll take care of this."

Yonker thanked him and climbed into his pickup truck. Williams watched as the truck turned onto the road.

"Hey, bud," Whitacre said as Yonker pulled away. "You don't think Terry will say anything, do you?"

Williams shook his head. "No, I don't think so."

Sighing, Whitacre leaned his head down. "Pull the car back into the garage."

Williams protested, but Whitacre interrupted. "Bud, pull the car back into the garage," he said. "Pull it back in before somebody sees me."

Nodding, Williams climbed into the front seat, drove the car into the garage, and turned it off. Even with the door open, the air was thick with fumes. With the car off, Williams figured that the garage would air out quickly.

Williams turned around and looked at Whitacre.

"Mark," Williams said gingerly, "why did you do it?"

No answer.

Then Whitacre exploded. "You fucking God!" he shouted, his eyes fixed on the ceiling. "You owe me!"

"Mark—"

"You fucking God! You owe me! After everything I did! You fucking God! You owe me!"

Williams didn't understand what was going on. This was a side of Whitacre he had never seen. He told Whitacre to wait in the car. He needed to find Ginger. He headed for the phone and called her at her parents' house.

"Ginger," Williams said, trying to sound calm, "could you come to the house?"

"Why? Rusty, what's wrong?"

"I just need to talk to you."

Ginger got testy. "I'm not coming over unless you tell me what's wrong."

Williams took a breath. "Mark just tried to kill himself, and—"

Ginger's piercing screams echoed on the line. Williams tried to calm her, but it was too late.

She had hung up.

Within minutes, a car raced up the Whitacre's driveway. Ginger was behind the wheel, with her mother in the passenger seat. The two women jumped out of the car, almost before it came to a stop, and ran toward the garage.

Everyone was screaming. The women pulled Whitacre out of the car to get him into the fresh air. As he struggled his way out, a family picture dropped off his lap, clattering to the garage floor. Whitacre scrambled to the ground.

"Give me that picture!" he screamed. "It's the only thing I have left!"

Ginger, with the help of her mother and Williams, took Whitacre over by the pool and walked him around. He staggered but seemed all right. Within minutes, the Whitacre children arrived, hysterical. They jumped out of the car, and Whitacre gagged, as if about to vomit. They ran over and wrapped their arms around their father.

"Rusty," Ginger said, "can you walk Mark around for a few minutes? Let me look after the kids. And I've got to make some arrangements."

Williams walked Whitacre back to the pool.

After talking with her children, Ginger was at a loss. If she called an ambulance, ADM would find out about the suicide attempt, and it might be used against him. She walked into the garage and picked up the phone. She decided to call a few people and look for help.

Over by the pool, Whitacre seemed well enough to be on his own. Williams sat him down and headed back to the garage. He found Ginger on the telephone.

"My dear God, Tom, the worst thing has happened," Ginger was saying into the phone. "That goddamn Dwayne Andreas. He did this to him. He ought to be killed."

After a few minutes, Ginger hung up, considering what she should do next. Finally, she reached a decision. Picking up her address book, she flipped through the pages, looking for Jim Epstein's home number.

She needed to let the lawyer know that his most famous client had just tried to kill himself.

CHAPTER 15

By 7:30 that morning, Dr. Derek Miller had showered and dressed for work. The psychiatrist's commute to the North Shore Treatment Center in suburban Chicago was fairly easy, but on this day Miller wanted to make rounds at the hospital. If he was going to be on time for his first scheduled appointment, he needed to leave a bit early.

Before he had the chance to head out, Miller heard the rhythmic chirping of his pager. He glanced down at the screen. The answering service, as expected.

Miller walked over to the phone and returned the call. In a soft, genial tone, the elderly psychiatrist identified himself to the operator, who told him that someone named Jim Epstein had left an urgent message. Miller knew Epstein well; the lawyer had contacted him several times when he represented people with psychiatric trouble.

Miller dialed Epstein's home in nearby Evanston.

"Derek, thanks for calling back so quickly," Epstein said. "I've got a client who needs help. He was a mole in a federal investigation of a food company. This morning, he shut himself in the garage with his car and tried to kill himself."

Epstein explained that the attempt had failed because the man had been found by his gardener. The client clearly needed psychiatric care. Would Miller see him? Epstein asked.

"Of course," Miller responded. "I can meet with him today and evaluate him."

Within fifteen minutes, the arrangements were set. Ginger agreed to drive Mark from Moweaqua to Chicago. Miller would meet them at his office in Highland Park.

At that moment, Gert Borasky, the Tennessee real-estate agent, was making final preparations for the closing on the Whitacres' new home.

Thinking the family might need help before the move, she called Moweaqua to offer her assistance. Ginger answered.

"Hello, Mrs. Whitacre, this is Gert Borasky in Tennessee. I was just calling about the house closing—"

Ginger cut her off. "I don't care what happens to the closing!" she barked. "My husband is half dead! Our gardener just found him in the garage! Do you think I care about some stupid house closing?"

Borasky backpedaled, but Ginger hung up. Stunned, Borasky placed the phone back in its cradle. What was happening? Was the family all right? Was the deal off?

She flipped through her phone listings, looking for Joseph Caiazzo, the lawyer representing the lender in the deal. She told Caiazzo of her call with Ginger, asking if he had heard anything about a suicide attempt. Caiazzo knew nothing but promised to make a few calls.

A few hours later, a fax from Caiazzo arrived for Borasky. The lawyer wrote that the Whitacres' mortgage lender had withdrawn the offer to finance the house.

"Mr. Whitacre has informed the mortgagee that he and his family will be entering the federal witness protection program," Caiazzo wrote.

Borasky stared at the fax. She needed to notify the realtor representing the seller, Paul Myer.

The news was conveyed later that day to Myer, and it sent him into a rage. There had been another offer for the house that he had turned away, and his family had already packed to leave. Whitacre had told Myer he could afford the purchase, that Washington was going to help out. And now the government was putting him into witness protection, leaving Myer hanging?

No, sir. He wouldn't stand for it.

Before he was done, Myer planned to teach everyone involved— particularly Whitacre—a very harsh lesson.

The Whitacres arrived later that morning at the North Shore Treatment Center, on the first floor of a Highland Park office complex. Dr. Miller appeared in the waiting room, a hint of a smile on his face. Mark looked disheveled; Ginger was obviously frazzled. The drive had been harrowing, with the couple getting lost three times. Ginger agreed to stay in the waiting room while Miller spoke with Mark. She seemed grateful for the break.

Whitacre walked in the office, dropping into a chair.

"Well, then," Miller said. "How are you feeling?"

The words rushed out. Whitacre's speech was rapid and unnatural, spilling from one topic to the next. Still, he managed to tell the story of his work with the FBI.

"But now, but now I've been accused of stealing $2.5 million," he said quickly. "That's what they said. That I stole $2.5 million."

"Did you?" Miller asked.

"Yeah," he said, adding that he had been taking kickbacks for the past four years.

"I get paid five hundred thousand a year, but it hasn't been enough. I've been spending about two hundred thousand more."

Whitacre explained that he owned foreign bank accounts in Switzerland, Hong Kong, and the Cayman Islands.

"Did you give any of the money to your wife?"

"No," Whitacre said, shaking his head. He had done very little to cover his tracks.

From what Miller heard, Whitacre behaved like a man who thought he would never be caught. Risk-taking was evident in many of his actions. Whitacre told of bringing jewelry back from overseas without paying customs duty. He often spirited thousands of dollars in undeclared cash in and out of the country, without so much as a worry.

"What would you have done if your suitcase had been searched?" Miller asked.

Whitacre blinked. "That never occurred to me. I mean, I look respectable. Why would they search me?"

As Whitacre ranted, Miller jotted down the words *circumlocutory and vague* to describe the monologue. But he saw little sign of the depression that Ginger and Epstein had led him to expect.

Whitacre said he had always succumbed to pressure from his environment. And, at ADM, the environment was corrupt. Executives fixed prices. And they took kickbacks. Whitacre had only fallen into wrongdoing, he said, because everyone else did it. He just wanted to be part of the gang.

"Was that true when you were a child?" Miller asked.

Whitacre nodded. "Yes."

He had always been something of a show-off; it had always been important to him to be on top of the heap.

"What do you remember about that?" Miller asked.

"Well, one time when I was a kid, I got a new, top-of-the-line bicycle," Whitacre said. "And I bragged to everybody about it. I told everybody how much it cost."

He looked at Miller. "It cost ninety-nine dollars."

"How did you end up working with the FBI?"

"They came to me," Whitacre responded.

"Did they know you were fixing prices?"

"No, that wasn't happening yet. They were just approaching a number of junior executives at ADM. They came to me because of that. I was a junior executive, and they were approaching the junior executives."

That didn't sound true. Why would the FBI approach people at ADM if no crime was taking place yet?

Whitacre's conversation was laced with mania. Miller decided that his new patient needed a complete medical and psychiatric work-up.

"What I would like to do is have you checked into the hospital," Miller said. He would conduct some psychiatric tests and also make sure there was no lasting effect from the suicide attempt.

Whitacre agreed, warning that there was a need for precautions. ADM was very powerful, he said. He was the main witness against the company's executives, and they would do anything to win. They might break in to Miller's office, maybe rifle through hospital files. If he used his insurance, ADM might find out about the hospitalization and use the information to discredit him further.

Miller told Whitacre not to worry. He would take every precaution. He would call the hospital and arrange for Whitacre to pay by credit card. No one would know.

Once Whitacre seemed stable, Miller called in Ginger. She told Miller how Mark had changed in recent years, becoming grandiose and intolerant. He bought things without regard to cost, she said; the family owned eight cars, including three sports cars that were almost never used.

But, she continued, the interview with prosecutors a few days back seemed to have pushed him further over the edge. He had told Ginger that one prosecutor—Mary Spearing—had been particularly hard on him. He had said that he never wanted to see Spearing again, that she frightened him.

Once he finished, Miller told Ginger of his decision to hospitalize Mark. Ginger nodded. She seemed relieved.

In Washington, Special Agents Bassett and D'Angelo took a cab straight from the airport to Bureau headquarters. They were supposed to be briefed in preparation for their meeting with Whitacre, and time was short. The agents headed first to the office of Charles Owens, chief of the Bureau's Financial Crimes Section. Owens was busy, so D'Angelo and Bassett took seats in a waiting area outside his office. He appeared minutes later.

"Sorry to keep you waiting, guys," he said.

They were going to have a busy day, Owens said. They would meet Ed Herbst for a briefing about the last Whitacre interview and then head over to the Justice Department for discussions with the Fraud Section prosecutors.

As Owens turned toward his office, the agents stopped him. When would they meet with Whitacre?

"Oh, hasn't anyone told you yet?" Owens asked. "He's not coming. He tried to kill himself this morning."

The *Washington Post* newsroom is a vast sea of cubicles and computers, with hundreds of reporters clicking on keyboards or tethered to telephone headsets. In an area of the newsroom designated for the paper's business section, Sharon Walsh was hitting the phones, chasing down a story. Walsh, a *Post* reporter of nine years, had been following the unfolding events at ADM for more than a month, already publishing a few scoops on the case.

Weeks before, she had been intrigued by the story in the *Chicago Tribune* that Whitacre had faked his educational background in a resume submitted to Millikin University. Walsh had already followed up with calls to Whitacre, and had heard a series of changing stories. First, he had blamed ADM, saying that the company had changed his resume without his knowledge. Later, he amended the answer, saying he had allowed ADM to inflate his credentials, but only because other executives there lied about their education.

The changing stories had convinced Walsh that she needed to dig deeper into Whitacre's background. Over days of calls, she tracked down his friends and acquaintances from various stages of his life, as far back as childhood. Many of them mentioned Whitacre's energy and intensity; he was a nonstop workaholic who, friends often joked, should not be allowed to drink coffee or other stimulants.

But for Walsh, the most compelling part of Whitacre's past was the tragic tale of his childhood, when he was orphaned and later adopted by a wealthy family. A number of people close to Whitacre had heard the story and had been impressed by his ability to overcome the trauma of losing his parents.

Clearly, the death of his parents would have a profound impact on

Whitacre—indeed, it may have been the formative event of his life. Walsh wanted to know more and phoned a cousin of Whitacre's, Leslie Demoret, who attended junior high and high school with him in Ohio. During her interview, Walsh mentioned Whitacre's adoption.

Demoret paused.

"That is absolutely not true," she said. Whitacre had never been adopted.

After that conversation, Walsh tracked down the people who had raised Whitacre—Marion and Evelyn Whitacre. She reached Marion, known among friends as "Farmer." After some introductory questions, Walsh veered the conversation to the main topic.

"I've heard Mark was adopted. Is that true?"

On the other end of the line, Farmer laughed.

"No," he said. "He's not adopted."

Bassett and D'Angelo walked across Pennsylvania Avenue toward the Justice Department, the muggy August day causing their shirts to stick to their skins. They were accompanied by Ed Herbst, the Supervisory Special Agent who had just finished briefing them about his interview with Whitacre. Now, Herbst was set to hand them off to the Fraud Section.

The group met in a conference room at the department. The agents were introduced to Mary Spearing, Don Mackay, and Jim Nixon. Mackay did most of the talking, explaining details of the case. ADM's lawyers, he said, were putting pressure on the department to wrap up the investigation.

"Fucking Williams & Connolly is demanding that Whitacre be prosecuted immediately," Mackay said. "They keep telling us that any third-year law student could indict this case today. Well, I told them to go get a fucking third-year law student."

Mackay explained that Williams & Connolly had already supplied the department with a binder full of documents, as well as a letter instructing the prosecutors to move quickly. He handed the materials over to the agents.

Bassett read the lawyer's letter, and couldn't believe their demanding tone. *Who the hell do these people think they are?*

More questions popped up as the agents reviewed the banking and corporate documents in the binder. How were Whitacre's crimes figured out so quickly? The timing seemed awfully fortuitous for ADM. Did they know about it beforehand? The agents knew these were questions to keep in mind, if not answer, during their investigation.

"Listen," Mackay said, handing them a piece of paper. "Here's Aubrey Daniel's number. Call him and coordinate the investigation with him. We want to talk to the employees who found these documents. We want to talk to Whitacre's associates. And we want the rest of the records."

Mackay showed the agents to an empty office where they could place the call.

Aubrey Daniel could not have been more soothing on the phone.

"Oh, it's nice to hear from you guys," he said when the agents identified themselves. "What can I do for you?"

Bassett and D'Angelo interviewed Daniel casually, asking him about the Whitacre documents. How had they been discovered? Daniel explained about the Ajinomoto lawsuit and the file review by an ADM lawyer.

The agents flipped to one document where Williams & Connolly had referenced a wire-transfer record from a Swiss bank account. This was hardly a record from ADM's files. How had the lawyers obtained it?

Daniel said that his firm had hired a Swiss lawyer named Christophe Buchwalder. On ADM's behalf, Buchwalder had filed a criminal complaint against Whitacre with Swiss law enforcement. Under Swiss law, the complainant had the ability to review documents obtained in the investigation.

"There's a Swiss investigation?" D'Angelo asked.

"Yes," Daniel said. "Run by a district attorney there, someone by the last name of Triet. They're looking into the wire transaction and provided the pertinent information to Buchwalder, who in turn told me about it."

The agent asked about interviewing ADM employees, and Daniel said he would be happy to make the necessary arrangements. And if the agents needed more documentation, he said, they should call him.

"Let's speak in a day or two and start setting it up," the lawyer said pleasantly.

Daniel paused. "By the way," he said, "did you two have anything to do with the antitrust investigation?"

No, the agents replied. That had been the Springfield division; they were from Chicago.

"Fine," Daniel said.

Bassett and D'Angelo hung up and headed back over to the fraud prosecutors.

"Well," D'Angelo said, "it looks like we're going to get access to everything we need."

Mackay laughed, with a look of astonishment.

"No shit?" he said. "That SOB's been giving us a hard time since day one."

Well, D'Angelo said, it looked like Williams & Connolly was willing to be cooperative from this point on.

The District Attorney's office in Zurich was making fast progress in its investigation of Mark Whitacre and Beat Schweizer, the man given power of attorney over a Whitacre account. Now, the prosecutors, led by Fridolin Triet, were hunting for Whitacre accounts at local banks.

The same day that Whitacre was found in his garage, Triet called Rolf Brüggermann at the legal department of the Union Bank of Switzerland. The trail to the bank had been easy to track; its name was stamped on the canceled $2.5 million check for the bogus ABP contract. From there, it wasn't hard to find an account at UBS controlled by Whitacre and Schweizer in the name of ABP Trading. Triet explained to Brüggermann that he was freezing the account's assets; no checks or wires could be issued from it. He also requested copies of the account's bank statements.

Brüggermann agreed. If Triet would fax over a request, he said, UBS would get the process started.

Herndon was still on vacation that night when he received a message to call Mutchnik at home. He phoned from his hotel. Mutchnik's wife answered, and, after asking about Herndon's vacation, put her husband on the line.

"Hey, what's going on?" Herndon asked.

Mutchnik mumbled a response. Something was wrong. His tone was somber, unusual for Mutchnik.

Mutchnik paused. "Mark tried to kill himself," he said slowly.

"You're kidding."

No, Mutchnik said. He told the story, explaining that at this point, Whitacre was hospitalized near Chicago.

After hanging up, Herndon called Shepard at home.

"Hey, I've talked to Jim; he gave me the story about Mark," Herndon said. "I can't believe it."

"Yeah, I know."

"Are you okay?"

Shepard answered without pausing. "Yeah," he said. "I'm okay."

The next day, Mary Spearing headed into an office at the Justice Department with Don Mackay and Jim Nixon. The case was far enough along that they needed to contact federal prosecutors in Springfield, for protocol if nothing else. After all, the crime had taken place in the jurisdiction of the Springfield U.S. Attorney, Frances Hulin.

Pushing the button on a speakerphone, Spearing called Hulin, who was unavailable. Instead, the call was transferred to Rick Cox, her First Assistant. Spearing described the Whitacre investigation, explaining that the department had decided her section would handle the case.

"Why?" Cox asked, sounding perplexed.

"Look, we've got the Antitrust Division involved," she said. "And the determination has been made that the Criminal Division is going to handle this."

Cox was unconvinced. There was no reason his office couldn't prosecute a case involving criminal activities that occurred in their district, he said.

"There are other issues," Spearing said. "Allegations have been raised that the agents in the price-fixing case may have been complicit in Whitacre's crimes. So there's concern about turning the case back over to Springfield."

"What?" Cox shot back. "That's outrageous!"

Mackay shifted in his seat, feeling uncomfortable. While Spearing hadn't meant to offend, Mackay thought she had gone too far. It wasn't necessary to call the home district of the Harvest King agents and suggest they had been involved in a multimillion-dollar fraud—particularly when the allegation was still based on just anonymous letters. This was going to cause trouble.

At the Springfield office of the FBI, emotions were raw. The supervisors were outraged when they heard about Spearing's call to Cox. Were Shepard and Herndon under investigation, as she seemed to be implying? If so, where was the FBI's Office of Professional Responsibility, which investigates possible wrongdoing by agents? Why was no one telling Shepard and Herndon that they needed lawyers?

The supervisors called Washington, demanding an OPR inquiry. If the Fraud Section thought there was something worth investigating, then they should follow procedure. They shouldn't casually toss around allegations—damaging the careers of these agents—*without even opening a case against them*. But inexplicably, the demand for a full investigation of the agents was refused.

It was beginning to seem like Washington took the matter seriously only when justifications were needed for cutting out Springfield— even if the allegations weren't enough to merit an actual criminal inquiry.

It all seemed like politics, pure and simple.

Late on Thursday, August 10, Dr. Derek Miller was at his desk, dictating two days' worth of notes about Mark Whitacre. Already, he had spent four and a half hours with Whitacre, as well as interviewing Ginger and Jim Epstein.

Some of Whitacre's story sounded like classic delusions. *A giant corporation is out to get me! I've been a spy for the FBI!* But in this case, the story was true. It made sifting fact from fiction a particularly nettlesome task.

The second Whitacre meeting had been difficult. That time, he had clearly been depressed. Miller had confronted him about his dishonesty, saying that he believed Whitacre had not yet told him the full truth and had been lying to Epstein. Whitacre reluctantly agreed.

Miller looked through his notes of the meeting as he continued his dictation.

"We talked about his dishonesty with his attorney and his dishonesty with me," he dictated. "It is really quite clear that he really does not feel the implications of this. There is a shallowness to his affect in this area."

Miller discussed his potential diagnosis.

"The differential diagnosis is clearly between a bipolar illness, which has been brought on by the stress of his behavior, or it is possible that he has a frontal lobe lesion which is slow-growing and has led to a deterioration of his ethical attitude," he dictated. "Until three or four years ago, he was apparently an honest man, and there was no evidence of any antisocial behavior in his youth or heretofore. In addition, there is some suggestion that he might be organically damaged."

Miller listed a series of other possible diagnoses, including organic mood disorder, mixed bipolar disorder without psychotic features, adult antisocial behavior, and narcissistic personality disorder.

Finishing his dictation, Miller paused for a moment. Whitacre's warnings about ADM had frightened him. Perhaps it was true that this company would burglarize his office, looking for Whitacre's files. Miller decided to be careful.

He filed the records under the pseudonym of Patrick O'Brien.

The next morning, Miller walked down the quiet hospital hallway, passing a few nurses and orderlies. Visiting hours had not begun; the throngs of family and friends had yet to arrive. He reached Whitacre's room, tapping on the door as he opened it.

Whitacre seemed wrung out and disoriented. His emotions flew from peak to valley, from excited highs to tears. Miller gently asked Whitacre some questions, first delving into the suicide attempt.

Whitacre swallowed but couldn't hold back the sob. "One of the reasons for that was because Ginger told me I would be better off dead. And I told her that."

Miller's face showed no surprise. "Why?" he asked.

"I thought that by telling her, I could maybe relieve her guilt."

Glancing up from his notepad, Miller studied Whitacre. *Was this true?* He couldn't tell. Certainly, it was hard to believe. Miller changed the subject. Had Whitacre told his attorney the truth about all of his foreign bank accounts?

"No," Whitacre said. "But I don't need to. The other assets I have weren't acquired illegally. Definitely not."

"Where are these assets?"

A million dollars or so was entrusted to another lawyer, Whitacre answered, and there was more money hidden away with other people elsewhere.

"But I got all this money legally," he repeated, almost as an afterthought.

"You need to tell your attorney," Miller said.

Whitacre shrugged. He wasn't sure he trusted Epstein enough to tell him the truth.

Don Mackay glared at his pager, annoyed. He had just come off his flight to the Springfield International Airport and hadn't been in the terminal for a minute when he heard the pager beep. It was his boss, Mary Spearing. He made his way through the crowds, hunting for a pay phone.

Mackay had come to Springfield with plans to speak with Shepard and Herndon about Whitacre's confession to taking $500,000 in kickbacks. He had read the 302 of that interview, but the story had since changed dramatically. Mackay wanted details; maybe there were bits of truth in Whitacre's original statement that might help the fraud investigation. Mackay knew this would be a tough meeting; already, word had filtered back that Springfield was blaming the Fraud Section for Whitacre's suicide attempt.

When he finally found a phone, Mackay dialed Spearing.

"Did you talk to the agents yet?" Spearing asked.

"I just got here, Mary," Mackay responded.

"Oh, good. Well, don't interview them."

Mackay was floored. "What do you mean?"

"My God, we've started World War Three," Spearing said. "The SAC is in on the act, Bureau headquarters is raising hell, they're even trying to get Louis Freeh involved."

"What!"

"You can't interview the agents."

"I'm not interviewing the agents! I just want to talk to them! *You* wanted me to talk to them."

Well, now, Spearing said, the Bureau was raising concerns that the agents were targets of a criminal investigation and perhaps needed a lawyer present.

Mackay burned. He had hoped that this meeting would be a chance to mend fences, to make it clear that despite Williams & Connolly's allegations against the agents, no evidence had ever been presented. But Spearing said that Mackay was to speak only with the supervisors, not the case agents. They wanted to see him the next morning. Chastened, Mackay hung up the phone, muttering curses to himself.

Oh, my God, he thought. *This is really escalating.*

Mackay did little to hide his consternation the next morning as he slumped onto the couch in the office of Don Stukey, the Springfield SAC. The more he thought about Springfield's reaction to his arrival, the more suspicious he had become. *What did these agents do or not do that was making everybody act like this?*

Sitting on a corner of his desk, Stukey appeared nonchalant. A few other supervisors arrived, one with a pad and pen. This encounter, Mackay realized, was going to end up on a memo somewhere in the bowels of the Bureau.

"So why do you want to interview the agents?" Stukey asked bluntly.

"It's not an interview," Mackay protested. "I just want to talk to them."

"So why do you want to talk to them?"

Mackay threw up his hands. "Because I need to find out everything I can about Mark Whitacre, that's all. I need to know what Whitacre said the last time they met. I've got a 302, but I need flesh on the bones. I need to know, if you look back with the benefit of what we now know, if there are things that happened that might seem different now."

"But why did you need to come here for that?"

The conversation went in circles. Stukey kept asking for assurances that Shepard and Herndon were not targets of the investigation, and Mackay kept swearing that he had no evidence that they had engaged in any wrongdoing. Springfield wanted OPR involved; Mackay said it wasn't necessary.

Already annoyed when he walked in the room, Mackay was becoming infuriated. *They're interrogating me like some drug-dealing dirtbag,* he thought.

After about twenty minutes, Mackay had had enough. He glanced at his watch and stood.

"Nice seeing you folks," he said. "I've gotta go."

With that, he headed out the door.

D'Angelo was in the FBI's Chicago office when he ran into Ed Worthington, the acting SAC. Something had come up on the ADM case, Worthington said.

"Williams & Connolly wants you off the case," he said. "ADM is arguing we're too close to Springfield."

There had also been some objections from people at Justice, Worthington added, who seemed to believe that the case would be better run by agents from the Washington Field Office.

D'Angelo telephoned Bassett with the news. They couldn't figure out why things were changing. Maybe, Bassett theorized, there were concerns at ADM because of his work in the commodities-exchange investigation.

Regardless of the reason, in a matter of days Bureau headquarters overruled everyone's objections. ADM could not pick and choose the investigators. Bassett and D'Angelo were seasoned agents. They would handle the case.

While the dispute was resolved, Bassett and D'Angelo had no trouble interpreting this new shot across the bow. Despite Aubrey

Daniel's friendly tone in their call, no new documents had been produced, and no interviews had been scheduled. The promise of amiable
cooperation from Williams & Connolly was almost certainly a thing of
the past.

Around the globe, private investigators retained by Williams &
Connolly were digging up more dirt on Mark Whitacre. No possibility
for information was ignored. Some detectives—under instructions
never to reveal that they were working for ADM—had even been
stationed outside the offices of a moving company, to conduct surveillance on the parked tractor-trailers loaded with the Whitacres' belongings for the long-aborted move to Tennessee.

Meanwhile, three detectives—Steve Vickers, Deepak Bhawnani,
and Eric Hui—were busy in Asia, tracking down phone numbers that
appeared on Whitacre's calling-card bills and hotel records. On one
expense form, they found a stay in Thailand at the Shangri-La Hotel;
the investigators called there trying to learn what movies Whitacre
may have rented—perhaps it would be pornography. But no such luck.
The hotel didn't offer such services.

The majority of their time, though, was spent tracking down corporations that did business with Whitacre at ADM. The theory was
simple: If he had used a bogus company once, he would do it again.
The investigators were tearing apart his records in search of companies
that didn't exist.

Whitacre had hired one purported regulatory consulting firm—Far
East Specialists, or FES—that appeared to be located in Bangkok, according to information in ADM's files. The investigators made numerous calls to local contacts. Nothing by that name could be found in
Thailand. Following up invoice information, an investigator checked a
local address for FES, but the site didn't exist.

Finally, they dialed a Bangkok phone number listed in the files. A
woman answered.

A few questions made it clear the woman did not work for FES.
Instead, the investigators had just telephoned a site in Bangkok's noto-
rious red-light district.

The ADM directors who assembled at the offices of Williams &
Connolly for a meeting that August were a confused and anxious
group. As members of the special committee, they were still uncertain
of their responsibilities. Were they supposed to only deal with the

tornado of lawsuits brought by shareholders and customers accusing ADM of price-fixing? Or were they supposed to resolve the criminal case as well?

Until now, most of the directors' communications had been by conference call, with Aubrey Daniel leading the conversation. In fact, the calls often became a monologue for Daniel as he described the state of the case. The committee itself was making few—if any—decisions. Some members were beginning to feel like figureheads.

But today's meeting might go differently. This would be the directors' first chance to meet Dick Beattie, the Simpson Thacher lawyer who had flown back from his Montana vacation to take the assignment. Beattie arrived at the conference room, accompanied by Charles Koob, his firm's top antitrust expert. As the two lawyers walked in, one director, Ross Johnson, broke into a wide smile and stood. He hadn't seen Beattie since the lawyer had helped best him in the takeover fight for RJR Nabisco.

Johnson walked to Beattie and threw an arm around him, turning him toward the other directors.

"Here's the best goddamned lawyer in the country," Johnson boomed. "And he's an old friend of mine."

Beattie smiled, pleased at the effusive endorsement from a one-time adversary.

The room was packed with lawyers. In addition to Simpson Thacher, Daniel and some of the other Williams & Connolly lawyers were in attendance. Jim Shafter, the longtime lawyer for the Andreas family, was seated to one side. Beattie suggested that the other lawyers leave the room, so that Simpson Thacher could discuss matters with its client. The Williams & Connolly lawyers were incensed at the suggestion but eventually agreed to step out.

The directors asked a few questions about the background of Beattie and his firm. Then, they pressed Beattie with questions about their responsibilities. Most spoke with concern about their respect for the Andreas family. Beattie answered each question, making it clear that the committee had a lot of work ahead.

"This is going to be a long process," Beattie said. "And eventually, you may have to make some very, very difficult decisions."

In the Chicago bureau of the *Wall Street Journal*, Burton and Kilman—the reporters who had broken the story of Whitacre's role with the FBI—were hard at work. They had learned of Whitacre's attempted suicide and were preparing an article for the Monday paper. During the day, Kilman checked his mail. He found a letter addressed to him from Whitacre, postmarked August 9. He tore it open and started to read. One portion stopped him.

"Regarding overseas accounts and kickbacks; and overseas payments to some employees," it said. "Dig deep. It's there! They give it; then use it against you when you are their enemy."

Letter in hand, Kilman went to find Burton. This had to go in the story.

In Washington, fear was setting in that the antitrust case might be in peril.

While lysine seemed secure, Whitacre's troubles were almost certain to bog down other cases—particularly citric acid. On a Saturday in Washington, Gary Spratling and Jim Griffin met for five hours to discuss the problem. By day's end, they reached their decision.

The lysine case would remain in Chicago. But the citric investigation would be sent to agents and prosecutors in San Francisco, while high-fructose corn syrup would be pursued in Atlanta.

The Harvest King team was off those parts of the case.

The press release from *Fortune* magazine arrived that same afternoon in newsrooms around the country.

FORTUNE EXCLUSIVE, it blared. FAST-TRACK EXEC BARES INSIDE SECRETS AT ARCHER DANIELS MIDLAND.

In the release, *Fortune*'s publicity department boasted that the magazine had snagged Mark Whitacre's first-person account of his experience as a government mole, with a story that included many of the confidential details from the price-fixing investigation. All this, the release said, from a man "who many say was in line to become president of the company." The magazine itself, according to the release, would be hitting the newsstands in nine days.

"If this story were not on the pages of *Fortune*," it read, "you'd swear you were reading a John Grisham novel."

Monday morning, law-enforcement offices in Chicago, Springfield, and Washington buzzed with concern about the *Fortune* article. Everyone was making calls, trying to find a copy so that they could gauge how much damage Whitacre had done. Finally, someone succeeded, quickly faxing the article to everyone involved in Harvest King.

To the agents and prosecutors in the case, errors in Whitacre's

story were apparent, always skewed to make him look good. The sabotage allegations that led to the FBI's arrival were portrayed as widely
suspected at ADM—not something Whitacre had raised himself. His
early attempts to walk away from the FBI were glossed over. Still, there
were plenty of accurate details, from the evidence that had been collected to the identities of targets.

The only government official mentioned in the article was Brian
Shepard, a fact that led to some good-natured teasing of the agent by
Herndon and the antitrust prosecutors. Repeatedly, Whitacre under-
scored his admiration for Shepard, saying that the agent's personality
had played a big role in his decision to cooperate.

"We met Brian Shepard, the head of the FBI in Decatur—a super-
nice guy," Whitacre told the magazine. Shepard "was a very trustworthy guy. I really hit it off with him well."

In the article, Whitacre also addressed a question that had vexed
many government officials: Why had he revealed the price-fixing
scheme in the first place?

"I did not feel comfortable lying to the FBI," Whitacre was quoted
as saying. "Definitely not."

The next day, Tuesday, Daniel Briel of the Swiss Bank Corporation's
Zurich office received a fax. For some reason, the one-page handwritten note was dated from a week before, August 8. Despite that, the
Swiss banker had seen the penmanship enough times to identify the
writer without reading the signature—it was from Mark Whitacre.

"I hope all is well," it began. "Please sell some bonds because I
need some *checks* written."

The instructions were unusual for Whitacre, but Briel knew it was
not his place to question a customer. As requested, he arranged for an
overnight package to be shipped by DHL. It was addressed to Mike
Gilbert in Ohio, a name Briel had not seen before. Inside, Briel included envelopes containing three checks—one each in the names of
Ginger Whitacre, Marion Whitacre, and Reinhart Richter.

Briel thought nothing of the transaction. No one had told him
that the Zurich district attorney was freezing Whitacre's assets in
Switzerland. After all, the prosecutors from that office had not yet
found Whitacre's account at Swiss Bank Corporation.

About twelve o'clock that afternoon, Herndon was walking toward his
desk when he noticed that the small red light on his phone was glowing. He dialed the voice-mail system and scribbled down the message.

It was Craig Dahle, the agent from Mobile in charge of the methionine investigation, asking Herndon to call back immediately.

Before he had a chance, a clerk dropped off a teletype. Herndon hung up; hand-delivered teletypes are classified *immediate,* the FBI's highest priority.

Glancing at the top, Herndon saw that the teletype had been sent to Springfield and Bureau headquarters by Craig Dahle. Herndon quickly reviewed the contents.

He nearly dropped the teletype.

"This is to advise that in preparation for grand jury indictment of captioned matter, it has been determined that Mark E. Whitacre, co-operating witness in Springfield's case, should be charged," the tele-type said. "The case is expected to be presented to a federal grand jury on Wednesday, August 16."

Floored, Herndon read through the teletype again.

Wednesday, August 16? That was tomorrow!

Herndon reached for the phone. He needed to call Jim Griffin at the Chicago antitrust office. The prosecutors should know that their already troubled witness was twenty-four hours away from being charged with corporate espionage.

In minutes, antitrust prosecutors were on the phone, calling Mobile, Washington—anyplace there was somebody who might derail the pending indictment of Mark Whitacre.

Griffin was the first to telephone Scott Lassar, his new co–lead counsel.

"It's Jim," Griffin said in his soft voice. "We've got another plot twist."

At 1:20 that day, a call came for Mary Spearing at her office in the Fraud Section.

"Ms. Spearing, this is Kate Killham with the FBI in Springfield. I wanted to let you know that I strongly believe that Bob Herndon and Brian Shepard should be the agents handling Mark Whitacre, and no-body else."

Spearing was dumbstruck. *This* again?

"This issue has already been discussed and resolved," Spearing said.

"Still, I believe that Bob and Brian should have that responsibility."

The call ended quickly. Outraged, Spearing phoned Chuck

Owens, the head of the FBI's Financial Crime Section, to complain. The Bureau needed to bring Springfield in line, she demanded, explaining the bizarre call she had just received. Owens said he would look into the matter.

In a matter of minutes, Owens learned some disturbing news. Kate Killham had never placed the call. Whoever had just spoken with Spearing was an impostor.

That same day, Beat Schweizer was in his home office in Steffisburg, Switzerland. Since striking out on his own after years at Swiss Bank Corporation in the Cayman Islands, Schweizer had been able to take a more relaxed attitude to his work. Now, he spent his workday dressed mostly in blue jeans; handling money for private clients also gave him the chance to spend more time parachuting, his passion. But he no longer could keep banker's hours. His office was always open, twenty-four hours a day.

That afternoon, Schweizer heard a call come in on his fax machine. A handwritten letter, several pages in length, rolled out. It was from Mark Whitacre, his odd but wealthy client from America. Since July, Whitacre had been calling Schweizer at all hours, jabbering about work he had done for the FBI. To Schweizer, the man was beginning to sound deranged.

This fax only reinforced that opinion. In it, Whitacre asked Schweizer to get a five-hundred-thousand-dollar check to his wife, Ginger.

"Please move it from my account to another account first, *not* directly from my account," it read. "Send it regular mail; *not* Federal Express; and with no return address."

Whitacre instructed Schweizer to include a typed anonymous letter inside the same envelope, with no names and no signatures. "It should say 'Dear Mrs. Whitacre, From a friend of Mark's who cares. Please take care.' "

He then asked Schweizer to write a one-hundred-thousand-dollar check to his parents, with another anonymous note. He also asked Schweizer to move his account "where it is safer," and also to "get the money back from Joseph." However, $250,000 was to be left with Joseph for a loan to Ginger.

"Please promise me on this," Whitacre wrote. "It's so important. You are a great friend. But my life is threatened due to putting these ADM guys in jail."

At the close he wrote, "I'm counting on you."

Finishing the letter, Schweizer shook his head. Most clients sent terse wiring instructions, no more than a sentence. But this one sounded positively insane.

Schweizer filed away the letter. He decided to ignore it. He didn't want Whitacre as a client anymore.

A package arrived by DHL courier early the next morning in Blanchester, Ohio, to the home of Mike Gilbert. The last few weeks had been unusual for Gilbert, to say the least. First, he had learned that his brother-in-law, Mark Whitacre, had worked with the FBI. Then Gilbert had received a call from his sister Ginger, asking if he would allow the Whitacre family mail to be sent to his house. Ginger feared that someone—probably ADM—was tampering with their letters and packages. Gilbert agreed to help.

When the latest small package arrived, Gilbert peeled it open. Inside, he found three envelopes, each addressed to Mark Whitacre. He set the envelopes aside, glancing at the mailing slip before throwing it away. It had been sent from Zurich, Switzerland. Gilbert cracked a smile.

"Hey, this one's from Switzerland," he laughed to his wife. "I wonder if it's money or something."

The distress from the Harvest King team about the imminent indictment of Mark Whitacre set off a series of meetings and phone calls to Washington and Mobile.

Despite Whitacre's apparent deceptions, he was still potentially a key witness in the price-fixing case. Indicting him *now,* just as the Fraud Section was starting its investigation, made no sense. Once indicted, Whitacre would have the right to go to trial quickly, making him the government's unquestioned adversary—ending whatever limited use he still might have in the lysine case. Plus, a prosecution at this point opened up the slight chance that evidence from Harvest King might come public in *his* trial, even before any charges were brought in the price-fixing case.

Then there was the embarrassment factor. If there's anything that federal law enforcement hates, it's looking stupid. How would it be explained that the government had simultaneously relied upon and investigated Whitacre?

No one argued that Whitacre shouldn't be indicted, just that it should be managed properly. If he had arranged to steal information from Degussa, he could be charged later as part of a broad indictment involving all of his crimes.

With so many arguments against immediate indictment—and so few for it—the decision was easy. Peter Clark, the Washington prosecutor who had locked horns the summer before with the Antitrust Division, ruled against presenting a Whitacre indictment to the grand jury that day. Senior Justice Department officials would review the rest of the Degussa case to determine how to proceed.

The Harvest King team heaved a sigh of relief. Only a few hours before Whitacre's scheduled indictment, the bullet had been dodged.

Two FBI agents arrived that same day on Twelfth Street at Metro Center in Washington, ready to surprise the lawyers at Williams & Connolly. Originally, just one agent, Charles Stuber Jr., had been expected to handle this assignment, but Ed Herbst had decided to tag along. After all, it wasn't every day that the Bureau subpoenaed Washington's most politically powerful law firm.

The promised cooperation from Williams & Connolly had slowed to a trickle. D'Angelo and Bassett were already objecting that selective presentation of evidence could easily skew facts—in ways, of course, most favorable to ADM. Even now, more than two weeks after Aubrey Daniel had raised allegations of agent wrongdoing, the government had not seen the anonymous letters that sparked the suspicions. The time had come to remind Williams & Connolly that the government had the power to force answers.

The agents walked into the twelve-story Edward Bennett Williams Building. On one side of the lobby, they saw the entrance to the Williams & Connolly reception area. The place was austere; unlike many Washington law firms, no cut marble or slate adorned the offices.

Identifying themselves to a receptionist, the agents said that they needed to serve a subpoena to Aubrey Daniel. The receptionist placed a call, and in a few minutes, a young lawyer named John Schmidtlein appeared. The agents presented the lawyer with two subpoenas.

"Mr. Daniel isn't here right now," Schmidtlein said.

"Well," Herbst replied, "is there anyone here who can accept these on behalf of the firm?"

Schmidtlein seemed uncertain. "Well, we're trying to get Mr. Daniel on the phone, but he's not here."

Herbst again pushed for anyone else who could accept the subpoenas. Finally, William McDaniels, another lawyer at the firm, showed up at the reception area. After reviewing the subpoenas, he accepted them without comment.

Their job done, the two agents left the office.

The crowds at the Illinois State Fair surged forward, with many extending hands toward Bob Dole, the Senate majority leader. Dole had arrived at the fair in Springfield, ostensibly to give a speech promoting the use of ethanol, the government-subsidized fuel additive that had brought ADM so many millions of dollars. But everyone knew that the senator was also there to advance his candidacy for the 1996 Republican presidential nomination.

During the day, a crowd of reporters approached Dole with questions. One asked if Dole believed the price-fixing case against ADM would hurt his old friend Dwayne Andreas.

"It's only an investigation," Dole said. "We have to wait and see what happens."

Paul Myer's complaints about his unsold Tennessee home were heard by official Washington within days.

A call placed to the staff of Tennessee congressman Bob Clement resulted in inquiries from Capitol Hill to the Justice Department, eventually reaching the office of Gary Spratling, a deputy chief of the Antitrust Division. Brenda Carlton, the division's congressional liaison, followed up with a phone call to Myer.

With little questioning, Myer detailed his dealings with Whitacre. He mentioned the claim from Joseph Caiazzo that Whitacre was in witness protection.

"The next day, that same lawyer called to say Whitacre was not competent to enter into a contract," Myer said. "I hired a lawyer, and he called Caiazzo. But all Caiazzo would say was that he no longer represented Whitacre."

There was no financial reason that prevented them from proceeding, Myer said. The Whitacres had obtained a mortgage. He had seen papers proving it.

"What was the name of the lender?" Carlton asked.

"I don't know," Myer said. "But we were satisfied the papers were valid."

After the call, Carlton typed her notes for Spratling, who in turn forwarded the information to the fraud prosecutors. Probably, he figured, the FBI would want to know about a Whitacre transaction of almost $1 million.

Since his suicide attempt, Whitacre seemed to have all but disappeared—at least, as far as the government was concerned. The fraud prosecutors were beginning to worry that things were becoming *too* quiet; Whitacre, they feared, might be planning to flee. Bassett and D'Angelo were instructed to contact Whitacre's lawyers for an update.

The agents placed a conference call on August 17. Epstein was out of town, so his partner Bob Zaideman took the call. He had few answers. On Dr. Miller's recommendation, the lawyers had not spoken much with Whitacre. Still, Zaideman assured the agents that Whitacre was not a flight risk. Just in case, he said, the lawyers had already taken Whitacre's passport from him.

The next day, Bassett telephoned Dr. Miller for an update. While Miller described nothing about Whitacre's condition or his treatment, by that point the doctor had placed him on lithium, a medication to treat manic depression. He explained to Bassett that Whitacre had been released from the hospital earlier that day and was no longer considered a risk to himself.

"Do you think he is any sort of a flight risk?"

"I am virtually certain that he's not," Miller replied. "He's not going anywhere."

"We still need to conduct further interviews," Bassett said. "Is he up to that?"

"Not yet," Miller replied. "It's too early."

Miller cleared his throat. "At this point, I believe any contact by the government could have a negative impact on Mr. Whitacre's health."

In Steffisburg, Beat Schweizer walked to the table where his wife and children were eating breakfast and kissed them good-bye. Rushing to make a seven o'clock doctor's appointment, the money manager walked out the front door and headed down the steps to his garage.

Partway down, Schweizer stopped. Two men in suits were waiting at the bottom of the steps. They approached him.

"Excuse me, who are you, please?" one of the men asked in German.

"Beat Schweizer. Who are you?"

The men brought out badges. They were police detectives, a special team that had driven the two hours from Zurich that morning. They had come to take Schweizer to Zurich for an interview with prosecutors. He knew that he would probably not be jailed, just released after the interview. But Schweizer was frightened nonetheless.

The detectives escorted Schweizer back to his home office. He stood by in shock as they collected his files and floppy disks and then downloaded data from his personal computer. Once they'd seized the evidence, they brought the material and Schweizer out to their car. They placed him in the backseat and drove away.

Two hours later, an anxious Schweizer was escorted to the prosecutor's office. People were everywhere; a group of men in suits sat at a long table. Schweizer was shown a seat. A man who had been working behind a desk stood and approached him.

"Herr Schweizer," the man said in German, "my name is Fridolin Triet. I am with the Special Crimes Unit."

Triet stepped closer.

"I want to ask you about Mark Whitacre."

For Shepard and Herndon, most days presented another reason to be miserable. Stories of Whitacre's lies were washing in so fast that it was hard to take them seriously anymore. The *Washington Post* had revealed the fictitious adoption, and now the agents were hearing rumors that Whitacre had told some story about being in witness protection just to get out of a house closing.

And it seemed that as Whitacre sank, so did the case. Nobody in Washington mentioned the tapes anymore, or seemed to recognize the potential of Harvest King. As far as the agents were concerned, splitting off citric and high-fructose corn syrup was the ultimate indignity. No one had consulted them before making such a huge strategic decision. Springfield was becoming a third-class citizen.

Herndon decided to put his anger into words. He banged out a teletype, criticizing many of the decisions that had been made at the Department of Justice.

"It appears," Herndon wrote, "that the actions of DOJ are unduly influenced by the headlines of the day and/or the statements of defense counsel."

To the casual reader, the words might have seemed restrained. But by the standard of the gray, bureaucratic language of Bureau communications, Herndon's statements bordered on a jeremiad.

In most cases, such strong words would be reworked—or even

spiked—by supervisors. But everyone in Springfield agreed with Herndon. On Monday, August 21, the teletype was sent to head-quarters almost unchanged.

That same morning, Mike Bassett picked up a copy of the *Wall Street Journal* from a table at his squad's office. On page two, the headline on an article stopped him cold.

ADM ASSERTS EX-OFFICIAL DIVERTED OVER $9 MILLION.

Bassett read the article quickly. There weren't a lot of details, al-though it said that the $9 million had been sent to a Swiss bank ac-count in the name of ABP Trading. Among the more telling parts of the article was a quote from Jim Epstein, given when he was called for comment.

"I'm not going to have anything to say for a long time."

To Bassett, the statement strongly suggested that Epstein had been just as surprised by the news as the FBI was.

D'Angelo was in a hotel room on Route 7 in Leesburg, Virginia. It was his first day of an "in-service," the term for an FBI training session used to teach agents new skills—in this case, for a possible future assign-ment teaching in Eastern Europe. As D'Angelo prepared to leave, the telephone rang. It was his new partner.

"You won't believe this," Bassett said. "It just came out in the *Jour-nal*. ADM says Whitacre stole nine million dollars."

D'Angelo shook his head. "Holy . . . ," he started. "Unbelievable."

"No kidding."

"This case is getting stranger and stranger. This is just really, really weird."

The agents griped for a minute. Williams & Connolly hadn't let them know anything about this money. In some ways, they feared the firm might be sending a warning by taking the information to the press first.

"We're being set up," Bassett said. "If they're going public with nine million dollars, they probably know a lot more."

"Probably."

"Yeah," Bassett sighed. "They're going to hold back just to make us look bad."

That same day, Ed Herbst left the Hoover Building, headed to Twelfth Street for another visit to Williams & Connolly. The first response to the subpoena served days before was ready to be picked up.

He walked into the reception area and identified himself. A small sealed envelope—addressed to Mary Spearing—was waiting. Herbst took it to his office and unsealed it. He needed to record the arrival of each item.

There was a cover letter to Spearing from Aubrey Daniel. One copy of the anonymous note from Tennessee that had been mailed to Dwayne Andreas, alleging wrongdoing by the agents. One copy of the same note to Randall. A copy of each envelope used to send the anonymous notes.

That was it.

On a day that ADM was boasting to the world about finding $9 million in Whitacre thefts, the only records its lawyers were willing to show the government were a couple of anonymous notes that proved nothing.

On the morning of Friday, August 25, Tony D'Angelo pulled up at the curb in front of a house in Reston, Virginia. From his rental car, he double-checked the address. No question; this was the Virginia home of Paul Myer, the man who had sold his house to Whitacre.

D'Angelo walked up the path to the house. It was a nice neighborhood, but this was no million-dollar residence. Obviously, the Tennessee house had been Myer's big home. He reached the front door and rang the bell.

A man answered, dressed in khakis and a white shirt. He glared at D'Angelo.

"Mr. Myer?" D'Angelo said. "I'm Special Agent Tony D'Angelo. We spoke earlier."

Myer hesitated, seeming to size up D'Angelo.

"Is Whitacre in witness protection?" he growled. "That's what he told me."

From that moment, every look, every sound communicated Myer's anger—at Whitacre, at the government, at *D'Angelo,* for that matter. He bitterly said Washington was responsible for his problems in selling his house. Somebody, he said, was going to compensate him.

"Wait, let's take this back a step," D'Angelo said. "I came here to get all the facts."

"Listen, I know how Washington works," Myer said. "I've worked at the White House. I know how the FBI works, and if I have to go public to embarrass you, then I will."

D'Angelo held up a hand. "That's fine," he said. "I'm not here to

dissuade you, I'm here to get the facts and get your story to my superiors who have decision-making authority. But we still don't know what
happened yet."

"Is Whitacre in witness protection?" Myer repeated.

"I really can't talk to you about the case," D'Angelo responded.
"But you know, I wouldn't be surprised if some of the things Mr.
Whitacre told you weren't true."

Myer nodded. He understood what D'Angelo was saying. He
showed the agent to the kitchen and served coffee. Then, as they sat at
the table, Myer told of his experiences with Whitacre. The mysterious
mortgage lender, the expectation of financial help from the government, the story about witness protection. D'Angelo took it all down.

Near the end of the interview, Myer spoke again of his anger, repeating that someone needed to compensate him.

"And if I don't get satisfaction," he said, "I'm taking my case to the
media."

One at a time, the lawyers for the potential defendants in the Harvest
King case had been visiting the prosecutors at the Antitrust Division.

The tactics of each were markedly different. John Bray, the cere-
bral and aggressive Washington lawyer hired for Mick Andreas, had already demanded a target letter for his client and the right to interview
Whitacre. Reid Weingarten, representing Terry Wilson, seemed to be
making noises about possibly cooperating—but, of course, only after
being allowed to review the tapes.

In late August, lawyers from the firm of Cleary, Gottlieb, Steen &
Hamilton, which represented Ajinomoto, came to visit the prosecutors. Hoping to persuade the defense team to cut a deal, the government lawyers allowed them to view some videotapes.

But even afterward, the defense lawyers played hard to get.
Ajinomoto was unwilling to consider guilty pleas for individual
executives—even Mimoto was off the table.

Besides, they cautioned, the prosecutors shouldn't push too hard.
After all, there were those allegations about wrongdoing by the FBI
agents who ran Harvest King.

The two ADM corporate lawyers stared down at the secretary. They
wanted answers.

The secretary, Liz Taylor, glanced anxiously at her hands. The
situation at ADM had grown uncomfortable for her ever since the

company learned that her former boss, Mark Whitacre, had worked with the FBI. Some executives treated her with suspicion, perhaps for good reason. While Taylor said nothing, she had known about Whitacre's role in the case for about two years. He had told her how, once the investigation went public, he was going to clean up ADM. But now he was gone, and she was left behind, an unfortunate stand-in for the object of the company's paranoia.

Until today, no one had questioned Taylor. She had watched in silence as two in-house company lawyers, Scott Roberts and David Smith, had searched Whitacre's office, digging through drawers and cabinets in search of—*what?*

But apparently, they had found something. Whitacre had maintained an off-site voice-mail account through a private vendor. The lawyers figured out that Taylor probably knew the access code. Now, they wanted it.

"Liz," Roberts said, "you're an employee of ADM. You have to answer our questions. We need to know that code."

Taylor shook her head. "I'm uncomfortable telling you. It has nothing to do with ADM. It's private."

"Liz, you don't have a choice. You have to tell us."

The conversation went in circles. Taylor didn't know what she was *supposed* to do, so she stuck with what she thought was right and refused. Frustrated, the lawyers asked her to think through her decision during lunch. She left the building, agonizing over her dilemma.

She telephoned Jim Epstein and described the situation. Epstein contacted Whitacre, who immediately called Taylor. The voice mail was a private number, he said, urging her to keep the code a secret.

Finally, Taylor headed back. Her decision stood, she told the lawyers. She was not revealing the code.

About two hours later, Taylor was at her desk when the telephone rang. It was Brian Peterson, Whitacre's successor as head of the Bioproducts Division.

"Liz," Peterson said, "I'm afraid we're going to have to transfer you out of the division. We're moving you over to a secretarial job in the plant."

Taylor was shocked. "Why?" she asked. "Why can't I stay at my regular job?"

There was little choice, Peterson replied.

"In the main office, sensitive information would cross your desk," he said. "And ADM doesn't trust you anymore."

• • •

In an unassuming office building in downtown Chicago, a swarm of law-enforcement officials stood outside the unmarked door to room 1603. They pushed the buzzer and waited, keenly aware that someone was most likely watching them with the camera embedded in the ceiling. The wait dragged on, and the prosecutors were getting ready to buzz again when someone answered. The officials walked inside the room, one of the office sites for the Chicago FBI.

It was the morning of September 5. The officials—Spearing, Mackay, and Nixon from the Fraud Section, along with Ed Herbst from the FBI—were shown to a conference room. They were joined by D'Angelo and Bassett, as well as their supervisor on the Whitacre case, Dave Grossman.

After almost a month of delay, Whitacre was finally going to sit down that day for another interview. The air in the room was electric. Grossman was particularly annoyed. There were seven people here, all to interview one guy. D'Angelo and Bassett were top agents, he thought—they didn't need prosecutors holding their hands. Grossman felt sure it would prevent them from gaining Whitacre's trust—the first step toward getting a confession. Grossman had voiced his concerns to Washington earlier, yet now everyone was here, as if he had never said a word.

Grossman looked around the conference room. "How many are going to this interview?" he asked.

"All of us," Spearing responded.

"That's ridiculous," Grossman said. "These are two experienced agents. You don't need to be here."

"It's important for us to be here," Spearing said.

"Who's running this investigation?" Grossman said sharply. "Is it the FBI?"

Spearing spoke slowly. "This is a very sensitive case and has very large ramifications. DOJ is going to help run this investigation."

The meeting quickly became heated. Grossman demanded that the agents be allowed to do their work unhindered, while Spearing insisted with equal vehemence that the prosecutors would be part of a Whitacre interview. D'Angelo and Bassett took it all in, saying nothing.

"Look, this is our investigation!" Spearing finally lashed out. "If you don't want to work on it with us, fine. We'll get agents who will."

Grossman was on his feet. "Fine!" he snapped. "We're out of it!"

With that, Grossman was gone.

Still at the conference table, D'Angelo and Bassett looked meekly at the prosecutors.

D'Angelo shrugged. "Hey," he said softly, "I still want to work on this, guys. It's a great case."

Herbst nodded and pushed back from the table, leaving the room to find the SAC. Soon, he was back with a ruling. The case was too important for diversions. D'Angelo and Bassett would remain the case agents.

But Dave Grossman was out as case supervisor. He would be replaced by Supervisory Special Agent Rob Grant.

It was a brilliant September afternoon with a perfect sky and a cool breeze. The agents and prosecutors strolled on a bridge crossing the Chicago River, heading toward Epstein's office on South Riverside. As they walked, D'Angelo and Bassett discussed the impending Whitacre interview, inviting the prosecutors to jump in with questions at anytime.

After everyone arrived at the law firm, it took a few minutes to assemble around a conference-room table.

"All right," Spearing said. "This is another interview with Mark Whitacre. You've met Agents D'Angelo and Bassett; they're conducting the interview."

She looked at Whitacre sternly, warning that if he planned to lie, he might as well not speak.

Epstein spoke up. "My client is cooperating and plans on continuing his cooperation. If there's anything you want to ask, he's here to tell you about it."

D'Angelo took over. He wanted to reiterate the importance of being truthful.

"This is your chance to put everything out on the table," he said. "This is the chance to redeem yourself, if you tell us every single thing that you've done—even things that might be in a gray area. We would rather it come from you than from ADM or another source, because you can still help yourself, if you're truthful."

Whitacre nodded. "I understand that," he said. "And I want to tell you, I feel bad. I'm so sorry, and I feel the worst about letting down Brian Shepard and Bob Herndon. I want to try and make that right."

He glanced around the room.

"The last time we talked I was under a great deal of stress," he said. "I said some things that weren't true. I'd like to clear that up right now."

• • •

His opening words were promising. Some things he had described before, Whitacre said, had never happened. Plus, he had failed to disclose several frauds, as well as the names of other co-conspirators.

He began, again, with his friend Sid Hulse and the 1992 deal involving Eurotechnologies. At the last interview, Whitacre had said that Hulse was a representative of Eurotechnologies and had paid a two-hundred-thousand-dollar kickback on a contract with ADM. But that wasn't completely true. Hulse, in fact, was the *owner* of Eurotechnologies and had kept $466,000 from the deal. Whitacre's share, he said, had been wired to his bank in the Cayman Islands.

"When did you set up that account?" asked D'Angelo.

"In the fall of 1991," Whitacre replied. "I went there 'cause lots of ADM employees have accounts there. That's for sure. Mick and Dwayne Andreas, too."

Whitacre said he opened his account during a vacation, in anticipation of receiving money from frauds.

"Why did Hulse receive the bigger portion?"

"ADM was trying to hire him as an employee. They wanted to use the kickback as an incentive."

Whitacre glanced around at the circle of faces.

None of this was his idea, he protested. This was standard procedure at ADM, a way of giving executives under-the-table compensation.

"Mick knew all about this kickback, the one with Eurotechnologies," Whitacre said. "I talked to him about it several times in the second half of 1991. He didn't have any problem with it. He told me, in fact, that there would be plenty of opportunities for me to take kickbacks on European and Asian contracts, for like ten or twenty-five percent of each contract."

"Did Mick help you set up the Caymans account?"

"No, I did that myself. But Mick told me what bank to use. In fact, I also set up an account later at the Union Bank of Switzerland. Mick told me about that, too. It was a place I could deposit money, so I wouldn't have to pay taxes. Every top ADM executive does it, though."

"All right," D'Angelo said, glancing through his notes. "Anything else involving Sid Hulse?"

"Yeah, well, something I mentioned last time," Whitacre replied. There was a fake loan agreement, where a one-hundred-thousand-dollar kickback was disguised to look like money Whitacre had borrowed from

Hulse. That way, he could deposit the money in a domestic bank account, but wouldn't have to report it as income. It would be tax-free.

"Anything else?"

Whitacre nodded. Another fraud he had left out before, he said, involved a company named something like Far East Specialties, also known as FES. The deal took place in March 1992 and involved bogus invoices submitted to ADM.

"For how much?" D'Angelo asked.

"Well, that one was for $1.2 million."

"Did you get all that money yourself?"

"No. A guy named Ron Ferrari took three hundred thousand dollars."

Ferrari was a friend who had played pro football with the San Francisco 49ers. It was Ferrari, Whitacre said, who had set up the FES account at a Hong Kong bank.

"How do you know Ferrari?" D'Angelo asked.

"He worked at ADM," Whitacre said. But the FES deal took place after Ferrari had left the company, he said.

Whitacre continued, saying that Ferrari was knowledgeable about kickback schemes and knew other ADM executives who had received money in such deals.

D'Angelo circled back to FES. Whitacre explained that once the money arrived in Ferrari's Hong Kong account, it had again been wired to the Caymans.

"Did you tell Mick Andreas about this transaction?"

"Well, I told him about the kickback, but I told him I was only receiving five hundred thousand dollars," Whitacre said.

"Why did you lie?"

Whitacre shrugged. "I thought he would consider $1.2 million to be excessive."

"Who else knew about this?"

"I'm not aware of anybody else knowing about this deal," Whitacre said. "Just me, Ferrari, and Andreas."

Whitacre looked around the room. "You know, it's really obvious that they knew about these deals. How do you think they found them so fast?"

Days before allegations were first raised against him, Whitacre said, he had been warned what was coming.

"I got a phone call from a guy at ADM named Lou Rochelli. He told me Randall was ordering everybody to pull invoices on the kickbacks. He knew exactly where to look. He said, 'We're going after

Whitacre for embezzlement.' He said that before they even had the records pulled."

The agents listened carefully. ADM's rapid discovery of its evidence against Whitacre had left them suspicious. And here, Whitacre was naming a potential witness, someone who might be able to testify about what had happened inside the company. If Rochelli backed up this story about Randall, this case could go in a whole new direction—against ADM.

"Did Randall know about these two kickbacks beforehand?"

"Not that I know of," Whitacre said.

D'Angelo changed the subject, asking about Whitacre's relationship with the FBI. It had begun, Whitacre said, in the fall of 1992—a few months after the FES transaction.

"Did you ever divulge these illegal activities to the FBI?" D'Angelo asked.

"No. I never thought ADM would divulge them or challenge them. They had too much to lose. They approved the deals, and everybody else was doing it, too. I just never thought they would risk bringing it up."

After starting his cooperation, Whitacre said, he did not commit any more frauds until May of 1994. That was when he arranged the $2.5 million ABP transaction involving Beat Schweizer, the Swiss national who helped move his money. In the last interview, Whitacre had said that Schweizer knew nothing of the illegal activities, although the prosecutors suspected that the man was a money launderer.

"Schweizer set up the bank account for ABP at the Union Bank of Switzerland," Whitacre said. "We always thought ABP would be a two-deal company."

"Did Schweizer know that the money was illegal?"

"I told him. He knew it was obtained illegally."

Ed Herbst, who had conducted the last Whitacre interview, sat back. *So much for protecting Beat Schweizer.*

"How did you meet Schweizer?" D'Angelo asked.

"He was supposed to be a banking expert, and I became aware of him when I was working with Degussa in Germany."

"Do other ADM executives use Schweizer?"

Whitacre looked back blankly. "I don't know."

"Did you use Schweizer while you were at Degussa?"

"Definitely not. I didn't do anything like this at Degussa. I was never exposed to it until I came to ADM."

The second ABP deal occurred earlier in 1995.

"Around February, Brian Shepard told me that my FBI work would be coming to an end soon," Whitacre said. "So I decided to do one more transaction."

That fraud was his biggest ever, Whitacre said—totaling $3.75 million. Again, he had used an ABP contract. After receiving the money, he hid it in his accounts in Hong Kong, Switzerland, and the Caymans. For the second time, he said, he had relied on Schweizer to move the money around.

"How much was Schweizer paid?" D'Angelo asked.

"I don't know, something like $750,000. If I could review some records, I could give you better answers."

D'Angelo flipped through his notes. "Anything else?"

"Well, those are the ones that *I* did."

"All right, Mark," D'Angelo asked, "how much are we talking about? How much money did you obtain illegally?"

Whitacre glanced to the ceiling, as if he was calculating the number in his head.

"About $7.7 million," he finally responded.

D'Angelo wrote that down. "Why did you take it?"

Whitacre shrugged. "I was looking for security, and I didn't think ADM would ever disclose it."

"Why not?"

"Because this stuff was part of the culture. They disclose the money I got, you guys are going to find out about what they got. I didn't think they'd risk that."

"Was Mick Andreas aware of all these transactions?"

Whitacre paused thoughtfully. "Not after the first two," he said. "Mick told me at the beginning that it wasn't necessary to tell him about every time I did this."

"But you still say Mick approved this?"

"For sure. Definitely. From my conversations with him, I know he wouldn't have disapproved of what I was doing."

D'Angelo watched Whitacre carefully. "But did he approve of the size of these transactions?"

"No, probably not," Whitacre said. "He probably would have thought five hundred thousand dollars for each was more acceptable."

Whitacre blinked through his glasses and shrugged.

"He probably would have thought some of these were excessive," he said. "He would have thought, with the bigger ones, I was being greedy."

• • •

There were other, smaller deals, Whitacre continued. Some involved Marty Allison, the ADM executive he had mentioned in his first interview. The total amount was more than the $40,000 he had identified then, he said. One deal was small, involving a ten-thousand-dollar cash kickback on a twenty-thousand-dollar computer contract.

"There was no wire transfer for that," Whitacre said. "Allison came to meet me at The Blue Mill. That's a Decatur restaurant. And while we were there, he gave me an envelope filled with hundred-dollar bills."

"Why would Allison share his money with you?"

"I was his boss," Whitacre said. "He gave it to me as insurance, in case anybody ever started asking questions."

"What else did you do with Allison?"

"There was another one where Allison set up an account in the name of Nordkron Chemie, to receive the money."

"Where was that account set up?"

Probably in Hamburg, Germany, Whitacre said. But $220,000 was wired to that account, with $110,000 then sent to a Whitacre account at Swiss Bank Corporation.

"Now, there was one other transaction you should know about, in 1991 or 1992," Whitacre said. "That involved a guy named Reinhart Richter."

Whitacre said that Jim Randall had wanted to hire Richter away from Degussa to head ADM's division in Mexico.

"So he came up with a way to pay Richter like $190,000 to $200,000 in bogus invoices," Whitacre said. "They set up some Mexican company to do it. I don't remember the name, but it had *Amino* in the title."

"Why do it that way?" D'Angelo asked.

"That's how they do it," Whitacre responded. "Like I told you before. They do it so they can pay extra money to the people they hire without alerting the shareholders."

Lots of ADM people talked about the money schemes, Whitacre said. Howard Buffett was concerned about it. Mick Andreas had groused that the company was giving out too much in under-the-table money after one executive retired early. A friend of Mick's, Tom Frankel, had taken money. Mick himself used a company called Amylun—or something like that—for his own kickbacks on bogus invoices.

Whitacre stopped speaking. He had reached an endpoint.

"Well, Mark, thank you for your help so far," D'Angelo said. "But now I want you to think. Are there any other illegal activities that you know about?"

Whitacre nodded eagerly. There were plenty of other misdeeds at ADM, he said. The company had stolen microbes by hiring competitors' employees and paying them to bring along the proprietary bugs. ADM had even hired hookers to hang around a plant in Eddyville, Iowa, in hopes of finding an employee willing to steal microbes.

There were also illegal payments to both American and foreign politicians, Whitacre said, as well as the widespread use of cocaine. ADM executives misused the corporate jet for personal purposes. They dumped genetic waste into animal feed. They secretly taped competitors who stayed at company apartments at the Decatur Club.

"You can ask Liz Taylor and Sue Lines about that," Whitacre said. "They're ADM employees who know all about it. They're the ones who type up the transcripts."

D'Angelo finished, and Bassett took over, reviewing Whitacre's bank accounts. Whitacre revealed a dozen accounts, both foreign and domestic. Next, Bassett returned to the money. Had he made any purchases with it recently?

"Well, I negotiated to buy a house in Tennessee from somebody named Paul Myer," Whitacre said. "I planned to use nine hundred thousand of my money for that."

Beat Schweizer, Whitacre said, was supposed to wire the money to an account set up by a New York lawyer named Joseph Caiazzo. The transaction had been structured to appear as if Whitacre was receiving a loan from an offshore institution. That way, Whitacre would owe no taxes. D'Angelo nodded; now he knew why the lender's identity had been so secret.

Not much later, the interview ended. Whitacre said he would be willing to meet again. Everyone stood.

"Thank you very much, Mark," D'Angelo said. "We appreciate your time."

D'Angelo and Bassett walked out onto South Riverside feeling pretty good. They had arrived with little documentation, and Whitacre had given them plenty of leads.

For the most part, Whitacre had impressed them. His body language had been open; he had smiled a lot. His demeanor was that of someone telling the truth, although both agents assumed he was holding back. The prosecutors were more skeptical. Spearing had been particularly annoyed by the agents' low-key style with Whitacre.

"I think you guys did a nice interview," she said. "But you were way too nice."

D'Angelo shrugged. "We're not going to beat up on him unless we have something to show that he's lying."

"Well," Spearing said, "*I* don't believe him."

Nearby, Don Mackay nodded in agreement.

"I'll tell you, this authorized stealing sounds nuts to me," he chimed in.

Mackay laughed.

"But, hell," he said with a smile, "if what Whitacre's saying is true, the government will end up *owning* ADM."

CHAPTER 16

At first glance, the man walking with the crowd of disembarking airline passengers was far from impressive. He was short with an average build and dark, close-cropped hair. His suit was in need of a pressing, and his shoes looked like they had been polished with a Hershey bar. If the man appeared to be just another weary business traveler—perhaps in town for a sales meeting—then that suited him fine. Louis Freeh, the Director of the FBI, was not the type to stand on pretense or pageantry.

Freeh came through the arrival gate alongside John Griglione, a forty-seven-year-old former defensive tackle with Iowa State who served as his driver and bodyguard. Just past the waiting area, Freeh saw four suited men. He recognized Don Stukey, the Springfield SAC, and headed toward him. Stukey extended his hand.

"Welcome to St. Louis," Stukey said. "You know my ASAC, John Hoyt?"

"Sure, I remember John," Freeh replied.

Stukey introduced the other two men accompanying him— an agent from a nearby Resident Agency and an airport police officer. After thanking the officer for his help, the group headed to their cars, parked just in front of the terminal.

It was early on the morning of September 7, 1995, a Thursday. For the first time since assuming the director's post two years before, Freeh was here to inspect the Springfield Field Office, coming by way of St. Louis, an hour-and-a-half drive from his final destination. Stukey asked Freeh if he wanted to be driven by Griglione; the Director shook his head, saying he would ride with the SAC.

Stukey walked to the front passenger side of his blue Mercury, opening the door for Freeh while Hoyt piled into the back. Griglione headed to a neighboring car, driven by the senior resident agent. The two cars pulled into traffic, headed to Springfield. As they drove onto the highway, Stukey tried striking up conversation.

"How was your flight?" he asked.

"Okay," Freeh responded.

Pause.

"You had to get up pretty early to catch it."

"Yup."

Pause.

"Are you going directly back tonight?"

"Yup."

Pause.

"How's the family and kids?"

"Okay."

An eerie discomfort settled in. Stukey launched into an overview of the Field Office. At times he would pause, hoping for a question. But Freeh would say nothing, and Stukey would continue his monologue—or fall silent for five to ten minutes at a stretch.

Shifting uneasily in the backseat, Hoyt watched the two men, unsurprised at how badly this was going. He had heard about inspections at other offices; Freeh never fraternized with the SAC or ASAC until after he had met alone with the agents. Word was that the Director didn't like chatting until he decided—based on the agents' comments—whether the supervisors would keep their jobs.

Hoyt sat back. This, he felt sure, would be one of the longest drives of his life.

Hours later, Freeh sat at a large conference table in Springfield, looking out at the faces of a small group of Special Agents. He brought out a sheaf of notes.

"It's good to be here," he said. "I've read about some of your cases, and you guys are doing a great job."

He glanced down at his notes.

"Scott Easton, I've read about your work on the Gangster Disciple case," Freeh said, looking at the agent. "Is there anything you want to add?"

For twenty minutes, the conversation continued. The agents were strongly impressed; Freeh was able to speak knowledgeably about most every major case in the office. Few of them had ever seen a Director show such an interest in their daily work.

Freeh looked down the middle of the table, where Shepard and Herndon sat on either side.

"Well, I know Bob and Brian are working on the ADM case," he said. "You had some good success going overt back in June. But I understand there are some issues with the cooperating witness. Anything you want to tell me about?"

Herndon spoke first. "Is there anything we can do to make sure that the field is consulted before decisions are made?" he asked. The Justice Department hadn't consulted them on rulings, such as sending parts of the case to San Francisco and Atlanta.

Freeh looked surprised. "I agree, the field should be consulted on big decisions."

The agents followed up, mentioning their concerns about being cut off from Whitacre. He was the person best able to help them with conversations when a tape was unclear, they said, but they were forbidden from even contacting him for *that*.

Freeh nodded. "I understand your concerns," he said. "But, for now, I do believe it's a good idea for you guys to remain separated from the CW until he pleads."

After a few more comments, the discussion on Harvest King was done. Freeh moved on to the next case.

Early that afternoon, Freeh was back in the car with Stukey and Hoyt, ready for the return trip to St. Louis. From the moment they pulled away, Freeh was a different man than the one who had been in the car that morning.

"Boy, you guys really have some good stuff going," he buzzed. "You need people on this ADM case. It's big."

Whatever the agents had said, obviously Stukey and Hoyt had passed the test.

Freeh looked at them. "What else do you need to push this case ahead?"

This, the two supervisors knew, was the time to bend Freeh's ear about the troubles with Harvest King.

"That case is frustrating," Stukey said. "Bob and Brian have knocked themselves out, and the only impression we get from DOJ is *them* wanting to prosecute *us*."

The supervisors explained about the allegations that had been raised—apparently with no evidence—of wrongdoing by the agents. They also described the "Chinese wall" between the fraud and antitrust investigations. Perhaps there was a reason to keep the Harvest King agents away from Whitacre for now, but there was no reason to treat them like suspects. Information from the two investigations should be shared. All the bureaucracy was slowing both cases, to the benefit of the real criminals.

"ADM and its managers are being ignored, while DOJ is concentrating their efforts looking into allegations against Whitacre and our agents," Hoyt said. "They appear intent on catching goldfish while Moby Dick swims away."

Freeh nodded. "This needs to be resolved," he said.

The conversation continued until Stukey pulled up in front of the airport terminal. They walked Freeh inside, where he was joined by Griglione. Once the plane was called, Freeh thanked the supervisors, congratulating them and then heading through the departure gate.

As they watched Freeh leave, Stukey and Hoyt felt giddy. Not only had things gone well, but Freeh seemed set on fixing the problems with Harvest King.

Perhaps soon all the craziness would be over.

At his house outside Mexico City the next Sunday morning, Reinhart Richter dialed the phone, hoping to send a voice-mail message to two ADM colleagues.

Richter, president of ADM Mexico, was overwhelmed with dread. Williams & Connolly had contacted him, instructing him to fly to Washington for a meeting on Wednesday, September 13. Somehow, they had found records of the bonus he had received in his earliest days at ADM. It was his worst nightmare. Since seeing the news stories about Whitacre, Richter had feared it would be only a matter of time before someone started asking about his own money.

Once in the voice-mail system, Richter pushed the buttons on his keypad to leave a confidential message. He had heard that his friends from the Bioproducts Division, Sid Hulse and Marty Allison, were in similar situations. He wanted to talk, maybe discuss what they should say. At 9:01, Richter heard a beep telling him to begin recording.

"This is a confidential message, message to Sid and to Marty," Richter said. "I hope you had a great weekend."

He paused. "See, my friends, I'm in trouble. When I started at ADM as an employee—not as a distributor, an employee—I got a startup bonus and, uh, some payments to me which now seems to complicate my life."

Richter sighed.

"I got, uh, money through two invoices," he said. But the invoices were for work that had never been done.

"ADM told me to do it, uh, I think," he said. "ADM was Mark for me at that time, of course. And, uh, I don't know whether and with whom he discussed this, but that's the way Mark, uh, told me how to do it. So I've got two invoices, and uh, I would appreciate hearing from you."

Richter mentioned that Williams & Connolly had contacted him, saying he believed that they wanted to speak with him about the invoices and the payment.

"Man, it's just crazy; it's just stupid," he said. "All right, guys. I hope you dream well, and uh, I would appreciate your call. Thank you. Bye now."

Early the next morning in Atlanta, Sid Hulse called his voice mail. Pressing the number three on the keypad, he heard the header of a message from Sunday.

Hulse pushed another button and listened to the message. His mind raced as he heard Richter's words. The man was actually *confessing*. At the end of the message, the system instructed Hulse how to delete it. But before he did anything, he decided to call his lawyer, Sheldon Zenner. In recent days, FBI agents had been pushing for an interview with Hulse and were scheduled to meet him that week. Maybe they would be interested in hearing this voice-mail message from his friend.

Two days later, the government's interview with Sid Hulse took place in a cramped conference room at the Fraud Section's Fourteenth Street offices in Washington. Bassett had a scheduling conflict, so Rob Grant, the new supervisor on the case, accompanied D'Angelo to the meeting. The agents arrived an hour early, giving them time to prepare with the fraud prosecutors, Don Mackay and Jim Nixon.

The group was already at the conference table when Hulse arrived, accompanied by Zenner and another lawyer, Sean Berkowitz. Hulse, a huge man, appeared nervous. Zenner swapped stories with the agents about some high-profile Chicago cases and cracked a few jokes.

Zenner sat back. "All right," he said. "I'm just here to meet you guys. I'm not taking part in this interview. I think you want to hear from Sid."

First, the ground rules. Hulse was appearing pursuant to a proffer agreement—a deal in which he promised to tell the truth so long as none of his statements could be used against him at trial. Both sides agreed.

D'Angelo started with Hulse's background. Hulse told how he had joined Degussa in 1982 as a sales representative for methionine. Shortly afterward, he met an energetic young nutritionist from Ralston Purina named Mark Whitacre. Hulse had been impressed and soon was suggesting that Degussa hire Whitacre. During the Degussa years, Hulse and Whitacre became friends. So in 1989, when Whitacre left for ADM, he quickly invited Hulse to come with him.

"Mark didn't leave Degussa on friendly terms and was prohibited from hiring Degussa employees," Hulse said. "To get around that, he told me to set up my own company, and he would pay me as an independent contractor."

Hulse became an ADM lysine salesman, drawing $13,500 a month as he helped the company break into the market.

"Did you ever pay kickbacks to customers for lysine orders?" D'Angelo asked.

"Never," Hulse replied. "There were no irregularities on any lysine contracts."

As time went on, Hulse said, ADM turned to him for assignments outside of his normal duties. For example, he said, there was a time when ADM was thinking about buying a competitor's division and asked Hulse for an analysis of the business and a recommendation on the purchase.

D'Angelo tried not to show disbelief. With teams of investment bankers on hand, ADM turns to a lysine salesman for a corporate analysis? *That's pretty weak,* he thought.

"Because of that extra work, Mark told me in mid-ninety-one that he had been authorized to pay me a bonus," Hulse continued. "But it was going to be paid outside the normal channels. And Mark was getting a bonus, too. So Mark and I would both receive one hundred thousand dollars, and an additional hundred thousand would be paid to me to cover taxes for both of us."

This made little sense. "Why would Whitacre receive a bonus through you?"

Hulse turned up his hands. "That was the way they wanted it done."

To make it work, Hulse said, he set up a shell company called

JT Technologies. Then, following Whitacre's instructions, a three-hundred-thousand-dollar invoice was sent to ADM, using a different bogus company name. That money—which was actually used for the bonus—eventually was deposited with JT Technologies.

"Why did you use a different company name for the invoice?" D'Angelo asked.

"To keep it secret from other people at ADM, including other people who worked for Whitacre," Hulse said. "Whitacre didn't want other people knowing about it."

Hulse looked at the uncomprehending faces of the government investigators.

"He said this was common practice at ADM," Hulse protested. "He told me that lots of bonuses like this were paid to high performers."

"Why pay it like this?"

"Well, besides stock options, ADM doesn't normally pay bonuses, and Whitacre didn't want the bonus looked at too closely by the board's compensation committee."

D'Angelo glanced at his notes. Whitacre was the only ADM executive being mentioned. Did others at the company know about the payment?

"Well," Hulse said, "I was under the impression that Mark's superiors knew."

"Who did he say approved it?"

"Mark never said specifically," Hulse shrugged.

"What did the invoice say that the payment was for?"

"Consulting fees."

"Anything specific about what these consulting fees were supposed to be for?"

For a moment, Hulse thought. "The only thing Mark said was not to relate the consulting fees to methionine."

After the invoice went in, Hulse said, the full $300,000 was sent to his Atlanta bank account. Whitacre was worried about taking back $100,000, so he told Hulse to prepare documents to make the payment look like a loan. That way, if needed, they would have a cover story.

"How did you feel about trying to make it look like a loan?" D'Angelo asked.

"I was uncomfortable with it," Hulse said. "I mean, I think the three hundred thousand from ADM was legitimate, but I'll admit the loan documents looked funny. But Mark wanted them, so he couldn't be linked to the bonus payment."

D'Angelo decided to press him with the central question.

"Ever think Mark might be using the bonus to divert money from ADM?"

Hulse looked back at D'Angelo blankly.

"That never occurred to me," he said.

D'Angelo reviewed his notes again. He realized there was one question about the JT Technologies transaction that he had not yet asked. He looked up at Hulse.

"What happened to your share of the money?" he asked.

Hulse's face flushed. He glanced over at Sheldon Zenner, who leaned in.

"Before Sid says anything, you know, of course, about these schemes with the Nigerian letters?" Zenner asked.

The investigators and prosecutors knew what Zenner meant. The "Nigerian Advance Fee Fraud"—also known as a "419 Fraud" after the relevant portion of the Nigerian penal code—had in recent years become one of the most infamous swindles combated by international law enforcement. Each year, Nigerian con men send out thousands of letters, largely to executives whose names appeared in trade journals and professional directories. The letter writers claim to be Nigerian bureaucrats who successfully overbilled the country's oil-rich military government for tens of millions of dollars by inflating contracts of foreign companies. The letter asks the executives to send corporate letterheads, invoices, and other documents that could be used to prove completion of the padded foreign contracts. In addition, the executives are asked to provide an offshore bank account, since the supposed bureaucrats need some place to send the money. Once the paperwork goes through, as much as $60 million will be wired to the account, with the executive promised some 30 percent of the illicit cash as a commission.

When an executive responds by sending the letterheads and invoices—which are actually used to write letters of recommendation to other targets—the Nigerian criminals know they have hooked another potential victim. Promises are made that money will soon be wired to the bank account. But inevitably, tales of problems arise—money is needed for taxes, bribes, or fees. Without it, the Nigerians claim, the illicit millions will never be released. They beg the executive for cash, all the while dangling the prospect of a multimillion-dollar payday. If the executive sends money, more stories of problems emerge, again requiring cash. And so the scam continues, until the executive is either drained of every dime or realizes that it is a con. Oftentimes, the victims—embarrassed or reluctant to reveal their willingness to participate in the illicit arrangement—do not report the crime.

But Zenner's casual reference to the Nigerian fraud seemed out of place. What did that have to do with Hulse?

"You always wonder who would be dumb enough to fall for something like that?" Zenner asked.

"Sure," D'Angelo said, curiosity in his voice.

Zenner broke into a smile, and gestured toward Hulse.

"My client," he said grandly.

Everyone laughed. *That's* where the money went?

"This is so embarrassing," Hulse said.

In 1991, Hulse explained, he and Whitacre had entered into a venture together. ADM was being deluged with faxes from Nigeria. As Hulse described the contents, it was clear that the letters were part of the Nigerian fraud.

"Now, Mark told me that other people at ADM had been involved in Nigerian deals like this and had made sizable profits," Hulse said. "And he guaranteed I wouldn't lose any money I invested. He was very excited about it."

Hulse said that he agreed to participate, and on two occasions wired a total of $120,000 to a bank in New York designated by the Nigerians. Whitacre had invested the same amount, and possibly more.

D'Angelo found this particularly interesting. In his interviews, Whitacre had never mentioned the Nigerians.

"Who did Mark identify at ADM who successfully invested with the Nigerians?"

"He told me Mick Andreas and some others had done these deals before."

"Did Mark give you the instructions on what to do?"

Hulse shook his head. "No, those all came from the Nigerians."

"Did you ever see any records of Mark's investments?"

"No, but I do think he put in more than me."

Still, Hulse said, he and Whitacre grew suspicious when the Nigerians kept pushing for more. Finally, they realized that they were being cheated.

"Now, remember," Hulse said, "Mark guaranteed my money. So when it fell apart, I went to him to collect."

"How did Mark respond?" D'Angelo asked.

Hulse shrugged.

"He told me it was time for another bonus."

Recouping the losses from the Nigerian fiasco was fairly easy. This time, Hulse said, he set up a shell company called Eurotechnologies, using his home computer to write bogus invoices to ADM of more than $600,000. For tax reasons, Whitacre wanted the money sent to Switzerland. So Hulse flew to Europe and opened a Eurotechnologies account at Swiss Bank Corporation.

"Anyone else know about this transaction?"

"No. Just Mark and me."

"What happened to the money sent to Switzerland?"

"Well, some time before, Mark and I went to the Cayman Islands, and we both set up bank accounts there. And after we got the money in Switzerland, Mark told me to transfer it to the accounts in the Caymans."

"How much did each of you get?"

"Well, I got something like $170,000 to $190,000, which included the money I lost to the Nigerians, and some extra to pay taxes. The remainder of it, like four hundred thousand dollars, went to Mark in his Caymans account."

D'Angelo asked a few more questions about how the Caymans accounts had been set up. "Now, what happened to the money you received?"

Hulse looked down at the table again, almost laughing.

"I took a bunch of it out of the account in 1992 to invest in a company called something like American National Securities, some brokerage firm about to go public."

Hulse said he invested $50,000 in the brokerage, while Whitacre put in $150,000.

"Where are the shares now?"

Hulse said he didn't know. Someone named Jerome Schneider was involved in the deal and was supposed to have transferred the shares to a New York brokerage. But now, Hulse said, he didn't know where the shares were.

"Who knew Schneider?" D'Angelo asked.

"Whitacre found him," Hulse said. "He saw some advertisement from Schneider in an airline magazine, like Delta magazine. Schneider advertises in those publications about how to set up offshore bank accounts."

"Okay. What happened to the rest of the money?"

"In late 1993, I moved about $141,000 from my Caymans account to Mark's."

D'Angelo blinked. "You sent it to Mark?"

"Yeah," Hulse said, nodding. "Mark was getting big returns because he had a managed account, you know, where somebody's making investments for him. But I didn't have enough for that type of account. So Mark let me put my money in his account for larger returns, and promised to give it back later, whenever I wanted."

"So how did you do?"

Hulse made a face. "Not well. Mark told me in 1994 that I had only earned like five or six percent."

D'Angelo wrote down the percentages. He wondered if Whitacre had been skimming money from his friend. Who was managing the account? he asked.

"In the Caymans? A guy name Beat Schweizer."

Beat Schweizer? The investigators were jolted. Whitacre had said he met Schweizer in Germany, while working for Degussa. What was the man doing in the Caymans?

"Schweizer eventually left the Caymans bank and set up his own business in Switzerland," Hulse said.

"Did you have any other contact with him?"

"No. He tried to solicit my business when he went out on his own. But I didn't do any other business with him."

D'Angelo brought out documents provided by Williams & Connolly. Hulse identified many of them as being bogus invoices and letters he had created.

After reviewing the documents, Hulse assured the investigators that he had told them about all of his transactions with Whitacre.

"Do you know about other ADM employees doing similar transactions?"

Hulse looked nervously over to his lawyer, and nodded.

"Reinhart Richter," he said softly.

"How do you know about him?"

Breaking in, Zenner explained about Richter's call on the voice-mail system.

"Do you have a copy of the message?" D'Angelo asked.

Zenner reached for the telephone on the table.

"Why don't we call his voice mail right now?" Zenner asked. "He saved it."

• • •

Once they learned that Richter's voice mail still existed, the investigators wanted a copy. One prosecutor hustled out of the room, coming back with a tape recorder.

Hulse looked down at the table, shaking his head.

"I don't feel right about this," he told Zenner. "Reinhart's a friend."

"You don't have a choice here, Sid," Zenner said. "They need to hear this."

The investigators watched, unmoved. If Hulse didn't want them to hear this, it never should have been mentioned. Finally, Hulse relented. They called the ADM voice-mail system on a speakerphone. As Richter's words filled the room, tears streamed down Hulse's face.

"I feel terrible about this," he muttered. "Just terrible."

After listening to the message twice, D'Angelo asked if Hulse knew of any other wrongdoing at ADM. Hulse repeated rumors he had heard from Whitacre. He had been talking to Whitacre a lot, he said.

"I called him when I saw that story in the newspaper about the $2.5 million theft," Hulse said. "I was worried that some of my money was tied up in that."

"What did Whitacre tell you?"

"He said not to worry," he sighed. "He told me ADM is in trouble."

Hulse and his lawyers left about fifteen minutes later. By the time they were on the elevator, the prosecutors and agents were whooping it up.

A *taped confession!* It wasn't often that any of them had come across evidence this strong so quickly. Richter apparently had been trying to coordinate his story with Hulse and Allison, and in the process had cooked himself.

"This is great," Don Mackay giggled.

Mackay looked over at D'Angelo and Nixon.

"Well," he said, "looks like we need to go down and speak with Mr. Richter."

Reinhart Richter was potentially the key to everything. Of that, the Williams & Connolly lawyers felt sure. With Richter's help, Mark Whitacre would be beyond redemption.

By early September, the defense lawyers—using investigators coordinated by Kroll Associates, the renowned corporate detective agency—had tracked down money that went to Richter, Hulse, and Allison. Now ADM held all the cards. On September 13, the day after Hulse's FBI interview, Williams & Connolly offered Richter a deal.

In exchange for Richter's cooperation in the investigations of

Whitacre, ADM would keep him as an employee. He would be required to repay, on mutually agreeable terms, the money traced to him—$180,966. Williams & Connolly would then work to make sure that Richter received immunity from the Justice Department.

The terms seemed fabulous. But Richter demurred. He would have to think about it, he said.

Hulse and Allison were not treated quite so gently.

That same morning, the two were notified that they were being fired, and were immediately barred from the office. Their passwords to the voice-mail system were deleted. They would never be allowed access to ADM again.

At Emory University's business school, Ross Johnson strode to a podium, ready to take questions from the assembled students, faculty, and alumni. Johnson had come to give a speech about his old company, RJR Nabisco, and the famous takeover battle that had engulfed it. But one member of the audience wanted to know about Johnson's work as an ADM director. What could he say about events unfolding there?

Johnson smiled.

"It's a pretty exciting experience when you find out that one of your top division presidents has been recording everything you've said for two and a half years," he said. "It's a mystery."

The idea that Whitacre was a Boy Scout who went to the FBI with stories of price-fixing made no sense, he said.

"The FBI—who have got some good scumbags in there too; it's almost a criminal mentality—they came in and got the goods on this guy," Johnson remarked. "For immunity, he signed this great, long agreement."

But once the case went public, the company found that Whitacre had shoved his hand deep into the till, Johnson said.

"Then, you know, he tried to commit suicide," Johnson continued. "But he did it in a six-car garage, which, I think, if you're going to do it, that's the place to do it."

The audience laughed.

In the end, Johnson said, he had no idea how everything would come out.

"But certainly we feel a lot better about it today than when it came over the air and the seventy FBI agents arrived in Decatur," he said.

"But they love to do that; they like to extort. Their technique is to get the gun on somebody and then put the pressure on. And then that puts the pressure on somebody else."

Johnson smiled. "Stay tuned," he snickered.

As he spoke, Johnson thought nothing of the nearby video camera, recording his every word. But soon, transcripts of that tape would appear in magazines and newspapers. Anyone in the country would be able to read his description of the nation's premier law enforcement agency as being little more than a bunch of hoodlums.

Dick Beattie of Simpson Thacher listened thoughtfully to the latest idea from Williams & Connolly. The government was responsible for Whitacre's actions, and he stole money. His cooperation agreement prevented him from reporting wrongdoing—part of his fiduciary obligation. ADM had been harmed. The next move was obvious, Aubrey Daniel argued. ADM should sue the Justice Department for damages.

The presentation ended. Beattie smiled, his blue eyes twinkling. And then he laughed out loud.

Before taking his seat, Whitacre glanced around the Chinese restaurant in downtown Ithaca, New York. He looked at the two men accompanying him, telling them that he needed to sit facing the door. With everything that was happening with ADM, Whitacre said, he had to be prepared for anything.

The two men, Dr. Colin Campbell and his son, Nelson, nodded appreciatively. Dr. Campbell, a professor at Cornell University, had served more than a decade before on Whitacre's doctoral thesis committee.

Their dinner this night had come about through serendipity. A few weeks before, Dr. Campbell had been contacted by Sharon Walsh of the *Washington Post* as she was preparing her article about Whitacre's background. The reporter's questions had raised his curiosity, and Dr. Campbell had decided to reach out to his former student.

As he spoke with Whitacre, Dr. Campbell was struck with an idea. He and his son were operating a small start-up company, which was working on a system to identify predictors of disease in human blood. But neither man had much business experience. And now, this former ADM executive—a man who had fought to do the right thing—was available. It seemed a perfect match, and Dr. Campbell had invited Whitacre to Ithaca to discuss the idea.

Just the first few minutes of their dinner at the Chinese restaurant left the Campbells awed at the events swirling around Whitacre. He declined their offers to meet other Cornell professors; better, he said, to keep a low profile.

As they enjoyed their meal, Whitacre said that ADM was out to get him for something he hadn't done, and explained the circumstances surrounding his suicide attempt.

By the end of the meal, the Campbells were a little frightened, but also excited. Whitacre seemed to have great ideas. If he could run ADM's giant Bioproducts Division, he certainly could handle their tiny company, which would soon be christened Future Health Technologies. Enthralled, they offered him the job of chief executive.

Whitacre's first day would be October 1. He would open offices for the company just outside Chicago.

Tired from his travels, Reinhart Richter sat at the dining table in the Whitacres' kitchen in their new suburban Chicago home. Richter had not flown home since his meeting with Williams & Connolly. Even though his lawyer had told Richter to stay away from Whitacre, he could not resist visiting his old friend.

So far, the visit had been odd. Whitacre had picked up Richter at O'Hare Airport that afternoon and then stopped on the way home for a psychiatrist's appointment. Richter had puttered around the waiting room until Whitacre emerged.

Sometime later, after they settled at the family's kitchen table, Whitacre pulled out a slip of paper.

"Listen, I've got what I promised," he said, passing the paper to Richter.

Richter glanced down. It was a check for $425,000 written to him on a Swiss bank account, one of the three checks that Daniel Briel had sent weeks before through Mike Gilbert, Whitacre's brother-in-law in Ohio. Richter felt elated; he had begun to worry that he would never see this money.

"Thank you, Mark," he said. The two men always spoke in English; Richter thought Whitacre's German was poor.

"Hey, I promised," Whitacre said. "But it's getting hard. ADM's trying to freeze my account in Switzerland."

The conversation continued on for some time. Whitacre mentioned how he had been pursued by ADM. Mick Andreas himself had called, Whitacre said, threatening to kill him if he disclosed the company's other dirty secrets. As Richter listened, the questions in his mind became overwhelming. He decided to broach one, about a lie that Whitacre had told him personally.

"Mark," he said softly, "what about this story of the adoption? Why did you come up with it?"

Whitacre waved his hand dismissively. "I had my reasons," he said. "It's not important, anyway."

On September 21, Jim Epstein called Agent Bassett with interesting news. Whitacre had spoken several times with Reinhart Richter. And Whitacre was telling Epstein that Richter was backing up his story.

Richter had been interviewed by ADM about the diversion of almost $200,000, Epstein said.

"Mark told me that Richter indicated to the lawyers he had obtained the money with the full knowledge and approval of Jim Randall, ADM's president," Epstein continued. "The ADM lawyer asked Richter to drop Randall from the story."

But when Richter refused, he was placed on leave. "Mark says that Richter believes that happened because he wouldn't change his story."

Richter could also back up other information, Epstein added. Richter had been present two years before when Whitacre had spoken with Howard Buffett about the offshore payments received by many ADM executives. Whitacre was saying that Richter was also present when Dwayne Andreas offered a Mexican politician a two-million-dollar bribe.

"There was one other thing," Epstein said. "Mark says that Richter heard Randall offer four million dollars to Dr. Chris Jones of Kronos, so that he would leave the company and start a methionine plant for ADM in Mexico."

Bassett wrote that down, not quite familiar with the name. He didn't immediately realize that Jones was the central player in the methionine criminal investigation being handled in Mobile.

For more than a week, the antitrust prosecutors were finally feeling optimistic. A plea deal with Terry Wilson seemed imminent. To move it along, they had allowed Wilson's lawyer, Reid Weingarten, to review videotapes. He seemed impressed, particularly with the Hawaii tape.

Cooperation from Terry Wilson would change everything. He could probably testify about price-fixing in other products; he could even serve as the prime witness in the lysine case if Whitacre's frauds proved fatally damaging.

But on September 27, the bubble burst. Weingarten informed

prosecutors that his client might take a plea in a normal case—but this was not a normal case. Wilson was fiercely dedicated to the Andreases and would never turn on that family. Wilson also had a son who was very sick, who needed him. The Andreases had been very supportive of Wilson and his family. He owed them. Put simply, Wilson loved ADM and wanted the company to win.

Mann accused Weingarten of tricking the prosecutors into showing him the tapes when no deal was possible. But Weingarten dismissed that, saying he had acted in good faith. Still, the prosecutors had their answer. The only way Terry Wilson would be testifying in this case was if he chose to do so—as a defendant.

In Hunt Valley, Maryland, David Page pushed through the glass door at the front of a Marriott Hotel. He followed the prearranged instructions, and in no time located Laurie Fulton and Bill Murray, the two lawyers from Williams & Connolly who had come to town to speak with him.

As he met the lawyers, Page exuded confidence. Even though he had been hired at ADM while continuing to work at another company, Page believed he and Whitacre had been clever. No one would figure out what they had done.

The lawyers asked a few opening questions. What, specifically, had been Page's responsibilities at ADM?

Page smiled. And then he lied and lied.

Early on the morning of October 10, Bassett and D'Angelo drove from downtown Chicago to Prospect Heights, a suburban town that is home to Household International. The agents found the finance company and parked in the lot. They walked to the building, knowing the next few minutes were sure to be interesting. Ron Ferrari, the person they had come to interview, had no idea the FBI was on the way.

The list of easy interviews in the case had rapidly dwindled to Ferrari, the former San Francisco 49er who was Whitacre's friend. Richter and Schweizer were out of the country, and Allison had already retained a lawyer. That left Ferrari as the last person mentioned in Whitacre's interview who could still be confronted without hassles.

Inside, the agents asked a receptionist for Ferrari.

"We're here to see him about a confidential matter," Bassett said.

A few minutes later, Ferrari showed up in the waiting area, looking nervous as the agents identified themselves.

"Oh," he said anxiously, "I'm surprised you guys came to see me already."

Interesting. Apparently, at some level, Ferrari expected them. He showed the agents to a private room.

"We want to talk to you about Mark Whitacre from ADM," Bassett said. "We're just here to get at the truth on this. We're hearing a lot of different things from different people. And we want to give you an opportunity to tell your side of the story."

Ferrari nodded. "Okay."

"First," Bassett said, "why don't you give us your background."

For several minutes, Ferrari told the agents about his education and profession. The story jumped around, with Ferrari repeatedly mentioning that he had "played ball." Whitacre never mentioned the professional football, so the agents had no idea what Ferrari was talking about.

"Yeah, I was a farm boy," Ferrari said at one point. "And I probably got my job at ADM because I played ball."

That's something like four times, D'Angelo thought. "Where'd you play baseball?" he asked.

"Uh, no, football," Ferrari responded. "I played with the San Francisco Forty-niners from 1982 through 1987."

The agents gave Ferrari the once-over. He didn't *look* like a football player.

"Yeah, I'm really lucky," Ferrari said, as if he had read the agents' minds. "I wasn't that great a player, but I got to play six years with the Forty-niners, and they won a Super Bowl championship. I'm the luckiest guy in the world."

Ferrari's story continued to circle around. The agents were pleased; people *this* nervous tended to make mistakes. Soon, a new phrase took the place of "played ball," as Ferrari repeatedly mentioned how he had "talked to Joe." The agents let it go the first few times without comment.

"You know, before I went to ADM, I always wondered what I would do in life," Ferrari said later. "And so I talked to Joe, and he gave me a lot of advice."

D'Angelo held up a hand. "Who's this 'Joe'?"

Ferrari blinked. Joe Montana, he said. The famous 49ers quarterback.

The agents nodded. As best they could figure, Ferrari was trying to impress them with casual references to having "played ball" and "talked to Joe." It wasn't working.

The conversation steered to Ferrari's friendship with Whitacre. The two joined ADM at about the same time, working in different divisions. Whitacre was higher on the corporate ladder, but they had become good friends.

"Did you ever have any business deals with Whitacre?" Bassett asked.

Ferrari shook his head. "No, never."

The agents let a moment pass. They had seen the paperwork showing Ferrari had done a deal with Whitacre involving a company called Far East Specialists, or FES.

Bassett leaned in. "Did you ever have a company called FES?" he asked.

Ferrari's face flushed with shock. "Yes," he said softly.

Under questioning, Ferrari gradually described the formation of FES. He had joined another company after ADM but decided to simultaneously use his skills in international marketing to find consulting work with Asian companies. So he had incorporated FES.

"How did you get that done?" D'Angelo asked.

"I saw an ad in an airline magazine that specialized in forming companies in Delaware. I don't remember the name of it. Maybe the Corporation Company?"

After a few other questions, Bassett tried to determine how real FES had been.

"Did FES have any officers or directors?"

"No, just me."

"Did you rent office space or hire any employees?"

Ferrari shook his head.

"Print any business cards or any stationery?"

"Umm, no, I don't believe so."

The agents let a few seconds pass. They had some FES stationery in a briefcase.

"Did you do *anything* with this business?" D'Angelo asked.

"Well, I traveled to Hong Kong to make a presentation to a foreign distributor."

"How did you first meet him?" Bassett asked.

"I don't remember."

"Pick his name out of a phone book, or what?" D'Angelo asked.

"We corresponded by mail and arranged a meeting."

The agents said nothing. Ferrari's story, of course, meant there were no phone records to prove any of this.

"What was the distributor's name?" D'Angelo asked.

"I really don't remember."

"Name of his company?"

Ferrari paused. "Sorry, I don't remember that, either."

Sounds like a really active company, D'Angelo thought.

"I might be able to find his card, or maybe the letters we wrote," Ferrari said.

Bassett removed a letter written on FES stationery from a brief-case. It had been used in support of a bogus invoice of $1.5 million to ADM.

"Do you recognize that stationery?"

Ferrari appeared even more nervous. "This isn't mine," he said. "We never did this kind of business."

The records referred to a Hong Kong bank account. Did Ferrari know it?

"Yeah, that's my account," he said. "I opened an FES account at the Swiss Bank Corporation while I was in Hong Kong for that meeting."

Again, Swiss Bank Corporation. Did everyone have an account there?

"Why Swiss Bank Corporation?" D'Angelo asked.

"It was in the same building where I had my meeting."

The agents barraged him with questions. Did he make an initial deposit? Did he receive bank statements? Did he open an American account? Each time, Ferrari answered no.

"I mean, it really didn't do any business," Ferrari said. "I just opened the account because I thought I might need it. But we didn't do any commission work."

"What did you do?"

"Well, I had some leads and put together proposals."

"Can you get us copies of those?"

"Sure, I'll try."

The agents paused. "And no money ever went through the Hong Kong account?"

"No," Ferrari said. "Except for that $1.5 million you have on those papers there. That was the money Mark wired into the account."

Nervously, Ferrari told his tale of the $1.5 million. After setting up FES, he had called Whitacre. When he told his friend that he was in the market for consulting work, Whitacre promised to keep his ears open. Then, Whitacre mentioned that he would be receiving a commission soon for some consulting he had done with a Pacific Rim company.

"Did you find it odd that he was doing consulting while working at ADM?" Bassett asked.

"I asked that. He said it wasn't only acceptable, but common and encouraged."

"How much did he say the commission would be?"

"He didn't tell me. But I expected it would be forty thousand dollars or fifty thousand. He didn't say, but that's what I thought."

At that point, Ferrari said, Whitacre told him he wanted to receive his commission offshore—without explaining why. Whitacre said he had no overseas account and asked Ferrari if he had access to one.

"So I told Mark about the FES account in Hong Kong," Ferrari said. "He was happy to hear about it, and I agreed to let him use it to receive his commission."

"Why didn't he open his own account?" D'Angelo asked.

"Well, he was going to, but he wanted to use mine in the meantime."

"And you thought that was fine?"

"Yeah. I had an account, he's a friend. Sure."

The agents asked about the money, but Ferrari said he had been in the dark. He didn't know where it was coming from, and wasn't receiving any of it. Whitacre even offered to pay him for his help, Ferrari said, but he had refused.

"About two weeks later, the bank notified me that my account had been credited with a $1.5 million wire transfer. That was the first I knew about it. I had no idea it was going to be that much."

"What was your reaction?"

"I called Mark that day," Ferrari replied, his voice rising. "I told him, 'You gotta get that money out of here. What the hell is going on?' I told him I couldn't believe such a large payment was related to a commission. He gave some long, complicated explanation."

"What was it?"

"I don't remember. But it calmed me down. Still, I demanded that he get all the money out of my account. Mark told me to wire like $160,000 to $180,000 to the account of another ADM executive, a guy named Reinhart Richter."

He wired the money to Richter and had retained the wire instructions. Afterward, Ferrari said, Whitacre promised to tell him where to send the balance. About sixty to ninety days later, Whitacre gave him instructions to wire the money to a Cayman Islands account. Ferrari said that he never kept a dime.

"You know, Whitacre is telling us something completely different," D'Angelo pointed out.

"I don't know what Whitacre is telling you. But this is the way it happened."

"Whitacre's saying that you helped create these letters and invoices."

Ferrari looked stunned. "I can't help what he's saying. I didn't do it."

"How long after you set up this account did you receive the $1.5 million?"

Ferrari shrugged. "Like a month."

"So this happens a month after you set up the account, and nothing else ever happens with the account. But you didn't set it up to receive this money?"

Ferrari nodded. "That's right."

"Did Whitacre tell you to set up the account?"

"No, that was my idea. Mark had nothing to do with it."

Still, once he began reading in the newspapers about Whitacre's money problems, Ferrari said, he began to fear the $1.5 million might be part of it.

"I called Mark, but he said, 'These things have nothing to do with you,' " Ferrari said. "He told me the allegations all had to do with an unrelated transaction."

The interview wound down after several hours, with the agents pounding on the portions of Ferrari's story that seemed to make little sense. Eventually, Ferrari volunteered that he had other dealings with Whitacre. Around 1994, he said, Whitacre had loaned him $25,000, which he had received in three checks of less than $10,000 each. Ferrari explained that he had repaid the loan about twelve months later.

"Did you repay it after the disclosure of the criminal investigation at ADM?"

"No, that wasn't why. Mark asked for it back in a phone call, and I paid it."

Had Ferrari ever heard of an illegal ADM bonus plan to pay executives offshore?

"Well, through the grapevine while I was in London, I heard something like that, about ADM executives receiving overseas compensation," Ferrari said.

"Who did you hear that from?" Bassett asked.

"I don't recall. But I do remember it had something to do with kickbacks and acquisitions of companies."

The agents discussed the records that Ferrari might have, and he agreed to put them together. They served him with a subpoena, requiring his testimony before the grand jury and the production of records.

"Think about what you told us," D'Angelo said. "This is a long time ago; maybe you can't recollect exactly how it happened. Let's talk again. We'd like to be able to go into the grand jury and say that you're cooperating. The worst thing you can do now is lie."

Ferrari nodded. "Yeah, I'll think about it."

The agents prepared to leave. Ferrari stopped them.

"Uh, one other thing," he said. "When you look through my records at Wells Fargo Bank, you're going to find a twenty-five-thousand-dollar deposit from earlier this year. I used the money to pay down debt on our family farm."

The agents listened.

"The money came from my Wells Fargo safe deposit box. My wife and I are big savers; we're very conservative, and we've always saved cash. But that money has nothing to do with Whitacre, ADM, or FES."

"Where did this cash come from?" Bassett asked.

"Just from savings. You know, I accumulated a lot of it before I was married."

This, the agents knew, was a topic they would have to revisit. But for now, the interview was over. They said their good-byes and left.

In the parking lot, the agents got into the car and shut the doors.

"This guy's full of shit," D'Angelo said.

"Yeah," Bassett agreed. "He's lying. His explanations aren't good."

Bassett turned the key and drove out of the lot. Both men knew that they were far from done with Ron Ferrari.

In the days that followed, Reinhart Richter finally appeared—at least in the press.

After more than a week of haggling with ADM's lawyers, Richter had been fired on September 22. Now, he was explaining to reporters that it was all part of a cover-up. Whitacre was telling the truth, Richter said, about ADM's under-the-table bonuses designed to help its executives evade taxes.

In the interviews, Richter admitted receiving $190,000 in secret payments when he joined ADM. But, he maintained, Jim Randall, ADM's president, had authorized it.

"He said to me, 'What are you going to do with all that money? Are you going to buy a Ferrari?' " Richter told *Fortune* magazine.

Now, said Richter, he was feeling misused and bitter. When he told ADM's lawyers about Randall's involvement, Richter claimed that they had refused to listen.

"The lawyers ignored the truth," Richter told *Fortune*. "They were just looking for ways to dump things on Mark and his colleagues."

Rapidly, the Chicago agents were facing a new problem: Relations with the prosecutors were deteriorating.

The first signs of trouble had been obvious during the summer, when the fraud prosecutors were pushing to wrap up the investigation quickly. What mattered, the agents had argued, was thoroughness, not speed. During the fall, the problem emerged again, at a meeting in Washington.

"This is an important case," Spearing told the agents. "We need Whitacre indicted by Thanksgiving."

"We're going to do a complete and thorough investigation," Bassett responded. "And if it takes us past Thanksgiving, it takes us past Thanksgiving."

The agents argued that if they failed to follow up Whitacre's allegations of corporate-wide wrongdoing, it would be his ultimate defense. The FBI investigation would be attacked for simply concentrating on him.

"We don't care about that," one of the prosecutors said. "We want Whitacre prosecuted. We can deal with these other allegations later."

This all seemed absurd. They hadn't been allowed to interview any ADM executives. Records were still dribbling in. How could they close the case without all of the information? Still, by the end of the discussion, the agents agreed to focus their efforts on Whitacre.

But as the 302s came in, prosecutors grew annoyed. What was all this with Ron Ferrari? The 302 of that interview made it seem as though they were going after *him,* not after Whitacre. Finally, on October 13, Don Mackay and Jim Nixon called Rob Grant, the case supervisor with the FBI.

"Listen," Mackay said, "we're concerned you guys are deviating from the Whitacre investigation into other areas. Remember, at our last meeting we agreed that the focus would be Whitacre and everything else would be put aside."

"That's what's happening, Don," Grant said. "Whitacre remains the focus. Everything that we're developing that isn't directly related to the frauds of him and his co-conspirators is not being addressed right now."

The two sides discussed access to information, with Grant spelling out some of the problems that were occurring between Springfield and Chicago because of the still-present Chinese wall. Springfield had interviewed Howard Buffett earlier, but wanted to speak with him again. Whitacre had told the Chicago agents information about Buffett. But, under the rules, none of that could be shared with Springfield before those agents sat down with him.

"Why is that a problem?" Mackay asked.

"It's a fundamental desire on the part of all investigators to know as much as possible about an interview subject," Grant responded.

Well, Mackay said, he didn't like the restrictions, either, but they had been put in place by high-level officials in the Justice Department.

Abruptly, Mackay changed the subject.

"What's going on with Scott Lassar?" Mackay asked. "What's he up to? Is he pumping Mike and Tony for information? He's only supposed to be getting it from us."

Grant took a breath. The bureaucracy was getting ridiculous. The prosecutors didn't even trust each other.

That morning, Jim Epstein stood among a crowd of commuters at the Evanston station, watching as a train to Chicago rumbled to a halt. The doors opened, and Epstein moved forward with the crowd, finding his way to a seat.

Epstein hadn't bothered to pick up a paper that day; he had plenty of work to review during his commute. He was reading a document when the man beside him brought out a copy of that day's *Chicago Tribune*. Epstein's eyes wandered over to check what was going on in the world.

And he froze.

Staring back at him from the top of the front page was a full-color picture of Mark Whitacre, dressed in a suit and seeming to be adjusting his glasses. Panicked, Epstein glanced at the headline that went with the photo.

ADM MOLE DISCLOSES A CACHE OF $6 MILLION; OFF-THE-BOOKS SCHEME ENDORSED BY BOSSES, FORMER EXECUTIVE SAYS.

Oh, my God.

"Excuse me," Epstein said to the man beside him. "Can I see that a moment?"

The man handed Epstein the paper, and the lawyer skimmed it quickly. It was worse than he imagined. In the first two paragraphs, Whitacre admitted acquiring millions of dollars through bogus invoices and then parking the money in overseas accounts.

Epstein sagged in his seat. The only way to save Whitacre from a long prison term was to keep him valuable to the government as a witness in the price-fixing case. But that meant keeping a low profile, not handing ADM more ammunition for cross-examination. And now, right there on the front page of the *Tribune*, his client had just publicly confessed to a multimillion-dollar fraud.

Later that day, Whitacre arrived for a scheduled appointment with his psychiatrist, Dr. Derek Miller.

"So," Miller said after Whitacre took his seat, "I see that you've been talking to the newspapers."

Whitacre nodded. He seemed achingly depressed.

"Didn't come out the way I expected," he said. "I thought they were just going to write about my new company."

Things had been slipping out of his control, Whitacre explained. He was beginning to feel the way he had before his hospitalization. He recognized that his behavior had become grandiose. He was being secretive with everybody, he said.

"That's how it's always been," Whitacre said. "Even when I was a kid, I would constantly disobey my father, but he never found out. He never found out."

At the end of the session, Miller told Whitacre that he wanted to increase his lithium levels. And from now on, he said, they needed to meet two times each week.

That night, Ron Ferrari was sitting on a living-room chair in his suburban Chicago home when he heard a knock at the front door. He glanced down a hallway. Through some glass, he saw his old friend Mark Whitacre on the stoop.

Ferrari felt a rush of anxiety. The FBI had rattled him; until then, he had been satisfied with Whitacre's assurances that the government had no interest in him. Now, he was under investigation. After his first disastrous interview, Ferrari had moved quickly to fix things. He had hired Jeffrey Steinback, a defense lawyer who commanded a good deal of respect from Chicago law enforcement.

Since then, Whitacre had tried contacting Ferrari; today alone, he had left several messages. But Ferrari had decided to cut off contact for a while. Now Whitacre was on his doorstep, and Ferrari didn't know what to do.

"Susan," Ferrari called to his wife. "It's Mark."

"What does he want?" she replied.

"I have no idea," Ferrari said.

Ferrari walked to the door, stepping outside before Whitacre could say a word. He shut the door behind him. He would not let Whitacre in.

"Hi," Ferrari said.

"Why haven't you called?" Whitacre said rapidly. "I've left lots of messages."

"I know you've left messages."

"But why haven't you called? I've left messages. Why haven't you called?"

Ferrari stared at Whitacre. "We don't have anything to talk about," he said.

"Well, wait, what happened?" Whitacre said. "Have you met with anybody? Have you met with anybody?"

Ferrari scowled. "Hell, yes, I've met with somebody. The Federal Bureau of Investigation came to visit me. It's quite interesting what they had to say."

Whitacre held up his hands. "Hey, listen, this isn't about you. Ron, listen to me, bud, they don't want you. They want ADM. I know these guys."

"Well, that's interesting. Because they're asking *me* questions. Why are you saying I created invoices?"

Whitacre babbled a response that made little sense.

"But listen," he continued, "they don't care about that. They want ADM."

Whitacre turned his hands as he spoke. "We've got to spin this thing. We've got to turn it back on them. Spin this thing. You've got to show it's compensation. You know these guys were taking money. You know that."

Whitacre listed other executives who had taken money, saying Ferrari knew all about them. Ferrari started to get scared. Whitacre was wild-eyed, out of control.

"I don't know about any of this," he said. "I never told you this. I didn't know anyone was taking money."

"You've said it!" Whitacre protested. "You've said it! You've got to spin this! This isn't about you; I didn't want to get you involved. This isn't about you. This is about them. They want ADM; they don't want you."

Ferrari held up his hands. "I'm done. I don't have anything else to talk about."

Whitacre blinked. "Does Susan know?"

"No," Ferrari lied. "She has no idea."

Ferrari opened the door. "We're done, we're not talking about anything else."

"Bud, I wouldn't do this to you. You know me. I've been in your shoes. I wouldn't do this to you."

Ferrari said nothing.

"You can't say we ever met here," Whitacre said suddenly. "You can't say I was here to see you."

Ferrari stared at him. "We are done."

He closed the door.

From the entryway, Ferrari could see Whitacre still standing outside, obviously thinking his friend would return. Ferrari reached for the switch for the porch light and flicked it off, leaving Whitacre in the dark.

Ferrari walked back to the living room. This whole experience had thrown him off. His hands were trembling. Taking a breath, he headed to the phone. He wanted to call his lawyer, to tell somebody what had just happened.

As Bassett and D'Angelo questioned an ever-widening circle of potential witnesses, echoes from their investigation were beginning to find their way into the media. For weeks, a series of news reports had appeared, saying that the government was indeed investigating Whitacre's allegations of an illegal, corporate-wide scheme to pay off-the-books bonuses to senior ADM officers.

The stories enraged the company and Williams & Connolly. The defense lawyers met with prosecutors, pounding the table and demanding that something be done. Finally, on October 18, reporters received calls from an ADM spokesman. If they phoned the Justice Department press office, the spokesman said, they would be given a statement.

As the calls came into the Justice Department, the statement was repeated, again and again.

"ADM is not a target or subject of a criminal investigation by the Criminal Division of the Department of Justice."

What the hell is going on?

D'Angelo and Bassett read the Justice Department's words in the newspaper the next morning. They had never seen anything like it before—a statement appearing to clear a company *before* an investigation was over. Worse, as far as they were concerned, the statement *wasn't true.* The investigation wasn't far enough along to know if Whitacre was lying. *This,* they felt sure, was politics at its worst.

After discussing it with Bassett, D'Angelo decided to make sure his boss knew about the latest outrage from Washington. He called Rob Grant.

"Hey, Rob," D'Angelo said. "You're not going to believe this."

"What's up?"

"Justice Department has come out with a statement saying ADM is not a target in the fraud investigation."

"What do you mean ADM is not a target?" Grant shot back.

"That's what it says. We don't know anything more."

"Wait a minute. What about Randall? What about Mick?"

"Just says ADM is not a target," D'Angelo repeated. "Can you believe that?"

"Why would they come out with something like that? What prompted that?"

"We don't know, Rob."

"Did you talk to anybody yet about it?"

"No, we decided to call you first."

"I'll call," Grant said.

Calls went back and forth throughout the day. But the release of the bizarre and misleading statement would forever remain a mystery to the Chicago FBI.

Later that day, Rick Reising, ADM's general counsel, stood on a blue-draped stage in a converted school, looking out onto a crowd of angry and concerned shareholders. In the wake of the raids, ADM's stock price had plummeted. Now, many shareholders were arguing for new directors, independent of the Andreas family.

But on this, the day of ADM's annual meeting of shareholders, little was mentioned about price-fixing. Instead, the executives issued explanations for Whitacre's thefts. Still, there was good news, Reising said.

"The Department of Justice has confirmed that there is no credible evidence that Mr. Whitacre's thefts were part of a plan by ADM to funnel compensation to its executives," he said.

The statement went far beyond anything Washington had actually said. But there was no arguing with the ADM executives running the meeting, as shareholders soon learned. At one point, Edward Durkin, a representative from the carpenters' union, launched into a speech critical of the company. From the podium, Dwayne Andreas ordered that Durkin's microphone be shut off.

Outraged, Durkin invoked Robert's Rules of Order, the standard text for governing procedure at official meetings. Andreas was un-moved.

"This meeting, sir," he snapped, "runs according to my rules."

In Chicago, Dick Beattie pushed through a revolving door, heading to the elevator that would take him to the Antitrust Division's Midwest office. He was accompanied by two colleagues, including Charles Koob, Simpson Thacher's top antitrust expert. Koob was going to be needed. For on this day, the government was, for the first time, going to play the Harvest King tapes to a representative of ADM.

The idea had been a gambit conceived by Scott Lassar. ADM had been riding high since the Whitacre mess had emerged. Perhaps if the case depended on Whitacre, they would have good reason for confi-dence. But everyone was forgetting the tapes—the foundation of the case.

Williams & Connolly seemed determined to fight to the end. That made sense; the firm appeared, in many ways, to be shouldering the battle for the Andreas family. A corporate plea would imply the guilt of Mick Andreas. Striking a deal for the company seemed as if it would be awfully difficult for Williams & Connolly.

But Simpson Thacher was another matter. Beattie represented only the special committee. He seemed more likely to push a settle-ment if the evidence called for it. Once the tapes became public, the directors would be hard pressed to explain why they hadn't resolved the case. Lassar had proposed making an approach to Simpson Thacher, in the hopes of persuading them to deal.

The lawyers were shown to a small room, where a television was already plugged in. For hours, as the tapes played, they took about 250 pages of copious notes.

By the end of the first day of viewing, any illusions that Beattie and Koob may have had about the price-fixing case were gone. For months, Beattie had been hearing arguments from Williams & Connolly that the tapes would never see the light of day. But from what he had just seen, Beattie was certain that was pure fantasy.

Walking out the door, Beattie glanced at Koob.

"There is no way things like that stay hidden," he said. "Those are going to be used in every law-school antitrust class for years."

The following day, November 1, a conference was held at FBI head-quarters in Washington to decide what to do about the Chinese wall. For months, Shepard and Herndon had worked under a cloud, at times tripping over the feet of D'Angelo and Bassett as they attempted to do their jobs. The situation had become untenable.

Most every prosecutor and supervisor from the two cases presented their views. As the reality of the Chinese wall was laid out, it became obvious that the rules needed revision. By the end of the meeting, Jack Keeney, Deputy Assistant Attorney General for the Criminal Division, announced that the wall was coming down.

Beginning that day, Shepard and Herndon could meet with Whitacre, if a prosecutor was present. Even better, Chicago and Springfield agents could share information. Hopefully, that would bring the two cases to a rapid close.

The new spirit of cooperation took hold in less than a week. Reinhart Richter had let it be known that he was willing to provide evidence in both the fraud and antitrust cases, so the two sides decided to coordinate their interview with him in Mexico City. On November 7, Herndon, Mutchnik, Bassett, and D'Angelo all flew down to Mexico.

That night, the four gathered at a restaurant. They compared notes about planned interviews and found that many involved the same people. The Chicago agents griped about their relationship with the Washington prosecutors; Jim Nixon, who had arrived on a different flight that same day, didn't even join the group for dinner. Herndon and Mutchnik razzed the two agents a little. The Harvest King team was not only working well together, they had become good friends.

Bassett leaned in to Herndon.

"You know, I never agreed with these walls," he said. "That was Justice."

Herndon nodded. "I know."

Before the night was over, the agents had put the problems of the past behind them. Now, they were just law enforcement again, all on the same team.

The next morning, after being cleared for entry, Richter walked past a Marine Corps guard into the American Embassy in Mexico City. He had just driven almost fifty miles, from his home in Cuernavaca, and was ready to talk. He was escorted to the office of the legal attaché, where the agents and prosecutors were waiting.

Richter shook everyone's hands. With his goatee and casual appearance, he looked more like an artist than a corporate executive. The group told Richter that the fraud investigators would conduct the first interview, followed by Herndon and Mutchnik. Richter agreed and sat at a table. Bassett, D'Angelo, and Nixon took their seats while Herndon and Mutchnik left the room.

Richter spoke in heavily accented English, the result of being a German national who spent most of his days in Latin America. He described meeting Whitacre when they both worked in Germany for Degussa. But soon Whitacre left to take his big position at ADM.

"While I was still at Degussa, I spoke with Mark by phone," Richter said, sitting stiff and straight. "He told me that he had received an up-front bonus to work at ADM."

The statement came out of nowhere; Whitacre had never mentioned an up-front bonus before. It sounded rehearsed.

Richter said that he had stayed in contact with Whitacre, and in January 1991, was hired by his friend as an ADM consultant. Once the plant was operating, he was to become ADM's lysine distributor in Mexico. For that, he was to receive $200,000 a year plus a start-up bonus of $50,000.

"I went to a meeting with Mark and Jim Randall," Richter continued. "They agreed to pay me an additional start-up bonus other than the fifty thousand dollars. Randall said the bonus would be paid in a special way so other ADM employees would not be aware of it. Randall told Mark to handle the bonus so it would not appear on the company books."

The statement directly contradicted Richter's taped phone message to Sid Hulse, which the agents had with them in a briefcase on the floor. If Richter kept going with this story, they were going to have to play it for him.

"Randall joked that I was to receive so much money I probably would want to buy a Ferrari," Richter said.

Richter described in some detail the negotiations that led to the amount of the bonus—with $190,000 paid off the books and $50,000 on the books.

"Mark told me to send an invoice to ADM from Aminac, which is a business I own," Richter said.

"How did you send those invoices?" D'Angelo asked.

"Either by fax or directly to Mark."

The Aminac invoice amount—$93,500—was wired to his account in Houston at the Post Oak Bank, Richter said. For the second wire transfer, Richter used the company of a friend named Adolpho Acebras. That company, Komven, sent the second invoice, for $87,466, and again the money was wired to Post Oak. A portion of that money, Richter said, may have gone to Acebras.

"What did you tell Mark about Acebras?"

"Nothing. He knew none of the particulars."

Richter never thought much about those 1991 payments until a few months before, when ADM went public with its allegations against Whitacre. Richter related how Williams & Connolly had contacted him and how he had flown to Washington to meet with the lawyers.

"They told me the payments related to these invoices were not authorized," Richter said. "I told them that Randall and Mark knew all about them."

The agents nodded, letting Richter speak without challenging him. They wanted him locked into his story before pointing out the problems.

"Later, I phoned Howard Buffett, another friend of mine from ADM," Richter said. "I told him that ADM could only have found those invoices so quickly because Randall and others knew about them. He told me to speak with Marty Allison and Sid Hulse, because they were in the same position I was. He also told me about other ADM executives he knew who may have received suspicious payments."

Bassett nodded, then calmly removed a spreadsheet from his briefcase. It showed money transfers at the Post Oak Bank account, where the invoiced payments had been wired.

"Now, from what we see here," Bassett said, laying out the records, "there is a good deal of money going from this account to Mark Whitacre."

Richter blinked. "Those are loans," he said stiffly.

"Loans?"

"Yes."

Bassett flipped through the records. "This is a loan?" he said, pointing to one transfer from the account to Whitacre. "And this, too?"

"Yes. Mark was going to repay me in 1996 or 1997. We wrote loan agreements for this. I still have them, if you want to see."

"Let's just keep looking at these," Bassett said. The records showed hundreds of thousands of dollars going to Whitacre, Ginger, even Whitacre's parents.

"These are all loans?"

"Yes," Richter said, his confidence wavering.

D'Angelo shook his head.

"Nobody's going to believe this," he said. "Other people have told us it isn't true. Hulse is telling us other things about this."

Not completely true, but it caught Richter's attention.

"Look, we know you're sticking up for Mark," D'Angelo said. "But Mark may ultimately cooperate. He's told us different things about these payments already."

Another bluff.

"To be blunt," Bassett joined in, "your story doesn't sound true."

The agents kept up the pressure. Finally, Richter slumped in his chair.

"You're right," he muttered. "It isn't true."

The agents paused. "What isn't true?" Bassett asked.

"All the loan documents, everything about these being loans. That is not true."

The agents stopped. Richter had just flipped.

"I feel terrible doing this to Mark," he said. "But he told me to say these things."

"All right," Bassett said. "So what really happened?"

Richter stared at the table, gently shaking his head.

"Mark never intended to pay these loans back," he finally said. "We just put the paperwork together in case anybody ever came back, asking questions."

"So what was this money that went to Mark from the account?"

Richter rubbed his temple, then looked at the agents. "This was the whole idea."

The agents were confused. What did he mean?

"From the beginning," Richter said. "All this money we said was a start-up bonus for me. It was for Mark."

Richter swallowed and looked at the agents.

"Everything went to Mark."

The dam had burst. For the rest of the interview, Richter poured out a new story.

Again, it involved Nigeria. Richter said that Whitacre had lost large sums of money there and thought of the bonus scheme as a way to recoup his investment. Whitacre believed that since Richter was a nonresident alien, his Houston account was the perfect place to hide the money, tax-free. Richter said he agreed to let Whitacre use it.

"Mark called me immediately before any funds were going to be wired to the account," Richter said. "He also told me what to do with the money once it arrived."

"How did you disburse the money?" Bassett asked.

"By wire, by check. Sometimes in cash."

"How much cash?"

Richter thought for a moment. "I remember one time coming to the United States, and I paid Mark twenty-five thousand or thirty thousand dollars in cash. Something like that."

"Anything else?"

"Yes, well, I sometimes gave Mark blank checks from the account, checks that I signed."

"Would you be able to identify cashed checks that weren't filled out by you?"

"Yes, I could do that."

Bassett showed Richter the spreadsheet of transactions in the Post Oak account. Using a blue pen, Richter marked each one that involved Whitacre. He also noted the purported bonus—totaling almost $226,000.

In time, most every disbursement was marked with a blue dot, although some of the money he identified as his own—almost all of it coming from the sale of his home in Germany. He had eventually deposited that $250,000 in Whitacre's Swiss bank account, Richter said, so that he could obtain a higher return on a managed account.

"I didn't have the five-hundred-thousand-dollar minimum for such an account," Richter said.

Weeks before, he had received a check for $425,000 from Whitacre, written on a Swiss bank account. Richter didn't know it, but this was one of three checks sent by the Swiss Bank Corporation to Mike Gilbert, Whitacre's brother-in-law in Ohio.

"Why did you receive that money?" Bassett asked.

"Some of it was money from my house that I had given to Mark. Probably fifty thousand to seventy thousand dollars was for the repayment of real loans I gave him. And the rest was compensation for services I provided through the Post Oak Bank account."

Richter sighed. He seemed weary.

"I must stop," he said. "I have a scheduled meeting I must attend."

The agents looked at him. Would he be willing to meet again? Bassett asked.

"Of course," Richter answered. "But now, I must go."

The agents and Nixon set down their pens. The interview was over.

Outside in a hallway, Herndon and Mutchnik looked up when Richter stepped out of the room. The two men stood, ready to begin. Richter shook his head.

"I'm tired," Richter said. "I have another meeting, and I need to get home."

The two suggested meeting in the morning.

"No," Richter said. "I can legally drive only on even days in Mexico City."

"What?" Herndon said, surprised. "Well, why don't you stay the night, then?"

"No," Richter said. "I need to get back."

This was getting tough. Herndon and Mutchnik knew that if they pushed Richter too hard, they might lose any chance for an interview. So they casually agreed to meet at the embassy in two days. Richter said good-bye and left.

That evening, Richter was at his home in Cuernavaca, when the telephone rang. His wife answered, and called to her husband. Richter quietly picked up the extension.

"Hey, how you doin'?" a voice said. "It's Mark."

The day of unexpected vacation was wonderful for Herndon and Mutchnik, offering a chance to visit Mexico's pyramids and other tourist spots. But by Friday, they were ready to meet with Richter.

Around eight-thirty that morning, Herndon was in his hotel room, preparing to walk to the embassy. The phone rang.

"This is Reinhart Richter. I have just learned that the embassy is closed today due to a federal holiday."

Herndon grabbed a pen. He needed to keep notes.

"Well, yes," he said, sitting down on the bed. "The embassy *is* closed, but I've made arrangements for our interview. They're going to let us in. We have a room."

"Oh," Richter said, pausing. "Well, um, I have a very important business meeting, very important for my future. I have made some phone calls trying to cancel, but I can't. I cannot reach anybody. I just can't meet you today."

What's going on here? Herndon thought. Richter had given them the runaround for days, and now he's coming up with excuse after excuse. A horrible thought popped into Herndon's mind.

"Did Mark Whitacre tell you not to talk to me?"

Richter paused. "I spoke to Mark since I saw you. But that was to talk about my meeting with the other agents."

"And did he tell you not to talk to me?"

"No, Mark told me that he knew you, and he agreed I should speak with you."

Richter said he might be willing to talk over the telephone in coming days, and the call came to an end. Herndon hung up and finished jotting down his notes.

Herndon felt certain that Richter was lying. Although he couldn't understand why Whitacre would do it, the agent was convinced that his old cooperating witness had persuaded Reinhart Richter to ditch the interview.

Glancing at his watch, Herndon realized Mutchnik was probably waiting in the lobby. He headed to the door, eager to find the prosecutor. He wanted to let him know that Whitacre may have just tampered with a witness.

CHAPTER 17

That same morning, Tony D'Angelo was at his desk in shirtsleeves, his suit jacket hung on a nearby coat rack. The Chicago Field Office was relatively quiet, with most agents using the early hours to pore over newspapers or review case files. D'Angelo, on his first day back from Mexico, had barely settled in when the phone rang. It was Herndon, calling from the embassy.

"Tony," Herndon said, "we've had a problem."

D'Angelo took notes as Herndon described the Richter call. Everything indicated that Whitacre had told Richter to stop talking.

"Could you call Whitacre and find out if he told Richter to cancel?" Herndon asked. "Urge him to call Richter back; tell him to reconsider."

D'Angelo put down his pen. "Okay, let me get on it right away."

He clicked off the line and telephoned Bassett.

"Mike, it's me," D'Angelo said. "Come on over. We need to talk to Jim Epstein."

Epstein returned the message from the agents at around nine-twenty that morning.

"Jim, hold on, okay?" D'Angelo said.

D'Angelo transferred the call to the speakerphone in his squad leader's office. He and Bassett headed to the office and punched a button on the console.

"Okay, Jim, we've got problems," D'Angelo began. "One, your client is lying to us."

"Whoa," Epstein said. "What do you mean?"

The two agents described how Richter had lied and then changed his story. Now, he was contradicting Whitacre.

"He told us the first version was something Whitacre cooked up," D'Angelo said. "So again, problem one, Whitacre is lying to us. And problem two, he's obstructing justice because he's telling witnesses to lie to us."

Epstein sighed. "Ah, damn it."

But there was more, D'Angelo continued. They had just heard from Herndon in Mexico, and now it seemed that Whitacre had persuaded Richter to stop talking.

"Basically, Whitacre's becoming more and more worthless every day in the antitrust case," D'Angelo said. "You know this is all discoverable. He's supposed to be telling the truth, Jim, and he's lying."

"Guys, I don't know what to say," Epstein replied. "I've been telling him to tell the truth."

"And you've got to tell him to stop talking to witnesses, too," D'Angelo said.

"I'm trying! I've told him not to call these people, but I can't baby-sit the man twenty-four hours a day."

"Talk to him again," D'Angelo urged. "If he's directing Richter not to talk, have him change his tune."

"Yeah, okay. Are you going to be there for a while?"

Both agents said they would.

"All right, I'll call him. Let me get back to you."

Minutes later, Epstein called back. "I've got Mark on the line," he said.

D'Angelo again transferred the call to his squad leader's office and headed there with Bassett. He punched the speakerphone button.

"Okay . . . ," D'Angelo began.

"I didn't tell Richter not to talk!" Whitacre sputtered. "He called *me*. He called me, very upset about his interview. He said you weren't interested in information against others at ADM. He was really upset, really upset by the interview and how he was treated."

Bassett glanced at D'Angelo. This made no sense. "What did he say specifically?"

"He said it was all just 'dump on Mark Whitacre.' He told me he tried to give evidence against other ADM executives, and Jim Nixon kept saying you guys weren't interested. You only wanted evidence against me!"

"Mark, that's the furthest thing from the truth," Bassett said. "We gave Richter every opportunity to tell his story. We asked lots of questions, not only about possible wrongdoing by you, but by other current or former employees of ADM. It was explored very extensively."

"Look, Mark," D'Angelo said. "Herndon is down there right now, and wants to talk to Richter. Is there anything you can do to facilitate that? They want to talk about the antitrust case. We already finished the fraud interview."

"I'll see what I can do," Whitacre said.

Whitacre called back within the hour with little to report. He had reached Richter's wife, he said. Her husband was at a dentist's appointment and would not be back for hours. No price-fixing interview could take place that day. But again, Whitacre said, he was convinced that the real problem was Richter's dismay about his first interview.

"He told me that the FBI and the Justice Department are working hard to protect ADM and the Andreases and Jim Randall," Whitacre fumed. "He said talking to you was like talking to Williams & Connolly."

"Did he tell you we didn't listen to his other allegations?" Bassett asked.

"He said you did a little, but without enthusiasm."

"Well, what didn't we hear about?"

For ten minutes, Whitacre ticked off a series of items, including allegations of a two-million-dollar bribe paid by Dwayne Andreas to a Mexican politician and a four-million-dollar under-the-table payment by Jim Randall to Dr. Chris Jones.

D'Angelo wrote down the information, although it sounded familiar. Epstein had told them weeks before that Richter was eager to spill these stories to the FBI. But, Richter had never said a word about any of it. Either Whitacre was lying, or Richter was holding back.

And both agents already suspected that they knew which of those options was most likely to be true.

The Monadnock Building rises above West Jackson Boulevard in downtown Chicago, its sixteen stories straining thick masonry walls. Completed in 1891, the Monadnock had once been the world's tallest building; now it was dwarfed by steel-structured giants. Standing just catty-corner from the Dirksen Federal Building, the architectural masterpiece had become a popular site for some of the city's top defense lawyers, including Jeff Steinback, the attorney hired by Ron Ferrari. For weeks, Steinback had been trying to arrange another interview with the government in hopes of staving off a possible prosecution. Ferrari had more to say, Steinback promised. Finally, an agreement was reached to meet on December 6.

That day, D'Angelo and Bassett walked with Jim Nixon through the Monadnock's shoe box of a lobby, toward a polished aluminum staircase. Old-fashioned light-filament bulbs, attached to tentacles adorning the walls and ceiling, battled feebly against the ground floor's Victorian darkness. The three men headed to an elevator that took them upstairs, where a woman met them in the waiting area of Steinback's office.

"Hey, Tony," the woman said as the group walked in. "How are you doing?"

"Okay, Carol. How've you been?" D'Angelo replied. The agent had dealt with Steinback many times before.

The group followed Carol into Steinback's office. Shafts of sunlight filtered through the windows, illuminating walls adorned with images of professional boxing, Steinback's passion. The lawyer was at his desk; beside him, Ferrari was in a chair, looking cowed. Steinback stood and broke into a smile.

"Hey, come on in," he said. "Take a seat."

The agents and Nixon settled into chairs facing the desk. After some opening chitchat, Steinback took control.

"Ron's here to cooperate," Steinback said. "He is ready to fully and truthfully answer your questions to the best of his ability."

Steinback glanced at Ferrari. "Isn't that right?"

Ferrari nodded silently.

Steinback continued his lecture, saying Ferrari understood the ramifications of failing to tell the truth. The agents wrote it all down, impressed. Steinback was a class act; he had clearly beaten up Ferrari on the importance of honesty before they arrived. If he lied, Ferrari was going to dig himself in deeper.

"Now," Steinback said, "I've looked over a copy of the 302 from your first meeting with Ron, and there are a few things that need to be clarified."

Clarified. In this game, the agents knew, that was a defense code for a client who wanted to change his story.

First, Steinback said, there was the matter of when Ferrari had wired all of the $1.5 million in his Hong Kong account to Whitacre in the Caymans. It hadn't been in sixty to ninety days, as he had maintained. In fact, money from ADM had remained in the account for at least eleven months.

D'Angelo wrote that down. Ferrari's story about desperately trying to move the money out of his account as soon as he heard about it had just fallen apart.

Another problem, Steinback said, was that Ferrari had taken longer to pay back the $25,000 loan from Whitacre than he had said in the first interview. Finally, there was the matter of the $25,000 in cash in Ferrari's safe-deposit box—the money that Ferrari said he and his wife had worked so hard to save. Ferrari hadn't told the whole story about that, either, Steinback said. He looked toward his client.

Ferrari picked up the dialogue.

"That money was from unofficial bonuses I received when I was playing football for the Forty-niners," he said.

"What do you mean?" D'Angelo asked.

Ferrari fumbled with an answer, glancing at his lap. Steinback leaned up, a sly grin on his face, and broke in.

"You know, sometimes things happen in football games that aren't officially sanctioned or aren't supposed to be officially sanctioned," Steinback explained.

The agents listened, uncertain where this was going.

"So, let's say there's an unpopular player on the other team. Sometimes, there are these little bonus payments that the coaches pay for a particularly vicious hit on one of those unpopular guys."

The agents stared at Steinback, incredulous. Professional football players were being paid money under the table to *hurt* one another?

Steinback smiled. He clearly enjoyed this story.

"They call it 'head-hunting,'" he said. "Basically for money paid when you take somebody's head off."

Steinback coolly glanced at Ferrari, checking his condition before tossing out the next bit of damage. "Now, the rest came from money he was paid for charity events. He'd attend, and they'd slip him a few hundred dollars honorarium, all cash."

The lawyer turned to Ferrari.

"Did I describe it accurately, Ron?"

Ferrari nodded, saying nothing.

The agents laughed.

The interview shifted to the $1.5 million payment in Ferrari's Hong Kong account. Again, Ferrari said that Whitacre had asked to use the account for a consulting commission.

"What did you know about the amount of money coming in?" Bassett asked.

"Like I said, I didn't know," Ferrari replied. "I expected it would be in the forty-thousand- to fifty-thousand-dollar range."

"You sure you didn't think it was more?"

"No, that's what I thought at the time."

Bassett pulled a file from his briefcase, removed a photocopy of a handwritten note, and handed it to Steinback.

"I think this might help his recollection," Bassett said flatly.

Steinback read the document as an expression of surprise flashed across his face. Without a word, he passed it to his client. Ferrari studied it in silence.

It was a moment for the agents to relish. The note was signed by Ferrari and sent to the Hong Kong bank days before the wire transfer from ADM. It informed the bankers that a large sum of money—precisely $1.5 million—would be deposited into Ferrari's account in two to three days. Not only did it prove Ferrari knew the amount of money coming, but also that he had worked to be sure the bank was prepared for it. His story was destroyed.

"That's your handwriting?" Bassett asked.

Ferrari's eyes stayed glued to the paper. "Yes."

"So, you sure you didn't know how much was coming?"

Ferrari said nothing. Then he looked up at the agents.

"Mark called beforehand," he said. "He told me $1.5 million was on the way."

"Why did you write the note?" Bassett asked.

"I was doing Mark a favor. But I was concerned about the size of the deposit and didn't know anything about where it came from."

"If you were so upset about the amount, why accept the money? Why didn't you tell the bank to send it back?"

Ferrari looked flustered. "I was just doing Mark a favor," he repeated.

The agents hammered on the inconsistencies in the story. Ferrari repeated that he had never received any of the money. He became defensive and dug in. D'Angelo decided to try a change-up and switched topics.

"You ever hear anything from Whitacre about Nigeria?"

"Yeah," he said. "He told me he had previously done some Nigerian deal, sending money there."

"What did he tell you about it?"

"It was strange. He'd send them money, and they would make up invoices or something. Mark told me that he expected them to return the initial investment plus more."

"Did he tell you how he knew about these deals?"

"Yeah. He said he learned about it from Mick Andreas, who had done something like this in the past."

Ferrari shook his head. "I thought it sounded crazy."

"When did you learn about it?"

"I don't know, I guess around 1991."

Ferrari seemed lost in thought for a second.

"I'll tell you, I really thought the whole thing was nefarious," he finally said. "And I was under the impression that Mark had invested a lot of money in it."

"Did you think the $1.5 million might have anything to do with the Nigerians?"

"I was very concerned about that," he said. "You know, I kept worrying that if this money had been generated through one of those deals that I might get a visit from these Nigerians sometime."

Ferrari glanced from the agents to Nixon. "That really worried me," he said.

The interview lasted almost two more hours. The agents returned to questions about the $1.5 million wire, but Ferrari kept playing the same notes. He had received no money and didn't know how Whitacre had obtained it.

The agents asked Ferrari if he knew about thefts of technology by ADM. He replied that he had heard stories from Whitacre about the company trying to steal microbes by sending people into the sewers near competitors' plants. But he cautioned that he had no personal knowledge of thefts. Everything was from Whitacre.

The interview ended and the agents put away their documents. With Nixon, they stood and made their exit. Within minutes, the three were back on the street, quietly discussing the interview. Both agents thought Ferrari was in trouble; the note to the bank crippled his story.

Nixon was not so sure.

A week later, on December 13, Mike Bassett saw the familiar colors of a Federal Express envelope in his box. He removed it and glanced at the shipping label. It was from the Fraud Section. Bassett headed back to his desk and pulled the cardboard strip along the envelope's top.

After reading the letter, Bassett reached for the phone. He needed to talk to D'Angelo right away.

"Tony, I just got a letter from the prosecutors," Bassett said. "You've got to see it. Goddamn it! I've never seen anything like it."

Within fifteen minutes, D'Angelo was reading the same letter. It struck him as strange right off the bat; most communications from prosecutors would go through supervisors, not directly to the case agents. But as D'Angelo read, what at first seemed odd struck him as far more worrisome.

The letter, signed by Mackay and Nixon for Mary Spearing, opened with a chatty "Dear Mike and Tony." From there, it launched into an assessment of the fraud investigation. It listed the interviews conducted and the amount of money traced so far. Records of companies and accounts in five parts of the world were still being sought. The prosecutors were also still attempting to arrange interviews through Aubrey Daniel with several ADM officers, including Randall and Andreas.

The prosecutors wrote that when the investigation began, they had hoped to finish by November. That proved impossible, but a new deadline was now being set.

"We would like to have the investigation completed by the end of January 1996," the letter read.

That's a little more than a month, D'Angelo thought.

To accomplish that, they needed to confront Whitacre soon.

"Some aspects of the investigation may not be fully completed until we have obtained access to individuals and records in foreign jurisdictions," the letter read. "Nonetheless, we believe the domestic part of this investigation can be substantially completed by this date."

The prosecutors wanted to indict before reviewing all the evidence? What was the rush?

To meet the deadline, the letter stated, the agents needed to focus on a few tasks. Those included interviewing seven people, completing a net-worth analysis for Whitacre, obtaining and reviewing his tax returns, tracing the fraud proceeds, and analyzing his phone records.

But the prosecutors were also clearly suspicious of the agents. At one point in the letter, they asked why they had not received 302s from conversations with defense lawyers. D'Angelo and Bassett both laughed. Agents don't write 302s for lawyers—those are reserved for witness statements. And, while they did write memos of those contacts, such records were rarely shared with prosecutors—after all, the *prosecutors* were supposed to be in frequent contact with the defense lawyers, not the *agents*.

Then, a sentence appeared that stopped D'Angelo cold.

"Please note that it is not an objective of this investigation to turn

Whitacre into an informant for the investigation of others who are involved in the improper activities of Whitacre."

He read the sentence again.

*It is not an objective of this investigation to turn Whitacre into an in-
formant for the investigation of others. . . .*

D'Angelo felt a chill. Was the FBI being ordered to ignore
Whitacre's leads, to ensure a quick indictment?

He set the letter down and looked at Bassett.

"What the hell is this?" he said.

Bassett folded his arms across his chest. "I was wondering how
long it would take you to see that."

Neither agent knew what to do. Their job was to pursue every lead
to the end of the earth; now, it seemed, they were being told to limit
their investigation to ensure the indictment of only one particular person.

They couldn't shake the feeling that they were witnessing a potential obstruction of justice—only this time, by the Department of
Justice itself.

Later that day, Bassett and D'Angelo were eating lunch in the rear of a
Chicago deli, stewing about their options. Bassett swallowed a bite of
his turkey sandwich.

"Goddamn it, this is bullshit!" he fumed.

"I've never seen anything like this," D'Angelo said. "We're not
putting up with this; we're going on record."

The Justice Department *had* to be bowing to the demands of
Williams & Connolly, the agents said. First, there was the false announcement that ADM was not a target; now it seemed that they were
being told to take out the chief witness against the company as fast as
possible. This was becoming some Washington influence game, they
railed.

"The fix is in, man," D'Angelo said. "Williams & Connolly is running this investigation."

The conversation shifted to hypotheticals. What if they did it?
What if they ignored Whitacre's leads?

"That one's not hard to figure out," Bassett said. "We could be
prosecuted for obstruction."

D'Angelo nodded and took a bite of his club sandwich.

"You know one thing is true," he said. "Once Whitacre's indicted,
they're not going to do anything against these other people."

"We've got to finish everything at the same time," Bassett said. "Once Whitacre's gone, DOJ is out of it."

Bassett took another bite of his sandwich and chuckled. He was expecting a transfer to Albany soon.

"I'll probably be out of here before this is over," Bassett said. "Then this will be all your problem."

"Thanks a lot," D'Angelo laughed.

The next step was sending this matter up the line in the Bureau. The agents agreed that this one might end up going all the way back to headquarters.

"Let's see if the Bureau backs us," Bassett said.

"Yeah, but Mike, what if they don't?"

The agents fell silent for a moment.

"I'll tell you, Mike," D'Angelo said, "if they tell us, 'Don't follow leads, don't go after co-conspirators, don't go after ADM,' that's it. I'll leave the job first."

"I feel the same way."

D'Angelo took another bite.

"And Mike," he added, "if that happens, I think we should go public."

Bassett nodded. That would be an enormous step for an agent, something almost never done. But he saw the logic.

"I agree," he said.

By the end of the meal, the agents were decided. If they were told to ignore Whitacre's leads—*if they were told to obstruct justice*—they would resign that day.

And afterward, they would call *60 Minutes*.

There had been no need to worry.

In the days that followed, the Bureau reacted with muted outrage to the extraordinary letter from the Justice Department. Their supervisors not only fell squarely behind Bassett and D'Angelo, but they took up the battle for them.

After hearing about the letter, their supervisor took the matter to Ed Worthington, the Chicago ASAC. Worthington agreed to sign the response to the prosecutors that D'Angelo had written. It oozed diplomacy, although a dig at the prosecutors occasionally slipped through.

The letter went through the prosecutors' requests one at a time. Regarding the net-worth analysis for Whitacre, it stated that requests for foreign-bank information had gone out, but that the analysis could not be completed before the data was delivered. As for obtaining

Whitacre's tax records, the response pointed out this was not usually handled by the FBI, since it required a court order—something the prosecutors needed to obtain.

"The U.S. Attorney's office for the Northern District of Illinois routinely procures tax information via such orders," it read, dripping condescension. "An example can be made available to your office if necessary."

Regarding the matter of the 302s of defense lawyers, the response explained that lawyer contacts are written up in memorandums, not 302s. Still, in the future those would also be shared with the prosecutors.

At the bottom, the response addressed the expectation that Whitacre would not be an informant against others.

"All potential criminal activities revolving around Whitacre's fraud scheme will be thoroughly investigated prior to the culmination of this case," the response stated. "The FBI will endeavor to complete these investigative tasks as expeditiously as possible. However, thoroughness should not be sacrificed to accomplish this goal."

In the days and weeks that followed, the Chicago Field Office sought support from headquarters for their decision to disregard the prosecutors' instructions. D'Angelo and Bassett briefed Neil Gallagher, Deputy Assistant Director for the FBI's Criminal Investigative Division. Afterward, Gallagher told the agents to ignore any instruction to take shortcuts.

"Keep doing what you're doing," he told them.

Signs of strain were emerging in what had been a united front by potential defendants in the price-fixing case. While ADM and its executives still seemed to stand steadfast against a plea, the foreign competitors were wavering—and obviously ready to fall.

Miwon's lysine division—now known by its new corporate name, Sewon—seemed the most geared up to cut a deal. In a series of discussions, Lawrence Kill, a lawyer representing the Korean company, said that Sewon was hoping for a fine of a few hundred thousand dollars; the prosecutors insisted on millions. But as they negotiated, several good signs emerged. First, Kill dangled the tantalizing news that Sewon had maintained documents relating to price-fixing. On top of that, he almost never mentioned J. S. Kim, the Sewon executive most involved in the scheme. Apparently, there would be none of the usual sticking points about the fate of executives.

That did not hold true for other conspirators. On December 19, lawyers for Ajinomoto called with a proposal. The company would plead nolo contendere—essentially a statement that Ajinomoto did not contest the charges, but was not pleading guilty. The lawyers also hinted that a plea might be possible from Kanji Mimoto, who had collected numbers for the volume agreement. But they said a plea from Kazutoshi Yamada, the managing director, was off the table.

The prosecutors listened but were unwilling to cut Yamada free. Still, this was Ajinomoto's opening bid. Before long, the prosecutors felt confident, the company would come back with a better offer—probably when indictment seemed inevitable.

On December 18, as a driving rain fell in Greenville, North Carolina, a car pulled off the road into the parking lot of a small chiropractic clinic. The driver, Vernon Ellison, a local private detective, maneuvered into a spot near the clinic door and shut off the engine. The swishing wipers that had been fending off the cold rain came to a stop. Ellison glanced toward his passenger, Andrew Levetown from Kroll Associates, the corporate investigative agency that was coordinating the search for Whitacre's millions.

"Ready?" Ellison asked.

"Let's go," Levetown said, throwing open the door.

Levetown had just arrived from Kroll's Washington office. Weeks before, Swiss lawyers had obtained many of Whitacre's records from his bank accounts in that country, and now agents were fanning out wherever money had been sent by wire or check. One name in the records was that of Patti McLaren, who appeared to have received a check for about $8,000 from Whitacre earlier in the year. Kroll detectives tracked McLaren to Greenville, but still didn't know who she was. Levetown had volunteered to confront her. Ellison, a licensed investigator in the state, was hired to tag along.

The two detectives walked toward the clinic door in the rain, pulling their trench coats tight. Inside, the waiting room was filled with patients flipping through old magazines and generally looking bored. Levetown glanced around the run-down office. It seemed the last place that might be associated with a Swiss bank account.

Near the front of the office, a woman sat behind a reception desk. The detectives approached her.

"Excuse me," Levetown said. "I'm looking for Patti McLaren."

The woman looked up. "That's me," she said.

Levetown identified himself and handed over his card.

"I wanted to ask you a few questions about some money you received from Mark Whitacre," he said.

McLaren eyed the men suspiciously.

"Well," she said, standing, "this would be awkward right here. Let me find a place where we can talk."

McLaren walked to the back of the office, out of sight. Levetown figured she was probably calling a lawyer. Minutes later, McLaren returned, her face deadly serious.

"I've got nothing to say to you," she said crisply.

"Well . . . ," Levetown began.

"I've got nothing to say to you," McLaren repeated.

She pointed to the door. "You have to leave now."

The detectives headed toward the exit. Levetown glanced back at McLaren. He decided to press her.

"Do you want to tell us why Mark Whitacre gave you eight thousand dollars last May?" he asked.

McLaren's anger and contempt showed in her face.

"We're a close family!" she snapped. "That's none of your business!"

McLaren's last words provided the necessary clue to her identity. Within hours, Kroll detectives figured out that she was Ginger Whitacre's sister. Whatever the reason Whitacre had given her money, there was probably little in the story that would help ADM. Levetown headed home.

The next day, Levetown returned to Kroll's offices at Eighteenth and M Streets in downtown Washington. His mind was already on other work; beyond the McLaren noninterview, he didn't expect to have much involvement in the case.

During the day, a call arrived at the switchboard. Janine Hightower, an office receptionist, answered.

"Kroll Associates."

"Andrew Levetown," the man on the line requested.

"May I ask who's calling?"

The caller's voice turned angry.

"I'm looking at his business card right now, the one he gave Patti McLaren. I know what he did. I know he's offering money to get people to tell stories about Mark Whitacre. I want you to get him a message for me. You tell him he not only just made the biggest mistake of his career, but the biggest mistake Kroll has ever made."

The caller clicked off the line.

Hightower found Levetown and told him about the bizarre call. He passed the message up the line. Eventually, a decision was made by Kroll's top officers to notify Williams & Connolly of the call.

The news deeply alarmed the defense lawyers. The anonymous Lamet Vov letters, which had stopped months before, had seemed vaguely threatening. Now this call raised those worries again. Something had to be done, they decided. Over the objections of the detective agency's founder, Jules Kroll, Williams & Connolly ordered the investigation cut back. Kroll operatives were instructed to conduct no further interviews of potential witnesses.

No one knew it, but the Lamet Vov—the man who had called to Kroll's offices—had just won a big round.

Outside of Yokohama, Japan, a letter arrived by overnight mail at the home of Masaru Yamamoto. For six months, Yamamoto, from Kyowa Hakko of Tokyo, had watched helplessly as the American investigation of the lysine price-fixing scheme unfolded. He could hardly believe that Whitacre had been taping their conversations all those years. He felt ashamed and frightened.

And now, the letter on this day, January 9, 1996, was telling Yamamoto to cut a deal.

The writer was David Hoech, an American consultant who for years had provided Yamamoto with market intelligence about the agricultural industry. Frequently, his information had been on target— particularly details of ADM's plans, which he had often learned about during conversations with Whitacre. But this time, Hoech was writing with a different type of inside dope. The government, he wrote, appeared to have strong evidence—and Yamamoto needed to be prepared.

"If the Department of Justice did not have a solid case, they would not have ceased the covert operation using Mark Whitacre," Hoech wrote. "Since June 27, 1995, they have been interviewing other people."

While Yamamoto was out of the reach of American law enforcement, Hoech said that the tapes would almost certainly be damaging and would likely appear in the Japanese media. Then, the consultant offered some blunt advice.

"I would make a deal with DOJ for immunity from prosecution first for myself, and second to try and protect the company," he wrote. "Please accept my advice and thoughts as one friend to another."

Yamamoto set down the letter. He faced a lot of tough decisions.

• • •

The government cast a wide net of subpoenas as Shepard and Herndon turned to some of the more bizarre allegations raised by Whitacre during his cooperation. Even with their witness's credibility in shambles, the agents could not ignore his charges. Besides, evidence of other crimes—from stealing proprietary microbes to illegally recording competitors—might give them the leverage they needed to obtain more evidence from ADM in the price-fixing case.

Some allegations seemed to hold little promise. One of the first to fall through was the claim that ADM had surreptitiously taped conversations at the Decatur Club. Whitacre had said that his information was secondhand, from secretaries who transcribed the tapes. But, when interviewed, the secretaries seemed to know nothing about it. With only unproven rumor, there was little to do other than hope that subpoenas might bring in real evidence.

Other allegations seemed to be supported by Whitacre's tapes, so the agents focused their efforts there. In an early recording, Jim Randall appeared to have been caught saying that he had paid $50,000 to someone named Mike Frein for a proprietary bacitracin bug. Herndon conducted a nationwide computer search, tracking Frein down and calling him. The agent asked broad questions; Frein steadfastly denied any wrongdoing and readily agreed to an interview. Herndon was delighted; this was moving quickly.

Days later, Herndon received a voice-mail message from Frein, telling him that the interview was off. Instead, Frein said, Herndon should telephone Aubrey Daniel. Herndon dialed the law firm's main number and asked for Daniel. He was surprised when the call was put right through.

"This is Bob Herndon. I'm an FBI agent on the ADM case. And I have a message from Mike Frein to call you."

"Yes," Daniel replied. "I don't represent him, but you'll be getting a call shortly from someone who does."

The call arrived quickly from William Joseph Linklater, who begged off the interview. He had only recently been hired to represent Frein, he said, and wouldn't even know his client yet if he saw him. Herndon sighed. With lawyers involved, hopes for an easy Frein interview were over.

Then, out of nowhere, a breakthrough.

A former ADM executive who had received a subpoena agreed to talk to Shepard. On January 17, Shepard met with the former executive, Joseph Graham.* In longhand, Shepard took notes of Graham's

*A pseudonym.

statements and was excited by what he heard. The new witness said that he had specific knowledge of ADM's attempts to steal competitors' technologies—even confirming some things that Whitacre had first described.

Graham said that he knew about ADM's attempts to use prostitutes to obtain information from competing companies and to find disgruntled employees. He also said that ADM had tracked down two prostitutes to work near a competitor in Eddyville, Iowa, before Randall pulled the plug on the whole operation.

There were other technology schemes, Graham claimed. For example, he was aware that ADM sent people into the sewers near competitors' plants, in hopes of finding proprietary microbes that had accidentally washed away. The allegation sounded exactly like something Whitacre had told Ferrari.

Graham also claimed to know about other schemes that Whitacre had never mentioned. He told Shepard that ADM had offered a Nebraska security firm $100,000 to pose as janitors on a competitor's premises for the purpose of stealing bugs. But the firm turned down the offer, he said.

Once Graham finished his story, Shepard asked for corroboration such as expense statements. Graham promised to search for the records.

Shepard hopped on the new information. He immediately flew to Nebraska to meet with the security firm that Graham had mentioned. But the interview was a bust. The firm's director denied knowing about the one-hundred-thousand-dollar proposal. The director seemed credible to Shepard—but so did Graham.

On September 24, Graham contacted Shepard with news. While he had been unable to locate the expense statements, something else had turned up. In one box, he had found a sealed envelope dated June 3, 1991. It was something he had hidden away years before and forgotten. Tearing it open, he had found two folded sheets of paper.

It was, he said, the list of questions that ADM had prepared for the prostitutes.

Herndon nodded a greeting to the radio operator for the Springfield office as he walked toward a fax machine. Shepard had called minutes before with the latest on the prostitute questions, promising to fax over a copy of them right away. Within minutes, a blurry, handwritten list scrolled out. Herndon picked up the sheets and headed back to his desk, reading as he walked.

"Questions for Girls, Eddyville," the top read.

Glancing over the first question, Herndon chuckled. *What is current grind—bushels per day?*

The other questions, given the circumstances when they would have been asked, seemed ridiculous. *Is Pepsi-Cola a big customer? Are they planning to add more fructose capacity? Who is the fastest growing wet miller?*

Herndon reached his desk and called over some fellow agents. Several had already heard about the discovery of the question list.

"You guys have got to hear this," Herndon said. He read out a few questions to the laughs of his colleagues.

"I can see it now," one agent chuckled. "Some bimbo's humping away with a Japanese guy who barely speaks English, and she blurts out, 'Is Pepsi-Cola a big customer?' "

The agents roared.

The laughter continued throughout the day. Herndon faxed a copy of the questions to the antitrust prosecutors. He also sent a copy to Rodger Heaton in the Springfield U.S. Attorney's office, since he was likely to handle the case if Antitrust took a pass—a likely prospect, since there really weren't provisions in the Sherman Act against prostitution or espionage.

The questions deflated whatever eagerness existed for the case. They seemed so ridiculous; the prosecutors worried that someone at ADM had been kidding Graham years before, and the man simply didn't get it. Either that, or whoever had put this idea together was a real buffoon. Topping it off, with Graham insisting that Randall had put a stop to the plan, there was a good chance that no crime had ever been committed—even if the questions were real.

Herndon and Shepard were told to keep pursuing the investigation, but they had few illusions about the chances for prosecution. After all, it's awfully hard to win a conviction for a crime that leaves the jurors in stitches.

Faxes and letters from the anonymous Lamet Vov had begun stacking up again at Williams & Connolly starting in November. The writer—purporting to represent an organization called the ADM Shareholders' Watch Committee—was no longer just sending them to the offices of ADM directors and managers; now, they were arriving at their unlisted home-fax numbers.

The letters criticized the board for being misled by ADM management and raised a series of unrelated claims, such as accusations that one executive had been involved in a hit-and-run. A January letter listed allegations that the writer claimed could be proved with Whitacre's tapes. That same letter attacked Kroll Associates for the attempted interview of Patti McLaren, claiming that the detectives had offered money to Whitacre's sister-in-law.

"The shareholders are well-equipped to see this battle through," the letter concluded. "No, Dwayne, we are not some politicians that you can buy off or frighten!"

As far as Aubrey Daniel was concerned, the letters amounted to illegal threats, almost certainly coming from Whitacre. Lawyers and investigators were dispatched around the country, trying to piece together information about the Lamet Vov—information that they hoped would prove useful in ADM's war against Whitacre.

The first assignment was to learn the meaning of *Lamet Vov*. That proved relatively easy; a lawyer digging through a reference book found the term under a slightly different spelling, *Lamed Vav Zaddikim*. The Hebrew phrase referred to a concept from the Babylonian Talmud about a group of thirty-six anonymous, righteous men who live in the world during each generation. There seemed little doubt that the writer of the Lamet Vov letters was making an allusion to this group of hidden saints.

Figuring out the Lamet Vov's identity proved more difficult than cracking the code of the pen name. With the first group of letters, the sender had altered the telltale, the line at the top of a fax that identifies the phone number of the transmitting machine. But finally, a fax with a telltale arrived. Williams & Connolly tracked it down to a Kinko's copy center in Kentucky and located the center employee who had handled the transmission. The employee had some vague memory of the man who had sent the letter, but the description sounded nothing like Whitacre.

As soon as the lawyers were set to concentrate more on Kentucky, another Lamet Vov letter arrived by Federal Express. This one was traced to a FedEx station in St. Louis, but that lead also proved to be a dead end. With the original letter in hand, though, Williams & Connolly had the chance to dig up some solid evidence. The letter was sent out and dusted for fingerprints—but none were found. Whoever sent the package had planned ahead and worn gloves.

In hopes of finding more leads, the letters were turned over to an expert who specialized in psychological profiles based on writing samples. The expert found similarities in sentence structure between the Lamet Vov letters and some of Whitacre's writings, but also found significant deviations in style. The expert concluded that, while Whitacre may have played some role in the Lamet Vov letters, another writer or writers had to be involved.

Stumped, Aubrey Daniel and his partner, Barry Simon, met at the Justice Department with Mackay and Nixon on January 31. The lawyers presented their findings to the prosecutors and requested that the government include the Lamet Vov letters in the investigation of Whitacre. The next day, the prosecutors sent a fax to Bassett and D'Angelo, describing the Williams & Connolly briefing and enclosing the Lamet Vov letters turned over by the lawyers.

"We request that the FBI initiate an investigation to determine the person or persons responsible for these letters," the prosecutors wrote. "Please call so that we may discuss your intended plan of action."

The agents laughed. Weeks before, they had been told to rush the investigation and put aside all of the other allegations of wrongdoing; now they were supposed to waste time figuring out who was writing a bunch of poison-pen letters?

"Who cares?" D'Angelo said in a call to Bassett. "What's the violation?"

The agents put the letters in the case file, and promptly forgot them.

But ADM and Williams & Connolly could not. Soon, reporters were calling the company asking questions about the allegations raised in the letters. The final straw came on February 12, when Bonnie Wittenburg, a stock analyst with Dain Bosworth, put out her latest report analyzing ADM stock. Wittenburg repeated her previously issued opinion that investors should sell the stock, listing several reasons. But one of her rationales stood out from the rest.

"Shareholders' Watch letters raise serious questions," she wrote.

The following day, a Tuesday, Scott Lassar headed into the conference room at the Chicago U.S. Attorney's office. He was joined by Herndon and Kevin Culum, an antitrust prosecutor. They had come together that day for the first full interview of Marty Allison, the former ADM vice president accused of participating in frauds with Whitacre. But this day, Allison was meeting with the government to be quizzed about his knowledge of price-fixing.

Allison arrived accompanied by his attorney, Michael Monico. The thirty-eight-year-old Allison was handsome, just over six feet tall, with blond hair and hazel eyes. From his first instant in the room, he seemed contrite.

Lassar told Allison that his cooperation would be reported to the fraud prosecutors. He then passed a proffer letter across the table, providing the commitment that Allison's truthful statements would not be used against him as direct evidence at trial. Monico and Allison read the document and signed it.

With the legal matters aside, Herndon took over.

"When did you first hear about price-fixing in lysine?" the agent asked.

Allison took a breath and nodded.

"I've known about price-fixing activities in the lysine market since approximately 1992," he began.

Marty Allison was a dynamite witness. His answers were direct, his demeanor unwavering. He fully responded to any question put to him, with little need for Herndon to tease out details. Unlike other witnesses in this case, his expressions of remorse seemed sincere, not self-pitying.

Best of all, Allison had extensive knowledge. He described Whitacre's concerns in 1992 about Terry Wilson's sudden assignment to work with his division. It coincided with Whitacre's story of how Wilson came in and began directing price-fixing. Allison also provided a window on regional price-fixing meetings held among lower-level lysine executives. Prior to his interview, Allison had even prepared a list of every regional meeting, based on records in his electronic calendar.

Some of Allison's information was disturbing. For example, he told of the 1994 ADM sales meeting in Scottsdale where Whitacre had presented competitors' secret sales figures to his rather astonished colleagues. As Allison described the event, Herndon felt his blood boil again. Whitacre had never told the FBI he had done this, and had not recorded the meeting.

Late in the interview, Michael Monico raised a hand. "Guys, we've only got a few minutes before we have to leave."

"We still have more questions," Lassar responded.

"We'll come back whenever you need," Monico said.

"Wait," Herndon said.

Monico had mentioned earlier that Allison knew about technology thefts by ADM. "Could we spend a few minutes on that before you leave?" the agent asked.

"Sure," Monico said. "Go ahead."

The story unfolded quickly. Allison described a 1990 meeting where Randall mentioned that Mike Frein had brought the bacitracin bug with him to ADM from his previous employer. Herndon's ears picked up. This was the kind of confirmation he was looking for.

"Randall made comments when I was first hired that really led me to believe that ADM was a different kind of company," Allison said.

For example, he described how Randall had once brought a competitor's bag into Whitacre's office, asking if they would be able to obtain the other company's microorganism by examining its contents. He had asked if ADM could go into the sewers near a competitor's plant to obtain a bug. He had also heard rumors that the company had placed listening devices on some of its own executives' phones and had even tried to use prostitutes against a competitor in Iowa.

As he wrote down the information, Herndon suppressed a smile. Allison, this great witness, had information on most everything he wanted to know about.

The next day, D'Angelo received a call from Scott Lassar about the Allison interview. The man, Lassar said, was an extremely promising witness.

"I think he could be very useful to you," Lassar added. "You ought to try to schedule an interview through his lawyer, Mike Monico."

Changing the subject, Lassar mentioned that he had been reviewing some of Whitacre's old 302s during the covert stage of the price-fixing case and had stumbled across something interesting. Back during the flare-up of the Mobile investigation involving methionine, Whitacre had been interviewed about former Degussa employees, including one named Chris Jones. Whitacre had said that he had arranged to pay Jones a monthly retainer of between $10,000 and $20,000.

"That just sounded too familiar to me," said Lassar.

"What do you mean?"

"I think you guys ought to check out whether these payments were utilized by Whitacre to divert other money from ADM for himself."

After skimming page 236 of the green paperback novel, Jules Kroll stopped to write down some notes for his ADM file.

The Whitacre investigation had been eating at Kroll for months. Since founding Kroll Associates in 1972, the fifty-six-year-old private detective had developed a reputation as a man who got the job done.

But not this time. Since Williams & Connolly had ruled out any more interviews, Kroll was muzzled. Still, nobody could stop Jules Kroll from thinking about the case. And now, Kroll was working on his most inventive investigative theory:

Mark Whitacre was playing out some sort of delusional version of John Grisham's book The Firm.

For days, often as Kroll puffed his cigars, he and a few associates had thumbed through copies of the book, looking for similarities between Whitacre's story and Grisham's tale of a young lawyer working at a corrupt law firm.

The most obvious comparison was between ADM and Grisham's fictional firm, Bendini, Lambert & Locke. Both hired employees from big cities to work in out-of-the-way towns. And while the fictional firm was in Memphis, it was really controlled by the Mafia from Illinois—ADM's home state. The firm used corporate jets as a centerpiece of a scheme to evade taxes; the Lamet Vov letters had made accusations about corporate jets and taxes. The head of security at Bendini, Lambert was a former cop who tapped phones, threatened people, and committed other crimes; the head of security at ADM was a former cop who Whitacre said had done those very same things.

There were also striking parallels between Whitacre and Mitch McDeere, the hero of Grisham's story. McDeere's father had been killed when he was seven; Whitacre falsely claimed that his father and mother had been killed when he was about the same age. McDeere faced death threats; Whitacre had publicly proclaimed that he had, too. Both cooperated with the FBI after being threatened with indictment. Both played a hero role by turning over evidence of colleagues' crimes. Both felt betrayed by the FBI. Someone leaked word of McDeere's cooperation; Whitacre claimed the same thing had happened to him.

The same American locations also cropped up in the two stories. The wives of both cooperators fled or tried to flee to suburban Nashville. There were random trips in *The Firm* to Knoxville and St. Louis; anonymous letters had already been traced to those two cities.

There were even bizarre similarities that Whitacre could not have controlled, including some between the real-life and fictional case agents. In *The Firm*, Special Agent Wayne Tarrance had been stationed at the New York City Field Office before being transferred to the smaller town where the big investigation unfolds. The same was true for Special Agent Brian Shepard.

And then . . .

And then there were the financial transactions. The fictional firm ran dirty money through companies with names like Dunn Lane Ltd., Eastpointe Ltd., and Gulf-South Ltd. ADM money had been run through companies with names like Aminac, Eurotechnologies, and FES. In real life and in fiction, there were wire transfers between New York money-center banks and banks in the Caribbean. McDeere set up accounts in the Caribbean and in Zurich; so did Whitacre. In the book, money that arrived in a Caribbean bank account was moved to Switzerland; Whitacre often laundered his cash the same way. The central locale for many of the fictional crimes was the Cayman Islands; same thing in real life. McDeere and his associates ended the book with eight million dollars in offshore accounts; Whitacre and his co-horts did a bit better, with slightly more than nine.

When the list was finished, Kroll looked it over. It went on for two pages, with forty-six similarities between the true and fictional stories. The detective had little doubt that this seemingly crazy theory was right on target.

Larry Kill picked up a stack of papers from a conference table and set them on his lap. The defense lawyer representing Sewon looked up from the documents, ready to make the presentation that he hoped would win his client a deal. Sitting across from Kill were Robin Mann and Jim Mutchnik, along with a paralegal from the Chicago antitrust office. Everyone had pens and paper for notes. Kill leaned back as he began.

"I want to be clear that we're coming forward with such detailed information in the hopes of obtaining a reduced fine," he said.

A smile flashed across his face.

"Not only can we provide you with records from Kim and other employees," he continued, "we've even got paper from Ajinomoto. You'll be very happy."

Kill flipped through the documents on his lap. The first price-fixing meeting attended by Sewon occurred in 1986, he began. From there, Kill delivered details of every meeting—where they had been held, who had attended, what had been said. Everything was documented, including—as Kill promised—with records that Sewon had received over the years from Ajinomoto. By the time Kill reached meetings in March 1992, Mann and Mutchnik not only were ready for a break, but also needed to place a call.

Mutchnik walked to the law-firm lobby, where he found a telephone. He knew that Jim Griffin was planning to make some final decisions involving Ajinomoto that day. For months, the Japanese company had been maintaining that ADM had dragged it into price-fixing. But now, thanks to Sewon, the ground had shifted. The records showed that, even before ADM came along, Ajinomoto had fixed lysine prices. Mutchnik punched in Griffin's office number.

"Jim," Mutchnik said, "wait for us to get back. They've got tons of info on Ajinomoto. They're up to their eyeballs in it."

Just after ten o'clock on the morning of March 3, a Sunday, Ginger was puttering around the house in suburban Chicago. Earlier that morning, Mark had driven the three miles to his office to check his e-mail account. The home computer wasn't working, he had told Ginger, and now she was waiting for him to come home.

Sometime later, Mark called. As soon as she heard him, Ginger knew that something horrible had happened. His voice was shaky, his breathing heavy.

"My God, Mark," she said. "What's wrong?"

He breathed deeply several times.

"A couple of guys just abducted me," he said.

A few hours later, Ray Goldberg and his wife Thelma were enjoying a lazy Sunday afternoon in their Cambridge apartment. Goldberg, a Harvard professor and member of the ADM board's special committee, had received publicity of late, thanks to a study he spearheaded to review the company's corporate governance. But this day, as the Goldbergs relaxed, ADM was far from their minds.

The phone rang and Thelma answered. The caller asked for Ray Goldberg.

"Who's calling?" she asked.

"My name is David Hoech," the caller said. "I'm from the ADM Shareholders' Watch Committee, and we need to talk."

Thelma told her husband who was calling. Goldberg didn't recognize the name; he knew nothing of Hoech's work as an industry consultant. He picked up the phone and said hello.

"Let me introduce myself," Hoech said. "I'm one of the leaders of the ADM Shareholders' Watch Committee, and everything that's ever been written is true and verified. I'm going to tell you some alarming things."

Hoech's tone was emotional and angry. Goldberg already vaguely understood that this caller played some role in the strange letters he had been receiving from the Shareholders' Watch Committee, and signed by the Lamet Vov.

"This morning Whitacre was abducted in the parking lot of his office, taken on a little ride for an hour and a half," Hoech continued. "His life was threatened. He was told, 'Tell your buddies at the Watch Committee that they shouldn't say any more things or talk to any more reporters, or you're all going to be dealt with.' "

Goldberg glanced around by the phone. He wanted to take a few notes. All he could find was a round piece of paper emblazoned with the words *I'd Rather Be Playing Tennis*. He flipped the paper over and picked up a pen.

"We're going on national television, and we're going to hang everybody out!" Hoech said, his voice rising. "You get hold of the rest of the members, and you call a goddamned special meeting and remove these people. This is ludicrous! This is America! What the hell is going on? Do you think we write this stuff because it's a lie? Do you think we spend $3.5 million to dig this shit up—and you people are sitting there listening to Dwayne, who's a dictator? This is a disgrace to democracy!"

Goldberg wrote down "$3.5 million to dig up this shit," and drew a box around it.

"You're going to have the blood of Whitacre, myself, and some other members on your hands because you people are standing around doing nothing!" Hoech raged.

In the background, Hoech's wife interrupted, telling him to calm down. Goldberg could not understand what was being said, but thought he was hearing children playing.

Hoech breathed deeply. "I'm sorry, but I'm upset, Goldberg."

This was Goldberg's chance to respond. "We are investigating—"

"Investigating, my ass!" Hoech yelled. "Get these people out of there! You're spending our money! They spent thirty million dollars! Goddamned Aubrey Daniel says last week, he says, 'All we've got to do is kill Whitacre, and we don't have a case.' "

Hoech's wife again told him to calm down.

"I'm sorry," Hoech said. "I'm not yelling at you, Goldberg. I'm just unloading. I'm tired of this. My life's been threatened."

"Who are these people threatening you?"

"Who are these people?" Hoech shot back. It was those criminals at ADM, he said, listing a series of allegations against company executives, ranging from drug use to being part of a hit-and-run.

"You don't know how rotten these people are!" Hoech yelled. "They're a disgrace to humanity!"

"Well," Goldberg said, "I'm sorry to hear that."

Hoech again mentioned the Lamet Vov letters.

"Everything you've read in those letters is factual. I'll go on national TV with it. And the reason we've stayed underground is because we know what we're up against."

"You're afraid of being hurt, is that it?"

"He's already threatened our life this morning; they've been down here," Hoech said. "I live in Florida, and they've been down here checking on me, and my phone is wired up; my fax machine I've had to unjam, and I know what we're up against. It's like with Marcos in the Philippines. You try to stay alive until you get the job done."

"Have you gone to the FBI or—"

"Come on! For what, Ray? Wake up!"

Goldberg almost sighed. "I guess I'm naïve."

"You are. Wake up!"

Hoech launched into a tirade, telling Goldberg that ADM management had lied, that the company was dirty, and that directors had abandoned their duties.

"It's gone too far now, Ray. You've gotta get hold of these people. You've gotta remove Dwayne, Mick, Randall, Terry Wilson, and Barrie Cox. If you don't, the blood is going to start flowing because these people are sick!"

Hoech started in again, repeating that ADM executives were dangerous. Goldberg realized he needed to bring this call to a close.

"I appreciate your calling," he interrupted.

Hoech stopped. He provided his phone number and repeated his name, asking that it be kept confidential. Goldberg asked a few questions. He learned that Hoech had never worked for ADM, although he claimed his group had owned three million shares of the company, which were sold the day of the raid.

"Now here's what I recommend," Hoech continued. "If they don't want to call a special board meeting, you resign. I'll get you all the press you want. I'll put you on national TV. ABC, NBC, and CBS."

Goldberg said he didn't want publicity but would continue working in the interests of ADM shareholders. Hoech promised to help in any way he could, including by writing more letters.

"Well, I appreciate your call," Goldberg said.

"You keep my name to yourself."

"I will."

Hanging up, Goldberg ran through his notes, now covering both sides of the paper. He decided to telephone his attorney. He needed advice on what to do, now that he had learned the identity of the mysterious Lamet Vov.

That same week, Williams & Connolly contacted the antitrust prosecutors with what at first sounded like big news: ADM wanted to cut a deal.

Then came the details. The lawyers offered for ADM to plead *nolo contendere* to charges of fixing prices for lysine and citric—allowing the company to dispose of the criminal case without giving evidence of guilt to the plaintiffs suing in civil court. In addition, the lawyers demanded immunity for all ADM officers. In exchange, ADM would turn over evidence that could be used to convict other companies in the two schemes. The government would have its victory and would be able to diffuse the almost certain legal attack that ADM was planning against the FBI.

"Otherwise, there's going to be a bloody war," Aubrey Daniel said in presenting the offer. "Let's avoid it."

The proposal was dismissed. What Williams & Connolly did not know was that the prosecutors were becoming very confident about their hand. That same week, all of the major lysine conspirators were knocking on the door, offering far better deals. Griffin and Mutchnik had just returned from Korea, where they had reviewed Sewon documents. Ajinomoto was already offering to pay $10 million in fines. And Kyowa Hakko was willing to plead guilty, if prosecutors passed on indicting Masaru Yamamoto.

At this point, Lassar and Griffin were turning aside the offers, demanding tougher terms. But the desperation of the other lysine producers let the prosecutors know that they didn't need ADM's silly little deal.

Dick Beattie slid into the backseat of the chauffeured sedan, headed to the airport. The Simpson Thacher partner warmly greeted the driver, a man he considered a friend. The driver was well known among the corporate elite; in addition to Beattie, he chauffeured Ross Johnson. But his best customer was Dwayne Andreas, who years before had trusted the driver to buy a stretch limousine for the ADM chairman's use when he was in New York.

The scandal at ADM had been difficult on the driver. Now, several customers were on different sides of the same issue. Since reviewing the tapes, Beattie had been blunt in advising the directors to consider a corporate plea. But Dwayne Andreas, who heard through the grapevine about Beattie's push, remained vehemently opposed. Much to the driver's discomfort, the brewing dispute had been a frequent topic of conversation among Andreas and his associates.

As they pulled onto the highway, the driver mentioned that he had heard talk about Beattie in his car.

"Watch out, be very careful," the driver said. "They're very nervous about you. And there's a lot of plotting against you."

Beattie thanked the driver for the warning, while figuring there was little that he could do about it.

But in Decatur, the suspicions about Beattie's intentions continued to grow. Dwayne Andreas, convinced that neither his son nor ADM could ever be convicted of price-fixing, began to suspect a complex conspiracy in the works. Beattie, he became convinced, was acting as the Trojan Horse for ADM's true enemy—Henry Kravis, the corporate buyout king who was the lawyer's premier client. In calls with Bob Strauss, Zev Furst, and other advisors, Andreas raged that Beattie was pushing a settlement to weaken ADM and set it up for a Kravis takeover. Strauss and Furst visited with Beattie, but walked away convinced of his good faith. Still, Andreas would have none of it.

Eventually, Beattie heard by phone from Ross Johnson.

"You ain't gonna believe what they're doing to you," Johnson chuckled.

A fax had been sent from Dwayne's office to some directors, Johnson said. It was an excerpt from a recent, highly critical book about Kravis and his firm, Kohlberg Kravis Roberts & Co. The excerpt was all about Beattie, portraying him as a man who had manipulated others for Kravis's benefit. Decatur's message was easy to decipher: Beattie was a bad guy who could not be trusted.

"The troops are coming, old buddy," Johnson laughed. "They're out to get you."

Sunday morning was relatively calm at the offices of ADM. Phones were mostly quiet, and the usual frantic hustle of the workday was muted. With few other distractions, the one-page, anonymous fax that arrived that morning in the legal department was noticed quickly.

"Be careful of *Fortune* Magazine. They are working closely with Whitacre," the note began.

The note lapsed into incoherence about some fax supposedly sent between ADM and Ron Henkoff, the *Fortune* magazine reporter covering ADM. In an apparent reference to David Hoech—the Lamet Vov—it mentioned that people at ADM were speaking with a man from Miami who was briefing Ray Goldberg about wrongdoing.

The fax closed with a warning about spies in ADM. "They see and hear more than you think," it said. "They even spent the weekend at the Whitacres' a few weekends ago. After that, Whitacre convinced them to talk to a reporter on background."

The ADM employee studied the fax. It was unsigned; there was no fax telltale. Then, he glanced at the fax machine. The AT&T Caller-ID device that had been installed appeared to have worked perfectly. Not only did it capture the phone number that sent the fax, but it also listed the name registered to that line. The employee read the screen.

"Whitacre, Ginger," it said.

On the morning of Monday, March 22, Robin Mann arrived at the office and saw the message light already glowing on her phone. Dialing into the voice-mail system, she retrieved a panicked message left the previous day by Ginger Whitacre. Someone had abducted her husband and threatened him weeks before, Ginger said. She was terrified; her family needed protection.

Mann returned the call and listened as Ginger spilled details of the story. Mark had gone to the office to check his e-mail on March 3, she said. Two men in a Dodge Dynasty had followed him into the parking lot.

Mark was thrown into their car, she said. He couldn't get out; the door locks had been sawed off. The men hopped in front and pulled away. For twenty minutes, Ginger said, the men drove Mark around, warning him to forget everything about ADM that wasn't on tape. These other allegations he raised should never be mentioned again, they told him.

"Did he file a police report?" Mann asked.

"No, we told Jim Epstein," Ginger replied. "But no police report. Mark was afraid of the publicity."

This was tearing up her family, Ginger said. Her fourth-grader was terrified; at one point they had found the child hiding in the closet. They had changed the locks on the house, but it wasn't enough. The family needed protection. Ginger said that she wanted someone to get back to her with information about what was going to be done.

Details of the call were relayed to Shepard and Herndon. Since Whitacre had already told Epstein about this abduction, the agents called the lawyer. Herndon explained the situation and asked for details.

"I'm sorry, I can't talk about this," Epstein replied. "This is an attorney-client conversation."

"Well," Herndon said, "can you call Whitacre and get a waiver of the privilege on this issue?"

Epstein paused. "Always an adventure. Do I have to?"

"Yeah," Herndon laughed. "You do."

That same afternoon, Herndon received a voice mail in reply from Jim Epstein.

"Mark Whitacre has not authorized me to talk to you about the matter we discussed," Epstein said stiffly on the message. "Furthermore, I would ask that I receive no further contact from the FBI regarding these threats."

This was beginning to sound to Herndon like another one of Whitacre's games. Instead of being a matter of concern, the episode quickly devolved into fodder for jokes. By the end of the day, it would forever be known among the investigators and prosecutors in Harvest King as the time Mark Whitacre had been abducted by aliens.

The sun was shining in Hallandale, Florida, on April 5, as Bassett and D'Angelo pulled up in a rental car to a guardhouse in the front of a condominium complex. Bassett rolled down the window as the guard approached.

"We're here to see David Hoech," Bassett said.

The guard told the agents to park their car. They maneuvered into a spot as the guard phoned Hoech's condo.

In the weeks since Hoech had revealed himself as the Lamet Vov, there had been a flurry of activity from Cambridge to Washington to Chicago. Ray Goldberg's information had been relayed to Williams & Connolly, and in no time, Bassett was interviewing the ADM director about his call with Hoech. The agents had since telephoned Hoech himself, who had agreed to an interview.

Hoech appeared at the guardhouse and escorted the agents toward his first-floor condo, which served as both his home and the headquarters of his company, Global Consultants. Inside, the agents were impressed. In the back, a sliding glass door led directly to the beach. This was a man who clearly led a comfortable life. Hoech introduced the agents to his wife, Carol.

"My wife would like to sit in," Hoech said. "Do you have a problem with that?"

"No, that's not a problem," Bassett replied.

Everyone took seats around a table.

"Just to start, are you taping this conversation?" Bassett asked.

"No, I'm not taping," Hoech said. "Are you?"

"We don't tape interviews," Bassett replied.

The interview began with Hoech describing his background. He had fought in Vietnam and then lived in Japan for about a dozen years. During that time, he developed clients in the agricultural industry. After returning to the United States in 1982, he consulted for both American and Japanese companies. By 1995, his business was doing well enough to earn him $200,000 that year.

"But," Hoech said, "I recently lost all of my clients because of my work with the Lamet Vov letters."

Hoech claimed that the Shareholders' Watch Committee consisted of about one hundred members who utilized moles throughout ADM to obtain secret information. Under questioning from Bassett, Hoech said he had known Whitacre since about 1990, and that the two had become friends. Whitacre had told him about the under-the-table bonuses sometime after the raids, Hoech said, and had identified other executives who received illegal compensation, including Mick Andreas.

"Did Whitacre play any role in writing the Lamet Vov letters?" Bassett asked.

"None whatsoever," Hoech said. "I have full responsibility for the creation and dissemination of the Lamet Vov letters. And I have no ulterior motives. I am simply seeking to change through all legal means the structure of ADM's corrupt leadership."

Hoech stressed that nothing in the letters was intended as a threat, and that the letters were not an effort to support Mark Whitacre.

"Approved or not, Whitacre defrauded the shareholders," he said. "He should be held accountable."

At the end of the conversation, the agents asked if Hoech would identify his sources. He declined.

"Many of my sources, particularly those within ADM, do not trust the FBI or the Department of Justice," Hoech said. "Dwayne is too powerful, and wields too much influence in Washington. Look at that unprecedented press release that DOJ put out saying ADM was not a target of the fraud investigation. What more proof do they need?"

Still, Hoech said that he would try to persuade his sources to speak with the agents. He promised that they could provide significant evidence of fraud.

The interview over, Bassett and D'Angelo gathered their things. Hoech accompanied them to the door.

"Where are you fellows staying?" Hoech asked.

They had reservations at the Embassy Suites up the road, but D'Angelo wasn't comfortable with the idea of telling a witness how to reach them.

"We don't have anything yet," he lied. "But we'll probably go north someplace."

"Let me help you get a place," Hoech said, suggesting a few locations.

The agents thanked him for his hospitality and drove to the Embassy Suites in Fort Lauderdale. Bassett and D'Angelo headed to their separate rooms.

The next morning, Bassett found an envelope under his door. It was a fax that had just been sent to the hotel. Inside was nothing important, just a news article about Andreas and Bob Dole in Florida. What left Bassett stunned was the attached personal note. He called D'Angelo.

"Tony," Bassett said. "You're not going to believe this. I got a fax from Hoech."

"What?"

"Yeah," Bassett said. "The guy somehow figured out where we're staying."

Supervisory Special Agent Kate Killham sat down at her computer in the Champaign Resident Agency, ignoring the sound of a train rumbling past her corner office window. Since taking responsibility for overseeing Harvest King, Killham had faced a lot of unpleasant moments. But this one, right now, was surely one of the worst.

For months, Killham had watched as the case tore at Brian Shepard. By any standard, Shepard was an emotional, pessimistic type who keenly felt attacks on his own character—and Harvest King had been loaded with plenty of those. Killham knew Shepard was paying a price in Decatur. He and his family had lost friends, particularly those who worked at ADM. The Shepards had felt snubbed by neighbors and had received the cold shoulder more than a few times. Everything

Shepard feared in the first days of the case had come to pass. His home, his commitment, his entire persona as an FBI agent was under attack. He wanted out of Decatur.

Then, a break. A position opened at the St. Thomas Resident Agency, which reported through the San Juan Field Office. With Shepard's experience and seniority, he was certainly a strong candidate for the job. If he won the transfer, the Shepards could move to St. Thomas and start over. Whenever Shepard was needed on the price-fixing case, he could fly back. It seemed the perfect solution. All Shepard needed was a recommendation from his supervisors, and he could probably start packing his bags.

Stukey and Hoyt turned the job of drafting the recommendation over to Killham, telling her specifically what to write. Now, with her shoes kicked off under her desk, she stared at the computer screen, feeling unsettled. She began by describing Shepard and his background, highlighting his work on Harvest King.

"He is tenacious, hardworking and dedicated," Killham typed. "He is a mature, seasoned agent with a strong investigative background and a deep commitment to the FBI."

She reread the memo so far. This recommendation was sure to win Shepard the transfer. She took a deep breath. Now, as ordered, she killed Shepard's chances. "Recommendation of SA Shepard for transfer to St. Thomas at this time is tempered by his crucial, ongoing contribution to the Harvest King investigation," she typed.

Killham felt terrible. In a few days, that sentence would be sharpened, to ensure no one misunderstood its meaning: Shepard could not be recommended for the job. It seemed so unnecessary. Herndon was topflight; he could manage the case alone. Plus, Shepard could have handled any issues by phone, and flown back for the trial.

Clicking the mouse on her computer, Killham saved the memo and printed it out. An agent's mental health had been sacrificed to Harvest King. It was, Killham thought, a horrible decision. Brian Shepard deserved better.

As the television cameraman turned on his portable lights, Mark Whitacre slid into a chair beside a potted fern. In front of him, a run-of-the-mill art print adorned the white wall of the conference room at Biomar International. The cameraman asked Whitacre to say a few words for a sound check. He nodded and spoke for a moment.

Across the table, Steve Delaney from *WAND News* in Decatur was in shirtsleeves, ready for his big scoop. For all of Whitacre's press statements, this would be his first television interview. Even Ginger had agreed to speak on camera. In Decatur, Delaney's report was sure to be huge.

For more than five hours, Whitacre, dressed in a blue suit with a red tie, took every question Delaney threw at him. Ginger, in an orange dress, looked calm and comfortable when Delaney directed his questions to her.

Sometime during the interview, Whitacre decided to drop his latest bombshell. On a Sunday morning in early March, he told Delaney, he had gone to the office to check his e-mail. In the lot, two men in a car called him over.

"I walked over, and they threw me in the backseat of the car and took me around for twenty minutes," he said.

"Threw you in the backseat of the car?" Delaney repeated.

"Oh yeah, very much so, and in a very aggressive way," Whitacre said, a wisp of a smile on his lips. "And they took me around for a twenty-minute joy ride and basically warned me that I better forget everything besides what's on—this was March third—warned me that I better forget everything besides what's on tape."

Delaney pressed for supporting evidence. But there were no witnesses and no security cameras outside. Still, Whitacre offered vivid details, from the make of the car to the way the back-door locks had been sawed off to ensure that he could not escape.

As Whitacre told the tale, the subtle smile flashed across his face several times. It was an old habit, something Whitacre often did when he was lying.

The entire abduction story was a phony. Whitacre had made it up—telling it to his family, to David Hoech, and now to all of Decatur—as part of a bizarre plan. He was feeling desperate and frightened. He wanted somebody to worry about him, to take charge of the mess he had made. He knew that if he told his lie to Delaney, it would be broadcast across Decatur. Whitacre's intended audience would almost certainly hear his cry for help.

For Whitacre knew that Brian Shepard watched *WAND News*. Despite everything that had happened, once Shepard heard the frightening but fictitious tale of the abduction, he might fear for Whitacre's safety. Then, Whitacre hoped, Brian Shepard might feel driven to reach out to him again.

And help.

CHAPTER 18

Through the expansive windows of his home office in Steffisburg, Beat Schweizer gazed toward the Castle of Thun, its Romanesque towers dwarfed by the majestic Swiss Alps in the distance. It was a breathtaking image, a vision from a childhood fairy tale come to life. But on this day, April 9, 1996, the panorama barely registered with him. The money manager's mind was racing, caught up in the harsh realities of his life. His dealings with Whitacre had come at a terrible price, costing him security, opportunities, and freedom. Even the once pleasurable prospect of traveling to America was now tainted with fears of arrest.

As computer screens around him flashed the movements of world markets, Schweizer reached a new resolve. He would not allow himself to remain imprisoned in his own country. He wanted to confront his accusers. Schweizer telephoned his lawyer, Kurt Sieger, asking for the names and numbers of American officials involved in the case. In minutes, Schweizer was on the phone with the Office of International Affairs for the United States Department of Justice.

"Hello," Schweizer said in accented English. "My name is Beat Schweizer. I'm calling about the American investigation of Mark Whitacre and ADM."

Schweizer's call seeking a meeting with American investigators signaled a potential break in the fraud case. Until now, he had remained out of easy reach. And, as the man who ran more than $6 million through Whitacre's bank accounts, he was sure to know more secrets than Hulse, Richter, or the others. There was even the chance—if Whitacre's story of a corporate-wide scheme was true—that Schweizer moved money for other ADM executives.

Even so, government fumbling almost cost investigators the interview. Schweizer said that he would come to the United States only if he received assurances that he would not be arrested while in the country; the Fraud Section sent back word that they could not guarantee safe passage. Under pressure from Bassett and D'Angelo, the prosecutors reversed themselves, but then informed Schweizer that he needed to speak through his attorney—the *last* thing the FBI wanted. Finally, Bassett became involved in the arrangements with Schweizer, and the money manager agreed to sit down for an interview without his lawyer present.

The meeting took place on May 13 in a conference room at the Fraud Section's Washington offices. Schweizer arrived alone, dressed in jeans and a sports coat. He took a seat on the far side of the conference table, warily eyeing the agents and prosecutors across from him.

Bassett handled the questioning. Schweizer said he worked at Swiss Bank Corporation in the Cayman Islands before striking out on his own in 1993.

"Have you managed money for many ADM executives?"

"No. Just Mark Whitacre and Sid Hulse."

"How did you meet them?"

"Hulse was a longtime customer of the bank. He introduced me to Whitacre sometime around 1991."

"What did you know about Whitacre's assets?"

Schweizer shrugged. "He said he had accounts in Europe, the Far East, Australia, and the Caymans."

Australia. That was new. Bassett brought out some bank records and showed them to Schweizer. They seemed to indicate that Whitacre had accounts in Monaco and Germany, Schweizer said.

"I had assumed he spread his assets around for diversification. But I know nothing about the banks other than the geographic locations. I never confirmed their existence."

"What did Whitacre tell you about these accounts?"

Schweizer thought for a moment. "I remember him telling me that his father had been employed in Australia and that his family was very wealthy."

Bassett nodded gently with each statement.

"How did Whitacre end up as a personal client?"

"Around January of 1994, I was contemplating leaving the bank and solicited Whitacre for his business," Schweizer said. "During that time, I also helped him open an account at Swiss Bank Corporation in Zurich."

"Why?"

"I was hoping he would transfer all his assets to Swiss Bank."

Methodically, Bassett guided the interview toward the $2.5 million transaction with ABP International—Whitacre's first deal involving Schweizer, and the one first discovered by ADM.

Schweizer said that when the deal came about, he had not suspected any problems. Whitacre had told him that he and some partners controlled a company called ABP Trading, which was involved in technology transfers.

"Everything about this company sounded appropriate," Schweizer said. "He promised me that his superiors at ADM knew all about it. He said he was dividing his work time eighty percent with ADM and twenty percent with ABP."

"What did he want you to do with ABP?"

"In 1994, he asked me to incorporate a company in Switzerland that would be related to ABP. I tried to persuade him to incorporate offshore, since it would be easier and less expensive. In Switzerland, the government requires a capital deposit of $100,000 before incorporation. But he insisted on Switzerland."

Bassett wrote that down.

"Swiss law requires corporations to hire auditors," Schweizer said. "He instructed me to hire Ernst & Young, because it was the same auditing firm used by ADM."

Schweizer shook his head. "There is something wrong with this man Whitacre," he said. "Why take this risk, hiring the same auditors as ADM? It makes no sense."

"What did you do next?" Bassett asked.

Schweizer said he helped Whitacre open a corporate account for ABP Trading at Union Bank of Switzerland. Later, Whitacre delivered the $2.5 million check from ADM, filled out to ABP International of Sweden.

"But the check did not have an endorsement from an official of ABP International," Schweizer said. "Union Bank would not accept it. The people in Sweden needed to endorse it. So Whitacre left and took the check with him. It came back to me with the signature. Then I signed it as an officer of ABP Trading, and the bank accepted it."

The investigators already knew that the signature on the back—for Lennart Thorstensson of ABP—was a forgery. Now, if Schweizer was telling the truth, it seemed that Whitacre was the forger.

All but $100,000 of the money was wired to the Caymans on Whitacre's instructions, Schweizer said, to an account called SPM&C

at the Caledonia Bank. From there, it was instantly wired back to Switzerland, to Whitacre's personal account. It sounded like classic money laundering.

"What did you think was going on?" Bassett asked.

"I assumed he was hiding money from his partners," Schweizer said.

"Now, your signature's on the Union Bank account along with Whitacre's. Was the one hundred thousand dollars left behind in that account as a fee for you?"

"No, no," Schweizer said, shaking his head. "That was Whitacre's."

Bassett pressed on the SPM&C account, but Schweizer refused to discuss it, saying the account was private. Money went into it that had nothing to do with Mark Whitacre or any other client, he said.

The words struck Mackay as laughable. He glanced at Nixon and rolled his eyes. This guy was mixing client money into other accounts for no reason? *This was money laundering.*

Bassett studied some documents. There was a second ABP transaction, he said, netting Whitacre $3.75 million.

"That occurred about a year later," Schweizer said. "Whitacre came to me just weeks before. He showed me the documentation, and I noticed it again involved ADM."

Schweizer stroked his chin.

"I had a bad feeling about it," he said. "He told me again and again that ABP would be doing business with many companies, that there were going to be drug companies and others. But again, it was ADM. I told him I would not accept any more transactions associated with ADM."

Once more, Schweizer said, the money was moved around in several accounts, including one on the Isle of Jersey.

"What were you paid for your services?"

"We agreed I would receive a management fee based on the size of the account, about one percent," Schweizer said. "I was probably paid fifty thousand Swiss francs."

A few minutes later, Schweizer mentioned his interviews with Fridolin Triet of the Zurich District Attorney's office.

"I have spoken to Swiss prosecutors three times, for a total of about twenty-four hours," he said. "I was questioned by Mr. Triet and by lawyers for ADM."

The room fell still. "Lawyers for ADM?" Bassett asked.

"Yes," Schweizer said. "They were the ones who provided the

questions. The translations were very sloppy. Even Triet had trouble understanding them."

Bassett asked Schweizer to identify which ADM lawyer had attended the interview. Schweizer said he didn't know, so the agent began listing names of lawyers.

"That one," Schweizer said after hearing a name.

Bassett took a breath. Schweizer had just identified Aubrey Daniel.* ADM's lawyers were interviewing these witnesses before the government had a chance.

At that point, Bassett brought out a 302 from one of Whitacre's interviews. Schweizer said he had seen the document before, during a meeting with Swiss prosecutors. That was no surprise; a copy of the confidential document had been sent to Triet for that reason.

Schweizer studied the faces of the assembled group.

"I saw it in the hands of the Williams & Connolly lawyer," he said.

The room went numb with realization.

ADM had been obtaining American law-enforcement records from the Swiss—right at a time when company executives were still potentially targets.

The investigation had been compromised.

News of the Swiss leak hardened attitudes in the government against ADM. For months, the company's lawyers had been dragging their feet, seeming to produce documents only when they felt like it. It had been good lawyering and had seemed hardly worth a battle. But now, everything was *backward*. The company had government documents, but the government didn't have records it needed from ADM. Even ADM's accountants, Ernst & Young, were refusing to comply.

The agents were particularly suspicious. The subpoenas covered records of ADM subsidiaries in the Cayman Islands, with names such as ADM Feeds Vietnam and ADM Animal Health and Nutrition Ltd. Perhaps, the agents thought, these documents might prove Whitacre's story of a corporate-wide illegal bonus system. Williams & Connolly filed a motion to quash the subpoena; a secret proceeding on the motion was scheduled before a federal judge in Peoria.

This time, the company could not be allowed to win. This was going to be war.

*While ADM lawyers were in the room for Schweizer's interview, Swiss officials said that Aubrey Daniel was not among them.

. . .

For three days, beginning on May 30, more than one hundred world leaders gathered on the outskirts of Toronto at the CIBC Leadership Center. They had come to the elegant converted spa for the forty-fourth annual gathering of the Bilderberg Group, an alliance of some of the world's most influential people. David Rockefeller was there; so was William Perry, the American defense secretary. Joining them were an assortment of monarchs, prime ministers, and industrialists, all invited for secret and frank talks about the direction of world economies and governments.

One executive in attendance, Dwayne Andreas, was keeping his eyes peeled for another invitee—Henry Kravis of KKR—in hopes of being able to confront the buyout specialist. Despite his advisors' skepticism, Andreas remained convinced that Kravis was working through Beattie to cripple ADM with a price-fixing settlement—leaving it vulnerable to an easy takeover. He wanted to personally tell Kravis that ADM would not be such easy pickings.

Eventually, he cornered Kravis. In a suspicious tone, he spelled out a few details about Beattie.

"Do you want ADM?" Andreas asked. "Are you after my company?"

Kravis stared at Andreas evenly. He had no idea what the man was talking about.

"No," Kravis replied. "I've got no interest in ADM."

A few minutes later, Kravis disappeared into the crowds of the powerful. Andreas was left behind, uncertain.

By June, Shepard and Herndon were ready to wrap up the investigation into ADM's possible technology thefts. No new evidence had been developed in the months since Shepard had obtained the purported list of questions for prostitutes from Joseph Graham, the former ADM executive. It was beginning to look like a dry hole.

Other problems seemed insurmountable. For one, the most recent potential crime appeared to have taken place five years before, in June 1991. But prosecutors faced a five-year statute of limitations, probably leaving them out of luck if charges weren't filed immediately. Topping it off, some of the purported activities might not have been crimes, such as trolling for microbes in sewers near competitors' plants. After all, garbage was public domain.

Prosecutors pushed the agents to drop the theft investigation and work exclusively on the more promising price-fixing cases. Before shutting down the effort, Shepard and Herndon decided to polygraph Graham. Herndon felt sure the witness would fail. Then, at least he could be comfortable with the knowledge that ADM had not escaped the possibility of being charged on a technicality.

On June 4, Graham sat down with a Bureau polygrapher. During the interview, the polygrapher asked two relevant questions: Did Graham lie when he said that ADM executives had met with a security firm about stealing microorganisms from a competitor? Did he lie when he said that the executives had discussed using prostitutes to gather information about competitors?

Both times, Graham answered that he had not lied.

When the test was done, the examiner called Shepard and Herndon into a room alone.

"He passed," the examiner said.

Graham was apparently telling the truth. And, largely because of statute of limitations problems, there was little the government could do about it.

Anxiety was spreading at Biomar International about the start-up's finances. Since October, when Whitacre had joined as chief executive, the company—then called Future Health Technologies—had burned through its reserves quickly. A new cash infusion was needed desperately.

In a meeting with Nelson Campbell, a company cofounder, Whitacre raised an idea. His elderly mother, Evelyn Whitacre, had some retirement money. She might be willing to lend as much as $100,000 to Biomar, he said.

"But listen, Nelson," he said. "My parents don't have a lot of money, and it would be a pretty big risk for them. So really, I don't think they could give us a loan unless we paid them fifty percent in interest."

"Fifty percent?" Campbell said, surprised. That was far higher than the rates the company usually paid.

"I know it's a lot, but I need to protect my parents."

Desperate for cash, Campbell accepted the terms. Whitacre agreed to write up the loan documents and have his mother sign right away.

Sometime later, Whitacre printed out the finished loan agreement on his computer. With no one around, he reached for a pen and signed his mother's name to the papers.

On another day at work, Whitacre called Campbell.

"My mother signed," he said. "Everything's done."

Days later, with the loan documents finalized, Whitacre approached a teller at a Chicago bank where Biomar kept an account. He handed over a one-hundred-thousand-dollar check, from his account at Swiss Bank Corporation. It was made out to his mother, not Biomar. But her name was signed on the back.

The teller accepted the check—sent from Switzerland almost a year before to Mike Gilbert, Whitacre's brother-in-law in Ohio—and deposited it in Biomar's account.

Cash from the ADM frauds was now financing Whitacre's new company. And neither Campbell—nor Whitacre's mother, who had never seen the check—had any idea.

The Fraud Section's battle for ADM documents was finally heard by the judge in Peoria on June 12. The hearing could scarcely have gone better for the prosecutors. ADM was ordered to produce most everything that the government wanted—invoices and related records, journals from the Bioproducts Division, correspondence, as well as wire transfers and other documents relating to the company's Cayman Islands corporations.

Victory in hand, Mackay and Nixon began to leave the courtroom. Vince Connolly, a lawyer for ADM's accountants, Ernst & Young, approached. Given the ruling, Connolly said, the firm would drop its opposition to showing the government its ADM documents. That afternoon, the accountants agreed to work out a schedule for the FBI to review any document covered by the subpoena.

The game of hardball had paid off.

In Springfield, Lou Rochelli found his seat before the twenty-three grand jurors, held up his right hand, and swore to tell the truth.

Rochelli, a former ADM controller, remained central to Whitacre's claims that the company knew all about his financial dealings. Whitacre maintained that Rochelli had called him shortly after the raid with word that Jim Randall was on a tear around ADM, telling the controller to pull specific invoices that would prove the company's newfound enemy was an embezzler. That, Whitacre insisted, was the evidence that ADM's top managers knew all about the bogus invoices. How else would they know exactly where to look?

As the grand jurors listened on that Thursday, June 20, Don Mackay led Rochelli through a description of the confusion that reigned inside ADM after the raid—followed by the shock when Whitacre's role in the case emerged. Still, Rochelli said, he maintained contact with Whitacre for a while, simply because he considered the man a friend.

Mackay glanced at his notes. "Do you recall having any discussions with Whitacre in which you indicated to him that you had heard Jim Randall, president of ADM, had asked people to start pulling files on transactions that Whitacre had been involved in?"

Rochelli looked only at Mackay.

"I believe we did, in one conversation, discuss the fact that I had heard people were being told to pull expense reports, things like that regarding trips Whitacre had taken and I informed him of that," he said. "Again, understanding Mark is a friend, I wanted him to be aware of what I knew and what was going on and whether that came from Jim Randall, I don't recall. Jim Randall certainly never discussed that with me."

Expense reports—the first stop for any company looking to discredit a former executive. No mention of invoices. Another critical support under Whitacre's story had collapsed.

Sounding its horn, the ferryboat from the Star Line slowly approached the dock on Kowloon Peninsula, across the harbor from Hong Kong's main island. On board, a group of Americans—including Brian Shepard, Bob Herndon, Scott Lassar, Jim Griffin, and Jim Mutchnik—gathered their belongings for the short walk along the waterfront to the elegant Kowloon Shangri-La Hotel. There, over the next few days, the Harvest King investigation would obtain its most critical evidence since the Whitacre tapes.

By June, negotiations with Ajinomoto and Kyowa Hakko had resulted in tentative plea deals. Both agreed to pay $10 million, and one executive from each company—Kanji Mimoto of Ajinomoto and Masaru Yamamoto of Kyowa Hakko—would also plead guilty and pay fines. No resolution had been reached on Kazutoshi Yamada, the powerful managing director of Ajinomoto whose meeting in California with Mick Andreas had resulted in the illegal volume agreement. The government was free to indict him.

Now, the Harvest King team had come to Hong Kong to hear the stories of the Japanese executives. If the statements and evidence offered over the next few days proved worthwhile, the agreements would be finalized.

The American team, dressed casually in sport shirts and slacks, headed into the lobby of the Shangri-La. Light from a huge chandelier spilled across the starburst design in the lobby's marble floor. The group came to a stop; they had no idea where to go. Before anyone was able to ask a question, David Westrup, a lawyer for Yamamoto, appeared.

"Welcome to the Shangri-La," Westrup told the group. "We've got you set up in a room over this way."

The group paraded through the lobby behind Westrup, toward the hotel's twenty-four-hour business center. The offices dripped elegance. The walls were polished cherry wood; luxurious carpeting lined the floor. A smartly dressed Chinese woman typed on a computer at the front. The lawyers and agents traipsed past her, toward a cramped conference room. They were joined by two other defense lawyers, James Kennedy and A. Paul Victor. Westrup took out an accordion folder, removing several books and stacking them across the narrow conference table.

"These are Mr. Yamamoto's personal diaries and calendars," Kennedy said. "The diaries include notes and observations of meetings and phone calls. The calendars also have notes in them, but are largely just schedules."

The defense lawyers left the room, and for hours the government team pored through documents. The leather diaries and calendars seemed particularly interesting. Though written in Japanese, Yamamoto used many proper names; numbers from the conspiracy appeared throughout. It was obvious that the documents were a perfect record of price-fixing, going back further than any of the Whitacre tapes.

The next morning, the Americans broke up, conducting separate interviews in conference rooms located two floors below the lobby. During a break, the group that had been questioning Yamamoto was near the hotel's Japanese restaurant, waiting for the others. Kevin Culum, a young antitrust lawyer known as "K.C.," bounded out of a room where another Kyowa Hakko executive was being interviewed.

"Hey, my guy's been giving up Wilson right and left," Culum raved. He pumped his fist. "Yeah!" he said. "We've got Wilson!"

The group stared at Culum, then broke out laughing. Culum seemed to have forgotten that Wilson was already featured on several dozen tapes.

"Hello? K.C.?" Herndon laughed. "We've *had* Wilson."

Still, the day proved to be a watershed in the investigation. With the benefit of his diaries and calendars, Yamamoto was almost a perfect witness. His recall of events was encyclopedic; his demeanor and style were inviting.

He would be stellar in a courtroom. Despite all of the troubles, the antitrust case was back on track.

The proffer meetings came to an end after more than a week, and the antitrust team flew home, delighted with the state of their once troubled case. The prosecutors didn't need Whitacre anymore. Now, they had other witnesses.

The air was stale and hot inside the dingy room where Jhom Su Kim, the president of Sewon America, had come to confess his crimes.

Herndon, Mutchnik, Mann, and a half dozen others—including Susan Booker from the antitrust office and Peter Hwang, a Korean-speaking Illinois state policeman who was assisting in the investigation—sat uncomfortably in the dimly lit conference room of a New York law firm, preparing their questions for Kim. It was the morning of August 12, a Saturday. No one had figured on the firm's air-conditioning being off for the weekend, particularly on such a humid day. Worse, Kim and one of his lawyers were chain-smokers; the room reeked of tobacco. No one was happy to be there.

Sewon was joining its Japanese competitors in striking a deal. Under the terms, both its American division and Kim would plead guilty and pay fines. But again, before signing off, the government wanted to hear Kim's information, to be sure it was worth the break he and Sewon were receiving.

The meeting started on a note as unpleasant as the setting. Translations of some Korean documents that the prosecutors had been expecting were not yet available. Kim grimaced when he saw the government's official translator was a woman, saying that she would be unable to understand business terms. Herndon and the prosecutors continued with their interview, dismissing the complaint.

Kim sucked down cigarettes at a rapid clip as he answered questions. With the translator speaking simultaneously in English, Kim explained that it was common for Korean competitors to have discussions about stabilizing prices and volumes. It was during the meetings, he said, that he learned he was violating American law.

Hours later, Mutchnik wrapped up with a final question. "Mr. Kim, we appreciate your help. How do you feel about all this?"

The question was translated. Kim said nothing, staring at the table as he took a long draw on his cigarette. Then, without warning, tears ran down his face. Unable to speak, Kim rushed out of the room, heading to his lawyer's office. The antitrust team was momentarily stunned.

What just happened?

Mutchnik looked toward Peter Hwang, the Illinois policeman who spoke Korean. "Peter," he said, "you've got to go find out what's going on."

Hwang met with Kim and his lawyer behind closed doors. When he returned, Hwang explained that Kim had misunderstood. The Korean executive knew he would be pleading guilty and believed—now that the interview was over—that he was heading to jail. In the weeks before, Kim had even traveled to Korea to bid his family goodbye.

Shaken, Kim was brought back into the room. The prosecutors slowly explained that he was finished, that he now could return to Korea, that he was going home. His deal, they explained, allowed him to avoid jail in exchange for his testimony. He would simply be paying a seventy-five-thousand-dollar fine. Slowly, the information sank in. Overjoyed at the reprieve, Kim thanked the prosecutors again and again.

That day in Chicago, Jim Epstein met with Don Mackay, Scott Lassar, and Jim Griffin to discuss Whitacre's fate.

Whitacre faced an array of charges; his sole defense that ADM managers had approved the illegal money transfers made no difference to his own criminal culpability. He had paid no taxes, he had laundered the money, he had submitted bogus invoices. All of it was illegal.

Mackay said that Whitacre faced up to four counts of conspiracy, six of wire fraud, sixteen of money laundering, and five more for filing false income tax returns.

"He's also going to have to pay restitution," Mackay said. "He'll have to forfeit his house and all his cars."

But Whitacre's exposure didn't end there. After the successful Hong Kong trip, the government had sent target letters to Mick Andreas and Terry Wilson, informing them that they faced imminent indictment. About the same time, Lassar and Griffin had tentatively decided that Whitacre would be joining his former ADM colleagues as a defendant.

His immunity gone because of his frauds, Whitacre now faced possible indictment for price-fixing.

• • •

On August 27, the Justice Department announced the plea agreements of the Asian companies and executives in the price-fixing case. ADM's strategic game board was thrown into disarray. With the sudden capitulation of its competitors, ADM now stood alone as the last giant lysine producer in the prosecutors' sights.

Settlement talks had reached a standstill. The government issued a deadline to the company: Settle the case by September 17—or be indicted.

Still, Dwayne Andreas remained torn; the legal dilemma facing his company was seen through the prism of whether his son would go to jail. He was working to ensure that the special-committee members knew his concerns, seemingly to little avail. For the first time in his life, Dwayne Andreas's skills at negotiating deals were failing him, as the stakes climbed with each passing day.

Andreas was pulled from all directions. Williams & Connolly assured him that Mick would be helped if the company fought the government and destroyed its case in court. But some board members, having heard descriptions of the tapes from Beattie, were demanding that Mick be tossed out of ADM immediately. Even Mick ripped into his father, alternately telling him to stay out of the case and accusing him of bungling everything.

Bob Strauss, the Washington superlawyer who was both an ADM director and a friend to Dwayne Andreas, was incensed. He thought Williams & Connolly's scorched-earth strategy was a foolish blunder; the lawyers were in danger of cutting off possible solutions. Strauss, confident of his skills in Washington backrooms, suggested that he contact prosecutors to negotiate a deal; Aubrey Daniel scuttled the idea. By the summer of 1996, Strauss was out of patience. He and other advisors suggested to Dwayne Andreas that it might be time to replace Williams & Connolly.

"They're a bunch of assholes," Andreas responded.

Still, after hashing it through, the group decided that it would be foolish to switch lawyers so late in the game. Instead, a plan was launched to gain control over the legal strategy. ADM's war against the government had to end. At that point, only one person seemed to be in the position to accomplish that: Dick Beattie, the legal advisor to the special committee, the man so distrusted in Decatur.

Strauss brokered a summit between Beattie and Andreas. The night of the meeting, Beattie arrived at 810 Fifth Avenue in Manhattan and made his way to Andreas's apartment. Andreas was waiting in the living room with Zev Furst, his longtime advisor. For hours, the three talked, with Andreas pushing Beattie to explain the reasons that ADM should settle. Beattie handled the situation delicately.

"I understand what you're going through," Beattie said. "I know your son is facing serious problems. He's in the crosshairs of the government."

Andreas listened, his face revealing nothing.

"But I saw the tapes—" Beattie continued.

"You saw the tapes they wanted you to see," Andreas interrupted sharply.

"That's true," Beattie said. "I've seen tapes selectively played by the government. But they are very powerful evidence."

Beattie explained the implications of the tapes for the publicly traded company, and the difficulties ADM and its shareholders would face at a trial, where the recordings would undoubtedly be made public.

"It's in the company's interest to settle this," Beattie said. "And I believe that by settling it now, you'll be able to help Mick later."

By evening's end, Andreas's opinion of Beattie had shifted dramatically. Never one to hold lawyers in high regard, he developed a level of trust for Beattie's judgment. As the days wore on, Andreas began to wonder if the answer to his problems had been with Beattie all along.

Andreas relayed a message to the lawyer. Concerns about ADM shareholders were largely behind the push for a settlement. But if ADM was no longer a public company, the shareholders would be out of the equation. Was it possible, Andreas wondered, that Henry Kravis of KKR might want to purchase ADM and take it private?

After the call, Beattie laughed; the enemy had now become the savior. Later, he phoned Kravis.

"Dwayne Andreas wants to know if you'd be interested in ADM," Beattie said with a bemused tone.

"Should I be?" Kravis asked.

Beattie didn't miss a beat. "No," he said.

September 10. Seven days until the scheduled indictment of ADM.

With the deadline looming, lawyers for the company and its executives met with prosecutors in Washington to feel out where everyone stood. John Bray, the lawyer representing Mick Andreas, held firm that his client would never plead. He thanked the government for the tapes; his team had found nuggets that they believed proved Mick's innocence.

"My client was set up by Mark Whitacre," he said.

Terry Wilson's lawyer, Reid Weingarten, argued that his client was simply a hostage. Wilson would never testify against the Andreas family, Weingarten said. As long as Mick Andreas refused to plead, Terry Wilson would, too. He would never turn his back on ADM.

Negotiations with the company were more direct. Gary Spratling, Deputy Assistant Attorney General for the Antitrust Division, spelled out the government's terms: ADM would plead guilty to price-fixing in both lysine and citric acid. Barrie Cox, who ran the citric business, would receive immunity and testify about conspiracies in that market. In exchange, ADM would be fined $125 million—far lower, the prosecutors said, than the company would face at trial. Williams & Connolly reacted with indignation; $125 million was exorbitant, they argued, some ten times the next highest price-fixing settlement.

As the negotiations stalled, Spratling and his team ended the meeting. On the way out the door, Spratling turned to Aubrey Daniel.

"Just so you know," he said, "the $125 million is negotiable. But not by much."

Four days left.

At 10:00 on the morning of September 13, the ADM special committee gathered in a windowless conference room on the twenty-sixth floor at 425 Lexington Avenue in Manhattan, the offices of Simpson Thacher & Bartlett. Aubrey Daniel opened with a briefing on the negotiations; in the past three days, the government had dropped the fine demand to $120 million. Other terms were unchanged: ADM would still have to plead guilty to two price-fixing conspiracies.

The terms left the committee shaken. One director, Glenn Webb, argued that the amount of money being sought was simply too high. Ross Johnson, Brian Mulroney, and several others voiced their agreement. The directors instructed Williams & Connolly to head back to the bargaining table and haggle over the price.

As the lawyers left, the same thought hung over the room. This was the end of something bigger than a criminal case. ADM was throwing in the towel; once a settlement was in place, Dwayne's succession plans for his son, so carefully nurtured over the years, would be destroyed.

John Daniels, the former ADM chairman who was cochairman of the group, leaned forward in his chair.

"I think we're all aware here of the tragedy being faced by Dwayne and his family," he said.

The other directors murmured their agreement.

Daniels glanced around the room.

"We're probably looking at the end of an era," he said.

September 17. Deadline.

During heavy negotiations, the government had agreed to drop the fine to $100 million, cautioning that the offer would not go any lower. It was $100 million or indictment.

Negotiations continued into the night. An endless series of details remained to be resolved. Finally, Aubrey Daniel had enough. He stood.

"We are not going to be railroaded into an agreement," he said sharply. "Before we agree to any settlement, we want to review every document. And you're not speaking to Barrie Cox until everything is done."

The evening ended without resolution. But the two sides were so close, prosecutors extended the deadline by one week. The clock started all over again.

Two days later, Aubrey Daniel and Barry Simon received a letter from the Antitrust Division that spelled out the terms of settlement. Daniel thought it was outrageous.

Under the terms, everyone at ADM would be granted immunity from prosecution, with a few exceptions. As expected, Mick Andreas and Terry Wilson still faced indictment. But in addition, Dwayne Andreas and Jim Randall would not receive immunity, either. Instead, ADM would have to cooperate fully, even as its chairman and president remained open to prosecution. The defense lawyers thought it was like putting a target sign on the backs of both men.

Daniel almost smiled. The government, he thought, had overstepped. The board would never accept this. He contacted Spratling.

"Thanks," Daniel said, "the letter makes this easier to reject."

"What are your concerns?" Spratling said.

"Bottom line, I want all investigations of Dwayne Andreas and Jim Randall off. They're done. Second, we're not going to pay one hundred million dollars. We'll pay twenty-five million for lysine, ten million for citric. But that's it."

Spratling paused.

"It's one hundred million," he said. "Or it's off."

The members of the special committee who met that morning at Simpson Thacher were incensed by the government's latest terms. It sounded too much like the prosecutors wanted to make a case against Dwayne Andreas and Jim Randall by rooting around inside the company. Unanimously, they rejected the proposal. The lawyers were instructed to tell the government that everyone at ADM was to receive immunity, except for those already targeted for indictment. Anything else was a deal breaker.

But the directors made it clear that the time had come for a deal. "The stock price is depressed," Ross Johnson said. "And it will stay depressed until we get this over with. We've got to clean up the mess."

Aubrey Daniel nodded. He understood.

At 11:05 the next morning, September 20, Gary Spratling's telephone rang. It was Aubrey Daniel.

"ADM says yes to one hundred million," Daniel said. "Don't tell anyone. Keep it on a need-to-know basis for now."

There were some conditions, Daniel said. Dwayne Andreas and Jim Randall had to receive immunity. That was not negotiable; if the government refused, the case was going to trial. Spratling took a few notes, saying the government would examine the issue. The lawyers agreed that they would work out the details in the coming days.

Spratling hung up and called Jim Griffin in Chicago. ADM, he said, appeared ready to cut a deal.

The answers to many of the remaining questions in the fraud case arrived—coincidentally—that same morning.

After months of negotiations, the fraud team had scheduled to meet Marty Allison, Whitacre's first hire at ADM. His lawyer, Michael Monico, had tried mightily to cut an immunity deal in exchange for testimony, but the government balked. Finally, Allison offered to submit to an interview under a proffer agreement, in hopes of leniency.

They met at the U.S. Attorney's office in Chicago. The full team on the case—Bassett and D'Angelo from the FBI, Mackay and Nixon from Justice—were there, pens in hand. Monico and Allison took seats on one side of the conference table. Allison seemed calm and embarrassed.

After introductions, Bassett began the questioning. Allison explained that he had first met Whitacre at an industry conference in the spring of 1989. At the time, Allison worked with Kyowa Hakko's lysine division; Whitacre was with Degussa, and spent their first meeting pumping Allison for information about the lysine business. Then, later that year, Whitacre called, saying that he had been hired to run ADM's lysine division and was looking for a salesman. Allison was hired after one interview with Jim Randall, starting work at ADM in January 1990.

Bassett decided to move into the frauds.

"What led to the first financial involvement with Whitacre?" he asked.

Allison nodded and took a deep breath. "It started my first year at ADM, when Mark got a letter from Nigeria."

The second floor of ADM was bristling with activity on that day in 1990. The low roar of orders from the trading room echoed around the office. No one ambled or loitered about. At ADM, it seemed, there was always work to be done. Marty Allison, the first new executive hired for Mark Whitacre's division, was still awed by the pace of the company. He remained astonished at how quickly he had been hired and how easily Randall had agreed to his salary demands. He was glad that Whitacre had told him to inflate the number.

Allison was approaching the elevators when he heard Whitacre call out behind him. His boss was excited, his face beaming with delight.

"Hey, Marty," Whitacre said. "Come to my office for a second. I want to show you something."

With Allison inside, Whitacre shut the door to his office and fished a sheet of paper out of his desk drawer. He thrust it toward his salesman.

"Look at this," he said.

Allison studied the paper. It was a strange letter, from someone claiming to be connected to the Nigerian Ministry of Petroleum Resources. The writer said that, through some complex fraud, he had gained access to millions of dollars that could be freed up with the help of someone like Whitacre.

Allison looked up. Whitacre was watching him eagerly.

"Is this for real?" Allison asked.

"Absolutely, absolutely. It's a great opportunity. My stepfather did this same thing, and he made a lot of money off of it."

Allison nodded. At the time, he had no idea that Whitacre didn't have a stepfather.

"I've been talking to them," Whitacre said. "The Nigerians. They want me to give them company letterheads, a bank account to send the money, and some bogus invoices."

"Wait a minute," one of the prosecutors interrupted. "What bogus invoices?"

"At the time I didn't know," Allison replied. "But he eventually told me that the Nigerians directed him to make the invoice related to the oil industry since he was supposed to be dealing with the oil ministry."

Bassett wrote that down. Whitacre had sent bogus invoices to Nigeria, apparently before ever using them at ADM. *Had he picked up the idea of invoice fraud from the Nigerians?*

"What did you think about this Nigerian transaction?" Bassett asked.

"I was skeptical, but I had a lot of confidence in Mark. He's very respected in the industry."

"Did Whitacre ever tell you anything about his dealings with the Nigerians?"

"Yeah, at one point I was on a business trip with him, and he told me that he had been in contact with the Nigerian representative and had faxed him documents."

"Did you ever become more involved in the Nigerian transaction?"

Allison nodded. "Yes," he said.

The dealings with Nigeria continued for months. Allison discussed the arrangements with an old college chum, Milos Lee Covert. At times, when Whitacre was traveling for ADM, he would telephone Allison or Covert, asking for help in faxing documents to the Nigerians. As a sign of good faith, Whitacre even asked Covert to send some watches to Lagos. Whitacre kept making noises about how Covert and Allison would share in his good fortune once the money finally arrived. Then, one day, Whitacre came by Allison's office with a proposal.

"Marty, you should invest with the Nigerians," Whitacre said excitedly. "It's going to be a big payoff."

Allison made a face. He didn't even like sending the faxes; he sure didn't want to send his own money.

"I don't know, Mark," he said. "The whole thing makes me a little uncomfortable."

"Marty, we're almost there. All we need is one more payment, just twenty thousand dollars, and the money's ours. You'll get your own portion. We'll all be rich!"

Allison didn't like being pressured by his boss. Still, he held his ground.

"I don't think so, Mark," he said. "I can't afford to lose that kind of money."

Whitacre smiled. "None of it's gonna be lost, Marty! We're going to make a fortune!"

"I don't know . . ."

"Listen, I'll guarantee your money. You won't lose anything. I'll take all the risk."

Allison thought about it for a moment.

"All right, Mark," he said.

"So you invested in the Nigerian deal?" Bassett said.

"No, not at all," Allison protested. "I viewed this as nothing more than a loan to Whitacre."

"You didn't see this as giving you a better chance for financial gain?"

"No. He was already promising me a portion for my help with the faxes. I didn't think this changed things much."

"So what happened with the money?"

"I wired it from my bank to a New York account. Whitacre gave me all the wiring instructions."

"Okay. What did Whitacre say about that?"

"He was all excited," Allison said. "He kept saying, 'We'll be rich.' "

Allison glanced at the faces around the room.

"That ended in a couple of days," he said.

Whitacre appeared at Allison's desk, obviously harboring some inner alarm.

"Something's wrong," he said. "The money hasn't shown up in the account."

"Have you talked to the Nigerians?" Allison asked.

"I can't find them."

Neither man made a sound or a movement.

"I think the money's been lost," Whitacre said, sounding shaken.

In the months that followed, Allison rarely raised the issue of Whitacre's guarantee of his $20,000. But in December 1991, Allison was preparing to buy a new house. He needed money to close the deal. He went to see Whitacre.

"So, Mark," Allison said, after explaining the situation, "I really need my money. I'm sure it's tough, but I need it back."

Whitacre nodded, deep in thought.

"We'll figure something out," he said casually.

Allison left Whitacre's office, concerned. The tone of his comment bothered him. It was obvious he didn't have the money; how would they figure something out?

A few days later, Whitacre told Allison that he had come up with a so-lution.

"Listen, here's what I'm going to do," Whitacre said, sounding electri-fied. "I'm going to put together an invoice for twenty thousand dollars and submit it to ADM. They'll pay it, and that'll get your money back. Maybe even Lee Covert would help here. We could disburse the money through him."

Allison stared at his boss. This proposal sounded very familiar. It was the fraud that the Nigerians had claimed in their letter to have perpe-trated against their government. Only now, Whitacre was suggesting that he, Allison, and Covert do it for real, against ADM.

"I don't know, Mark," he said. "I thought the money would come from you."

Whitacre held up his hands.

"Hey, Marty," Whitacre said. "Listen, you're not going to be alone here. I've lost more than two hundred thousand dollars to the Nigerians, and I need to recover some losses, too."

Still, Allison felt uncomfortable. What if somebody found out?

Whitacre smiled.

"Marty, I'm the division president," he chuckled. "Nobody will ques-tion me."

"What happened after that meeting?" Bassett asked.

"I agreed to contact Lee Covert to get this going," Allison said. "I told him we needed to do it to recover the losses from the Nigerian transaction."

Covert agreed to help. Under the plan, Whitacre would submit a bogus invoice for slightly more than $80,000. Whitacre and Allison would each receive $20,000; Covert would keep the rest and pay all the taxes. Covert formed a company, Covert & Associates, which sub-mitted the bogus invoice. On January 9, 1992, following Whitacre's written instruction, ADM sent Covert & Associates $81,250.

"What happened to the money?" Bassett asked.

"In January or February of that year, I met several times with Covert," Allison said. "Over the course of those meetings, he delivered forty thousand dollars in cash to me."

"Why to you?"

"I was living in St. Louis by then. I was nearby."

"What did you do with the money?"

"I kept twenty thousand, and delivered the rest to Mark."

"Delivered how?"

Allison swallowed. "Cash in a briefcase," he said.

The agents showed Allison a series of documents from the Covert & Associates transaction. He pointed out his own handwriting, as well as Whitacre's.

"All right," Bassett said. "What led up to your next financial transaction with Whitacre?"

In the summer of 1993, Allison replied, he was transferred to London.

"Now, I was hearing rumors around the office about executives receiving off-the-books bonuses," he said.

"Rumors from who?"

"I don't remember. People besides Whitacre. But I always assumed the rumors were true, and that ADM was making the payments to keep leverage on executives because of the price-fixing at the company."

Bassett wrote that down. He was not surprised; by that time, Whitacre had already told Hulse and Richter about such bonuses, and sent illegal payments to both men.

"Anyway, before I left for London, Whitacre came to see me."

Whitacre was smiling as he headed into Allison's office and shut the door.

"Hey, bud," he said. "I've got some news for you."

Standing in front of his desk, Whitacre explained that Allison was about to receive an off-the-books payment. Allison felt flattered; he assumed it was increasing his status in ADM's management.

"Now, I'll tell you what you need to do," Whitacre said, handing him a slip of paper. "Call this 800 number. They'll help you set up a corporation in Delaware. I want you to call it Nordkron Chemie."

Whitacre wrote out the name. Allison looked at it.

"Why Nordkron Chemie?"

"It's close to the name of a real company in Hamburg."

Smiling, Whitacre explained that the money paid through Nordkron Chemie would include a bonus for him as well. Allison didn't mind sharing with his boss. He was a team player.

As instructed, Allison set up the corporation and opened an account at Dresdner Bank during a routine visit to Germany. He heard nothing more about the transaction until August, when Whitacre called him in London.

"Well, Marty," Whitacre said, "a $220,000 bonus is almost on its way to Nordkron Chemie."

Allison was excited to hear the news.

"Now, you understand, most of that is mine," Whitacre said.

"Yeah, I remember."

"Okay, here's how it breaks down. When the money arrives, $140,000 of it is mine. I'll tell you how to get it to me. And the other eighty thousand is yours."

"Okay," Allison said. The money sounded great.

"Now, this is all going to be tied to some bogus research trials in Europe," Whitacre said. "But don't worry about that. I'll take care of it."

Whitacre instructed Allison to mail him an empty envelope from Germany the next time he was there. Then, he could attach the postmarked envelope to the bogus contract before submitting it for payment.

Allison didn't understand. If this was approved by management, why the subterfuge?

"It's just for the accounting people," Whitacre said. "Even though senior management knows about these payments, the accounting department doesn't."

Allison relaxed. That sounded reasonable.

The money arrived in three installments; as promised, it totaled $220,000. Whitacre first requested his share in April 1994, asking for a sixty-thousand-dollar check in the name of Union Bank of Switzerland. Allison did not know that this check was part of the money Whitacre was using to establish the ABP Trading account at Union Bank—the account where a $2.5 million ADM check would be deposited in a few months.

In June of that year, Whitacre asked Allison for three more checks totaling $140,000—in the names of Stiner, DMJ, and Sloan Implement. Despite all the money flowing out, the remaining $80,000 suited Allison fine. But he had some concerns. He called Whitacre, asking how to handle the taxes on these bonuses.

"Well," Whitacre said, "some people claim the payments, some people don't."

"What do you think, Mark?"

"Hey, Marty," Whitacre said amiably. "Whether you pay taxes is up to you."

By the end of Allison's interview, the full truth seemed to have finally emerged.

The key to the case was Nigeria. In his interview, Sid Hulse—the beneficiary of the first bogus invoice—seemed to have thought that the Nigerian investment had popped up as an idea *after* he received his illegal money. But Allison made it clear that Whitacre had been scrounging up cash for Nigeria many months before. Whitacre had started the old-fashioned way, by borrowing money. But when that ran out, he appeared to have applied the Nigerian's invoice fraud to ADM, all in the search of the money he needed for his big payoff. Once everything fell through, Whitacre knew that no one at ADM had noticed the outflow of cash. He returned to the corporate till, grabbing cash to compensate himself and his friends for their foolish losses.

The 1991 transactions told the whole story. Of the $530,000 in illegal transfers that year to Hulse and Richter, almost 85 percent ended up in Lagos—not counting the twenty-thousand-dollar loan from Allison and whatever Whitacre invested. The agents and prosecutors were certain that the Nigerian fraud had been the driving force behind this entire enterprise.

The approved bonus plan no longer made any sense. Records from ADM and its accountants proved to be a dry hole; even the corporation's Caymans subsidiaries were nothing important. Plus, it was hard to believe that each payment coincided so closely with the financial demands of the Nigerians—and later of Whitacre's friends who wanted their money back.

Making Whitacre's story less credible, none of the initial money ever went directly to him. Instead, for his fraud allegations to be true, ADM would have to be wiring illegal bonuses to its executives through third parties—including people who didn't work for the company. Why would sophisticated executives create so many unnecessary witnesses to their crimes? Why not simply wire money directly to Whitacre's offshore accounts, as was done later in the scheme?

To the agents and prosecutors, there was only one explanation: The use of other executives helped to hide that most of the money was going to Whitacre. In the earliest days of the scheme, he had used his friends and associates to create a wall between himself and ADM. But it was telling that, once money started going to Whitacre personally, his compatriots—who had been paid so much under-the-table cash in their earliest days at the company—never received another dime.

That day, the agents and prosecutors emerged from the Allison interview confident that they had finally figured out the whole truth behind the fraud schemes at ADM.

They had no idea that at least one more piece of the puzzle was still missing.

D'Angelo found it the next week, in the pages of a lawsuit.

ADM had sued Mark Whitacre the previous Thursday, just as it was wrapping up negotiations for the outlines of its plea agreement. The forty-page complaint accused Whitacre of defrauding ADM with a group of associates—including Allison, Ferrari, Hulse, and Richter. But it also named Whitacre's family members who turned up in the banking records—his wife, his mother, and his in-laws.

D'Angelo looked at the long list of defendants on the first page. All the names were familiar. Except one.

David Page.

Just as the agents had expected, ADM had been holding back. D'Angelo flipped through the suit, and found the name on page 19. The suit said that Whitacre had hired David Page in 1993 but that throughout his employment, Page had continued working for another company, Vanetta USA.

"Page was something of an illusory employee at ADM," the suit said. "Most employees in the Bioproducts Division did not know that David Page was an ADM employee. Page did not hold himself out to others as an ADM employee, and Page did not conduct business on behalf of ADM."

What the hell?

Lower down, another sentence jumped out.

"Page also received at least $30,000 from Whitacre's personal bank account at the Swiss Bank Corporation."

D'Angelo reached for the phone to call Bassett. They needed to track down David Page, and find out what Whitacre had been doing with him.

Page turned up in Pennsylvania, and a local FBI office sent an agent to interview him. But when the 302 of the interview came back to Chicago, D'Angelo was convinced the man was lying. The interviewing agent had not known enough about the case to catch the discrepancies. D'Angelo started making plans to visit Page in person.

Page hired a lawyer and agreed to meet the FBI again. By then, Bassett's transfer to Albany had come through; for the most part, he was off the case. D'Angelo and the case supervisor, Rob Grant, flew to Washington to meet with Page at the Fraud Section.

Page told of being interviewed by Whitacre for a job that paid $120,000 a year, with a thirty-thousand-dollar signing bonus. The interview took place at a Decatur Mexican restaurant in 1993, just as Harvest King was picking up steam.

"I asked Whitacre what my responsibilities would be at ADM," Page said. "And he responded, 'Nothing.' "

It was a scam, Page said. Whitacre told him to kick back one-third of his salary each year; Page could keep one-third and use the other third to pay taxes. Whitacre even received one-third of the thirty-thousand-dollar signing bonus.

"Whitacre assured me that no one would ever know about our relationship or the kickbacks," Page said. "He told me that he was president of the division and no one was looking over his shoulder."

Eventually, Page said, he took on a new role. Whitacre was having trouble bringing his overseas cash back into the United States and wanted an untraceable method for obtaining the money—after all, those millions were doing him no good sitting in Switzerland or the Caymans.

So Whitacre asked Page to open a Swiss account of his own. Then, beginning in the fall of 1994, Whitacre periodically wired $10,000 from one of his offshore banks to Page's foreign account. Simultaneously, Page withdrew $10,000 in cash from his American bank account and passed the money to Whitacre. With that system, Page helped Whitacre launder $30,000 into the United States.

"Usually we would meet at a hotel," Page said. "And I would just pass him an envelope stuffed with cash."

After almost three hours, the interview ended. The investigators and prosecutors gathered their papers, tossed them in their cases, and made their way to the exit. As soon as the door closed behind them, they began laughing.

"I'll tell you, Whitacre has *no* credibility," D'Angelo said. "I can't believe his greed! With all his millions, he's setting up this guy for a few thousand!"

Mackay shook his head. "This tops them all."

Something about the petty nature of the Page fraud—and the complexity of the laundering—eliminated any remaining doubts about the deceit in Whitacre's story. The frauds had never been about a corporate scheme. They had been about greed. Pure and simple.

The group spent the rest of the day marveling at Whitacre's machinations. But the humor ended when Don Mackay voiced the concern slowly dawning on all of them.

"When you get stuff like this popping up out of nowhere," Mackay said, "you know we'll probably never figure out everything Whitacre did."

CHAPTER 19

"So, where do we stand?" John Daniels asked his fellow directors.

It was shortly before noon on Tuesday, October 8, the day of the last gathering of the ADM special committee. Williams & Connolly had finally hammered out the final details of a plea agreement with the government. Now, the directors had returned to Simpson Thacher to vote the deal up or down.

In the room, four ADM directors, three Simpson Thacher lawyers, and the company's general counsel listened as Aubrey Daniel spelled out the terms of the settlement. Several directors, including Brian Mulroney and Ray Goldberg, listened in by speakerphone. On one side of the conference room, coffee and pastries loaded on a buffet table remained largely untouched.

For more than twenty minutes, Daniel described the deal. The price tag stood at $100 million. Dwayne Andreas and Jim Randall would now be part of the immunity deal, he explained, although both were expected to testify before the price-fixing grand jury. When Daniel finished, the room was silent for a moment.

"All right," Mulroney said over the phone. "Let's poll the vote."

Glenn Webb, a director who headed an agricultural company, spoke up. "No. It's too early in the process to make a decision of this magnitude."

The size of the settlement left Webb troubled. "This is a terribly high price," he said. "At this amount, I would think we could get a lot more concessions."

Several directors nodded in agreement. Their friendship with Dwayne Andreas weighed on them. Some directors looked to Beattie for his opinion.

"No, that's not our place," Beattie said. "This is one of those hard decisions we've been telling you about that you're going to have to make."

Ross Johnson leaned up. "We have to stay focused on the shareholders. An indictment would really hit the value of the stock. We need to move on."

At one point, Aubrey Daniel suggested that he could perhaps negotiate the price of the settlement down.

"Aubrey!" John Daniels snapped, pounding the table. "I don't want any more negotiation. We've got to come to grips with this. Let's not prolong this process."

Aubrey Daniel nodded, saying nothing.

The discussions continued for hours. Finally, John Daniels had had enough. He shot a look at Beattie.

"Let's bite the bullet and accept this," he said. "It's in the best interest of the shareholders."

"Let's poll the vote," Mulroney said.

Ray Goldberg, who was calling from Harvard and had only a few minutes before he was scheduled to teach a class, was the first to respond.

"We've got to put this behind us," he said. "If this is what it takes, I vote yes."

Daniels glanced toward Rod Bruce, a former ADM executive. "Roddy?"

"Yes," Bruce said evenly.

Brian Mulroney, who was calling from an airport where he was waiting for a flight, was next. Everyone knew that this moment—effectively turning against the Andreas family—would be difficult for him.

"Brian?" Daniels said.

A moment's hesitation.

"We need to do the right thing for the company and the stockholders," Mulroney said. "We've done a terrific job as a special committee. It's now the time for us to make the right decision for all those involved."

A few directors nodded in agreement.

"And I regret that the U.S. government treated people the way they treated the ADM people, that they would have a father testify against his own son," Mulroney continued.

The next words rushed out without even a breath.

"I'm sorry, I have to run," Mulroney said. "I'm giving my proxy to Glenn Webb."

Mulroney was gone. He never voted.

The conference-room door opened. A waitress wheeled in a buffet lunch of salmon, boneless chicken, and pasta salad, distracting the directors. As the waitress laid out lunch, Daniels looked to Webb, the man with two votes.

"Well, Glenn. How do you vote?"

Webb threw up his hands. "I vote in favor."

Daniels turned to Ross Johnson, who had already made it clear where he stood.

"Yes," Johnson said.

One more to go. Daniels faced John Vanier, a quiet man who was chief executive of his own agricultural company.

"Jack?"

Vanier chuckled. "Of course I vote yes."

Unanimous. The case was over.

Their official duties out of the way, the remaining directors turned to lunch. Beattie addressed the group.

"There's one other important issue we have to discuss," he said. A decision needed to be reached about the future of Mick Andreas and Terry Wilson.

On October 17, two days after the record price-fixing settlement with ADM was announced, company shareholders gathered in Decatur for the annual meeting. Those who remembered the company's combative approach the previous year were surprised to see a subdued Dwayne Andreas take to the stage this time around. No longer did he silence critics; instead, he complimented even vociferous detractors. Most surprising, he issued an apology for ADM's crimes.

"I consider this a serious matter, which I deeply regret, and I acknowledge to you that this occurred on my watch," he said. "You have my apology and my commitment that this will never happen again."

Whitacre was never mentioned directly, but neither were Mick Andreas and Terry Wilson. As the ceremonies ended, reporters surrounded Brian Mulroney near the stage. With ADM pleading guilty to price-fixing, one reporter asked, what was the future of Mick Andreas and Terry Wilson?

"They no longer work here," Mulroney said simply.

Terry Wilson had retired, and Mick Andreas had gone on leave. Their once stellar careers at ADM were over.

• • •

Providing psychiatric treatment to Whitacre had been a whirlwind for Dr. Derek Miller.

It had taken months to find a lithium level that controlled Whitacre's manic periods. But, in early October, Whitacre showed signs of trouble, writing a letter to his lawyer that accused the government of being communist. It was the worst time for him to spin out of control. Not only was his case heading toward indictment, but he was leaving Chicago for Biomar's offices in Chapel Hill, North Carolina—away from his regular sessions with Miller.

On October 16, Miller dictated progress notes for Whitacre, whom he still referred to as Patrick O'Brien.

"Mr. O'Brien is really being quite manic, and it is clear that he is not taking his lithium," Miller said. "He denied that he was not taking it to me. But he told his attorney that he was not taking it because he enjoys how he feels when he is not taking it."

Miller planned to refer Whitacre to a North Carolina psychiatrist. He could only hope that Whitacre followed up with the new doctor before he did something self-destructive.

The teams of prosecutors clustered at a Justice Department conference room, surrounding Jim Epstein. The defense lawyer had come to Washington to take the first steps in the settlement dance for Whitacre. Until now, Epstein thought that the government's fears of Williams & Connolly had driven decisions in the prosecution of his client. But today, he wanted Washington to understand there was a price to be paid for mishandling Whitacre as well.

"It's these guys from ADM who stole hundreds of millions of dollars, defrauding people worldwide," Epstein told the group. "Mark not only told you about it, but he gave you unprecedented evidence to prove it. He helped you stop a multimillion-dollar fraud. He gave you the chance to show that multinational price-fixing is going on."

Epstein looked down the row of faces.

"When agents go undercover for the FBI, they get trained for the stresses of living a secret life, of having nobody who is really their friend," he said. "We hear this all the time from you guys, about how difficult that is and how easy it is for trained agents to crack."

Not a sound or a movement interrupted the moment.

"And here was Mark, a civilian with no training. He didn't choose this as a career. But you guys just shove him in there, you tell him 'go for it.' You send him in there without training, without support, without anything to make sure he doesn't crack under the pressure."

Epstein's words were having a visible effect.

"Mark committed a crime. It was indefensible. He stole nine million dollars. But that's opposed to helping you stop a multimillion-dollar fraud many times that."

Now, Epstein said, because of vagaries of the sentencing guidelines, Whitacre faced more prison than did the executives whose price-fixing involved much more money.

"Now, we're not looking for the earth, the sky, and the stars," he said. "We're looking for something in the area of three years, which is about what the guidelines are for these guys who stole hundreds of millions of dollars."

The option, Epstein said, was a sentencing hearing.

"We'll be at a public hearing covered by the world's press, and I'll lay out everything Mark did, good and bad. I'll talk about the lack of training and everything that happened to him because he came forward. Your future whistle-blowers will pick up the *New York Times* and the *Wall Street Journal*, and read what Mark's life has been like because of his decision to cooperate."

Epstein spread his arms.

"And then," he said, "you'll never have one of these guys pick up the phone and call you ever, ever again."

Jack Keeney, the Acting Assistant Attorney General in charge of the Criminal Division, was the first to speak.

"Well," he said, "we have a formidable person across the table from us."

Epstein left with no agreements, but he had made headway. He would have to return a few times to nail down a deal. In the end, he figured Whitacre would receive a five-year sentence, with the potential that the judge could depart downward. It was the best outcome he could imagine. But Whitacre was outraged when he heard that his lawyer was even *considering* a plea deal.

"This isn't right!" Whitacre moaned. "ADM's the bad guys! The Justice Department is covering for them. It's just 'dump on Mark Whitacre!' "

Rather than negotiate, Whitacre said, they should sue the government. The FBI had mistreated him. A lawsuit might make them back down. Epstein barely listened. He had heard Whitacre complain many times about being persecuted. The man was disconnected from reality.

"What do you want me to do, Mark?" Epstein asked, exasperated. "You've got to focus here. You stole nine million dollars, and basically admitted it on the front page of the *Tribune*. I'm just doing damage control. We've got very few cards in our hand, and I'm going to play them the right way to give you the least possible time."

Epstein hit the same points again and again, until Whitacre finally seemed convinced. But a few days later, a fax arrived at the office for Epstein. It was a letter from Whitacre, on Biomar stationery.

"Ginger and I have spent many hours in discussions the past few weeks about which direction we would like to go," he wrote. "We have decided to go a different direction than you had planned and recommended."

Epstein finished the letter and set it on his desk.

He'd just been fired. And he couldn't have been happier.

Fine, go, Epstein thought. *You're not my problem anymore.*

Whitacre had already been searching for new lawyers and was quick to name replacements. The first was Richard Kurth, a lawyer from Danville, Illinois, whom Whitacre trusted. The two had grown close after Kurth had provided advice on selling the house in Moweaqua. During that time, the two had discussed Whitacre's situation, and Kurth had offered his input. From what he had heard, Whitacre had little doubt Kurth was just the kind of lawyer he needed.

But Kurth, a specialist in bankruptcy and personal-injury cases, needed help. So he told Whitacre about a friend he had known since law school. The lawyer, Bill Walker, a hulking man with a shock of white hair, ran his own practice in Granite City, Illinois. He was aggressive and loud; he expressed outrage that the government would even *consider* indicting Whitacre. Walker's style appealed to Whitacre, and the lawyer was hired immediately.

One of the most complex white-collar cases ever was now being handled by a personal-injury lawyer and his friend, a small-town solo practitioner.

At 10:25 on the morning of November 6, a single-page fax arrived in ADM's legal department. It was addressed to Rick Reising, the general counsel.

Reising read the fax quickly. It was another unsigned letter relating to Whitacre, one of many ADM had received in recent years. But this one was the most stunning of all.

"I used to work for the United Brotherhood of Carpenters, the pro-
ponent of a shareholder proposal on director liability brought before
the Archer Daniels Midland shareholders," the letter read. "The UBC
is also a strong supporter of Dr. Mark Whitacre and has helped him,
with the help of Cargill, find stronger counsel."

There was one important item, the letter said, that ADM needed
to know.

"Dr. Whitacre discharged Mr. Epstein due to the fact that he
would not tell the government about certain tapes that were not in the
FBI's favor."

After Whitacre began taping ADM, it said, he had grown uncomfortable with the local FBI agent running the case.

"The local agent would tell Dr. Whitacre to take several of the
tapes that he felt were in ADM's favor back home with him and to destroy them," it read. "Whitacre became disenchanted with the FBI,
and started taping several meetings with the agents, unknown to them,
because of the trust factor. He built a strong file of tapes that the FBI
told him to discard and also several tapes of the FBI telling him to discard them. These are the tapes that Mr. Epstein would not let him use
because of the strong chance of weakening the government's case
against ADM."

The caller ID device on the fax machine was checked. The sender
had tried to block the number, but failed.

The fax had come from the North Carolina offices of Biomar International.

Mark Whitacre's employer.

The Harvest King team was sharply divided on a single question: What
should be done with Mark Whitacre?

Since July, Lassar and Griffin had been set on charging Whitacre
with price-fixing. The evidence from the Japanese and Koreans proved
that the conspiracy started many months *before* Whitacre began cooperating, and showed Whitacre was central to the scheme during that
time. Since he had blown his immunity, the prosecutors argued, the
jury would be angered if Whitacre wasn't charged.

Shepard and Herndon were unconvinced. They couldn't accept
the idea of indicting the man who brought them the case.

"This is wrong," Shepard said in a conference call. "We wouldn't
have anything if it wasn't for Whitacre."

Lassar explained his reasoning, adding that even if Whitacre were convicted, his sentence would likely run concurrent with his prison term in the fraud case.

"Then what difference does it make, Scott?" Herndon asked. "It seems unfair."

"He's not going to be able to handle it," Shepard said. "He's too fragile. If we indict him, there's no telling what he'll do."

In the end, the agents lost the argument. On December 15, 1996, a federal grand jury in Chicago handed up indictments against Mick Andreas, Terry Wilson, and Mark Whitacre, as well as Kazutoshi Yamada of Ajinomoto, charging them each with one count of violating the Sherman Act.

After flying from North Carolina, Whitacre arrived for a visit to Dr. Miller, seeming agitated and out of control. He had come with his new lawyers, and, with Whitacre's permission, Miller told Walker and Kurth about their client's bipolar illness. They had known nothing about it and asked for a book on the subject.

For a time, Miller sat with his patient alone. He had no doubt that Whitacre's lithium levels were low. He was manic, babbling about some lawsuit he was planning that he thought would solve all of his problems.

"When I'm finished with this court case," Whitacre told Miller, "I'm going to become the new CEO at ADM."

Brian Shepard walked into the mail room in the Decatur Resident Agency on the morning of January 9 to check the office answering machine. The digital display showed that there was a message waiting, and Shepard pushed the button.

"This is Ron Henkoff from *Fortune* magazine. I have something important to talk with you about, if you could return my call."

Shepard knew of Henkoff; he was the reporter who had written the Whitacre cover story in *Fortune*. At 11:20, Shepard returned the call. Henkoff got right to the point.

"I was calling to get your comments regarding some allegations by Mark Whitacre," Henkoff said.

"I'm sorry," Shepard replied. "I can't comment."

"Well, I'm giving you the opportunity to comment because of the nature of the information."

Henkoff said that he had heard a tape of what purported to be a conversation between Shepard and Whitacre. In the tape, Henkoff said, someone who sounded like Shepard could be heard playing a recording of Mick Andreas, and then instructing Whitacre to destroy it.

The bad news kept coming. Henkoff said that Whitacre was planning to sue Shepard. The suit would accuse the agent of hitting him with a briefcase and forbidding him from contacting a lawyer or a doctor during the investigation.

Shepard felt his insides tearing out.

"I can't comment, I'm sorry," he replied.

Hanging up, Shepard called Mutchnik. "We need to talk," he said.

Mutchnik patched in Herndon in Springfield.

"Okay, Brian, what's up?" Mutchnik asked.

"I was contacted by a reporter from *Fortune* magazine, the one who did that first article," Shepard said. "Mark's saying he's going to file a lawsuit against me. He's saying I told him to destroy tapes."

"Ahh, jeez," Herndon moaned. "What a jerk."

Shepard was beside himself. How could Whitacre's new lawyer file this suit based on his word? There couldn't be a tape—none of this had ever happened.

"What do we do?" Shepard asked, distraught. "Can we just go to court and get him to take it back?"

"Brian, it doesn't work that way," Mutchnik replied. "I don't know what court it's going to be filed in, but you can't just make it go away. Once it's filed, you have to go through a process. It'll take time."

Shepard seethed. "This isn't right!" he shouted.

"Brian, don't worry," Herndon said. "It's crap. It's just Whitacre. Nobody will believe it."

Shepard wasn't persuaded. "I told you!" he said bitterly. "I told you something like this would happen."

He breathed in heavily. "I knew we never should have indicted him for price-fixing," he said. "I knew it."

Two days later, *Fortune* magazine sent out a press release with a copy of its latest article, under the headline BETRAYAL. It was based on another Whitacre interview, but this time with a far different spin.

"The mole has turned," it read, saying Whitacre was blowing his whistle again. "Now, Whitacre is fingering the FBI itself, accusing one of its agents of ordering him to destroy evidence, denying him access to lawyers and doctors, and driving him to the brink of suicide. And once again, he says the charges are backed up by tapes."

The article quoted Whitacre saying that Shepard had told him to get rid of tapes that were favorable to ADM. Out of concern, Whitacre said, he had begun taping the agent, several times recording him as he gave instructions to destroy evidence.

"I was realizing the FBI was not much different than ADM," Whitacre said in the article. "They had their own conspiracies. And I was stuck in the middle."

The article did not quote any tapes, and said that the recordings were no longer in Whitacre's possession. But, it added, sources were saying the tapes still existed.

The magazine cautioned that there were reasons to be skeptical of Whitacre's new claims—particularly since they contradicted his earlier praise for Shepard. But the article said that Whitacre had been in secret anguish for months about agent wrongdoing. It referenced a July 1995 letter to Jim Epstein, in which Whitacre laid out his concerns. In the article, Whitacre said that Epstein had persuaded him not to take on the government as an enemy. But now, he told the magazine, he could no longer bear holding back.

That same day, a faxed copy of the article arrived at my home. I had been covering the bizarre ADM story for the *New York Times* since the fall of 1995, and was familiar with its frequent twists. This new article, I knew, accurately portrayed Whitacre's latest allegations. For weeks, Whitacre had been telling me tales of FBI corruption; to support his claim, he had provided me with two documents—the Epstein letter later cited in the *Fortune* article and a letter apparently signed by his psychiatrist. Both, Whitacre said, proved that he had been discussing FBI wrongdoing since 1995.

Whitacre had also played a recording for me, which he said showed that Shepard had ordered him to destroy evidence. While I could recognize the voices on the tape as belonging to Whitacre and Shepard, their words were largely incomprehensible. Whitacre had provided a transcript, but would not give me a copy of the tape.

After reading the *Fortune* article that Sunday, I telephoned Whitacre.

"Mark, I need to come visit you right away."

Whitacre sounded leery. "Why?" he asked.

"Why do you think? The *Fortune* article!"

After a pause, Whitacre consented to a meeting in North Carolina. He understood how reporters felt when they were beaten on a big story. I asked him to bring Ginger, who had been mentioned in the *Fortune* article as well. He agreed.

• • •

The next evening in Chapel Hill, I met Mark and Ginger in Biomar's lobby and was escorted to a conference room. I took a seat at the head of the table, while the Whitacres sat across from each other. Mark looked at me expectantly.

He didn't know that I had come with a script.

"Mark," I said, "before I ask anything, I want to talk to you for a minute."

Whitacre nodded. "All right."

"For the last four years, everyone who met with you has wanted something," I said. "The FBI wanted your help on an investigation. Prosecutors wanted your help to get a conviction. Reporters wanted your help to get a story."

Whitacre stared back blankly. He had no idea where this was going.

"I'm not here tonight because I want anything from you," I said. "I'm here because I'm worried about you."

Whitacre blinked.

"What do you mean?" he asked.

Reaching into my briefcase, I brought out a manila folder filled with documents.

"These are the records you gave me," I said. "I've looked them over very carefully."

"Okay."

I set the documents on the table.

"And they're not real. They're forgeries."

The room was silent.

For weeks, I had struggled with concerns about the bogus documents. Whitacre's allegations against Shepard had been built on fraud. The barely audible tape he had played for me was also fake; while it was clearly Shepard's voice, the background static on the recording repeatedly changed pitch depending on who was speaking—a strong sign that it had been spliced together from different recordings.

At the time, it had hardly seemed newsworthy that someone had lied to a reporter. But then, rumors circulated that *Fortune* would be printing the allegations against Shepard. My editors ruled, and I agreed, that we could not tell *Fortune* about the forgeries, since we didn't know whether the magazine had obtained other material to support the story—or was even, in fact, planning an article.

Aware by that time that Whitacre had been diagnosed with a bipolar condition, I spoke with several psychiatrists. Laying out the scenario, I asked what would happen if the *New York Times* revealed the forgeries after a *Fortune* article appeared. Most agreed that such a disclosure ran a significant risk of prompting another suicide attempt. It was an impossible situation, a choice between watching the destruction of an agent's career or potentially prompting the death of a witness. Troubled by those options, I had consulted with another expert, who had devised the third alternative that was being pursued on this night: confrontation.

As planned, I brought out the letter purportedly written by Dr. Miller in 1995. In it, the psychiatrist appeared to discuss Whitacre's allegations against Shepard. It was Whitacre's proof that his claim was not something he had thought up once he faced price-fixing charges.

I showed Whitacre a second Miller letter I had obtained, pointing out dramatic differences between them. The typeface changed. The format was different. The 1995 letter was addressed to "Dr. Mark Whitacre" and opened with "Dear Mark"; the second, later letter was addressed to "Mark Whitacre" and began, "Dear Mr. Whitacre."

Mark brushed away these concerns, saying that a new secretary could account for the change. I pointed out other problems with the 1995 letter; as planned, each discrepancy was more difficult to explain than the last. I glanced at Ginger; her face showed doubt. It was time to pull out the stops.

"Another problem is the letterhead," I said. "The office has an area code of 847. But the letter was written on November 14, 1995. That area code wasn't in use yet."

Whitacre didn't hesitate.

"Well, everybody knew about that area code coming," he said. "Lots of people ordered it early when they bought new stationery. That's probably what Dr. Miller did."

"I thought about that," I said, pulling out another document. "So I asked the phone company, Ameritech."

I slid the document across the table to him.

"This is the press release they issued in 1995, when they first announced the 847 area code. It's dated November twentieth, six days after this letter was written."

Ginger looked shocked.

"So, Mark," I said, "how did Dr. Miller know the new area code before it was announced?"

Whitacre stared at the press release, saying nothing. Finally, he looked up.

"Well, I don't understand why you're having all these problems," he said sharply. "Ron Henkoff called Dr. Miller, and he told him that this letter is real."

Whitacre was lying. This was the turning point I had been told to expect.

"Well, I called Dr. Miller, too. And after I persuaded him there's no doctor-patient privilege for fake documents, he told me that he's never seen this letter before."

Whitacre didn't move.

"He also said that he's very worried about you and wants to speak with you right away," I said.

I slid a piece of paper with a phone number toward Whitacre. "He's at home right now, waiting for your call."

My conversations with Miller had taken place days before. We skated on the edge of the doctor-patient relationship; without ever mentioning Whitacre's name, I explained my dilemma. The charade continued with Miller instructing me generally on how to handle this type of situation with a severe manic-depressive—and then arranging for the call to his home. Everything—from the words I had chosen to the request that Ginger be present as a witness—had been planned with Miller's input.

In the next few minutes, Whitacre tearfully confessed that the Miller letter was a forgery. I told him that Jim Epstein was at home and had agreed to comment on the authenticity of the letter cited by *Fortune*, if Whitacre would give permission. Shaken, Whitacre admitted that the Epstein letter was also fake. Ginger covered her face with her hands, telling her husband he was damaging himself with his lies.

We remained in the conference room for another hour. Eventually, the Whitacres went alone to another room, where they phoned Dr. Miller. Thirty minutes passed. When they returned, Mark looked chagrined.

"Looks like I'm going back to the hospital," he said.

Our meeting continued; we eventually moved to the Whitacres' house so that Ginger could pack for the hospital. There, Mark assured me that his story of FBI corruption was true, even if the documents were fakes. I told the Whitacres that I would be writing an article about his confession, and that it would be appearing as soon as possible. Past one in the morning, there was nothing left to say. I left their home. It was the last time I would speak with Mark Whitacre for several years.

• • •

Thirty hours later, Bill Walker, Whitacre's new attorney, was making his way through a hectic swirl of crowds at O'Hare Airport. He had picked up a copy of the *New York Times* and was reading it as he headed for his plane. Then he saw a headline that brought him to a halt.

ARCHER DANIELS INFORMER ADMITS RECENT DECEPTION.

Oh, shit! Walker thought.

Whitacre had given him no idea this was coming.

That same day, a federal grand jury in Springfield indicted Whitacre on forty-five felonies, including wire fraud, tax evasion, and money laundering. His nighttime visit to Ron Ferrari's home in October 1995—when he had urged his friend to confirm his story of a corporate-wide scheme—led to an obstruction-of-justice charge. There were no other mentions of the under-the-table bonus story.

For once, there was no public comment from Whitacre. He remained under psychiatric care in a Chapel Hill hospital, where he would stay for much of the week. He was not allowed access to newspapers or television news. His doctors believed that they might worsen his condition.

In the months that followed, the job of negotiating a plea for Whitacre fell to his new lawyers, Bill Walker and Richard Kurth. But unlike Epstein, who had already made headway with the Justice Department, the new lawyers started from several yards back. Not only did they arrive with no cache of trust, their decision to file the Shepard suit had crippled their credibility with the government.

Neither lawyer seemed to recognize the incalculable damage caused by their gambit. At meetings with fraud prosecutors, Walker rambled about Shepard's purported misdeeds that were raised in the lawsuit. But there were also new, more incredible allegations. Walker told prosecutors that Shepard had forced Whitacre to join other ADM executives in a tryst with prostitutes at New York's Waldorf-Astoria Hotel; the lawyer claimed that Shepard feared Whitacre would be ostracized by other ADM executives if he did not participate. This had torn apart the family, Walker said, since Whitacre had recently confessed the indiscretion to Ginger and explained Shepard's role in it.*

---

*Whitacre's story is not true. Expense records show that the only time the executives mentioned by Whitacre stayed at the Waldorf together was in early 1992, before he met Shepard.

At the end of each monologue, Walker would look knowingly at the prosecutors, informing them that, of course, many of these allegations could be proved with the evidence that Whitacre had gathered on tape.

But those supposed tapes were elusive. Whitacre claimed that in the summer of 1995, he had sent the Shepard recordings to a friend for safekeeping. The friend's name was familiar to the government. It was David Hoech, the now-infamous Lamet Vov. To prove his new claim, Whitacre produced a tape of a phone conversation with Hoech. In it, Hoech told Whitacre that he had received the material and destroyed it. But Whitacre insisted that the tapes still existed.

Walker also claimed that there was taped evidence from Harvest King proving that ADM had authorized the payments to Whitacre. The recording, he said, was from the spring of 1994, and had captured Mick Andreas openly discussing the $2.5 million payment to Whitacre. When the FBI had questioned Whitacre about it at the time, Walker said, his client had explained the matter away as merely a discussion of a salary boost. The fraud prosecutors told Walker's claims to Herndon, who reported back that no such recording existed.

Eventually, Walker presented his terms for a plea agreement. They were difficult to understand. But as best as Mackay could tell, Walker was hoping for a plea that would allow his client to keep at least some of the money from ADM and serve no prison time. Mackay telephoned and rejected the offer.

Weeks later, Walker arrived for a meeting in the Fraud Section conference room. Mary Spearing was there, along with Mackay and Nixon. Walker, in short sleeves and no tie, took a seat on the far side of the table. As the meeting began, he brought out a sheet of paper from his shirt pocket. It was his original terms for a settlement. He asked about them again. Spearing gave Mackay a look.

"Didn't Don get back to you on this?" she asked.

"Yeah, he did," Walker said.

Spearing stared at him for a moment. "We're not here to negotiate this," she said.

But Walker wouldn't drop it. Spearing left the room as Walker listed his terms again, explaining the reasoning for each. Eventually, Mackay had enough, and held up his hands.

"All right, Bill," he said. "Thank you. I get it."

Walker stared at the prosecutors.

"You know, you've been around Mr. Mackay," he said slowly. "This all goes back many years, probably before you were born. This is bigger than any of us, and it's ongoing. And I know who's behind it."

For several minutes, Walker weaved tales of mysterious conspiracies, driven by powers he would not describe.

"I know you're skeptical, but I've seen it. I know who they are. But I can't tell you who right now."

Mackay suppressed a smile. "Is that because you're afraid for your safety?"

"Well, no," Walker said. "I'll tell you someday when this is all over."

Walker looked Mackay in the eye. "I'll tell you the identity of the Master Puppeteer," he said.

Mackay blinked. "Who?" he finally stammered.

"The Master Puppeteer. I know who it is. And no, it's not who you're thinking."

"Who am I thinking?" Mackay asked.

"It's not Dwayne Andreas. He's just small fry."

Mackay knew that if he looked at Nixon, he would crack up.

"I can't tell you now," Walker said. "But I promise, I'll reveal the identity when this is all over."

"Well, I guess this is somebody who's alive, then."

Walker raised his hands. "I'm not saying any more."

The prosecutors rushed Walker through the rest of the meeting. After seeing him out, they headed back into Mackay's office. There, they both collapsed in laughter.

Whitacre's allegations against Shepard set off a series of new problems for the price-fixing prosecution. Lawyers for Mick Andreas and Terry Wilson demanded a hearing to determine whether the FBI had destroyed exculpatory evidence. Federal Judge Blanche Manning, who had been assigned the case, granted the motion.

In preparation for the hearing, the prosecutors launched a series of meetings with Shepard and Herndon, reviewing the investigation. At one session, the group met in a large conference room at the Antitrust Division's Chicago office. Boxes of documents were piled around. Scott Lassar led the discussion from the head of the table.

"Okay, Brian," he said. "Walk me through the beginning of the investigation."

Shepard nodded. "All right," he said.

Starting with the first phone call, Shepard described the earliest days of Harvest King—the first interview with Mick Andreas, the delay as he waited for Whitacre that same night, the Fujiwara allegations.

"Of course," Shepard said, "nothing came from the Fujiwara investigation."

Lassar shrugged. "Well, that was just part of Whitacre's fraud," he said simply.

What? The words hit the agents hard.

"What are you talking about, Scott?" Herndon said.

"That whole Fujiwara episode was part of Whitacre's fraud," Lassar repeated. "Think about it. He's telling ADM there's a saboteur who can be stopped if they pay millions of dollars, wired to Swiss and Cayman Islands accounts."

Lassar looked from Herndon to Shepard.

"There's only one person we know of who had accounts there. It was Whitacre. He was trying to steal the money."

The agents were shaken.

"Wait," Herndon said. "That makes no sense. This isn't like the other frauds. It doesn't involve invoices."

"Yeah, Scott, I don't know," Shepard said. "He did nothing else like this."

Lassar held up his hands. "Guys, we've all got to be on the same page. One big question in this hearing is going to be what Fujiwara was all about. What other explanation is there? Who was going to get that money?"

"But Scott," Herndon said, "ADM isn't going to hand Whitacre ten million dollars and say, 'Drop it off with the extortionist. See you at work tomorrow.' That money isn't going to go out the door easily. They'd trace it."

"No, they wouldn't," Lassar replied. "It was going to Swiss and Caymans accounts. They'd never figure it out."

Shepard shook his head. "I don't agree with this."

"Yeah, Scott," Herndon said. "I'm not saying you're wrong. But I'm not going to be able to testify to that. We don't have any evidence to prove that."

Shepard and Herndon left the meeting unconvinced, even a little angry. The idea required them to readjust everything that they had believed about the investigation.

But over time, logic overpowered their emotional resistance. Lassar's theory explained so much—why Whitacre had been so nervous in the first days, why he had stressed that the price-fixing was more important than the Fujiwara threats, why he had been so volatile.

The agents had always thought that Harvest King had, indirectly, led to the discovery of Whitacre's frauds. But eventually, they understood that the opposite was also probably true: The frauds had indirectly led to the FBI's discovery of price-fixing.

By the fall of 1997, the fraud investigation was effectively finished. The FBI and the prosecutors had interviewed scores of witnesses, hunted the Caymans for records, and reviewed thousands of documents.

Most of Whitacre's stories were chased down, but invariably, the person portrayed as the source of the rumor told a markedly different version. While ADM's financial controls were clearly slipshod, nothing had emerged to prove the existence of a corporate-wide fraud scheme.

Even though he was the last main witness to speak with the government, Marty Allison was granted the first plea bargain. He was charged with one count of conspiracy, signing the agreement a month after his critical interview. In consideration of his cooperation, he received no jail.

A grand jury indicted Reinhart Richter, but the charges remained under seal for many months. During that time, he met with the FBI again to clarify a few issues. He had never heard of an illegal bonus plan while working at ADM, he said; the money sent to him was used solely for recouping Nigerian losses. He also told investigators that he had partially misled them about the $425,000 check he had received from Whitacre—a portion of that was accrued salary that Whitacre had withheld from him. Eventually, Richter pleaded guilty to two conspiracy counts, but also received no prison time because of his cooperation.

To the dismay of the case agents, the prosecutors declined to pursue indictments against Ron Ferrari, Beat Schweizer, or David Page. Mackay and Nixon did seek approval to charge Sid Hulse, but their presentation to an indictment review committee was so poor that the request was denied.

D'Angelo was particularly outraged. Marty Allison had cooperated and was now a felon; Hulse, he thought, had tailored his story to limit his culpability, and would escape without a blemish. D'Angelo demanded a chance to appear before the indictment review committee himself. The unusual presentation by an FBI agent was so impassioned and well-prepared that the committee reversed itself. Indictments of Hulse for fraud and tax violations were approved.

The only major target left was Mark Whitacre.

. . .

The staff at Biomar crowded into a conference room, where Whitacre sat at the head of the table. Following his indictment and confession to manufacturing documents, Whitacre had been asked to step down as chief executive, but had been allowed to continue working with a smaller sister company called Clintech. But now Whitacre wanted to tell everyone that he would be out of the office for months.

"My lawyers and I have decided that it's time for me to put forward my side of the story more aggressively," he said. "For the next few months, I'm going to be involved in a media tour, involving television and newspapers."

Already, Whitacre told the group, his lawyers were making arrangements for appearances on NBC and ABC; an interview with Barbara Walters, the *ABC News* correspondent, had already been set up, he said.

"So, I just wanted everybody to know I'm not going to be around much in the next few months. I'm going to be out there, fighting to prove my innocence."

Whitacre finished his speech. Several longtime staff members crowded around him, wishing him luck.

There would be no media interviews. Instead, plea negotiations with Whitacre moved into high gear. Walker sought a maximum of five years in prison; the prosecutors were unwilling to go below a minimum of seven.

Days before Whitacre's trial was scheduled to begin, a tentative deal was struck. Whitacre would plead guilty to thirty-seven felonies, including money laundering, wire fraud, and tax evasion. In exchange for his cooperation, the prosecutors would ask the judge to sentence him below the usual range dictated by the federal guidelines. Under those terms, Whitacre could expect a seven-year prison term.

After reaching the tentative agreement, on October 7 Mackay called Jim Griffin, letting him know the developments. Later that afternoon, Mackay and D'Angelo were working in the "war room" they had reserved in the Urbana federal courthouse in preparation for the Whitacre trial. The phone rang and Mackay put it on speaker.

"Don, it's Scott Lassar."

Lassar was on a speakerphone in Chicago, joined by the rest of the antitrust team. They had heard about the Whitacre plea agreement, he said, and had concerns.

"What we'd like is to try and combine the two cases, and arrange for a global plea," Lassar explained. "And—"

"His lawyer doesn't want to combine the cases," Mackay interrupted gruffly. "He's saying the antitrust case really isn't high on his radar screen."

"Well, Don, there's a possibility that the judge might not accept a plea if it doesn't resolve everything."

Mackay interrupted again with an objection. Lassar pressed forward.

"In our case, this deal is going to make it look like Whitacre got twenty years off his sentence. It will look sneaky, like we're trying to put something past them."

Mackay listened, annoyed. He wanted nothing to do with wrapping the cases together. *His* trial was about to begin. This plea agreement would be a victory. It had been approved up the line in the Justice Department. Now, as far as he was concerned, the antitrust team was trying to mess everything up to compensate for their own mistakes.

Lassar continued his explanations. Mackay's face twisted in rage. Too much coffee and nicotine had combined badly with the stresses of trial preparation. He exploded.

"Cocksuckers!" he screamed in a high, shrill voice.

Everyone went silent.

"I'm sick of you!" Mackay screeched. "We'll go to trial without your fucking cooperation! Good-bye!"

Mackay slammed the speakerphone, cutting off the call.

Back in Chicago, the assembled group heard an audible click. The room remained quiet.

"Well," Lassar finally said, "I think that went pretty well."

In Urbana, Mackay was on a tear. His face was cherry red, his breathing labored. D'Angelo and Nancy Jardini, a new prosecutor on the case, stood back as Mackay ranted. D'Angelo feared that the prosecutor was on the verge of a heart attack.

"Those goddamned cocksuckers!" he raged. "You know we're going to have to try this case because they can't get their fucking act together! This is all their fault!"

The storm clouds passed after ten minutes. Mackay knew that he had handled the situation badly, but remained angry with the antitrust team. The Fraud Section wanted the plea. So soon, the prosecutors came up with a plan.

The Whitacre plea would proceed. But until that time, the prosecutors told D'Angelo, the antitrust team was to be kept largely in the dark about what was happening.

"Case 97-20001," the court clerk announced to a packed courtroom. "United States of America versus Mark Whitacre."

The government and defense lawyers stated their names. Judge Harold Baker, from the federal district court in Urbana, looked out over the courtroom. Whitacre, dressed in one of his best suits, sat calmly beside Bill Walker.

"The clerk informs me this is a change-of-plea proceeding, is that right?" Judge Baker asked.

Walker stood. "Correct, your honor."

Judge Baker glanced toward Whitacre. "Will you come and stand before the court, Mr. Whitacre?"

Whitacre walked to a podium.

"Mr. Whitacre, is it correct that you want to enter a plea of guilty to some thirty-five counts?"

"Yes, your honor."

Walker interrupted. The real number in the plea was thirty-seven, he said. Baker asked a series of questions, to ensure that Whitacre was capable of making a decision to plead. Whitacre told the judge that he had been diagnosed as a manic-depressive, was taking lithium, and had been hospitalized for the condition twice.

Judge Baker looked over the plea agreement.

"The government has agreed not to bring any additional charges against you, is that right?" Judge Baker asked. "Provided you haven't hidden information from them?"

"I think it's limited, your honor, to the Tax Division of the Justice Department and the Fraud Division of the Justice Department," Walker said.

Why would Whitacre leave himself exposed to another charge? If he pleaded guilty to everything, the possible jail time wouldn't change.

"I want to talk to you guys about that," Baker said, looking at the prosecutors. This agreement wasn't binding on other agencies of the government? he asked.

Nancy Jardini stood. "We don't, as the Fraud Section of the United States Department of Justice, do not have the authority to bind the Antitrust Division or an individual district," she said. "The defendant understands that."

Turning to Whitacre, Judge Baker asked pointed questions; did he know that this plea would have no effect on the other criminal charges against him? Whitacre said he understood. Judge Baker was satisfied.

"The court accepts the pleas of guilty," he said. "The court finds the defendant guilty as charged."

Judge Baker continued Whitacre's bail and called a recess. Crowds of reporters and observers filed out of the courtroom. Many received copies of Whitacre's printed, official statement, acknowledging that he had reviewed and signed the plea agreement. Near the bottom of the single page, one phrase stood out in bold italics.

"I regret participating in the money conspiracies **that were approved by upper management**," it read.

Thirty minutes later, D'Angelo called Herndon.

"Look, I know this is going to be awkward, but you're the first person I've called," D'Angelo said. "Whitacre entered a plea today at two-thirty."

"What?"

"Sorry. I was ordered not to say anything."

Herndon thanked D'Angelo and hung up, annoyed. Even if Whitacre wouldn't work out a price-fixing deal, both Shepard and Herndon had wanted to be at the plea. Now, the bickering with the Fraud Section had cost them the opportunity. They had lost a chance for closure.

Reaching for the phone, Herndon called Shepard, who was taking a day off at home. He wanted to let his partner know about the Justice Department's latest low blow.

Months later, two Chicago lawyers pushed through the door to the lobby of a La Quinta Inn near Raleigh, North Carolina. They headed for the front desk.

"My name's Sheldon Zenner," the older lawyer said to the clerk. "I'm looking for Bill Walker."

It was December 28, a Sunday. Zenner and his colleague, Sean Berkowitz, were preparing for the trial of their client, Sid Hulse. For months, they had pushed Walker for an interview with Whitacre—the man Hulse said had approved everything. Whitacre was key to Hulse's defense.

Walker arrived in the lobby dressed in sweats, with shoes but no socks. He led the lawyers to a sitting area, near a buffet table offering a continental breakfast. Zenner and Berkowitz hesitated. This was not the right place for a private discussion. The moment seemed surreal.

"I've been using this as my office away from my office," Walker said. "Lets me work near Dr. Whitacre."

The Chicago lawyers sat.

"Dr. Whitacre is very supportive of Sid Hulse," Walker said. "He feels terrible about getting Sid involved in this and will certainly do what he can to help out."

For more than an hour, the lawyers discussed ground rules for the interview. Then, Whitacre arrived, looking relaxed and chipper, and found a seat. Hotel guests walked nearby, carrying cereal and muffins to their tables.

"Okay," Whitacre said. "What do you want to know?"

Two months later, on February 6, the fraud team met with Whitacre in the same hotel lobby. They listened angrily as he described his discussions with Hulse's lawyers; Whitacre had canceled a meeting with the government about the same time, claiming to be too busy. But the biggest problem now was that just weeks before trial, Whitacre was changing his story about Sid Hulse.

As Walker rested on a nearby couch, Whitacre told a jumbled tale, contradicting himself from one sentence to the next. Mackay and D'Angelo had no doubt that he was once again adjusting his story, this time to protect Hulse.

Whitacre said he had advised Hulse that there was no need to pay taxes on the illegal money until he brought it back to the United States; then, he claimed to have no memory of discussing taxes with Hulse. The cash that Hulse had kicked back to Whitacre from the first three-hundred-thousand-dollar payment was a loan, he said— apparently forgetting that he had already admitted this was a cover story cooked up years before. Other money that went to Hulse from ADM included the repayment of the loan, Whitacre said.

"Wait a minute," D'Angelo said. "If you owed one hundred thousand dollars, why was Hulse recouping that money through ADM?"

Whitacre blinked, pausing. "I don't remember the reason," he said finally.

The contradictions continued for hours. Whitacre would change the meaning behind a payment again and again, struggling to extract Hulse from his thicket of crimes.

When the interview ended, Don Mackay headed for the exit,

fuming. How could Whitacre be so stupid? He had cut a deal to cooperate, he hadn't been sentenced, and now—on the eve of Hulse's
trial—he was *changing his story*?

"Can you believe this shit?" Mackay growled.

"It's pretty unbelievable, Don," D'Angelo said.

At that moment, Mackay shelved any plans of seeking a reduction
of Whitacre's sentence. *Let him do the max.*

Mackay looked at D'Angelo.

"We're gonna hammer that SOB," he said.

Packages and letters from Whitacre began arriving in government and
corporate offices around the country. Some simply contained a letter;
others came with a packet of supporting documents. Some even included audiotapes.

Copies of the same letter went to Janet Reno, Jim Griffin, and
Robin Mann. In three short paragraphs, Whitacre acknowledged making mistakes during his time as a cooperating witness and apologized.

Some prosecutors also received copies of an affidavit signed by
Whitacre. On page 5 was a section that stopped all of them in their
tracks.

"Regarding Brian Shepard," it was headed.

In the next five paragraphs, Whitacre confessed—in a roundabout
way—that he had made up the allegations that Shepard had instructed
him to destroy tapes.

"I did turn in every tape of ADM and its competitors with no exceptions," he wrote. "Furthermore, no tapes were altered at any time."

Whitacre explained that the idea for lying about Shepard had
come from a former ADM executive. This person, he said, had persuaded him that ADM would drop its lawsuits against Whitacre if he
told the Shepard story. Whitacre wrote that no record of his conversations with this executive would exist, since they had only spoken on
pay telephones, using untraceable phone cards.

At the same time, other packages arrived for staffers at Biomar.
Whitacre's relationship with his new employer had ended after he had
pleaded guilty in the fall. Biomar had then canceled certain stock
awards given to Whitacre, saying that he had failed to work there long
enough to vest.

Nelson Campbell, a company cofounder, knew that the move had
made Whitacre furious, and the new package alerted him that his former chief executive would not give up his stock so easily. Campbell

first heard from a distraught employee who had received a thick envelope from Whitacre; others phoned him soon afterward. One at a time, Biomar staffers who by then were aware of the contents brought their packages to Campbell unopened.

Warily, Campbell popped one open. Inside was a twenty-four-page affidavit and a cassette. Campbell read the affidavit but became so distressed that he was unable to continue. Whitacre was accusing him of a series of wrongdoings. Not only that, but Whitacre said he had been secretly taping his Biomar colleagues, using the recorder he purchased during Harvest King. Copies of the material, Whitacre wrote, had been sent to the Justice Department and the Securities and Exchange Commission for investigation.*

Campbell shook his head as he read the document. *Every criminal accusation was a lie.* Some allegations had some vague basis in truth. The company had talked with its lawyers about complying with laws forbidding the bribery of foreign officials; in Whitacre's version, that became part of an effort to hand out bribes. Eventually, Campbell listened to the tape that Whitacre had secretly recorded at Biomar.

As he heard himself speak, in conversations many months old, Campbell felt overwhelmed. The words on the tape were not proof of wrongdoing. They were innocuous, meaningless. But as he listened, Campbell thought that the conversation did not play back the way he remembered it. Periodically, there were clicks and stops on the recording, as it seemed to jump around. Campbell shut off the recorder as the realization overtook him.

Whitacre, he thought, had spliced the tape.

At 7:34 on the morning of February 26, the day of Whitacre's scheduled sentencing, Truck 72 from the Chapel Hill Fire Department raced down East Franklin Street with its lights flashing and siren blaring.

Making a turn, the truck pulled to a stop at a house on Deming Road. Jerry Blalock, a firefighter, hopped out of the driver's seat and hustled up the driveway, toward a burgundy Lincoln Continental. As he approached the car, Blalock saw two garden hoses, taped to the car's dual tailpipes and threaded through to the driver's side window.

Sitting in the backseat was a blond, baby-faced man who appeared unconscious. A bible rested in the front seat. Nearby were copies of *Fortune* magazine and other news articles. The firefighters

*None of the allegations were deemed worthy of pursuit.

pulled the man out of the car and gave him oxygen. He seemed alert almost immediately.

"What's your name?" one of the technicians asked.

The man blinked.

"Mark Whitacre," he said.

Hours later, Judge Baker looked out at the lawyers sitting in his court. "Where is the defendant?" he asked.

Bill Walker stood. "Your honor, it's believed he tried to commit suicide this morning at his home."

The prosecutors wanted Whitacre arrested immediately, Walker said. But instead, Walker offered to fly to North Carolina, to bring his client back.

Baker rejected the proposal. He issued a warrant for Whitacre, instructing the U.S. Marshal's Service to take him into custody and bring him back to Urbana.

Whitacre's apparent suicide attempt damaged him greatly. The Chapel Hill police concluded that it had been staged, probably to gain sympathy. The detectives found his demeanor and symptoms were inconsistent with a real attempt, and informed the prosecutors and Judge Baker. Whitacre's sentencing was rescheduled for March 4, 1998.

That day, Bob Herndon pushed open the heavy wooden door to Judge Baker's courtroom, holding it for his wife, Raelene. Herndon had almost decided to stay home. A beloved family pet had died in his arms hours before, and he was emotionally fragile. But Raelene had encouraged him to go; her husband needed to see the case through.

Reporters and onlookers packed the courtroom. The Herndons walked in unnoticed, finding seats near the wall on the right side. The agent saw Ginger Whitacre, up in the first row. He said nothing to her.

He checked his watch. The hearing was scheduled to begin any moment, and Brian Shepard, as usual, was running late. Herndon kept his eye on the door until Shepard walked in. He waved; he had saved his partner a seat.

Minutes later, the lawyers arrived, along with Whitacre, who was escorted by federal marshals. His appearance shocked the agents. His cocky self-confidence was gone. He seemed frightened and small.

Herndon leaned toward Shepard. "He doesn't look very good," he whispered.

"No," Shepard replied, "he doesn't."

The hearing began, with the lawyers arguing about Whitacre's pre-sentence report. Walker objected to the report's conclusion that Whitacre had failed to accept responsibility for his crimes by insisting on the existence of an illegal bonus scheme. Walker said there was even a tape from Harvest King that proved Whitacre's story.

"The government has possession of that tape," he said. "They know that tape exists."

Back in the gallery, Herndon leaned over to Shepard.

"What tape is he talking about?" he whispered.

"I have no idea," Shepard said.

Mackay responded by denying the existence of not only the tape, but of *any* evidence of Whitacre's claims. Once the legal jousting finished, Baker looked to Whitacre.

"Do you want to come stand before the court?" he asked. "You have a right to make a statement if you wish."

Whitacre stood. "I would like to, your honor."

Taking his place at a podium, Whitacre glanced down at his prepared statement. "I appreciate the opportunity to say a few words," he said. "It's been a long five years."

He wanted to be clear that he accepted responsibility for his actions, he said. For a moment, he seemed to glance around the courtroom.

"I apologize to a lot of people in this room," he said. "And to a lot of them who are not in this room for my actions. I apologize greatly."

Whitacre looked back at Judge Baker.

"Your honor, I am here to accept my punishment. That's all."

Judge Baker told Whitacre to remain standing, asking Walker to join his client. Once they were in place, the judge spoke in somber tones.

"This is a task that I approach with sorrow. To observe that Mr. Whitacre is not the usual felon who comes before this court is, of course, a gross understatement."

Most of the defendants he saw, Judge Baker said, were poorly educated, with few opportunities. Yet here was Whitacre, well educated with a supportive family. He had built ADM's Bioproducts Division; his success was meteoric.

"It is not inconceivable that in due course he might have become the CEO of ADM. But interlaced with his success is a tale of mendacity, deceit, coercion, and theft."

Whitacre had manipulated friends and associates, Judge Baker continued. "His motivation was just garden-variety venality and greed."

Whitacre showed no reaction.

"The court can find no clear connection between Mr. Whitacre's bipolar disorder and his criminal conduct. At times, he displays what could easily be characterized as sociopathic behavior. It is difficult to know when Mr. Whitacre is lying and when he is telling the truth."

Throughout the case, Judge Baker said, Whitacre had changed his story; most recently, he had contradicted his earlier statements regarding Sid Hulse.

"What his motivations may be for these contradictory statements to the government is unclear. The result has been greatly to his detriment. He had bargained for a seventy-eight-month recommended sentence, and now faces a possible sentence of double that period of time."

Judge Baker looked at Whitacre.

"It's the judgment of this court that the defendant be committed to the custody of the Attorney General of the United States or her authorized representative for the term of one hundred and eight months," Judge Baker said. "That's the minimum guidelines sentence in this case, and the court feels that under all of the circumstances, that's adequate."

One hundred and eight months. Nine years in prison. The rest of the sentence seemed insignificant; Whitacre was ordered to make restitution to ADM. With interest, the total came to more than $11 million.

Still, Whitacre showed no reaction. Judge Baker recessed the hearing and left the courtroom. The marshals approached Whitacre to take him back to jail. Shepard and Herndon watched as their former cooperating witness was escorted through the courtroom's back door. For years, they had anguished over this man. But now, their emotions were a jumble. Their feelings were torn between the friend they had known and the liar they had come to know.

The agents left the courtroom. Reporters surrounded Mackay, as Shepard and Herndon passed largely unnoticed. In the lobby, they donned sunglasses and headed outside. An alert television cameraman saw them, and began filming as they walked to their cars parked at a neighboring shopping mall. Eventually, the cameraman went on his way.

In the dimming light of the late afternoon, the agents and Raelene stood by Herndon's minivan and talked. About Whitacre, how he looked, how he seemed, what he said.

"Hey," Herndon said. "What did you think about it when Mark said he had hurt people in the courtroom?"

Shepard shook his head. "Mark doesn't realize how many people he's hurt," he said softly.

About the same time, Whitacre ducked his head as marshals placed him handcuffed in the backseat of the car that would return him to the Decatur County Jail, where he was being held. As the car pulled away, Whitacre glanced out the window and saw a television camera. He waved.

At the jail, the marshals checked Whitacre back in. As they waited, another prisoner noticed them. The sentencing had already been all over the television news. The prisoner recognized Whitacre's face.

"Hey," the prisoner said. "That's you! Ain't you the guy I just saw on TV?"

Whitacre turned to the man, a smile on his face.

"Yes," he replied happily. "I am."

EPILOGUE

Opening arguments in the criminal price-fixing trial of Mick Andreas, Terry Wilson, and Mark Whitacre were heard on July 15, 1998, in courtroom 2125 of Chicago's Dirksen Federal Building. Scores of spectators attended, seated in rows of curved benches separated from the well of the courtroom. Television monitors were scattered around the space, allowing for easy viewing of the many videotapes that prosecutors promised would be featured during the trial.

Jim Griffin walked to the front of the jury box, facing the twelve jurors and six alternates. Behind him, many of the major participants in the case sat at four crowded counsel tables. Mick Andreas, dressed in a blue suit with a multicolored tie, brought his hand to his chin as Griffin prepared to speak. Nearby, a haggard Terry Wilson listened as he sat beside his lawyers, sucking on a tic tac. But Yamada of Ajinomoto was nowhere to be seen; although he remained under indictment, he had not returned to America to face the charges.

Another person was also conspicuous in his absence. Against the advice of his lawyer and the trial judge, Blanche Manning, Mark Whitacre had chosen not to attend. During the many weeks of trial, Whitacre, who was only a few months into his sentence for fraud, would have been housed in a maximum-security prison near the courtroom. The day before, he had told Judge Manning that he wanted to return to his minimum-security facility in North Carolina, where he felt safer and the food was better.

At the prosecution table, Herndon and Shepard sat beside each other, ready to assist with any last-minute questions. This was the moment both agents had lived for during the past three years—the chance for vindication. The flood of accusations against them—by ADM, by Whitacre, by the government itself—had taken a toll. Even

Judge Manning, ruling against a defense motion to throw out the tapes, had condemned the agents for failing to better control Whitacre. But now, just being in the courtroom was the personal testament that they had survived the attacks on their professionalism and character. They were on the government's team; they were the experts. As they listened to Griffin detail the prosecution's case to the jury, the agents felt a growing sense of redemption. This trial would be the living affirmation of their work.

"Michael Andreas and Terrance Wilson were caught red-handed on audio- and videotape, committing the crime that they're charged with," Griffin said to the jury. "Because Mark Whitacre cooperated, we have several different types of evidence, of taped evidence."

But, Griffin told the jurors, Whitacre had committed his own crimes by stealing money from ADM, and so he, too, had been charged with price-fixing. The defendants would be talking a lot about Whitacre, he said, and attacking the investigation. But the jurors could trust the case.

"As so often happens when there's a mountain of evidence against you, you better attack something, and that's what you're going to hear," Griffin said. "We're going to put these agents on the stand so they can tell you how they conducted this investigation. They followed the rules, and they collected this mountain of evidence."

Griffin finished shortly before two o'clock, and Judge Manning called a lunch recess. The lawyers then met in the judge's chambers, to debate a motion submitted by the defendants. Shepard and Herndon were not invited to attend.

The trial resumed at 3:00 sharp. Before the jury arrived, lawyers sparred for a few minutes about a new defense objection. Judge Manning dispatched the matter quickly, overruling the defense. She turned to a marshal.

"Get the jury, please," she said.

Mark Hulkower, one of Wilson's lawyers, stood. The defense wanted to renew its motion to preclude Shepard and Herndon from attending the trial, he said. They were both scheduled to be government witnesses. Their reliability and credibility would be a central part of the defense. Neither should be allowed the benefit of hearing other testimony, Hulkower argued—implying that the agents might change their statements to match those of other witnesses.

Judge Manning, standing behind her chair in a blue robe, looked to the prosecutors.

"At this time what I'm going to do is I will abide by the ruling that I made in chambers," she began. "The government can elect one of these two."

For a second, there was silence. The courtroom's overhead fluorescent lights flickered.

Mutchnik stood. The prosecutors had considered this a possibility, but he knew that neither agent had been properly prepared for it.

"Your honor," he began, "could the government propose that during the opening statements, since it's not evidence, it's not likely to affect either of their testimony—"

"No, counsel," Manning interrupted. "I have ruled. Make your selection."

Mutchnik stood in the center of the courtroom. He was out of options.

"We'll elect Agent Herndon," he said.

"To remain?" Judge Manning asked.

"To remain."

"Okay."

Mutchnik began to ask whether the ruling might be reconsidered, when Judge Manning interrupted him.

"Agent Shepard?" she said simply. "You may leave the courtroom."

Shepard blinked. The courtroom was silent. Herndon shook his head. It took every ounce of Shepard's strength to stay silent, to contain his outrage at Judge Manning's ruling. He gathered his belongings and stood.

"I'm sorry," Judge Manning said.

As he walked through the gallery, Shepard could feel hundreds of eyes on him, the eyes of strangers and of friends. All searching his character, looking for the flaw that led to his ejection from the courtroom. It seemed like a public branding, a statement to the world that somehow, Brian Shepard had done something improper.

After all he had sacrificed to this case—his family time, his career opportunities, even his reputation—Shepard's chance for redemption had been turned on its head. He felt humiliated and betrayed before the entire world. Only this time, he thought, it was the people he counted as friends who had abandoned him.

That afternoon, Shepard was on a couch in his hotel room, reading *The Partner*, a Grisham thriller. He was doing his best to control his emotions. But he was failing.

A knock came at the door. It was Herndon and Mutchnik, the two people who had grown closest to Shepard during the turbulent years of Harvest King. Both felt devastated. It was as if they had gone to war and left a man behind. Mutchnik, as the prosecutor responsible for handling the issue, in particular felt that he had let down his friend. The choice had not been meant to condemn Shepard; Herndon, who had spent so many long hours summarizing the tapes, had an almost encyclopedic recall of their contents. It was a critical skill that the prosecutors needed for trial.

Their dismay about Shepard only worsened when he came to the door. His eyes were red; he appeared to have been crying. Worse, since he was now a sequestered witness, Shepard could not be told about the day's testimony. It was as if he was not a member of the team at all.

In the hotel room, Shepard raged about the ruling.

"How could she make this decision?" he asked. "What's wrong with having two agents, if you can have one?"

Mutchnik tried explaining the legal issues, but his words rang hollow. "Listen," he finally said, "why don't we take you out? Maybe grab some pizza and beer."

Shepard agreed, and the three headed behind the hotel to Giordano's, a well-known Chicago pizza maker. But any hopes that dinner would improve things rapidly collapsed. Shepard could not get past his pain. Watching their friend suffer, both Herndon and Mutchnik started to cry.

"Brian, I'm so sorry," Mutchnik said tearfully. "This was my job. I feel like I failed you."

Herndon wiped his eyes. "I didn't just lose a partner in there. I feel like I've lost my best friend."

The emotional dinner ended, and Mutchnik headed off to catch a train home. Shepard and Herndon walked back to the hotel, taking the elevator to their rooms.

The doors opened on Shepard's floor. Herndon swallowed, and patted his friend on the back.

"Have a good night's sleep," he said. "I'll see you tomorrow morning. We'll walk over to Antitrust together."

Shepard nodded, and walked away.

In the morning, as Herndon was getting ready to leave his room, Shepard called. He would not be coming with him.

"I've been up all night," Shepard said. "I really didn't get much sleep."

"Okay," Herndon said. "So what do you want to do?"

"I want to get packed," he replied. "I just want to go home."

• • •

With his return to Decatur, Shepard's anger worsened. He came to suspect—wrongly—that Herndon had played some role in the outcome, to ensure he stayed at the trial. After all the damage done to Shepard by this investigation, he was unable to deal with the disappointments anymore.

He cut off communications. He refused to answer telephone calls from the antitrust team to the Decatur R.A.; if they left a message requesting material, he would fax it to them without comment. Calls to his home were answered by his wife, Diana, who refused to put Shepard on the line.

Herndon sought out Jim Griffin and told the prosecutor that he wanted to trade places with Shepard. He wanted to look out for his friend; after seeing Shepard so devastated, he was willing to give up his spot at the prosecution table, no matter how gut-wrenching the decision. But Griffin turned aside the request. The decision, he said, had been made in the best interest of the case.

Distraught, Herndon sat down at a computer during a trial break and typed out a letter to his friend.

"Brian," he wrote, "Jim tells me we are now communicating with you via fax. What is up with that? I don't know what happened to you since you left, but obviously you (and Diana) now harbor a belief that I and maybe others conspired behind your back to keep you out of the trial. Nothing could be further from the truth."

Before it happened, he had no idea that only one agent would be allowed to stay in the courtroom, Herndon wrote.

"This non-communication is killing me," he typed. "We are friends. I did not do whatever you think I did. I have been sick over this decision from the moment it was made. I hope that you can work through your emotions."

Herndon faxed the note to Decatur. He returned from trial, hoping to find a message from Shepard in response.

It did not come that day. Or the next.

Early on September 14, Fritz Dujour, a sixty-eight-year-old native of Haiti, slipped on his familiar brown suit and walked from his home on Chicago's southeast side to a nearby bus stop. Later, as the Number 6 rumbled downtown, Dujour wondered if he might have dressed too formally. But he had worn a suit every day during his thirty-five years as a city engineer; he could certainly do the same this morning, when he was expected to vote on the guilt or innocence of three ADM executives charged with crimes.

The price-fixing trial had finally gone to the jury, almost two months after opening arguments. For all the cautions issued by the lawyers about the case's complexity, for the most part the issues seemed pretty simple. Hard to believe at times, but simple.

At the federal building, Dujour took the elevator to the twenty-first floor, walking the familiar path to the jury room. The smell of freshly brewed coffee greeted him in the hallway; someone had obviously put to use the Kitchen Gourmet coffeemaker that he had brought in weeks before. Opening the door, Dujour bid good morning to two jurors who had arrived earlier in the sterile jury room. He poured some coffee into a Styrofoam cup, and slid into a leather chair at the head of the table.

Within a few minutes, all twelve jurors had arrived. Janet Hale, a bubbly, exuberant woman who had been elected foreperson, brought the deliberations to order. For days, they reviewed tapes, debated, and cajoled. The first vote they took was on Whitacre; for some reason, the jurors agreed that his role was the easiest to address. The discussion about him lasted about an hour.

"We're all satisfied," Hale said. "We might as well vote."

In alphabetical order, she called on each juror one at a time. The first vote was unanimous.

Two more times, the jurors repeated the procedure. Review, debate, and vote. By Wednesday afternoon, they had reached verdicts on all three defendants. They chose to sleep on their decision for one day. The next morning, they returned to the jury room and reviewed what they had done. Everyone remained satisfied. Hale summoned the marshal who was seated outside the jury room.

"We've reached a unanimous verdict," she said.

In the antitrust office, prosecutors and agents were in the middle of a game of Nerf basketball. Shepard was there; a series of meetings had finally been held with him, where he had been assured that Herndon had played no role in excluding him from the trial. Shepard still felt deeply wounded by the slight, but had ended his self-imposed exile. He did not want to miss the verdict.

Overhead, the group heard a page for Jim Griffin and then Marvin Price, his deputy. Instantly, they understood. There was a verdict. The Nerf ball was tossed aside, and the players grabbed their suit jackets.

The lawyers, agents, and defendants found their seats in the packed courtroom. Forty-five minutes passed, until finally the marshal brought in the jury. Several jurors felt intimidated by the size of the crowd. They stared at the ground as they found their seats.

Herndon studied the faces, looking for a sign, a clue.

Nothing.

"Good afternoon, ladies and gentlemen," Judge Manning said to the jurors. "I received your note indicating that you have reached verdicts. Who speaks as foreperson?"

Hale identified herself.

"Ms. Hale, has the jury reached unanimous verdicts as to all three defendants?"

"Yes, we have."

"All right," Judge Manning said. "Would you please hand the verdict forms to the court security officer?"

The papers were passed from Hale to the officer, who handed them up to Judge Manning. She glanced over them. A look of apparent surprise registered on her face.

"All right," Judge Manning told the jurors. "I want you to listen very carefully because afterwards you will be polled as to whether or not this is and was your verdict."

The judge looked down at the sheets in front of her. Several prosecutors stared straight ahead, motionless. Herndon, his heart pounding, looked at Mick Andreas. Judge Manning began to read.

"We, the jury, find the defendant Michael D. Andreas guilty as charged in the indictment."

Herndon turned his eyes away from Andreas, looking at the back of Mutchnik's head. He swallowed and heard the word *guilty* two more times. All three men had been convicted. Herndon whispered his thanks to the jurors, then glanced toward Shepard.

His partner, his friend, looked back and gave him a nod. The hearing wrapped up in a matter of minutes. Everyone remained in place until the last juror filed out. Herndon and Shepard stood, emotional and shaky, and walked toward each other.

And there, in the center of the courtroom, the two agents embraced.

Sunlight cut through the morning haze, flickering in the passing trees. Just past a Chevrolet dealership, I turned left off of Route 25 north. Mobile homes lay scattered on the side of the road, amidst lush greenery. A water tower loomed over the trees. To the left, a brown sign appeared, reading, "U.S. Department of Justice, Federal Bureau of

Prisons." I had reached the Federal Correctional Institution in Edgefield, South Carolina. Mark Whitacre's new home.

In the months before my visit that day, the decisions that Whitacre made over the years had largely finished playing out. Mick Andreas and Terry Wilson were both sentenced to two years in prison. Whitacre received two and a half years, but Judge Manning allowed six months of that to run concurrent with his term for fraud. In her ruling, Judge Manning found that Whitacre was a leader of the price-fixing conspiracy, which increased his time under the sentencing guidelines. No such finding was made for Andreas and Wilson.* Manning explained the apparent discrepancy, saying that Bill Walker had been the only defense lawyer not to object to the designation.

The FBI agents whose lives had been affected by Whitacre returned to their jobs. Brian Shepard remained as senior resident agent in Decatur, where he frequently spoke of retiring. Bob Herndon received a transfer back to Kansas City, where he worked on a squad that handled health-care and securities-fraud cases. Tony D'Angelo stayed with the Chicago Field Office and found himself involved in a price-fixing investigation with some of the Harvest King prosecutors. His partner, Mike Bassett, continues to live and work in Albany, New York.

Many of the prosecutors also saw changes in their lives. Jim Griffin, partly as a reward for his work in Harvest King, was promoted to a position in Washington and was eventually named a Deputy Assistant Attorney General for the Antitrust Division, replacing Gary Spratling, who moved to private practice. Scott Lassar was named United States Attorney for Chicago immediately before the price-fixing trial, leading the prosecutions of federal crimes in that district for years. Robin Mann continued working as an antitrust prosecutor; Jim Mutchnik took a job with a Chicago law firm. In the Fraud Section, Mary Spearing left for private practice, while Jim Nixon joined the National Association of Securities Dealers. Don Mackay continued at the Justice Department.

People associated with Whitacre during his career experienced varying ripple effects on their lives. Just days after Whitacre's sentencing, Sid Hulse gave up his fight, pleading guilty to conspiracy and tax fraud. He was sentenced to ten months in prison. David Hoech—the Lamet Vov—continued his letter-writing campaign against ADM,

---

*In a ruling issued June 26, 2000, the Seventh Circuit Court of Appeals declared Manning in error in this decision, and ordered her to resentence Andreas and Wilson to longer prison terms.

often accusing the government of selling out Whitacre and the shareholders by cutting the plea deal with the company.

The Zurich district attorney kept open the investigation of Beat Schweizer, although Whitacre now steadfastly maintains that the Swiss money manager knew nothing of his crimes. The Mobile investigation was ended with no charges brought against Chris Jones or Tim Hall, the former Degussa employees, and no evidence that either knew anything about Whitacre's frauds.

Biomar International recovered from the Whitacre whirlwind. It has since changed its name and is planning a public offering of stock. Colin and Nelson Campbell have told associates that the Whitacre experience has steeled their commitment to business ethics; both men are now exploring methods of contributing their stock in the company to a philanthropic foundation they hope to form.

Some of the most dramatic repercussions were felt by people in other industries, many who never knew Whitacre. ADM evidence of price-fixing in the citric-acid market led to guilty pleas from numerous multinational corporations—including giants like Hoffman-LaRoche and an affiliate of Bayer AG—which had participated in the conspiracies. That, in turn, indirectly helped provide evidence used in a criminal investigation of price-fixing in the huge multibillion-dollar market for vitamins. Several executives pleaded guilty in the vitamins case, including Kuno Sommer, the Hoffman-LaRoche official whom Whitacre had tried to record discussing the citric-acid conspiracy. Eventually, about thirty different grand juries investigated price-fixing in almost every corner of the food and feed industry; by 1999, the government had obtained more than $1 billion in fines. In the wake of Harvest King, it has become apparent that price-fixing was a workaday endeavor around the globe, involving scores of corporations and executives.

And yet.

The only person to step forward and reveal these crimes—despite his bizarre reasons for doing so—was Mark Whitacre. It took someone as deeply troubled as he—a man so reckless he would steal millions of dollars while working for the FBI—to tip the first domino in what has emerged as a multibillion-dollar criminal enterprise.

Cooperating witnesses rarely are without flaws. In the 1970s, Detective Robert Leuci—the so-called Prince of the City—exposed corruption on a grand scale in New York's legal system, from the police station to the courthouse. And yet, in the end, it was Leuci himself who emerged as perhaps the most corrupt of all, having committed numerous crimes and then perjuring himself about them. In recognition of his assistance, Leuci was never indicted. But in that instance, the same prosecutors who ran the case helped investigate their witness. Unlike in the Whitacre case, no artificial separations were imposed for political or bureaucratic reasons. Prosecutors could judge Leuci based on the whole picture. They understood that few cooperating witnesses are pure—an unreasonable expectation that could easily cripple law enforcement's ability to obtain evidence of crimes.

It is hard to argue that Whitacre should never have served time in jail; his unending lies and flip-flops as he desperately tried to avoid responsibility for his actions guaranteed a substantial prison term. But it does seem that the length of Whitacre's sentence was driven more by his self-destructive tendencies than by the magnitude of his illegal acts. In the end, it appears the same recklessness that led Whitacre to become a cooperating witness helped to more than double the length of his time in prison.

I met with Whitacre at the Edgefield prison in a small room just off the visitors' area. He looked fit; he had lost weight and had been exercising. The hairpiece that had given him such a youthful appearance was gone now. If not for his green prison jumper, he would have looked more like a corporate executive than he ever had before.

For hours, we reviewed his experiences. He frequently contradicted the written record—at times, he even contradicted other statements he made in the same interview. Despite the findings of two psychiatrists—and the evidence from his own actions—Whitacre is no longer medicated for psychiatric conditions; he says the Bureau of Prisons has found him in perfect mental health.

Even from prison, he had continued to insist that the money he stole was part of a vast corporate conspiracy. For the second time, I confronted him with the evidence of his deceptions. There was nothing to support his story of an under-the-table bonus scheme; everything pointed toward the probability that he had simply stolen the money.

Whitacre argued, bringing up various events that he said supported his story. Point by point, we discussed them.

Finally, he nodded. "All right, I'll tell you the truth," he said. "The only other person who knows this is Ginger. But I'll tell you."

For more than four hours, Whitacre confessed. Shortly after arriving at the company, he said, he had heard rumors that some executives had engaged in corporate frauds—yet no one seemed to care. And indeed, just two years after Whitacre's arrival at ADM, the corporate treasurer left the company amidst allegations of financial wrongdoing, yet no criminal action was ever taken.

Stealing seemed to pose little risk of punishment. And so, Whitacre stole. "They're criminals," he said. "What are they going to do if they catch me? How could they risk having a criminal case?"

Was he admitting that there were no approvals by senior managers for his money transfers?

"The bottom line," he said, "is that I started taking money for my own personal use from shareholders, with no approvals whatsoever."

The later multimillion-dollar thefts, he said, only came about when he believed the investigation was coming to a close. He feared that the case put his finances at risk and decided to steal more to protect himself.

"If I was never working under cover, I never would have taken so much," he said. "It was my way out. It was my severance, you know? I wrote my own severance."

Still, Whitacre denied that the Fujiwara episode had simply been another attempt to defraud ADM of millions—he never would have taken money that way, he said. He also disagreed with the conclusion of FBI investigators that the Nigerian fraud had been a driving force behind his thefts. Even without it, he said, he would have stolen the money.

Of course, it's impossible to know whether Whitacre is actually telling the truth. Much of his story remains incomprehensible. Just because he thought he could steal, why did he do it? And once he was caught, why didn't he simply confess?

"I don't know," he responded. "If I could explain that, I probably wouldn't be here."

Whitacre said he maintained the lie to everyone, including his wife. He only told Ginger the truth about his thefts during one of her many visits to prison. She understood, he said, and forgave him.

During our conversation, he often spoke lovingly of his family. Ginger and the children have moved nearby so that they can visit him every weekend. Both Mark and Ginger said their marriage is as strong as ever. In fact, he said, almost everything about prison was better than the years that followed his decision to become a cooperating witness.

"I felt like when I was at ADM, I lived so many lives," he said. "I wasn't sure who I was. Does that make any sense? If I was with Brian

Shepard, I was an informant. If I was with Mick and Terry, I was Mr. ADM. It was pretty stressful, no doubt about it."

Whitacre said that he has spent his jail time studying, earning multiple degrees by mail in law and psychology. If he could spend the rest of his daylight hours with his family and at school, he said, he wouldn't mind returning to prison every night.

"Today, I know more who I am and what I really want out of life," he said. "I've gained my life back. I feel the way I want to feel. I sleep better in prison than I have since I don't know how long. My mind's at ease."

"So," I asked, "if you could push a button, and it would let you come out of prison and be back at ADM?"

Whitacre smiled. "I wouldn't push it, ain't no way," he said. "I'm happy now."

Bob Strauss stood before his fellow ADM directors, smiling as he looked toward his friend, Dwayne Andreas. They had gathered in Miami to honor Andreas, who was stepping down as ADM chairman after a quarter century.

"This is a man I cannot praise highly enough," Strauss said. "He has always had the miraculous ability to move through different worlds—agricultural, political, international. And he has left his mark on them all."

The tributes to Andreas continued for hours, even as the directors celebrated his replacement. Allen Andreas, Dwayne's nephew, was assuming the top job, taking the position that his cousin Mick had been groomed for during most of his life. In many ways, it was an odd closing of the circle. It was Allen who had placed the original call to the CIA in 1992 about possible saboteurs at ADM—the call that set in motion the events that led to Mick's downfall.

After three hours, the meeting broke. The directors headed downstairs, where limousines waited. Dwayne climbed into the front seat of a car; in the back were mostly family members who came for the big day. As the car headed to the airport, a sense of tragedy hung over the group. An era was passing, in a way no one had planned. Mick, Dwayne's son, his chosen successor, was now a convicted felon. This was a turning point where the reality of everything that had been lost could not be shunted aside.

The limousines arrived at the airport, driving to the tarmac where corporate planes were ready to whisk board members back to their homes. A number of the directors were already out of their cars, waiting for their friend. Dwayne emerged from the front seat, taking a moment as others in his car climbed out. Among them was his daughter, Sandy. The emotional moment was proving to be too much for her. Tears filled her eyes. She looked into her father's face.

"Oh, Dad," she said.

Andreas opened his arms and clutched his daughter. Together, they stood near the car, both sobbing with an overwhelming sadness.

Standing nearby, the directors and family friends averted their eyes, not wishing to intrude on so private a moment. Then they turned, leaving Dwayne Andreas and his daughter alone in their tears, as they made their way across the tarmac to the awaiting planes.

POSTSCRIPT

By 2000, Mark Whitacre appeared to have achieved a new sense of balance in his life, finally seeming more comfortable with the truth than with lies. Following the publication of *The Informant*, Whitacre would admit his deceits again and again, in television interviews and in communications with the government. As he wrote in a letter to me, by having admitted the truth in our final interview, he was finally able to get beyond his bizarre experiences of the past.

With encouragement from government officials, Whitacre applied for executive clemency from the President. He seemed a strong candidate. His self-destructive history, driven by his psychological difficulties, had left him with a sentence that took no account of his unprecedented cooperation in exposing one of the largest corporate conspiracies in history.

The application received substantial support. FBI agents spoke publicly about their discomfort with the sentence, or wrote letters to the Justice Department expressing their belief that Whitacre should be released. United States senators, including John Ashcroft, the future Attorney General, asked the department to consider the application carefully. For the first time in years, Whitacre and his family felt hopeful.

On January 7, 2001, President Bill Clinton appeared at a policy forum in New York's Waldorf-Astoria hotel. There, a number of important figures, including Dwayne Andreas, were being honored. And on that evening, Clinton made clear that politicians would not be backing away from Andreas despite the revelations of widespread corruption at his company.

"I want to congratulate Dwayne Andreas, my good friend," Clinton said, "and thank him for his many kindnesses to me."

Twelve days later, on his last day in office, Bill Clinton signed 176 pardons and commutations—bestowing executive mercy on two fugitives, a felon under active criminal investigation, and a drug dealer. Many of the controversial recipients had connections to campaign contributors or others with influence at the White House—a fact that led to congressional hearings and a criminal investigation.

But Mark Whitacre was passed over. He remains in federal prison.

AFTERWORD

This is a book about the malleable nature of truth. As the story shows, reality can serve as the handmaiden of fiction—real phone records may document a call, yet the substance of a conversation can be twisted into any meaning. Throughout these pages, I've tried to play upon that line between fact and fantasy. While everything described in this book occurred, the story was intentionally structured to lend temporary credence to some of the many lies told in this investigation. Essentially, I was attempting to put readers in the same uncertain position as the investigators, all while dropping hints—admittedly subtle at times—about where reality began.

Even the title, *The Informant*, was a bit of a deception. While prosecutors and reporters often used the term, under FBI rules, Whitacre was technically not an informant in Harvest King—rather, for reasons of little consequence, he would be classified as a cooperating witness. Instead of alluding to Whitacre's work in the price-fixing case, the title was a reference to his character, one seemingly influenced by mental illness. While he turned in the price-fixers, he also turned on the FBI and his subsequent employer. He informed on possible ADM saboteurs, knowing that the threat was a lie. He repeated rumors against others. He was willing to inform on the failures and crimes—both real and imagined—of everyone other than himself. But in the end, it was Mark Whitacre—a man who remains as puzzling as he is tragic—who was most damaged by his falsehoods.

It is said that truth can set you free. But as this story shows, a corollary also holds true: Lying can leave you imprisoned—in every possible meaning of that word.

Kurt Eichenwald
June 2000

NOTES AND SOURCES

This book grew out of my five years of coverage in the *New York Times* of the scandals at the Archer Daniels Midland Company. It is based on more than eight hundred hours of interviews, many of which were tape-recorded, with more than one hundred participants, as well as thousands of documents. Every person who appears in a significant role in these events was contacted—either directly, through a repre-sentative, or both—and offered an opportunity to be interviewed.

The documents include investigative notes of interviews, internal government teletypes and e-mails, personal diaries and notes, sched-ule books, expense and travel records, telephone logs, filings with the Securities and Exchange Commission, confidential corporate and gov-ernment memos, grand jury testimony, sworn statements, books, and news clippings. Among the most important documents I relied on were transcripts of the tapes recorded during Harvest King, as well as copies of certain of the audio- and videotapes themselves.

Many of the interviews were conducted on condition of ano-nymity. However, none of the participants in any of these interviews will be named. That is because, in a book, identifying those who spoke on the record makes it far easier to determine those who did not.

To ensure accuracy in a story involving so many people who have lied, I established a "pyramid of credibility." Tapes and transcripts were at the base; they trumped all other recollections or documents. Sec-ond were contemporaneous documents—teletypes, expense records and travel documents, contemporaneous diaries, notes and memos, schedule books, phone logs. Just above that were 302s, but only for establishing what was said at an interview, not necessarily for the underlying truth of the statements. Third were sworn statements and testimony. Last were interviews. In essence, the story was built on a foundation of documents, then fleshed out with information from interviews that was corroborated by those records.

Most taped dialogue appears as it did in the transcripts. However, the conversations are not presented in their entirety. A transcript of a single conversation can take up hundreds of pages, enough to fill this entire book. So, in the taped dialogue, I have edited the conversations down to portions that communicate the essence of the discussion. Such editing was usually done in blocks—in other words, whole sections were kept together for both fairness and accuracy.

At times, participants made statements that, even in context, were difficult to interpret. It is the nature of conversation that a few participants will wander away from the main point, or throw out an idea that is simply off the topic. If I could not understand the point of a statement, and the speaker was unable or unwilling to explain to me its meaning, the statement and all surrounding dialogue were not used.

Finally, some taped dialogue was edited for clarity. Oftentimes, speakers would interrupt each other, repeat themselves midsentence, use confusing grammar, or break up their conversation with frequent nonverbal sounds. If the statement could be easily understood without editing out those unnecessary elements, it appears in this book exactly as it was spoken. In those rare instances where cluttering, meaningless elements made the statements too hard to easily understand, they were edited out. In two instances, recollections from interviews were used to fill in a word or two that were unintelligible on the tapes. None of the words recalled by participants were incriminating in any way, and fit perfectly in context.

The transcripts themselves are not sacred texts; transcripts of tapes from two different devices that recorded the same meeting sometimes contained different interpretations of what was said. In such instances, I have gone with the fullest transcript whenever possible. Twice, the transcripts clashed with what sounded to me like clear words spoken on the actual tape. This only happened in instances where the transcribed statements made no sense in context. Those two instances are explained in these notes.

All other dialogue and quotations come from participants or witnesses to conversations, or documents that describe the discussion. In a few instances, secondary sources were informed of events or conversations by a participant. If those secondary sources agreed on what they were told—and it was corroborated by documents—the information was used. Such dialogue and events were never incriminating.

Because of the many sources used in reconstructing dialogue, readers should not assume that any individual participant in a conversation is the source of the statement or even among the sources. When the text describes someone as having thought or felt something, it comes either directly from that individual, from a document written by that individual, notes or other records of that individual's comments to a third party, or others to whom the people in question directly described their experience.

Of course, I am not claiming that this is a perfect transcript of everything that was said and done during this eight-year story. It does, however, represent the best recollection of these events and conversations and more accurately reflects reality than mere paraphrase would. Invariably in the course of my interviews with participants, they would find that my pressing them for specific details and words led to greater recall of the events, or of ideas for records that might help them to better remember what happened. People who began an interview claiming a poor memory often were eventually able to reconstruct tiny details of events, which matched the recollections of others.

In some instances, I was unable to determine the precise date that an event occurred. In those cases, I have presented the relevant scene at the point in the narrative that is most consistent with the apparent timing in other documents and interviews. When that occurs, I give no indication of the event's date.

Descriptions of individual settings come from interviews, documents, or personal observation. Most details of weather conditions come from records on file with the National Climatic Data Center.

PROLOGUE

1 Some details of the Country Club of Decatur from personal observation, as well as a series of 1995 photographs included with some of the organization's promotional materials. Also from Robert W. and Maxine Kopetz, *The History of the Country Club of Decatur*, 1993.

1–4 Some details of Wilson interview from FBI notes of interview, known as an FD-302 for case #60A-SI-46290.

4–6 Dialogue between Whitacre, Wilson, and Mick Andreas from a transcript of FBI tape #1B138, dated June 27, 1995.

6–7 Some details of Whitacre's meeting with the FBI on the evening of June 27, 1995, from an FD-302 of that date. Other details from an FD-504b from that night, an FBI document that describes the chain of custody for an original tape recording.

CHAPTER ONE

11 The 1992 visits to Decatur by Gorbachev and Quayle were described in a history of the Decatur Airport, which can be found on the Internet at http://www.decatur-airport.org/html/history.html.

11 Details of Andreas's political contributions from Jill Abramson and Phil Kuntz, "Antitrust Probe of Archer Daniels Puts Spotlight on Chairman Andreas's Vast Political Influence," *Wall Street Journal*, July 11, 1995, p. A18; "Hedging Bets," *Wall Street Journal*, May 29, 1992, p. A1; "Archer Daniels Tops List of Political Contributors," *Wall Street Journal*, August 14, 1991, p. A10. Also, Andreas was featured in a 1998 *Frontline* broadcast, "So You Want to Buy a President." See www.pbs.org/wgbh/pages/frontline/president/players/andreas.

12 The laundering of Andreas's twenty-five-thousand-dollar contribution into the account of a Watergate burglar was described by Bernard Gwertzman, "GAO Report Asks Justice Inquiry into GOP Funds," *New York Times*, August 27, 1972, p. A1. Andreas's indictment for the one-hundred-thousand-dollar Humphrey contribution was described in "Cox Charges Illegal Gift to Humphrey," *New York Times*, October 20, 1973, p. 17.

12 The description of the Reagan statue and the other information about Decatur and ADM's role there from E. J. Kahn Jr.'s detailed 1991 book about the company entitled *Supermarketer to the World* (Warner Books, 1991), pp. 9–14.

12–16 Some details of the September 10, 1992, visit by Ajinomoto to the ADM headquarters from the trial testimony of Kanji Mimoto, in the case of *United States of America v. Michael D. Andreas et al.*, number 96CR762, as well as in the testimony of Hirokazu Ikeda from the same trial, and the FD-302s of Mimoto, Ikeda, and Fujiwara dated July 1996.

13 Two excellent books analyzing the Japanese negotiating styles and the psychology of Japanese businessmen were written by the same man, Robert M. March. They are entitled *The Japanese Negotiator* (Kodansha International, 1991) and *Reading the Japanese Mind: The Realities Behind Their Thoughts and Actions* (Kodansha International, 1996).

13–14 Randall's professional background from Kahn, *Supermarketer to the World*, pp. 126–27.

14 Details of the use of ADM's products and its growth from a variety of internal corporate documents, including "Amazing Grain: A Guide to the Wonders of Corn," "Archer Daniels Midland: An Overview," "ADM Bioproducts: Lysine," and "ADM Bioproducts: Threonine/Tryptophan," as well as the annual reports from the company dated from 1992 through 1998.

15 ADM's investment in its lysine plant from *Chemical Marketing Reporter*, "ADM Board Approves $150 mm Plunge Into Fine Chemicals," May 1, 1989, p. 7.

15 ADM's lysine capacity in 1992 from a company press release of October 23, 1991, "ADM to Expand Lysine Production."

15 The production problems in the lysine plant are described in the FD-302 of Michael D. "Mick" Andreas, dated November 4, 1992, for case file number 192B-SI-45899.

16 The tour by Ajinomoto executives of the ADM lysine plant and the attempt to steal the lysine technology was described in Mimoto's trial testimony in *U.S. v. Michael D. Andreas et al.* Additional information from the FD-302s of Mimoto and Ikeda, as well as from notes taken during the tour by one of the participants.

16–17 The author reviewed contemporaneous phone logs that recorded this and other calls placed to Mark Whitacre by some of the Japanese executives who toured the ADM plant.

17–19 Some details of the meeting between Whitacre and Mick Andreas from the Andreas FD-302, November 4, 1992, as well as the first FD-302 of Mark E. Whitacre, dated November 4, 1992, for case number 192B-SI-45899.

19 Andreas's decision to call his father, Dwayne, about the Fujiwara allegations is described in his 302 of November 4, 1992.

19 Details about the death of Shreve Archer from the *New York Times*, November 11, 1947, p. 27. Information about the early days of Archer Daniels Midland from Marion E. Cross, *From Land, Sea and Test Tube: The Story of Archer-Daniels-Midland Company*, an unpublished 1957 corporate biography.

20 Details about Thomas Daniels's background from Kahn, *Supermarketer to the World*, pp. 152–53.

20 Details about Andreas's early days at Cargill from Wayne Broehl Jr.'s in-depth history *Cargill: Trading the World's Grain* (Dartmouth College, 1992), pp. 682, 687–88, 708–9.

20 Details of Andreas's youth from a series of original family papers obtained by the author, and from *Fortune* magazine, "Oh, How the Money Grows at ADM," October 8, 1990.

20 Dwayne Andreas's height and weight from *Current Biography*, March 1992.

20–21 Descriptions of the paranoia and fear of the early 1950s are provided in Fred J. Cook's *The Nightmare Decade* (Random House, 1971), a fabulous exploration of the history and psychology of the anti-Communist hysteria of that time.

21 Details of Andreas's trip to Moscow, and the reaction at Cargill, from Broehl, *Cargill: Trading the World's Grain*, pp. 762–64.

21–22 Details of the evening of Humphrey's nomination from Theodore H. White, *The Making of the President: 1968* (Atheneum, 1969), p. 354, and *Boston Globe*, "Hubert All Smiles at TV Set," August 29, 1968, p. 28.

22 Andreas was deemed part of the Humphrey brain trust by James Younger in "The Humphrey Brain Trust," *Chicago Tribune Magazine*, October 20, 1968, p. 65.

22 The details of Andreas's contribution to Humphrey's 1948 senate campaign from Hubert Humphrey, *The Education of a Public Man: My Life and Politics* (Doubleday & Co., 1976), p. 295.

22 Humphrey's vacations with Andreas and his selection as Michael Andreas's godfather from Carl Solberg, *Hubert Humphrey: A Biography* (W.W. Norton & Co., 1984), p. 231.

22 Andreas's relationship with Thomas Dewey from Kahn, *Supermarketer to the World*, pp. 105–10.

22 Andreas's world travels from Peter Carlson, "Chairman across the Board," *Washington Post Magazine*, July 14, 1996, p. 14. Also from Solberg, *Hubert Humphrey: A Biography*, pp. 219–20, 414–15, and Kahn, *Supermarketer to the World*, pp. 85–94.

23 Details of Andreas's bid to sell butter to the Soviets from the *New York Times*, "Sales of Butter to Soviet Barred," January 20, 1954, p. 1.

23 The method Andreas used to deliver oil to the Soviets was described in Carlson, *Washington Post Magazine*, July 14, 1996, p. 16.

23 Andreas's and Humphrey's encounter with Bobby Kennedy at the Mayflower from Solberg, *Hubert Humphrey: A Biography*, p. 231.

23 Andreas's fear of wiretaps from a series of letters from his brother Osborne Andreas to Professor George Vetter of New York University. The letters, written throughout the 1960s, were obtained by the author and are not publicly available.

24 Nixon's invitation to Andreas to join his cabinet from Kahn, *Supermarketer to the World*, p. 108.

24 Andreas's twenty-five-thousand-dollar cash contribution into the safe-deposit box from Theodore H. White, *The Making of the President: 1972* (Atheneum 1973), p. 297. Andreas's one-hundred-thousand-dollar cash contribution at the White House from Charles R. Babcock, "Soft Money Is Like the Man Who Came to Dinner," *Washington Post*, June 24, 1994, p. A4.

24–25 Andreas's effects on federal policy from Carlson, *Washington Post Magazine*, July 14, 1996. Also, see Timothy Noah, "Ethanol Boon Shows How Archer Daniels Gets Its Way in Washington with Low-key Lobbying," *Wall Street Journal*, December 29, 1993, p. A10.

25 Dialogue from the O'Neill/Gorbachev conversation from Kahn, *Supermarketer to the World*, p. 39, and Tip O'Neill with William Novak, *Man of the House* (Random House, 1987), p. 293. The dialogue in the books differs in some minor ways. The dialogue in this book is a combination of those two descriptions.

26 Andreas's role in back-channel communications between Gorbachev and Reagan from Carlson, *Washington Post Magazine*, July 14, 1996, p. 13.

26 Andreas's role in briefing White House and State Department officials from a personal letter written by his brother, Osborne Andreas, to Professor George Vetter of New York University, on December 24, 1961. The author also obtained copies of summaries of conversations forwarded by Andreas to other departments of the government.

27 The federal price-fixing case against ADM on fructose would be dismissed in 1991 by a federal judge in Iowa for lack of evidence.

27 ADM's history of legal problems from Carlson, *Washington Post Magazine*, July 14, 1996, p. 28.

27 ADM's role in training FBI agents for the sting at the commodities exchanges from Sue Shellenberger, *Wall Street Journal*, "Grain Maverick," February 9, 1989, p. 1; Greg Burns, *Chicago Sun-Times*, "ADM Helped Undercover Agent Learn CBOT Ropes," October 17, 1990, p. 35.

27 Mick Andreas's reaction on learning of ADM's role in sponsoring the FBI from Paul Craig Roberts, *Washington Times*, "Price-fixing Fabricators?" January 31, 1997, p. A16.

27 In a letter to the author, Thomas Frankel essentially denied everything I have written in this book about him, describing my references to him as "misleading, inaccurate, and incorrect." However, much of the information comes directly from government records, and every portion of the book related to Frankel—with the exception of the direct quotes from government records that appear below—was shown to representatives of ADM or its executives, who did not dispute the accuracy of what appears here.

The public story about the resignation of Frankel was reported by Scott Kilman, "Archer-Daniels Treasurer Resigns after Securities Losses Are Discovered," *Wall Street Journal*, September 16, 1991, p. A8. The following day, a criminal investigation into possible wire fraud was opened at the FBI's Chicago Field Office, case file number 196B-CG-82508. Several financial institutions and ADM were subpoenaed in the course of the investigation. ADM's cooperation in the case, however, was limited. Without the eager participation of the victim in the case, the investigation was closed without prosecution in July 1993. But ADM officials told me that the circumstances surrounding the Frankel affair were far broader than were ever publicly revealed. Afterward, the head of the board's audit committee stepped down for failing to detect the transactions, a director involved in the situation said.

A July 23, 1993, letter written by Special Agent Gregg Schwolback to a prosecutor in the Chicago U.S. Attorney's office details the specifics of the investigation into Frankel's activities. It stated, "By way of background, the investigation involved a $14.6 million loss to Archer Daniels Midland Company, Decatur Il., which had been caused by the Treasurer, Thomas H. Frankel, between 1984 and August 1991. The loss resulted to ADM because Frankel failed to place a $26 million hedge position to offset the company's $350 million short position, a position which ADM had held since 1984. Since the hedge position had not been placed by Frankel, ADM began to incur losses as interest rates declined over the seven-year period. By August 1991, the cumulative loss to ADM totaled $14.6 million. Frankel prevented detection of the loss by creating fictitious internal trading documentation and other records to make it appear as if the hedge position existed throughout the seven-year period. On August 30, 1991, Frankel resigned after other ADM officials discovered the loss and the fictitious trading documentation and other records which he had created."

The Frankel investigation was impeded by several factors in addition to ADM's reluctance to cooperate, according to government records and interviews. According to the July 23 letter, a review of documents subpoenaed from ADM "failed to reveal any violations of federal law that occurred in the Northern District of Illinois," which is covered by the Chicago office. The letter mentioned that the proper venue for the Frankel investigation was with the Springfield division, but that it was unlikely to be pursued there because Springfield "was presently conducting an investigation of ADM for price-fixing."

On July 20, 1993, Agent Schwolback contacted Special Agent Joe Weatherall, who by that time was a co–case agent on the price-fixing investigation. Schwolback asked about the possibility of conducting a joint interview of Frankel when the price-fixing case was more fully developed. According to a memo of the call written by Schwolback that day, Weatherall said that "because of the progress being made in their case, they did not want Frankel to be interviewed at this time." According to the memo, Weatherall indicated that Frankel would have to be interviewed at some point in the price-fixing investigation, but that interview never took place.

One important question in the investigation was what had happened to the $26 million that government records say was supposed to have been used to create a hedge position. ADM officials said that the company believed some of the money may have ended up with Frankel himself. According to interviews with the government, that was considered by the FBI as a possible "theory of the crime," but the case was closed before the question could be adequately pursued. According to investigative notes reviewed by the author, information developed later in the related ADM cases showed that a bank account linked to Frankel had attracted the attention of bank compliance officials because of large sums of money moving through it. It is not clear whether this account was linked in any way to possible wrongdoing since, ultimately, no further information about it was ever developed, and no charges were ever brought against Frankel.

28–29 Allen Andreas has never before been publicly disclosed as the executive who contacted the CIA. However, his conversations with Dwayne and Mick Andreas were described—without mentioning Allen's name—during the trial of *U.S. v. Michael D. Andreas et al.*

CHAPTER TWO

31–32 Some details of Worthington's call to John Hoyt from an internal teletype, from FBI-Springfield to FBI headquarters, dated November 5, 1992.

32–34 Some details of Shepard's personal history from *U.S. v. Michael D. Andreas et al.*

33 Shepard's residence in Matawan from local real-estate records. The time of the commute from that town from the *New York Times*, "If You're Thinking of Living in: Marlboro," July 12, 1987, section 8, p. 11. Marlboro residents relied on the Matawan train station.

35–38 Some details of the FBI interview of Michael Andreas from his 302 dated November 4, 1992, for case file number 192B-SI-45899.

37 The statements by the FBI that ADM could keep any "superbug" that the company obtained from Fujiwara was supported in testimony of Mark Cheviron before the Special January 1996 Grand Jury, on November 12, 1996, in the case titled "In Re: Grand Jury Investigation," court caption number 95 GJ 573.

38 The stories Whitacre told at ADM of his personal history were described in *Macleans*, "The Mole Who Cracked a Conspiracy," February 22, 1999, p. 49. Also from a sworn deposition from Reinhart Richter of May 18, 1998, in the civil case *Archer Daniels Midland Company v. Mark Whitacre et al.*, case number 96-2237, filed in the United States District Court for the Central District of Illinois.

38–40 Whitacre's anxiety about speaking with the FBI has been described in several documents. First, Shepard discussed Whitacre's general anxiety at the time in his court testimony in *U.S. v. Michael D. Andreas et al.* It is also mentioned in the grand jury testimony of Mark Cheviron, before the Special January 1996 Grand Jury, on November 12, 1996, in the case titled "In Re: Grand Jury Investigation," court caption number 95 GJ 573. Finally, Whitacre alluded to it himself in *Fortune*, "My Life as a Corporate Mole for the FBI," September 4, 1995, pp. 56–57.

39 Some details of Mark and Ginger Whitacre's personal history from "Little Miami High School 15th Year Reunion Information Sheet," dated June 8, 1991. A copy of the document was provided by a former classmate of the Whitacres.

40–41 Shepard described the delay in speaking to Whitacre during his court testimony in *U.S. v. Michael D. Andreas et al.*

The plan of action for the Fujiwara investigation was described by Shepard in a teletype to FBI headquarters, dated November 5, 1992.

42–43 Shepard's first interview with Mark Whitacre is described in several documents, both confidential and publicly available. The foremost record of the meeting is the FD-302 dictated by Shepard for file #192B-SI-45889. Shepard also described the meeting in his testimony during *U.S. v. Michael D. Andreas et al.* Details were also contained in an FBI teletype prepared by Shepard on November 5, 1992. Finally, additional information about the meeting was described by Mark Cheviron in his testimony before the Special 1996 Grand Jury.

Some of this information conflicts. Neither the 302 nor the teletype indicates where the meeting took place. In his court testimony, Shepard said that the interview took place at the FBI office in Decatur. In his grand jury testimony, Cheviron insisted that was incorrect, and that the meeting took place at Jim Shafter's office. After cross-checking as much information as possible, I have concluded that Agent Shepard's recollection is in error, since it is not consistent with any other information that was obtained. Cheviron's recollection is consistent with all of that other information. This is simply a mistake that can easily be expected with the passage of years.

43–44 Some details of Whitacre's false story about the threat to his daughter from the FD-302 of his interview with Brian Shepard on November 6, 1992, as well as from Ronald Henkoff, "The ADM Tale Gets Even Stranger," *Fortune*, May 13, 1996, p. 113.

44–46 Cheviron described the events of November 5, 1992, in his grand jury testimony of November 12, 1996.

48 Details about the history of Moweaqua from records and news clippings on file with the Moweaqua Coal Mine Museum, Moweaqua, IL.

48–53 Some details of the November 5, 1992, interview of Mark Whitacre by Brian Shepard from two FD-302s of that date. Other information comes from an internal FBI teletype, prepared by Bob Anderson, a Springfield squad leader, on November 6, 1992.

Shepard also described many of the details in his testimony during *U.S. v. Michael D. Andreas et al.* His most detailed description came in his testimony of August 12, 1998. During that day's testimony, Shepard described how Whitacre told him about being coached by Cheviron and Mick Andreas immediately before their first meeting. No evidence emerged in this investigation that Mark Cheviron had any personal knowledge of the price-fixing activities at ADM. He was never charged with any other wrongdoing either.

Shepard also testified that Whitacre had described conversations with James Randall about efforts to steal microbes from competitors. Those efforts, Shepard testified, included paying Michael Frein $50,000 for stealing a bacitracin bug, and using prostitutes who were hired by Mark Cheviron to get information from employees of competitors.

Later in his testimony, Shepard was asked specifically if any of these separate allegations turned out to be true. Shepard replied, "In my opinion, they are true."

Through his lawyer, Jeff Cole, Randall denied any involvement in such activities. Also, through his lawyer William J. Linklater, Michael Frein firmly denied that he had ever improperly taken any microbes from his former employer. I am also aware that, in a short discussion with an FBI agent, Frein denied any involvement in wrongdoing. According to notes I have reviewed, officials from IMC told the FBI that they had no knowledge of any microbe thefts, although they said that at the time in question, they had no means of determining whether any bugs were missing.

Another ADM executive, Marty Allison, informed the government during an FBI interview that he had also personally heard from Randall that Frein had brought the bacitracin bug with him from his previous employer. Allison's statement to Special Agent Herndon was recorded in a 302 dated February 13, 1996. Allison later pleaded guilty to charges in an unrelated criminal case involving actions he took while working for ADM.

The case was still under investigation in 1996, documents show. A January 30, 1996, letter to Frances Hulin, the United States Attorney in Springfield, from Special Agent Robert Herndon, described elements of the investigation to that point, including the allegations pertaining to Frein and Randall. No charges were ever brought against either man.

Finally, a December 23, 1992, teletype prepared for Bureau headquarters by Special Agent Joe Weatherall detailed many of the allegations that were the subject of the Springfield FBI's investigation, including the possible interstate transportation of stolen property and what it described as "a pattern of obstruction of justice concerning the Springfield division matter." Again, no charges were ever brought in either case.

No charges were ever brought by the government involving the Corn Refiners Association, and no substantive evidence was ever developed indicating that the association itself was involved in price-fixing.

CHAPTER THREE

54–56 The meeting and attendance at the Springfield meeting in Stukey's office from a private calendar maintained by one of the participants.

56–58 The history of the Sherman Antitrust Act comes from a variety of sources. The law's legislative history and early years of performance comes from Ron Chernow's towering biography *Titan: The Life of John D. Rockefeller Sr.* (Random House, 1998). Other details of the law, and of the Progressive Era, come from H. W. Brands, *The Reckless Decade: America in the 1890's* (St. Martin's Press, 1995), pp. 58, 158; Steven J. Diner, *A Very Different Age: Americans of the Progressive Era* (Hill and Wang, 1998), pp. 14–75; and William Manners, *TR & Will: A Friendship that Split the Republican Party* (Harcourt Brace & World, 1969), pp. 43, 191. Details on the use of the law in price-fixing cases from A. D. Neale and D. G. Goyder, *The Antitrust Laws of the United States: A Study of Competition Enforced by Law* (Third Edition), and Thomas W. Hazlett, "The Legislative History of the Sherman Antitrust Act Re-examined; Economics and 100 Years of Antitrust," *Economic Inquiry*, April 1992, p. 263.

58–59 Whitacre's call on the morning of November 6, 1992, was described in Cheviron's grand jury testimony, as well as in the 302 of Mark Whitacre, for the investigation of that same day.

59 Copies of the ABP contract, and the note faxed by Harald Skogman to Mark Whitacre, were obtained by the author.

60–62 Cheviron's afternoon meeting with Shepard and the FBI is described in several records. They include Cheviron's grand jury testimony of November 12, 1996, and Shepard's trial testimony in *U.S. v. Michael D. Andreas et al.* It is also referenced in the testimony of Donald Stukey, at a pretrial hearing in that same case held on November 5, 1997.

62–63 The episode involving the call from Regina from the Inland Telephone Company is described in several records. They include Cheviron's grand jury testimony of November 12, 1996; a transcript of a recorded conversation between Cheviron and Special Agent Brian Shepard that took place on November 9, 1992; an FBI 302 of Ginger Whitacre, dated November 6, 1992; and a 302 of Mark Whitacre taken that same day.

63–65 The meeting between Whitacre and Shepard on the night of November 6, 1992, was described in several 302s. They include two 302s prepared by Shepard, based on his notes of that night. At the time, Shepard was dividing his notes into separate 302s based on different possible crimes. That same night, he also interviewed Ginger Whitacre, and her comments were also recorded in a 302.

64–65 Shepard described his reaction to Whitacre's story about the threat to his daughter in his testimony during *U.S. v. Michael D. Andreas et al.*

65–71 Some details of the meeting between Whitacre, Shepard, and Paisley on November 8, 1992, from two 302s prepared by the agents from Shepard's notes of that meeting. Also, Shepard discussed this meeting in his testimony in *U.S. v. Michael D. Andreas et al.*

71–73 Cheviron discussed his conversation with Whitacre on the morning of November 9, 1992, as well as his subsequent telephone call with Shepard, in his grand jury testimony of November 12, 1996.

72–74 Cheviron described his November 9 conversation with Reising in a telephone conversation with Shepard that same day. The conversation was recorded, and a transcript was reviewed by the author. Shepard also described the conversation in his trial testimony in *U.S. v. Michael D. Andreas et al.*

73–74 The conversation between Paisley and Cheviron on November 9, 1992, from a transcript of the FBI tape 1B2 for case #60A-SI-46290.

74 Details of Paisley's filing of the Cheviron tape, as well as its log number, from an FBI 504B of November 9, 1992.

75 The location and other details of the first recorded conversation were revealed by Shepard in his testimony during *U.S. v. Michael D. Andreas et al.*
    Some details of the appearance of the hotel from personal observation, as well as interviews with people who remembered the location's look in 1992.

76 Details of the signing of the FD-472s and FD-473s from the documents themselves.

76–78 The conversation between Whitacre and Yamamoto from the transcript of the recorded conversation, government file number 1B1. While portions of this tape were played at the trial of *U.S. v. Michael D. Andreas et al.*, the full transcript has never been publicly released.

78 The description of the calls to Ikeda and Mimoto, as well as the other failed calls, from the transcript of the recorded conversation, government file number 1B1.

78 Details of the signing of the FD-504b from the document itself.

78–79 Some details of the conversation between Whitacre and Shepard on the night of November 9, 1992, from three 302s prepared by Shepard.

CHAPTER FOUR

80 The description of the weather on the road from Decatur to Springfield comes from records on file with the National Climatic Data Center in Asheville, North Carolina. The records include the hourly surface weather observations for November 10, 1992, from both the Decatur and Springfield stations maintained by the U.S. Department of Commerce.

80 The time frame of Paisley's trip to Springfield was established by an FD-504b, a document that describes the chain of custody for tape-recorded evidence maintained by the FBI. The document shows that Shepard turned over the tape to Paisley at 10:25 that evening. Other information developed by the author showed that Paisley left his meeting with Shepard within five minutes of receiving the tape. Getting onto the highway from downtown Decatur could take anywhere from ten to fifteen minutes. So, by the time that Paisley had reached the open fields on Interstate 72, it would have been shortly before eleven o'clock.

82 Weatherall's military history from documents on file with the National Personnel Records Center in St. Louis, MO, including the agent's record of assignments from 1961 through 1970.

83–85 The meeting between Whitacre, Shepard, and Weatherall on the night of November 13, 1992, was described in three separate 302s from that day. Also, references were made to the discussions in a teletype prepared for FBI headquarters by Weatherall on November 19, 1992. The room number from hotel expense records.

85–87 Details of Whitacre's phone conversation from Colorado with Shepard come from several different sources. A small amount of information comes from a 302 Shepard prepared, which described only the price-fixing discussion. Other notes Shepard wrote down were not recorded in a 302, although the agent did maintain the information in a case file. Those notes were later transcribed into an undated document called "FBI File Information." Finally, references were made to the discussions in a teletype prepared for FBI headquarters by Weatherall on November 19, 1992.

89 Whitacre's excuses for not taping were detailed in a 302 with Shepard, dated November 13, 1992.

89–90 Karen Sterling's sense of intimidation and fear involving Sid Hulse—as well as her concerns about sexual harassment—were described in a 302 from an interview with Special Agents Thomas Simon Jr. and Anthony D'Angelo on March 9, 1997. In that interview, Sterling described how she had begun carrying a gun in her purse out of concerns for her safety around Hulse. Sterling told the FBI that she reported Hulse's conduct to his boss, Mark Whitacre, but that Whitacre told her he would not do anything about it because Hulse was an important person to ADM.

A secretary who subsequently worked for Hulse, Mary Hodge, told a similar story about her boss's behavior and sexual harassment to the FBI. That was described in a 302 of her interview, dated June 27, 1997, and written by D'Angelo. Again,

Hodge told the FBI that she reported the conduct to Whitacre, who again declined to take action. Hodge ultimately filed a formal complaint at ADM.

Sterling brought a sexual-harassment suit in the state court of Fulton County, Georgia, naming ADM and Hulse as defendants. Hodge filed a case against the company and Hulse in the federal district court in Atlanta. According to their FBI statements, both women's cases were settled with requirements that the terms remain confidential.

90 The conversation between Whitacre and Hulse is described in a 302 of Hulse's interview with Special Agent Robert Herndon, dated May 10, 1996.

91 Some details of the Regal McCormick Ranch from Patricia Myers, "Soothing the Sizzle: Cool Oases Spell Relief to the Summer-Weary," *Arizona Republic*, August 30, 1996, p. 1.

91 Whitacre lunch location and time at the Regal McCormick Ranch from a record obtained by the author of his expense statements, travel schedules, and telephone calls.

91 While the FBI file information says that Whitacre told Shepard he was at a motel in Phoenix, records of his expense statements, travel schedules, and telephone calls show that he was only at the McCormick Ranch that day.

91–94 Details of the November 18, 1992, Whitacre conversation with Shepard from two sources—the undated record of "FBI File Information" and Weatherall's teletype of November 19, 1992.

94 Whitacre's travel schedule and his November 23 meeting with Jones and Hall, from the records of his expense statements, travel schedules, and telephone calls obtained by the author.

94 Details of the FBI's November 24 meeting with Whitacre from a 302 prepared by Shepard and a teletype to headquarters, written by Weatherall and dated December 2, 1992.

95–96 The price war in the world lysine market took effect in late 1992, lasting through early 1993. It is demonstrated in government exhibit 43A, introduced in *U.S. v. Michael D. Andreas et al.*

96 Kanji Mimoto described his 1992 conversation with Whitacre in an interview with Shepard in Hong Kong on July 2, 1996. Details of that conversation come from the 302 prepared of that interview. In the interview, Mimoto does not know the month that the conversation took place. However, based on Whitacre's records of expense statements, travel schedules, and telephone calls, it could only have occurred in late November.

96–99 Some details of Whitacre's first meeting with Cudmore from a 302 prepared from that meeting, as well as a teletype to headquarters written by Joe Weatherall on December 2, 1992.

99 The conversation between Kevin Corr and Richard Reising from a transcript of FBI recording 1B4 for case #60A-SI-46290. Reising's conversation with Shepard from a transcript of recording 1B37 for the same case. The call was also described in Weatherall's December 2 teletype.

99–100 Details of Whitacre's telephone call on December 1 from a 302 prepared by Shepard, and Weatherall's December 2 teletype.

100–101 Details of Whitacre's stay in Frankfurt from his expense reports, as well as information about the hotel that can be found on the Internet at www.sheraton.com.

100–102 Details of Mimoto's conversation with Whitacre from Frankfurt are contained in the 302 of July 2, 1996.

102–103 Whitacre's meeting with Shepard and Weatherall where he recounts the Fujiwara story and mentions Brasser from a 302 of the meeting, dated December 10, 1992.

103 The conversations with the Behavioral Science Unit were described in a teletype written by Shepard, dated December 14, 1992. Shepard also made reference to those conversations in his trial testimony at *U.S. v. Michael D. Andreas et al.*

103 The room number for the meeting where Special Agent Hamara first appeared from hotel expense records.

CHAPTER FIVE

105–107 Details of the lie detector test given to Whitacre on December 21, 1992, from the polygraph report of Special Agent Edward T. Hamara, dated December 28, 1992, field file number 192B-SI-45899. Other details from a teletype prepared by Special Agent Weatherall dated December 28, 1992. Also, Weatherall described some events that took place on the day of the polygraph in his testimony at a pretrial hearing in *U.S. v. Michael D. Andreas et al.*, on December 16, 1997.

107–108 Details of Whitacre's statements to Shepard and Weatherall on December 21, 1992, from a 302 of that day.

108 The sodium gluconate price-fixing scheme, plus the details of Wayne Brasser's firing and the roles of Barrie Cox and Terry Wilson in the activities, are supported by a 302 of Cox by Special Agent Louis F. Caputo Jr., from an investigation on October 11–12, 1996.

108–11 Dialogue from the Whitacre-Brasser call of December 21, 1992, from a transcript of FBI recording 1B6 for case #60A-SI-46290.

112–15 The December 22, 1992, meeting between Whitacre, Shepard, and Weatherall was described in a 302 of that day, as well as in a December 28, 1992, teletype to FBI headquarters written by Weatherall.

114–15 Kataro Fujiwara denied making any of the calls described in these pages in an interview with the FBI in July 1996. Whitacre's stories about contacts with Fujiwara after an initial call have not been consistent.

116 Whitacre's purchase of the cans of caramel popcorn from his expense reports. According to the reports, they were purchased for executives at a company called Biosys, Inc.

116–117 Whitacre's second meeting with Cudmore is described in a 302 of December 29, 1992. A copy of the cooperation agreement was also obtained by the author.

117–18 Details of the discussion between Whitacre and the FBI from a 302, dated January 4, 1993. The tape was also discussed by Whitacre in a 302 dated January 7, 1993.

118 Some details of Whitacre and Randall's trips in January 1993 from a report obtained by the author on Whitacre's expenses, travel schedules, and telephone records.

118–20 The conversation between Whitacre and Randall from a transcript of FBI tape number 1B13 for case #60A-SI-46290. Shepard described his opinion of the tape, and the allegations, in his court testimony for *U.S. v. Michael D. Andreas et al.*

Shepard was not alone in his interpretation of the tape. During the Andreas trial, Scott Lassar, the U.S. Attorney in Chicago, also stated that the tape supported Shepard's belief. "The theft of bacitracin, the use of prostitutes, they are confirmed on tape," he said.

But Jeff Cole, Randall's lawyer, disputed Shepard's interpretation, saying in an August 20, 1998, article in the *New York Times* that he did not believe tapes proving such allegations existed. "These allegations are preposterous," Mr. Cole said. "I don't believe there is any tape that when fairly and impartially heard supports the conclusion that Mr. Randall knew about prostitutes or theft of technology." Again, through his lawyer, Frein denied any wrongdoing.

121 Whitacre's trip to the Cayman Islands during the week of January 9 from two sources: his expense and travel records, which show him as traveling to Grand Cayman from January 13 to January 16, and records of entry at the Cayman Islands, which confirm those two dates.

121 The added statement to the cooperation agreement from a copy of the original document.

121–22 Dwayne Andreas's consideration of firing Mark Whitacre—and how he was persuaded not to by Jim Randall—from notes of his 1996 sworn testimony before the price-fixing grand jury.

122 Details of Chicago's decision to keep up the Christmas lights on Michigan Avenue throughout January of 1993 from *Chicago Tribune*, "Lights Out Isn't Here Yet for Christmas Die-hards," January 22, 1993, p. 6.

122–23 The Ajinomoto executive's opinions of ADM were described in a series of notes taken at meetings of the Japanese company by one of the participants.

123 Mimoto described the failed efforts to find the lysine bug in the handkerchief in his trial testimony at *U.S. v. Michael D. Andreas et al.*

122–24 The January 22 meeting between Whitacre, Ikeda, and Mimoto is described in two records: a July 1996 302 of Ikeda prepared during the Hong Kong visit and a March 16, 1993, 302 of Whitacre. The two records conflict as to whether the meeting occurred in the evening or the morning, and so the timing of the meeting is not mentioned.

124 Williams described this encounter with Whitacre in sworn testimony on November 4, 1997, at a pretrial hearing in the case of *U.S. v. Michael D. Andreas et al.*

125 Whitacre's repeated efforts to describe Brasser's job search and other matters from a series of Whitacre 302s from 1993, dated January 25, January 28, February 1, February 3, February 8, and February 10. The attempt to interview Brasser is described in a January 12, 1993, teletype written by Weatherall.

125–26 Details of the lie detector test given to Whitacre on March 10, 1993, from the polygraph report of Special Agent Edward T. Hamara, dated March 22, 1993, field file number 192B-SI-45899. Also, Special Agent Weatherall described some events that took place around the time of the polygraph in his testimony during a pretrial hearing in *U.S. v. Michael D. Andreas et al.* on December 16, 1997.

127 The Behavioral Science Unit instructed the agents to avoid interrogating Whitacre if he failed the lie detector test, according to Hamara's March 22 polygraph report.

127–28 Some details of the March 11 meeting between Whitacre and the FBI from a 302 of that date.

CHAPTER SIX

131–34 The dialogue and certain other descriptions from the March 17 discussions between Whitacre, Wilson, and Randall are from a transcript of tape 1B20—as well as of an enhanced version of the same tape, numbered 1B63—for case #60A-SI-46290.

134–36 The dialogue and certain other descriptions from the March 18 discussions between Whitacre, Andreas, and Wilson are from a transcript of tapes 1B21, 1B22, and 1B61 for case #60A-SI-46290.

The exact date that Whitacre received the notebook and briefcase recorders could not be established. Recollections on that fact differed, as did the documentary evidence. However, everyone involved agreed that he had obtained those devices by the spring of 1993, sometime after he signed the cooperation agreement and before his second polygraph. But this was the first documented time that either of the devices was identified as having been used.

135 Information regarding Tommy Thompson's 1994 campaign-finance drive, and its national implications, from "Outsiders Aiding Thompson," *Wisconsin State Journal*, July 21, 1993, p. 1D.

137 Some details about the architecture of the federal plaza in Chicago from Paul Gapp, "A Unified Front for the Government: The solid Metcalfe Building fits right in with its federal neighbors," *Chicago Tribune*, November 10, 1991, p. 26.

139–40 Some details of the nighttime visit to ADM by Special Agent Tom Gibbons from notes of a briefing that was provided subsequent to the event.

141 Details of Hoech's conversation with Whitacre from an April 1993 letter summarizing the discussion. The letter was written by Hoech to Masaru Yamamoto of Kyowa Hakko. Additional details about Hoech's relationship to Kyowa Hakko from Yamamoto's testimony in *U.S. v. Michael D. Andreas et al.*

143 Williams described the "014" episode with Whitacre in sworn testimony on November 4, 1997, at a pretrial hearing in the case of *U.S. v. Michael D. Andreas et al.* The exact date this occurred is unclear, although it occurred shortly after the FBI provided Whitacre with the briefcase. The story appears here in the narrative because it is by this point that Whitacre definitely received the briefcase.

143–44 Dialogue from Whitacre's "marching orders" meeting with Mick Andreas from a transcript of tape 1B32 for case #60A-SI-46290.

144 In this one instance, I have chosen to edit something of substance from Whitacre's full quote, because I cannot substantiate that it is a truthful reflection of what had just occurred. His full statement on returning to the office was, "Eight-thirty A.M., Thursday morning, the fifteenth. And just saw Jim Randall and Mick Andreas. Eighty-thirty A.M., April fifteenth. Two hours before our flight to Chicago. Saw Mick Andreas and Jim Randall. For the . . . for the marching orders." While he did speak with Randall for a moment, there was no conversation in the transcript of tape 1B32 indicating that the ADM president had said anything pertaining to the Chicago trip.

Absent any evidence that Randall had given marching orders in this conversation, I have removed his name from the statement.

145 The room number at the Chicago Marriott Downtown from hotel expense records.

144–45 Details of FBI surveillance at the Yamamoto meeting from surveillance 302s for April 15, 1993.

146–47 Dialogue and other details regarding the Yamamoto meeting of April 15, 1993, from a transcript of videotape 1B33 for case #60A-SI-46290.

148–50 Some details of the meeting between the antitrust prosecutors and Springfield FBI from contemporaneous notes of the event.

150 The location of the Whitacre meeting with Shepard and Gibbons from a hotel receipt for that day from the Best Western Shelton Inn.

151–52 The comments made by Shepard and Gibbons when the body Nagra was turned on at the Best Western were recorded on tape 1B43 for case #60A-SI-46290.

152 The identity of the plane used on April 28, 1993, its passengers, and its route from an internal ADM flight log for that day. Additional information about the plane from its registration statement on file with the Federal Aviation Administration. While the name being used in this book is technically correct for the airplane, it is more commonly referred to as the King Air 350, according to Blair Sullivan, product manager for Raytheon Company, which manufactures the plane. I have chosen to go with ADM's own identification to the FAA.

152–56 The dialogue and many details of Wilson and Whitacre's trip to Chicago on April 28 from transcripts for tape 1B43 (the body Nagra) and 1B44 (the briefcase) for case #60A-SI-46290. Other details of the meeting from a preparatory teletype by Weatherall, dated May 5, 1993.

153–54 Details of the Gaslight Club from personal observation and from Mike Michaelson, "Lobbying for a Good Time," *Chicago Daily Herald*, April 2, 1999, p. 27.

156 Ultimately, Whitacre submitted an expense report that was illegible, according to an analysis of his expense reports obtained by the author.

157 The timing of Whitacre's subsequent meeting with Shepard at the Best Western from the 504b chain-of-custody documentation for tape 1B43.

158 Timing of the agents' filing and copying of tape 1B43 from the 504b chain-of-custody form.

159 Hoyt's inscription in his daily planner from the original document.

CHAPTER SEVEN

162 Certain information regarding the investigation involving First Financial of Louisiana from "Louisiana Broker Gets Three-year Term," *National Mortgage News*, September 10, 1990, p. 5. Details of the case against the federal judge, Robert F. Collins, from "U.S. Judge Is Convicted in New Orleans Bribe Case," *New York Times*, June 30, 1991, p. A13.

163 Details of the meeting in Decatur between Yamada and Andreas from a transcript of tape 1B47.

163 The date of the ADM trip to Vancouver was established by an analysis of Whitacre's expense statements that was obtained by the author.

163 The attendance at the Vancouver meeting from "Government's Proffer of Co-conspirators' Statements," filed on May 6, 1998, in the case *U.S. v. Michael D. Andreas et al.*

164 Details of the Vancouver meeting from several sources, including contemporaneous notes of the discussion maintained by Jhom Su Kim of Miwon, which coincided with 302s of Whitacre taken by Weatherall on June 24, 1993, and by Shepard on June 28, 1993.

165 Page described his meeting with Whitacre in a 302 with Special Agent Anthony D'Angelo and Supervisory Special Agent Rob Grant on November 25, 1996. Other information from the complaint filed in *ADM v. Mark E. Whitacre*. While the Page meeting definitely took place in the summer of 1993, dating it precisely proved difficult. In his 302, Page remembered the discussions as taking place in August of that summer, but a review of Whitacre's expense statements showed that it occurred in June. Page officially began his employment with ADM in October. Because of these conflicts, I have chosen to present these events with no dates specified. However, the documents make clear that they occurred at about the time they are presented in the narrative.

165 Details of Whitacre's expense statement from a confidential analysis of those reports obtained by the author. The relationship between Vanetta USA and ADM from the complaint filed *ADM v. Mark E. Whitacre*.

165 Whitacre's interest in avoiding questions about David Page is evident from two sources—the misrepresentation of Page's employment on his expense report; this, of course, could have been the result of error. But, in his 302, Page said he was told by Whitacre to lie about where he worked in his employment application, a clear sign that the original misrepresentation was an intentional effort to avoid drawing attention to Page.

166 Details about Forsyth and its history from *Decatur-Forsyth: Visitor's Guide*, Spring-Summer 1999.

166–70 Details of Whitacre's meeting with the FBI on July 13, 1993, from a 302 of that date.

168–69 The dialogue from Whitacre's July 13 phone call with Mimoto from a transcript of tape #1B21.

170 Some details of the meeting in Budapest from a 302 of a June 30, 1996, FBI interview with Kota Fujiwara, an executive with Kyowa Hakko. This is not the same person as Kotaro Fujiwara, whose name was used by Whitacre in his fictitious story about the extortion threat.

171 The change in price of lysine from June to July 1993, from "Government's Proffer of Co-conspirators' Statements," filed on May 6, 1998, in the case *U.S. v. Michael D. Andreas et al.* Also from ADM internal company records.

173 Details of the August 24, 1993, meeting between Whitacre and the FBI from an FBI 302 of that day.

173–75 Dialogue from *The Firm* was transcribed from a video of the movie.

175 Whitacre's statements that he believed he had met his obligations under the co-operation agreement from a document entitled "FBI File Information," produced by the government in the case *U.S. v. Michael D. Andreas et al.*

175–76 Details of Whitacre's September 26, 1993, phone call with Shepard from a 302 of that day.

176 Details of the September 28, 1993, meeting between Whitacre and the FBI from a 302 of that day.

177 Whitacre continues to publicly maintain that he taped the agents during this case, and there are a number of reasons to believe him. First, I have heard excerpts of one of the tapes, which contains extended portions with Brian Shepard's voice, making statements that do not coincide with the timing and tenor of other comments of Shepard's that were recorded accidentally during the price-fixing case. Secondly, there came a point during the investigation when the agents began to suspect that Whitacre was in fact taping them, based on his refusal to remove his jacket even when the room they were in was extremely hot. Finally, Whitacre made it a habit of surreptitiously recording a number of people, including reporters and his subsequent employer. There is no reason to believe that he would not do the same thing with the FBI. His actions, plus the existence of a tape, has led me to conclude that Whitacre did indeed record the agents occasionally during Harvest King.

177 Details of the events in the Paris hotel lobby on October 5, 1993, from 302 created following an FBI surveillance by Shepard.

177–78 Some details of Whitacre's conversation at the American Embassy in Paris from an FBI 302 of October 5, 1993.

178 The room number and location for the morning meeting in Forsyth from hotel expense records.

179–83 Dialogue and other details regarding the Andreas meetings of October 12, 1993, from a transcript of audiotapes 1B43 and 1B46 for case #60A-SI-46290. Other information from a 302 resulting from Whitacre's meeting with the FBI that same night.

183 For privacy reasons, the name "Debbie" was substituted throughout this book for the actual name spoken by Andreas and Whitacre. The same thing was done for every other woman mentioned in a sexually inappropriate way. These women are the unknowing victims of this verbal abuse; I saw no reason to risk subjecting them to public embarrassment.

183–85 Dialogue and other details regarding the Ikeda phone call of October 12, 1993, from a transcript of audiotape 1B44 for case #60A-SI-46290.

185–87 Dialogue and other details regarding the Andreas meetings of October 13, 1993, from a transcript of audiotape 1B47 for case #60A-SI-46290.

187 Information regarding Weatherall's call from Whitacre of October 13 from a 302 of that day.

CHAPTER EIGHT

183–84 Some descriptive details of the John Wayne Airport from its Web site at www. ocair.com. Some descriptive details of the Irvine Marriott from its Web site at www.marriott.com. Other information from a series of hotel bills and related expense records from the meeting.

The location of the meeting was determined from bills attached to Whitacre's expense report covering October 25, 1993, and hotel expense records, including an "audiovisual event order" through MVP Visual Presentations at the hotel.

189 The type of plane flown to Irvine was determined from the company log of air travel. Descriptive details of the jet from the company's aircraft registration, on file with the Federal Aviation Administration. Weather conditions for the flight were described on the recording that day.

189 The price of the easel from the audiovisual event order.

189–97 Details of the October 25, 1993, Irvine meeting from FBI videotapes, as well as transcripts for FBI tapes 1B56, 1B57, and 1B58 for case #60A-SI-46290.

197–98 Some details of Whitacre meeting with Herndon on October 25 from an FD-504b, a chain-of-custody record, for tapes collected that night.

200 Details of Whitacre's expenses from the original bills. Whitacre's travel out of the United States documented by immigration records from a foreign country.

200–201 Details of Japanese negotiating strategies from March, *The Japanese Negotiator*. The intention of Ajinomoto is apparent from a translation of the discussions in Japanese of those executives at the Irvine meeting. They are also evident in Whitacre's many discussions with Mimoto and Ikeda, which are described in transcripts of tape 1B66 (November 8 and 11), 1B69 (November 30), and 1B74 (December 1) for case #60A-SI-46290.

201 Whitacre's discussions with Andreas and Wilson from a transcript of tape 1B74 for case #60A-SI-46290.

201–202 Some details of Hulin's nomination and background from "Simon, Moseley-Braun Expect White House to Nominate Hulin," States News Service, October 8, 1993; "White House Nominates Hulin," States News Service, October 12, 1993; and "Hulin Sworn in as First Female U.S. Attorney for Central Illinois," United Press International, January 7, 1994.

203–204 Details of Whitacre's purchase from Radio Shack from a copy of the original bill, dated December 2, 1993.

204 Details of Wilson and Whitacre's travels to Tokyo on December 7 from receipts for their expenses on that day.

204–206 Dialogue from the December 8, 1993, meeting at the Palace Hotel from a transcript of tapes 1B75, 1B76, and 1B77 for case #60A-SI-46290.

208 Whitacre's meeting of February 2, 1994, is described in a 302 by Shepard and Weatherall from that day.

CHAPTER NINE

209–11 Herndon described many of the problems during the setup for the Hawaii meeting in his sworn testimony during the trial of *U.S. v. Michael D. Andreas et al.*

211–12 Herndon described the use of the F-Bird in his sworn testimony in *U.S. v. Michael D. Andreas et al.*

214–23 The dialogue and events described from the Hawaii meeting comes from transcripts of tapes 1B94, 1B95, 1B96, 1B98, and 1B101 for case #60A-SI-46290. Some descriptive elements come from my own observations from the Hawaii videotapes.

222 Wilson's statement, "I wanna be closer to you than I am to any customer, 'cause you can make it that I can make money or I can't make money," comes from my own listening to the Hawaii videotape. This interpretation differs from the government's transcript. In its transcript, the government records Wilson's words as "I wanna be closer to you than I am to any customer. 'Cause you can make us, I can make money. I can't make money." I have chosen to go with my interpretation for several reasons: First, the words seemed clear when I listened to them. Second, they make perfect sense in context. Third, the words from the government's interpretation mean nothing and don't seem to fit in context.

224–25 The dialogue of Whitacre's conversation with Wilson as they walked across the parking lot from a transcript of tape number 1B93 for case #60A-SI-46290.

227 Whitacre described the citric discussions at the Andreas birthday party in a 302 dated March 7, 1994.

227 The timing of the meeting between the agents and the prosecutors from a scheduling book of one participant.

228–29 The status of the regional price-fixing meetings from the February 13, 1996, 302 of Marty Allison. A copy of notes from the meeting was reviewed by the author.

228–29 The preparation and expectations surrounding the ABP check request comes from several sources. First, I obtained a copy of the original document. The document does not contain the personal note written by Whitacre, but it was described in a 302 of James Kirk Schmidt on January 24, 1996. Schmidt said that, after he read the note, he covered it with white-out tape. The tape is visible on the copy. Other elements of this section come from Schmidt's 302. In addition, the surrounding circumstances are described in the 302 of Beat Schweizer on May 13, 1996. Whitacre's travel plans from an analysis of his expense reports.

230–31 Timing and other details of Weatherall's retirement from copies of items presented to him at his farewell reception.

231 Details of the Degussa investigation from a June 20, 1994, memo written by James Baker, a trial attorney for the Justice Department's Fraud Section, to an official with the economic crimes unit of the FBI. Dahle's trip to Washington was described in a teletype from FBI-Mobile to FBI headquarters, dated June 23, 1994. The identity of Kyle Rountree as the cooperating witness in this case was learned from a nongovernmental source.

CHAPTER TEN

232 The July 12 contact from Supervisory Special Agent Dan Larkin of the fraud unit is described in a teletype, dated July 15, 1994, from the Springfield Field Division to FBI headquarters.

232 The document described is the Baker memo, dated June 20, 1994.

233–37 Some details of the August 1 meeting with Whitacre from a 302 of that meeting.

237–39 The August 10 meeting between the Fraud Section and the antitrust team was described in an August 12, 1994, teletype from FBI-Springfield to FBI headquarters.

239 Some details of the Players Riverboat Casino, as well as the state ordinances on casino gambling boats, from David Snyder, "Lake Charles Bets on Its Boat," *New Orleans Times Picayune*, December 6, 1993, p. A1; and Richard Stewart, "Lake Charles Casino Takes Care and Cash of Senior Gamblers," *Houston Chronicle*, January 8, 1995, State section, p. 1.

239–40 The August 24 conversation with Rountree, the cooperating witness in the Mobile case, was described in limited portions of a 302 from that date reviewed by the author.

240–41 Dialogue from the September 12, 1994, meeting between Whitacre and Andreas from a transcript of tape 1B118 for case #60A-SI-46290.

241–42 Details of Howard Buffett's experiences involving Congressman Durbin and the football tickets from a 302 of Buffett's first FBI interview, conducted by Special Agent Robert Dale Schuler on June 27, 1995. Durbin was not mentioned by name in the 302, but his identity was determined and confirmed by the author. Through a spokeswoman, Durbin said that he recalled attending a Bears football game with Buffett, but added that he had never requested any tickets and would not do so. Nothing in the text is intended to imply that Durbin made such a request.

242 The Espy problems were described by David Johnston, "Agriculture Chief Quits as Scrutiny of Conduct Grows," *New York Times*, October 4, 1994, p. A1.

242–44 The October 11 meeting between Whitacre and the FBI is described in a 302 of that date.

244–50 Details of the Chicago trip of Whitacre, Wilson, and Andreas—as well as the meeting at the Four Seasons and the return trip—from transcripts of tapes 1B121 and 1B124 for case #60A-SI-46290.

245–46 The description of the cab taken by the ADM executives from a receipt of the trip.

246 Observations of the ADM executives from FBI surveillance 302s written by Herndon and Shepard, dated October 13, 1994.

250 Details of the October 14 phone discussion between Whitacre and Shepard from a 302 of that date. Whitacre's location when he made the phone call was established by the author through time stamps on his receipts from that day.

250–52 Details of the Scottsdale sales meeting from the February 13, 1996, 302 of Marty Allison.

251 Richter described talking with Whitacre about his background in his sworn deposition of May 18, 1998, in the case *ADM v. Mark E. Whitacre et al.*, case number 96-2237. This was the first of three days in Richter's deposition.

252–53 Timing and some other details of Whitacre's visit with Daniel Briel from a faxed memo from Whitacre to Briel, dated October 25, 1994, that was kept on file at the Swiss Bank Corporation's office in Zurich. Whitacre's hotel was determined by copies of the bill, which included time stamps.

253 Whitacre's news of the Atlanta meeting was described in his 302, dated November 2, 1994, and written by Shepard and Herndon.

253–54 The discussion about the possible arrest of the foreign executives during the Atlanta meeting was detailed in a December 8, 1994, teletype from the Springfield FBI to headquarters.

256–57 Details of the GE case, and the subsequent reaction, from William W. Horne, "GE Crushes the Trustbusters," *American Lawyer*, January-February 1995, p. 57.

259 Details from the Kuno Summer tape of December 12, 1994, from a summary of recording 1B127 for case #60A-SI-46290.

259 The relationships between Coca-Cola and the Buffetts in that time from a proxy statement of Berkshire Hathaway, Warren Buffett's investment vehicle, that was filed with the Securities and Exchange Commission on February 23, 1995.

259–60 Howard Buffett's intention—prior to his knowledge of the FBI investigation—to resign from ADM in December of 1995 from a July 10, 1995, teletype from FBI-Springfield to FBI headquarters, which summarized statements made by Buffett in an FBI interview of June 29, 1995.

CHAPTER ELEVEN

263–64 Herndon described the problems with the briefcase recorder in his testimony during *U.S. v. Michael D. Andreas et al.*

264–67 Details of the Atlanta meeting from a transcript of recordings 1B30 and 1B31, dated January 18, 1995, for case #60A-SI-46290.

266 The transcript of Chaudret's statement in response to Whitacre's story about receiving his briefcase from a hotel employee quotes him as saying: "Very funny, huh," and adding, "In Paris, it would have already been sold." The author listened to the videotape recording on headphones, and also played it to someone who is fluent in French. Both of us concluded that the transcript was wrong. Since the words we heard made more logical sense than the quote from the transcript, I chose to rely on them in the dialogue.

269 Some details of Whitacre's call with Chris Jones from a 302 of Whitacre, dated January 31, 1995, and written by Shepard. Also from a 302 by Craig Dahle, from his interview of February 1, 1995.

269–70 Some details of Whitacre's call with Shepard from the 302 of January 31, 1995.

270–72 Some details of Whitacre's interview with Dahle from a 302 of February 1, 1995.

272–73 Herndon's talk to Bureau headquarters from a written copy of the speech.

277 Some details of the Hulin meeting were described in an undated E-mail, written by Anne Bingaman to the Chicago antitrust office.

278–79 Details on Hulin's plan to go overt from a routing slip prepared for supervisors in the Springfield FBI and dated February 28, 1995.

279 Details of Bingaman's e-mail from the original message.

279 Details of the Chicago antitrust office's e-mail from the original message.

284–85 Some details of Mimoto's April 8 conversation with Whitacre from the Ajinomoto executive's 302, dated July 2, 1996.

285–86 Some details of the Oklahoma City bombing from "Terror in the Heartland," *U.S. News & World Report*, May 1, 1995, p. 28.

286 Whitacre described his tendency of carrying thousands of dollars in cash in his briefcase in statements to his psychiatrist, which were recorded in an admission note by Dr. Derek Miller dated August 9–10, 1995. Also, Marty Allison of ADM made reference to that in his FBI interview dated September 20, 1996.

286–87 Bruch described the April 27 calls on the "hello" line and the main office line in a written communication reviewed by the author.

CHAPTER TWELVE

290 Details of the FBI National Academy event, as well as of Cheviron's memo to Claudia Manning, from the original memo.

292 Details of the strategy behind the raid from an internal FBI teletype, dated June 22, 1995.

293–97 Some details of Whitacre's meeting of June 26, 1995, with the FBI from a 302 of the interview.

298 Details of the flight to Washington by Hoyt and Kilham from the tickets and expense logs.

300–305 Some details of the June 27, 1995, FBI interview of Mick Andreas from the 302 prepared by Shepard and Herndon, as well as a summary teletype dated June 28, 1995.

307–308 Details of the Dwayne Andreas interview of June 27, 1995, from a 302 of that day, written by Special Agents Alec Wade and Steven Nash.

308 Details of the Barrie Cox interview of June 27, 1995, from a 302 of the investigation and a summary teletype written the next day.

308 Details of Buffett's FBI interview of June 27 from the 302.

308 Details of Kirk Schmidt's interview of June 27 from the 302.

310 Details of the witnesses known by the FBI to have been informed by Whitacre of his role as a cooperating witness from a summary FBI teletype of June 28, 1995.

311–13 Some details of the meeting between Whitacre and the FBI in the parking lot of the Holiday Inn from a 302 of that encounter.

314 The background of Aubrey Daniel III from James Warren, "Back in the Limelight: My Lai Prosecutor Pops Up in Archer Daniels Midland Case," *Chicago Tribune*, July 16, 1995, Tempo section, p. 92. Other background on Williams & Connolly from S. H. Lawrence, "The Passing of Power at Williams & Connolly," *Washington Post*, September 19, 1988, p. F1.

314–15 Details of Buffett's day on June 28, 1995, from a 302 of the following day.

316 Details of Whitacre's phone call to the FBI about having hired a lawyer from a 302 dated June 28, 1995.

316–18 Whitacre described certain events that took place at Shafter's office in a 302 prepared by Herndon and Shepard on June 30, 1995. Shafter described those events in a November 10, 1995, letter to Thomas C. Green, a lawyer for John Dowd.

CHAPTER THIRTEEN

321 Some details of Whitacre's nighttime call with Shepard on the day after the raids from a 302 dated June 28, 1995.

322 Some details of Aubrey Daniel's late-night call to Whitacre and Whitacre's subsequent conversation with Shepard from a 302 prepared by Shepard and dated June 29, 1995.

322–24 Some details of Whitacre's morning at ADM, plus his subsequent experiences at the Decatur R.A., from a 302 prepared by Herndon and Shepard, dated June 29, 1995.

328 Shepard described his conversation with Whitacre, including the mixed-up paging message, in a 302 dated July 1, 1995.

328–29 Scott Roberts described his discovery of the bogus ABP International contract to the FBI on January 24, 1996. Some details from this scene come from a 302 of that interview prepared by D'Angelo and Bassett. Other details from original copies of both ABP contracts, as well as signed affidavits from James Randall and Lennart Thorstensson, dated July 29, 1995, and July 17, 1995, respectively.

329 Rochelli described his conversation with Mark Whitacre several days after the raids in testimony before a federal grand jury on June 20, 1996. Other details come from a 302 of Rochelli's interview with the FBI on January 24 of that same year.

329–30 Details of Whitacre's July 2 conversation with Shepard were recorded in a 302 of the same date.

330–31 Some details of the meeting between Epstein, Daniel, and Simon from notes taken during the meeting by one of the participants.

331–32 Some details of Whitacre's encounter with the *Wall Street Journal*, and his subsequent lies to Shepard, were recorded in a document entitled "FBI File Information."

332 Details of the original *Wall Street Journal* report from Thomas M. Burton and Scott Kilman, "Seeds of Doubt: An Executive Becomes Informant for the FBI, Stunning Giant ADM," *Wall Street Journal*, July 10, 1995, p. 1.

333 Information regarding the WAND broadcast on the morning of July 11 from a summary transcript of that newscast.

333 Ron Ferrari's professional football career background from Tim Rosaforte, "Ferrari Prepared for the Long Haul," *Orlando News Sentinel*, January 19, 1985, and the *1986 Media Guide*, p. 39, published by the National Football League.

333–34 Details of Ferrari's conversation with Whitacre from Ferrari's sworn testimony of January 27, 1998, in the case of *ADM v. Mark E. Whitacre et al.*

334 Mark Whitacre also reported receiving threatening calls to the FBI a series of times.

334 Headline of *Wall Street Journal* article of July 13 from the original news story.

334–35 Whitacre's conversation with Herndon on July 13, 1995, was recorded in a 302 of that same date.

335 Details of the anonymous letters that arrived at ADM on July 18, 1995, from copies of the original letters and their envelopes.

336 Background of Franklin, Tennessee, from Don O'Briant, "Walking in a Victorian Wonderland," *Atlanta Journal and Constitution*, November 17, 1999, p. 6G. Also, from Donna Dorian, "Franklin: The Best Small Town in Tennessee," *Colonial Homes*, February 1995, p. 62.

336 Some details of Gert Borasky's conversation with Ginger Whitacre from the 302 of her interview with D'Angelo in 1995.

336–37 Details of the first Lamet Vov memo from the letter itself. The timing of the letter's arrival, and the other details about where it was sent, from itemized AT&T phone records for David Hoech.

337–38 The makeup of the ADM special committee of directors was detailed in Burton and Kilman, "Archer-Daniels Names 9-Member Panel on U.S. Criminal Probe and Civil Suits," *Wall Street Journal*, July 20, 1995, p. 4.

338 Details of the *Chicago Tribune* article from Michael Arndt and George Gunset, "Mulroney Heads ADM Probe 'Response': Discrepancies Emerge in Reported Mole Whitacre's Academic Record," *Chicago Tribune*, July 20, 1995, Business section, p. 1.

339 Some details of the original negotiation between Whitacre and Myer for the house from a copy of their contract of sale, dated on the first page as July 20, 1995, but signed by both parties on July 21.

339–40 Myer described his run-in with Whitacre on July 21 in several documents. His most detailed description was provided in his July 17, 1996, deposition in the case *Paul J. Myer and Carole A. Myer v. Mark Whitacre et al.*, case number 23547, filed in the Chancery Court for Williamson County at Franklin. Other information from the 302 of his 1995 interview with D'Angelo at his home in Reston, Virginia.

340 Details of the anonymous note from San Francisco to Aubrey Daniel from a copy of the original.

340–41 Details of Aubrey Daniel's letters to Attorney General Janet Reno from the original documents.

342–43 Some details of Whitacre's interview with Henkoff, as well as the topics of discussion, from Mark Whitacre and Ronald Henkoff, "My Life as a Corporate Mole for the FBI," *Fortune* magazine, September 4, 1995, pp. 52–63.

343 Borasky's conversations with Whitacre and Caiazzo are described in her 302 from the summer of 1995. Details of Caiazzo's letter of July 26, 1995, to Borasky from a copy of the original.

343 Rochelli's conversation with Mark Whitacre was described in his June 20, 1996, testimony before a federal grand jury and the 302 of his January 24, 1996, interview with the FBI.

343–344 Whitacre's complaints to Shepard are described in a 302 of the conversation, dated July 27, 1995.

344 Details of the Lamet Vov letters during the summer of 1995, including the July 30 letter, from copies of the originals.

346 Details of the state-of-severance negotiations between ADM and Whitacre as of August 2, 1995, from a memo describing a meeting the following day at the Justice

Department, where Williams & Connolly presented a copy of the tentative severance agreement. The memo, dated August 16, 1995, was written by Scott Hammond, an attorney in the Antitrust Division.

347–55 Some details of Whitacre's first confession and the related conversation from a 302 prepared by Shepard and Herndon and dated August 2, 1995.

353 No substantive evidence ever emerged indicating that Frankel received money as part of an ADM bonus plan. Again, Frankel has denied all wrongdoing and was never charged.

CHAPTER FOURTEEN

356–58 Details of the meeting between Williams & Connolly and the antitrust attorneys from the detailed August 16, 1995, memorandum written by Hammond.

356 Details of the handwriting expert's findings from the original document report of July 24, 1995, by Lyndal L. Shanefelt.

357 In the presentation to the Justice Department, Williams & Connolly incorrectly described these letters as saying that the Whitacre embezzlement amounted to $2.5 million—essentially rounding it to the nearest half million dollars. The actual amount of $2.35 million comes from a copy of the original letter.

358–59 Details of Whitacre's phone call to Shepard on August 3, 1995, from one of two 302s of their conversations on that day.

363 The Chicago city corruption case with the informant who committed crimes while working for the FBI was Operation Silver Shovel. Details of that investigation and the informant's troubles from Matt O'Connor, "Silver Shovel Dirt Piles Up," *Chicago Tribune*, January 11, 1996, News section, p. 1.

365–66 Details of the meeting between Williams & Connolly and Seth Waxman on August 4, 1995, come from a memo to the file written by Waxman immediately after the lawyers left his office.

368–71 Some details of the August 4 meeting between the Whitacres, Shepard, and Kate Killham from the 302 prepared of those discussions.

372 Some details of Page's meeting with Whitacre from the 302 of his FBI interview, dated November 25, 1996.

372 Details of the I.O.L.A. account set up by Caiazzo from two documents in Whitacre's Swiss bank records, including a statement of account for account number PO-50,933.0 at the Swiss Bank Corporation in Zurich, as well as a copy of the original wire-transfer order, dated August 4, 1995.

372–73 The confrontation between Mark and Ginger Whitacre was described separately by the couple in their subsequent interviews with Dr. Derek Miller, and were described in Dr. Miller's notes of the interview dated August 11, 1995.

373 The news of Whitacre's thefts from the Associated Press, "ADM Fires Mole, Says He Stole at Least $2.5 Million," August 7, 1995.

374 Epstein described the last-minute change in Whitacre's story to his client's psychiatrist, Dr. Derek Miller of Chicago. Some details from this scene from the doctor's notes of that discussion, dated August 9, 1995.

374–80 Some details of Whitacre's August 7 interview with the FBI and the Fraud Section from a 302 prepared by Supervisory Special Agent Edward Herbst.

381 Details of Bassett's role as Michael McLoughlin from Christopher Drew and William B. Crawford Jr., "Indictments Name 46 Traders," *Chicago Tribune*, August 3, 1989, p.1.

382–86 Rusty Williams described the events on the morning of August 9, 1995, in an interview with Special Agent Shepard on June 24, 1996. Some details from the 302 of that interview.

CHAPTER FIFTEEN

387 Some details of Dr. Derek Miller's contacts with Epstein and the Whitacres from his admission note for Patrick O'Brien, the alias he used for Mark Whitacre, dated August 9–10, 1995.

387–88 In subsequent recollections of these events to government officials, the precise timing of the Borasky call to Ginger Whitacre was in dispute, with some people claiming it had occurred on August 10, 1995, rather than August 9. However, everyone agreed that subsequent to that call, Borasky received the fax from Joseph Caiazzo. I have established the timing through a copy of that original fax, which carries an electronic "telltale" that clearly establishes the transmission time of the document as being on August 9, 1995, at 11:28 in the morning. Some details of this scene are from that letter, as well as from the 302 of Borasky's interview with D'Angelo, and an August 16, 1995, memo by the Department of Justice of an interview with Paul Myer by Brenda Carlton. Other details are from Myer's 302 with D'Angelo, from August 25, 1995.

388–90 Details of Dr. Derek Miller's first meeting with Whitacre from his admission note of August 9–10, 1995.

391–92 Some details of Walsh's hunt for the truth about Whitacre's adoption history from "Whistle-blower Leaves Trail of Contradictions: Former ADM Executive Mark Whitacre's Life Includes Puzzles, Inconsistencies," *Washington Post*, August 11, 1995, p. D1.

393–94 Some details of Daniel's conversation with D'Angelo and Bassett from a memorandum recording an attorney contact, written by D'Angelo on August 11, 1995.

394 Details of the Swiss investigation as of August 1995—including the conversations with Rolf Brüggermann, from a series of faxes sent by Triet to Swiss bankers in Zurich during that month, including a letter of August 10, 1995, to Brüggermann.

396–97 Details of Miller's conversations up through August 10 from his admission note of August 9–10, 1995.

397 Details of Miller's conversations with Whitacre of August 11 from his progress note of that day for Patrick O'Brien, the alias he used for Mark Whitacre. Other information from Miller's notes of an interview with Ginger Whitacre on that same day.

400 Details of the work by private investigators in Thailand from an August 14, 1995, memorandum prepared by Steve Vickers, Deepak Bhawnani, and Eric Hui regarding the "Williams & Connolly case."

401–402 Details of the letter sent to the *Wall Street Journal* from Kilman and Burton, "Ever More Serious: ADM Informant Faces Widening Allegations; He Attempts Suicide," *Wall Street Journal*, August 14, 1995, p. A1.

402 *Fortune* press release from the original document sent out over PR Newswire on August 12, 1995.

403 Whitacre's quotes in *Fortune* from "My Life as a Corporate Mole for the FBI," *Fortune*, September 4, 1995, p. 52.

403 Details of the fax sent to Briel from a copy of the original document. While the document is dated August 8, there is no doubt it was sent the following week. Not only is that confirmed by the fax telltale, but also by the dates of when the three checks were written on Whitacre's Swiss bank account.

403–404 Some details regarding Herndon's notification of the pending Whitacre indictment from the August 15, 1995, teletype.

405–406 Details of Whitacre's note to Beat Schweizer from a copy of the original document.

406 Some details of Gilbert's receipt of the package from Switzerland from his sworn testimony, given December 20, 1997, in *ADM v. Mark E. Whitacre*.

406–407 Some details of the resolution of Whitacre's pending indictment from an August 22, 1995, memo from Peter Clark to George Martin, an Assistant United States Attorney in Mobile, and Special Agent Craig Dahle.

407–408 Some details of the scene where the FBI serves Williams & Connolly with a subpoena come from a 302 written by Herbst and Stuber on August 16, 1995.

408 Bob Dole's comments at the Illinois State Fair from Anthony Man, "Senator Predicts Probe Won't Hurt Company's Clout in Washington," *Decatur Herald & Review*, August 17, 1995, p. 1A.

408–409 Details of Brenda Carlton's interview with Myer from a memo she wrote to Gary Spratling, dated August 16, 1995.

409 The conversation between Bassett, D'Angelo, and Zaideman was recorded in an internal FBI memo written by the agents on August 21, 1995. Other details from an August 17, 1995, memo written by Zaideman to Jim Epstein. Details of the August 18, 1995, conversation between Bassett and Miller from a 302 written September 8, 1995.

410–11 The quote from Herndon's August 21, 1995, teletype from a copy of the original document.

411 Details of the *Journal* article from Kilman and Burton, "ADM Asserts Ex-official Diverted Over $9 Million," *Wall Street Journal*, August 21, 1995, p. A2.

411–12 The items obtained from Williams & Connolly on August 21, 1995, were described in a 302 written by Herbst on that date.

412–13 Details of D'Angelo's interview with Myer from a 302 of August 25, 1995, for case file number 196D-CG-99593.

413–14 Some details of Liz Taylor's meeting with ADM lawyers and the subsequent outcome from the 302 of her interview with Bassett and D'Angelo, dated January 18, 1996.

416–22 Details of Whitacre's interview of September 7, 1995, from a 302 written by D'Angelo and Bassett for case file number 196D-CG-99593.

421 Again, while Frankel was investigated for financial wrongdoing, no evidence ever emerged that the company had paid him an under-the-table bonus. No charges were ever brought against him.

422 Joseph Caiazzo has said that he had no idea the money for the house mortgage was coming from Whitacre himself. His statement appeared in "Records Show Flows from Archer Executive's Account," *New York Times*, October 24, 1995. To the best of my knowledge, that article was the first time it was publicly disclosed that Whitacre had used the house mortgage as a method of bringing money from a foreign account back into the country, tax-free. Asked about the transaction, Caiazzo expressed surprise. "I'm as shocked as anybody," he said in the article. "I had reason to believe that it was absolutely not his money." Caiazzo was never charged with any wrongdoing.

CHAPTER SIXTEEN

427–28 The timing of Richter's message to Hulse and Allison, as well as the words he used, from a transcript of the voice mail.

428 Hulse's decision to save Richter's message from a 302 of his interview of September 12, 1995, as well as a September 15 memorandum of a subsequent discussion between Sean Berkowitz and D'Angelo.

428–35 Some details of Hulse's interview with the FBI on September 12 from a 302 written by D'Angelo and Grant for case file number 196D-CG-99593.

431–32 Descriptions of the Nigerian swindle from copies of fraud letters, as well as a 1998 briefing paper by the International Organization of Black Security Executives and information posted on the Web site for the Securities and Exchange Commission. Additional information from transcripts of a December 11, 1994, broadcast of *60 Minutes* and an August 17, 1994, broadcast on *Morning Edition* with National Public Radio.

433 Jerome Schneider's background from Kate Berry, "Is It Still Smart to Keep Your Money Offshore?," *Investor's Business Daily*, July 9, 1996, p. A1. Also, from a transcript of an April 11, 1997, broadcast on *20/20*, the television program.

435–36 The deal offered to Richter by ADM on September 13 was described in a letter two days later from Steve Urbanczyk of Williams & Connolly to Scott Roberts of ADM's legal department.

436 The termination of Sid Hulse was described by Sean Berkowitz in his conversation with D'Angelo that night, which was recorded in the memorandum of September 15.

436–37 A partial transcript of Johnson's speech at Emory was printed in "ADM and the FBI 'Scumbags,' " *Fortune*, October 30, 1995, p. 116.

437–38 Whitacre's new job at Future Health Technologies was described by Bloomberg Business News, "ADM Whistleblower Whitacre Has New Job," *Springfield State Journal-Register*, October 10, 1995, p. 23.

438–39 Richter described his conversations with Whitacre in his sworn testimony of May 18, 1998, in *ADM v. Mark E. Whitacre et al.*

439 Details of Epstein's September 21 call to Bassett from a memorandum written by Bassett dated September 26, 1995.

440 Details of Page's interview with Williams & Connolly from the 302 of his November 25, 1996, interview with D'Angelo and Grant for case file number 196D-CG-99593.

440–46 Details of Ron Ferrari's first FBI interview from a 302 dated October 10, 1995, and written by D'Angelo and Bassett for case file number 196D-CG-99593.

446–47 Richter's comments appeared in several reports, including Henkoff, "Checks, Lies and Videotapes," *Fortune* magazine, October 30, 1995, p. 109, and Bloomberg Business News, "Fired ADM Exec: Firm OK'd Secret Payments," *Decatur Herald & Review*, October 12, 1995, p. 1A.

447–48 Grant described his October 13 phone call with Mackay and Nixon in an electronic communication to Bureau headquarters, written on October 21, 1995.

448–49 Details of the *Tribune* article from Nancy Millman, "ADM Mole Discloses a Cache of $6 Million: Off-the-Books Scheme Endorsed by Bosses, Former Executive Says," *Chicago Tribune*, October 17, 1995, p. 1.

449 Details of Whitacre's meeting with Miller on October 17 from the psychiatrist's notes of that day's session.

449–51 There are several documentary sources for the story of Ferrari's encounter with Whitacre, two of which are contemporaneous. A memorandum by Bassett written on October 20, 1995, described a phone call of the previous evening with Jeff Steinback, Ferrari's lawyer, in which the encounter is described. In addition, immediately after the event, Ferrari prepared a memo for Steinback, describing the events as they unfolded. Finally, Ferrari described the event in his sworn testimony of January 27, 1998, in the case of *ADM v. Mark E. Whitacre et al.*

452 The Justice Department statement appeared in several publications. Relevant articles are from Nancy Millman, "ADM 'Not Target' of Criminal Probe," *Chicago Tribune*, October 18, 1995, Business section, p. 1, and "Archer-Daniels Is Not Subject of One Investigation by U.S.," *New York Times*, October 18, 1995, p. D10.

452–53 Richard Reising's statement at the ADM shareholders meeting from Henkoff, "ADM Takes the Justice Department for a Spin," *Fortune* magazine, November 27, 1995, p. 35. Other details, including the contretemps between Andreas and the union official, are from my own observations and notes.

455–59 Details of Richter's November 8 interview with D'Angelo and Bassett from the 302 of that encounter written by the agents for case file number 196D-CG-99593. Additional details from his sworn testimony in *ADM v. Mark E. Whitacre*, as well as from Whitacre's 2004 examination on December 3, 1997, in the bankruptcy case *In re: Mark Edward Whitacre and Ginger Lynn Whitacre*, case number 97-14541 (Chapter 7), filed in the United States Bankruptcy Court for the Middle District of North Carolina, Durham Division.

Adolpho Acebras was never charged with wrongdoing in the case. Richter discussed the role of Acebras in greater detail during his testimony in *ADM v. Mark E. Whitacre et al*. Supporting material comes from the original documentation in the transaction, including: an undated letter from Komven to Richter, bearing the signature of Acebras; an internal ADM "accounts payable check/distribution request," which shows that the check was made out to the same address and individual listed in the undated letter; and a copy of a December 1, 1991, check from ADM in the amount of $87,466, payable to Acebras.

459–60 Herndon's encounter with Richter by phone was described in an electronic communication written by D'Angelo, regarding his phone call with Herndon immediately following those events.

CHAPTER SEVENTEEN

461–63 Some timing and related issues involving the phone calls on the morning of November 10, 1995, from a billing-account statement from Epstein, Zaideman & Esrig.

461–63 Some details of the conversations of November 10, 1995, between Herndon and D'Angelo; D'Angelo and Bassett; D'Angelo, Bassett, and Epstein; and D'Angelo, Bassett, Epstein, and Whitacre from an electronic communication written by D'Angelo on November 14.

463 Some details of Whitacre's follow-up call on November 10, 1995, from a 302 from that date written by Bassett and D'Angelo for case file number 196D-CG-99593.

463 Some information about the history of the Monadnock Building from Adam Davidson, "Chicago Is a Showcase for Architectural Landmarks," *Chicago Tribune*, June 21, 1999, Metromix section, p. 1.

463–67 Some details of Ferrari's interview of December 6, 1995, from a 302 of that day written by D'Angelo and Bassett for case file number 196D-CG-99593.

467–69 Quotations from the December 12, 1995, letter from Spearing, Mackay, and Nixon to Bassett and D'Angelo come from the letter itself.

470–71 Quotations from the December 12, 1995, letter from Worthington to Spearing come from the letter itself.

472–74 The run-in between Patti McLaren and Andrew Levetown was described in some detail by Nancy Millman, "Private Investigators on Trail of Whistle-blower at ADM," *Chicago Tribune*, February 4, 1996, Business section, p. 1; as well as by Henkoff, "Of Gumshoes, Gardeners and ADM," *Fortune* magazine, March 4, 1996, p. 31. In both of those articles, the writers referred to allegations by McLaren that Levetown had indicated his firm might provide her with money for information about Whitacre. While such an offer is perfectly legal—and indeed, common among private detectives—Kroll Associates has vigorously disputed that it ever occurred. So, in the narrative, I have chosen to place the break immediately before the events in dispute. Whether it occurred, I believe, is of no consequence and does not affect the story. While these allegations are raised later by the Lamet Vov, they are not being described for their truth, but rather for the impact the charges had on Kroll's efforts.

474 Quotes from Hoech's letter to Yamamoto from the actual document.

475 The failure of the secretaries to bring up the Decatur Club allegations from their 302s taken during the ADM investigations.

475–76 Statements of the new witness, identified with the pseudonym of Joseph Graham, regarding possible frauds at ADM from a subsequent memo describing the information written by Herndon for Frances Hulin, dated January 30, 1996.

476–77 The "prostitute questions" from the actual document.

477–78 Details and quotes of the Lamet Vov letters from the following communications: July 18, 24, 30, and November 26, all in 1995. Also, from January 3, 1996.

478 Background of the term *Lamed Vav Zaddikim* from C. G. Montefiore and H. Lowe, *A Rabbinic Anthology* (Meridian Books, 1960), and Rabbi Stephen Pearce, "Kee Tissa: On imagining each person as the Messiah," *Torah Thoughts*, March 8, 1996.

478–79 Some details of Williams & Connolly's hunt for the Lamet Vov from a letter written by Jim Nixon to Bassett and D'Angelo on February 1, 1996.

479 Quotes of Daniel and Simon's letter from the original document addressed to Mackay and Nixon, dated January 31, 1996.

479 Dain Bosworth research quote from Wittenburg's original report.

479–81 Some details of Marty Allison's interview from a 302 of February 13, 1996, written by Herndon.

482 Details of Lassar's conversation with D'Angelo on February 14 from a memo of the discussion written by D'Angelo.

482–83 Some details of Kroll's comparisons of the ADM case from John Grisham, *The Firm*, 1991.

484–87 Details of Goldberg's conversation from Hoech from several sources. The first and most important is a tape recording of the discussion made by Hoech. Second is a 302 of Goldberg, written by Bassett, following a March 19, 1996, interview about the call. Details of Goldberg's notes during the phone call come from the original document.

488 The pages about Dick Beattie that were sent around to ADM directors were from Sarah Bartlett, *The Money Machine* (Warner Books, 1991), pp. 287–300.

488–89 Quotes from the anonymous letter faxed to ADM are from the original document. Some other details of the event from a letter from Barry Simon of Williams & Connolly to Jim Nixon at the Justice Department, dated March 21, 1996, and from information contained on a Polaroid picture taken that day of the caller-ID box.

489–90 Some details of the efforts to confirm the abduction story from a memorandum written by Mike Bassett on March 27, 1996.

490–92 Some details of the Hoech interview from a 302 prepared by Bassett and D'Angelo.

492–93 Details of Killham's recommendation for Shepard's transfer to St. Thomas from the original draft.

493–94 Details of Whitacre's interview with Steve Delaney of WAND from a videotape of the event.

CHAPTER EIGHTEEN

495–96 Beat Schweizer's call to the Justice Department, and the subsequent difficulties in arranging his interview, are described in an electronic communication to Bureau headquarters written on April 18, 1996, by Bassett, as well as an electronic communication from the same date relating to Bassett's contact with Kurt Sieger.

496–99 Some details of Schweizer's interview with the government from a 302 of May 13, 1996, written by Bassett and D'Angelo. Also, from an electronic communication to Bureau headquarters, written by D'Angelo on May 15.

498–99 The Justice Department confirmed that the Swiss prosecutors were sharing information with ADM attorneys. That is documented in an electronic communication, written by Bassett on May 20, 1996.

499 The reaction to the news of the Swiss leak is described in the electronic communications of May 15 and May 20.

500 A listing of the attendees to the 1996 Bilderberg conference was obtained by the author. Some details of the CIBC Center from a press release issued by the company on January 13, 1994.

500–501 Some details of the final interview with Shepard's new witness from records of the polygraph.

501–502 The Biomar transaction involving the one-hundred-thousand-dollar Swiss check is described in several documents, including the depositions of Evelyn Ann Whitacre on March 23, 1998, and of Marion E. Whitacre on March 24, 1998, in the case of *ADM v. Marion E. Whitacre*, case number C-1-98-100, filed in the U.S. District Court for the Southern District of Ohio, brought since Whitacre's parents' names appeared on checks written from their son's foreign bank accounts. The case was later dropped. Additional information from the original documents, including the loan agreement and the Swiss check, as they correspond to the testimony of Mark Whitacre on October 24, 1997, in the bankruptcy case *In re: Mark Edward Whitacre and Ginger Lynn Whitacre*, case number 97-14541.

502 The court fight in Peoria is described in an electronic communication by D'Angelo, written on June 14, 1996.

502–503 Details of Rochelli's grand jury appearance from a transcript of the proceedings, dated June 20, 1996. This also corresponds with Rochelli's interview with the FBI, as documented in a 302 written by D'Angelo and Bassett, dated January 24, 1996.

504–505 Details of the Yamamoto documents from copies of the original records. Some details of Yamamoto's interview from a 302 written by Herndon, dated June 30, 1996.

505–506 Some details of the August 12, 1996, interview with J. S. Kim from a 302 prepared by Herndon.

506 The discussions with Jim Epstein about possible charges were recorded in an electronic communication to Bureau headquarters, written by D'Angelo on August 16, 1996.

511–518 Some details of the government's interview with Marty Allison from a 302 written by D'Angelo and Bassett, dated September 20, 1996.

518 The total amounts of the money stolen in 1991 that went to Nigeria from records prepared by the Chicago FBI for the fraud investigation.

518–19 Details of the lawsuit from the original complaint in *ADM v. Mark E. Whitacre et al.*

519–20 The hunt for and subsequent interview of David Page from a series of documents, including a 302 prepared by Special Agent James Halterman from the first interview conducted with Page; a 302 by Bassett from September 23, 1996, which described the hunt for Page; and the 302 of the final interview on November 25, 1996, prepared by D'Angelo and Grant.

CHAPTER NINETEEN

521–23 Some details of the final meeting of the ADM special committee from the official minutes.

523 Descriptions from the 1996 ADM shareholders meeting from my own personal observations.

524 The difficulties in treating Whitacre from progress notes written by Dr. Derek Miller, October 11–16, 1996.

526 Details and quotes from the letter terminating Epstein from the original document, dated November 3, 1996.

526 Kurth's background and specialty from his entry in Martindale-Hubbell.

526–27 Quotes from the "Carpenter's Union" letter from the original document. Other details from a November 8, 1996, letter by Aubrey Daniel, written to John C. Keeney, acting Assistant Attorney General of the Criminal Division.

528 The meeting between Whitacre, his lawyers, and Dr. Miller was documented in a progress note, dated December 19, 1996.

528–29 Some details of the Henkoff call and subsequent contacts were described in a detailed electronic communication, prepared by Shepard on January 9, 1997.

529–30 Quotes and details of the *Fortune* article from Henkoff, "Betrayal," *Fortune* magazine, February 3, 1997, pp. 82–91.

530–33 I had certain advantages in recognizing the forgeries. Months earlier in 1996, at the time I was beginning to express doubts about some of Whitacre's stories, an old press release issued by him reappeared at my office. It had what appeared to be a fax telltale at the top with my office fax number on it. David Hoech, the self-proclaimed Lamet Vov, told me that this document had been filed in court by ADM and was evidence that I had been sending information to the company. As a result, I was told, Whitacre was planning to sue the *New York Times* and me for millions of dollars. I did not know how to take this, since Whitacre himself was not saying any of this to me—and in fact, when asked, discounted it. On checking the court records, I found the same document filed as an exhibit, but it did not contain a telltale for my fax number.

The document that I had been sent was a forgery. The telltale was the number for the receiving fax machine at the *Times*, not the machine used to send documents. Moreover, phone bills showed that no call had ever been made from the number on the telltale. Finally, the telltale itself was printed in a font that is not used in any fax machine, although it is the default font for a popular word-processing program. From then on, I knew to study every record in this case for evidence of forgery.

Around the time of the publication of *The Informant*, David Hoech again relied on this forgery to begin falsely suggesting to reporters that I had been forwarding documents to Williams & Connolly. I decided to find out, once and for all, who had created the forgery. Subsequently, in a telephone conversation with Whitacre, I asked if he had, in fact, forged the document. Whitacre admitted doing so, although he said he could no longer explain his motivation. I would point out, however, that the fall of 1996 was when Whitacre's psychological state was at its most confused.

Finally, I want to stress that in the course of this story, almost every reporter—including me—made mistakes. Mine came early in my coverage, in 1995, when I incorrectly reported that Whitacre had reached a plea agreement with the government. While at that point Whitacre had agreed to plead guilty and cooperate, the government had not accepted the offer. No one gave me bad information; rather, I had simply misunderstood, and, as a result, misrepresented the truthful details I had learned and confirmed. Of course, everyone involved in the case recognized my error, and so it had no impact on these events. I wrote a corrective article the next day. I bring this up to underscore, while the situation with the bogus documents worked out well for me, that did not unfailingly hold true.

532–33 The bogus Miller letter was dated November 14, 1995, but was obviously prepared sometime after that. The actual letter, from Miller to Whitacre, was dated December 16, 1996. The bogus letter from Whitacre to Epstein was dated July 17, 1995, but was also prepared sometime later. The Ameritech press release was dated November 20, 1995.

534 Details of the *New York Times* article from "Archer Daniels Informer Admits Recent Deception," *New York Times*, January 15, 1997, p. D1.

534 Details of Whitacre's charges from the indictment filed in *U.S. v. Mark E. Whitacre*, case number 97-20001, filed in the U.S. District Court in the Central District of Illinois, Urbana division.

538 Details of the dual appearances before the indictment review committee from an electronic communication prepared by D'Angelo on February 6, 1998.

541–42 Details of Whitacre's plea from the transcript of the proceedings dated October 10, 1997. Quotes of statement handed out after the plea from the original document.

543–44 Some details of Whitacre's final interview with the government from a 302 prepared by D'Angelo, dated February 6, 1998.

544–45 Details of the Whitacre affidavits from the original documents, both dated

January 26, 1998. The cancellation of the stock certificate resulted in a number of disputes between Whitacre and Biomar, now known as BioSignia. A partnership, including Ginger and the children, sued BioSignia and the Campbells in May 2000, claiming that one million shares of the stock—which the suit contends had been paid to Whitacre in lieu of salary—had been improperly canceled by the company. In an earlier discussion of the dispute, J. William Koegel Jr. wrote a letter to Bill Walker dated October 28, 1999. In it, Mr. Koegel said that the company was surprised by Whitacre's claim that he was owed stock, since the stock never vested. According to the letter, Whitacre testified that he had no claim to the stock during his bankruptcy proceedings, and indeed, no claim of ownership by either Mark or Ginger was made during the course of the bankruptcy. However, the new lawsuit claims that the partnership holds assets on behalf of the Whitacre children.

545–46 Details of Whitacre's second apparent suicide attempt and the subsequent investigation from written reports on the incident from the Chapel Hill Police Department, listed under case number 9805666, dated February 26, 1998. The report also includes written statements by members of the Chapel Hill Fire Department.

546 Details of the first Urbana hearings from personal observation and a transcript of the proceedings, dated February 26, 1997.

546–49 Some details of the day of Whitacre's sentencing in the fraud case from personal observation and a transcript of the proceedings, dated March 4, 1998.

EPILOGUE

551–53 Details from the day of opening arguments in the price-fixing case from personal observation and a transcript of the proceedings, dated July 15, 1998.

552 Manning's criticism was contained in a memorandum and order, filed in April 1998 in *U.S. v. Michael D. Andreas et al.*

555 Quotes from Herndon's fax to Shepard from the document.

556–57 Some details of the verdict in the price-fixing case from a transcript of the proceedings, dated September 17, 1998.

558 As of this writing, Yamada of Ajinomoto remains under indictment, and American officials told me that the Japanese executive will be arrested if he attempts to come into the United States. No effort has been made to deport him from Japan— partly, I am told, out of concerns for international relations and also because of the difficulty in proving he had been adequately served notice of the case. Ajinomoto did plead guilty and paid a ten-million-dollar criminal fine. While only Mimoto pleaded guilty to the charges, Ikeda was granted immunity and testified about his participation in the criminal conspiracy during the trial of Mick Andreas, Terry Wilson, and Mark Whitacre.
    Among the other participants, Kyowa Hakko also pleaded guilty and agreed to pay a ten-million-dollar criminal fine. Again, only one company executive—Masaru Yamamoto—pleaded guilty, paying a fifty-thousand-dollar fine. Sewon America Inc., a Paramus, New Jersey, subsidiary of Sewon in Korea, pleaded guilty and agreed to pay whatever fine was deemed appropriate by the court. J. S. Kim also admitted his guilt and was fined $75,000. No other Sewon executives were charged. Finally, Cheil

Jedang pleaded guilty and agreed to pay a $1.25 million fine for its involvement in the conspiracy. None of its executives were charged.

The litigation between ADM and Mark Whitacre dragged on for years. The company eventually settled or dropped its complaints against everyone but Whitacre himself. That case resulted in a court order that Whitacre pay back $1.7 million in salary and benefits he received from ADM, because of what the court said was his failure to faithfully perform his corporate duties. ADM, in turn, was ordered to reinstate certain stock options that had been awarded to Whitacre. But in the end, the battle was mostly pointless: Whitacre was already on the hook to pay ADM $11 million, and the new judgment was uncollectable, Bill Walker, his lawyer, told reporters at the time.

The patent infringement suit between Ajinomoto and ADM also dragged on for some time. A trial was held in 1996, eventually resulting in a judgment on March 13, 1998. In that judgment, Judge Sue L. Robinson of the Federal District Court for the district of Delaware found that ADM had infringed on Ajinomoto's valid patent for its threonine microbe. As a result, ADM was ordered to pay Ajinomoto a royalty rate of $1.23 for every kilogram of threonine sold since May 1993. The court also entered an injunction prohibiting ADM from continuing to infringe on the Ajinomoto patent.

559 The plans of the Campbells to donate their stock to charitable endeavors was described in an April 4, 2000, letter to their company's shareholders and employees.

ACKNOWLEDGMENTS

As always, there are many to thank.

At the *New York Times*, Chris Bockelmann and Brent Bowers offered generous amounts of their time reviewing the manuscript and sprinkled their magic throughout these pages. Their suggestions were invaluable. I am also indebted to my boss and friend, Glenn Kramon, who allowed me the freedom to follow my nose on this story and always backed me up. And I owe thanks to John Geddes, who first let me pick up the ADM story and stayed with me whenever the going got rough.

Others at the *Times* offered help at important junctures, including Diana Henriques, David Barboza, Mark Landler, Alison Leigh Cowan, Barnaby Feder, Gina Kolata, Laura Holson, and Adam Liptak. Donna Anderson helped dig up news articles, and Karen Cetinkaya provided photo research. Dylan McClain handled graphics.

I was unusually fortunate to work with three talented researchers— Michael Brick and Jamie Paton, both now reporters in the joint newsroom at the *New York Times* and TheStreet.com; and Geanne Rosenberg, now a contributing editor at the *National Law Journal*. Their skills never ceased to astonish me. Remember their names— they will each do big things in journalism.

My savior, as always, was Diane Obara, a hardworking assistant who was always ready to go the extra mile whenever the work piled up. Also helping out were Jacqueline Durham and Anna DiLegge.

I owe particular thanks to Alison Comas, a friend who agreed to read the manuscript in its roughest form to help me determine if I was on the right track. Julianna Patrick saved my life more times than I can count, coming by to help out whenever my schedule proved to be too much. Antonia New provided me with desperately needed suggestions at a critical juncture—and as a result, unknowingly had an effect on the events described in this book. And Jamie Moss of Newspros Strategic Communications once again proved her talent with an endless stream of brilliant suggestions.

I also want to thank Peter Comas, Alan Wachtel, Allan Naarden, Scott Burbine, Edward Beja, Kathy Paul, and Errington Thompson. The guys from Gravy—particularly John Fischer, Scott Friesen, Eric Lambert, Adam Payne, Colin Trevorrow, and Brian Ullman—were all amazingly patient with my frequent absences and never complained. Scott once again proved his diverse talents as he led me on an expedition of the Internet. And, for helping me as only a musical cybergenius can, special thanks go to Wes Carroll, the man of a thousand projects and the driving beat behind the House Jacks (www.housejacks.com), one of America's most talented rock bands.

My agent, Freya Manston, was the first person to hear about the idea for this book and was always its biggest cheerleader. Without her support, this project would never have been completed.

I also want to thank everyone at Broadway Books, who provided an incredibly supportive and professional experience. In particular, I want to thank my editor, Suzanne Oaks, who once again guided me on my voyage into publishing. Suzanne was assisted by Claire Johnson, who was always ready to answer my endless questions with patience and a smile. Debbie Stier and Suzanne Herz were both a delight; as marketers, they are what authors' dreams are made of. When the time came for the heavy lifting—that is, the copyediting of this book—Deirdre Hare put in an amazing performance, snapping the manuscript into shape in nothing flat. Supervising the entire production schedule and organization was Bette Alexander, who seemed able to accomplish any request within moments. Lauren Field spent endless hours conducting a legal review with me, making the book all the better with each suggestion. And those are just a few of the people at Broadway who made this experience so wonderful. I thank you all.

Above all, I want to thank my wonderful family. My wife, Theresa Eichenwald, was always there for me—to cheer me on, to get me through the tough days, to lessen the other loads. She was, again, my first reader, my best editor, and my best friend. But this time, she had three helpers: our sons, Adam, Ryan, and Sam. All of them displayed endless patience and support. In truth, this book could not have been written without my family and the contributions they made.

But now, it's finished. So guys, I'm home.

INDEX

Kurt Eichenwald has written about white-collar crime and corporate corruption for the *New York Times* for more than a decade. A two-time winner of the prestigious George Polk Award for excellence in journalism and a finalist for the 2000 Pulitzer Prize, he has been repeatedly selected by *TJFR Business News Reporter* as one of the nation's most influential financial journalists. For the *Times*, he has covered some of the highest-profile news stories emanating from the business world, including the Archer Daniels Midland story, and he is the author of *Serpent on the Rock*. Eichenwald lives in Westchester County, outside New York City, with his wife and three children.